David C. Cook
Bible Lesson
Commentary

The Essential Study Companion *for* Every Disciple

David C. Cook
Bible Lesson
Commentary

NIV

David C Cook
transforming lives together

DAVID C. COOK NIV BIBLE LESSON COMMENTARY 2012–2013
Published by David C Cook
4050 Lee Vance View
Colorado Springs, CO 80918 U.S.A.

David C Cook Distribution Canada
55 Woodslee Avenue, Paris, Ontario, Canada N3L 3E5

David C Cook U.K., Kingsway Communications
Eastbourne, East Sussex BN23 6NT, England

The graphic circle C logo is a registered trademark of David C Cook.

Lessons based on *International Sunday School Lessons: The International Bible Lessons for
Christian Teaching*, © 2009 by the Committee on the Uniform Series.

ISBN 978-0-7814-0567-6

© 2012 David C Cook

Written and edited by Dan Lioy, PhD
The Team: John Blase, Doug Schmidt, Renada Arens, Karen Athen
Cover Design: Amy Konyndyk
Cover Photo: iStockphoto

Printed in the United States of America
First Edition 2012

1 2 3 4 5 6 7 8 9 10

022712

A Living Faith

Jesus Is Lord

Beyond the Present Time

God's People Worship

A Word to the Teacher

The twelve year old sat polishing his saxophone a few minutes before the morning worship service. That Sunday he was playing in the wind ensemble. He could hardly wait for the opportunity to arrive.

"What a shine on that instrument!" the group's director commented.

"Thank you!" the boy replied. "My grandfather's here this morning, and he's deaf. I thought if I put on a real good shine, he could at least enjoy the glow."

Somewhere that boy had stumbled upon one of the great foundations of human relations—the ability to care about others and to anticipate their needs.

The lessons presented in this year's edition of the *David C. Cook Bible Lesson Commentary* are taken from selected portions of the Old and New Testaments. We will learn not only about God's power but also about His ability to meet the humblest of needs. The Lord played His song of salvation (in a manner of speaking) to even the most tone-deaf and even the most hard of heart.

Isn't that one of the gifts we bring to our service for the Lord Jesus? It's to be patient and helpful when someone misunderstands us. It's to have such love for others that we do all we can to let them know about the Savior. It's to polish our communication style so that even the most unteachable person learns.

The joy of telling others about the Messiah beckons. Let our saxophones be shiny. Let our message glow!

Your fellow learner at the feet of the Master Teacher,
Dan Lioy

Using the *David C. Cook NIV Bible Lesson Commentary* with Material from Other Publishers

Sunday school materials from the following denominations and publishers follow International Sunday School Lesson outlines (sometimes known as Uniform Series). Because *David C. Cook's NIV Bible Lesson Commentary* (formerly *Peloubet's)* follows the same outlines, you can use the *Commentary* as an excellent teacher resource to supplement the materials from these publishing houses.

NONDENOMINATIONAL:

   Standard Publishing: *Adult*
   Urban Ministries
   Echoes Teacher's Commentary (David C Cook): *Adult*

DENOMINATIONAL:

   Advent Christian General Conference: *Adult*
   American Baptist (Judson Press): *Adult*
   United Holy Church of America: *Adult*
   Church of God in Christ (Church of God in Christ Publishing House): *Adult*
   Church of Christ Holiness: *Adult*
   Church of God (Warner Press): *Adult*
   Church of God by Faith: *Adult*
   National Baptist Convention of America (Boyd): *All ages*
   National Primitive Baptist Convention: *Adult*
   Progressive National Baptist Convention: *Adult*
   Presbyterian Church (U.S.A.) (Bible Discovery Series—Presbyterian Publishing House or P.R.E.M.): *Adult*
   Union Gospel Press: *All ages*
   United Holy Church of America: *Adult*
   United Methodist (Cokesbury): *All ages*

Faith Calls for Perseverance

Scripture

Background Scripture: *Hebrews 10:19-31*
Scripture Lesson: *Hebrews 10:19-31*
Key Verse: *Let us hold unswervingly to the hope we profess, for he who promised is faithful.* Hebrews 10:23.
Scripture Lesson for Children: *Matthew 8:5-13*
Key Verse for Children: *Then Jesus said to the centurion, "Go! It will be done just as you believed it would." And his servant was healed at that very hour.* Matthew 8:13.

Lesson Aim

To emphasize remaining faithful to the Savior regardless of the circumstances.

Lesson Setting

Time: Before A.D. 70
Place: Possibly Rome

Lesson Outline

Faith Calls for Perseverance

I.   Persevering in Doing What Is Right:
Hebrews 10:19-25
  A. *Being Confident to Enter God's Presence: vss. 19-20*
  B. *Recognizing Our Great High Priest: vss. 21-22*
  C. *Holding Resolutely to the Hope We Confess: vs. 23*
  D. *Encouraging One Another to Be Faithful:*
     vss. 24-25
II. Recognizing the Danger of Apostasy:
Hebrews 10:26-31
  A. *Willfully Persisting in Sin: vss. 26-27*
  B. *Callously Spurning the Messiah: vss. 28-29*
  C. *Recoiling from the Prospect of God's Judgment:*
     vss. 30-31

Introduction for Adults

Topic: *Steadfast Determination*

When we marry, we show that we have more than enough reasons to be faithful to our spouses. And the longer we are married, the stronger those reasons become, simply because we get to know one another better. Love is the best reason to be steadfast in our commitment.

The Letter to the Hebrews gives us a number of reasons to be resolute in our devotion to Jesus. The writer of this epistle did not tell us to grow in our love for Jesus. Instead, the author told us to consider the fact that Jesus is a "great priest over the house of God" (10:21). The more we fill our minds with Jesus' greatness, the more we will love Him and be faithful to Him.

Introduction for Youth

Topic: *Got Faith?*

If we had to pick one reason to have faith in Christ, what would it be? Would we choose His sovereign power and glory, His upholding the universe, or His being better than the angels? Probably not. We would declare our loyalty to Him because He is our "great priest over the house of God" (Heb. 10:21).

Behind this truth is the fact that the Son died on the cross so that we could have free and full access to the Father (vs. 20). Of course, our wickedness and our desire to have things our own way were the reasons Jesus had to sacrifice Himself on Calvary. How could Jesus love us that much? The fact is that He did and therefore we do not ever want to betray Him. He paid too much for us to turn our backs on Him.

Concepts for Children

Topic: *Great Faith*

1. When Jesus was in Capernaum, a soldier asked Jesus to heal his servant.
2. The soldier had great respect for Jesus.
3. The soldier also had great faith in Jesus.
4. Jesus was pleased to learn that the soldier trusted in Him so much.
5. Jesus wants us to put our faith in Him for salvation.

Lesson Commentary

I. Persevering in Doing What Is Right: Hebrews 10:19-25

A. Being Confident to Enter God's Presence: vss. 19-20

Therefore, brothers, since we have confidence to enter the Most Holy Place by the blood of Jesus, by a new and living way opened for us through the curtain, that is, his body.

The Letter to the Hebrews teaches that the Lord Jesus, as the mediator between God and humanity, has established a new and better covenant than the old one based on the Mosaic law. The new covenant is better precisely because it is established on "better promises" (8:6). If the first covenant had sufficiently met the needs of people and had adequately provided for their salvation, then there would have been no need for a new covenant to replace it (8:7). But the old covenant was insufficient and inadequate. It wasn't adequate in bringing people to God, and therefore a new covenant had to be established.

God had found fault with the chosen people under the old covenant (8:8), primarily because they did not continue in that holy compact (8:9). In turn, human failure rendered the old covenant inoperative. Although Ezekiel had written about God's establishing an "everlasting covenant" (Ezek. 16:60), only Jeremiah had spoken of a "new covenant" (Jer. 31:31). The prophet did not say that the covenant God made with the Israelites would be renewed. Rather, Jeremiah said that a completely new compact would be established (Heb. 8:8).

As Hebrews 8:10-12 and 10:15-17 reveal (see Jer. 31:33-34), the new covenant would be inward and dynamic. God's Word would actually have a place inside the minds and hearts of His people. The old covenant had been inscribed on tablets of stone and was external. But in regard to the new covenant, God vowed that His teachings would be internalized by His people. The new covenant would also provide a way for believers to have an intimate relationship with God. While Jeremiah echoed several Old Testament promises (see Gen. 17:7; Exod. 6:7; Lev. 26:12), the life, death, and resurrection of the Lord Jesus opened a completely new avenue for human beings to relate to their heavenly Father. Because of the salvation the Son provided, all believers could enter into God's presence.

Many Bible interpreters divide Hebrews into two parts: 1:1–10:18 and 10:19–13:25. This division is based on a shift in the author's emphasis that begins at 10:19, where the author's heavy doctrinal teaching was, for the most part, concluded. Now he instructed his readers on how to apply and live out the doctrines of the Christian faith that he had taught them up to this point in his letter. Based on the Son's saving work at Calvary, the author reminded his readers that they could now enter the Father's presence. To many of the Hebrews, this may have been a bold statement. As far as they had known, only the Jewish high priest was permitted into the most holy place. Yet the author issued an open invitation to all believers to confidently enter the presence of God because of the "blood of Jesus."

The author explained that the access the Son inaugurated into the Father's presence was "new and living" (vs. 20). The way was fresh in that it was based on the new covenant established by Jesus' sacrifice. And it was always present because it depended on the Son Himself, our eternally living Lord. In Jesus' day, the separating curtain between the holy place and the most holy place in the Jerusalem temple was 60 feet high by 30 feet wide and about 5 inches thick. Obviously, such a curtain could not have been torn easily, and yet when Jesus died, "the curtain of the temple was torn in two from top to bottom" (Matt. 27:51; see also Mark 15:38; Luke 23:45). In one sense, until that curtain was torn, access into God's presence had been limited to the Jewish high priest. But just as that curtain was torn, so Jesus' body was broken on the cross for us. As viewed symbolically by the author of Hebrews, the Son's sacrificial death was the way by which all believers were given access to the Father.

B. Recognizing Our Great High Priest: vss. 21-22

And since we have a great priest over the house of God, let us draw near to God with a sincere heart in full assurance of faith, having our hearts sprinkled to cleanse us from a guilty conscience and having our bodies washed with pure water.

Not only do we have a spiritual sacrifice enabling us to enter the Father's presence, but we also have a great High Priest "over the house of God" (Heb. 10:21). Scripture reveals that the Son of God became a human being so that He could purchase our salvation through His death on the cross. Nonetheless, He still reigned supreme over all God's people. The author of the epistle had made it clear that after the Son completed His work of salvation, He returned to heaven, where He now sat at the place of highest honor, namely, the right hand of God the Father (see 1:3). From there the Son interceded for us before the Father.

In light of what Jesus had done for believers, the author urged his readers to be proactive in living for the Messiah. Because of our provisions from the Son and our position in Him, we should claim what He has promised to us. In essence, the writer said that Jesus' work of salvation should spur His people into action. Moreover, in the exhortations that followed, the author numbered himself with his readers. Indeed, five times in 10:22-25 he used the phrase "let us" to introduce ways in which all believers were to respond to the Messiah's work.

The author invited his readers to draw near to God, and he encouraged them to do so with a "sincere heart" (vs. 22) and with the "full assurance" that "faith" brought. The author knew that it was important for God's people to be right inwardly when they entered the Father's holy presence. Therefore, the author stressed that only through faith in the Son could the redeemed be made acceptable and "draw near" to the Lord. (Lesson 2 provides a fuller discussion of what faith means.) Under the old covenant, the priests were made ritually pure by being sprinkled with blood. The writer made use of this Old Testament imagery when he said that believers were cleansed by having their "hearts sprinkled" and their "bodies washed." In this analogy, some think the author was referring to water baptism, while others say he meant an inner spiritual cleansing of the conscience from the guilt of wrongdoing. In either case, when we trust in the Son, our sins are pardoned and we are free to commune with the Father.

C. Holding Resolutely to the Hope We Confess: vs. 23

Let us hold unswervingly to the hope we profess, for he who promised is faithful.

The author of Hebrews encouraged his readers to hold firmly to the "hope" (10:23) in the Son they confessed. The writer also urged them to do so without doubt or hesitation. They could depend on God, for He was resolutely faithful to His promises. Therefore, even when believers were tempted to give up their Christian beliefs and return to their former ways of thinking and acting, they were to resist such enticements by confidently waiting for the fulfillment of God's promises.

D. Encouraging One Another to Be Faithful: vss. 24-25

And let us consider how we may spur one another on toward love and good deeds. Let us not give up meeting together, as some are in the habit of doing, but let us encourage one another—and all the more as you see the Day approaching.

The author of Hebrews encouraged his readers to give thought to how they could help one another be loving servants of the Son. The Greek noun translated "spur" (Heb. 10:24) is the same word from which is derived the English word *paroxysm*, which refers to a fit or tantrum. Acts 15:39 is the only other place in the New Testament where this Greek noun occurs. It describes how Paul and Barnabas sharply disagreed over whether to take John Mark on another missionary journey. Concerning the writer of Hebrews, he told his readers to provoke their fellow believers into loving each other and exasperate them (in a manner of speaking) toward doing good works. Admittedly, this would not be easy for them to do. Even so, they had plenty of incentive when they realized how much external pressure they encountered to renounce the Savior.

Outside influences were so corrosive that some of these believers were beginning to abandon their corporate times of worship. Verse 25 is often used out of context by those anxious to goad Christians into regular church attendance. Certainly, we should not give up meeting together. However, those to whom the author of Hebrews was referring were not just missing a worship service to go fishing on a nice summer Sunday. Rather, as verses 26-31 make clear, they were nonparticipants in church who were in danger of apostatizing.

The latter circumstance is why the author of Hebrews exhorted his readers to get in the habit of encouraging each other. They were especially to do so as "the Day" approached. Interpreters are unsure as to the writer's intent here. Some think he meant the coming destruction of Jerusalem, which occurred in A.D. 70 (see Matt. 24:1-2; Mark 13:1-2; Luke 21:5-6). Others believe he meant the day of judgment (see 1 Cor. 3:13). Whichever is the case, the author's main intent was to ensure that his readers were accountable to each other by urging one another along in the faith. Interestingly, Hebrews 10:22-24 contains the often repeated trio of Christian characteristics—"faith" (vs. 22), "hope" (vs. 23), and "love" (vs. 24; compare 1 Cor. 13:13; Col. 1:4-5; and 1 Thess. 5:8).

II. RECOGNIZING THE DANGER OF APOSTASY: HEBREWS 10:26-31

A. Willfully Persisting in Sin: vss. 26-27

If we deliberately keep on sinning after we have received the knowledge of the truth, no sacrifice for sins is left, but only a fearful expectation of judgment and of raging fire that will consume the enemies of God.

The Letter to the Hebrews was directed to believers who endured adverse circumstances and challenges to their faith (see 10:32-34). In the epistle, the author sought to encourage them to live wholeheartedly for the Lord Jesus. Evidently, some professing Jewish Christians who received this letter were on the brink of relinquishing their commitment to the Messiah. They were tempted to abandon the church and reintegrate fully into the Jewish synagogue worship of the day. In response to their situation, the writer urged them to remain firm in their Christian faith. From the text of this letter, we can surmise that these recipients were confronting a stark choice. Should they persist in following Jesus of Nazareth, or should they renounce their Christian beliefs and settle into a more conventional lifestyle? The author admonished them to make the best decision, namely, to persevere in their faith in the Son.

The author had written a warning against apostasy in 6:4-6, and he returned to that theme again in 10:26-31. Some claim that the people cited in these sets of verses were individuals who merely professed to be believers, not genuine Christians who later defected. Others maintain that these individuals were genuine believers who later lost their faith. Yet another view is that the people in mind were genuine believers who spiritually lapsed but didn't lose their faith.

In 10:26, the writer alluded to the sacrificial system under the old covenant, which made offerings for those who sinned unintentionally (see Num. 15:22-29; Heb. 5:2). For all that, no sacrifice was prescribed for those who sinned defiantly or blasphemously (see Num. 15:30-31). In a similar way, apostasy was a deliberate defection from the living God. Some equate apostasy with the unpardonable sin (see Mark 3:22-30). Others say it occurs when people believe for a while but fall away in a time of testing (see Luke 8:13). Still others say it happens when people make a shipwreck of their faith (see 1 Tim. 1:19-20), when people turn completely away from God (see Heb. 3:12), or when those who have known the way of righteousness turn their backs on it (see 2 Peter 2:20-22).

Those tempted with committing apostasy were people who understood the nature of Jesus' saving work, had been active in the church, and yet rejected the Messiah. By continuing their deliberate sin of renouncing the Lord, they were left with no other "sacrifice" (Heb. 10:26) for their transgressions. In essence, they had spurned their only means of redemption and therefore had no other person to whom they could appeal for forgiveness. The writer's words were filled with warnings of God's wrathful "judgment" (vs. 27). The author referred to the latter as a "fearful expectation" and a "raging fire" that would incinerate those who opposed God (see Isa. 26:11; Zeph. 1:18). In short, apostates would be punished for bearing sins for which they refused to be pardoned.

B. Callously Spurning the Messiah: vss. 28-29

Anyone who rejected the law of Moses died without mercy on the testimony of two or three witnesses. How much more severely do you think a man deserves to be punished who has trampled the Son of God under foot, who has treated as an unholy thing the blood of the covenant that sanctified him, and who has insulted the Spirit of grace?

In Hebrews 10:28-29, the author used an illustration from the Old Testament to emphasize the seriousness of the apostates' situation. In particular, those who rejected the Mosaic law were executed "without mercy" (vs. 28) based on the "testimony" offered by "two or three witnesses" (see Deut. 17:6). The writer reasoned that since such severity existed under the old covenant, even more severity under the new covenant would fall on those who were guilty of doing the following: treating the "Son of God" (Heb. 10:29) with contempt; profaning the Messiah's blood, which He shed to purify the apostates' from sin; and insulting the Spirit, who brought God's mercy to the defectors.

Previously, in 6:6, the writer warned that there was no way for those who fell away "to be brought back to repentance." Some think the author meant that repentance in such cases was "impossible" (vs. 4) for humans, but not for God. Others say the author meant that repentance was out of the question as long as the mutineers continued in their defiant defection. Still others assert that the writer literally meant what he said. In other words, it was an absolute impossibility for individuals to repent again after having enjoyed the Lord's saving grace (see vss. 4-5). In that way the latter interpretation equates falling away with blasphemy against the Holy Spirit (see Matt. 12:32; Mark 3:29). By renouncing the Son, the apostates crucified Him "all over again" (Heb. 6:6) and subjected Him to "public disgrace." In essence, those who did this demonstrated that they had come to despise the fact that the Messiah died for their sins.

C. Recoiling from the Prospect of God's Judgment: vss. 30-31

For we know him who said, "It is mine to avenge; I will repay," and again, "The Lord will judge his people." It is a dreadful thing to fall into the hands of the living God.

The author of Hebrews appealed to the Old Testament to reinforce his assertions. The first quotation in Hebrews 10:30 is from Deuteronomy 32:35, in which Moses said that God's vengeance against His enemies was a divine prerogative. The second quotation was from Deuteronomy 32:36 and Psalm 135:14. The writer of Hebrews wanted to leave no doubt in his readers' minds about God's intent to punish sinners. In case his readers did not yet regard God's judgment with proper trepidation, the writer appended a final dire warning. He said it was a terrifying prospect to be judged by the "living God" (10:31). The dread, of course, was for the unbeliever. Christians looked forward to receiving God's mercy and grace. But for a hardened, incorrigible apostate, "falling into the hands" of the eternal Lord would indeed be a horrible experience.

Discussion Questions

1. Why is it possible for believers to enter God's presence with confidence?
2. In what sense is Jesus the believers' great High Priest?
3. What are some excuses believers might give for not wanting to worship with other Christians?
4. What arguments did the writer of Hebrews use to urge His readers to remain faithful to the Savior?
5. What are some ways believers can deal with temptations they face to turn away from, rather than follow, the Lord?

Contemporary Application

We can never talk too much about Jesus. We learn the Good News and believe it so that we can receive forgiveness and eternal life. But how much do we learn about Jesus after that? How much time do we give to studying the four Gospels and the application of the salvation narrative in the epistles?

It has often been said that cults thrive on recruiting poorly educated Christians. Without a growing knowledge of Jesus, people can easily drift away and be deceived by false teachers. That danger is real and the best prevention is continual study of and reflection on the glories of Christ.

To ignore Jesus is to expose ourselves to mortal danger. Diligent study, praise, and testimony keep us fresh in our walk with Jesus. We need to depend on Him every day just as much as we need our daily swim, hike, or stint on the treadmill. In turn, He enables us to remain faithful to Him regardless of the circumstances.

Like the saints who are mentioned in the Old Testament, we might struggle from time to time with doubts. Instead of allowing uncertainty to control us, we should examine our fears in the light of what Scripture teaches. The truth of God's Word can calm us when we are feeling anxious about something. And the Lord's faithfulness to us and others can encourage us when we are going through difficult times.

Faith Is Assurance

Scripture

Background Scripture: *Hebrews 11:1-7; Psalm 46*
Scripture Lesson: *Hebrews 11:1-3, 6; Psalm 46:1-3, 8-11*
Key Verse: *Now faith is being sure of what we hope for and certain of what we do not see.* Hebrews 11:1.
Scripture Lesson for Children: *Mark 10:13-16; Psalm 23*
Key Verse for Children: *"Anyone who will not receive the kingdom of God like a little child will never enter it."* Mark 10:15.

Lesson Aim

To stress the importance of being strong in our faith in the Lord.

Lesson Setting

Psalm 46:1-3, 8-11
Time: Written sometime before the exile (586 B.C.)
Place: Jerusalem

Hebrews 11:1-3, 6
Time: Before A.D. 70
Place: Possibly Rome

Lesson Outline

Faith Is Assurance
   I. Faith Described and Exemplified: Hebrews 11:1-3, 6
      A. *Hope and Certainty: vs. 1*
      B. *Ancient Testimonies: vs. 2*
      C. *Creation of the Universe: vs. 3*
      D. *Importance of Faith: vs. 6*
  II. God's Readiness to Help the Faithful: Ps. 46:1-3, 8-11
      A. *Stability Found in God: vs. 1*
      B. *Convulsions within Nature: vss. 2-3*
      C. *God's All-Powerful Presence: vss. 8-9*
      D. *God's Reassuring Presence: vss. 10-11*

Introduction for Adults

Topic: *Steadfast Confidence*

How much faith is enough to constitute steadfast confidence in God? Biblical insight into this matter can be found in Hebrews 11 and Psalm 46. The Old and New Testaments never describe faith as the lever to demand things from God. Rather, faith is exemplified as enduring trust in the Creator's promises, which transcend the here and now.

Faith drives us to believe that biblical values are the most important. Also, we focus our hope on the eternal city of the sovereign King. While that heavenly abode is our enduring reward, we live by faith now according to God's standards of justice and holiness.

This means that our resolute trust in the Lord moves us out from the proclamation of the Gospel to help people in need. We bring help in the here and now because our hope is firm in God's promises. Faith prompts obedience, hope, love, and hard work.

Introduction for Youth

Topic: *What Is Faith?*

In his novel *A Walk to Remember*, Nicholas Sparks vividly tells how Jamie, a high school senior, brings an entirely new perspective into the life of her boyfriend. She does this not with high-pressure religion but by living out her own faith in God.

Eventually, not only Landon but also his family and his pals come to a new appreciation of the power of faith in the rough and tumble of high school life in a small town. Jamie moved them not by her preaching but by her living faith.

The possibilities of similar responses to faith arise almost every day. If our faith means anything (see Heb. 11:1, 6), we will put it on the line in front of our friends. We need to talk with one another about how to do this tactfully and lovingly. We need to talk about how to handle ridicule and possible loss of friends.

When our faith permeates our values and our conduct, others will see the difference. Some will be changed, and some will not. But we are called to be faithful at all times and in all places.

Concepts for Children

Topic: *Childlike Faith*

1. Jesus enjoyed spending time with children.
2. Jesus' loving and gentle touch helped children know that He cared for them.
3. Jesus' followers were not happy that He gave children His attention.
4. Jesus said that even children, when they believe, can enter God's kingdom.
5. Jesus wants us to believe in Him so that we can become part of His spiritual family.

Lesson Commentary

I. Faith Described and Exemplified: Hebrews 11:1-3, 6

A. Hope and Certainty: vs. 1

Now faith is being sure of what we hope for and certain of what we do not see.

In Hebrews 10:38, the writer quoted Habakkuk 2:4 to stress that the righteous person lives by faith. Based on that statement, Hebrews 11 is devoted to portraying the lives of Old Testament heroes who lived by faith. As a result, chapter 11 is probably the best-loved portion in Hebrews and is often called "The Hall of Faith." It furnishes us with brief biographies of belief and encourages us to fortify our faith in God as many who have gone before us have done. The original readers of Hebrews may have wondered if it would be easier simply to fade back into their former Jewish traditions and religious practices. To them the author gave a description of biblical faith. He said that faith is a present and continuing reality. It is the confident assurance that gives substance to what we "hope for" (vs. 1). Faith is also the evidence for our conviction of the certainty of "what we do not see."

In this discussion, "faith" is a key theological term. In one sense, it refers to a person's trust in God. In another sense, it is used in the New Testament to refer to the body of truths held by followers of Christ. Belief, or faith, can be understood as having four recognizable elements. First is cognition, an awareness of the facts; second is comprehension, an understanding of the facts; third is conviction, an acceptance of the facts; and fourth is commitment, trust in a trustworthy object. Popular opinion sees faith as irrational. It is supposedly believing in something even when your mind tells you not to. In contrast, the biblical concept of faith includes both reason and experience. Such faith, however, is not limited to what we can see. It makes unseen spiritual realities perceivable, not by willing them into existence, but by a settled conviction that what God has said about them is true.

B. Ancient Testimonies: vs. 2

This is what the ancients were commended for.

The writer implied by his remarks that there are realities for which there is no visible evidence; and yet those realities are no less true. It is through faith that we know those realities exist, especially God's promise of salvation, which cannot be physically seen or felt. How, then, can one recognize the presence of faith in the life of a believer? The author appealed to a long list of biblical examples to answer this question. God commended them precisely because of their faith in Him (Heb. 11:2). There are two problems some people have with the past. They either disregard it or forget it. Hebrews 11 stresses the importance of remembering the past and living by faith. We discover from the testimony of other believers who have gone before us that we can remain faithful to the Lord—despite the hardships we might be experiencing—because He will remain faithful to us.

C. Creation of the Universe: vs. 3

By faith we understand that the universe was formed at God's command, so that what is seen was not made out of what was visible.

The writer said it was the faith of the Old Testament saints that made them pleasing to God. Their trust in the Lord was well-founded, for He is the Creator and Ruler of the universe (see Ps. 146:6). We perceive with the mind that the temporal ages were set in order by the spoken "command" (Heb. 11:3) of God. Biblical faith also enables us to recognize and accept the truth that what is seen was made out of what cannot be seen. Despite all appearances to the contrary and despite all of the naturalistic explanations about the origin of the universe, God gave existence to the cosmos. We have nothing but the written Word of God to explain how life first began, and we believe what it has revealed to us. In this regard, Revelation 4:11 asserts that the all-powerful Lord "created all things." Furthermore, it is because of His sovereign will that they were "created" and existed.

D. Importance of Faith: vs. 6

And without faith it is impossible to please God, because anyone who comes to him must believe that he exists and that he rewards those who earnestly seek him.

The author of Hebrews began his list of those who lived by faith with the example of Abel (11:4). Both Abel and his brother Cain brought sacrifices to the Lord. But because of Abel's faith, his sacrifice was more pleasing to God than Cain's. The Lord thus commended Abel for being a righteous person (see Gen. 4:1-16). Righteousness by faith becomes a key theme in Hebrews 11. Though the upright actions of faithful people are referred to time and again, the author implied that faith was the wellspring of their righteous acts and that God commended them for their faith (see Gen. 15:6).

Numerous conjectures have been recorded as to why Abel's sacrifice was superior to Cain's. Some think God accepted Abel's sacrifice because, as an animal offering, it involved blood, whereas Cain's, as a type of grain offering, did not. Others note that Abel's sacrifice was living and Cain's was lifeless, or that Abel's grew spontaneously and Cain's grew by human ingenuity. Perhaps the strongest reason Abel's offering was accepted and Cain's was rejected lies in the attitude of both brothers. Abel offered his sacrifice willingly, and thus his was a demonstration of faith. Hebrews 11:4 reveals that, though Abel is dead, his faith speaks to all the generations that follow him.

Verse 5 next mentions Enoch, about whom Scripture says little. Because of his faith, Enoch did "not experience death." Instead, God took him away (see Gen. 5:24). The reason is that Enoch's life "pleased God" (Heb. 11:5). The author stressed that "without faith" (vs. 6) it is impossible to enjoy the Lord's favor. Those who approach Him must first believe that He is the true and living God. Moreover, they must accept the fact that He rewards those who "earnestly seek him." Put another way, we must believe that the Lord both exists and cares for us. Here we see that faith is so foundational to the Christian life that one cannot be in a relationship with God apart from it.

II. GOD'S READINESS TO HELP THE FAITHFUL: PSALM 46:1-3, 8-11

A. Stability Found in God: vs. 1

God is our refuge and strength, an ever-present help in trouble.

Psalm 46 is one of the "Songs of Zion" (along with Pss. 48, 76, 84, 87, and 122) due to its confident affirmation of God as the faith community's source of help and strength in times of trouble. It remains debated who wrote this poem and when. It's also unclear whether the author was referring to specific events in Israel's history or was just making a general statement. One suggestion is that the deliverance of Jerusalem from Sennacherib in 701 B.C. provides the chronological setting for the psalm (see 2 Kings 18–19; Isa. 36–37). While there is nothing specific in the biblical text to support this conjecture, it remains likely that Psalm 46 was written in Jerusalem sometime before the nation's exile in 586 B.C. Additionally, the hymn maintained an enduring relevance for God's people, especially with its emphasis on Jerusalem as the royal "city of God" (vs. 4) and the epicenter of His triumphant kingdom on earth.

The psalm's heading reads "for the director of music." This suggests the piece was originally meant to be a part of the worship liturgy performed in the temple by the leader of the Levitical choir. The members of the latter included the "Sons of Korah." Korah was a Levite who, along with Dathan, Abriam, and On, participated in a failed revolt against the leadership of Moses and Aaron while the Israelites were camped in the wilderness of Paran (see Num. 16:1-49). This treasonous act notwithstanding, David later appointed some of Korah's descendants to serve as ministers of music within the tabernacle and temple (see 1 Chron. 6:31-37).

Psalm 46 is composed of three symmetrical stanzas, with each containing three verses (vss. 1-3, 4-6, and 8-10). There are also two refrains, with each containing one verse (vss. 7 and 11). One proposed musical arrangement has the members of the Levitical choir singing the opening stanza (vss. 1-3) and the two refrains (vss. 7, 11), while the music director sang the second and third stanzas (vss. 4-6 and 8-10). Part of the superscription says "according to alamoth," in which the last term literally means "young women." However, the specific connotation here remains uncertain. One possibility is that "alamoth" designates a specific style of music—for example, one that called for female voices singing in the soprano range (see 1 Chron. 15:20). Another suggestion is that the term referred to young women who played timbrels (similar to modern-day tambourines) as they traveled with a procession of singers and other musicians heading to the temple for worship.

In Psalm 46:1, "refuge" translates a Hebrew noun that denotes a place of shelter from rain, storm, or other perils. Also, "strength" renders a noun that points to what is fortified and secure. Together these words depict God as the believers' impenetrable defense. Regardless of the adverse situation or anguishing circumstance, the Lord is always ready to help. Psalm 9:9 likewise declares that God provides safety for the oppressed and is a refuge in times of trouble. Moreover, we learn in 37:39 that the Lord protects the faithful even in the most challenging dilemmas. According to 61:3, God is comparable to a strong tower where the upright may flee when danger lurks. Even when the health of believers begins to fail and their spirit weakens, the Lord empowers them to cope with seemingly overwhelming conditions (see 71:23). Because He is their place of safety, they can find rest in the shadow of the Almighty (see 91:1-2) and have their eternal needs fully met (see 142:5).

B. Convulsions within Nature: vss. 2-3

Therefore we will not fear, though the earth give way and the mountains fall into the heart of the sea, though its waters roar and foam and the mountains quake with their surging. Selah

Because the believers' stability is found in God, the faith community deliberately chooses to forsake fear and completely trust in Him. A series of convulsions of nature are described in Psalm 46:2-3. Some think these probably were meant to symbolize the ferocity of a war. Another option is that a doomsday scenario involving naturally occurring disasters is being portrayed. The latter included a violent series of earthquakes that cause the mountains (the epitome of all that is stable and enduring) to crumble into the sea (vs. 2).

Furthermore, there's a succession of massive tsunamis that cause ocean-sized tidal waves to inundate the land. The "roar and foam" (vs. 3) of water is so intense that it even seems to cause the mountains to be shaken by the violence. The creation myths of many ancient Near Eastern cultures told about gods who subdued a chaotic ocean and formed the world from it. These people viewed large bodies of water as evil. While Israelite religion denied the reality of such myths, God's people nonetheless were familiar with them. Thus it was natural for the psalmists to compare encroaching evil with water that seems to engulf the land.

The Jordan River follows the Great Rift Valley, which is a fault in the earth's crust. Consequently, from earliest times, Israel has been subject to earthquakes. The psalmist evidently drew on his experience with such events. Seismic activity is terrifying enough in our day, even when we understand its cause. Earthquakes must have been far more unsettling at the time Psalm 46 was composed. Nevertheless, the poet said the people of God trust in Him and refuse to succumb to fear. Even though the waves may roar and the surging waters may rise, the Lord sits enthroned in majesty and watches over His people to preserve them (see 93:3-4). In 3:5-6, David declared that he would not be afraid of a multitude of people who attacked him from all directions, for the Lord sustained him.

C. God's All-Powerful Presence: vss. 8-9

Come and see the works of the LORD, the desolations he has brought on the earth. He makes wars cease to the ends of the earth; he breaks the bow and shatters the spear, he burns the shields with fire.

The imagery of upheaval introduced in Psalm 46:2-3 reappears in verse 6. This time, however, it is used with respect to nations and kingdoms of the world being locked in mortal conflict. Fallen humanity and its leaders might rage, but their dominions are doomed to one day fail. Moreover, when chaos ensues, their fiefdoms will crumble. God is the cause of this turmoil. The poet depicts His thunderous shout as the battle cry uttered by a mighty warrior that terrifies the nations and causes the kingdoms to be shaken (see Pss. 18:13; 68:33). In point of fact, at the sound of His voice, the entire planet dissolves (see Amos 9:5).

Psalm 46:7 reveals God to be full of power and grace. The verse is literally translated "the LORD of hosts is with us." The poet was indicating that God is like a mighty warrior-king who leads the armies of heaven into battle on behalf of His chosen people (see 24:10). The name translated "God of Jacob" (46:7) evokes the memory of one of the nation's greatest ancestors. The Lord—who graciously chose Jacob for a blessing instead of his older brother, Esau—protects the faith community (20:1). The Hebrew noun translated "fortress" (46:7) refers to a high place or elevated stronghold. The imagery is that of a mountaintop citadel that cannot be overcome by an army of invaders (see 9:9; 18:2). Because the mighty God is on the side of the upright, they experience His gracious hand of protection.

The final portion of Psalm 46 invites us to use the eyes of our imagination to examine the aftermath of a tremendous battle. The field is strewed with the broken and smoking instruments of warfare. This is a scene of terrible destruction. But this is not just the result of one group of armed fighters overcoming another. God Himself entered the fray on the side of His people. Thus the desolation on the battlefield is His work (vs. 8). He brought peace, but He did it by carrying the battle to a decisive end. This scene cannot represent only the conclusion of a battle in Israel's history, for the psalm says God brings an end to "wars" (vs. 9) that occur throughout the planet. Likewise, God destroys whatever fighters use in combat, including bows, spears, and shields. Most likely, the scene is a preview of God's end-time victory over evil.

D. God's Reassuring Presence: vss. 10-11

"Be still, and know that I am God; I will be exalted among the nations, I will be exalted in the earth." The LORD Almighty is with us; the God of Jacob is our fortress. Selah

Psalm 46 envisions a throng of hostile nations determined to wipe out God's chosen people. The redeemed, though, have nothing to fear, for the Lord protects them. Indeed, above the din of earth's wicked people, God cries "Be still" (vs. 10), meaning "Enough! Stop!" He calls all people to recognize Him as God, and He confidently declares that He will be exalted as the supreme King throughout the entire globe (see Pss. 18:46; 99:2; 113:4; 138:6). Despite the forces of evil attempting to spread chaos in the world, the Lord of heaven's armies remains unchallenged in His rule. Understandably, the righteous consider their Creator to be like a "fortress" (46:11), that is, a lofty stronghold where they find protection (see 9:9; 18:2).

Discussion Questions

1. What is the significance for you of the description of faith in Hebrews 11:1?
2. Why do you think our faith in the Son pleases the Father?
3. How has God been like a mighty warrior to you when you felt threatened by others?
4. Why is it important to look to God for hope when life feels chaotic?
5. In what ways can believers contribute to God's exaltation in the world?

Contemporary Application

Many of us have gained spiritual benefit, either directly or indirectly, from the ministry and writings of John Wesley. Wesley first exercised faith in Jesus while attending a small group where the leader was reading aloud from the writings of Martin Luther. Martin Luther, in turn, moved toward salvation while reading the Book of Romans. (It was Luther's commentary on Romans that Wesley heard on the night of his "heart-warming" salvation experience.)

In a similar way, the writer of Hebrews found his faith increased as he thought about Old Testament figures. The writer shared their accounts with his readers, hoping that the ancient examples of faith would inspire first-century believers. Today, our faith can be strengthened as we read the Letter to the Hebrews. Just as the Old Testament heroes of faith trusted and obeyed God, so must we. And as Psalm 46 makes clear, our obedience to the will of God should impact every area of our lives—from the office to the home.

Stepping out in faith requires our readiness to obey God's will. This, in turn, can lead us down unexpected paths. At first this might seem scary to us. But then we come to see that the sovereign Ruler of the universe knows what is best for us. We learn through life experiences to wait on His timing when it comes to enjoying the blessings of faith. Some of these come in this life, but most are received in eternity. One example of the clarity of God's will for us is His desire that we live holy lives and seek His guidance in every circumstance. Regardless of how many options lay before us, it is always the Creator's will that we act in harmony with His Word.

Faith Is Endurance

Scripture

Background Scripture: *Hebrews 12:1-11*
Scripture Lesson: *Hebrews 12:1-11*
Key Verses: *Let us throw off everything that hinders and the sin that so easily entangles, and let us run with perseverance the race marked out for us. Let us fix our eyes on Jesus, the author and perfecter of our faith. Hebrews 12:1-2.*
Scripture Lesson for Children: *Hebrews 12:1-11*
Key Verses for Children: *Let us run with perseverance the race marked out for us. Let us fix our eyes on Jesus, the author and perfecter of our faith. Hebrews 12:1-2.*

Lesson Aim

To become more holy as a result of experiencing God's discipline.

Lesson Setting

Time: Before A.D. *70*
Place: Possibly Rome

Lesson Outline

Faith Is Endurance

I. Running the Race: Hebrews 12:1-3
   A. *Persevering in the Faith: vs. 1*
   B. *Keeping Our Mind on Jesus: vss. 2-3*

II. Accepting God's Discipline: Hebrews 12:4-11
   A. *The Chastening of the Lord: vss. 4-6*
   B. *The Analogy of Human Parents: vss. 7-9*
   C. *The Benefit of God's Discipline: vss. 10-11*

Introduction for Adults

Topic: *Steadfast Fortitude*

A minister shared his experience as a small boy when he went to his first symphony orchestra concert. He marveled at the musicians as they came onto the stage and sat down. They all seemed so different. Some were young, while others were old. Some were thin and others were big.

One by one, the musicians picked up their instruments and began to play a few notes. It sounded like a dozen cats fighting on a hot night in the middle of the city. None of them were playing the same notes, let alone the same music. Then the boy saw a man in a long black coat walk to the center of the stage. When he raised a long, thin, black stick, the noise immediately stopped. With a sweep of this man's hand, the musicians began to play again and the sound this time was incredibly beautiful.

Jesus represents the Conductor who gives order and meaning to our lives. He is our Leader and Guide who watches over and provides for us so that we have the steadfast fortitude to make it through our life journey. Jesus alone is sufficiently qualified, capable, and trustworthy to do this for us. And that is why He is to be the sole focus of our faith (see Heb. 12:1-3).

Introduction for Youth

Topic: *Endurance to Run the Race*

For decades, athletes and scientists agreed that no human being would ever run a mile in less than four minutes. And their predictions proved accurate. No one did. But one young man believed that he could go beyond that limit. On May 6, 1954, Roger Bannister broke the four-minute barrier. Now, among world-class male runners, several athletes beat Bannister's one-time record in nearly every mile race. But it took someone of Bannister's determination to be the first. He set the pattern. He became a great leader whose example others follow.

This week's Scripture text reminds us that Jesus is the best example of what it means to be a great leader. As the supreme commander of our salvation, He endured the shame of the cross. And though the authorities executed Jesus as a criminal, the Father raised Him from the dead so that all who trust in Him can have eternal life. As the pioneer and perfecter of our faith, Christ alone demonstrates that He is a leader who can be trusted.

Concepts for Children

Topic: *Following Jesus' Example*

1. Jesus showed us how to live for Him.
2. Jesus wants us to follow His example.
3. Sometimes it might seem hard for us to live for Jesus.
4. Jesus is always present to help us live for Him.
5. We can thank Jesus for giving us the strength to do what is right.

Lesson Commentary

I. RUNNING THE RACE: HEBREWS 12:1-3

A. Persevering in the Faith: vs. 1

Therefore, since we are surrounded by such a great cloud of witnesses, let us throw off everything that hinders and the sin that so easily entangles, and let us run with perseverance the race marked out for us.

Chapter divisions, which were placed in the Bible centuries after it was written and compiled, can prove misleading. For instance, Hebrews 12:1-3 piggybacks perfectly onto chapter 11. In fact, the first word in 12:1 ("Therefore") alerts us to the fact that what we are reading proceeds directly from what comes before it. The writer said, "Therefore, since we are surrounded by such a great cloud of witnesses." Presumably, the witnesses were people of faith mentioned in chapter 11.

The term rendered "witness" in the Bible is filled with significance. The Greek word is *martus* and comes from the verb *martureo,* which means "to testify" or "to bear witness." The idea is one of affirming what he or she has seen or experienced. The New Testament writers sometimes applied *martus* to those believers in Christ who were attesting to their faith while enduring persecution. Thus, in time such believers came to be known as *martyrs,* that is, those who voluntarily suffered death as the penalty for their allegiance to Christ.

The writers of the New Testament often used *martureo* to refer to believers who personally testified to Jesus' work on earth, regardless of whether suffering was present. John noted the various witnesses who testified about Jesus. These included God the Father (John 5:31-32, 37; 8:18), the Holy Spirit (15:26), Jesus Himself (8:14, 18), Scripture (5:39), Jesus' own works (5:36), John the Baptizer (1:34), and Jesus' disciples (15:27). The concept of witness is prominent not only in the New Testament but also in the Old Testament. For example, Jacob used a pile of rocks to serve as a reminder that God was a witness to the patriarch's agreement with Laban (see Gen. 31:45-50). In addition, the Mosaic law required that at least two witnesses had to support a charge of wrongdoing (see Num. 35:30; Deut. 17:6).

This background information helps to clarify the reference in Hebrews 12:1 to the huge crowd of witnesses testifying to the life of faith. From the perspective of runners in a stadium, the spectators all around them in the stands might look something like a cloud of people. In a sense, Christians also have a cloud of people watching us: the saints in heaven. As "witnesses," they watch us and cheer us on in our race. They are also motivating examples of faithfulness.

In the ancient world, runners in a race competed without any clothing. They would strip themselves of anything that might weigh them down or entangle their arms and legs. Similarly, the Hebrew Christians were to rid themselves of every encumbrance that might prevent them from living for the Redeemer. While some of these hindrances were not inherently sinful (for example, longstanding religious traditions), others were. The latter included the fear of being persecuted, resentment toward others, and sexual immorality (10:38-39; 12:15-16).

In mentioning "the sin that so easily entangles" (12:1), the writer may have had in mind the danger of defection resulting from discouragement—in other words, apostasy. The presence of opposition from others tempted some first-century Christians to revert to their former way of life. In light of this possibility, the writer urged his readers to remain steadfast in their faith even when they encountered hostile forces. We are also to "run with perseverance" our race of faith. This goes to show that our spiritual race is more like a marathon than a sprint. We must have the determination and the fortitude to keep running a long time and not quit.

B. Keeping Our Mind on Jesus: vss. 2-3

Let us fix our eyes on Jesus, the author and perfecter of our faith, who for the joy set before him endured the cross, scorning its shame, and sat down at the right hand of the throne of God. Consider him who endured such opposition from sinful men, so that you will not grow weary and lose heart.

As was noted earlier, the author of Hebrews used an athletic metaphor in 12:1. Regardless of the nature of the race, every event has a definite goal, namely, a tape to break. The wise runner is one who keeps his or her eyes on the finish line and doesn't look back. As Christians, we, too, have a goal—we are heading for the Savior. And so the writer of Hebrews urged, "Let us fix our eyes on Jesus" (vs. 2). After all, the Redeemer is "the author and perfecter of our faith." While we must persevere in our running, it is Jesus who enables us to both begin and complete the race.

One way Jesus helps us to start, continue, and finish our race is by being the ideal example. He is the champion runner of the ages. As we struggle in our race, we can know that He has already been there and has shown that the race can be won. Just as we are to focus our attention on Jesus, so He kept His eyes fixed on the joy of completing the mission the Father had given to Him. And just as we are to persevere in the race marked out for us, so Jesus "endured the cross, scorning its shame."

The cross brought great suffering and disgrace, but the Son kept in mind that the glory of enduring the cross would be much greater. Despite facing the highest hurdle anybody has ever had—the cross—Jesus successfully completed His race. And instead of receiving the wreath of leaves awarded to a victorious runner in the ancient world, the Son was rewarded with supreme authority. He took His seat in the place of highest honor beside His Father's throne in heaven (see 1:3).

The writer of Hebrews, knowing that his readers would sometimes feel weary and lose heart because of opposition, urged them to reflect earnestly on what Jesus experienced (12:3). Throughout the course of His earthly ministry, the Lord had to endure terrible opposition from sinners, and yet He persevered until He won the victory. Taking inspiration from the Messiah, we can persevere in our race no matter what obstacles wicked people may place in our way. Jesus, the pioneer and perfecter of our faith, is our supreme example.

II. Accepting God's Discipline: Hebrews 12:4-11

A. The Chastening of the Lord: vss. 4-6

In your struggle against sin, you have not yet resisted to the point of shedding your blood. And you have forgotten that word of encouragement that addresses you as sons: "My son, do not make light of the Lord's discipline, and do not lose heart when he rebukes you, because the Lord disciplines those he loves, and he punishes everyone he accepts as a son."

The Hebrew Christians had endured persecution for their faith (Heb. 10:32-34), yet they had not suffered to the extent that Jesus had. They also had not gone through the horrors cataloged in 11:35-38. It is clarifying to note that the location of the people to whom this letter was written is almost as uncertain as who wrote it. There is included in the epistle no description of the recipient church, and only a few clues vaguely identify the letter's readers.

Some point to the author's greetings from "those from Italy" (13:24) as evidence that the epistle's recipients were Italians, perhaps living in Rome. Using the same phrase, however, others say the greeting is evidence that the letter was written from Italy. There is no way of verifying either interpretation. The believers who received this epistle evidently had faced adversity, though no one had yet met martyrdom (10:32-34; 12:4). Based on the topics addressed by the letter—sacrifices, the role of priests, and the function of the tabernacle, for instance—they were Jews who had converted to Christianity. And yet they may have been contemplating reverting to their Jewish traditions rather than maturing in their faith in the Messiah.

Like their Hebrew Christian predecessors, believers living from the first through the third centuries A.D. were repeatedly slandered and accused of wrongdoing by their opponents. In such an environment the behavior of Christians greatly affected the spread of the Gospel. In his work entitled *Annals,* the Roman historian Tacitus (A.D. 56–120) described Christianity as a "deadly superstition." He also wrote that the Emperor Nero (A.D. 37–68), in an attempt to silence rumors that he was responsible for starting the fire that destroyed much of Rome, blamed and punished Christians living in the city.

The early church leader Tertullian (A.D. 160–225) noted in his writings some of the false charges leveled against believers by their opponents: "Police and informers bring up accusations against the Christians as sex criminals and murderers, blasphemers and traitors, enemies of public life, desecraters of temples, and criminals against the religion of Rome." It was not until the reign of Constantine in the early fourth century A.D. that Christianity was officially sanctioned by the Roman empire. Prior to that time Christianity was held in suspicion by many government officials.

Pliny the Younger (A.D. 61–113), the governor of the Roman province of Bithynia in Asia Minor from A.D. 111–113, wanted to know what his official stance should be toward Christians. He thus wrote a letter to the Emperor Trajan (A.D. 53–117) in which he asked for instructions. Pliny's letter reveals the kind of attitude that many Roman officials had toward early Christians: "I thought it all the more necessary, then, to find out finally what was true by putting to torture two girls who were called serving girls. But I found nothing but a depraved and enormous superstition. Consequently, I adjourned the investigation and turned to you for advice."

The author of Hebrews realized that his harassed and beleaguered readers were tempted to return to their former way of life. Even so, the writer urged them not to give up. He reminded them that no matter how difficult their situation had become, it had not yet led to bloodshed. Expressed differently, none of them had died for their faith (12:4). A schoolmaster was once asked what would be the ideal curriculum for children. He answered, "Any program of worthwhile studies, so long as all of it is hard and some of it is unpleasant." The original readers of Hebrews had been experiencing what was hard and unpleasant in their "struggle against sin." Thankfully, however, none of them had so far been martyred.

Despite the fact that their struggle was not as bad as it could be, the Hebrews were being tempted to look on their suffering in the wrong way. Once more, the author referred to some Old Testament Scripture to validate his point. This time he focused on Proverbs 3:11-12. This passage teaches those being disciplined by the Lord to respond properly. We are not to err by making light of it. Neither are we to err by losing heart, taking the experience too seriously. Instead, we should recognize that discipline from the Lord is a sign that He loves us and considers us His spiritual children (Heb. 12:5-6). And therefore, we should accept His discipline and pay attention to what He's trying to teach us through it.

At first, it might be hard for us to accept the truth that God's discipline of us is a sign of His love. We might mistakenly assume that His chastisement is solely to punish us, not educate us. Nevertheless, His foremost purpose is to bring about our character formation. The Lord cares for us so much that He corrects us for our eternal good. The suffering He allows us to experience can cause us to stop and take another look at our lives. It can force us to reevaluate our priorities and put first things first. Through God's hand of discipline, we learn to renounce sin in our lives and to become more holy in our conduct and grow in Christlikeness.

B. The Analogy of Human Parents: vss. 7-9

Endure hardship as discipline; God is treating you as sons. For what son is not disciplined by his father? If you are not disciplined (and everyone undergoes discipline), then you are illegitimate children and not true sons. Moreover, we have all had human fathers who disciplined us and we respected them for it. How much more should we submit to the Father of our spirits and live!

The aim of the author of Hebrews was to make his audience aware of suffering as a teaching tool used by God; in other words, discipline is pedagogical. This insight makes the writer's statement in the first part of 12:7 all the more forceful. Believers are to patiently go through divine "discipline," for the Lord is treating them as His spiritual children. Since the dawn of time, good parents have been actively involved in disciplining their children. Likewise, God disciplines all His spiritual children.

In the first century A.D., many Roman nobles had illegitimate children to whom they gave financial support but made little effort to educate. Rigorous training was reserved for the children of the aristocrat's legal wife, for her offspring would bear the family name and inherit the nobleman's estate. When God subjects us to His hand of discipline, He shows that He cares even more for us, who are co-heirs with Christ (see Rom. 8:17). Also, when the Lord corrects us, it demonstrates that we are legitimate members of His heavenly family (Heb. 12:8).

Notice the way in which the writer argued from the lesser reality to the greater reality ("how much more")—from human parents upward to the heavenly Father (vs. 9). If we respect our earthly parents when they discipline us, we should much more "submit to the Father of our spirits and live." Discipline by God should not cause us to think worse of Him, but rather to respect Him all the more. When He corrects us, His wise and loving purposes undergird His actions.

C. The Benefit of God's Discipline: vss. 10-11

Our fathers disciplined us for a little while as they thought best; but God disciplines us for our good, that we may share in his holiness. No discipline seems pleasant at the time, but painful. Later on, however, it produces a harvest of righteousness and peace for those who have been trained by it.

In human discipline, there is always the element of imperfection, even though our parents disciplined us as well as they knew how (Heb. 12:10). By an upgraded contrast, divine discipline is always for our eternal benefit, in order that we might "share in his holiness." God's discipline is always prudent, and we can be sure it is needed and contributes to our spiritual growth. When we submit to the Lord's hand of correction, we experience greater moral fitness. We also become increasingly conformed in every aspect of our lives to the image of Christ.

The author admitted that no discipline is pleasant while it's occurring. In fact, it's downright painful. The benefit appears only later, when it yields the fruit of "righteousness and peace" (vs. 11) by allowing us to be spiritually trained in this way. The Greek verb rendered "trained" is based on the word from which we get gymnasium. We could say discipline gives us a tough workout but helps us get into tip-top shape.

On the surface, it might seem counterintuitive to imagine that the griefs springing from tragedies, persecutions, and conflicts can have any temporal or eternal benefit. Yet Scripture teaches that God uses these hardships to prepare us to be at peace in all situations and to respond rightly to Him and other people in the face of difficulties. For instance, sufferings can teach us humility and patience. Also, through hardships we learn to trust God more and draw upon His strength to endure the trials we're experiencing.

Because God is our loving heavenly Father, He never disciplines us for sadistic reasons. And He does not enjoy seeing us experience pain. When God disciplines us, His intent is to help us grow and succeed in our walk with Christ. When we try to avoid God's discipline, we sacrifice long-term spiritual maturity for short-term ease. The real joys and victories of the Christian life will elude us, unless we yield to God's loving hand of discipline in our lives.

The writer of Hebrews, perhaps returning to the running imagery, exhorted his readers to strengthen their limp hands and feeble knees (vs. 12). Verse 13 extends the imagery by quoting from Proverbs 4:26. The recipients of the epistle were to smooth out the racetrack (in a manner of speaking) so that even the lame could get around it without falling and hurting themselves. The idea is that, as we are running our own race, we should look out for our fellow believers and try to help them succeed in their races as well.

Discussion Questions

1. In your opinion, what is the relationship between Hebrews 11 and 12?
2. What kind of weight do you think prevents believers from running their race?
3. Why is it appropriate for God to discipline us as His spiritual children?
4. In what ways has God disciplined you? How have you responded?
5. What can you do to help other believers run their race of faith better?

Contemporary Application

You have probably heard sermons in which the speaker defined *holiness* as being set apart to God for His use. The basic idea is that we belong to God and exist to do His will. Because we are His children, He disciplines us so that we might become more holy in our thinking, in our acting, and in our witness for Him.

The way we respond to God's discipline can shape our view of life. For instance, we become more worldly in our thinking if we respond to God's discipline with bitterness and anger. In contrast, we become more holy in our thinking when we respond to His discipline with humility and trust.

Our growth in holiness can enhance our witness to others. By way of example, imagine a friend at church who gets angry with you over something you said. If you respond by lashing out in anger, you could worsen the situation. But by remaining calm and respectful, you give God the opportunity to enhance your witness and move you along to spiritual maturity.

As we run the race of Christian living with perseverance, we leave an example for others to follow. We encourage them to break with sinful habits and become more Christlike in their behavior. We also spur them on to spiritual maturity. As an outcome of our marathon of faith, we not only possess the fruit of an upright life but also assist those who are coming after us to grow in godliness.

Faith Inspires Gratitude

Scripture

Background Scripture: *Hebrews 12:14-29*
Scripture Lesson: *Hebrews 12:18-29*
Key Verse: *Therefore, since we are receiving a kingdom that cannot be shaken, let us be thankful, and so worship God acceptably with reverence and awe.* Hebrews 12:28.
Scripture Lesson for Children: *Luke 10:25-37*
Key Verse for Children: *"Love the Lord your God with all your heart and with all your soul and with all your strength and with all your mind"; and, "Love your neighbor as yourself."* Luke 10:27.

Lesson Aim

To remain faithful to the Savior as we eagerly wait for His return.

Lesson Setting

Time: Before A.D. 70
Place: Possibly Rome

Lesson Outline

Faith Inspires Gratitude

   I. Mount Zion Superior to Mount Sinai: Hebrews 12:18-24
      A. *The Mountain of Fear: vss. 18-19*
      B. *The Dread of the Israelites: vss. 20-21*
      C. *The Mountain of Joy: vss. 22-24*
  II. An Unshakable Kingdom: Hebrews 12:25-29
      A. *Being Diligent to Heed the Lord: vs. 25*
      B. *Taking Away the Created Order: vss. 26-27*
      C. *Offering Worship Pleasing to God: vss. 28-29*

Introduction for Adults

Topic: *Steadfast Thanks*

The author of Hebrews wrote to believers who were encountering challenges, frustrations, and opposition to their faith. Their decision to overcome their hardships gives us hope to remain steadfast in our faith and thankful to God for the strength He provides in the midst of our difficulties.

As we overcome our afflictions, we grow stronger in our walk with Christ. These steps to maturity resemble foothills that sometimes block the view of the lofty snowcapped peaks. But because the peaks are there, we, like a mountain hiker, can push onward and upward with the Lord's help.

In Romans 8:31-34, Paul declared that regardless of our struggles, no one can stand against us, for God is for us. This being so, the question is not whether God is on our side, but whether we are on God's side. In order for us to be spiritually victorious, it is important first for us to yield ourselves fully to God. To align ourselves on God's side, our desires and ambitions must bow to God's plan.

Introduction for Youth

Topic: *Fearful or Thankful Faith?*

Pastor Duane Scott Willis and his wife, Janet, dearly loved the nine children God had given them. But midmorning on November 8, 1994, a fiery automobile explosion claimed the lives of their six youngest children. Eight days later, the bereaved couple explained to the media how they could make it through the sudden and horrific tragedy with unwavering hope in the Lord.

"We must tell you that we hurt and sorrow as you parents would for your children. The depth of pain is indescribable. The Bible expresses our feelings that we sorrow, but not as those without hope.

"What gives us our firm foundation for our hope is the Bible. The truth of God's Word assures us that our children are in heaven with Jesus Christ. Our strength rests in the Word of God. The Bible is sure and gives us confidence. Everything God promises is true."

Concepts for Children

Topic: *Living Our Faith*

1. Jesus told a story about a good person.
2. This person helped someone who had been hurt by others.
3. The story is about being kind to others.
4. The story stresses how important it is to show God's love to people in need.
5. God wants us to help others, regardless of how different they might be.

Lesson Commentary

I. MOUNT ZION SUPERIOR TO MOUNT SINAI: HEBREWS 12:18-24

A. The Mountain of Fear: vss. 18-19

You have not come to a mountain that can be touched and that is burning with fire; to darkness, gloom and storm; to a trumpet blast or to such a voice speaking words that those who heard it begged that no further word be spoken to them.

Hebrews 12:14 pulls together two threads from the preceding verses (which were studied in last week's lesson). Verse 10 mentions "holiness," while verse 11 refers to "peace." Both words reflected strategic Hebrew ideas that, when taken together, carry the connotations of a life of wholeness. Both peace and holiness are to be goals for Christians. We are to strive to be at peace with everyone (vs. 14). That includes our fellow believers, our non-Christian neighbors, and even our enemies. We are also to seek personal purity. The author provided an incentive for seeking holiness when he said that those who are not holy will not see the Lord. God is all-holy, and He cannot tolerate moral impurity in His presence.

The twin virtues in verse 14 are the opposites of two vices mentioned in the following verses. First, the opposite of peace is the troublemaking of sinners (vs. 15). Second, the opposite of holiness is sinfulness, which includes immorality and godlessness (vss. 16-17). The author also explained some of the things involved in seeking peace and holiness. Verses 15 and 16 begin similarly: "See to it that no one . . ." and "See that no one . . ." Together, these two verses show us the responsibility believers have for helping one another become the people God wants us to be.

First, we are to guard against others turning back from the wonderful "grace of God" (vs. 15). The writer alluded to Deuteronomy 29:18 when describing the apostasy occurring in the midst of his readers. If someone in a church spurns the Messiah, that person's unbelief can have a poisonous effect on others in the congregation. Like a toxic root that grows underground and then puts out weeds that choke a crop, apostasy can spread and undermine the faith of many. Second, we are to help others avoid immorality and godlessness (Heb. 12:16-17). While Jacob takes his place in the honor roll of faith (see 11:20-21), his brother, Esau, became a classic case of impiety (12:16).

At the time of the Hebrew patriarchs, the firstborn son traditionally received more honor and benefits than his younger brothers. But the Bible shows that more than once an older brother lost the pride of place to a younger sibling. The most prominent case of such a switch involved Isaac and Rebekah's two sons, Esau and Jacob (see Gen. 25:21-34). These brothers were fraternal twins, with Esau being born shortly before Jacob. They were rivals from the womb, and their parents fueled their rivalry by each parent favoring one son over the other. When the two were grown, Esau foolishly agreed to sell Jacob his birthright. This belonged to

Esau, for he was the older son who was supposed to inherit the larger portion of his father's estate. Several years later, while Esau was preparing to receive his father's blessing, Jacob managed instead to steal the blessing by using deceitful and manipulative tactics (see 27:1-29).

Understandably, serious friction arose between Esau and Jacob (see vss. 30-41), though years later they were able to patch up their relationship (see 33:1-17). Esau became a powerful man and the founder of the Edomite nation (see 36:1-43). Nonetheless, from the Bible's perspective, he would always remain Isaac's disenfranchised son. Indeed, Esau became a prototype of the secular person, for by bartering away his birthright, he failed to value what God accorded a high price tag (Heb. 12:16). Esau had to live with the consequences of his error. He couldn't get back the firstborn's blessing after he had lost it, no matter what he did. The lesson in this for the original recipients of Hebrews—and for us—is that if a person persists in rejecting the Savior, he or she must eventually pay the price. After death, the godless will be filled with remorse, but they will no longer have the opportunity to repent.

As a way of encouraging his readers to persevere in their faith, the author reminded them of the superiority of the new covenant over the old one. He maintained that while Mount Sinai (where the Mosaic law was given) was great, Mount Zion (representing the Messiah's kingdom) is greater still. It would be incorrect to conclude that the writer was somehow discrediting Mount Sinai, for he affirmed the central role it occupied in salvation history. By way of example, when Moses was receiving the law from God on Sinai, the mountain was "burning with fire" (vs. 18) and covered with "darkness, gloom and storm." There was a trumpet blast and the sound of God's voice, to which the listeners could not bear to listen (vs. 19).

B. The Dread of the Israelites: vss. 20-21

Because they could not bear what was commanded: "If even an animal touches the mountain, it must be stoned." The sight was so terrifying that Moses said, "I am trembling with fear."

The sound of God's "voice" (Heb. 12:19) would not even permit animals to touch the mountain, since it had been made holy with the Lord's presence (vs. 20). The display of God's awesomeness was such that even Moses, God's prophet, was terrified (vs. 21). These historical details are confirmed in the Old Testament (see Ex. 19:12-13, 16-19; Deut. 9:19). The term "Zion" is used over 150 times in the Old Testament. Zion is first mentioned in 2 Samuel 5:7 as a Jebusite fortress on a hill. After being captured by David, this fortress was called the City of David. Here Israel's king brought the ark of the covenant, thereby making the hill a sacred site (6:10-12).

C. The Mountain of Joy: vss. 22-24

But you have come to Mount Zion, to the heavenly Jerusalem, the city of the living God. You have come to thousands upon thousands of angels in joyful assembly, to the church of the firstborn, whose names are written in heaven. You have come to God, the judge of all men, to the spirits of righteous men made perfect, to Jesus the mediator of a new covenant, and to the sprinkled blood that speaks a better word than the blood of Abel.

The historical eminence of Zion eventually came to be equated with Jerusalem itself (see Isa. 40:9; Mic. 3:12). For instance, Psalm 125:1 declares that "Mount Zion . . . cannot be shaken but endures forever." Indeed, in biblical thought, Zion was the place where the Lord resided and presided. This explains why Hebrews 12:22 refers to Mount Zion as the "heavenly Jerusalem" and the "city of the living God" (see 11:10, 13-16; 13:14). Previously, the members of the covenant community in the Old Testament era went to Mount Sinai. In contrast, new covenant believers have journeyed to Mount Zion. Also, unlike Mount Sinai, which "can be touched" (12:18), Mount Zion is impalpable. Furthermore, Mount Sinai is a physical mountain, whereas the end-time Mount Zion is not.

In Galatians 4:24-31, Paul constructed an allegory using Mount Sinai and Mount Zion (see vss. 21-23). The apostle endeavored to show that God's plan to give Abraham a son was fulfilled, not by human effort, but by God's keeping His promise in a miraculous way. The apostle figuratively interpreted Old Testament passages (for example, Gen. 16; 17:15-21; and 21:1-21) to illustrate the difference between law and grace. Paul considered Hagar's literal slavery to be symbolic of the spiritual slavery caused by the law given at Mount Sinai. Hagar corresponds to Jerusalem of the apostle's day, for it was the center of the Jewish religion and the hometown of the Judaizers (that is, religious legalists). The apostle personified the city of Jerusalem and said she was enslaved with her children, meaning the Jews. They were still bound to the law because they had not found freedom in the Messiah. In contrast, Jesus' followers are the children of another mother, namely, the Jerusalem that is above, and she is free. Paul quoted Isaiah 54:1 to show how the heavenly Jerusalem can be said to be the mother of all Christians.

With respect to Hebrews, the writer explained that in coming to Mount Zion, Jesus' followers had encountered several eternal blessings. The first one is "thousands upon thousands of angels in joyful assembly" (12:22). Second is "the church of the firstborn, whose names are written in heaven" (vs. 23). This "worshiping community" includes all Christians on earth. Because of Jesus, they will be treated like privileged heirs of heaven (see Rom. 8:17), where they already have their names enrolled. The third blessing is "God, the judge of all" (Heb. 12:23). As the end-time Judge of all creatures, the Father will not condemn, but rather justify those who believe in His Son.

Fourth is "the spirits of righteous men made perfect." These are probably believers from the Old Testament era, such as the people mentioned in chapter 11. They have been made perfect in the sense that their souls have been cleansed from sin through the Messiah (see vs. 40). The fifth blessing is "Jesus the mediator of a new covenant" (12:24; see 8:6). Moses was the mediator of the old covenant by receiving the law from God and delivering it to the Israelites. Similarly, the Son mediated the new covenant by teaching about faith and dying so that sinners can be reconciled with the Father. Sixth is "the sprinkled blood that speaks a better word than the blood of Abel" (12:24). The "sprinkled blood" is what Jesus shed on the cross. Whereas Abel's blood cried out for retribution (see Gen. 4:10), Jesus' blood makes forgiveness possible.

II. An Unshakable Kingdom: Hebrews 12:25-29

A. Being Diligent to Heed the Lord: vs. 25

See to it that you do not refuse him who speaks. If they did not escape when they refused him who warned them on earth, how much less will we, if we turn away from him who warns us from heaven?

The writer of Hebrews urged Jesus' followers not to "refuse him who speaks" (12:25), which is a reference to God. The author mentioned the Exodus generation as an example of what not to do. When God dwelt with the Israelites, He repeatedly warned them not to disobey Him. Despite this, they did rebel against Him, and so He punished them on several occasions. Moreover, virtually all of them died in the Sinai desert before the nation entered the promised land (see Num. 14:26-35). Given that this was the fate of those who refused to heed the divine message given by Moses, it is even less likely that people today will be able to escape God's judgment if they reject the Lord Jesus, who issues His warning from the throne room of heaven (Heb. 12:25). In short, the Messiah demands complete and unwavering faithfulness from His followers.

B. Taking Away the Created Order: vss. 26-27

At that time his voice shook the earth, but now he has promised, "Once more I will shake not only the earth but also the heavens." The words "once more" indicate the removing of what can be shaken—that is, created things—so that what cannot be shaken may remain.

Hebrews 12:26 reveals the dire consequence of renouncing the Savior. In the time of Moses, there was a violent earthquake at Sinai (see Ex. 19:18). But at the Messiah's second coming, God promised to upturn not only the earth but also the heavens (Heb. 12:26; see Hag. 2:6). This latter episode will be much more serious than the former one. At the end of the age, all of creation will be shaken, and only what is unshakable will survive (Heb. 12:27). The latter refers to the Savior's kingdom, which is unshakable and will survive the coming demise.

Second Peter 3:10 reveals that when God's patience with the ungodly is finally exhausted, "the day of the Lord" will come suddenly, as a thief who strikes in the darkness (see 1 Thess. 5:2; Rev. 3:3; 16:15). Jesus also taught that His second advent would be unexpected, like the unwelcome intrusion of a burglar (see Matt. 24:42-44; Luke 12:39-40). But unlike the housebreaker, Jesus will have every right to take whatever He wishes, for there is no power, position, or possession that does not already belong to Him. Second Peter 3:10 uses strong language typical of end-time passages to describe three events that will happen when the Messiah returns.

First, the heavens will vanish with a "roar" (see Isa. 13:10-13; 34:4; Rev. 6:14). The latter renders a Greek adverb that denotes the presence of a horrific noise similar to a whirling, rushing sound. Second, the "elements" (2 Peter 3:10) will melt away in a fiery blaze. The noun translated "elements" refers to the celestial bodies in the universe (sun, moon, and stars) as well as the chemical compounds out of which they are made (earth, air, fire, and water). Third, the planet and every deed done on it will be "laid bare." The latter renders a verb that points to the truth that one day every human creation will be entirely exposed and perfectly judged by God. Another textual reading uses a different verb that means "to burn up" or "be consumed by fire." In this case, the idea is that everything on earth will be obliterated. In turn, humanity will be left to stand exposed and accountable before God.

Peter spelled out in graphic terms the terrifying events that will take place when the Messiah returns. The apostle did not do so to produce a trembling fear in the hearts of his readers, for he had assured them of their hope in the Redeemer. Since eventually all earthly things will be completely destroyed, believers should want all the more to live in a manner that is pleasing to God. Specifically, they are to be "holy and godly" (vs. 11) in their conduct. Moreover, because death for any of us is but a heartbeat away, and because the Son could come soon, we should feel an urgency to glorify the Father in our daily living.

C. Offering Worship Pleasing to God: vss. 28-29

Therefore, since we are receiving a kingdom that cannot be shaken, let us be thankful, and so worship God acceptably with reverence and awe, for our "God is a consuming fire."

The writer of Hebrews noted that the future kingdom of God is unshakable (12:28). When the Bible talks about the divine kingdom, it is primarily referring to the Lord's rule over His creation. Two conclusions can be drawn from the truth that believers will inherit an unshakable kingdom (Heb. 12:28). First, they should "be thankful" that the Father, in His grace, allows them to be saved through faith in His Son (see Eph. 2:8-9).

Second, the writer of Hebrews encouraged believers to offer worship that is pleasing to God, namely, with "reverence and awe" (12:28). Put differently, before God's majestic presence, believers should exercise humility, especially as they offer Him praise. In support of his second conclusion, the author quoted Deuteronomy 4:24 (see Ex. 24:17; Deut. 9:3; Isa. 33:14), which says that "God is a consuming fire" (Heb. 12:29). The idea is that God tolerates no rivals, whether real or imaginary (see James 4:4-5). Ultimately, people must face God either as a purifying fire or as a punishing fire, that is, to be cleansed or to be consumed.

Discussion Questions

1. What contrast did the writer of Hebrews make between Mount Sinai and Mount Zion?
2. What sort of eternal future did the author say awaits believers?
3. What are some reasons you have heard the unsaved give for rejecting the Savior?
4. What will happen to the heavens and the earth at Jesus' return?
5. What are some things believers can do as they await Jesus' return?

Contemporary Application

As children, we looked forward to Christmas with great anticipation. The promise of what that special day would bring motivated us to be good. Later, as teenagers, we looked forward to getting our driver's licenses and to graduating from high school. The promise of new freedoms motivated us to demonstrate our trustworthiness. Then, as adults, we plan and look forward to special events and vacations as a means of personal renewal or as an escape from stress.

Without something to look forward to, most people get bogged down, even depressed. The problem is that earthly pleasures and rewards are temporary fixes. Christmas passes and so does the sense of excitement and wonder. Graduation is barely over before the hard realities of adult life march in. Vacations become past history, and all too soon, so do our memories of them.

Believers can certainly experience joy here on earth, but the struggle to live in a godly manner in a sinful and uncertain world is always present. The original recipients of the Letter to the Hebrews knew firsthand the stark reality of the preceding truth. That's why the author of the epistle stressed that this world is not our truest home and that looking forward to the Messiah's return gives believers hope. The writer also emphasized that this hope is not something Christians merely wish for. It is absolutely certain to happen. And that certainty puts their focus on the Savior. The confident assurance of Jesus' return also puts both the problems and the pleasures of yesterday and today into perspective. They are temporary.

Since so much time has passed, and since many of us live quite comfortably, it is understandable that Jesus' return does not impact us as it should. Yet, to the Father, the Son's return is imminent, and so it should be to us as well. We need to always look forward to Jesus' coming again because that thought will help us remain faithful to Him. If we truly love the Lord, none of us want Jesus to return right when we are sinning. Instead, we want Him to find us serving Him with "reverence and awe" (Heb. 12:28). Then, at His return, He will say to us, "Well done, good and faithful servant!" (Matt. 25:21). In light of these thoughts, what kind of fruit are we bearing in our witness?

Faith Requires Love

DEVOTIONAL READING

John 13:31-35

DAILY BIBLE READINGS

Monday September 24
Psalm 18:1-6 I Love You, O Lord

Tuesday September 25
Deuteronomy 7:7-11 Faithful Love

Wednesday September 26
Deuteronomy 5:6-10 Obedient Love

Thursday September 27
Deuteronomy 6:1-9 Taught to Love

Friday September 28
John 13:31-35 Love One Another

Saturday September 29
Luke 6:27-36 Love Your Enemies

Sunday September 30
Hebrews 13:1-3; 1 Corinthians 13 Faith, Hope, and Love

Scripture

Background Scripture: *Hebrews 13:1-6; 1 Corinthians 13*
Scripture Lesson: *Hebrews 13:1-3; 1 Corinthians 13*
Key Verse: *Now these three remain: faith, hope and love. But the greatest of these is love.* 1 Corinthians 13:13.
Scripture Lesson for Children: *Hebrews 13:1-3; 1 Corinthians 13*
Key Verse for Children: *Faith, hope and love. But the greatest of these is love.* 1 Corinthians 13:13.

Lesson Aim

To appreciate the role that Christlike love serves within the church.

Lesson Setting

Hebrews 13:1-3	*1 Corinthians 13*
Time: Before A.D. *70*	*Time:* A.D. *55*
Place: Possibly Rome	*Place: Ephesus*

Lesson Outline

Faith Requires Love

I. Love's Presence: Hebrews 13:1-3
    A. *Love Commanded: vs. 1*
    B. *Love Demonstrated: vss. 2-3*

II. Love's Importance: 1 Corinthians 13:1-3
    A. *Several Noteworthy Gifts: vss. 1-2*
    B. *Two Impressive Actions: vs. 3*

III. Love's Nature: 1 Corinthians 13:4-7
    A. *What Love Is and Is Not: vss. 4-6*
    B. *Love's Persevering Quality: vs. 7*

IV. Love's Permanence: 1 Corinthians 13:8-13
    A. *The Impermanence of Spiritual Gifts: vss. 8-10*
    B. *The Promise of Knowing the Lord: vss. 11-12*
    C. *The Greatness of Love: vs. 13*

Introduction for Adults

Topic: *Steadfast Love*

Anthony Campolo tells the story of a 13-year-old hydrocephalic girl living in a Haitian missionary hospital. The girl, brain-damaged and deformed, rocked nervously on her bed, day after day, year after year. The Haitian nurses, though very busy with more hopeful cases, lovingly tended this girl, feeding her, changing her diapers, and tending to her safety needs.

One day the girl accidentally rocked herself off her bed and onto the cement floor, seriously injuring herself. The nurses could have dismissed the fall as being "God's will" and cut down on her care. Instead, they chose to increase her care and to spend long hours in prayer for her.

Steadfastly loving the unlovely is a Christian's mandate and challenge (see 1 Cor. 13; Heb. 13:1-3). Will we love those we find physically and mentally repulsive? Will we care about and care for society's "hopeless"?

Introduction for Youth

Topic: *Show Some Love*

Pastor Jeff Wallace recalled the following incident involving his daughter, Gracie, when she was a young girl. It helps us to appreciate the role that Christlike love serves among believers.

"With my daughter's hand in mine, we walked out of the convention hall where we had heard a gifted preacher convey afresh the love and grace and mercy of the Lord. I had noticed Gracie's rapt attention as the preacher spoke. I, too, was greatly moved and impressed by his message.

"I thus wasn't surprised when Gracie looked up at me and asked, 'Daddy, did you think that was a good preacher?' 'Oh, yes, sweetheart, he is a great preacher,' I responded. 'Do you think he's a better preacher than you are?' 'Oh, yes, sweetheart, he's a much better preacher than I am.' 'Not really, Daddy,' she concluded. 'The only preacher better than you is Jesus!'

"Of course, my confidence in my preaching ability was little affected by my daughter's opinion. But my heart was overjoyed by her expression of pure love and devotion. Love does that. It always affects. It always brings joy. It always builds up."

Concepts for Children

Topic: *A Loving Faith*

1. God wants us to show the love of Jesus to others.
2. Jesus promises to give us the strength to be loving to others.
3. We show love to others by caring about them.
4. Showing love is the best gift we can give to others.
5. The love of Jesus will last forever.

Lesson Commentary

I. LOVE'S PRESENCE: HEBREWS 13:1-3

A. Love Commanded: vs. 1

Keep on loving each other as brothers.

Hebrews 13 communicates some 20 commands on 15 different subjects. Therefore, in its format this chapter is somewhat akin to the Book of Proverbs, which takes a rather scattershot approach with its many seemingly unrelated verses. Nevertheless, Hebrews 13 is far from being a haphazard wrap-up to the book, for it has a logical arrangement. The first four verses, for instance, have in common the fact that they all deal with social relationships. These verses tell how to treat Christian brothers and sisters (vs. 1), strangers (vs. 2), prisoners and the mistreated (vs. 3), and marriage partners (vs. 4). Then verses 5 and 6 deal with the related issue of greed versus contentment.

Perhaps verse 1 contains the most all-embracing of the commands in this section, for it tells the readers to keep on loving one another as brothers and sisters. Often in the New Testament we read that Christians are, in effect, members of the same family and should treat each other that way. The original recipients of Hebrews were already exercising kindness and compassion toward one another, but the writer of the letter felt a reminder would not be amiss.

B. Love Demonstrated: vss. 2-3

Do not forget to entertain strangers, for by so doing some people have entertained angels without knowing it. Remember those in prison as if you were their fellow prisoners, and those who are mistreated as if you yourselves were suffering.

Believers are not to relate only to one another, but to outsiders as well. In this regard, Hebrews 13:2 urges believers to show hospitality to "strangers," which most likely refers to itinerant Christian preachers. In the first century A.D., there weren't many inns, and those that did exist often had an unsavory reputation. So travelers had to rely on householders if they were to get good accommodations during a journey. As an encouragement toward being hospitable, the writer reminded his readers that some have unwittingly hosted "angels." Even today, entertaining in our homes can still be a way of ministering to others.

As we step back from the preceding information, we recognize the truth that the Bible never lets us be satisfied with insipid expressions of civility. Christian love goes the second mile by displaying kindness to others. Everybody of course loves friends, but Jesus urged us to love our enemies as well (see Matt. 5:41-44). For instance, in Hebrews 13:1, we learn that we should treat other believers as members of God's spiritual family. We also discover that travelers will visit our homes if we carry out the command of verse 2, but we ourselves will need to travel a bit in order to fulfill the command of verse 3. This directive is to remember two groups: prisoners and the mistreated.

Probably with both groups the author of the epistle had in mind Christians who were being persecuted for their faith. Thus visiting and identifying oneself with such people, as the writer urged, could have entailed considerable risk. But it was important for the Christian community to present a united front. By this is meant believers supporting one another and maintaining the links within the body of Christ, regardless of the danger. The recipients of the letter had already suffered persecution and had stood with others who were being persecuted (see 10:33-34), so they knew just what the author was talking about.

II. LOVE'S IMPORTANCE: 1 CORINTHIANS 13:1-3

A. Several Noteworthy Gifts: vss. 1-2

If I speak in the tongues of men and of angels, but have not love, I am only a resounding gong or a clanging cymbal. If I have the gift of prophecy and can fathom all mysteries and all knowledge, and if I have a faith that can move mountains, but have not love, I am nothing.

First Corinthians 13 has been called a "hymn to love." It is sublime in tone and powerful in content. In a sense, this chapter carries on the discussion of spiritual gifts that Paul had begun in the previous chapter. But chapter 13 primarily is Paul's description of Christian love. We learn that love is not a spiritual gift. Rather, it is the way in which all spiritual gifts should be used.

Paul began his discussion by naming certain representative gifts and actions, the first of which is speaking in "tongues of men and of angels" (vs. 1). There are a number of views regarding what Paul meant. One possibility is that these were actual languages or dialects being spoken by people and angels. A second possibility is that the tongues were unintelligible words of ecstasy spoken by the person or angel in praise to God. A third possibility is that the apostle was speaking in exaggerated terms to include every conceivable form of speech.

Paul presented a hypothetical situation in which he could speak those kinds of tongues. As impressive as this may be, apart from love, the apostle's speech would have been like the sound made by a noisy gong or a clanging cymbal. These were musical instruments used in pagan rituals. Put another way, his utterances would be just noise having little meaning. The absence of love would rob the gift of its value.

Paul next referred to three other spiritual gifts: prophecy, knowledge, and faith (vs. 2). Again the apostle spoke hypothetically, describing a situation in which he had these gifts in abundance. He might be able to deliver messages from God, have insight into all sorts of spiritual mysteries and truths of the divine, and have such a strong belief that he could dislodge mountains from their foundations. From a human standpoint, these gifts would be impressive. But if while Paul had these special abilities he was without love, then from the standpoint of God, the apostle would be an absolute zero. The absence of love would rob the gifted one of his value.

B. Two Impressive Actions: vs. 3

If I give all I possess to the poor and surrender my body to the flames, but have not love, I gain nothing.

Paul finally referred to two impressive actions that he might perform. The first of these would be giving everything he owned to the destitute (1 Cor. 13:3). Throughout the Bible we see the importance of helping those who lack what they need materially. The second action involves the apostle surrendering his body to be burned at the stake. This refers to martyrdom by means of the "flames."

Other early manuscripts read, "If I . . . give over my body to hardship that I may boast." In this case, Paul may have been referring to serving others without regard for one's welfare and to boasting in the Lord in a wholesome manner about the sacrificial act. Regardless of whether burning or boasting is to be paired with helping the poor, the apostle's point in verse 3 remains the same. He taught that if he did these actions and yet was devoid of love, he would not gain anything through what he had sacrificed. The absence of love would rob service of its value.

III. LOVE'S NATURE: 1 CORINTHIANS 13:4-7

A. What Love Is and Is Not: vss. 4-6

Love is patient, love is kind. It does not envy, it does not boast, it is not proud. It is not rude, it is not self-seeking, it is not easily angered, it keeps no record of wrongs. Love does not delight in evil but rejoices with the truth.

Using both positive and negative terms, Paul described for the Corinthians what he meant by love. The apostle had previously spoken hypothetically about himself, but now he personified love for his readers. Most likely, Paul chose his words carefully to implicitly condemn errors committed by his readers. First, the apostle noted that Christlike love is known for its patience and kindness. The first of these terms is passive, while the second is active. As believers, we are to have a long fuse (so to speak) to our temper. We must not retaliate when wronged. Rather, we are to remain steadfast in spirit, consistently responding to others in a gracious and considerate manner (1 Cor. 13:4).

Next, Paul described in a series of terms what love is not and does not do. Instead of envying people, love is thankful for God's blessing. Rather than arrogantly parading itself about, love is humble. Christian charity is never ill-mannered, disgraceful, or shameless to others. It does not seek its own interests or demand to gets its own way, but is concerned with the welfare of others (vs. 5). Love is not easily provoked to rage or irritated. Likewise, it is not resentful. Expressed differently, love does not keep score of the transgressions others have inflicted. In addition, love never finds pleasure in the misdeeds and evil schemes of others. This last quality is paired with another. Love does not praise iniquity and injustice, but exalts in the truth of God (vs. 6). Similarly, love is overjoyed when others promote what is right in God's eyes.

B. Love's Persevering Quality: vs. 7

It always protects, always trusts, always hopes, always perseveres.

Paul noted four things that Christlike love does in fullness (1 Cor. 13:7). It bears all things, which means it is always supportive and helpful. This also implies that godly charity has the ability to face trials and patiently accept them. Love believes all things, meaning it searches for what is finest in people and accepts as true the very best that they have to offer. Love hopes all things, meaning it maintains confidence in God's ability to turn evil circumstances into good. Finally, love endures all things, meaning it remains faithful to God to the end of all ordeals.

IV. LOVE'S PERMANENCE: 1 CORINTHIANS 13:8-13

A. The Impermanence of Spiritual Gifts: vss. 8-10

Love never fails. But where there are prophecies, they will cease; where there are tongues, they will be stilled; where there is knowledge, it will pass away. For we know in part and we prophesy in part, but when perfection comes, the imperfect disappears.

Paul noted that love will never fail or come to an end. Put another way, Christian charity will last forever (1 Cor. 13:8). The apostle's readers had become overly enamored with their Spirit-given abilities. They did not realize that love should have been infinitely more important to them than whatever gift they might have had. Their priorities would be aligned when they made the love of Christ a foremost concern in their lives. Paul next stressed that one day even the most spectacular of spiritual gifts will cease to be needed. For example, God will render prophecy inoperative, cause miraculous tongues to fall silent, and end the need for the gift of knowledge. Here the apostle was contrasting two periods—an earlier one in which the spiritual gifts are needed and a later one when they are not needed. Yet Bible interpreters differ over the time frame Paul had in mind.

One view is that the first period extended between Pentecost (when the church was established) and the end of the apostolic period (when the church supposedly reached spiritual maturity). With the completion of the New Testament canon, the second period has already begun. Another view is that the first period is the time between the Messiah's first and second comings, with the second period following after Jesus' return to earth. In either case, Paul used several examples to illustrate the difference between the two periods. First, the distinction is like the difference between the partial and the complete, or between the imperfect and the perfect (vss. 9-10). The gifts of knowledge and prophecy, for example, put believers in touch with God only imperfectly. But in the later period, believers will be in full and perfect contact with Him.

B. The Promise of Knowing the Lord: vss. 11-12

When I was a child, I talked like a child, I thought like a child, I reasoned like a child. When I became a man, I put childish ways behind me. Now we see but a poor reflection as in a mirror; then we shall see face to face. Now I know in part; then I shall know fully, even as I am fully known.

Paul next illustrated his meaning by drawing an analogy involving childhood and adulthood. The apostle said that when he was a child, he talked, thought, and reasoned as a child. But now that Paul had become an adult, he had set aside childish ways (1 Cor. 13:11). Childhood is like the first period, and childish ways are like spiritual gifts. Just as childish ways are appropriate for a child, so spiritual gifts are appropriate for people in the first period. But then (to follow the analogy further), adulthood is like the second period. It is a time in which we will put away our spiritual gifts, for they will not be appropriate any longer.

For his next illustration, Paul used an analogy involving a mirror (vs. 12). In that day, mirrors were made out of polished metal and provided a poor, distorted image of what they were reflecting. The glimpse of the Lord that we get as He is reflected in our spiritual gifts is like looking in such an imperfect mirror. In the second period, however, our vision of the Lord will not be mediated by our spiritual gifts, for we will see Him face-to-face. Bible scholars have disputed Paul's exact meaning here. Was the apostle saying that vision using a mirror is blurry or reflected? Expressed differently, does the exercise of our spiritual gifts provide us with a poor sense of who God is, or does it give us an indirect sense? In either option, the contrast between our vision of the Lord (involving spiritual gifts) in the first period and our vision of Him (not involving spiritual gifts) in the later period still stands.

The apostle switched from the language of sight to that of knowledge when he noted that he, like all believers in the first period, knew God only partially. But Paul looked forward to a time when he would know God fully. Of course, the apostle was not suggesting that human beings will ever have knowledge equaling that of God. Moreover, the Lord is not limited, as people are, by conditions of the first period. He already knows all people fully, completely, and perfectly.

C. The Greatness of Love: vs. 13

And now these three remain: faith, hope and love. But the greatest of these is love.

First Corinthians 13:13 contains Paul's summation of his teaching about love. He said that Christian charity is for now and for eternity. The apostle likewise mentioned that faith and hope abide together with love, though the latter was the greatest of the trio. These three characteristics, in a sense, sum up the Christian life. As was noted in lesson 2, "faith" denotes trust in the Savior and commitment to His teachings. "Hope" refers to an unshakable confidence that the promises of the Father will ultimately be fulfilled by the Son. Thanks to Paul we have already learned what "love" denotes.

Some interpreters have suggested that the apostle meant that faith and hope, like love, are eternal, since they can be considered manifestations of love. Paul, however, more likely included faith and hope in verse 13 to remind his readers that love is for now, just as are faith and hope. When the apostle went on to say that love is the greatest virtue, he probably meant that Christian charity eclipses faith and hope because it lasts forever. But the latter two virtues, like the spiritual gifts, are for this age only. Faith is not necessary in eternity because then we will be in the very presence of God. Likewise, hope is not necessary in eternity because then our expectations will have been fulfilled.

Discussion Questions

1. Why do you think the writer of Hebrews stressed the importance of showing Christlike love?
2. How is it possible for believers to be patient and kind when others are rude to them?
3. What was Paul's main purpose in stressing that spiritual gifts are temporary, but love is permanent?
4. What can you do to become more Christlike in your love?
5. How might you encourage your fellow believers to let the love of Christ permeate their attitudes and actions?

Contemporary Application

Scripture reveals that at the Savior's return, the need for spiritual gifts will cease, for the church will be perfected in Jesus' presence. Be that as it may, faith, hope, and love exist now for our spiritual benefit. And of these three, the greatest virtue is love, for it most expresses the nature of God as revealed at Calvary.

To love the way God does involves making a conscious decision. The Lord Himself is the best example of this. As Romans 5:8-10 teaches, God chose to reach out to us in love even when we were His enemies. Despite our sin, God decided to bring peace and wholeness to our relationship with Him.

There will be times when we do not feel like loving other people. It is in those moments that we need to look to God in faith for supernatural help. He is ready and willing to give us the strength to love in a Christlike fashion. But first we must submit ourselves to God's will.

In addition, when God enables us to love despite our desire at times not to, the unsaved will see the power of Jesus' love working through and in us. In a morally corrupt society in which people yearn for a power greater than what they have, so as to give them meaning and value, the love of Christ in us will draw them to Him. Here, then, is another reason to choose to love: to surrender our will to Jesus' will and thus be a beacon to others.

Stephen's Arrest

DEVOTIONAL READING

Proverbs 8:1-11

DAILY BIBLE READINGS

Monday October 1
  *Isaiah 59:1-8 Barriers
  between You and Your God*

Tuesday October 2
  *Jeremiah 8:22–9:9
  Falsehood, Deceit, and
  Deception*

Wednesday October 3
  *Zechariah 8:14-19 These
  Things You Shall Do*

Thursday October 4
  *Proverbs 8:1-11 My Mouth
  Will Utter Truth*

Friday October 5
  *John 16:12-15 Guided into
  All the Truth*

Saturday October 6
  *Acts 6:1-7 Full of Faith and
  the Spirit*

Sunday October 7
  *Acts 6:8–7:2 Full of Grace
  and Power*

Scripture

Background Scripture: *Acts 6:8–7:53*
Scripture Lesson: *Acts 6:8–7:2*
Key Verse: *Stephen, a man full of God's grace and power, did
great wonders and miraculous signs among the people.*
Acts 6:8.
Scripture Lesson for Children: *Acts 6:8-15*
Key Verse for Children: *[The people] could not stand up
against [Stephen's] wisdom or the Spirit by whom he spoke.*
Acts 6:10.

Lesson Aim

To recognize that the life-changing power of Jesus
enables us to be bold in our witness.

Lesson Setting

Time: About A.D. 35
Place: Jerusalem

Lesson Outline

Stephen's Arrest
  I. The Arrest of Stephen: Acts 6:8-15
      A. *The Miracles Performed by Stephen: vs. 8*
      B. *The Debate with Antagonists: vss. 9-10*
      C. *The Presentation of False Accusations: vss. 11-14*
      D. *The Countenance of Stephen: vs. 15*
  II. The Speech Given by Stephen: Acts 7:1-2
      A. *The High Priest's Question: vs. 1*
      B. *The Response Offered by Stephen: vs. 2*

Introduction for Adults

Topic: *Courage to Speak*

Evangelism is a word that scares many Christians. We think telling others about the Savior is the responsibility of religious experts. But this week's lesson reminds us that a relatively unknown convert named Stephen made a significant impact in witnessing for the Lord. It was possible because Stephen operated in the Messiah's life-changing power.

God gives us many opportunities to point others to Jesus. When we meet people at their deepest physical and social needs, for example, we gain opportunities to share that we serve in the name and power of the risen Lord.

Perhaps we fail to see beyond the outward appearance of many people. We think they don't need religious faith. But as we get to know them, they often admit to some glaring spiritual needs. As one woman told her friends, "The best gift I can give my family is to get my spiritual life straightened out." She has since that time come to faith in Christ!

Introduction for Youth

Topic: *Speak Up!*

Many Christian young people in your class will have personally encountered some level of harassment because of their faith. Some may have heard non-Christian family members joke about their walk with God. For others, their Christian ethics may have left them feeling like outsiders at school. The point is that your students can probably relate times when they may have asked themselves whether witnessing for the Lord was worth the conflict.

This week's lesson tells us that enduring hardship for the Savior is worth it. Being harassed is nothing compared to what Jesus is doing in the lives of your class members. Like Stephen, who didn't whine when he was persecuted, your students can rejoice when the power of Jesus touches their lives and the lives of others.

Concepts for Children

Topic: *Speaking of Faith*

1. Stephen was someone who believed in Jesus for salvation.
2. Jesus gave Stephen the ability to do many wonderful things for others.
3. Some people said mean things to Stephen for being a follower of Jesus.
4. Stephen would not let others talk him out of having faith in Jesus.
5. Jesus gives us the strength to believe in Him, regardless of what we go through.

Lesson Commentary

I. THE ARREST OF STEPHEN: ACTS 6:8-15

A. The Miracles Performed by Stephen: vs. 8

Now Stephen, a man full of God's grace and power, did great wonders and miraculous signs among the people.

In the earliest days of the church (Acts 1–5), the apostles remained in Jerusalem, proclaiming the Gospel to the Jews only. However, it was God's intention that the Good News be taken to all people throughout the whole world (see Matt. 28:19-20; Acts 1:8). Beginning in Acts 6, Luke recounted how God accomplished His plan for the church expansion and the spread of the Gospel through the persecution that followed Stephen's death. First, Luke explained that after Jesus ascended, the church experienced explosive growth. People were entering God's kingdom by the thousands, far more than the 12 apostles could possibly minister to.

At some point, a quarrel broke out between the Jewish believers who spoke Greek and the ones who spoke Aramaic or Hebrew. The first group complained that their widows were not given their share when the food supplies were distributed each day (6:1). There is some debate over the identity of the "Grecian Jews." Most likely they were Greek-speaking Jews who had become Christians. When Israel and Judah fell (in 722 and 586 B.C., respectively), the Jews were scattered throughout the Assyrian and Babylonian empires. This was known as the Diaspora, or the dispersion. The Hellenistic Jews were descendants of the scattered Jews, who had returned to Jerusalem for religious reasons. This explains the presence of Greek-speaking synagogues in the city.

The Jewish community had many food pantries for the poor, especially for widows who had lost their means of support when their husbands died. In addition, many of the older Jews of the Diaspora came to Jerusalem to be buried there. Since many of these older widows had left family behind them, the burden for support fell on the community. Those who had become Christians might have been disqualified from regular Jewish aid. Thus the early Christian church had to make provisions for them.

The Hellenistic Jews, however, felt like second-class citizens in the church. Apparently, their widows were being ignored when it came to the distribution of food and supplies for the poor. Since the apostles acknowledged the dilemma, the problem must have been real and not just a matter of perception. The situation possibly was a symptom of a much deeper problem—prejudice because of strong difference of opinion. It is also quite possible that a language barrier existed between the two groups, which increased the tensions between them. Clearly, there was a need for additional believers who were willing to wait on tables so that the apostles could devote themselves to praying and preaching the Word of God.

In Scripture, widows, orphans, and aliens are consistently depicted as the poorest and most helpless among the people. Often, they had no one but God as their patron and protector (see Ex. 22:22-23; Deut. 10:18; Isa. 1:17). In Bible times, there was no real social safety net to catch the dispossessed and homeless when their source of support was suddenly gone. Widows, orphans, and foreigners were often reduced to begging if there was no friend, relative, or patron to care for them (see Gen. 38:11; Ruth 1:8). Often they were ignored by their neighbors, but Job strongly rebuked those who "sent widows away empty-handed and broke the strength of the fatherless" (Job 22:9). Also, the law made provision for widows to glean grapes, grain, and olives out of the bounty of others (see Deut. 14:28-29; 24:19-21). In the early church, taking care of poor widows was regarded as a special duty of every congregation of believers. For example, Paul gave Timothy special instructions about caring for widows in the church (see 1 Tim. 5:3-16).

The Twelve responded to the crisis facing the Jerusalem church by calling a meeting of all the believers. The apostles could have assumed responsibility for overseeing the relief work. But they correctly saw this as a diversion from their main tasks of praying and preaching and teaching the Gospel. They thus decided to delegate to others the important job of administering the charitable distribution of food to the poor (Acts 6:2). The apostles were not interested in just filling a vacancy with willing bodies. Every duty needing attention in the body of Christ (the church) was important. If any of these tasks were done by believers who were not Spirit-filled, the entire church suffered.

Consequently, the apostles made it clear that those to be appointed had to be well-respected and "full of the Spirit and wisdom" (vs. 3). The Twelve would then put these believers in charge of the food relief program. More than one problem was solved in this way. Not only did the widows among the Hellenistic Jews receive needed supplies, but also the appointment of Hellenistic believers to positions of leadership helped erase the stigma of being second-class Christians among these people. In addition, the apostles would have greater freedom to pray and minister God's Word (vs. 4).

The apostles' solution to the complaint made by the Hellenistic Jews resolved a problem that could have become major. The Twelve allowed this group of believers to choose their own representatives (vs. 5). All seven Christians had Greek names, which suggests that they were Hellenists. Only one of the seven was described as a proselyte—a Greek Gentile who had become a Jew before becoming a Christian. Stephen is described as a believer full of faith and controlled by the Holy Spirit. We can assume that the other believers chosen also met these qualifications. In fact, Stephen and Philip would later demonstrate other spiritual gifts. The primary responsibility of these seven believers, however, was one of service to the Hellenistic Jews. In fact, we get the word "deacon" from the Greek term for service. The first recorded evidence that Paul recognized the role of deacon as an official position of leadership in the church was when he wrote his letter to the Philippians (Phil. 1:1; see also 1 Tim. 3:8-13). The duties of deacons, however, were performed long before the role of deacons became an actual office within the church.

Luke highlighted two things that the apostles did after the seven believers were chosen. First, the apostles prayed and laid hands on the seven. By following this Old Testament custom (see Num. 27:18, 23; Deut. 34:9), the apostles set apart the seven for their church duties. Second, the apostles delegated some of their church authority to Stephen and the other six believers (Acts 6:6). The ministry of the seven believers had immediate results. The church in Jerusalem grew rapidly. Even a large number of Jewish priests became followers of the Messiah. Instead of a few people trying to do everything, other believers contributed to the well-being of the community of faith (vs. 7). According to verse 8, Stephen did more than just wait on tables. The Holy Spirit so filled him with "grace and power" that he was able to perform amazing "wonders and miraculous signs" in the presence of others. For the first time, the ability to perform such great deeds extended beyond the apostles.

B. The Debate with Antagonists: vss. 9-10

Opposition arose, however, from members of the Synagogue of the Freedmen (as it was called)—Jews of Cyrene and Alexandria as well as the provinces of Cilicia and Asia. These men began to argue with Stephen, but they could not stand up against his wisdom or the Spirit by whom he spoke.

In addition to performing miracles, Stephen also proclaimed the Gospel, which disturbed the Jews who had come from different parts of the Roman Empire. One group was the "Synagogue of the Freedmen" (Acts 6:9). The word *synagogue* means "assembly," coming from a Greek verb that means "to bring together." The Jews probably established synagogues during the exile. The Babylonians had destroyed Jerusalem and its temple and deported most of the inhabitants of Judah. In order for the Jews to preserve their religious teachings and practices, they established synagogues as local places for worship and instruction. Most communities where Jews lived had at least one synagogue, and some had two or more. According to tradition, the Jewish leaders in a community were to establish a synagogue if at least 10 Jewish men lived in the town.

In New Testament times, Jews would meet in the synagogue on the Sabbath. During the worship service, men sat on one side and women on the other. The participants would recite the Shema (a confession of faith in the oneness of God, based on Deuteronomy 6:4-9), prayers, and readings from the Law and the Prophets. A speaker would deliver a message and then give a benediction (see Luke 4:16-21). The elders of the town selected laymen to oversee the care of the building and the property, to supervise the public worship, to choose people to read Scripture and pray, and to invite visitors to address the congregation. An attendant would hand the sacred scrolls to the reader during the service. After the reader finished, the attendant would return the scrolls to a chest mounted on a wall.

Not much is known about the "Synagogue of the Freedmen" (Acts 6:9). Archaeologists have found an inscription dedicating a synagogue of the libertines in Jerusalem. The founders of the assembly might have been released Roman slaves who had converted to Judaism. While freed slaves enjoyed a respectable social class in the Roman Republic, Jewish leaders ranked such converts below other proselytes (for instance, freeborn Gentiles who had become Jews). It is also possible that the Freedmen were Jews whom the Romans had enslaved and were later released in Rome. Their homes may have been in Rome, but they built a synagogue in Jerusalem, which they often visited. A third possibility is that the Freedmen were Jews who lived in the African city of Liberatum and had come to Jerusalem to worship in the temple.

The synagogue was attended by Jews from Cyrene, Alexandria, Cilicia, and Asia. Both the Cyrenians and the Alexandrians had come from major cities in North Africa. Cilicia was located in the southeast corner of Asia Minor, and "Asia" was a Roman province in the western part of Asia Minor. The Hellenist Jews were constantly battling an image of being "second class" to their Hebrew brothers and sisters. Even the Talmud (a collection of Jewish writings that predates the New Testament) said these people were not to be trusted. Since they wanted to be fully accepted as Jews, they no doubt repressed any behavior that challenged Jewish traditions. Perhaps just when the Hellenist Jews seemed to be making some headway, a young Greek-speaking Jew turned Christian came on the scene, preaching repentance and belief in Jesus as the Messiah. Though the Hellenist Jews were incensed with Stephen, they were no match for his Spirit-inspired "wisdom" (vs. 10). Indeed, despite their best efforts, they failed to refute his message by debating with him.

C. The Presentation of False Accusations: vss. 11-14

Then they secretly persuaded some men to say, "We have heard Stephen speak words of blasphemy against Moses and against God." So they stirred up the people and the elders and the teachers of the law. They seized Stephen and brought him before the Sanhedrin. They produced false witnesses, who testified, "This fellow never stops speaking against this holy place and against the law. For we have heard him say that this Jesus of Nazareth will destroy this place and change the customs Moses handed down to us."

Stephen's opponents on the sly instigated some rogues to testify that he had spoken slanderously against Moses and God (Acts 6:11). Naturally, what the false witnesses claimed alarmed the Jewish people and their rulers in Jerusalem. This prompted the religious elite—namely, the elders and scribes (that is, experts in the Mosaic law)—to authorize Stephen's arrest and appearance before the "Sanhedrin" (vs. 12). The latter was the Jewish supreme court of the day.

The antagonists found a group of individuals who were willing to tell blatant lies. These "false witnesses" (vs. 13) claimed that Stephen spoke against the cherished institutions and laws of ancient Judaism. In particular, he was accused of claiming that "Jesus of Nazareth" (vs. 14) would demolish the temple and throw out all the "customs" Moses had given to the chosen people. These were charges similar to those that had been brought against Jesus at His trial. Some think the indictment represents a garbled version of the episode recorded in John 2:19-22.

D. The Countenance of Stephen: vs. 15

All who were sitting in the Sanhedrin looked intently at Stephen, and they saw that his face was like the face of an angel.

As Stephen stood before the seated members of the high council, all of them stared at him "intently" (Acts 6:15). The reason for their fixed gaze is that the face of Stephen beamed as bright as that of an "angel." This suggests that the Spirit of God was uniquely manifesting His presence in Stephen's life at that moment.

II. THE SPEECH GIVEN BY STEPHEN: ACTS 7:1-2

A. The High Priest's Question: vs. 1

Then the high priest asked him, "Are these charges true?"

Stephen's opponents had accused him of slandering Moses, the law, the Jerusalem temple, and God. The high priest in office at the time (most likely Caiaphas) asked Stephen whether he thought his accusers were telling the truth or lying about him (Acts 7:1). The high priest was the person who presided over the meetings of the Sanhedrin, or Jewish national council. This assembly was made up of 70 members: the chief priests, professional teachers of the law, and the elders. Annas had been high priest from A.D. 6 to about A.D. 15, when the Romans removed him from office. Nevertheless, the Jews still recognized him as high priest. Caiaphas, Annas's son-in-law, served as the high priest from A.D. 18 to about A.D. 36. During his tenure, he condemned Jesus to death.

B. The Response Offered by Stephen: vs. 2

To this he replied: "Brothers and fathers, listen to me! The God of glory appeared to our father Abraham while he was still in Mesopotamia, before he lived in Haran.

Acts 7:2-53 contains the speech that Stephen gave to the Sanhedrin. It is the longest recorded public address in the book. Stephen followed Hebrew custom by surveying the history of Israel. He began by respectfully addressing his listeners as "brothers and fathers" (vs. 2) and enjoining them to heed what he had to say. Here we see that Stephen took seriously the charges that were brought against him and grounded his defense on the teaching of the Old Testament. Unlike his detractors, Stephen was characterized by "gentleness and respect" (1 Pet. 3:15) as he spoke.

Stephen directed the attention of the audience to the time when the all-glorious Lord manifested His presence to their ancestor Abraham while he lived in Mesopotamia. The religious elite of Stephen's day lauded the temple in Jerusalem as the place where God displayed His glory. Yet, when the Lord appeared to their esteemed patriarch, it was not even in Palestine, but in Mesopotamia. Stephen explained that this incident occurred before Abraham relocated with his family to Haran. This was a city in the northern part of Mesopotamia located on the Balikh River, which is a branch of the Euphrates. Terah (the father of Abraham), Nahor

(Abraham's brother), and the patriarch's extended family left Ur and migrated to Haran (see Gen. 11:31). We cannot be sure why God called Abraham and not someone else. But from later events in the patriarch's life, we know he had many fine qualities. This does not mean he was perfect. In fact, Joshua 24:2 reveals that at the time Abraham was living in Ur, his family was worshiping false gods.

Discussion Questions

1. What attributes of Jesus were present in Stephen's life?
2. Why did Stephen's opponents incite the false witnesses to make the particular claims they did?
3. What attitude do you think the religious elite had toward Jesus of Nazareth?
4. When you perform Christian duties, what risks might bother you the most? Why?
5. What might hinder you the most from serving in the church? What can you do to overcome this obstacle?

Contemporary Application

One of the clearest evidences of the Spirit's work was the conversion of many unbelievers. Before they put their faith in Christ, these individuals were self-focused and eternally lost. Then, after being spiritually reborn, they abandoned their sinful ways and became bold witnesses for the Lord Jesus.

Stephen would be a case in point. The Spirit of God not only brought him to a knowledge of the truth but also gave him the ability to witness boldly in Jerusalem for the Savior. Even when Stephen was challenged by the authorities, he unflinchingly remained committed to the Messiah.

In addition to being bold, Stephen resisted the temptation to take credit for the miracles he performed. Instead, he consistently focused the attention of his detractors on the Lord Jesus. Stephen's desire mirrored that of others in the early church, namely, that as many people as possible would abandon their sin and trust in Christ for eternal life.

The Spirit's power still changes lives. At times, the power is evident in health situations where medical science has no explanation for the apparent healing. The Spirit's power also brings changes in behavior, turning around those who once lived selfishly, so that their lives can focus on others.

Although many worldly forces are intent on removing the Lord Jesus from people's lives, they are feeble when they encounter the Savior's power. Thus we can rejoice, for His power is far greater than any earthly power. Moreover, His life-changing power enables us to be bold in our witness.

Stephen's Martyrdom

Scripture

Background Scripture: *Acts 7:1–8:1a*
Scripture Lesson: *Acts 7:51–8:1a*
Key Verse: *While they were stoning him, Stephen prayed, "Lord Jesus, receive my spirit."* Acts 7:59.
Scripture Lesson for Children: *Acts 7:51-60*
Key Verse for Children: *While they were stoning him, Stephen prayed, "Lord Jesus, receive my spirit."* Acts 7:59.

Lesson Aim

To evaluate the importance of being both courageous and gracious in letting others know about Jesus.

Lesson Setting

Time: About A.D. 35
Place: Jerusalem

Lesson Outline

Stephen's Martyrdom

I. The Indictment of the Religious Leaders: Acts 7:51-53
   A. *Resisting the Holy Spirit: vs. 51*
   B. *Persecuting the Prophets: vss. 52-53*

II. The Stoning of Stephen: Acts 7:54-60
   A. *The Indignation of the Sanhedrin: vs. 54*
   B. *The Heavenly Vision Experienced by Stephen: vss. 55-56*
   C. *The Capital Punishment of Stephen: vss. 57-58*
   D. *The Martyrdom of Stephen: vss. 59-60*

III. The Involvement of Saul: Acts 8:1a

Introduction for Adults

Topic: *Paying the Price*

Organizations in the West can be very competitive. This is evident from the sports teams that dominate athletics and the fierce rivalry that exists among businesses. Even the entertainment industry is marked by ruthless self-interest.

Individuals are also competitive. Students try to outdo their peers in terms of grades. Employees do whatever they can to climb to the top of their professions. Many people want to drive a better car and own a nicer home than their neighbors.

Being a faithful servant is a revolutionary concept to adults who are highly competitive. When you put the interests of others first, as Stephen did, you're not thinking of eliminating them to get to the top. Instead, you're cultivating relationships and showing love, even if it demands personal sacrifice. Isn't this what being a Christian is really all about?

Introduction for Youth

Topic: *Take a Stand*

There are many ideas of what constitutes effective leadership. And some of the more unsavory notions encourage using deceit and manipulation to get ahead. It should come as no surprise to the teens that the biblical view of leadership is entirely different. Consider Stephen. When threatened with the prospect of death, he did not lash out in anger. Instead, he endured the rejection and scorn.

Admittedly, the latter responses are some of the hardest things for believers to respond to graciously. It is natural for us to become defensive, especially when others disagree with our Christian beliefs. It is also easy to feel resentful when someone belittles the truths about the Lord Jesus that we hold most dear.

Nonetheless, the Savior can help us remain patient and calm throughout our ordeal. Also, regardless of what our peers might say, He can empower us to show Christlike love. He even undergirds our boldest expressions of faith with humility and compassion toward others.

Concepts for Children

Topic: *Stephen Faces Death*

1. Stephen told some leaders he was serving Jesus.
2. Stephen said the leaders were wrong for not believing in Jesus.
3. The leaders were angry when they heard what Stephen said.
4. Jesus helped Stephen deal with a hard situation.
5. Jesus is always with us, no matter what we are going through.

Lesson Commentary

I. THE INDICTMENT OF THE RELIGIOUS LEADERS: ACTS 7:51-53

A. Resisting the Holy Spirit: vs. 51

"You stiff-necked people, with uncircumcised hearts and ears! You are just like your fathers: You always resist the Holy Spirit!"

Last week we learned about a group of emancipated Jewish slaves who told the Sanhedrin that Stephen was preaching against the Mosaic law and the supremacy of the Jerusalem temple. Possibly Stephen's opponents decided to use accusations that had been successful before in eliminating Jesus. The allegations they used were undoubtedly inflammatory remarks that they knew would upset the Jewish leaders. Indeed, this is what happened, and it led to the Council authorizing Stephen's arrest and formal interrogation before the entire assembly (Acts 6:9-15). Caiaphas, who was the high priest at that time, asked Stephen whether he thought the charges being brought against him were correct and valid (7:1).

One of the ways to appreciate Stephen's witness is the Greek adjective rendered "full" (Acts 6:8). In other words, he was brimming with the "grace and power" of God. Such a Spirit-emboldened believer can do great things for the Lord. This was certainly true of Jesus and Stephen. Like the Messiah, Stephen found himself at the center of controversy over theological matters. And, like Jesus, Stephen confounded his detractors with a logic and disposition they could not deny.

In his formal response, Stephen followed Hebrew custom by surveying the history of Israel. He did so to emphasize that Jesus of Nazareth was Israel's promised Messiah and Redeemer. In particular, Stephen's address sets forth a refutation of the three points of reference on which some first-century A.D. Jews placed an idolatrous emphasis: the land, the law, and the temple. Concerning the Jews' veneration of the Promised Land, Stephen argued that while Judah remained important, God's activities in Israel's history often took place outside of Palestine. Also, wherever God is present, that locale is considered holy (7:2-36).

Moreover, the Jews revered the law and, in turn, the one who gave them the law—Moses. But Stephen reminded his listeners that this legendary figure clearly pointed to a coming Prophet who was greater than Moses and the law. Likewise, the people rejected Moses and embraced idol worship, just as they spurned Jesus (vss. 37-43). Finally, the Jews fixated on the Jerusalem temple as a symbol of God's past workings with the nation of Israel and the source of their future hope—so much so that they ended up worshiping the shrine rather than their Creator-King. Tragically, many also seemed to confine God's work to the sanctuary alone, instead of recognizing that He transcended any edifice made by people (see Isa. 66:1-2; Acts 17:24).

Stephen declared the religious leaders to be as "stiff-necked" (Acts 7:51), or stubborn, as an unyielding ox or donkey. Moreover, the members of the Council were "uncircumcised" in their thoughts, emotions, and will. By this declaration, Stephen meant that the Sanhedrin, though physically circumcised, were no different in their attitude and actions from the uncircumcised pagans they detested. Because the religious leaders refused to listen to God and rebelled against His Word, they were spiritually stubborn and unregenerate (see Ex. 32:9; 33:3, 5; Deut. 9:6; 10:16; 30:6; Jer. 4:4). Furthermore, instead of being genuinely devoted to the Lord, the Council was guilty of always fighting against the Holy Spirit. Stephen noted that this was the same offense their ancestors had committed.

B. Persecuting the Prophets: vss. 52-53

"Was there ever a prophet your fathers did not persecute? They even killed those who predicted the coming of the Righteous One. And now you have betrayed and murdered him—you who have received the law that was put into effect through angels but have not obeyed it."

Stephen rhetorically asked whether there ever was a spokesperson for God that the ancestors of the Sanhedrin did not mistreat. Stephen declared that the Council's predecessors were even guilty of murdering the prophets who foretold the advent of the "Righteous One" (Acts 7:52), which is a reference to Jesus of Nazareth. Of course, the religious leaders rejected His claim to be the Messiah. Also, rather than heed Him as their Redeemer and Lord, they schemed with the civil authorities to have Him crucified. The irony is that the Mosaic law the Council members so highly prized contained prophecies about the coming of the Savior. Put differently, it was the members of the Sanhedrin, not Stephen, who were guilty of violating the law and desecrating all that it stood for.

Here we learn that the Mosaic law was ordained or decreed by angels. Though angels are not mentioned as being instrumental in God's issuance of the law to Moses in Exodus 20, their presence at Mount Sinai is mentioned in several other New Testament passages (see Gal. 3:19; Heb. 2:2). Mention is also made in the Septuagint version of Deuteronomy 33:2, as well as in the *Antiquities* of the first-century A.D. Jewish historian Josephus. Apparently, the involvement of angels in the mediation of the law was widely accepted by the second century B.C.

Stephen was convinced that the Gospel was true, and this must have given him the courage to proclaim the Good News to others. His gratitude for what God had done in his life also may have given him the boldness to expose himself to danger, especially as he told people about the Lord Jesus. Most importantly, the Savior enabled Stephen to be courageous in his witness to others. Even when he stood before such an imposing and authoritative group as the Sanhedrin, the Spirit empowered him to be forceful in his witness.

II. THE STONING OF STEPHEN: ACTS 7:54-60

A. The Indignation of the Sanhedrin: vs. 54

When they heard this, they were furious and gnashed their teeth at him.

The natural reaction of the religious leaders was to become "furious" (Acts 7:54).

The latter renders a Greek verb that literally means to be "cut to the quick." The members of the Council also began to grind their teeth. This is an idiomatic expression to point to the presence of extreme rage. Stephen's speech was upsetting to the religious leaders because it was a stinging indictment of a history of unbelief for the nation and its chosen people. But more specifically, in the minds of the religious leaders, Stephen's claim of divinity for Jesus of Nazareth, the person whom they had schemed to be crucified, was a clear case of blasphemy. According to the Mosaic law, this offense was punishable by death (see Lev. 24:13-16).

B. The Heavenly Vision Experienced by Stephen: vss. 55-56

But Stephen, full of the Holy Spirit, looked up to heaven and saw the glory of God, and Jesus standing at the right hand of God. "Look," he said, "I see heaven open and the Son of Man standing at the right hand of God."

Despite the rage of the Sanhedrin, Stephen remained under the complete control of the Holy Spirit. At Jesus' trial, He had declared to the Council that they would see the "Son of Man sitting at the right hand of the Mighty One" (Mark 14:62). As Stephen fixed his gaze heavenward, he had a vision of the Father's glory and the Son standing at the Lord's right hand (Acts 7:55). While the "Son of Man" (vs. 56) is customarily pictured as seated at the Father's right hand, some have suggested that the Messiah had risen on this occasion to welcome the first martyr of the church. Others think Jesus was testifying on behalf of Stephen.

C. The Capital Punishment of Stephen: vss. 57-58

At this they covered their ears and, yelling at the top of their voices, they all rushed at him, dragged him out of the city and began to stone him. Meanwhile, the witnesses laid their clothes at the feet of a young man named Saul.

Stephen's words were so blasphemous to the religious leaders that they put their hands over their ears and drowned out his voice with their shouts (Acts 7:57). Perhaps with the fury of an uncontrollable mob, the Council rushed at Stephen, hauled him out of Jerusalem, and began to throw stones at him. Though he faced imminent death, Stephen demonstrated before his antagonists what it truly meant to honor the Lord. Stephen's desire was not to perpetuate a dead institution and its lifeless traditions. Rather, he sought to please God, regardless of the circumstances or the cost to himself. While these things were taking place, the official witnesses took off their outer garments and laid them at the feet of a young man named "Saul" (vs. 58) of Tarsus. (He is later called Paul in Acts 13:9.) He was a Pharisee and associated with the Sanhedrin (see Phil. 3:5). It's possible Saul was an instigator of Stephen's trial (see Acts 8:3; 9:1-2).

In ancient Israel, stoning was the most commonly prescribed form of execution for capital offenses. These offenses usually involved breaking particular Mosaic laws. Included among the crimes that carried the death penalty were child sacrifice

(Lev. 20:2), involvement with the occult (20:27), working on the Sabbath (Num. 15:32-36), worshiping false gods (Deut. 13:10), rebellion against parents (21:18-21), adultery (22:21-24; Ezek. 16:38-40), and blasphemy (Lev. 24:14-16; John 10:31-33). The men of a community normally carried out the sentence of stoning (Deut. 21:21). In cases involving capital crimes, the testimony of at least two witnesses was required, and those witnesses were obligated to cast the first stones (Deut. 17:5-7; John 8:7; Acts 7:58). Execution normally occurred somewhere outside the city or camp boundaries.

The members of the Sanhedrin, not Stephen, were guilty of rebelling against God. Years earlier, during Jesus' earthly ministry, He declared that in the day of judgment, He would not be the one to accuse His opponents of sinning against the Father. Instead, it would be their esteemed lawgiver, Moses, in whom the religious authorities of the day had pinned their hopes of salvation (John 5:45). In the future time of reckoning, the critics would not be able to look to Moses as their intercessor before God (see Ex. 32:30-34; Ps. 106:23), for ultimately what Moses penned concerned the Messiah. Jesus and Moses were so intertwined that to receive or reject Moses was to receive or reject Jesus (John 5:46-47). He who is the only mediator between God and humanity is also the same person the elite spurned (see 1 Tim. 2:5). In short, to reject the Son—the Father's only provision of salvation—was to leave oneself eternally condemned (see Heb. 6:4-8; 1 Pet. 2:7-8).

D. The Martyrdom of Stephen: vss. 59-60

While they were stoning him, Stephen prayed, "Lord Jesus, receive my spirit." Then he fell on his knees and cried out, "Lord, do not hold this sin against them." When he had said this, he fell asleep.

While Stephen was being stoned, he made two dying requests. First, he prayed that the Messiah would receive his spirit (Acts 7:59). The comparison to our Lord's dying prayer is too striking to be overlooked (see Luke 23:46). Just as the Son had committed Himself to the Father, so Stephen cast himself upon Jesus. Thus, to Stephen's dying breath, he confirmed the deity of the Messiah. Second, while Stephen knelt on the ground, he prayed for his enemies. He asked the Lord not to hold his executioners guilty for what they had done (Acts 7:60). This petition echoed Jesus' cry at His crucifixion (see Luke 23:34). Stephen, like his Master, ended his life by returning forgiveness for vengeance, and love for hatred.

Despite the terrifying prospect of death, Stephen remained calm and hopeful. Unlike his detractors, he had the assurance that God the Son—his Savior and Lord—would receive him into His glorious presence. The words "he fell asleep" (Acts 7:60) are a common euphemism for death in Scripture. The verse points to the peace with which Stephen died. His triumph was grounded in the risen Messiah. He, having conquered death, promised a future resurrection awakening for His disciples.

III. THE INVOLVEMENT OF SAUL: ACTS 8:1A

And Saul was there, giving approval to his death.

Earlier it was noted that a young Pharisee named Saul was standing with the clothing of the executioners (Acts 7:58). By doing so, Saul did not show mere passive approval of the stoning. Some have suggested that this act meant Saul was in charge of the proceedings. In any case, 8:1 shows Saul actively and wholeheartedly condoning the grizzly death of Stephen. Saul's statement about himself in 22:20 agrees with 8:1. The hatred he had of all believers before his conversion was manifested in his attitude toward Stephen. God would eventually use Saul's disdain for Jesus to lead the Pharisee to eternal life.

Acts 7:58 and 8:1 are the first mention of Saul in the book. He may have attended the synagogue where Stephen carried on his debate. Like Stephen, the Pharisee realized that Christianity was incompatible with the old religious order. Although Saul approved of Stephen's execution, he later was unable to forget his role in the martyr's death (see 22:20). Saul would soon find himself continuing the work Stephen and other like-minded believers had begun. Later, Saul realized he had been the worst of sinners. Because the Devil had blinded his mind to the truth, only the Spirit could enlighten his understanding and convince him of his need for the Messiah. God, in His mercy, allowed this to happen so that Saul, the foremost of sinners, might be a trophy of divine grace. The former persecutor of the church thus became an ideal display of the Messiah's unlimited patience. Saul would serve as an example to others who in the future would put their trust in the Son and receive eternal life (see 1 Tim. 1:16).

Until Stephen's death, Christian converts were content to remain in Jerusalem. But on the day when Stephen was martyred, "a great persecution" (Acts 8:1) erupted against the church. God providentially used this maltreatment to scatter believers everywhere, especially in Judea and Samaria, to proclaim the Gospel in those areas. The apostles, however, remained in Jerusalem to provide leadership there. Meanwhile, godly men buried Stephen amid great mourning over his death (vs. 2).

Discussion Questions

1. Why were the religious leaders so calloused to the truth about Jesus?
2. In what ways were the religious leaders like their ancestors?
3. How was it possible for Stephen to remain gracious in his witness while being mistreated by the Sanhedrin?
4. Describe a time when you were courageous in speaking about the Lord. What resulted from it?
5. How would an active, consistent prayer life strengthen a believer who is facing opposition?

Contemporary Application

Luke explained how Stephen rose to a leadership position within the church. In the process, Luke revealed that the most important qualification for Christian service is being controlled by the Holy Spirit. Stephen was a man who possessed this quality in a remarkable way. Through God's grace and power, this wise servant (Acts 6:3) became a great miracle worker (vs. 8), evangelist (vs. 10), and the first to give his life for the cause of Christ.

For many of us, the thought of telling others about our faith brings on sweaty palms and a suddenly vacant mind. We fear embarrassment, ridicule, and rejection. We also fear violating the rules of etiquette that religion should never be discussed in polite society. Perhaps we are ultimately afraid of failing, and the possibility of losing face as well as a soul for the kingdom of God. Stephen's testimony before the people and leaders of the Jews provides us with an excellent example of how to courageously witness to God's grace. Stephen spoke his mind straightforwardly and authoritatively, even when he encountered opposition.

Maintaining a courageous witness does not mean we are disrespectful, obnoxious, or overly aggressive. We are not trying to pick a fight with others or alienate them from the Lord Jesus and His Gospel. Our desire is to be persistent and make the truth known in a way that is biblically accurate and relevant. Doing this is not always easy, and without God's help, we will fail. That is why we should continue to trust Him to give us the wisdom we need to remain focused and godly as we maintain a courageous testimony.

We should also look to God for inner strength and clarity of mind to say the right words at the right time. God can and does empower His people to courageously present the truth of His grace in ways they never imagined. The key, of course, is to completely rely on Him.

Trying to Buy Power

Scripture

Background Scripture: *Acts 8:4-24*
Scripture Lesson: *Acts 8:9-24*
Key Verse: *When Simon saw that the Spirit was given at the laying on of the apostles' hands, he offered them money.* Acts 8:18.
Scripture Lesson for Children: *Acts 8:9-24*
Key Verse for Children: *Peter answered: "May your money perish with you, because you thought you could buy the gift of God with money!"* Acts 8:20.

Lesson Aim

To emphasize that God provides many opportunities for us to share the Gospel.

Lesson Setting

Time: Around A.D. *35*
Place: Samaria

Lesson Outline

Trying to Buy Power

  I. The Conversion of Simon the Sorcerer: Acts 8:9-13
    A. The Sorcery of Simon: vss. 9-10
    B. The Decision of Simon to Believe: vss. 11-13
 II. The Confrontation with Simon the Sorcerer: Acts 8:14-24
    A. The Dispatching of Peter and John: vss. 14-17
    B. Simon's Offer of Money: vss. 18-19
    C. Peter's Rebuke of Simon: vss. 20-23
    D. Simon's Repentant Response: vs. 24

Introduction for Adults

Topic: *Power Brokers*

In his book *Cultural Anthropology,* Paul G. Hiebert defines a social culture as an "integrated system of learned patterns of behavior, ideas and products, characteristic of a society." The social setting that we come from usually defines who we are as individuals. Most people are comfortable living and working around those with whom they are most familiar and with whom they share a social culture.

When Christ comes into our lives, He begins to replace our fear of other people with a love for them. Instead of fearing how they might harm or reject us, we are more able to think of their need for Christ, and, therefore, we will want them to experience God's forgiveness and love.

We see this perspective at work in Philip's evangelistic outreach in Samaria. He could have been put off by Simon the sorcerer, who acted as if he was the great power broker of God (so to speak). Despite Simon's swagger, Philip remained committed to sharing the Gospel with him. And the Lord used Philip to bring Simon to the place where he, too, "believed and was baptized" (Acts 8:13).

Introduction for Youth

Topic: *Not for Sale!*

The formation of cliques remains a prevalent phenomenon among teens. And with the existence of such groups can come the notion that people in one clique are unwelcome in another clique.

This adversarial mentality runs counter to the gospel of Christ. He wants saved teens to share the Good News even with those they might feel are their enemies. To be sure, this can be difficult. But it's amazing how the power of Christ can break down barriers between people.

The mission field of believing young people may begin with their families, then extend into their schools or neighborhood, and finally into the larger society. Regardless of whom the Lord brings into the lives of your students, they should be alert to the opportunities to tell others how much Jesus means to them. And as Peter emphasized to Simon, God's grace is offered freely to the lost and cannot be purchased at any price.

Concepts for Children

Topic: *Not for Sale!*

1. Philip went to Samaria to tell people about Jesus.
2. In Samaria, Philip did many amazing things.
3. God used Philip to encourage a famous person named Simon to believe in Jesus.
4. The church in Jerusalem sent Peter and John to help Christians in Samaria.
5. God wants us to tell people about Jesus.

Lesson Commentary

I. THE CONVERSION OF SIMON THE SORCERER: ACTS 8:9-13

A. The Sorcery of Simon: vss. 9-10

Now for some time a man named Simon had practiced sorcery in the city and amazed all the people of Samaria. He boasted that he was someone great, and all the people, both high and low, gave him their attention and exclaimed, "This man is the divine power known as the Great Power."

As was noted in last week's lesson, the stoning of Stephen unleashed a firestorm of hatred against the followers of the Lord Jesus. Among the believers scattered by the persecution was Philip (Acts 8:5). He was one of the persons previously selected along with Stephen to look after the Greek-speaking widows (see 6:5). Philip, like Stephen, illustrates how a person faithful in one ministry was given a wider sphere of service. His works recorded in chapter 8 were only the beginning of a long, fruitful span of service (see 21:8).

At some point, Philip decided to travel "down" (8:5; or downhill) from Jerusalem to the principal "city in Samaria." Samaria was a region in central Palestine first occupied by the tribe of Ephraim and part of the tribe of Manasseh. One of the region's most prominent centers, the ancient town of Shechem (near Mount Gerizim, Samaria's highest peak), became the capital of the northern kingdom of Israel under Jeroboam (931–910 B.C.; see 1 Kings 12:25). Later, a city named Samaria (begun by Omri around 880 B.C.) became the capital of the northern kingdom, and remained so through several kings until it fell to the Assyrians in 722 B.C. When the northern kingdom fell, most of its prominent citizens were deported to Assyria, Aram (Syria), and Babylon. The depleted Israelite population was then replaced with foreigners from Babylon and elsewhere (see 2 Kings 17:24). Through the intermarriage between the newcomers and the Israelites left in the land, the resulting people later known as Samaritans were formed.

Because of their mixed Jewish-Gentile blood, early pagan worship (vs. 29), and later religious ceremonies that centered on Mount Gerizim rather than the temple in Jerusalem (see John 4:20-22), the Samaritans were generally despised by the Jews throughout their history. This certainly remained true in New Testament times. In fact, the Jews of Philip's day were unrelenting in their view that the Samaritans were racially impure. The Jews also saw Samaritans as religious half-breeds since Samaritans rejected much of the Scriptures, accepting only the first five books. Moreover, despite their common ancestry, their equal regard for the law, and their shared hope for a Messiah, Jews and Samaritans usually refused to have anything to do with each other (see Luke 9:51-56; John 4:9).

There is some doubt about the exact identity of the city where Philip took up temporary residence (Acts 8:5). Some conjecture it was the region's capital, which also happened to be called Samaria. Regardless of which particular city Philip visited, it was there that he proclaimed the truth about the Messiah to the residents.

It is somewhat surprising that the Samaritans listened to Philip, for he was a Jew (vs. 6). It may have helped that he was a Hellenistic Jew (6:1), that is, a Jew who spoke Greek and was influenced by Greek culture. It also may have helped that Philip had recently endured Jewish persecution. Perhaps the Samaritans had heard about and approved of disputes about the temple that Christians such as Stephen had carried on with Jews (vss. 13-14).

At any rate, when the Samaritans heard Philip's message and saw the miracles he performed, they listened intently to what he proclaimed (8:6). They knew something unusual was happening among them. They watched wide-eyed as those with evil spirits were set free and as paralytics and cripples walked (vs. 7). The record of the miracles Philip performed reads like a list of the very signs Jesus Himself had earlier done. The Savior performed many miracles during His earthly ministry, some of which are not recorded in the Gospels. His miracles were extraordinary expressions of God's power.

When the Son performed a miracle, He directly altered, superseded, or counteracted some established pattern in the natural order. The miracles of Jesus served several purposes. First, they confirmed His claim to be the Messiah. Second, they validated His assertion that He was sent by God and represented Him. Third, they substantiated the credibility of the truths He declared to the people of Israel. Fourth, they encouraged the doubtful to put their trust in Him. Fifth, they demonstrated that the one who is love was willing to reach out to people with compassion and grace.

As Philip performed various miracles, God used these signs to give evidence of His presence and truth to a previously despised, neglected people. It is no wonder "there was great joy in that city" (vs. 8). From this information we see that supernatural power was impressive to the Samaritans. In turn, this explains why many Samaritans followed Simon, a sorcerer (vs. 9). In the ancient world, the kind of magic he practiced flourished. Luke recorded three incidents related to magic: the account of Simon (vss. 9-24), the account of Elymas (13:4-12), and the account of seven Jewish exorcists (19:13-20).

Details about the magic practiced by those magicians are mostly lacking. But more generally, we know that Greco-Roman magic combined ideas from a number of sources. Assyrian and Babylonian magic contributed knowledge of astrology. Egyptian magic contributed a belief in the power of secret names. Persian magic contributed ways of using spirits for good and evil ends. Israelite magic contributed a body of divine and angelic names thought effective in incantations (that is, magic spells).

The Greco-Roman magic practiced by Simon tended to be practical. On behalf of their clients, sorcerers tried to prevent or avert harm, to hurt enemies with curses, to inspire love or submission in others, and to gain revelations from the spirit world. Simon's own involvement with magic extended back a number of years. He beguiled people with his antics and claimed that he was someone important (8:9).

He was able to convince the Samaritans—from the least to the most prominent—that he was the great power of the divine (vs. 10). The idea probably is that Simon either claimed to be God or alleged to be God's chief representative.

B. The Decision of Simon to Believe: vss. 11-13

They followed him because he had amazed them for a long time with his magic. But when they believed Philip as he preached the good news of the kingdom of God and the name of Jesus Christ, they were baptized, both men and women. Simon himself believed and was baptized. And he followed Philip everywhere, astonished by the great signs and miracles he saw.

It was because of the magic Simon performed that he held such sway over the people of Samaria (Acts 8:11). But the arrival of Philip changed all that. He proclaimed the "good news" (vs. 12) about the divine kingdom, especially as it centered on Jesus the Messiah. As a result of Philip's evangelistic activities, many men and women put their trust in the Messiah. They also gave evidence of their decision to believe by being baptized. We learn in Scripture that the divine kingdom embraces all who walk in fellowship with the Lord and do His will. The kingdom is governed by God's laws, which are summed up in our duty to love the Lord supremely and love others as ourselves. Moreover, this kingdom, which was announced by the prophets and introduced by Jesus, will one day displace all the kingdoms of this world, following the return of the Lord Jesus.

Simon decided to put his faith in Jesus and get baptized. Simon did so because the amazing things God did through Philip enthralled him. The missionary's works of power were so superior to Simon's that the former sorcerer stayed close to Philip wherever he went (vs. 13). On the one hand, Simon marveled at the miracles he saw Philip perform. On the other hand, the evangelist's intent was not to make a name for himself. Instead, his goal was to confirm the truth he proclaimed, especially Jesus' ability to rescue people from their life of sin. It was the grace of God that enabled the Samaritans and Simon to give up their sinful attitudes and believe in the Lord Jesus. Similarly, when we come to faith in the Messiah, we must surrender our old life so that we can receive a new life. Our old sinful ways of thinking, our old attitudes and prejudices, and our old habits and lifestyles must all be given up so that God can do His work in us.

II. THE CONFRONTATION WITH SIMON THE SORCERER: ACTS 8:14-24

A. The Dispatching of Peter and John: vss. 14-17

When the apostles in Jerusalem heard that Samaria had accepted the word of God, they sent Peter and John to them. When they arrived, they prayed for them that they might receive the Holy Spirit, because the Holy Spirit had not yet come upon any of them; they had simply been baptized into the name of the Lord Jesus. Then Peter and John placed their hands on them, and they received the Holy Spirit.

In the persecution following Stephen's stoning, the apostles bravely maintained the church's presence at its original center, Jerusalem. There news of Philip's successes in evangelizing the lost of Samaria reached them. Peter and John, as representatives of the apostles, went to see for themselves what was happening in Samaria (Acts 8:14). Peter and John arrived at a city that had been transformed by the power of God. The two were able to build on the foundation laid by Philip. This included the apostles strengthening and developing the faith of the new believers. Thus, the first thing Peter and John did was pray that the new converts might be given the Holy Spirit (vs. 15).

Luke explained that the Spirit had not yet fallen on any of the converts. The reason is that the Samaritan believers had only undergone water baptism in Jesus' name (vs. 16). This statement raises an intriguing question. How was it possible for the Spirit not to be received by those who had believed the truth about "the kingdom of God and the name of Jesus Christ" (vs. 12)? Bible scholars differ in their answers to this question. Problematic is the notion that Peter and John's ministry conveyed a second, separate blessing of grace—a work of the Spirit beyond His initial indwelling. Some view the apostles' work as a sort of confirmation with the goal of bringing intellectual faith up to a higher level. The most likely explanation is that this was a unique occurrence in which God used Peter and John to communicate the Spirit in such a way that the Jerusalem believers would accept the Samaritans.

Peter and John clearly expected something more to happen in the Samaritans' lives. Thus, the apostles showed their affirmation, solidarity, and support for the new converts by laying their hands on them. When the apostles did so, the Samaritan converts were given the Holy Spirit (vs. 17). The laying on of hands was a common practice among Jews for blessing people or putting them into a ministry or service. Luke did not tell what followed the praying and laying on of hands, other than to say that the Samaritan believers were granted the gift of the Spirit. Luke had earlier described in greater detail signs that accompanied fillings of the Holy Spirit (see 2:2-4; 4:31). Though we are not told exactly what happened when the Spirit came upon the Samaritans, we know that some demonstration of God's power appeared. Those who looked on recognized this manifestation as a supernatural event.

B. Simon's Offer of Money: vss. 18-19

When Simon saw that the Spirit was given at the laying on of the apostles' hands, he offered them money and said, "Give me also this ability so that everyone on whom I lay my hands may receive the Holy Spirit."

Simon, the former sorcerer, was one of the observers. (The text gives no suggestion that he was a participant.) When he saw the demonstration of God's power that came when the apostles laid their hands on the Samaritan converts and prayed, something of his former ways stirred within him. This was supernatural ability like nothing he'd ever seen, an influence and control over people far better than any scheme he'd ever used. Simon, unable to hide his eagerness, "offered . . . money" (Acts 8:18) to Peter and John. Simon crassly reasoned that if he could manipulate the mysterious power to give others the Spirit by laying hands on them, he could then recapture his lost fame and influence (vs. 19).

C. Peter's Rebuke of Simon: vss. 20-23

Peter answered: "May your money perish with you, because you thought you could buy the gift of God with money! You have no part or share in this ministry, because your heart is not right before God. Repent of this wickedness and pray to the Lord. Perhaps he will forgive you for having such a thought in your heart. For I see that you are full of bitterness and captive to sin."

Peter saw through Simon's request. The apostle told him in no uncertain terms that since he tried to use money to acquire the "gift of God," both he and his precious silver could eternally "perish" (Acts 8:20). If such language seems too harsh, it is precisely what Peter intended. In telling Simon he might languish in hell, Peter used the same word Jesus used in saying, "Broad is the road that leads to *destruction*" (Matt. 7:13, emphasis added). Next, Peter firmly told Simon that he could not have any "part or share" (Acts 8:21) in the evangelistic work, for he tried to bargain with the Lord and bribe His ambassadors. Peter urged Simon to abandon his evil plan and turn away from his sinful motives. If he did so, God could forgive him of his warped thinking (vs. 22).

Peter described Simon's spiritual condition as being consumed by envy, resentment, and greed. Moreover, the apostle said that Simon remained in bondage to wickedness (vs. 23). There is a lingering question as to whether Simon was a genuine believer. While verse 13 seems to indicate that he was, verses 20-23 seem to suggest that he was not. There are several possible answers to this question. Some say Simon only appeared to believe when he saw and experienced Philip's power. Others say Peter used exaggerated terms, meaning only that Simon had sinned badly, not that he was an unbeliever. A third group maintains that Simon abandoned his faith when he tried to buy divine power.

D. Simon's Repentant Response: vs. 24

Then Simon answered, "Pray to the Lord for me so that nothing you have said may happen to me."

Although Peter's words were blunt, they remained appropriate and effective. Acts 8:24 reveals that Simon displayed a change of heart. He asked that Peter would petition the Lord, so that none of what the apostle said would take place in Simon's life. After this episode, Peter and John spent a little more time solemnly proclaiming the truth of God to the local residents. Then, as the two apostles journeyed back to Jerusalem, they declared the Good News in numerous villages in Samaria (vs. 25).

On one level, Simon desired a good thing, that is, to be able to impart the Holy Spirit to others. But on another level, Simon asked for the wrong reasons. In particular, he was more interested in serving himself than in serving the Lord or others.

Whenever we desire to do something good in service to God, we must take care that our motives are pure. It's easy to put selfish ambition into good works when sacrifice and commitment are needed instead.

Discussion Questions

1. How did Simon the sorcerer make a name for himself in Samaria?
2. What astonished Simon the most about Philip?
3. What did Peter and John do when they arrived in the Samaritan city?
4. What is the purpose of miracles, signs, and wonders in promoting the Gospel?
5. What can we do to let go of our own ways so that God can show us His ways?

Contemporary Application

Despite Jesus' command to witness to the ends of the earth, the church might have stayed comfortably in Jerusalem if the early Christians had not been persecuted (Acts 8:1-3). Thankfully, under God's direction, Philip was willing to be used in the proclamation of the Gospel to the Samaritans. The evangelist was not put off by their despised status in the Jewish society of the day.

We function better within our comfort zone, where people are familiar and circumstances are easy. Often, though, God sends us into unfamiliar or scary places because He has work for us there. A sign in a church, which people see as they leave, says, "You are now going out into the mission field." Where might God be sending you to share the Gospel? You might say, "I do not speak very well." Instead, you could smile and say "God loves you" to a very tired store clerk; or you could tell a peer at work or school that you are a Christian; or you could help a person carry heavy packages as a prelude to sharing your faith.

God may place you in an unusual situation. If so, submit to Him in the power of His Spirit. The Lord might want you to talk to and encourage a handicapped person. You could feed a child who comes to the local soup kitchen or join with others in your church to resettle a refugee family. Any of these contacts might open a door to share the Gospel.

You should prepare yourself to witness through Bible study and prayer. You will want to be friendly and show interest in the person before you launch into a spiritual discussion. If you sense the Spirit's nudging to talk with someone, be sure to pray first. Ask God for His words, not yours. If you obediently share as God provides opportunity, He will bless you for your faithfulness, not your eloquence.

The Ethiopian Eunuch

Scripture

Background Scripture: *Acts 8:26-39*

Scripture Lesson: *Acts 8:26-39*

Key Verse: *The eunuch said, "Look, here is water. Why shouldn't I be baptized?"* Acts 8:36.

Scripture Lesson for Children: *Acts 8:26-39*

Key Verse for Children: *Then Philip began with that very passage of Scripture and told him the good news about Jesus.* Acts 8:35.

Lesson Aim

To consider how to overcome social barriers in order to tell people about the Savior.

Lesson Setting

Time: Around A.D. 35

Place: The desert road going from Jerusalem to Gaza

Lesson Outline

The Ethiopian Eunuch

I. Philip Shares the Gospel: Acts 8:26-35
   A. *The Command of the Angel: vs. 26*
   B. *The Activities of the Ethiopian Eunuch: vss. 27-28*
   C. *The Question Asked by Philip: vss. 29-31*
   D. *The Scripture Passage Being Read by the Eunuch: vss. 32-33*
   E. *The Explanation Offered by Philip: vss. 34-35*

II. Philip Baptizes the Ethiopian Eunuch: Acts 8:36-39
   A. *The Request to Be Baptized: vss. 36-37*
   B. *The Fulfillment of the Request: vss. 38-39*

Introduction for Adults

Topic: *Erasing the Boundary Lines*

Imagine how different the situation would have been had Philip not heeded the prompting of the Spirit to share the Gospel with the Ethiopian eunuch. Thankfully, Philip did not let social and cultural differences he might have had with the government official stop him from being used by God in a special way.

Many of the personal prejudices of adults have been ingrained in them since childhood. On their own, they don't have the determination and strength to overcome their deep-seated intolerances. Only God can remove those biases.

If there is any doubt about prejudice in the church, ask yourself why the statement "Sunday morning remains the most segregated time of the week" still rings true. Possibly members of your class are extremely alike. Can it be that personal prejudices have made it uncomfortable for other kinds of people to feel welcome?

This week's lesson encourages your students to seek God's help in overcoming whatever prejudices they have. This in turn will enable them to present a truly Christian witness to others.

Introduction for Youth

Topic: *I Can Belong*

Perhaps you've heard the statement that all people are created equal, but some are more equal than others. Tragically, that's the way things often work in church youth groups. Some members seem to be more important and valuable than others. When this attitude prevails, it drives adolescents away from Jesus.

We don't know whether Philip had any reservations about sharing the Gospel with the Ethiopian eunuch, but if Philip did, the Spirit enabled him to overcome his biases. Likewise, there are times when the young people in your class will have to do the same, especially when new people show up at church activities. Let your students know that God plays no favorites, not even in church youth groups.

Because God wants all people to be saved, Christian youth should work hard to make everyone in their class feel accepted, welcomed, and loved. Yes, this is an act of faith on their part. Let them know they can trust the Lord to help them overcome their prejudices.

Concepts for Children

Topic: *Sharing the Faith*

1. An official from Ethiopia had gone to Jerusalem to worship the Lord.
2. While this person was returning home, the Holy Spirit had Philip go to the official and tell him about Jesus.
3. Philip explained to the official a passage from the Book of Isaiah.
4. The Lord used Philip to lead the official to faith in Jesus.
5. We can use the Bible to encourage others to trust in Jesus.

Lesson Commentary

I. PHILIP SHARES THE GOSPEL: ACTS 8:26-35

A. The Command of the Angel: vs. 26

Now an angel of the Lord said to Philip, "Go south to the road—the desert road—that goes down from Jerusalem to Gaza."

This week's lesson spotlights the conversion of a man from Ethiopia. In ancient times, Ethiopia was located in the region of Nubia, just south of Egypt, where the first waterfall of the Nile goes into the Sudan. The modern nation of Ethiopia is located farther to the southeast. Many Bible scholars equate Ethiopia with the land of Cush (see Gen. 2:13; Isa. 11:11). Cush was an enemy of Egypt for centuries, gaining and losing independence, depending on the pharaoh who was in power. After the Assyrians conquered the Egyptians in 671 B.C., Ethiopia maintained a strong center of trade.

The most influential Ethiopian leader, Tirhakah, aided Hezekiah when Sennacherib invaded Judah in 701 B.C. (see 2 Kings 19:9; Isa. 37:9). The capital, Napata, was abandoned around 300 B.C. The capital of Ethiopia then moved south to Meroe, where the kingdom continued on for another 600 years. Archaeological digs in Napata and Meroe have disclosed a number of pyramid tombs, as well as temples to the Egyptian god, Amun. During the New Testament era, several queens of Ethiopia bore the name Candace, which was probably a hereditary title, not a proper name. Modern Ethiopian Christians consider the eunuch of this week's text their country's first evangelist. In fact, many regard his conversion as the beginning of the fulfillment of Psalm 68:31.

As we continue the narrative in Acts 8, we learn that an angel of the Lord told Philip to leave the city and go south to the road that led from Jerusalem to Gaza (vs. 26). In ancient times, Gaza was a town located about 50 miles from Jerusalem. The original city was destroyed in the first century B.C. and a new city was built near the coast. Not knowing what he would find on the desert road, Philip obeyed. Leaving behind the excitement and action among the new Samaritan converts, he traveled into the desert. God's opportunities may not always excite us. We may think we see greater potential elsewhere. Obedience like Philip's, however, opens the door for God to do things we could never have imagined.

B. The Activities of the Ethiopian Eunuch: vss. 27-28

So he started out, and on his way he met an Ethiopian eunuch, an important official in charge of all the treasury of Candace, queen of the Ethiopians. This man had gone to Jerusalem to worship, and on his way home was sitting in his chariot reading the book of Isaiah the prophet.

Running through the desert south of Jerusalem was a well-traveled road, a main route toward Egypt. On the road was a "eunuch" (Acts 8:27) returning from

Jerusalem to his native Ethiopia. By the man's chariot and servants, Philip could see he was an important government official. It's possible, though, that the Greek noun rendered "chariot" (vs. 28) was little more than an ox-drawn cart that was going only slightly faster than walking speed.

In Scripture, the word "eunuch" usually denotes male attendants assigned to serve in a royal household. As a precautionary measure, male palace servants were castrated, especially if their area of work involved the king's harem (see 2 Kings 9:32). Eunuchs might also have been men who were born without the ability to reproduce. Because they were not subject to the drives of other men, eunuchs could be trusted to oversee the king's harem (see Est. 2:15). In fact, the Greek noun translated "eunuch" (Acts 8:27) means "keeper of the bed" or "superintendent of the bed chamber."

While eunuchs enjoyed high status in the royal court, they were nevertheless held in low esteem in social and religious circles. In some cases, however, the word *eunuch* seems to have been purely a governmental title, not necessarily applied to a castrated man. Some think the Ethiopian "eunuch" was of this type. They say this, for one thing, because the eunuch had been in Jerusalem for worship. Generally speaking, Jewish law prohibited the participation of eunuchs in the Jewish assembly (see Deut. 23:1), though there may have been exceptions to this ban (see Isa. 56:4-5). Moreover, the Ethiopian was in charge of finances, not a harem. Acts 8:27 states he was a sort of secretary of the treasury for "Candace." She was responsible for carrying out the secular duties of the reigning monarch, who was considered too sacred to perform such administrative chores.

While the Ethiopian eunuch sat in his chariot, he read aloud to himself. This was a common practice in those days for those who had reading materials. But scrolls and other reading materials, transcribed by hand, were not readily available to the average person. Only the wealthy and influential could afford literature. Even more rare was a non-Jew possessing Hebrew Scripture, as this court official did. Because the Ethiopian had managed to obtain a copy of Isaiah, and since he had traveled to worship at the temple in Jerusalem, we may conclude that he was a convert to the Jewish faith. If not, he must surely have been a "God-fearer." This was a label given to Gentiles who believed in the one true God of Israel but who had not been circumcised. In short, the Ethiopian worshiped the true God.

C. The Question Asked by Philip: vss. 29-31

The Spirit told Philip, "Go to that chariot and stay near it." Then Philip ran up to the chariot and heard the man reading Isaiah the prophet. "Do you understand what you are reading?" Philip asked. "How can I," he said, "unless someone explains it to me?" So he invited Philip to come up and sit with him.

Philip sensed the Holy Spirit urging him closer to the chariot (Acts 8:29). A simple but profound lesson for us here is that in order to receive this specific divine guidance, Philip first had to obey God's general command (vs. 26). Had the evangelist refused to go southward to this desert area, he would not have been available to receive this divine directive. Likewise, we need to make ourselves available to God by following the clear and basic principles of His Word. Philip obeyed by running up to the Ethiopian (vs. 30).

During this time, the presence of eunuchs from Africa and other places was common. Philip's conversation with the Ethiopian official, however, shows the inclusiveness of the Gospel. The Father's provision of salvation through faith in the Son is for persons of every race, kindred, and nation. In addition, Luke made it clear that the Lord had arranged for this meeting not only to expand the spread of the Gospel but also to give salvation to someone He loved. Since the Ethiopian was reading aloud, Philip knew the Scripture verses the eunuch was contemplating. Knowing that this passage referred to the suffering Servant, Philip asked the official if he understood what he was reading.

The Ethiopian did not try to hide his ignorance. As one who wanted to comprehend God's Word, he admitted that he needed another to explain the prophet's words. Perceiving that Philip was such a person, the official invited Philip to sit next to him in his chariot (vs. 31). While it is true that the meaning of many portions of Scripture is self-evident, some passages are difficult to understand. Even Peter found portions of Paul's letters difficult to comprehend (see 2 Pet. 3:15-16). In light of this circumstance, God has provided gifted believers who through study and the illumination of the Spirit can expound His Word for the benefit of others.

D. The Scripture Passage Being Read by the Eunuch: vss. 32-33

The eunuch was reading this passage of Scripture: "He was led like a sheep to the slaughter, and as a lamb before the shearer is silent, so he did not open his mouth. In his humiliation he was deprived of justice. Who can speak of his descendants? For his life was taken from the earth."

The Ethiopian had been mulling over Isaiah 53:7-8. This passage describes a person who submitted to affliction and death without objection. He would do so to atone for humankind's sin. He was willing to die for others because He loved sinners and wanted to remove their transgressions. By oppression and unjust judgment, this person would be taken away to His death. Isaiah asked who could speak of this person's descendants. The Jews believed that to die without children was a tragedy (see 2 Sam. 18:18). The suffering Servant would have no physical descendants, for His life would be "taken from the earth" (Acts 8:33). Indeed, He would be stricken for the sins of humanity.

If you turn to Isaiah 53:7-8 in whatever version of the Bible you are reading, you may notice that the passage the Ethiopian was said to be reading, as recorded in Acts 8:32-33, is not what you find printed in your version of the Old Testament. That is because Luke was quoting from the Septuagint version of the Hebrew sacred writings, which was the most common translation used in New Testament times. The Septuagint was a Greek translation of the Old Testament that was produced in Alexandria, Egypt, about 285–247 B.C. The word *Septuagint* is a Latin term for 70. It is based on the legend that 70 Jewish scholars from Jerusalem were brought to Egypt to make this translation. The Greek rendering of the Old Testament was needed, since many Jews outside of Israel knew Greek but did not know Hebrew. Incidentally, the Septuagint is the version that New Testament writers most often quote—either verbatim or with minor changes in translation.

E. The Explanation Offered by Philip: vss. 34-35

The eunuch asked Philip, "Tell me, please, who is the prophet talking about, himself or someone else?" Then Philip began with that very passage of Scripture and told him the good news about Jesus.

The eunuch asked Philip whether Isaiah was talking about himself or referring to someone else (Acts 8:34). What an opportunity this was to tell the Good News about the Messiah! Luke did not give the details of what Philip shared with the Ethiopian official. Nevertheless, we can assume that Philip at least expounded on Jesus as the suffering Servant, for that is what the Isaiah passage is about. In this case, the Bible prepared the eunuch's heart for the proclamation of the Gospel by creating a spiritual hunger to know about the identity of the suffering Servant. From this we see that studying God's Word often alerts people to their need for the Savior and gives them the desire to trust in Him.

Philip explained how Jesus fulfilled the prophecy, namely, how He had been condemned and crucified as the Lamb of God, and how He rose from the dead (vs. 35). This information is not the answer the Ethiopian would have received from non-Christian, first-century A.D. Jews. Most saw the passage as referring to Isaiah himself, or to the nation of Israel, not to a suffering Messiah, since that did not fit in with their idea of a conquering Savior who would deliver them from the Romans. Actually, Luke 22:37 indicates that Jesus first applied Isaiah 53 to Himself before His crucifixion, when He quoted verse 12 to the apostles at the Last Supper.

Even though Isaiah used the past tense in describing the Servant, He had not appeared in the prophet's time. Moreover, in Isaiah's descriptions we find seemingly contradictory pictures of the Servant. For example, He is both humiliated and glorious, both a sufferer and a conqueror. Who can combine these divergent roles? From the New Testament we discover that Jesus Christ fulfills the messianic prophecies recorded in Isaiah 52–53. In His first coming, He died on the cross to redeem people from sin. In Jesus' second coming, He will defeat His foes and set up His glorious kingdom (see Rev. 19:11–20:6).

Three times previously Isaiah had spoken about the Servant of the Lord (see Isa. 42:1-7; 49:1-13; 50:4-11). In 52:13–53:12, the prophet spoke explicitly about the Servant for a final time. Isaiah said the Messiah would be grossly marred and disfigured as well as despised and rejected. His death would be an atonement justifying those who have gone astray. Isaiah began by noting that the Servant would "act wisely" (52:13), which is a sign of His obedience to God's will. Also, the Servant would "be raised and lifted up and highly exalted." These words remind us of what Isaiah said about God the Father in the prophet's temple vision recorded in chapter 6. So the Servant, like God, is worthy of worship. In the New Testament, references to Jesus' exaltation often occur in contexts of people worshiping and extolling Him (for example, Phil. 2:9-11).

II. PHILIP BAPTIZES THE ETHIOPIAN EUNUCH: ACTS 8:36-39

A. The Request to Be Baptized: vss. 36-37

As they traveled along the road, they came to some water and the eunuch said, "Look, here is water. Why shouldn't I be baptized?" Philip said, "If you believe with all your heart, you may." The eunuch answered, "I believe that Jesus Christ is the Son of God."

Evidently, part of the conversation between Philip and the Ethiopian included the topic of baptism. It was the government official, not Philip, who noticed water along the way and proposed that he should be baptized (Acts 8:36). Verse 37 is not in the earliest ancient manuscripts of Acts and therefore is not printed in some contemporary versions of the Bible. Even so, the verse is consistent with the expectations the apostles had of those who put their faith in the Messiah. Specifically, trusting in the Son and being baptized go hand in hand (so to speak). Philip's statement and the official's affirmation of Jesus being the "Son of God" was indeed the fulfillment of Isaiah's prophecy.

B. The Fulfillment of the Request: vss. 38-39

And he gave orders to stop the chariot. Then both Philip and the eunuch went down into the water and Philip baptized him. When they came up out of the water, the Spirit of the Lord suddenly took Philip away, and the eunuch did not see him again, but went on his way rejoicing.

Since the Ethiopian now trusted in the Lord Jesus, the government official ordered his chariot to be stopped. Most likely the Ethiopian was part of a caravan journeying in the same direction and moving slowly down the road. Once the chariot was no longer moving, the eunuch stepped into some nearby water and allowed Philip to baptize him (Acts 8:38). The baptism could have taken place at any number of locations. Tradition identifies the spot as near the town of Bethsura. The baptism, however, may have taken place nearer Gaza.

Verse 39 says that once the two came out of the water, the Spirit of the Lord "took Philip away." Some see in this description a miracle in which the evangelist was transported from the site of the baptism to Azotus. Others, however, interpret this merely as Philip's abrupt departure under the compulsion of the Spirit. The biblical text leaves no doubt that Philip carried his preaching mission farther to the north (vs. 40).

Discussion Questions

1. How did Philip respond to the command he received from the angel of the Lord?
2. What did Philip do to engage the official in conversation?
3. What explanation did Philip offer to the Ethiopian's question regarding Isaiah 53:7-8?
4. How might you discern a particular encounter as God's opportunity to share the Gospel?
5. Why does boldness to witness come from God?

Contemporary Application

It is usually difficult to be one of the first to do something new. Philip was a groundbreaker. He went beyond the barriers of race and social class to tell the good news of Jesus to an Ethiopian official. Philip was obedient to God and overcame social barriers in the process.

Often Christians allow social differences to hinder their relationships with others. However, the command to spread the Gospel demands that we see all people as individuals of sacred worth and value, created in the image of God. Admittedly, venturing into new and unfamiliar social situations can be frightening. Feelings of inadequacy and fear of rejection can make us feel powerless in sharing our faith in the Lord Jesus. Nevertheless, we must never lose sight of the truth that God will be with us when we encounter social barriers. Through the indwelling presence of the Spirit we can overcome these barriers and share the Good News of Jesus with those who are different from us.

This requires us to be willing to tell unbelievers about the Savior wherever they may be. Indeed, it is often outside the church building that people are converted to the Son. Jesus preached in the synagogues (Luke 4:44), taught a multitude by the seashore (5:3), privately ministered to Nicodemus at night (John 3:1-2), and on a mountain explained principles of God's kingdom (Matt. 5:1-2). The Son ventured into different contexts to share the Father's love. Can we do less?

Our mission field may begin with our families, then extend into our neighborhood, and finally into larger society. Regardless of the individual or situation, we need to be alert to the opportunities to tell people how much Jesus means to us.

Paul before Agrippa

Scripture

Background Scripture: *Acts 25:23–26:32*
Scripture Lesson: *Acts 26:19-32*
Key Verse: *"I am not insane, most excellent Festus," Paul
replied. "What I am saying is true and reasonable."*
Acts 26:25.
Scripture Lesson for Children: *Acts 26:19-32*
Key Verse for Children: *"I am not insane, most excellent
Festus," Paul replied. "What I am saying is true and reason-
able."* Acts 26:25.

Lesson Aim

To recognize that our personal testimonies reflect the
Gospel of Christ in our lives.

Lesson Setting

Time: A.D. *57–59*
Place: Caesarea

Lesson Outline

Paul before Agrippa
  I. Paul's Defense: Acts 26:19-23
      A. *Paul's Obedient Response: vs. 19*
      B. *Paul's Ministry: vs. 20*
      C. *Paul's Affirmation of the Truth: vss. 21-23*
  II. Paul's Call for Decision: Acts 26:24-32
      A. *To Festus: vss. 24-25*
      B. *To the King: vss. 26-27*
      C. *The King's Refusal: vss. 28-29*
      D. *The Comments after the End of the Assembly:
         vss. 30-32*

Introduction for Adults

Topic: *Taking a Stand*

What constitutes "the call" mystifies many people. God called Abraham, Moses, Samuel, Isaiah, and Paul in rather dramatic fashion. Does He still do that today? Another bothersome question is whether "the call" is reserved for people going into the ministry. When a young man told his adult sponsor that he might like to be a missionary, the sponsor replied, "Have you been called?"

In a general way, the Father calls people to faith in the Son and to lives of obedient, faithful service. This remains the case regardless of their vocation. Thus, the primary career calling of all believers is to be faithful in taking a stand for Christ while living God-honoring lives.

No believer can ever doubt what God's will is in this regard. We do not need to see a bright light in the sky, like Paul did while he was traveling on the road heading into Damascus. We do need to study the Scriptures, pray, worship, and fellowship with other believers. In that context, God promises to make His way clear to all of us.

Introduction for Youth

Topic: *Standing by My Convictions*

A young man, new in his Christian faith, wondered how to decide what to do in an important matter. He had heard about asking God for guidance, but he didn't know what to do. So he conceived a simple test. If he got a letter with a certain stamp on it, this would indicate the matter one way. If not, he would choose the other option.

Sadly, this person's method was based more on superstition than faith. Yet so often when we are deeply perplexed, we wish Jesus would appear and tell us what to do, like He did for Paul. Of course, later on Paul wrote that "we live by faith, not by sight" (2 Cor. 5:7). We trust the Lord to direct our steps and help us to stand by our Christian convictions, even though we can't physically see Him.

Concepts for Children

Topic: *Paul Stands before the King*

1. When Paul was traveling with some people to Damascus, they saw a bright light and fell to the ground.
2. Paul heard the Lord say that He was the one whom Paul had been hurting.
3. Jesus called Paul to tell others about the Gospel.
4. Paul told a king named Agrippa that he had been faithful in sharing the Gospel with as many people as possible.
5. God wants us to let people know about the Good News concerning Jesus.

Lesson Commentary

I. PAUL'S DEFENSE: ACTS 26:19-23

A. Paul's Obedient Response: vs. 19

"So then, King Agrippa, I was not disobedient to the vision from heaven."

The Book of Acts presents several episodes in which Paul was able to share his background, conversion, and call to the Gentiles. One circumstance involved the apostle testifying before a formal inquiry attended by King Herod Agrippa II. When Agrippa gave Paul permission to speak, the apostle expressed his appreciation for the opportunity to address the charges some religious leaders had brought against him (26:1-2). Paul acknowledged that the dignitary had an intimate knowledge of Jewish matters (vs. 3). The apostle noted that he had been a Pharisee who meticulously observed the Mosaic law and Jewish customs (vss. 4-5). Paul declared that it was for the hope of Israel—namely, the resurrection of the dead—that he was on trial (vss. 6-8). The apostle related that at one point in his adult life he openly opposed Christianity (vs. 9). He had imprisoned many followers of Jesus (vs. 10). Paul had gone from synagogue to synagogue and city to city to find, arrest, and prosecute Christians (vs. 11).

Then one day, Paul was on such a mission to Damascus, armed with the authority and commission of the leading priests (vs. 12). Around noon, a light from heaven shone down on Paul and his traveling companions (vs. 13). All of them immediately fell to the ground. But only the apostle could make sense of the voice saying to him in Aramaic, "Saul, Saul, why do you persecute me?" (vs. 14). The heavenly voice then declared to Paul that it was hard for him to "kick against the goads." This statement reflected an ancient Greek proverb. A young ox, when it was first yoked, usually resented the burden and tried kicking its way out. Every time the animal kicked, though, it struck some sort of sharp object (such as a goad). The point of the adage was that the ox had to learn submission the hard way. In a similar manner, Paul before his conversion was resisting God, and he found it increasingly difficult to fight against the Lord's will.

Paul wanted to know the identity of the heavenly voice. Imagine how shocked he was to learn that it was Jesus, whose disciples Paul had been persecuting (vs. 15). What he had done to these believers was the same as if he had been doing it personally to the Messiah, their Lord. Despite the severity of Paul's many sins, Jesus revealed Himself in order to forgive Paul and commission him for Christian service. Jesus ordered Paul to stand up. The risen Lord then explained that He had appeared to this former persecutor of the church to appoint him as His servant and witness. In other words, Paul would serve the Messiah as the apostle proclaimed the Good News of salvation. The content of Paul's declarations would be twofold: his present experience of seeing Christ and subsequent revelations in which Jesus conveyed important truths to the apostle (vs. 16).

The hardship Paul had inflicted on other believers would now be experienced by him as well. Despite this, Jesus pledged to protect the apostle, especially as he witnessed to both Jews and Gentiles (vs. 17). No doubt at first the thought of ministering to non-Jews must have been a psychological jolt to Paul. Nevertheless, it was the Lord's will for the apostle to take the message of grace to unsaved Gentiles, for they needed to hear the truth. Jesus was specific about Paul's goal in sharing the Gospel. God would use him to open their spiritually blind eyes, to turn them from the darkness of sin to the light of God's holiness and from "the power of Satan to God" (vs. 18). By putting their faith in the Messiah, the lost would be pardoned and given a place among God's people, who were set apart because they believed.

Paul declared to King Agrippa that he remained true to the vision from heaven he had experienced (vs. 19). Here we see the essence of cosmic spiritual warfare as it is conducted on earth. Satan is the great perpetrator of sin and darkness. He blinds and holds people in his grip. Jesus broke Satan's power by His death and resurrection. Therefore, Jesus promised that those who believe in Him would be freed and forgiven. This was Paul's message from Christ and it is still the church's message today.

B. Paul's Ministry: vs. 20

"First to those in Damascus, then to those in Jerusalem and in all Judea, and to the Gentiles also, I preached that they should repent and turn to God and prove their repentance by their deeds."

The account of Paul's conversion from Christian hater to devout disciple is described in three places in Acts (9:1-19; 22:2-21; 26:9-18). The basic narrative is the same, though there are slight differences in the details in each summary. The consistent emphasis is that Paul had an encounter with the risen Lord on the road heading into Damascus, and this dramatically changed the direction and focus of the Pharisee's life. After the Savior revealed Himself to Paul in a vision, the new convert was left blinded. He received instructions to go into Damascus and find the house of Ananias on the street called Straight. For three days, Paul did not eat or drink anything.

Meanwhile, in Damascus, Ananias received his own vision from the Lord. The Savior directed Ananias to go to Paul (who at that time was known as Saul), restore his sight, and tell him about his new mission. Instead of persecuting believers, he would now join them. In fact, Paul would spread the Gospel even further, particularly among the Gentiles. Though Ananias was fearful of Paul because of what Ananias had heard about Paul's persecutions, Ananias did what the Lord directed. As a result, a new believer was baptized, filled with the Holy Spirit, and empowered to share the Good News with whomever would listen.

In time Paul regained his sight, and his strength returned following a meal. After only a few days with the believers living in Damascus, he began attending the synagogues of the Jews. In these places of worship, Paul declared the message that "Jesus is the Son of God" (9:20). This phrase, which occurs first here in Acts, was related to the messianic identity of the Lord Jesus (see 2 Sam. 7:14; Ps. 2:7). Later, preaching the Gospel first in Jewish synagogues became part of Paul's missionary strategy, especially as he heralded the Good News to the rest of the Roman world (see Acts 13:5; 17:1-2; 18:19).

By combining the information from Acts 9 and 2 Corinthians and Galatians, we discover that the time Paul spent preaching in Damascus after his conversion might have been as long as three years. During this period, the apostle ministered in the surrounding area of Arabia, that is, before he was forced to escape in the night from the city (see Acts 9:25; Gal. 1:15-18; 2 Cor. 11:32-33). It was then that Paul traveled to Jerusalem to see the other apostles (see Gal. 1:18-19). Acts 26:20 records Paul's summary statement of all his evangelistic efforts during these years of sharing the truth about Jesus. It did not matter whether the apostle was in Damascus, Jerusalem, or in the rest of Judea. His emphasis remained the same. Everyone had to abandon their sins and turn to God in faith. Also, they were to prove the reality of their commitment "by their deeds," that is, by the upright way in which they lived. The idea is that genuine repentance is evidenced by changed behavior.

C. Paul's Affirmation of the Truth: vss. 21-23

"That is why the Jews seized me in the temple courts and tried to kill me. But I have had God's help to this very day, and so I stand here and testify to small and great alike. I am saying nothing beyond what the prophets and Moses said would happen—that the Christ would suffer and, as the first to rise from the dead, would proclaim light to his own people and to the Gentiles."

Paul explained that some antagonistic Jews arrested him in the temple courts of Jerusalem because he proclaimed the Good News about the Messiah. These enemies of the faith charged the apostle with teaching against the Mosaic law and the temple. They also falsely accused him of defiling the holy place by bringing Gentiles into where they were not allowed to go (see Acts 21:27-36). For these reasons, religious fanatics in Jerusalem attempted to murder Paul (26:21). Despite their efforts, God protected the apostle (vs. 22).

Festus and other Roman officials could not quite grasp why the Jewish authorities had Paul arrested. The apostle hoped that Agrippa, who was a reputed expert in the Jewish faith, would understand how a message that gave an equal spiritual heritage to the Gentiles would enrage some Jews. Moreover, as Paul stood before Agrippa, he sought to make a connection between his calling on the road to Damascus and the reason for his subsequent arrest. The apostle's point was that his fellow Jews thought he was tearing down their faith, but they had misunderstood the reason and motivation for his obedience to his heavenly vision.

In reality, Paul was being consistent with the Jewish faith by declaring to both "small and great alike" what God had disclosed beforehand in the writings of the "prophets and Moses" about the suffering Messiah. Paul emphasized to Agrippa that the content of the apostle's message was in agreement with what was revealed in the Hebrew sacred writings. In other words, Paul taught nothing except what the Old Testament foretold would occur. To be specific, the apostle related that Scripture prophesied the suffering, death, and resurrection of the Messiah. In fact, Jesus' rising from the dead would be like a beacon of light shining the truth and glory of God "to his own people and to the Gentiles" (vs. 23).

II. PAUL'S CALL FOR DECISION: ACTS 26:24-32

A. To Festus: vss. 24-25

At this point Festus interrupted Paul's defense. "You are out of your mind, Paul!" he shouted. "Your great learning is driving you insane." "I am not insane, most excellent Festus," Paul replied. "What I am saying is true and reasonable."

It soon became clear to Agrippa that Paul was doing more than giving a bland recounting of his religious experiences. The apostle was actually trying to convince the king to become a follower of the Messiah. Agrippa was in a difficult spot. If he told those in attendance that he believed the Old Testament prophets, he would be affirming the truth of Paul's statements. On the other hand, to deny the prophets would have placed Agrippa in a bad light (so to speak) with his Jewish constituents.

As Festus listened to the proceedings, he grew increasingly uncomfortable with Paul's assertions. So, in an adroit maneuver, Festus interrupted the entire proceeding by suddenly retorting, "You are out of your mind, Paul!" (Acts 26:24). Festus also accused the apostle of becoming insane from excessive religious study. This tactic completely changed the psychological tone of the gathering by calling into question Paul's credibility. The apostle could have been paralyzed by fear or silenced by feelings of intimidation. Instead, he remained calm and respectful as he countered that his statements were accurate and rational (vs. 25).

B. To the King: vss. 26-27

"The king is familiar with these things, and I can speak freely to him. I am convinced that none of this has escaped his notice, because it was not done in a corner. King Agrippa, do you believe the prophets? I know you do."

Even though many of the Jewish scholars of Paul's day missed it, the prophets did speak about a Messiah who would suffer, die, be raised again, and be a light to the Gentiles (see Pss. 16:8-11; 22; Isa. 53; Luke 24:44-47; Acts 2:23-33; 1 Cor. 15:3-4). Paul's statement to Agrippa presumed that he was familiar with the truths the apostle was declaring. Furthermore, Paul spoke openly with the monarch about the Savior because the apostle was certain Agrippa was well aware of the facts concerning Jesus of Nazareth. After all, none of what happened to the Messiah took place in a "corner" (Acts 26:26), that is, outside of public view. Once more, Paul tried to bring Agrippa to the point of making a decision for Christ. That's why the apostle affirmed the king's belief in the Old Testament prophets. The apostle wanted to see Agrippa put his faith in the Messiah spoken of in the Hebrew sacred writings (vs. 27).

C. The King's Refusal: vss. 28-29

Then Agrippa said to Paul, "Do you think that in such a short time you can persuade me to be a Christian?" Paul replied, "Short time or long—I pray God that not only you but all who are listening to me today may become what I am, except for these chains."

Agrippa's interruption of Paul's statement indicates that the king wanted to end the exchange. The dialogue evidently was becoming too personal for Agrippa and thus it was expedient for him to redirect the focus back to the apostle. The monarch skillfully did this with a rhetorical question, which was worded more like an accusation. Agrippa conveyed strong doubt that during this brief exchange, Paul would be able to talk the king into becoming a "Christian" (Acts 26:28). Followers of Jesus were first called Christians in the city of Antioch (see 11:26). Evidently, the people in that city made a joke by calling Jesus' disciples "Christians," namely, followers and soldiers of Christ. The name *Christian* occurs three times in the New Testament (see Acts 11:26; 26:28; 1 Pet. 4:16), which indicates that the label took hold early in church history.

What originally was meant as an insult became a badge of honor. The name officially distinguished Christians from other Jewish sects and made it clear that the Lord Jesus was the object of His disciples' faith. In contrast, Agrippa's evasion of Paul's question with a question suggests that the king was not serious about becoming a genuine follower of the Lord Jesus. Paul evidently sensed this, but that did not seem to stop him from urging the king and the rest in attendance to commit their lives to the Savior. That's why the apostle responded so openly and frankly with his listeners. Paul wanted everyone in the chamber to become disciples of the Lord (Acts 26:29).

D. The Comments after the End of the Assembly: vss. 30-32

The king rose, and with him the governor and Bernice and those sitting with them. They left the room, and while talking with one another, they said, "This man is not doing anything that deserves death or imprisonment." Agrippa said to Festus, "This man could have been set free if he had not appealed to Caesar."

At that point in the proceeding, Agrippa and the rest of the dignitaries arose and left the auditorium (Acts 26:30). They jointly acknowledged that Paul had not done anything to warrant capital punishment or imprisonment (vs. 31). Agrippa noted to Festus that if Paul had not appealed to the emperor, he could have been set free (vs. 32). The dignitaries did not realize, however, that God was using these series of events to bring about the apostle's proclamation of the Gospel in Rome.

Discussion Questions

1. What was Paul focused on doing when he encountered the risen Lord?
2. What did Paul begin doing immediately after his conversion? Why?
3. How was Paul's message connected to the teachings of the Old Testament?
4. How do you think you would have handled King Agrippa's attempt to sidestep Paul's evangelistic appeal?
5. What are some ways we can creatively herald the truth about the Savior?

Contemporary Application

When Paul was brought before King Agrippa, the apostle gave an account of how he had encountered the risen Savior and how he had served Christ since that eventful day. Indeed, the apostle's life was a compelling testimony of the Gospel. Today, the Father still calls followers of His Son to mirror His life and teachings. If we are to be clear to others about the Good News, our lives need to clearly be like His.

In *Evangelism,* former Richard Nixon adviser Charles Colson told about having lunch with a non-Christian journalist who was intrigued by Colson's commitment to the Lord Jesus. Colson arrived at the restaurant braced for an argument. The journalist responded that it was wonderful that Colson had found this new peace and fulfillment, but he said he had friends in the New Age movement who had experienced similar feelings.

Having hit one obstacle, Colson shifted to the issue of eternal life because he knew that the man had experienced some health problems. The journalist, however, answered that death was just the end. He did not believe in an afterlife. Colson continued to try to talk about his personal faith despite the many obstacles this man set before him. By using different approaches, Colson kept the all-important issue of the Gospel at the forefront of the discussion.

Here we see that the individual lives of believers are really about the Savior. Our lives should tell His story and not be about us. Moreover, we should be ready, as Paul was, to tell how the truth about the Messiah intersects with our lives and how He has spiritually changed us.

Admittedly, part of our witness is how we came to trust in the Lord Jesus for our salvation. But our testimony also includes what role He has played in our lives this past year, this past month, and even this past week. No one else has that part of His story. Those who listen to us should see Jesus at work in our lives. This includes hearing and answering our prayers, taking us through the tough times, and guiding us in the way He wants us to go.

Paul Sails for Rome

Scripture

Background Scripture: *Acts 27*
Scripture Lesson: *Acts 27:1-2, 33-44*
Key Verse: *In this way everyone reached land in safety.* Acts 27:44.
Scripture Lesson for Children: *Acts 27:33-44*
Key Verse for Children: *Everyone reached land in safety.* Acts 27:44.

Lesson Aim

To look to God for strength to do His will with an uncompromising heart.

Lesson Setting

Time: A.D. *59*
Place: Adriatic Sea; Malta

Lesson Outline

Paul Sails for Rome
   I.   Setting Sail for Rome: Acts 27:1-2
        A. *The Decision Is Made: vs. 1*
        B. *The Ship Is Boarded: vs. 2*
   II. Being Shipwrecked: Acts 27:33-44
        A. *The Encouragement to Eat: vss. 33-38*
        B. *The Breakup of the Ship: vss. 39-41*
        C. *The Safe Arrival on Land: vss. 42-44*

Introduction for Adults

Topic: *Weathering the Storm*

Jonathan took the leadership of a Christian education ministry that was floundering. With boldness, wisdom, and faith he energized the work and took it to new levels of effectiveness. Then Lou Gehrig's disease struck him. Rather than quit and spend his time complaining, Jonathan attacked his work with renewed vigor. His cheerfulness and courage inspired many.

Jonathan gave an inspiring address to the congregation, many of whom were moved to tears. Despite the life storms he faced, he did not wallow in self-pity. Instead, he challenged his fellow Christians to persevere in faith, regardless of what setbacks might come their way.

Like Paul, Jonathan knew God so deeply that he accepted his hardship with graciousness. After several years, Jonathan succumbed to the ravages of the disease. Yet as Paul did in his life, Jonathan also left a powerful mark on his church, his family, and his ministry.

Introduction for Youth

Topic: *A Stressful Journey*

A young man named Mike began using drugs as a way to cope with the stresses in his life. Soon he became addicted to them. Sometime after that, he went through a recovery program in an effort to get his life back on track.

Part of Mike's effort included going door-to-door looking for odd jobs—washing windows, trimming bushes, and so on. One family asked him to spade a garden plot. This was tough work, because the twenty-by-thirty-foot area had been lawn for many years. Mike tore into his task but soon wearied of it because he had no idea how to use a spade. His enthusiasm did not make up for his inexperience.

The owner came back aghast as he saw huge holes appearing everywhere. He took Mike aside and showed him how to spade in a more orderly way. Once more, Mike tackled the plot. This time, he finished the work acceptably.

Most of us need practical help and wise counsel so that we can do God's work in His way. Growing things in God's spiritual garden is not easy. Paul was able to mature in his faith and become a discerning spiritual leader by looking to God for strength. Like the apostle, with the Lord's help, we can also join raw courage to a seasoned faith and finish our God-given responsibilities in a prudent manner.

Concepts for Children

Topic: *Keeping Calm in the Storm*

1. Paul traveled with others on a ship heading to Rome.
2. While the ship was out at sea, a big storm blew it off course.
3. Everyone feared that they were going to die.
4. God used Paul to help everyone remain calm.
5. Even in scary situations, God can give us the strength to do what He wants.

Lesson Commentary

I. SETTING SAIL FOR ROME: ACTS 27:1-2

A. The Decision Is Made: vs. 1

When it was decided that we would sail for Italy, Paul and some other prisoners were handed over to a centurion named Julius, who belonged to the Imperial Regiment.

In A.D. 35, while Paul was traveling on the road leading to Damascus, he encountered the risen Lord and became one of His most devoted followers. Right from the start, it was the Messiah's will that Paul would be His "chosen instrument" (Acts 9:15) to herald the Good News to the Gentiles, their rulers, and even Paul's fellow Jews. Furthermore, it was the Lord's will that the apostle would experience hardship and deprivation because he served as Jesus' personal ambassador (vs. 16). Later, during Paul's third missionary journey (A.D. 53–57), he noted that he was divinely compelled to proclaim the Gospel in Rome (see 19:21). Then, in A.D. 57, when the apostle wrote the Letter to the Romans, he stated his earnest desire to proclaim the Good News in the capital of the empire (see Romans 1:15). Later that same year, the apostle suffered the indignity of imprisonment in Jerusalem for his faith in Christ. While there, the Savior appeared to Paul in a vision and reassured him that it was the divine will for the apostle to bear witness in Rome (see Acts 23:11).

In A.D. 59, what Paul knew would happen actually occurred. For the past two years, the apostle had been incarcerated at Caesarea (see 23:33; 24:27). This was a seaport located on the Mediterranean coast about 23 miles south of Mount Carmel. Between 25 and 13 B.C., Herod the Great invested a considerable amount of time and effort to make the locale a first-rate port facility and adjoining city. In turn, he named the locale in honor of Caesar Augustus, whom historians consider the first emperor of Rome (27 B.C. to A.D. 14). Caesarea was largely Gentile, a center of Roman administration, and the location of many of Herod's building projects. It was from here that the civil authorities decided to place Paul and some other prisoners on a sailing vessel bound for Italy (27:1). This long, boot-shaped peninsula between Greece and Spain was the birthplace of the Roman republic, and its capital, Rome, was the epicenter of the sprawling empire.

A centurion named Julius was in charge of the prisoners, including Paul. Julius was a member of the Augustan Cohort (possibly stationed in Syria-Palestine). There is considerable disagreement over the exact identity of this contingent. Some think it was an elite imperial regiment, while others maintain the troops assigned to the cohort mainly served an auxiliary function. More generally, the Roman military was made up of five groups. The city of Rome was protected by the *imperial* guard. The seas were controlled by the Roman *fleet*. In outlying areas, units belonging to the *auxilia* and *numeri* had flexibility to adapt to local military needs and customs. But the backbone of the Roman military was the *legion*. In Paul's day, Rome had about 25 legions, with each containing about 6,000 soldiers. Each legion had ten *cohorts* (or 600 soldiers); each cohort had three *maniples* (or 200 soldiers); and each maniple had two *centuries* (or 100 soldiers).

Unlike aristocratic Romans, who aspired to higher offices, centurions like Julius usually began as regular soldiers and worked their way up through the ranks. *Centurion* was the highest rank that an ordinary enlisted soldier could attain and the equivalent of today's U.S. Army sergeant major. Promotion to the position of centurion was dependent upon battle experience and military savvy. Soldiers who achieved this rank generally stayed in that position for the remainder of their career. Army service for males typically began around age 17, and roughly half of the enlisters who survived the required 20 years of service were highly rewarded. If the superiors of a centurion thought well of him, he could serve throughout the Roman Empire. Centurions had other responsibilities besides maintaining order among the troops. They were given a great deal of autonomy on the battlefield and had to think well on their feet. Centurions often carried out executions for people convicted of capital offenses. Many times the Roman army would hire mercenaries, and centurions would be held personally responsible for these often reckless soldiers.

B. The Ship Is Boarded: vs. 2

We boarded a ship from Adramyttium about to sail for ports along the coast of the province of Asia, and we put out to sea. Aristarchus, a Macedonian from Thessalonica, was with us.

At this time, Paul was grouped with other prisoners. Some of them might have been convicted criminals who would eventually die as combatants before huge crowds in the games held at the Colosseum in Rome. All of them were placed on board a modest-sized, privately owned cargo ship (perhaps weighing less than 250 tons) that had originated from its home port of Adramyttium (Acts 27:2). This was a harbor on the west coast of Asia Minor between Troas and Pergamum. Adramyttium was also located in Mysia, a region that likewise included Assos, Pergamum, and Troas. Mysia was a crossroads for travel, trade, and conquest. Throughout the Medo-Persian and Roman periods, this region was strategic to the strength and stability of the area.

Once the vessel set sail, it was scheduled to make stops at various ports along the coast of the Roman province of Asia before finally heading to Rome. Paul was accompanied by a believer named Aristarchus, who might have functioned as the apostle's personal attendant (see Acts 19:29; 20:4; Col. 4:10; Philem. 24). Aristarchus's hometown of Thessalonica was located in the Roman province of Macedonia in Greece. The writer of Acts told about some of Paul's experiences using the plural "we," which indicates that the author was with the apostle during those occasions, including his voyage to Rome (see Acts 16:10-17; 20:5–21:18; 27:1–28:16). This clue points to Luke, who was a physician by profession (see Col. 4:14) and a co-laborer with Paul (see Philem. 24).

The ship sailed about 70 miles north to Sidon, and Julius was kind enough to permit Paul to visit his friends in the city (Acts 27:3). Once the vessel had set out to sea again, the contrary winds and choppy seas made sailing difficult. Thus the ship sailed north of Cyprus in hope that the island and the mainland of Asia Minor would break the force of the gale (vs. 4). The vessel eventually made its way to the port city of Myra in the province of Lycia, where the passengers boarded a larger Alexandrian grain ship (possibly weighing around 800 tons) heading for Italy (vss. 5-6). The prevailing winds made sailing to the port city of Cnidus difficult and slow. Though the pilot wanted to steer the vessel across the Aegean Sea to the coast of Greece, strong winds forced the vessel south. The ship sailed along the southern coast of Crete in an attempt to break the force of the gale (vs. 7). Nevertheless, the vessel still struggled to make it to a small port called Fair Havens (vs. 8).

With the passing of the day of Atonement, the sailing season was quickly drawing to a close (vs. 9). Paul warned that continuing the journey would be dangerous (vs. 10). But the pilot and owner of the ship wanted to harbor the vessel at the larger port of Phoenix, which was about 60 miles away. This would give them a better opportunity to sell the grain on board. Julius decided to disregard Paul's admonition and continue the journey to Phoenix (vss. 11-12). When a gentle southern breeze began to blow, the crew thought it would be a good time to set sail along the shoreline of Crete (vs. 13). However, a violent northeasterly storm suddenly appeared and forced the vessel south into the open sea (vss. 14-15).

The ship headed to a small island named Cauda, which barely broke the force of the wind long enough for the crew to take aboard a small boat that was being towed by the ship and that was hindering it from steering properly in the turbulent waters (vs. 16). The crew also passed strong ropes crosswise under the hull of the vessel to prevent it from breaking apart in the storm. As the ship continued on its treacherous course, the sailors began to fear the possibility that the vessel would run aground on the sandbars of Syrtis, which were just off the northern coast of Africa. In an attempt to slow the craft down, the crew lowered the sea anchor (vs. 17). As the storm continued to violently pound the vessel, the sailors threw cargo overboard to lighten the craft (vs. 18). In a desperate attempt to save the ship, the sailors threw its rigging overboard (vs. 19). As the storm continued to rage, the passengers eventually gave up all hope of being rescued (vs. 20).

II. BEING SHIPWRECKED: ACTS 27:33-44

A. The Encouragement to Eat: vss. 33-38

Just before dawn Paul urged them all to eat. "For the last fourteen days," he said, "you have been in constant suspense and have gone without food—you haven't eaten anything. Now I urge you to take some food. You need it to survive. Not one of you will lose a single hair from his head." After he said this, he took some bread and gave thanks to God in front of them all. Then he broke it and began to eat. They were all encouraged and ate some food themselves. Altogether there were 276 of us on board. When they had eaten as much as they wanted, they lightened the ship by throwing the grain into the sea.

In such a raging storm, there would have been a great deal of seasickness. Also, any kind of food preparation would have been unlikely. This explains why the crew had not eaten for days. Undoubtedly, they were exhausted from the ordeal. Paul stood up and admonished them for not originally heeding his advice (Acts 27:21). But he tried to encourage them with the good news that not one of their lives would be lost, though the ship would be destroyed (vs. 22). The apostle related that the previous night an angel of the God whom he served revealed that Paul would make it safely to Rome to present his case to the emperor and that none of the people on board the ship would die (vs. 23-24). The apostle asserted that he trusted in God's providential care, though he related that the vessel would run aground on some island (vss. 25-26).

After 14 days out at sea, the ship continued to be driven across the Adriatic Sea (which extended to southern Italy). Around midnight, the sailors sensed that they were drawing near to land (vs. 27). As they periodically took soundings (using a weighted line to measure the depth of the sea), they learned that the water was progressively getting shallower (vs. 28). To prevent the ship from possibly crashing against some rocks, the crew lowered four anchors from the stern (vs. 29). The sailors next pretended they were going to lower some more anchors from the bow to further slow the vessel down. But in reality, they were trying to escape from the ship (vs. 30). Paul warned the centurion that unless the sailors remained with the vessel to safely pilot it to shore, the rest of the passengers would lose their lives (vs. 31). The officer thus ordered his men to cut the ropes that held the lifeboat and let it fall to the sea (vs. 32).

As dawn of the fifteenth day approached, Paul noted that for the past two weeks his fellow passengers had been watching and waiting anxiously to see how their situation might turn out. During that extended period, none of them had eaten anything (vs. 33). Now the apostle urged everyone on board the ship to eat some food and increase their chance of surviving. In fact, Paul stated that all of them would make it through the ordeal without one hair on their heads being harmed (vs. 34; for this common Hebrew expression, see 1 Sam. 14:45; 2 Sam. 14:11; 1 Kings 1:52; Luke 21:18). Then the apostle took a piece of bread, openly thanked God for the provision, broke off a portion, and ate it (Acts 27:35). His action encouraged all 276 people on board to do the same (vss. 36-37). After that, the crew threw the bags of grain (most likely wheat) overboard to further lighten the ship so that it would venture farther into shore (vs. 38).

B. The Breakup of the Ship: vss. 39-41

When daylight came, they did not recognize the land, but they saw a bay with a sandy beach, where they decided to run the ship aground if they could. Cutting loose the anchors, they left them in the sea and at the same time untied the ropes that held the rudders. Then they hoisted the foresail to the wind and made for the beach. But the ship struck a sandbar and ran aground. The bow stuck fast and would not move, and the stern was broken to pieces by the pounding of the surf.

When it was daylight, the crew spotted a coast they did not recognize. Nonetheless, they noticed a cove with a smooth, sandy beach (what is now called St. Paul's Bay). They surmised that if they could safely navigate the ship between the rocks, the sheltered bay might turn out to be a suitable spot to ground the vessel (Acts 27:39). With that plan in mind, the sailors cut the anchors loose and let them sink into the sea. They also untied the ropes, which were used to hold the steering oars together and the stern rudders in place. Taking this action would help the crew better pilot the ship to shore. Next, they raised the mainsail at the front of the vessel so that the wind would blow it forward to the beach (vs. 40). However, the ship encountered adverse sea conditions, struck a reef, and ran aground. While the bow of the vessel remained firmly implanted in the shoal, the stern broke apart due to the violent force of the waves (vs. 41).

C. The Safe Arrival on Land: vss. 42-44

The soldiers planned to kill the prisoners to prevent any of them from swimming away and escaping. But the centurion wanted to spare Paul's life and kept them from carrying out their plan. He ordered those who could swim to jump overboard first and get to land. The rest were to get there on planks or on pieces of the ship. In this way everyone reached land in safety.

As chaos and panic ensued, there was the possibility that some of the prisoners might try to escape by swimming ashore. Also, if any prisoners got away, the soldier who was supposed to be guarding them would be executed for dereliction of duty (see Acts 12:19; 16:27). Thus to prevent this from happening, the soldiers decided to kill all the prisoners on board the ship (27:42). Evidently, however, Julius had come to respect Paul. And so, because the centurion wanted to prevent the apostle from perishing, the army officer stopped his men from doing what they had planned. Instead, Julius ordered everyone who could swim to dive first into the water and heard for shore (vs. 43). The remainder of the crew and passengers were to make it to shore by holding on to planks or other portions of the demolished ship. In this way, everyone made it to the beach unharmed (vs. 44).

It's easy to tell someone not to be afraid when everything seems to be going well, but when a friend comes down with a serious illness, that's a different matter. Automatically, it seems, fear kicks in. Fear has positive value when it keeps us from taking risky chances. However, fear has negative value when it begins to undermine our faith. When the trials of life seem overwhelming, we should fortify our souls, not with wishful thinking, but with truths about God revealed in His Word. We can't promise people that everything will be all right. But we can reassure them that God's love and care will be there when they need it. Much more than physical protection is in view here. The assaults of the world, the flesh, and the Devil are made against our souls, and thus we need God's protection in each of these arenas. It's reassuring to know that nothing escapes the attention of our loving Guardian and Keeper (see Pss. 23; 121).

Discussion Questions

1. What circumstances led to Paul's being taken to Italy?
2. Why had everyone on board the ship gone without food for two weeks?
3. In what ways did Paul show the traits of a natural-born leader?
4. How is it possible for believers to remain calm in life-threatening circumstances like the one Paul faced?
5. What are some noteworthy things God has done through you that He wants you to share with others?

Contemporary Application

Paul experienced a difficult situation on the voyage to Rome. Even though the circumstance was life-threatening, he did not lose heart. Instead, the apostle looked to the Lord for strength to do His will. In fact, Paul's unwavering reliance on God was the source of the apostle's courage.

The issues facing us in life are often complex. These include health complications, family problems, and financial challenges. In the midst of an unanticipated and unwelcome crisis, how should we respond? One option is to panic and lose hope. Another is to rely on the Lord to survive and overcome the ordeal. When we do the latter, a marvelous thing occurs. God empowers us to face each moment with joy and optimism.

As we have seen from this week's lesson, Paul's complete reliance on God became the underlying basis for his fellow travelers' being able to endure an intense storm, regain their composure, and make it through a harrowing ship-wreck. Similarly, regardless of the pressures we face, God can enable us to be victorious in carrying out His will. Also, as the Lord did with Paul, He will often work through our levelheaded thinking and clear understanding of Scripture to help us discern what is morally proper and improper.

As we turn to God in faith and commune with Him in prayer, He will help us to maintain an uncompromising heart. Moreover, this becomes the basis for our success in ministry. Admittedly, it's easy for us to allow events and problems to distract us from the core issues of life. Just as Paul had to remain focused on the Lord during the his traumatic circumstance, we also have to keep the eyes of our faith on God so that we do not become derailed by the challenges we face. With the Savior as our constant companion and guide, we have nothing to fear on our life journey.

Paul Ministers in Malta

Scripture

Background Scripture: *Acts 28:1-10*

Scripture Lesson: *Acts 28:1-10*

Key Verse: *Paul went in to see [Publius's father] and, after prayer, placed his hands on him and healed him.* Acts 28:8.

Scripture Lesson for Children: *Acts 28:1-10*

Key Verse for Children: *The rest of the sick on the island came [to Paul] and were cured.* Acts 28:9.

Lesson Aim

To affirm that God has gifted His people to do His work.

Lesson Setting

Time: A.D. *59*
Place: Malta

Lesson Outline

Paul Ministers in Malta

   I. A Rush to Judgment Concerning Paul: Acts 28:1-6

      A. *An Initially Warm Reception on Malta: vss. 1-2*

      B. *An Overly Negative Opinion Concerning Paul: vss. 3-4*

      C. *An Overly Positive Opinion Concerning Paul: vss. 5-6*

  II. An Opportunity to Minister: Acts 28:7-10

      A. *Experiencing Hospitable Treatment: vs. 7*

      B. *Healing Many People: vss. 8-9*

      C. *Being Outfitted for the Voyage: vs. 10*

Introduction for Adults

Topic: *Helping One Another*

Too often today churches get mired in arguments and division, not in spiritual unity. While the members of a congregation might embrace core theological truths, they obsess over peripheral, far less important matters. Meanwhile, the church's larger purpose and common bond in Christ gets lost in the fracas.

For instance, some churches are weakened because of a false dichotomy between so-called gifted believers and the rest of the ordinary Christians. We have to make room for all believers to exercise their God-given gifts for the common good of helping one another. We cannot afford to let some Christians think they are second-class because they do not have some of the more publicly recognized gifts.

While Paul was on Malta, he demonstrated oneness, unity, and harmony. He would not tolerate disputes over the talents and abilities believers have. After all, these are intended to be used in doing God's work. When the latter remains the primary goal, it leads to a vital, loving, growing, unified congregation.

Introduction for Youth

Topic: *A Stressful Journey*

Youth are introduced early to the values of working together. They work on class projects, participate in musical groups and plays, and join athletic teams. They all know that if any member slacks off, the team suffers. They also know that if any player tries to steal the show, the team is weakened. Clearly, the actions of every member are noticed and accounted for!

These are the kinds of illustrations teenagers can understand when applied to the church, which is Christ's team (in a manner of speaking). The beauty of the church is that faith in Jesus is the only requirement to be on the team. As Paul taught and displayed on the island of Malta, it doesn't depend on skill or experience. It only requires faith.

Faith is also required to accept the contributions of all other team members. Perhaps the final production will not be as professional as we would prefer, but we have to remember that the church is not only for professionals. The church is also for lifelong learners and followers of Christ. We all need to coach each other so that our team can use its gifts to do the Lord's work.

Concepts for Children

Topic: *Paul Heals Others*

1. Paul was on his way to Rome to tell powerful people about Jesus.
2. After surviving a storm, Paul spent some time on an island called Malta.
3. Various people on the island thought different things about Paul.
4. Paul used his time to help others with their problems.
5. God can help us find good things to do for others.

Lesson Commentary

I. A Rush to Judgment Concerning Paul: Acts 28:1-6

A. An Initially Warm Reception on Malta: vss. 1-2

Once safely on shore, we found out that the island was called Malta. The islanders showed us unusual kindness. They built a fire and welcomed us all because it was raining and cold.

As we learned last week, Paul and other prisoners at Caesarea were turned over to a Roman centurion to be taken to the capital of the empire. They boarded a ship and stopped in several ports along the way. Because the voyage was late in the season, bad weather made progress difficult. The ship's captain ignored Paul's advice and gambled that he could reach a better harbor in which to winter. But hurricane-strength winds blew them off course. Then, after riding the storm for two weeks, the travelers were shipwrecked. Paul's counsel, however, enabled all the crew and passengers to survive.

After everyone from the grounded ship had made it to shore unharmed, they discovered that the island on which they had arrived was Malta (Acts 28:1). Otherwise known as *Melite* in Greek, it is located in the Mediterranean Sea between Sicily and Africa. Malta is also about 90 miles southwest of Syracuse, which then was a Greek city on the southeast coast of Sicily (vs. 12). By 1000 B.C., Phoenicians had colonized Malta. In 218 B.C., the island was captured by Rome. This occurred at the start of the Second Punic War, which the Republic waged against Carthage (a city in North Africa). Rome granted Malta the status of *municipium,* which allowed the inhabitants a large measure of local autonomy.

Malta encompasses about 95 square miles and was a strategically located stopping point for commercial ships traveling east to west and north to south. The island's natural harbors provided shelter for ocean-going vessels from the stormy conditions of the Mediterranean Sea. A considerable portion of Malta was parched, agriculturally unproductive, and lacking any important natural resources. Be that as it may, the local residents were somewhat able to cultivate the eastern half of the island, which enabled them to produce olive oil and wool. Paul and the rest of the travelers remained on Malta for three months (vs. 11).

The Greek adjective translated "islanders" (vs. 2) is more literally rendered "barbarians" or "foreigners" and refers to non-Greeks and non-Romans who were presumed to be culturally primitive. In this case, the local inhabitants of Malta were descendants of the Phoenicians, and their native language was Punic (a Phoenician dialect used by the people of Carthage). But far from being uncivilized brutes, the Maltese showed themselves to be extraordinarily kindhearted and generous to Paul and the rest of the travelers. In fact, the inhabitants of the island greeted the shipwrecked victims with a fire they had kindled. This would have been a welcome sight on a cold, rainy day, especially after a forced swim in the Mediterranean Sea.

B. An Overly Negative Opinion Concerning Paul: vss. 3-4

Paul gathered a pile of brushwood and, as he put it on the fire, a viper, driven out by the heat, fastened itself on his hand. When the islanders saw the snake hanging from his hand, they said to each other, "This man must be a murderer; for though he escaped from the sea, Justice has not allowed him to live."

It seems that Paul could attract attention without even trying. On this occasion, the apostle gathered an armful of sticks to add to the fire the local inhabitants had made. And as he was placing the brushwood on the flames, the heat caused a poisonous snake that was hiding in the sticks to crawl out and attach itself to his hand (Acts 28:3). When the people of the island saw the viper gripping Paul's hand with its fangs, they immediately concluded that he was a "murderer" (vs. 4).

The Maltese superstitiously assumed that even though the apostle had eluded the wrath of the storm, a goddess named Justice would not permit him to survive any longer. This pagan deity was believed to be the daughter of Zeus (the king of the gods in the Greek pantheon who was said to preside over the universe). Supposedly, Justice, by enacting an oracle of judgment against Paul in connection with his guilt, was carrying out the will of another goddess named Fortune or the Fates. In other words, the local residents saw the snakebite as divine retribution for the apostle's presumed crime, which the civil authorities had failed to detect or punish.

C. An Overly Positive Opinion Concerning Paul: vss. 5-6

But Paul shook the snake off into the fire and suffered no ill effects. The people expected him to swell up or suddenly fall dead, but after waiting a long time and seeing nothing unusual happen to him, they changed their minds and said he was a god.

The Maltese must have been surprised when they saw Paul simply shake off the viper from his hand and drop it into the fire, where the creature died. In contrast, the apostle experienced no ill effects from the venomous bite of the snake (Acts 28:5). We don't know that Paul specifically prayed for God's help, but the apostle seemed quietly confident that the Lord was watching over him. Perhaps Paul recalled the Savior's visit and reassuring statement when the apostle was imprisoned in Jerusalem: "You must . . . testify in Rome" (23:11). Consequently, God would not let a snakebite stand in the way of His fulfilling His promise.

Some critics point out that no poisonous snakes are found on Malta today. The implication is that the incident recorded in 28:3-5 was not the miracle Luke made it out to be. However, today's circumstances on the island need not be the same as what prevailed almost two thousand years ago. We can be confident that the Maltese in Paul's day knew their island and its creatures sufficiently well. They also recognized the symptoms of those who had been bitten by poisonous snakes and lizards. In this case, the local inhabitants watched with bated breath to see those symptoms overtake the apostle. Luke, too, as a physician, would have had some knowledge of snakebites and their effects on people.

The Maltese expected Paul to swell up or experience a raging fever. They also assumed the apostle would suddenly collapse and die. Yet, after they had waited a long while, they noticed that no harm came to Paul. In light of this latest development, the local residents decided to revise their theory about the apostle. Since he had twice escaped death, they jumped to a new conclusion. This time the Maltese decided he had to be a "god" (vs. 6) or perhaps one of its favored human subjects. While presuming often causes us to judge people unfairly, sometimes it causes us to inappropriately honor people. Hero worship is no better than prejudice. Concerning the apostle, he was neither a murderer nor divine.

II. AN OPPORTUNITY TO MINISTER: ACTS 28:7-10

A. Experiencing Hospitable Treatment: vs. 7

There was an estate nearby that belonged to Publius, the chief official of the island. He welcomed us to his home and for three days entertained us hospitably.

A man named Publius was the chief Roman official, or local magistrate, of Malta. As such, he was responsible for maintaining peace on the island and ensuring that a sufficient amount of taxes were collected and sent to Rome. Publius occupied an estate containing fields and several buildings. Since the latter were in the general vicinity of the place where shipwrecked survivors swam ashore, it probably did not take long for him to learn about these new arrivals to Malta. The official invited the stranded crew and passengers to his spacious villa, where he provided for their needs for the next three days (Acts 28:7). This hospitable gesture on the part of Publius would ensure the health and safety of his guests and give them enough time to find suitable longer-term living arrangements for the winter.

B. Healing Many People: vss. 8-9

His father was sick in bed, suffering from fever and dysentery. Paul went in to see him and, after prayer, placed his hands on him and healed him. When this had happened, the rest of the sick on the island came and were cured.

At this time, the father of Publius was bedridden from a high "fever and dysentery" (Acts 28:8). Evidently, the elderly man was experiencing an inflammatory disorder of the intestine, particularly the colon, which was characterized by severe abdominal pain, diarrhea, and blood loss. If left untreated, the disease could have been fatal. When Paul heard about the man's illness, the apostle was granted permission to see him. Paul first prayed to God on behalf of the sick man. Then the apostle placed his hands on the infirmed gentleman and brought about his healing.

Some think the father of Publius might have had Malta fever (which is sometimes called Mediterranean fever and is similar in symptoms to malaria). In Paul's day, this ailment was common on the island, at Gibraltar, and in other Mediterranean areas until medical science developed a vaccine for it. The malady was an infectious bacterial disease transmitted by microbes in goats' milk. The cause of Malta fever was not discovered until the late nineteenth century. The ailment would usually last about four months, but occasionally someone would suffer for two or three years. Sore joints and nervous disorders could accompany the disease. Luke used the plural word for "fever" (literally "fevers"). This accurately describes the characteristic off-and-on attacks experienced by its victims.

The startling news of what Paul had done quickly traveled throughout Malta (which is only 18 miles long and 8 miles wide). In a relatively short time period, infirm residents from all parts of the island came to the apostle to be healed, and he responded by curing them of their afflictions (vs. 9). Succinctly put, Paul heard about someone who was sick, and he offered to do what he could. In a sense, the apostle created his own opportunity to do good. And so out of a shipwreck came a series of healings. Moreover, from a prisoner of Rome came physical and spiritual deliverance to others. We, too, can take the initiative in many situations. Likewise, with God's help we, too, can create our own opportunities by simply offering to do what we can for others in need. The incentive to do so comes from Galatians 6:10. There Paul encouraged believers to do good to everyone—whenever the opportunity arose—and especially to those who belonged to the household of faith.

The longer our Christian lives stretch on, the more likely we are to suffer fatigue and to hear the voice of discouragement whispering in our ears. Paul himself must often have thought, *I can't go on!* and *What's the use?* But he persevered to the end, and with God's help we, too, can persevere as long as necessary. In this regard, the Christian life is not a sprint but a marathon. God provides strategic opportunities for us to do good to others (vs. 10). We should try to discern these opportunities and eagerly act on them. Helping unbelievers is an excellent way to witness without words to God's goodness. But if anything, we should be more eager to help other Christians, since we are all part of God's family. Paul portrayed the reward awaiting the faithful—namely, an intimate relationship with God—as an incentive to renew their efforts at doing good (vs. 9).

Serving others in this way requires unselfishness and dependence on God's Spirit. But those who do not do the hard work of Christian living should not delude themselves that God will bless them (vs. 7). People who perform the acts of the sinful nature rather than bear the fruit of the Spirit will not be rewarded, for God will not be mocked. Unlike people, He cannot be fooled, and His justice is perfect. Furthermore, there is a simple relationship between how people live and how God judges and rewards them (vs. 8). By way of example, a farmer who sows barley cannot expect to harvest wheat. Similarly, those who obey the callings of the flesh (and thereby give evidence of their unregenerate state) cannot expect to receive eternal life from God. Instead, they will earn eternal destruction. Happily, though, the opposite of this truth is that if we live by the Spirit, we will enjoy eternal life.

C. Being Outfitted for the Voyage: vs. 10

They honored us in many ways and when we were ready to sail, they furnished us with the supplies we needed.

It's not difficult to imagine how grateful the Maltese felt in response to what Paul had done for their sick residents. In turn, the islanders bestowed many honors on the entire group of visitors. This included taking care of their short-term needs and outfitting them for the rest of the voyage to Rome (Acts 28:10). As noted earlier, Paul, Luke, and the others stayed for three months on Malta. Then in February, when the treacherous winter weather had passed, they sailed northward for Rome on an Alexandrian ship that had as a figurehead the twin gods named Castor and Pollux (vs. 11).

In pagan mythology, the twin sons of Zeus, Castor and Pollux, were believed to offer favor to those who navigated the seas. Mariners considered the twins (who were also called Gemini, after their constellation in the heavens) to bring good luck during a storm. It would not be unusual for the sailors and soldiers, having just endured a terrible shipwreck, to congratulate themselves on the good fortune of finding a ship with the Gemini as its figurehead. But of course it made no difference to Paul and Luke, who trusted in the living and true God for their safety at sea and on land.

As the ship headed northward, it made stops at Syracuse, on Sicily's coast, and Rhegium, at the toe of Italy's boot (vss. 12-13). Then the travelers set out for Puteoli, which was one of Rome's main ports (vs. 13). This remained the case despite the fact that Puteoli was located 75 miles from the capital. Some believers in Puteoli invited Paul and his companions to stay for a week. They had heard about Paul and wanted to host him. They desired to hear his testimony and teaching firsthand. The Roman centurion, Julius, who apparently was in no hurry, permitted the apostle to visit. Then the group headed for Rome along the Appian Way, which was one of Italy's main roads (vs. 14).

The news of Paul's arrival traveled from Puteoli to Rome ahead of him. The apostle had not founded the church in the capital. But as noted in the previous lesson, he had written to the believers living there to express his interest to visit them (see Rom. 1:15). The Roman church appears to have been an active one, and of course it was in the most strategic city in the empire. A group of believers from Rome set out to meet Paul on the way. Some stopped at the Three Taverns, a town about 35 miles south of the capital. A second group went as far as the Forum of Appius, another town 10 miles farther from Rome. Their welcome, like a red-carpet treatment for a dignitary, encouraged Paul. God used these believers to minister to the apostle and reassure him that he would not be alone in Rome. He responded by thanking God for their help (Acts 28:15).

Discussion Questions

1. How did God enable Paul and the rest of his fellow travelers to arrive safely on shore?
2. Why do you think the residents of Malta rushed to judgment concerning Paul?
3. How did Paul make the most of the situation to minister to others in the name of the Savior?
4. What are some ways you can serve others with the talents and abilities God has given you?
5. What is the greatest spiritual blessing you can imagine experiencing as a result of ministering to others for Christ?

Contemporary Application

Kim has volunteered at the homeless shelter in her town for several years. As a result, she has made friends with people she never would have known. Kim has befriended wayward teens doing community service there, as well as warm, caring retirees who have added a fresh perspective to her life.

One woman in her seventies has become a particular encouragement to Kim. Kim has also learned more about the social services in her community and has even taken advantage of the free mental health clinic herself. Best of all, Kim has been able to watch God work in the lives of destitute people and has become more grateful for the small but adequate apartment in which she lives.

In her own life, Kim has seen how God has gifted her to do His work. The Lord has graced us also with talents and abilities He wants us to use in ministering to others. When we let the Savior's concerns rank equal in importance with our own, as Paul did on Malta, our character changes. In turn, we're likely to experience the Lord's spiritual blessings.

It's not that Christian service earns God's blessings or erases our problems. Even Paul faced significant challenges in his life, including being taken as a prisoner to Rome to stand trial for his faith. Nonetheless, the apostle did see the greater purposes of God become fruitful, especially through his own work and the work of other believers.

We also must be careful not to dictate to God just what our spiritual blessings should be. Instead, our goal is to serve the Lord and let Him decide on how, when, and where His blessings will come. Perhaps we will be blessed by seeing someone we have been teaching really grasp what God is about. Or it might be seeing the career advancement of someone whom we helped get a job. It could even be receiving a positive report from a missions agency we have supported for years.

Paul Evangelizes in Rome

DEVOTIONAL READING

Deuteronomy 4:32-40

DAILY BIBLE READINGS

Monday November 19
*Exodus 6:6-13 Will They
Listen to Me?*

Tuesday November 20
*Deuteronomy 1:41-45 I Told
You So!*

Wednesday November 21
*Deuteronomy 4:5-14
Charged to Teach*

Thursday November 22
*Deuteronomy 4:32-40 The
Voice of Discipline*

Friday November 23
*Deuteronomy 30:6-14 The
Word Is Very Near*

Saturday November 24
*Acts 28:16-22 We Would
Like to Hear*

Sunday November 25
*Acts 28:23-31 Teaching
Boldly and without
Hindrance*

Scripture

Background Scripture: *Acts 28:16-31*
Scripture Lesson: *Acts 28:23-31*
Key Verse: *"I want you to know that God's salvation has
been sent to the Gentiles, and they will listen!"* Acts 28:28.
Scripture Lesson for Children: *Acts 28:23-31*
Key Verse for Children: *[Paul] welcomed all who came to
see him. Boldly and without hindrance he preached the king-
dom of God and taught about the Lord Jesus Christ.*
Acts 28:30-31.

Lesson Aim

To reflect on the importance of proclaiming the
Gospel to the lost.

Lesson Setting

Time: A.D. *59–62*
Place: Rome

Lesson Outline

Paul Evangelizes in Rome

  I. Proclaiming the Gospel to the Local Jewish
Leaders: Acts 28:23-27
    A. Presenting the Truth of the Gospel: vs. 23
    B. Encountering a Mixed Response: vs. 24
    C. Confronting Calloused Hearts: vss. 25-27
  II. Proclaiming the Gospel to a Wider Audience:
Acts 28:28-31
    A. Witnessing to the Gentiles: vss. 28-29
    B. Proclaiming the Kingdom of God: vss. 30-31

Introduction for Adults
Topic: *Spread the News*

The Bible is our best defense against evildoers, impostors, and deceivers. Therefore, just as Paul did while imprisoned in Rome, it's our duty to maintain our commitment to study, proclaim, and obey God's Word. At the same time, we must gear our families and churches for instruction in Scripture, both for salvation and for remaining steadfast in the face of various opponents of the Gospel.

Consistent with Paul's example, our Christian education programs must center on teaching salvation through faith in the Son. We dare not assume that just because people attend Sunday school and church—even those who come from Christian homes—they have necessarily come to personal faith in the Messiah.

We hope and pray that every child will respond favorably when they hear the Good News. Parents, teachers, and pastors committedly working together can help to bring salvation and faith to our children.

Introduction for Youth
Topic: *I'm Going to Tell It*

We only mislead people when we offer the joys and blessings of the Gospel without the hardships. In our culture, however, hardships are not so easy to define. Like Paul did in Rome, we might face some ridicule or lose some friends, but we still have many other choices.

Perhaps we look in the wrong place for the battle to maintain our commitment to Christ. Throughout his ministry, Paul warned about not just physical but also spiritual hardships. These arise when people choose contemporary myths and reject God's Word.

In today's culture, hardships could easily consist of rejecting ungodly, unwholesome elements in entertainment, literature, and sports. After all, Satan uses music, television, radio, the Internet, books, and magazines to lure us away from God's truth. For some youth, it's a hardship to let go of these things for the sake of following Jesus. We, teachers of God's Word, can encourage them to remain committed to following the Savior—even when they face hard times—to the very end of their lives.

Concepts for Children
Topic: *Paul Preaches in Rome*

1. Once Paul made it to Rome, he asked some Jewish leaders to visit him.
2. Paul's visitors asked him to share what he believed.
3. Paul told his visitors about putting their faith in Jesus.
4. Some of the visitors believed what Paul said.
5. The Lord can help us tell others that Jesus loves them.

Lesson Commentary

I. PROCLAIMING THE GOSPEL TO THE LOCAL JEWISH LEADERS: ACTS 28:23-27

A. Presenting the Truth of the Gospel: vs. 23

They arranged to meet Paul on a certain day, and came in even larger numbers to the place where he was staying. From morning till evening he explained and declared to them the kingdom of God and tried to convince them about Jesus from the Law of Moses and from the Prophets.

After Paul's arrival in Rome, he could have been placed in one of the city's civil or military prisons. That would not have been a pleasant way to await his trial. Instead, he was permitted to rent his own home, to receive visitors, and to preach the Gospel (Acts 28:16). Soldiers of the Praetorian guard, the emperor's bodyguard unit, took turns watching Paul while chained to him. Most likely these soldiers also heard the apostle's testimony, and we can imagine a number of Roman warriors put their faith in the Savior as a result. Because of Paul's presence in Rome, the Gospel penetrated the inner circles of Roman officialdom and affected influential people in the capital (see Phil. 1:12-14). It was also during this time that the apostle wrote the so-called "prison epistles" of Ephesians, Philippians, Colossians, and Philemon. Even while chained to a soldier, Paul remained productive.

Three days after Paul arrived in Rome, he took advantage of his freedom to have visitors by trying to establish relations with the city's Jewish community. He summarized for a group of their leaders the circumstances that brought him as a prisoner to the capital of the empire. He openly acknowledged his trouble with some Jews in Jerusalem. He insisted, however, he never did anything to hurt the Jewish people. Additionally, he said he never violated the "customs of our ancestors" (Acts 28:17). In Romans 3:2, we learn that the Jews had been trusted with the oracles of God (a reference to the Old Testament). A number of privileges are listed in 9:4-5 that belonged to Israel as God's chosen nation. These included worshiping Him in the Jerusalem temple and receiving His wonderful promises. The Jews were the offspring of the patriarchs and enjoyed the honor of the Messiah being an Israelite.

It's not by accident that in the early days of Paul's imprisonment in Rome, he first met with the resident Jews. In every place where Jews lived, the apostle spoke first to them before going to the Gentiles. Previously, most likely toward the end of his third missionary journey, Paul stated in 1:14 that he had a great sense of obligation to communicate the Gospel to as many people as possible. Indeed, as verse 15 indicates, this is the reason the apostle had been eager to come to Rome. Even though the present circumstances were less than ideal, this did not deter Paul from evangelizing the lost in the capital of the empire.

Verse 16 explains that the apostle was not ashamed to be associated with the Good News about Christ, for it represented the power of God that made salvation possible. Moreover, eternal redemption is available to all who believe, first to the

Jew, then for the Gentile. Since Jews were the heirs of the promises of Abraham and the people from whom the Messiah came, it was appropriate for the Gospel to be preached first to them. Eventually, when the Jews rejected the Good News, Paul turned to the Gentiles (see Acts 13:44-46; 18:5-6). According to Romans 1:17, the Gospel explains how unrighteous people can receive an upright standing before a holy God. Regardless of whether one was a Jew or a Gentile, he had to appropriate this righteousness by trusting in the Messiah (see Hab. 2:4).

Paul told the local Jewish leaders that the Roman government in Palestine had conducted a judicial hearing regarding his case. After cross-examining him, the officials determined that Paul had not done anything to deserve death or imprisonment (Acts 28:18; see 26:31). In fact, they struggled to delineate the charges being made against the accused (see 25:27). Even so, when the civil authorities sought to release the apostle, his opponents protested the decision. Moreover, when they continued to press their charges against him, Paul was forced to appeal his case to Caesar (which was his right as a Roman citizen). The apostle was careful to emphasize that he was not bringing any countercharge against his "own people" (28:19). He was appearing before the emperor as a defendant only. Paul's final statement demonstrated the link between Judaism and the Christian church. His ministry, which had led to his current predicament, was due to the "hope of Israel" (vs. 20).

In response to Paul, the local Jewish leaders claimed to have heard nothing "bad" (vs. 21) about the apostle. This included the absence of any written correspondence from Judea. There weren't even verbal reports against Paul from anyone who had come from Judea. While claiming not to know anything negative about Paul, the Jewish leaders admitted having heard unfavorable reports about the Christian church. They called the group a "sect" (vs. 22), which indicated that Christianity was still regarded as a splinter group of Judaism. In all likelihood, the resident Jews had heard that the followers of Jesus held a low view of the law and created disturbances (see 21:20-21). It's also possible that in this exchange with Paul, the Jewish representatives were exercising some diplomatic restraint to avoid trouble with the Roman officials. Some experts think that religious disputes with Christians, involving major disturbances, had caused the Emperor Claudius to order all Jews out of Rome about the year A.D. 49. Jews had returned to Rome sometime after Claudius died in A.D. 54.

Despite their suspicions, the local Jewish leaders agreed to return "on a certain day" (28:23) to hear what Paul had to say about Jesus of Nazareth and the religious movement connected with Him. It appears that on the surface of things, Paul's fellow Jews seemed open-minded. In fact, for an entire day the apostle reasoned with those who came to hear him. He testified from the Old Testament about the rule of God and the promise of the Messiah found in "the Law of Moses" and "the Prophets." Paul used the Jewish sacred writings to show how Jesus had fulfilled the prophecies in numerous ways. The apostle taught that the kingdom of God includes His rule in the hearts of believers. The divine kingdom was not merely limited to the nation of Israel, as the Jews had long believed.

B. Encountering a Mixed Response: vs. 24

Some were convinced by what he said, but others would not believe.

What the Jews had long hoped for was what Paul heralded as an accomplished fact: the advent of the Messiah. This was a consistent theme in the apostle's evangelistic preaching. For instance, while at Pisidian Antioch, during Paul's first missionary journey, he told about the one in whom God had most fully revealed His grace: Jesus the Savior (Acts 13:23). Jesus was the descendant of David who had been promised in such Old Testament prophecies as Isaiah 11.

Paul declared that the promises of Scripture had been fulfilled in the Messiah. The apostle quoted Psalm 2:7 in support of Jesus' divine sonship (Acts 13:32-33). Paul quoted Isaiah 55:3 and Psalm 16:10 to back up Jesus' resurrection (Acts 13:34-35). Those passages could not have been fulfilled ultimately in David, since the illustrious king died. But Jesus, David's descendant, was raised immortal. In Him the hopes of the prophets were fulfilled (vss. 36-37). When Paul met with the local Jewish leaders in Rome, he convinced some in his audience, but many others remained unpersuaded (28:24).

C. Confronting Calloused Hearts: vss. 25-27

They disagreed among themselves and began to leave after Paul had made this final statement: "The Holy Spirit spoke the truth to your forefathers when he said through Isaiah the prophet: 'Go to this people and say, "You will be ever hearing but never understanding; you will be ever seeing but never perceiving." For this people's heart has become calloused; they hardly hear with their ears, and they have closed their eyes. Otherwise they might see with their eyes, hear with their ears, understand with their hearts and turn, and I would heal them.'"

Animated debate continued among the Jews themselves, with some supporting the apostle's views and others denouncing them (Acts 28:25). The meeting finally broke up when Paul quoted an unflattering prophecy from the Septuagint version (an ancient Greek translation) of Isaiah 6:9-10. In doing so, the apostle declared that his listeners heard but did not understand God's truth. Likewise, they saw but did not perceive God's revelation. Their problem was that their hearts were calloused, insensitive, and unfeeling. The result was that they did not turn to God for spiritual healing (Acts 28:26-27).

Just as we have physical senses that enable us to understand and respond to our surroundings, we also have spiritual senses with which we can perceive God. But we must take care that our spiritual senses function better than the spiritual senses of those who rejected Paul's message. We might be able to see with physical eyes, but still be spiritually blind. We might be able to hear with physical ears, but still be spiritually deaf. We might be able to physically touch, but still be spiritually calloused.

II. PROCLAIMING THE GOSPEL TO A WIDER AUDIENCE: ACTS 28:28-31

A. Witnessing to the Gentiles: vss. 28-29

"Therefore I want you to know that God's salvation has been sent to the Gentiles, and they will listen!"
After he said this, the Jews left, arguing vigorously among themselves.

In response to the local Jews' refusal to believe the Gospel, Paul declared that the Father's saving message through the Son was also being offered to the Gentiles (Acts 28:28). Furthermore, they would hear and heed the Good News. After the apostle had made this statement, his fellow Jews departed. As they left, they heatedly argued with one another about what Paul had said (vs. 29).

B. Proclaiming the Kingdom of God: vss. 30-31

For two whole years Paul stayed there in his own rented house and welcomed all who came to see him.
Boldly and without hindrance he preached the kingdom of God and taught about the Lord Jesus Christ.

The city of Rome—where Paul now found himself under house arrest—was located on the Tiber River on seven hills, about 15 miles inland from the Tyrrhenian Sea. In the first century A.D., Rome was one of the two largest cities in the world (the other being Xian, China), with a population estimated at 1 million people. Rome was a walled city of less than 25 square miles. It boasted the royal palace; ornate fountains; elaborate baths (some of which housed libraries and social clubs); the Circus Maximus, used for chariot racing and other games; and the 50,000-seat Colosseum. The Forum, where citizens engaged in political, religious, and commercial enterprises, was where Paul likely defended himself and the Christian movement. Some 82 temples were built or remodeled in Rome in the first half of the first century A.D.

During Paul's day, Rome was the political capital of an empire that, by the first century A.D., extended from the Atlantic Ocean to the Persian Gulf, and from North Africa to Britain and northern Europe. As a booming metropolis, Rome was connected to other parts of the ancient world by an intricate system of highways. Also, Rome's communications system was unsurpassed at the time. In fact, during the first century A.D., the city was at the hub of trade and commerce. Because of its location and prestige, Rome was a strategic center for the spread of the Gospel. It's no wonder that people remarked concerning the city, "All roads lead to Rome."

While in the capital, Paul remained in detention in his own "rented house" (Acts 28:30) for "two whole years." He was not assigned a place to live by the government. Rather, he paid his own living expenses. Perhaps this indicates that the apostle earned a living by tentmaking even while in custody. In any case, Paul had considerable freedom to see people. Indeed, this "open-door" policy enabled many to visit him and discuss the Gospel. He did not hesitate to proclaim the truth about Jesus boldly and triumphantly in the heart of the empire (vs. 31).

The two-year period of house arrest is somewhat mystifying. According to one group of historians, Roman law required cases to be heard within 18 months or they had to be dismissed. Paul's two-year wait suggests to some that his prosecutors failed to press charges within the allotted time. With bureaucratic delays, they say, Paul finally stood before Caesar for formal release after being held two years. While some see the apostle's imprisonment ending with a death sentence passed by the despotic Nero (who was previously mentioned in lessons 3 and 10), many others maintain that Paul took one more missionary journey before being rearrested and executed in Rome about A.D. 62–67.

Paul's final words seem to be that of a believer who was content. He affirmed that he had been faithful to do all that God had assigned to him. The apostle had no regrets, for he had surrendered his life completely to the Lord (see 2 Tim. 4:7). Paul compared his life to the offerings the Old Testament priests made (see Phil. 2:17; 2 Tim. 4:6). They poured wine or oil on a sacrifice just before it was to be burned (see Num. 15:1-12). The apostle saw this as a picture of something that was irretrievable—once the wine was spilled, it soaked into the sacrifice, the wood, and the ground around the altar. It could not be picked up. It was gone. Eventually, Paul would be gone, the last drop of his life poured out for the Lord. How important it is to live our lives so that at the end we will have no regrets!

Concerning other prominent believers mentioned in the New Testament, Peter probably was martyred at about the same time as Paul, and in Rome as well. According to tradition, all the original eleven apostles were martyred, with the exception of John. It is presumed he died in old age after writing the Book of Revelation about A.D. 95. We know even less about the later years of other individuals, such as Barnabas, Silas, Apollos, and Luke. A few, including Mark and Timothy, are thought to have survived into the period when Romans began persecuting the church. Luke was Paul's last co-laborer (see 2 Tim. 4:11) and may have shared the apostle's fate.

The first Roman persecution began in the summer of A.D. 64, when Emperor Nero tried to shift the blame for the burning of Rome onto Christians (a point previously made in lesson 3). Revelation, which was penned during the reign of Domitian (A.D. 51–96), gives evidence of heated persecution at that time. Also, letters from Emperor Trajan (A.D. 53–117) indicate that a profession of faith in the Lord Jesus had become a capital offense. Many Christians, including the bishops Ignatius and Polycarp, were put to death around the mid-second century. Emperor Marcus Aurelius(A.D. 121–180) thoroughly disliked Christians and put many to death throughout the empire.

An unresolved issue is the reason why Luke concluded Acts as he did. Some think he wrote as far as the account had gone. Expressed differently, he couldn't tell the end because he was himself waiting to find out what would happen. Others conjecture that Luke had a grander scheme in mind, namely, that he wanted to emphasize that the church's work continues until Jesus returns. The last verse of Acts also has been viewed as a summary of the accomplishments of the early church as the apostles, especially Paul, spread the Gospel from Jerusalem to Rome: "You will be my witnesses in Jerusalem . . . and to the ends of the earth" (1:8). In that sense, we also can be part of the unfinished saga. We can be part of what God is doing in this age through believers everywhere who make up the Savior's church.

Discussion Questions

1. What set of circumstances led to Paul's being incarcerated in Rome?
2. Why do you think Paul asked the local Jewish leaders to meet with him?
3. What compelled Paul to request to be tried by the emperor?
4. If you were Paul, what would you have said to the Jewish representatives who met with him?
5. What responses have you encountered after sharing the Gospel with others?

Contemporary Application

How do we make the Gospel available to all people? We can use radio, television, films, books, and the Internet (to name a few things). We have more means available to us than ever before. At the same time we should not forget the important role that each of us serves in proclaiming the Good News.

Believers are critical to the success of evangelism because people want to see our love and compassion for them as individuals, not just as part of a mass audience. They want to see Jesus in us. They want to ask why our faith works for us. This reminds us that our personal witness for Christ can be just as effective as any other means of spreading the Gospel.

We should be careful not to assume that everyone has heard the message of salvation, despite the media we may use to disseminate the Gospel. We have to think about people from different backgrounds who may be bypassed by the media and by our churches. We dare not give the impression that the Gospel is anyone's private property. Paul made it clear that everyone who calls on the Lord will be saved and that part of the process includes their hearing and understanding the truth. That's where we come in.

When we rely on ourselves and not on God to do His evangelistic work, one of two things might result. On the one hand, we might become filled with pride. We imagine that God needs us and that His people cannot survive without us. On the other hand, we might experience frustration and failure. Despite initial appearances of progress and success, our self-energized attempts to do the work of the Lord will not succeed in the long run or have any lasting value.

Although God's power is always available, we seem to notice it more in our times of affliction. Undoubtedly, this proved to be true for Paul as he spent time under house arrest in Rome. It is when we see our own limitations that we are most inclined to turn to God, draw on His strength, and gain a renewed appreciation for His unlimited power in proclaiming the Gospel to the lost.

Spiritual Blessings in Christ

Scripture

Background Scripture: *Ephesians 1*
Scripture Lesson: *Ephesians 1:3-14*
Key Verse: *He predestined us to be adopted as his sons
through Jesus Christ, in accordance with his pleasure and
will—to the praise of his glorious grace, which he has freely
given us in the One he loves.* Ephesians 1:5-6.
Scripture Lesson for Children: *Ephesians 1:3-14*
Key Verse for Children: *[God] chose us in him before the
creation of the world.* Ephesians 1:4.

Lesson Aim

To encourage believers to praise God for every spiritual
blessing.

Lesson Setting

Time: A.D. *60*
Place: Rome

Lesson Outline

Spiritual Blessings in Christ
  I. Blessings in Christ: Ephesians 1:3-10
    A. *Praise to the Father: vs. 3*
    B. *Chosen by God: vss. 4-6*
    C. *Redeemed by God: vss. 7-8*
    D. *God's Plan Centered in Christ: vss. 9-10*
  II. Brought Together in Christ: Ephesians 1:11-14
    A. *Jewish Believers in Christ: vss. 11-12*
    B. *Gentile Believers in Christ: vs. 13a*
    C. *Sealed by the Spirit: vss. 13b-14*

Introduction for Adults

Topic: *Chosen and Claimed*

According to folklore, General Eisenhower rebuked one of his generals for referring to a soldier as "just a private." Eisenhower reminded the general that the army could function better without its generals than it could without its foot soldiers. "If this war is won," Eisenhower said, "it will be won by privates."

In the same way, the church needs more "privates" than "generals." These are believers who have a genuine appreciation for the fact that the Father has chosen and claimed them in His Son. Moreover, the Father has identified them as His own by sealing them with the Holy Spirit (see Eph. 1:13).

Indeed, God has appointed ordinary people—including the saved adults in your class—to do the work of ministry. Meanwhile, He appoints some to be pastors and teachers to equip these "privates" so that they can win people for Christ.

Introduction for Youth

Topic: *Too Blessed to Be Stressed*

As adolescents progress through high school, the necessity of making plans for the future can cause them a lot of stress. Upon graduation, some will head off to college, while others will enter the workforce. Their common goal is to claim the best opportunities that life offers them.

One young man had his heart set on playing professional baseball. But when none of the major league teams drafted him, his dream was smashed. What should he do? Because he was a Christian, he sought God's will. This person decided to obtain more schooling in theology and began an internship working with his church's youth. Two years later he was on his way to a foreign country to coach baseball and to introduce kids to Christ.

Most important was this young man's basic decision to follow God's will. The same is true for all of us. The Father has chosen us in the Son to be His spiritual children. Also, in Christ we have received all we will ever need for our spiritual growth and welfare. In light of these blessings (and many others), we can accept and do God's will with supreme confidence.

Concepts for Children

Topic: *Adopted into the Family*

1. The Father loved us before we were born.
2. The Father gives us many blessings in His Son, the Lord Jesus.
3. One of these blessings is being forgiven.
4. Another blessing is becoming a member of God's family.
5. The Father wants us to thank Him for all He has done for us.

Lesson Commentary

I. BLESSINGS IN CHRIST: EPHESIANS 1:3-10

A. Praise to the Father: vs. 3

Praise be to the God and Father of our Lord Jesus Christ, who has blessed us in the heavenly realms with every spiritual blessing in Christ.

Ephesus was located at the intersection of several major east-west trade routes and became a vital commercial, political, and educational center of the Roman Empire. The size of the city is shown by its theater, which could seat over 24,000 people. The city was perhaps best known for its magnificent temple of Diana, or Artemis, one of the seven wonders of the ancient world. (Diana was the Greek goddess of the moon, forests, wild animals, and women in childbirth.) More importantly, Ephesus figured prominently and dramatically in early church history, for Paul used the city as a center for his missionary work in that region.

The apostle evangelized Ephesus toward the end of his second missionary journey (Acts 18:18-21). When he departed, he left a Christian couple named Priscilla and Aquila to continue his work (vs. 26). When Paul wrote the Letter to the Ephesians, he was no longer an evangelist on the move. Instead, he was a prisoner in Rome. And the church he was now writing to was not opposing him and his teaching. Rather, it was basically a sound congregation that was ready to receive advanced instruction in theology and ethics. Paul began the epistle by identifying himself as an apostle. Although Paul was always ready to admit his unworthiness to receive grace, he never underrated his role as an apostle, or ambassador, for Christ since it had been given him "by the will of God" (Eph. 1:1).

It bears mentioning that not all early Greek manuscripts of this letter have the words "in Ephesus" in verse 1. Bible scholars have explained this omission in various ways. But most likely the letter was sent to the church in Ephesus and then passed around to other congregations in the Roman province of Asia Minor (now western Turkey). Also, the general nature of the majority of the epistle's teaching may indicate that from the start Paul meant for the letter to be read by more than one church. In any case, the apostle called his recipients "saints"—literally, "holy ones." Paul was not addressing certain Christians who were holier than others. Instead, he was addressing all his readers. Evangelicals believe that all Christians are saints because Jesus has set us apart as His own special people. He has also made us holy with His own righteousness.

Furthermore, Paul called his readers "the faithful in Christ Jesus." They were faithful in the sense that they had expressed faith in the Son for their salvation and also in the sense that they were faithfully following Him. The apostle concluded his greeting with a blessing on his readers. He wished them "grace and peace" (vs. 2). The essence of the Gospel is the grace of God given to undeserving people. Peace is the harmony felt by those in a restored relationship with the Lord.

115

The general nature of Ephesians makes it difficult to determine the specific circumstances that gave rise to the letter. Nevertheless, it is clear that the recipients were predominately Gentiles (3:1) who were estranged from citizenship in the kingdom of Israel (2:11) but devout followers of the Lord (1:1). Now, thanks to the gracious gift of the Father, they enjoyed the spiritual blessings that come through faith in the Son, including peace with the triune God.

Ordinarily in Paul's letters, he followed up his greeting to his readers with thanksgiving for them. In this epistle, however, he delayed the thanksgiving so that he could offer extended praise to the Father (vss. 3-14). The apostle extolled the Father for the spiritual blessings He has given to the Son's followers (vs. 3). The Father has blessed us, among other ways, by choosing us (vss. 4-6), redeeming us (vss. 7-8), and revealing His eternal plan of redemption to us (vss. 9-10). The Father sometimes blesses His people materially as well as spiritually, but in verse 3 Paul chose to focus on spiritual blessings. These are certain, for they have been secured for us "in the heavenly realms." They flow from the Father, through the Son, to us.

Verse 3 is only one of many places in Scripture where the word "blessing" appears. It refers to an act of declaring (or wishing) favor and goodness upon others. In the Old Testament, important people blessed those with less power or influence. For example, the patriarchs declared God's favor upon their children (Gen. 49:1-28). Leaders frequently blessed their subordinates, especially when preparing to leave them (for instance, Moses and Joshua, Deut. 31). The Lord's people bless Him by showing gratitude and singing songs of praise (Ps. 103:1-2). God also blesses His people through spiritual and physical enrichment. For instance, He showers them with life and fruitfulness (Gen. 1:22, 28). Of course, God's foremost blessing is turning people from their wicked ways and pardoning their sins (Acts 3:25-26). The atoning sacrifice of the Son is the basis for the Father's favor and goodness to believers (Eph. 1:3).

B. Chosen by God: vss. 4-6

For he chose us in him before the creation of the world to be holy and blameless in his sight. In love he predestined us to be adopted as his sons through Jesus Christ, in accordance with his pleasure and will—to the praise of his glorious grace, which he has freely given us in the One he loves.

The first spiritual blessing Paul mentioned is that the Father "chose us" (Eph. 1:4) and "predestined us" (vs. 5). These terms are parallel but have different shades of meaning. Just as the Father chose the Jewish nation to be His own and to receive the promised land as an inheritance, so He chose Christian believers before He made the world to be His own people and to receive the inheritance of eternal life. It can "never perish, spoil or fade" (1 Pet. 1:4), for it is "kept in heaven" for us eternally.

There are at least two distinct views of what predestination means when it is discussed in Scripture. Some think that people are so debased by sin that they are unable to respond to the offer of salvation made available in the Son. It is argued that those who believe have the ability to do so only because the Father previously chose them for redemption. In other words, He gives them grace, and this enables them to believe the truth. Others think that the Father gives all people enough grace to accept the offer of salvation. This remains true even though many reject His grace. In this way, the Father predestines some for redemption in the sense that He knows beforehand those who will choose to believe the truth of their own free will.

Regardless of which view is preferred, it remains clear that the Father chose believers "to be holy and blameless in his sight" (Eph. 1:4). To be holy means to be distinctly different from the world so that the Father can use us for His purposes. Our holiness is the result of our having been chosen, not the reason we were chosen. To be "blameless" means to be free of the immoral and selfish lifestyle that marks people who are apart from God. The Father also predestined believers "to be adopted as his sons" (vs. 5). Through Jesus Christ, the Son, we become spiritual children of the Father. Under Roman law, adopted sons enjoyed the same standing and entitlements as natural sons. Similarly, the Father reckons believers as His true children and as recipients of all the benefits that go with that status. It's no wonder that believers give the Father praise for the wonderful grace He has poured out on them in His Son, whom the Father dearly loves (vs. 6).

C. Redeemed by God: vss. 7-8

In him we have redemption through his blood, the forgiveness of sins, in accordance with the riches of God's grace that he lavished on us with all wisdom and understanding.

Despite the magnificence of our having been chosen by the Father, this spiritual blessing is not the only one we receive. Paul also mentioned the blessing of redemption (Eph. 1:7-8). Through redemption the Father makes His choosing effective in our lives. The Greek noun translated "redemption" (vs. 7) refers to a ransom. It was used in ancient times to describe the buying back of someone who had been sold into slavery or had become a prisoner of war. The noun also described freeing a person from the penalty of death. Because we were born with a sinful nature, the Father was not attracted to us due to any goodness He saw in us. Despite our sinful condition, He rescued us from our state of separation from His holiness. The Father did this by sending His Son to become the sacrifice for our sins. By His blood, the Messiah ransomed us from slavery to sin and from the sentence of death under which we languished.

Closely related to redemption is "forgiveness." The Greek noun Paul used had a variety of meanings, including "to send off," "to release," "to give up," "to pardon," and "to hurl." The basic idea is that when we receive the effect of the Son's redemption through faith, the Father releases us from the penalty of our sins and casts our sin debt far away from us. What the Father did for us through His Son was in harmony with the riches of the Father's grace. In addition to showering us with His unmerited favor, the Father has also lavished us "with all wisdom and understanding" (vs. 8). Before we believed, we did not have spiritual insight. But since coming to a knowledge of the truth, we can now see how things really are and can get an idea of how the Father wants us to live.

D. God's Plan Centered in Christ: vss. 9-10

And he made known to us the mystery of his will according to his good pleasure, which he purposed in Christ, to be put into effect when the times will have reached their fulfillment—to bring all things in heaven and on earth together under one head, even Christ.

Another spiritual blessing Paul listed is our ability to know the "mystery of [God's] will" (Eph. 1:9). The Greek noun rendered "mystery" generally denotes that which is hidden or secret. For the apostle, a "mystery" is a truth that was once hidden but has now been revealed through the Messiah. The Father's disclosure to us of His will was in accordance with His good pleasure, which He centered in His Son. Paul declared that the Father's eternal plan was to head up all things in the Son at the divinely appointed time (vs. 10). This includes everything "in heaven and on earth." The Greek verb translated "bring . . . together" means to sum up. In Paul's day, when a column of figures was tallied, the total was placed at the head of the column. In a similar fashion, at the end of history all things will be seen to add up to the Son.

From eternity, the Father has intended to give the Son possession of all things. But from our viewpoint within history, we can see that the Father set His plan in motion at just the right time, namely, when the Son came into the world at His incarnation. Moreover, the Father will bring His plan to a glorious conclusion at just the right time, namely, when the Son comes into the world at His second advent. On that day, our sorrows will be over, our conflicts will be at an end, and our weakness will be replaced by strength.

II. BROUGHT TOGETHER IN CHRIST: EPHESIANS 1:11-14

A. Jewish Believers in Christ: vss. 11-12

In him we were also chosen, having been predestined according to the plan of him who works out everything in conformity with the purpose of his will, in order that we, who were the first to hope in Christ, might be for the praise of his glory.

Previously, in Ephesians 1:4-5, Paul mentioned the Father's plan for believers. Now the apostle returned to that theme. He noted that the Father causes all things to happen in accordance with "the purpose of his will" (vs. 11). This included Jews such as Paul coming to faith in the Son. The language of Ephesians (particularly the first half) is richer and more effusive than the language in other letters Paul wrote. The apostle's style is demonstrated in this phrase: "the plan of him who works out everything in conformity with the purpose of his will" (vs. 11). The phrase contains an inclusive term ("everything") and several synonyms ("plan," "works out," "purpose," "will"). This style suits Paul's subject of the Father's grand plan for believers, the church, and the universe.

The divine purpose was that the conversion of Jews to the Son would bring the Father eternal praise (vs. 12). Similarly, according to Romans 8:28, "in all things God works for the good of those who love him, who have been called according to his purpose." The historical record is that the apostles and other Jews were the first to trust in the Son. Admittedly, the majority of Jews who were contemporaries of Paul rejected the Messiah. Nevertheless, a remnant of that generation of Jews formed the nucleus of the church. Through them, the Gospel went out to the entire world. Those early Jewish believers were walking testimonies of the Father's glory.

B. Gentile Believers in Christ: vs. 13a

And you also were included in Christ when you heard the word of truth, the gospel of your salvation.

With Ephesians 1:13, Paul changed pronouns from "we" to "you." He was now specifically referring to the Ephesian believers. Although Jewish Christians had been chosen for their role in starting the church, this should not make the Ephesians feel like outsiders. They, too, were included in the Son's spiritual body. Expressed differently, Jewish and Gentile believers formed one united church. Paul delineated the stages of development by which the Gentiles had become "included in Christ." It is the same process through which anyone is born again. First, the Gentiles had "heard the word of truth" when Paul or others had proclaimed the Gospel to them. Then they "believed" the truth they heard. The result was their spiritual regeneration.

It's clarifying to note that all three persons of the Trinity are involved in this salvific process. The Father has blessed us because of our spiritual union with His Son. Furthermore, the gift of the Spirit identifies us as God's spiritual children. Moreover, the Spirit is the believers' guarantee that they belong to the Father and that He will do for them what He has promised in His Son. The Spirit's abiding presence confirms that one's faith is genuine and that one's adoption into God's family is real. These are excellent reasons for us to give unending praise to God!

C. Sealed by the Spirit: vss. 13b-14

Having believed, you were marked in him with a seal, the promised Holy Spirit, who is a deposit guaranteeing our inheritance until the redemption of those who are God's possession—to the praise of his glory.

Paul noted that when his readers trusted in the Son, they were "marked . . . with a seal" (Eph. 1:13), which is the Holy Spirit. In other words, the Father identified believers as His own by giving them the Spirit, whom He promised long ago. By calling the Spirit a seal, Paul may have raised a number of images in the minds of his readers. At that time, seals were put on documents to vouch for their authenticity. They were also attached to goods being shipped to indicate right of possession and safeguard protection. Sometimes they represented an office in the government. Any of these uses of seals might symbolize a part of the Holy Spirit's work in the lives of those who follow the Messiah.

But for Paul, the Spirit is not only a seal. He is also a "deposit" (vs. 14). In the apostle's day, a deposit was an initial payment or first installment assuring a retailer that the full purchase price would be forthcoming. At the end of time, believers will receive the final installment of eternal life from the riches of the Father's grace. During the interim, the Spirit's presence in our lives assures us of coming glory. This giving of the Spirit is also to "the praise of [God's] glory" (compare vs. 12).

Discussion Questions

1. What did Paul say that God had bestowed on the believers in Ephesus?
2. To what extent did Paul say that God has blessed us as Christians?
3. Why is it so difficult at times for us to accept God's spiritual blessings?
4. When did Paul say that the Father would bring all things under the headship of the Son?
5. What role does the Spirit serve in the life of believers?

Contemporary Application

How quickly our culture saturates our minds with so-called "truths" that affect our wills and emotions. Every day we are bombarded with messages about how to stay well, how to get rich, how to succeed, how to be popular, and so forth. When things don't work out the way these messages suggest, we wonder what's wrong with us.

As Christians, we can't escape these messages about the world's values, so we have to fortify our minds with the facts God has revealed to us. His truths include our having been chosen for salvation and adopted into His spiritual family. Moreover, the Father has disclosed that through His Son our sins are forgiven and we have been set free from sin's bondage. The Father has made known to us that as a result of our decision to trust in His Son, we have the abiding Holy Spirit as the Father's stamp of ownership.

Each day we can pick up our Bibles and build our faith. We can read texts like Ephesians 1 and rejoice in the goodness of the Lord. We can realize that the genuinely important things in life are centered around His incomparable blessings in the Messiah and the divine guarantee of an eternal inheritance. When we think about these truths, somehow what the world tells us fades into insignificance. Our lives achieve purpose, order, and composure. And, in the process, we find God's enduring grace and peace.

One in Jesus Christ

Scripture

Background Scripture: *Ephesians 2–3*
Scripture Lesson: *Ephesians 2:11-22*
Key Verse: *In him the whole building is joined together and rises to become a holy temple in the Lord.* Ephesians 2:21.
Scripture Lesson for Children: *Ephesians 2:1-10*
Key Verse for Children: *God, who is rich in mercy, made us alive with Christ.* Ephesians 2:4-5.

Lesson Aim

To bring to peace all the differences with our fellow believers.

Lesson Setting

Time: A.D. *60*
Place: Rome

Lesson Outline

One in Jesus Christ

   I. The Messiah—Our Unity and Peace: Ephesians 2:11-18
      A. *Excluded from the Community of Faith: vss. 11-12*
      B. *Included in the Community of Faith: vs. 13*
      C. *Peace between Saved Jews and Gentiles: vss. 14-15a*
      D. *Unity among Saved Jews and Gentiles: vss. 15b-16*
      E. *Joint Access to the Father: vss. 17-18*
  II. The Messiah—Our Cornerstone: Ephesians 2:19-22
      A. *Members of God's Family: vss. 19-20*
      B. *A Holy Temple for the Lord: vss. 21-22*

Introduction for Adults

Topic: *Unity, Not Uniformity*

We sometimes mistakenly imagine a great hardwood sending down roots deep into the soil. But naturalists point out that a healthy tree is one whose roots go sideways, not deep down. And the roots don't just protect that one tree, but rather are woven together with the roots of other trees in order to hold up the entire forest.

Like a healthy growth of trees in a forest, Jesus' followers do not consider merely protecting themselves. They realize that the loneliness, meaninglessness, and alienation in the world stem from the refusal of people to relate to God and to one another. Indulging in self-interest and self-preservation produces an unstable person who, like a poorly rooted tree, will be weak and easily toppled. As Paul emphasized in his teachings, all believers must be rooted together in Christ!

Introduction for Youth

Topic: *Unity in the Community*

Differences among people in a community are a fact of life, and we spend most of our lives trying to accommodate them. Of course, some people never do. In extreme cases, people fight and die to keep their distinctives alive. Even when our differences do not lead to bloodshed, they cause unhappiness and despair.

Looking at how hard it is to resolve problems brought on by racial, religious, national, and economic differences, we are tempted to say there is no hope. But as Paul reveals in this week's Scripture text, the Gospel of Christ offers us the only hope we have to bring people together, despite their differences.

Our mission as believers is to help people understand who Jesus is and what He can do. Of course, we have to claim our new status as part of God's family. We have to demonstrate how we can overcome our differences in the body of Christ. We must never give up on the Father's plan to bring people together in peace and harmony under the Son's lordship.

Concepts for Children

Topic: *Love Brings Us Joy*

1. Grace is a gift that comes to us freely from the Father, not because of anything we have done.
2. The Father's love for us is shown by sending His Son for us.
3. When we trust in Jesus, we are saved.
4. The Father has given us a new way of life through faith in His Son.
5. In response to the Father's love in His Son, we should love one another.

Lesson Commentary

I. THE MESSIAH—OUR UNITY AND PEACE: EPHESIANS 2:11-18

A. Excluded from the Community of Faith: vss. 11-12

Therefore, remember that formerly you who are Gentiles by birth and called "uncircumcised" by those who call themselves "the circumcision" (that done in the body by the hands of men)—remember that at that time you were separate from Christ, excluded from citizenship in Israel and foreigners to the covenants of the promise, without hope and without God in the world.

Ephesians 2:8-9 reveals that the Father saves all believers by His grace. This is His free act of doing something good for us, even though we don't deserve it. Put another way, the grace Paul referred to is the Lord's favor that He shows without regard to the recipient's worth or merit. God bestows His kindness despite what the person deserves. This is possible because of what Jesus did at Calvary. The Father's grace is activated in our lives through faith. Paul said that when we put our trust in the Messiah, we become the recipients of His grace, and so we enjoy salvation.

God's grace is one of His key attributes. For instance, Exodus 34:6 reveals that the Lord is "the compassionate and gracious God." His redemption of His people from Egypt and His establishment of them in Canaan was a superlative example of His grace. He did this despite their unrighteousness (Deut. 7:7-8; 9:5-6). The Son is the supreme revelation of the Father's grace. Jesus not only appropriated divine grace but also incarnated it (Luke 2:40; John 1:14). The Son died on the cross and rose from the dead so that believing sinners might partake of the Father's grace (Titus 2:11). Even their entrance into the divine kingdom is not based on their own merit.

Although our good works did not produce salvation, as believers our salvation is intended to produce good works (Eph. 2:10). The Greek term rendered "do" is the same word translated "live" in verse 2. It means "walk about." While unbelievers walk about doing evil deeds, believers are to walk about doing good deeds. Through grace, we are God's "workmanship" (vs. 10). He created us, and He created the tasks He wants us to accomplish. We need not go about our lives aimlessly but can seek to discover and fulfill God's plan for our lives. When we do the will of the Father as His obedient servants, we show the world that we are His work of art, namely, those whom He has created anew in the Son to the Father's eternal praise.

After Paul reminded the Ephesians about their former need for God to raise them from spiritual death to spiritual life by His grace (vss. 1-10), the apostle went on to recount their former disadvantages in contrast with the Jews (vss. 11-13). The Jewish people are the descendants of Abraham, Isaac, and Jacob. God entered into a covenant with them to make them the channel through which His truth would be declared to the world. Gentiles are all peoples other than Jews. Old Testament law permitted Gentiles to become members of the covenant community if they were circumcised and agreed to obey the law. Even so, Gentiles never joined the Jewish faith in large numbers.

Admittedly, some Jews considered themselves superior to Gentiles, not because of what God had done for the Jews but simply because of who they were. This prejudice carried over into the early church, as Jewish believers reckoned Gentiles to be second-class Christians unless they adopted Jewish practices. Paul had to deal with this problem often. The apostle taught that the Jews' privilege was due solely to God's grace in making a covenant with them, but many Jews identified their privilege with their circumcision, which was merely a sign of the covenant.

In Paul's day, the Jews called themselves "the circumcision" (vs. 11) and used the insulting term "uncircumcised" of Gentiles, such as the Ephesians. The apostle stated the use of this contemptuous term without meaning any disdain himself. In fact, Paul affirmed that, under the Gospel, circumcision holds no spiritual significance. As he said elsewhere (see Rom. 2:29), true circumcision is of the heart. Many Jews went too far in elevating their privileges. Nevertheless, it is true that Gentiles—such as those living in Ephesus—were under some disadvantages. The apostle proceeded to describe the Ephesians' condition before they were saved.

First, Gentiles had been without the Messiah (Eph. 2:12). The promises of the coming Redeemer had been made to the Jews, and so Gentiles did not expect Him. Second, Paul's non-Jewish readers had been alienated from the citizenship of Israel and strangers to the covenants of promise. While membership in the commonwealth of Israel was not a guarantee of salvation, it was of significant value, for God had made promises of blessing to the physical descendants of Abraham and Isaac. Third, the Ephesians previously had no hope and were without God in the world. Though God had not forgotten the Gentiles, most of them knew nothing about Him. Their pagan religious practices did not put them in touch with Him and so left them with no hope of finding peace and immortality.

B. Included in the Community of Faith: vs. 13

But now in Christ Jesus you who once were far away have been brought near through the blood of Christ.

Paul next turned from the dismal picture of the Ephesians' former condition of once being far away from God. Now, by means of the Son's shed blood, they had been brought near to the Father (Eph. 2:13). The Son was the meeting point with the Father for all who believed the Gospel. So then, the Father's grace in the sacrifice of His Son was the reason for the Ephesians' change in status.

It is helpful for us to appreciate what an astonishing fact it was for Jewish believers in the church to accept and assimilate Gentile Christians. Early church leaders argued over this point. Peter received a vision from the Lord to convince him to preach to the Gentiles (see Acts 10). Then he had to defend his actions before leaders of the church in Jerusalem (see 11:1-18). Moreover, the Jerusalem Council debated the issue (see chap. 15). However, their decision to welcome Gentile believers into the church without requiring adherence to the laws of Moses was not well received by everyone in the church.

The barriers and hostilities between Jews and Gentiles were rooted in thousands of years of tradition. Admittedly, God had told His chosen people, Israel, to stay away from the gods and immoral practices of the surrounding Gentiles. The Lord also prohibited intermarriage. But at the same time, God instructed members of the covenant community to be hospitable to Gentile aliens. Furthermore, the prophets foresaw a time when God's kingdom would include Gentile believers.

Regrettably, by the time of Jesus and Paul, the concept of Jewish separation had become so warped that it amounted to racial and religious prejudice. For instance, Jews were not permitted to enter Gentile homes, and strictly observant Jews erected an impregnable social wall around themselves. So, instead of bringing spiritual light to the Gentiles, the Jews ended up consigning them to outer darkness. Part of the Gospel's power includes taking radically different people and making them one.

C. Peace between Saved Jews and Gentiles: vss. 14-15a

For he himself is our peace, who has made the two one and has destroyed the barrier, the dividing wall of hostility, by abolishing in his flesh the law with its commandments and regulations.

When the Ephesian believers were reconciled with God (Eph. 2:11-13), they were also brought together with Jewish believers (vss. 14-18). Of course, Jews and Gentiles were still distinct groups. But as far as the church was concerned, the Son had merged the two groups (vs. 14). Previous religious and ethnic backgrounds did not matter to their status in the church, for all were equals in the Messiah. Paul described this union as the Son tearing down the middle wall of partition, a barrier of hostility, which once separated Jews and Gentiles.

The physical arrangement of the shrine in Jerusalem was the dominant image in verse 14. Paul may have been thinking about the wall at the temple mount that separated the court where anyone was welcome from the courts where only Jews could go. The Court of the Gentiles, in particular, permitted non-Jews to come near the sanctuary and worship God. But a barrier separated this enclosure from another section where only Jews could go. There were also signs that threatened punishment by death for any Gentiles who entered the Holy Place. This was the spot where it was thought that God dwelt. This locale was also where sacrifices for sin were offered.

Paul was saying that in the church, Jewish believers and Gentile Christians could mingle freely. Regardless of one's religious or ethnic background, all stood in need of divine grace. Because sin entered the human race and controlled the lives of people, God in His pure righteousness could not permit human beings in His presence. Also, sin caused people to rebel against God and live without any consideration of their Creator. Because of the Son's work on the cross, the Father has dealt with sin and entered into a relationship with believers. For reconciliation to be applied individually, it is necessary that each person accept the Son's work for herself or himself.

Paul stressed that Jesus, through His atoning sacrifice, united believing Jews and Gentiles. The apostle noted in verse 15 that the Son's death nullified, or rendered inoperative, the commandments and ordinances of the law of Moses. This does not mean that the Father had cast off the moral principles of the law. Rather, the Son makes it possible for the righteous standards that people could never achieve to be attained. The Mosaic law had been given to the Jews, and because of that many felt superior to Gentiles. But Jesus, by dying on the cross, became the means of salvation for all people. Thus salvation by faith in the Messiah superseded the law.

D. Unity among Saved Jews and Gentiles: vss. 15b-16

His purpose was to create in himself one new man out of the two, thus making peace, and in this one body to reconcile both of them to God through the cross, by which he put to death their hostility.

Paul personified Jewish and Gentile believers and said the Messiah had made one new body out of those two groups (Eph. 2:15). From a spiritual perspective there were no longer Jews and Gentiles. A new body had come into existence—the church—resulting in peace. Here we see that God's grace has been poured out on all of us—no one has been left out. The Lord, in turn, wants us to imitate Him and to embrace all people with His love and acceptance. The apostle noted that the Son's death reconciled Jews and Gentiles to the Father as well as to each other (vs. 16). The Son brought an end to the hostility between sinners and the Father as well as to the hostility between Jews and Gentiles. Because the Son died on the cross, the enmity between people and the Father can die there too.

E. Joint Access to the Father: vss. 17-18

He came and preached peace to you who were far away and peace to those who were near. For through him we both have access to the Father by one Spirit.

Since the Son never made Gentiles the prime focus of His earthly ministry, Ephesians 2:17 must refer to the spread of the Gospel to Gentiles. The apostles and other Christians were responsible for this evangelistic effort. Thus, through the Son's early followers, He proclaimed peace through the Gospel to Gentiles (who were far away from the Father) and to Jews (who were somewhat nearer to Him). Centuries earlier, Isaiah had foretold a day when the peace of God would be proclaimed to those near and far (see Isa. 57:19). Paul declared the fulfillment of Isaiah's prophecy through the Messiah and the proclamation of the Gospel.

As the Good News was heralded, the Spirit brought Gentiles—those "far away" (Eph. 2:17)—and Jews—those "near"—together before the Lord in a community of faith. Jews had been, in a sense, nearer to God than Gentiles because they had the Old Testament revelation and because the Messiah had ministered among them. But now, both Jews and Gentiles—indeed, all people—have equal access to the Father through the same Holy Spirit because of what the Son has done at Calvary. All three persons of the Trinity make this possible (vs. 18).

II. THE MESSIAH—OUR CORNERSTONE: EPHESIANS 2:19-22

A. Members of God's Family: vss. 19-20

Consequently, you are no longer foreigners and aliens, but fellow citizens with God's people and members of God's household, built on the foundation of the apostles and prophets, with Christ Jesus himself as the chief cornerstone.

After all that Paul had written about the new status of both Gentiles and Jews in Christ, the apostle next drew his conclusion. To do this, he used a construction metaphor. He said Gentiles and Jews form a single building, with the Savior as the cornerstone. In ancient times, it was common practice for builders to place a stone at the corner where two walls of an edifice came together. The intent was to bind together and strengthen the intersecting walls. This practice was augmented by the fact that builders made their more permanent structures out of stone that was precisely cut and squared. Jesus, as the "chief cornerstone" (Eph. 2:20), is the foundation of the believer's faith.

Paul told the Ephesians that they were no longer outcasts. The Greek adjective rendered "foreigners" (vs. 19) refers to transients who had no rights or privileges. Also, the adjective rendered "aliens" describes residents who, by the payment of a minor tax, received protection but not full citizenship. Both terms indicate an inferior status. This was the standing of Gentiles before coming to faith in the Messiah. Instead of being inferior, the Ephesians were now fellow citizens with the saints (that is, all of God's holy people) and members of God's household (that is, His spiritual family). In other words, like Jewish believers, saved Gentiles were now in a personal relationship with God. The Lord's household of believers is like a building that is being erected on the foundation of the New Testament apostles and prophets (see 3:5). The Messiah is the cornerstone, or capstone, of the entire structure (2:20). This means that the church is based on the Son and the work He performed through the leaders of the church.

B. A Holy Temple for the Lord: vss. 21-22

In him the whole building is joined together and rises to become a holy temple in the Lord. And in him you too are being built together to become a dwelling in which God lives by his Spirit.

Like a cornerstone joining two walls together, the Messiah is the one in whom the entire structure (namely, the community of the redeemed) is united. Moreover, Jesus enables it to continuously grow into a holy temple for the Lord (Eph. 2:21). In Paul's day, construction workers would shape and move huge blocks of stone until they fit each other perfectly. Similarly, through faith in the Son, Gentiles are joined together with Jews to form the Messiah's spiritual body. The Greek noun for "temple" that Paul used did not stand for the entire sanctuary complex, but only for the inner sanctum where God's presence dwelt. In keeping with this designation, the apostle told the Ephesians that they, as well as the Jewish believers, were part of a dwelling—the church—in which God lives by His Spirit (vs. 22).

Discussion Questions

1. What was the reason for the change in status of the Ephesians?
2. What is the basis for spiritual unity between believing Jews and Gentiles in the church?
3. What is the basis for the removal of enmity between people and God?
4. What things can you do to promote harmony and eliminate prejudice within the church and society?
5. In what sense is Jesus the cornerstone of your church?

Contemporary Application

Jesus takes total strangers and makes them into a family. Our church life is intended to reflect this truth. Indeed, Jesus has done everything possible to make good family relations a reality within the church. That said, we have to confess that sometimes we fall short of achieving His will.

Moreover, to our disappointment, we have to admit that our divisions stand out more than our oneness. In the church, we sometimes treat fellow believers as though they were our enemies. How tragic it is when we verbally attack one another, spread gossip, and create division.

In light of the above shortcomings, we all need to receive a fresh reminder of God's ideal. In conjunction with the Son, the Father has brought us together and broken down the barriers between us. The church is supposed to work like a unified body, not a splintered group of individuals. The reason is that Jesus' death on the cross reconciled both Jews and Gentiles to God. Because of the Son's redemptive work, there is an ending to the hostility between sinners and the Father. Likewise, through the Messiah all people have come together in offering worship and service to the Father.

How, then, can we achieve the Father's purpose of unity and peace for the church? We do so by listening to the Son instead of giving in to our selfish desires. Now that the Father has spiritually cleansed and forgiven us due to the atoning sacrifice of His Son, we are free from sin's divisive power. Also, the Messiah enables us to be built up into a spiritual temple—that is, a dwelling place for God, where He lives and reigns through His Spirit.

Unity in Christ

Scripture

Background Scripture: *Ephesians 4:1-16*

Scripture Lesson: *Ephesians 4:1-16*

Key Verse: *There is one body and one Spirit—just as you were called to one hope when you were called—one Lord, one faith, one baptism.* Ephesians 4:4-5.

Scripture Lesson for Children: *Ephesians 4:1-16*

Key Verse for Children: *Speaking the truth in love, we will in all things grow up into . . . Christ.* Ephesians 4:15.

Lesson Aim

To recognize that we are each responsible to build up other believers.

Lesson Setting

Time: A.D. *60*
Place: Rome

Lesson Outline

Unity in Christ

   I. Living in Unity: Ephesians 4:1-6
      A. *The Characteristics of a Christlike Life: vss. 1-3*
      B. *The Common Aspects of the Believers' Faith: vss. 4-6*
  II. Serving in Unity: Ephesians 4:7-13
      A. *Spiritual Gifts from Jesus: vs. 7*
      B. *Jesus' Authority to Bestow Spiritual Gifts: vss. 8-10*
      C. *A Diversity of Spiritual Gifts: vs. 11*
      D. *A Common Purpose for the Spiritual Gifts: vss. 12-13*
 III. Growing in Unity: Ephesians 4:14-16
      A. *Spiritual Instability: vs. 14*
      B. *Spiritual Stability: vss. 15-16*

Introduction for Adults

Topic: *Living Together*

An officer parachuting off a plane was so intent on leaping out at the right coordinates that he ordered silence to the lower-ranking soldier beside him. "But, Lieutenant—" continued the private. "Not another word!" snapped the officer. As the lieutenant made ready to jump, the private pulled him to the floor. "Like I've been trying to tell you, your chute's torn!" shouted the soldier to his now-grateful superior.

Although this story is fictional, it isn't too far-fetched. In real life, words heard and heeded can and do make tremendous differences in our being able to live together within the body of Christ (see Eph. 4:2-3). Have you ministered beneath or beside someone who, because he or she "knew it all," would not listen to others? Worse, have you exhibited that kind of behavior yourself?

Building others up in love requires us to graciously listen to them. God wants our work with fellow believers to edify, not diminish, the body of Christ (see vss. 15-16).

Introduction for Youth

Topic: *We Are One*

"All for one and one for all" is a great rallying cry for French musketeers, political movements, and football teams. It sounds so wonderful. It assumes that each individual will lay aside his or her own preferences for the sake of others.

But when we allow Jesus to break down barriers, we do much more than paper over our differences. We have to confess and acknowledge that hostility does exist. We also have to admit that unless we allow Jesus to change us from within, we won't be able to achieve oneness in human relationships.

Because Jesus gives each of us a new heart and new motivation, we can seek His help and power to get along with everyone, regardless of our differences. We accept people as they are and see them as objects of God's love in the Gospel. We also show humility and love—demonstrating Christlikeness to people who are very different from ourselves—so that we can all become one family in Christ (see Eph. 4:2-6).

Concepts for Children

Topic: *Working Together*

1. Jesus wants us to be gentle and kind to others.
2. Jesus wants us to work together in helping each other.
3. Jesus welcomes all of us into His church.
4. Jesus has a special job for us to do in His church.
5. Our love for others can encourage them to trust in Jesus as their Savior.

Lesson Commentary

I. LIVING IN UNITY: EPHESIANS 4:1-6

A. The Characteristics of a Christlike Life: vss. 1-3

As a prisoner for the Lord, then, I urge you to live a life worthy of the calling you have received. Be completely humble and gentle; be patient, bearing with one another in love. Make every effort to keep the unity of the Spirit through the bond of peace.

While under his first house arrest in Rome, Paul had the time to write numerous letters. He seems to have penned epistles to the churches in Ephesus and Colossae, as well as to Philemon of Colossae, at about the same time. Paul's colleagues, Tychicus and Onesimus, could have dropped off one letter at Ephesus on their way to delivering the other two in Colossae (see Eph. 6:21-22; Col. 4:7-9; Philem. 10-12).

Ephesians has been called "The Heavenly Epistle" and "The Alps of the New Testament." In it the apostle takes the reader from the depths of ruin to the heights of redemption. The letter contains two distinct, though related, parts. Chapters 1–3 remind the readers of their privileged status as members of Christ's body, the church, which occupies an important place in God's plan for the universe. Chapters 4–6 appeal to the readers to live in a way consistent with their godly calling rather than to conform to the ungodly society in which they lived.

The apostle's status as an evangelist imprisoned for the cause of Christ lent weight to his appeal to the Ephesians. Since Paul had been faithful to the point of being imprisoned, they (who were under less pressure) could be faithful too. Specifically, the apostle urged his readers to live a life worthy of the calling they had received (4:1). Having been given saving grace, they should do no less than respond to the Lord by living faithfully. This does not mean that believers were to earn their salvation by leading a worthy life. Rather, they conducted themselves uprightly as a result of their spiritual rebirth.

So that the Ephesians would know what he meant by a life worthy of their calling, Paul mentioned four virtues that ought to be theirs (and ours as Christians): humility, gentleness, patience, and forbearance (vs. 2). Each of these terms is worth considering further. The Greek noun translated "humble" was adapted by Christians to describe an attitude of lowliness. The noun rendered "gentle" refers not to weakness but to submission to others for the sake of Christ. The noun translated "patient" indicates the refusal to avenge wrongs committed against oneself. Finally, the phrase "bearing with one another" refers to putting up with others' faults and peculiarities.

The four virtues Paul cited can all contribute to the church's harmony. This goal was uppermost in the apostle's mind. In his day, Jewish and Gentile believers sometimes did not understand one another. Also, Gentile Christians from different backgrounds or with different temperaments sometimes did not get along. Paul wanted to see all believers united and harmonious. Nonetheless, unity is something we must work at. As the apostle noted in verse 3, we are to "make every effort to keep the unity of the Spirit through the bond of peace." Here we see that Christians are united through the Spirit, but our unity can be damaged if we allow our relations to become hostile rather than peaceful. That is why it is sensible to add peacemaking to the list of virtues believers ought to possess.

B. The Common Aspects of the Believers' Faith: vss. 4-6

There is one body and one Spirit—just as you were called to one hope when you were called—one Lord, one faith, one baptism; one God and Father of all, who is over all and through all and in all.

After exhorting the Ephesians to preserve spiritual unity, Paul went on to show the role that unity plays in various aspects of the Christian faith. In fact, the apostle's mention of the "unity of the Spirit" (Eph. 4:3) prompted him to give more attention to the matter. First, Paul noted that there is one spiritual body of Christ and that its members have the same Spirit. Believers also have been called to the same glory-filled future (vs. 4). The "body" is the church. Just as a human body has many parts but is one entity, so the church has many members but is one group. Indwelling all members of the church is the Holy Spirit. As we learn from 1:14 (which we considered in lesson 1), the Spirit's presence in our lives is the guarantee of our common hope to live eternally with God in heaven. This became our hope and expectation when we accepted the call to faith.

Second, there is only "one Lord, one faith, one baptism" (4:5). All believers serve one Lord, namely, Jesus Christ. We serve this Lord because we have made the same profession of faith in Him. Also, baptism identifies us with the Messiah. The reference to baptism could either be to water or the Spirit (see Rom. 6:3-4; 1 Cor. 12:13). Third, there is only "one God and Father" (Eph. 4:6), who alone is sovereign over us all, in us all, and living through us all. In a culture that recognized many gods, Paul affirmed that there is only one true God whom Christians worship and serve. He is the Father of all who believe in Him. In His relationship to His people, He is both transcendent ("over all") and immanent ("through all and in all"). Paul's mention of all three persons of the Trinity in verses 3-6 shows us that the Godhead harmoniously works together to bring about the unity of believers in everyday life.

If we were to make a sign indicating the major characteristic of the church, it might simply say "ONE." Seven times in these three verses Paul used the Greek numeral rendered "one" to describe who we are as believers. But do Christian people appear to be one? The fact that we sometimes fail does not alter the truth of God's Word. To reiterate what was said above, there's supposed to be one body (the Savior's church), one Holy Spirit, one hope of eternal salvation, one Lord (Jesus Christ), one common faith, one baptism into the Son's body, and one God and Father. These theological truths are the great foundation stones of our spiritual unity. Also, these are the reasons why we are called to keep the unity of the Spirit. Without these truths, there is no way to live in unity.

Moreover, these truths supersede our denominational distinctives and our historic church traditions (distinguished though they might be). While we are free to choose the local church that we want to join, we are not supposed to emphasize its distinctives over what God has revealed in His Word. When we do otherwise, we end up fracturing the spiritual body of Christ. We have to confess that we are Christians first, and Presbyterians or Methodists or Baptists or whatever second. To look at the matter another way, there are not many bodies of Christ, not many Holy Spirits, not many Saviors, not many faiths, not many baptisms, and not many deities. Because unbelievers sometimes get a false impression from us, we have to redouble our efforts to show that we really are one in the Messiah, that is, despite our different church labels.

II. SERVING IN UNITY: EPHESIANS 4:7-13

A. Spiritual Gifts from Jesus: vs. 7

But to each one of us grace has been given as Christ apportioned it.

Paul followed up his strong message about church unity with an equally strong message about gift diversity. The apostle noted that Jesus supplies His followers with grace, making some Christians leaders who prepare the rest for ministry so that the whole church may achieve unity and maturity. When Paul said that the Messiah gives "grace" (Eph. 4:7), the apostle was referring to the divine blessing by which believers are equipped, or enabled, to perform ministries in the church. We do not earn grace. We are given it. Neither can we pick the kind of grace we will receive. The Son assigns it as He sees fit. We are to receive this grace thankfully and use it for the Father's glory.

B. Jesus' Authority to Bestow Spiritual Gifts: vss. 8-10

This is why it says: "When he ascended on high, he led captives in his train and gave gifts to men." (What does "he ascended" mean except that he also descended to the lower, earthly regions? He who descended is the very one who ascended higher than all the heavens, in order to fill the whole universe.)

To support what he had said about Jesus giving grace, Paul cited Psalm 68:18 in Ephesians 4:8. The picture is one of a triumphal procession in which the victor both received and distributed gifts. When applied to Jesus, this verse reveals that through His redemptive work on Calvary, He prevailed over Satan and his hosts (see Col. 2:15). Ephesians 4:8 also declares that the Messiah has given gifts to His followers ever since His ascension. Lest anyone doubt that the one who "ascended on high" was the Lord Jesus, Paul added a parenthetical explanation in verses 9 and 10. The apostle noted that the person who ascended had previously descended "to the lower, earthly regions" (vs. 9). The main emphasis is that Jesus completely conquered sin, death, and Satan through His resurrection and ascension.

Despite the clarity of emphasis, scholars have different opinions about what Paul actually meant. Some think the apostle was referring to Jesus' entrance into Hades after His crucifixion (specifically, the saved portion of the underworld or realm of the dead) to take saints to heaven when He rose from the dead (see 1 Pet. 3:19-20; 4:6). Others say that the Messiah's descent refers to His death and burial in the grave. Still others claim that Paul was talking about Jesus' incarnation, in which He came to earth as a human being (see John 3:13). This person "who descended is the very one who ascended" (Eph. 4:10). Expressed differently, Jesus is not only a man who lived on earth but also the Lord whose eternal dwelling is in heaven. Jews of the day believed there were seven heavens. But Paul said that the Son ascended "higher than all the heavens." In fact, now He fills "the whole universe." This means Jesus' lordship over the universe is absolute and complete because of His resurrection and ascension. He thus has the power and authority to be generous in bestowing gifts of grace to His followers.

C. A Diversity of Spiritual Gifts: vs. 11

It was he who gave some to be apostles, some to be prophets, some to be evangelists, and some to be pastors and teachers.

All believers have at least one spiritual gift (see 1 Pet. 4:10). But in Ephesians 4:11, Paul focused on those who have received special abilities to be leaders in the churches. He mentioned apostles, prophets, evangelists, pastors, and teachers. The Greek noun rendered "apostle" is used in various ways in the New Testament. In this case, Paul was probably using the term in a restricted sense, to refer to a group of people (including himself) whom Jesus had personally chosen to found the church.

The "prophets" Paul had in mind were probably not Elijah, Isaiah, and the other Old Testament spokespersons. The church of Paul's day had its own prophets. These people delivered messages from God and sometimes foretold the future. Before the New Testament books were written, about the only way God communicated directly to the church was through His special speakers. The other three kinds of leaders have related functions. "Evangelists" in the early church were people who conducted outreach in areas where the church had not yet been established. Put another way, they were pioneers for the faith. In the wake of the evangelists, "pastors and teachers" served already established congregations. Pastors shepherded churches, while teachers instructed them. Of course, these two roles could be combined in one person.

D. A Common Purpose for the Spiritual Gifts: vss. 12-13

To prepare God's people for works of service, so that the body of Christ may be built up until we all reach unity in the faith and in the knowledge of the Son of God and become mature, attaining to the whole measure of the fullness of Christ.

At the outset, it's worth noting that the Greek noun often rendered "gifts" (see 1 Cor. 12:4) is *charismata.* The singular form of this word is *charisma.* Both terms relate to the word *charis,* which means "favor" or "grace." While *charisma* denotes a personal endowment of grace, *charismata* refers to a concrete expression of grace. The main idea is that the Spirit bestows His gifts of grace on Christians to accomplish God's will. Paul listed three categories of spiritual gifts through which the Holy Spirit manifests Himself in the church. There are "different kinds of gifts," "different kinds of service" (vs. 5), and "different kinds of working" (vs. 6).

Despite the diversities and differences, all spiritual gifts have the same source— the triune Godhead: the Spirit (vs. 4), the Lord Jesus (vs. 5), and God the Father (vs. 6; see 2 Cor. 13:14; Eph. 4:3-6). Moreover, despite the presence of different, uniquely gifted believers, they all have a common goal. The Lord wants them to equip believers to do God's work so that the church might be strengthened (Eph. 4:12). Christians use their gifts to help one another become united in their faith and intimate in their knowledge of God's Son. The entire body benefits when each of its members is mature, fully grown in the Lord, and measuring up to the full stature of Christ (vs. 13).

III. GROWING IN UNITY: EPHESIANS 4:14-16

A. Spiritual Instability: vs. 14

Then we will no longer be infants, tossed back and forth by the waves, and blown here and there by every wind of teaching and by the cunning and craftiness of men in their deceitful scheming.

Children tend to be gullible, vulnerable, and easily victimized. This is true both in the physical and spiritual realms (see Acts 20:29-30; Col. 2:8). As long as believers remain immature, they will be like a ship tossed on a stormy sea. As the winds of opinion blow in one direction, some Christians are easily swayed by it. Then as another gust of ideas blasts across their bow, they change their mind about what they believe. According to Ephesians 4:14, Jesus' followers are not to be characterized by spiritual immaturity and ignorance. Paul's frequent sea voyages, including his harrowing trip to Rome (see Acts 27:1–28:14), may have prompted the seafaring metaphor he used in Ephesians 4:14.

B. Spiritual Stability: vss. 15-16

Instead, speaking the truth in love, we will in all things grow up into him who is the Head, that is, Christ. From him the whole body, joined and held together by every supporting ligament, grows and builds itself up in love, as each part does its work.

Paul did not want God's people to be fooled by the cleverly worded lies of religious imposters. Instead, the apostle urged believers to hold to the truth in love (Eph. 4:15). Expressed differently, honesty, veracity, and compassion should characterize all that believers say and do. Believers are also to become more like the Savior in every area of their lives. This is as it should be, for He is the Head of the church. Under His direction, this spiritual body is fitted together perfectly.

By calling Jesus "the Head," Paul was returning to his familiar analogy between the church and the body. Believers make up the members of Christ's body, with

Him as our Head. Paul liked this analogy because it indicates the organic connection between Jesus and His followers. As each part does its own unique and special work, it helps the other parts to grow (vs. 16). Each member of the Messiah's spiritual body is to work together in harmony to promote the growth and vitality of the church. As a result, the entire body becomes healthy, mature, and full of love. Every believer should operate with one another so that all might mature and come to know the Son more fully.

Discussion Questions

1. What connection is there between humility, gentleness, and patience? Why must all three virtues be present in the believers' lives?
2. In what way are believers joined together in the body of Christ?
3. How do evangelists, pastors, and teachers fit into the divine plan?
4. What enabling grace has the Savior given you to share with others?
5. In what way is the body of Christ to be built up? Why is this important?

Contemporary Application

Our culture emphasizes individuality and personal fulfillment. Not surprisingly, the concept of having things in common or working for the larger good is hard to achieve. However, Jesus, the Head of the church, endows individual believers with spiritual gifts, not for their own sakes, but for the sake of His body.

That's why Paul's picture of how we work together to build up the church is so instructive. The church body the apostle had in mind is alive and bursting with productive activity. Paul urged all believers to do their "works of service" (Eph. 4:12). The apostle also believed that the spiritual body's functions are enhanced because "every supporting ligament" (vs. 16) works together.

In this scenario of unity and cooperation, there is steady growth from infancy to adulthood and maturity in Christ. The Redeemer's spiritual body pulses with the heartbeat of mutual love and unity. And the entire body throbs with the vital warmth of the Father's love in the Son.

The key to making this picture a reality is the Head, the Lord Jesus. Each member "ligament" grows in Him with ever-deepening fellowship, worship, and obedience. From Him members draw on His fullness for all their needs, especially as they use their spiritual gifts for God's glory.

Live in the Light

Scripture

Background Scripture: *John 1:1-14; Ephesians 4:17–5:20*
Scripture Lesson: *John 1:1-5; Ephesians 5:1-2, 6-14*
Key Verse: *Be imitators of God, therefore, as dearly loved children.* Ephesians 5:1.
Scripture Lesson for Children: *Matthew 2:1-11*
Key Verse for Children: *[The Magi] bowed down and worshiped [Jesus] . . . [and] presented him with gifts.* Matthew 2:11.

Lesson Aim

To strive to emulate the Son in our personal relationships.

Lesson Setting

Time (John 1:1-5): Around A.D. *85 or later*
Place: Possibly Ephesus
Time (Ephesians 5:1-2, 6-14): A.D. *60*
Place: Rome

Lesson Outline

Live in the Light

I.   Encountering the Son: John 1:1-5
   A. *God's Eternal Word: vss. 1-2*
   B. *Creation through the Word: vs. 3*
   C. *Life and Light in the Word: vss. 4-5*

II. Emulating the Son: Ephesians 5:1-2, 6-14
   A. *Following the Son's Example: vss. 1-2*
   B. *Shunning All Forms of Immorality: vss. 6-7*
   C. *Living as Children of Light: vs. 8-10*
   D. *Exposing the Unfruitful Deeds of Darkness: vss. 11-14*

Introduction for Adults

Topic: *Living by Example*

When *Animal Kingdom,* Walt Disney World's newest Orlando, Florida, attraction, was under construction throughout most of the 1990s, park developers struggled with some unique problems. One was dealing with the intelligence of their new residents.

Although nearly all of the animals would be free to roam vast spaces during the day, at night they were all brought into their pens for safekeeping. Despite being well cared for, these animals yearned to be free. And they realized that one way to attain that freedom was to imitate the actions of their human caretakers with the intent of exploiting any weaknesses they could find in their captors' behavior.

In Ephesians 5, Paul indicated that believers should also have a strong desire to be truly free from all forms of immorality. Unless we wish to remain captive to the evil that surrounds us, we need to emulate the Savior in every aspect of our lives (see vss. 1-2).

Introduction for Youth

Topic: *Go Light!*

Christmas recalls the birth of Jesus, the Light of the world (see John 1:4-5). The season reminds us that He first loved us by coming to earth as a human being. In turn, we have the privilege of knowing and loving the Savior. What better opportunity is there than than this holiday to create a meaningful celebration to honor Him?

So, how can we celebrate? We can call some of our friends together to have a simple time of commemorative worship. Or we can be alone and, in a creative way, let Jesus know how glad we are that He chose to be among us. In doing these sorts of things, we can draw near to the Messiah. Furthermore, through meaningful celebration, we can deepen our relationship with Him.

Concepts for Children

Topic: *The Best Gift of All*

1. The magi asked Herod where Jesus, the King of the Jews, had been born.
2. The magi searched for and found Jesus by following the star.
3. The magi discovered that Jesus was worth seeking.
4. When the magi found Jesus, they worshiped Him and gave Him gifts.
5. Jesus is pleased when we choose to worship and serve Him.

Lesson Commentary

I. ENCOUNTERING THE SON: JOHN 1:1-5

A. God's Eternal Word: vss. 1-2

In the beginning was the Word, and the Word was with God, and the Word was God. He was with God in the beginning.

Christian tradition has consistently affirmed the apostle John as the author of the Gospel that bears his name. Clearly, this Gospel was written by an eyewitness of the events he described. The Gospel's details about the topography of Palestine and the towns that relate to Jesus are all accurate. The author's familiarity with Jewish customs and religious practices are also dramatically evident in this Gospel. Most importantly, however, the fourth Gospel provides us with unparalleled insights into the Lord Jesus. It is only in this account that we learn about the marriage feast at Cana (2:1-11), the Lord's discussion with Nicodemus (3:1-21), the raising of Lazarus (11:1-44), the washing of His disciples' feet (13:1-17), and the great "I am" declarations (6:35; 8:12, 58; 9:5; 10:7, 9, 11; 11:25; 14:6; 15:5). John also gave memorable glimpses of Thomas (11:16; 14:5; 20:24-29), Andrew (1:40-41; 6:8-9; 12:22), and Philip (6:5-7; 14:8-9).

John stated his purpose for this Gospel in 20:31. He affirmed that Jesus is the Messiah and the Son of God. According to John, Jesus was not merely a human being, a man possessed with a type of Christ spirit, or a spirit being who merely appeared human. Jesus is God, who came in the flesh and now rules in heaven. Throughout this Gospel, John constantly showed Jesus to be the Son of God. John's presentation of Jesus' miracles, teachings, and experiences all point to Him as the Messiah. John's Gospel was intended to convince people to place their trust in the Lord Jesus as the Son of God, who died for their sins and will one day come again.

John 1:1-18, which is known as the Prologue, helps set the stage for the rest of the fourth Gospel. The Prologue is foundational to what we understand about Jesus, for it addresses the issues of His deity and humanity, His preexistence and incarnation, and His glorification by the Father and rejection by humanity. Because of the poetic quality of the Prologue, some believe it was used as an ancient Christian hymn. Matthew and Luke began their accounts of Jesus' life with His birth and genealogy. Mark began with the ministry of John the Baptizer, who paved the way for the Messiah. In contrast, John's opening words echo the first words of Genesis. Indeed, the apostle takes us back to the dawn of creation with the phrase "in the beginning was the Word" (John 1:1). John clearly identified the "Word" (or in Greek, *logos*) as Jesus in verse 14.

In 560 B.C., Heraclitus, an Ephesian philosopher, taught that everything was constantly changing. Despite this continuous state of flux, there was a design and order in the universe under the control of the Logos. Heraclitus held that the Logos not only governed events and patterns in the world but also enabled humans to know right from wrong and to recognize truth. In Greek thought, the Logos created and sustained the universe. Later, in the first century A.D., an Alexandrian Jewish philosopher named Philo borrowed this Greek term and identified the Logos with God's creative powers. Philo said that the Logos was God's mind stamped upon His creation and the vehicle by which we can know God. Interestingly, the phrase rendered "Word of God" is found hundreds of times in the Old Testament and, in many of these instances, is given personal creative attributes. Being familiar with the Greek and Jewish views of the Logos is key to understanding the nature of the Messiah as described by John. It also helps us see why the apostle used the concept of Logos to communicate the nature of the Son to those familiar with the term.

In essence, John said to his Gentile and Jewish readers, "For centuries you have attributed creative and divine powers to the Logos. In fact, the Logos is Jesus Christ, the Son of God, and now He has become a human being just like you." Though John did not again use the Greek term rendered "Word," the idea of Jesus as the Word of God is woven throughout the narrative of the fourth Gospel. Since the Word existed "in the beginning" (vs. 1), the Word could not be a created being. In reality, the Word was God and with God at the same time. Though distinct persons, God the Father and God the Son share the same divine nature (along with God the Holy Spirit). In short, the one whom we call Jesus was with the Father from the very beginning (vs. 2).

B. Creation through the Word: vs. 3

Through him all things were made; without him nothing was made that has been made.

John 1:3 reveals that the Father brought all things into existence through the Son. Likewise, Colossians 1:16 affirms that all things in heaven and on earth were created by the Son. This includes whatever is visible or invisible, along with all principalities and powers. Similarly, Hebrews 1:2 adds that even the temporal ages owe their existence to the Son, through whom the Father has spoken in "these last days."

C. Life and Light in the Word: vss. 4-5

In him was life, and that life was the light of men. The light shines in the darkness, but the darkness has not understood it.

The Son's provision of life—both physical and spiritual—is another major theme in John's Gospel. The apostle tied life in the Son to the metaphor of light (1:4). John often contrasted the darkness of sinful humanity with the light of the Messiah—not only in his Gospel but also in his first letter (see 1 John 1:5; 2:8). The Son dispels the darkness and reveals the Father's truths by the light of His Word (John 1:5). For this reason, darkness is hostile to the light. In Scripture, light symbolizes all that is wholesome and genuine, while darkness portrays the opposing qualities of error and evil. Both the Old and New Testaments equate light with the truth of the Word. For instance, Psalm 119:105 says that God's Word of truth is a lamp to the believers' feet and a light for their path. Also, in 2 Corinthians 4:4, Paul said that the Devil had blinded the eyes of unbelievers so that they could not see "the light of the gospel" that displays "the glory of Christ."

II. EMULATING THE SON: EPHESIANS 5:1-2, 6-14

A. Following the Son's Example: vss. 1-2

Be imitators of God, therefore, as dearly loved children and live a life of love, just as Christ loved us and gave himself up for us as a fragrant offering and sacrifice to God.

When people encounter the Son revealed in John 1:1-5, it should bring about a profound change in the way they think and act, especially in comparison to the unsaved. This includes emulating the Son in their attitudes and priorities. We find this emphasis in the Letter to the Ephesians, where Paul urged his readers to put off their old sinful selves and put on new righteous selves (4:17-24). To illustrate what he meant, the apostle explained in verses 25-28 that the Christian's life should be marked by speaking truth instead of falsehood, avoiding sins associated with anger, and laboring honestly instead of stealing. Verses 29-32 deal with some of the issues involved in replacing the old self with the new self: unwholesome talk versus edifying talk and malice versus love.

Next, in 5:1, we read about how we ought to imitate God. Paul's injunction is more than just in the matter of forgiveness. Christians are to reflect the holiness of God in all aspects of their lives. As children try to copy their parents, so we should try to copy our heavenly Father. And to imitate God means to walk in the way of "love" (vs. 2). This implication is that our entire existence should be characterized by acts and signs of love shown to family, friends, and strangers. Paul referred to the example of the Son to illustrate how we should love. Jesus showed us His love by giving Himself up as a sacrifice for our sins. Just as Old Testament sacrifices of animals sent up a pleasing aroma to the Lord (see Ex. 29:18), the Messiah's death was a fragrant offering. It was an acceptable sacrifice to the Father because of the Son's perfection of love. In brief, His love is unselfish, pure, and active.

B. Shunning All Forms of Immorality: vss. 6-7

Let no one deceive you with empty words, for because of such things God's wrath comes on those who are disobedient. Therefore do not be partners with them.

A life filled with God's love will not include the sins that the Ephesians saw in their pagan neighbors and that, indeed, they themselves had committed before coming to faith. In Ephesians 5:3-4, Paul named some of those sins. Then, in verse 5, the apostle stated that these and other vices are marks of people who will not enter the kingdom of God. The present aspect of the divine kingdom is the Lord's everlasting rule and the working out of His loving and wise plan for the ages. As such, God's kingdom is not always apparent and unbelievers do not always acknowledge it. However, one day the divine kingdom will come in all its fullness and be evident to all (see Matt. 6:10; 25:31-34). At that time, God's glorious power will conquer the forces of evil and unbelief.

Evidently, Paul expected some people in the Ephesian church to say that his standards of morality were higher than necessary. The apostle called the arguments employed by such individuals "empty words" (Eph. 5:6). The moral standards Paul taught were not his own but God's, and the Lord does indeed judge those who disobey His standards. Thus the Ephesians were not to be deceived by people with low moral standards or "be partners with them" (vs. 7) by joining in their sin.

C. Living as Children of Light: vs. 8-10

For you were once darkness, but now you are light in the Lord. Live as children of light (for the fruit of the light consists in all goodness, righteousness and truth) and find out what pleases the Lord.

Paul once more called upon his readers to remember their past without the Son. The apostle told the Ephesians that before putting their faith in the Messiah, they had not only lived in moral and spiritual "darkness" (Eph. 5:8) but also been darkness. Now, after becoming followers of the Savior, they not only lived in moral and spiritual "light" but also were light. Since the Ephesians had been enlightened and were themselves Christ-reflecting lights, Paul made two demands on them. Both of these requests amount roughly to the same thing: the Ephesians were to shun evil and do good.

First, the apostle's readers were to "live as children of light." This means they were to follow the light of the Son and do what the Father approves. They were to consistently show by their attitudes and actions to which kingdom they belonged— the Savior's kingdom of light, not Satan's kingdom of darkness. Paul added a parenthetical statement to provide examples of the conduct of those who live in God's light. The apostle said that the "fruit" (vs. 9), or product, of this light is "all goodness, righteousness and truth." The Greek noun rendered "goodness" refers to kindness, generosity of spirit, and moral excellence. The noun translated "righteousness" describes justice and fairness. The noun rendered "truth" stands for genuineness and honesty. As for Paul's second demand, he told the Ephesians to try to learn what is pleasing to the Lord (vs. 10). In every situation that comes up, and every time we have a decision to make, we should seek the Father's will. Once we have discerned what God desires, we should determine to follow His leading.

D. Exposing the Unfruitful Deeds of Darkness: vss. 11-14

Have nothing to do with the fruitless deeds of darkness, but rather expose them. For it is shameful even to mention what the disobedient do in secret. But everything exposed by the light becomes visible, for it is light that makes everything visible. This is why it is said: "Wake up, O sleeper, rise from the dead, and Christ will shine on you."

In Ephesians 4:11, Paul directed his readers not to be participants in the unfruitful works of "darkness." Instead, followers of the Messiah were to "expose" the deplorable nature of these sordid acts. On the one hand, believers were not to commit sins. On the other hand, they were to unmask iniquity for what it truly is, namely, disobedience to almighty God. Unlike light, which produces wholesome spiritual fruit such as goodness, righteousness, and truth, darkness is barren and leads to nothing good, whether temporal or eternal.

What the "disobedient" (vs. 12) did "in secret" was so disgraceful that Paul thought some of its shamefulness putrefied believers who spoke unnecessarily about these degenerate activities. Be that as it may, the apostle's statement did not conflict with what he said in verse 11 about believers exposing the true nature of wickedness. Specifically, it is God working through us who unmasks sin. The apostle compared the process to "light" (vs. 13) shining into the darkness and making "visible" what was previously concealed. It is God's Word operating in the lives of Jesus' followers that discloses evil deeds so that their true character can be seen by everyone (vs. 14).

Exposure by the light of Christ is just what the unsaved require, especially if they are to be convinced of their need for change. To support his point, Paul quoted a fragment of poetry, which appears to have been based on Isaiah 9:2 and 60:1. The immediate source of the quote is not known. It might have been from a chorus addressed to Christian converts during their baptismal service. Whatever its source, the poetry urges the unregenerate to wake up from their sleep by putting their faith in the Messiah. As a result, they would be regenerated. The image is that of a corpse being given new life and rising from its casket. The poetry emphasizes that the Messiah shines His light so that sinners can see a way out of the darkness.

The Son is continually available to light the path of life for His followers. For this reason, we are to make a habit of watching our conduct. To do otherwise would be imprudent and irresponsible (Eph. 5:15). In Paul's day, immorality seemed far more common than morality. Consequently, he exhorted his readers (and likewise us) to seize every "opportunity" (vs. 16) to do good, not evil. Life presents itself with many confusing and conflicting choices that can lead people in "foolish" (vs. 17) directions. Nonetheless, the apostle believed that if believers made the effort, they could come to know what the Father wanted of them.

One kind of imprudent act against which Paul warned is becoming intoxicated with "wine" (vs. 18). Drunkenness is a sin in itself, and it often leads to other transgressions. The latter included "debauchery," or wild living. The apostle set up an intriguing contrast to inebriation. Rather than believers putting themselves under the control of alcohol through excessive drinking, they should put themselves under the control of the Holy Spirit, especially by submitting to Him. At the moment of salvation, we received the Spirit. And at different times in our walk with the Lord, we can receive a fresh filling of the Spirit.

Believers who are controlled by the Spirit desire to worship the Lord. In verse 19, Paul associated worship with music. In particular, his readers were to communicate among themselves with "psalms, hymns and spiritual songs." The first item in this list probably referred to the Psalms recorded in the Old Testament. "Hymns" were melodies composed by believers to honor God. "Songs" might have been called "spiritual" either to distinguish them from similar compositions by the unsaved or because the ballads referred to spontaneous singing in the Spirit. In addition to communicating with one another by means of music, the Ephesians were to "sing and make music" in their hearts to "God the Father" (vss. 19-20). This was one way Paul's readers (along with us) could give thanks to the Lord for all He has given believers in union with His Son, the Messiah.

Discussion Questions

1. According to the apostle John, who is Jesus?
2. What aspects of God's character are we to imitate?
3. What are some definite steps believers can take to be more loving toward others?
4. What does it mean for us to walk as "children of light" (Eph. 5:8)?
5. What are some ways that believers can "expose" (vs. 11) wicked deeds?

Contemporary Application

We are called to emulate the Savior in our relationships (see Eph. 5:2), but some people seem impossible to get along with. They just rub us the wrong way or maybe even go out of their way to make our lives difficult.

For instance, whenever Claire got to church on Sunday morning, there was Arnold right in her face. He was overbearing and hardly gave her space to talk to anyone else. Claire endured him because Arnold was part of a ministry team in which Claire also served.

Though on the surface Claire appeared to be kind, inside she was seething with rage at Arnold's inability to take what she was sure were obvious clues— verbal and otherwise—that she was not comfortable with his attentiveness. After church, Arnold would become the target for Claire's mocking remarks and jeering comments as she related to a friend the latest happenings at church.

However, Claire became increasingly guilt-ridden about being nice to Arnold and then ridiculing him behind his back. Claire knew she should do what Jesus did in His relationships with people—be honest and forthright with Arnold, but with gentleness and respect. Also, Claire needed to end her cruel remarks to others about Arnold.

After resolving to do what was right, Claire talked to Arnold the following Sunday. While it was a difficult discussion to initiate, Claire felt relief as she was able to understand Arnold's intentions and relate her own discomfort. As the truth came out, Claire felt her resentment leaving. In its place was a new respect and appreciation for Arnold, who graciously received her message.

Christ's Love for the Church

Scripture

Background Scripture: *Ephesians 5:21–6:4*
Scripture Lesson: *Ephesians 5:21–6:4*
Key Verse: *Submit to one another out of reverence for Christ.*
Ephesians 5:21.
Scripture Lesson for Children: *1 John 3:18-24*
Key Verse for Children: *This is [God's] command: to . . .
love one another.* 1 John 3:23.

Lesson Aim

To maintain an unwavering commitment to our church
and individual families.

Lesson Setting

Time: A.D. *60*
Place: Rome

Lesson Outline

Christs Love for the Church

   I. Showing Mutual Respect: Ephesians 5:21-33
      A. *The Overarching Responsibility: vs. 21*
      B. *Responsibility of Wives to Husbands: vss. 22-24*
      C. *The Responsibility of Husbands to Wives: vss. 25-30*
      D. *The Profound Mystery: vss. 31-33*
  II. Nurturing Good Parent-Child Relationships:
      Ephesians 6:1-4
      A. *The Responsibility of Children: vss. 1-3*
      B. *The Responsibility of Parents: vs. 4*

Introduction for Adults

Topic: *Family Matters*

When it comes to claiming our family responsibilities as believers, not under-standing what they are isn't the problem. The Savior's commands are clear and straightforward. Our difficulties arise when, knowing what we are supposed to do, we lack the courage, faith, and will to act.

We have not genuinely understood the nature of spiritual warfare and how important basic spiritual training is for us. We have not invested sufficient time and energy in growing our faith, studying God's Word, praying, and being filled with the Spirit.

We can read Paul's guidelines for happy marriages and family life. Yet, for these guidelines to help us, we need to maintain a vital faith in the Savior. We can't abide by our responsibilities if we have a weak faith. Jesus must be Lord of every-thing in our lives. Our supreme desire must be to please Him.

Introduction for Youth

Topic: *It's Not about You!*

Sociologists tell us we have yet to see the fruit of family breakdown in the United States. But anyone in touch with children and teenagers knows very well how bitter that fruit is in their lives. They begin to doubt their personal worth and self-identity, and question whether there remains any safe and secure place for them.

What we used to call the traditional family barely survives. Many adolescents live with single parents, or as part of "blended" families. They are trying to make some sense out of separation and divorce and where they fit in.

Against this stark backdrop, Paul's picture of marriage and family life reads like a fairy tale. We need to take a lot of time, in groups and one-on-one, to try to rebuild these shattered lives and dreams. Above all, we need to offer teenagers the good news that there is a place for them—and everyone—in the family of God.

We do not abandon God's Word just because so many today have violated His design for the family. Instead, we continue to love, serve, teach, and train. We do so, not only by words, but also by the integrity of our own commitment to the Savior and His will.

Concepts for Children

Topic: *Love Is the Way*

1. God wants us to show love in what we say and do.
2. We love others because God loves us.
3. The Spirit helps us to show love to others.
4. We show love by being available to others in their time of need.
5. Even when it seems we can do nothing, we can pray for those who are hurting.

Lesson Commentary

I. SHOWING MUTUAL RESPECT: EPHESIANS 5:21-33

A. The Overarching Responsibility: vs. 21

Submit to one another out of reverence for Christ.

As we learned in last week's lesson, Paul stated in Ephesians 5:15-20 that living for the Son in a corrupt environment requires us to make a habit of watching our conduct. We're to live in a wise, judicious manner, governed by the Father's will. Such a Spirit-led life expresses itself in thankfulness and music-filled worship. Paul continued his instructions on specific lifestyle issues by directing all believers to submit to one another (vs. 21).

The Greek verb rendered "submit" was used in literature outside of the Bible in the sense of soldiers subordinating themselves to their superiors, or of slaves yielding to their masters. Here, the verb does not mean a forced submission, but rather voluntarily giving up one's rights and will. Because of our selfish human nature, we do not naturally want to yield or adapt to anyone. But since we love and respect the Savior, and since He asks us to submit to one another, we must do so. Paul developed what he meant about submission by discussing three sets of household relationships—those between wives and husbands (vss. 22-33), between children and parents (6:1-4), and between slaves and masters (vss. 5-9).

B. Responsibility of Wives to Husbands: vss. 22-24

Wives, submit to your husbands as to the Lord. For the husband is the head of the wife as Christ is the head of the church, his body, of which he is the Savior. Now as the church submits to Christ, so also wives should submit to their husbands in everything.

At least as early as Aristotle, Greek writers—especially Stoic philosophers—offered rules for governing households. They hoped to build a stable society. Hellenistic (Greek-influenced) Jewish teachers frequently made lists of household rules. They believed that these moral laws applied equally to Jews and Gentiles. Probably, early Christian writers were influenced by the Hellenistic Jewish teachers. Besides Ephesians 5:22–6:9, household codes can be found in Colossians 3:18–4:1; 1 Timothy 2:8-15; 6:1-2; Titus 2:1-10; and 1 Peter 2:18–3:7. Several Christian leaders from the post-apostolic period also listed household codes.

In Ephesians 5:22, Paul offered his first example of submission among Christians by stating that wives are to submit to their husbands. He did not, however, provide a detailed explanation of what he meant. Since this instruction has given rise to widely differing interpretations, we might wish the apostle had said more. Perhaps it is helpful to consider what Paul did not mean by his statement. He was not saying that women are inferior to men or that all women must submit to all men. And even though the apostle said wives should submit "in everything" (vs. 24), the teaching of

Scripture as a whole indicates that a wife should not submit when her husband wants her to act in a way that is clearly contrary to God's will (compare Acts 5:29).

Interpreters of Ephesians 5:22-33 tend to take one of two views concerning what this passage says about marriage. One group thinks that wives should submit by obeying their husbands, and husbands should submit to God by loving their wives. Advocates of this view note that Jesus' sacrifice and love for the church establishes His authority. They conclude that while husbands should be kind and considerate toward their wives, they should also exercise authority when necessary. Another group says that Paul's command for wives to submit to their husbands is essentially equivalent to his command for husbands to love their wives. Proponents of this view emphasize Jesus' abandonment of authority on the cross and the mutuality of love between the Savior and the church. They conclude that in a marriage, both partners are equals and should equally share authority.

Instead of explaining what he meant by wifely submission, Paul made a comparison in verses 23 and 24. He said a wife is to submit to her husband just as she—indeed, just as all the church—submits to the Savior. That's because a husband is the head of his wife just as the Messiah is the Head of the church. This comparison helps us only if we understand what Paul meant by the Son being the Head of the church. New Testament scholars have taken different positions on this. According to one group of experts, Jesus is the Head of the church in the sense that He is the church's source and origin. On the basis of this interpretation, these scholars conclude that a wife must honor and love her husband, but the two may share decision making equally. According to another group of experts, the Messiah is the Head of the church in the sense that He is its leader and authority. Based on this interpretation, these scholars suggest that a wife should honor and love her husband, but he should oversee family decisions.

C. The Responsibility of Husbands to Wives: vss. 25-30

Husbands, love your wives, just as Christ loved the church and gave himself up for her to make her holy, cleansing her by the washing with water through the word, and to present her to himself as a radiant church, without stain or wrinkle or any other blemish, but holy and blameless. In this same way, husbands ought to love their wives as their own bodies. He who loves his wife loves himself. After all, no one ever hated his own body, but he feeds and cares for it, just as Christ does the church—for we are members of his body.

The wife is not the only partner in a marriage who has a duty to the other. While she is to submit to her husband, he must love her sacrificially and unconditionally (Eph. 5:25). In a male-dominated Roman society, the news that husbands owe their wives any duty must have sounded revolutionary. Once again, Paul put husbands in the place of the Savior and wives in the place of the church to help clarify his meaning. A husband is to love his wife even as Jesus loves the church.

Verses 25-30 contain the apostle's description of how the Son loves the church and how husbands should love their wives. The Greek verb translated "love" in these verses is *agape.* Generally speaking, the term refers to an unselfish and active concern for another. This is the appropriate word, since Jesus' love for us motivated Him to give up His life for us (vs. 25). Throughout this passage, Paul used wedding and marriage terms to picture the Savior's love for the church. Before a wedding ceremony in ancient times, the bride would carefully wash herself and put on clean clothes. Similarly, the Messiah cleanses His bride, the church, "by . . . washing with water through the word" (vs. 26). (Some think this statement is part of a reference to early baptismal practices.) After this washing, the bride of Christ is "radiant . . . without stain or wrinkle or any other blemish" (vs. 27). Expressed differently, the redemption the Son won on the cross cleanses members of the church of sins, making us "holy and blameless" in the Father's sight.

In modern wedding ceremonies, it is traditional for the bride's father to present the bride to the groom. But in ancient weddings, ordinarily a friend of the groom would present the bride to the groom. According to Paul's description, neither the modern nor the ancient traditions will be followed in the Messiah's wedding ceremony with the church, which will take place at the end of time. Jesus will act as both the presenter and as the groom, since He will present the church to Himself. Why does the Savior love the church so much? He gave Himself up for it, washes it, and will present it to Himself. It's because the church is His spiritual body (vs. 30). A person naturally loves his or her own physical body and shows that love by taking care of it (vs. 29). Similarly, a husband should love his wife as much as he loves himself. Indeed, by loving his wife in this unselfish manner, a husband "loves himself" (vs. 28).

D. The Profound Mystery: vss. 31-33

"For this reason a man will leave his father and mother and be united to his wife, and the two will become one flesh." This is a profound mystery—but I am talking about Christ and the church. However, each one of you also must love his wife as he loves himself, and the wife must respect her husband.

In Ephesians 5:31, Paul quoted Genesis 2:24 to show how a married couple are joined. Adam realized that Eve was, quite literally, bone of his bones and flesh of his flesh. Eve had been made from Adam. This illustrates that the bond of marriage is strong. In fact, the Greek verb translated "united" (Eph. 5:31) literally means "to glue upon." Paul's implication was that a man must love the woman to whom he is joined (in a manner of speaking) by marriage.

Genesis 2:24 has a dual implication. People have always known that it refers to the relationship between husbands and wives. But only after the Savior's coming to earth did some realize that it also refers to the relationship between Jesus and the church. That's what Paul meant when he called it a "profound mystery" (Eph. 5:32). As noted in lesson 1, the apostle was referring to a deep secret that had been disclosed through the Redeemer. In verse 33, Paul summarized his instructions to husbands and wives. Husbands are to love their wives as they love themselves, and wives are to respect their husbands. The lordship and example of the Son is the basis for such a mutually loving and submissive relationship.

The state of marriage today would not be so bleak if partners would learn to follow Paul's advice. How many marriages have gone sour because wives, for selfish reasons of their own, have failed to give their husbands the respect due them? And who can count the marriages that have disintegrated because husbands have been too self-absorbed to show their wives the love that's in their hearts? If a wife cares as much for her husband as for herself, and if a husband cares as much for his wife as for himself, their marriage will be the lifelong union God meant it to be.

II. NURTURING GOOD PARENT-CHILD RELATIONSHIPS: EPHESIANS 6:1-4

A. The Responsibility of Children: vss. 1-3

Children, obey your parents in the Lord, for this is right. "Honor your father and mother"—which is the first commandment with a promise—"that it may go well with you and that you may enjoy long life on the earth."

The second set of household relationships Paul addressed included children and their parents. We may not often think of children reading the apostle's letters (or listening as they were read aloud) along with adults in the churches. But Ephesians 6:1-3 is one place where the apostle addressed children directly. He told them plainly that it is proper for children to obey their parents (vs. 1). This obedience by children is to take place "in the Lord." Paul imagined a family in which both parents and children believe in the Savior. Neither mother nor father, but Jesus is the family's ultimate authority. Therefore, the parents make rules consistent with Christian principles, and the children obey their parents as they would obey Jesus.

This instruction for children to obey their parents was hardly unusual. The same instruction may be found at several places in the Bible. Paul quoted the fifth commandment to back up his instruction (vss. 2-3; compare Ex. 20:12; Deut. 5:16). How can the fifth commandment be the "first" (Eph. 6:2) with a promise if the second commandment also seems to have one (Ex. 20:5-6; Deut. 5:9-10)? The fifth may have been "first" in the sense that it was the initial (and primary) one taught to children. Or the fifth is at least one of the first divine injunctions in importance. Perhaps to make the requirement of child obedience sound less like a duty and more like an opportunity, Paul drew attention to the promise attached to the fifth commandment: "That it may go well with you and that you may enjoy long life on the earth" (Eph. 6:3). The promise does not give absolute assurance that those who are obedient to their parents will have a long and easy life on earth. But generally, the promise indicates that God blesses those who honor their parents.

B. The Responsibility of Parents: vs. 4

Fathers, do not exasperate your children; instead, bring them up in the training and instruction of the Lord.

After telling children to be obedient, Paul turned his attention to fathers (Eph. 6:4). Here Paul's teaching was truly countercultural. According to the Roman law of *patria potestas* (Latin for "power of a father"), the male head of a family exercised nearly absolute authority over his children, the extended descendants in the male line (regardless of their age), and those adopted and reared in the family. Only the male head was entitled to any rights in private law, and even property acquired by other family members was owned by the father. He could murder an unwanted newborn, make his children work in the fields wearing chains, sell his children into slavery, or impose capital punishment on a family member.

Far from advocating such parental tyranny, Paul told fathers—and by implication, mothers—they didn't have absolute power over their children. The apostle taught that while parents have the right to require obedience from their children, parents should not make such severe demands on their children that the latter become exasperated. Provoking children to anger creates discouragement and resentment and often leads to outright rebellion. Instead of frustrating, enraging, or ridiculing their children, parents should adopt rules and policies that are objective, fair, and sensible.

When parents operate under the lordship of the Savior, they will consider their children's feelings and provide them with godly instruction. The Greek noun rendered "training" refers to the discipline and nurture parents give their children to cultivate their minds and morals. The noun rendered "instruction" refers to the correction, admonition, and encouragement that parents give their children. Together, these terms emphasize that parents should use all appropriate methods to teach their children about God, with the goal that they will put their faith in the Savior and become His faithful disciples.

In stepping back from the preceding emphases, we have to admit that we bristle at the idea of submission, especially because it seems to inhibit our freedom. When we apply what Scripture teaches, we run smack into popular ideas that tell us to please ourselves first and not allow ourselves to be restrained by others. Because mutual submission is a distinctively Christian concept, we should not be surprised when it is met with hostility and ridicule. After all, we live in a world of self-indulgence, not sacrifice for the sake of others. It's clarifying to recognize that the biblical notion of submission has nothing to do with subjugation, inferiority, or servitude. Rather, it means loving and blessing others in a generous and humble manner. Our constant concern must be the welfare and feelings of others, not our own self-fulfillment.

In the context of the church, we look for ways to help others to grow spiritually. We also put their physical and social needs ahead of our own priorities. In the family context, mutual submission means that parents and children submit to the loving requirements of each other, depending on their circumstances and needs. It has to be worked out in terms of personal priorities. Family members voluntarily relinquish something they want, or their time, for the sake of another family member. While the stability of the family is at stake, so is the honor of the Savior and the integrity of God's Word. If we fail here, we confess to unbelievers that scriptural teaching concerning mutual submission and Christlike love doesn't work. If we can trust the Lord for our eternal salvation, we can also depend on Him to take care of our marriages and children.

Discussion Questions

1. What is the motivation for our submitting to one another?
2. What did Paul mean when he said that wives should submit to their husbands?
3. In what sense is Jesus the Head of the church?
4. What was Paul illustrating by his comments regarding Jesus' love for the church?
5. How should we who are parents treat our children?

Contemporary Application

According to God's Word, responsible Christian living starts in the family. In the church family, we are called to love and purity. In our physical families, we are called to mutual submission, respect, love, and obedience. Paul's teaching will not win secular approval in a society based on "personal rights." This means that believers have to stand out not only by what they say but also by how they live.

In short, the best defense of these principles is a godly example. So, when we see Christian families crumble, it is a wake-up call to the church. And when we see conflicts, it's a summons to prayer and wise intervention. It will take great courage for the church to stand publicly for God's design for marriage and family life. But our culture desperately needs Christians who will not yield to popular culture.

Believers choose to live this way because they reverence, or honor, the Savior and want to please Him. In turn, they are committed to follow His example. Our mutual submission is based on the Messiah's submission to the cross for us. He came not to be served but to serve (see Matt. 20:28; Mark 10:45).

We need to embrace this perspective if mutual submission is to work. Also, being aware of the biblical basis for submission helps us to avoid some of the nasty arguments that often arise over our rights, especially when it comes to husband-wife and parent-child relationships. Family rights, separation, and divorce could in large measure be avoided if we understood and practiced mutual submission.

Proclaiming Christ

Scripture

Background Scripture: *Philippians 1:12-30*
Scripture Lesson: *Philippians 1:15-26*
Key Verse: *In every way, whether from false motives or true, Christ is preached. And because of this I rejoice.* Philippians 1:18.
Scripture Lesson for Children: *Matthew 5:13-16*
Key Verse for Children: *You are the salt of the earth. . . . You are the light of the world.* Matthew 5:13-14.

Lesson Aim

To find purpose, hope, and joy in living for the Messiah.

Lesson Setting

Time: A.D. 61
Place: Rome

Lesson Outline

Proclaiming Christ

 I. Proclaiming the Messiah: Philippians 1:15-18a
   A. *Discordant Reasons: vs. 15*
   B. *Sincere and Insincere Motives: vss. 16-18a*
 II. Exalting the Messiah: Philippians 1:18b-26
   A. *Anticipating Deliverance: vss. 18b-19*
   B. *Living and Dying for the Savior: vss. 20-24*
   C. *Rejoicing in the Savior: vss. 25-26*

Introduction for Adults

Topic: *Motives and Messages*

One day a Christian writer asked a graduate student what was his motive for living. The student said he wanted to finish school and get a good job. "Then what?" the writer asked. Well, the student said he would get married and raise a family. "Then what?" the writer asked a second time. The student said he would like to have a successful career and make enough money to take care of his family and retire comfortably.

"Then what?" the writer asked a third time. "What do you mean?" the student asked, bewildered. The writer challenged the student, "Is that all there is to life? And what about the life to come after you die? Then what?" Like many people, the student had never thought about a higher purpose in life, or about his eternal future.

Christians, too, must check their reasons for living, since it is easy for them to follow the world's values and goals. If we really believe the message that "to live is Christ" (Phil. 1:21), we will devote ourselves to more than successful careers, money, and retirement. Jesus will determine our interests and how we spend our time, energy, and money.

Introduction for Youth

Topic: *Truth Is Truth*

During a high school wrestling match, Caleb "the underdog" appeared on the verge of losing. The state champion was about to pin him. But suddenly, in what seemed like a miracle, Caleb threw off his opponent and defeated him. How? Because Caleb never gave up hope in the midst of hardship.

Wrestling is a picture of the Christian life. Paul reminded his readers of the truth that they wrestled with powerful spiritual opponents. He himself demonstrated what it was like. The apostle never quit, despite physical beatings, abuse, and imprisonment. Rather than succumb to defeat and despair, he came up rejoicing. He refused to be pinned.

The same spiritual principles can work for saved teens. As they pray for one another and the Holy Spirit helps them, good can come out of their most difficult moments (Phil. 1:19).

Concepts for Children

Topic: *Salt and Light*

1. Jesus teaches His followers that obeying God will bring true joy.
2. Just as salt makes food taste better, so Jesus' followers bring out the best in others.
3. Jesus wants His followers to show others the way to Him by their actions.
4. Jesus wants His followers to share His love and goodness with others.
5. Jesus wants His followers to bring joy and hope wherever they go.

Lesson Commentary

I. PROCLAIMING THE MESSIAH: PHILIPPIANS 1:15-18A

A. Discordant Reasons: vs. 15

It is true that some preach Christ out of envy and rivalry, but others out of goodwill.

Philippi was an ancient town that was originally called Krenides. The latter means "springs," which was probably a reflection of its abundant water supply. The city was renamed by King Philip II of Macedonia when he subdued it around 356 B.C. Later Philippi became a strategic Roman colony since it was situated on a major road (called the Via Egnatia) that linked Rome with the continent of Asia. This Greek city was located about 10 miles north of the Aegean Sea and was coveted for its gold mines and fertile soil.

During Paul's second missionary journey, he planted the first European church in Philippi (see Acts 16:9-40). This probably occurred around A.D. 50. A few of the converts of Philippi, such as Lydia, became some of his dearest friends. The dramatic conversion of a jailer and the exorcism of a slave girl also occurred in this city. Some Bible scholars suggest that the physician, Luke, was from this town, since it had a well-known school of medicine and because he noted its prominence (vs. 12). In any case, the Philippian church always held a cherished place in Paul's heart. He came back to visit this city on his third missionary journey around A.D. 55–56. In fact, he may have passed through the city twice on this particular trip.

After the Philippian believers sent Paul a generous gift while he was under house arrest in Rome, the apostle wrote this letter to thank them for their kindness and to report on his current situation. At the same time, Paul took this opportunity to urge them to remain strong and united in their faith in the Messiah, even though many external and internal elements may have been discouraging them. The apostle was referring to his house arrest when he spoke about himself as being "in chains for Christ" (Phil. 1:13; see Acts 28:30-31), not of his later imprisonment in the Mamertine dungeon prior to his execution. The circumstances relating to his house arrest around A.D. 60–62 were certainly more agreeable to his physical well-being than the brutal incarceration he suffered in Rome at the end of his life around A.D. 66–67. It was during this final imprisonment when he wrote Second Timothy (see 1:17; 4:6-7).

Undoubtedly, the Philippian Christians knew that Paul was under house arrest and was awaiting his trial before Caesar on serious charges. The consequences of those charges could be terribly grievous for the apostle, at least physically. It was possible that he could be sentenced either to death or a long, harsh imprisonment for sedition against Rome. His friends in Philippi probably prayed fervently that God would comfort and deliver him from his unpleasant and precarious situation. Aware of their concern for his welfare and safety, the apostle wanted to assure them in this letter that God was not only caring for him but also bringing unexpected and marvelous fruit to his ongoing ministry (Phil. 1:12).

Paul was especially excited about the Lord's work among the emperor's guards, for everyone there knew that the apostle was under arrest because of his unswerving faith in Jesus and courageous defense of the Gospel. Some of them had received the Son as their Lord and Savior. It was clear to everyone that the apostle was not under house arrest because he had violated a civil law or because he was a political agitator. The sentries who were responsible for guarding Paul probably observed how he lived out his faith in the Messiah. Some may have listened to the apostle's teachings about the Savior and shared what they learned with other palace guards, noting that Paul's characteristics were nothing like those of most other criminals they guarded. Moreover, the Gospel was advanced not only among these guards but to many other people as well (vs. 13).

Furthermore, Paul attributed the proclamation of the Gospel by other Christians in Rome to his being "in chains for Christ." Whether Paul was describing an actual condition in which he was chained to a guard or was referring to his imprisonment and sufferings in general is not clear. In any case, he was elated that his example encouraged other Christians to be brave and bold in declaring the Word of God (vs. 14). There was the possibility that all of Paul's believing readers might also come under the iron fist of the Roman authorities. If the Lord could still bring fabulous fruit to the apostle's ministry while he was under house arrest, they, too, could be fruitful for the Lord whether in or out of prison.

Although believers were courageously proclaiming the Gospel in Rome, Paul was not ignorant of the rationale behind their preaching and teaching. Some were doing it for the right reasons, which he praised, but others were doing it for the wrong reasons. They were not preaching the Savior to nonbelievers "out of goodwill" (vs. 15) but "out of envy and rivalry." Yet why would believers be impelled in these ungodly ways? They were certainly members of the Christian community. Most of these were probably jealous of the prestige Paul had earned within the Christian community and competed for the same authority he held among them.

B. Sincere and Insincere Motives: vss. 16-18a

The latter do so in love, knowing that I am put here for the defense of the gospel. The former preach Christ out of selfish ambition, not sincerely, supposing that they can stir up trouble for me while I am in chains. But what does it matter? The important thing is that in every way, whether from false motives or true, Christ is preached. And because of this I rejoice.

Unlike Paul's rivals, his friends in Rome preached the Good News about the Messiah with unimpeachable motives. Their evangelism sprang from the love they had in the Savior—a love that empowered them to tell nonbelievers about the compassion Jesus has for the lost. In addition, they understood why Paul was under house arrest—not because he was an outlaw, but because he stood up for the

Gospel of Christ. Knowing this also instilled in these believers the courage to boldly stand up for the Lord Jesus as well (Phil. 1:16).

When Paul said of his imprisonment that he was "put here for the defense of the gospel," he was specifically saying that God had brought him to Rome for a particular purpose. It was no accident or quirk of fate that the apostle was there. In the approximately 30 years that had passed from Jesus' resurrection to Paul's imprisonment, the Gospel had been carried through incredible means from an obscure province of the Empire—Judea—to the court of Caesar himself. The Father had chosen the apostle to defend the truth about His Son in front of the most powerful and influential leaders of Paul's time. The Roman world could reject the life-giving message the apostle brought, but it could no longer ignore it.

Evidently, Paul's rivals were not content just to operate apart from the apostle's ministry. They were also motivated by the desire to intensify his dilemma while he was under Roman custody. They may have figured that their preaching would place Paul into further jeopardy with the civil authorities, perhaps even contributing to his conviction. With the apostle out of the way, they could enhance their standing within the Christian movement in Rome. Thus it was clear to Paul that these preachers were insincere in proclaiming the Gospel and that selfish ambition was their underlying motive (vs. 17).

Despite the malevolent intentions of the apostle's rivals, he didn't care about their ill will toward him as long as the Gospel was preached. If nonbelievers were hearing the Good News about Jesus Christ and receiving Him as their Lord and Savior, that was all that counted to Paul. He didn't care what happened to him as long as people were coming into the kingdom. Therefore, he was not concerned about the motives behind the preaching of selfish competitors. The apostle only wanted to be sure that people were receiving the right message about the Savior. Evidently they were, for Paul was overjoyed at knowing that Christians were advancing the Gospel even within the capital of the Roman Empire (vs. 18a).

II. EXALTING THE MESSIAH: PHILIPPIANS 1:18B-26

A. Anticipating Deliverance: vss. 18b-19

Yes, and I will continue to rejoice, for I know that through your prayers and the help given by the Spirit of Jesus Christ, what has happened to me will turn out for my deliverance.

Paul was confident that he was securely in God's hands. The apostle believed that whatever befell him would bring glory and honor to the Father because He was in control of Paul's life and the circumstances that affected his existence. Therefore, though the apostle was under house arrest in Rome, he could rejoice and keep on rejoicing, for the Lord was with him and sustaining him (Phil. 1:18b). Also, Paul knew that his Philippian friends were praying for him. A unique intimacy had developed between the apostle and the Christians in Philippi, and Paul naturally cherished their deep concern for him.

What is more, the apostle coveted the prayers of other Christians, for he appreciated the distinctive power that believers' prayers had in enlisting God's aid (vs. 19). Paul likewise valued the strengthening he received from the Spirit of Christ, which supplied him with the courage, determination, and hope to persevere joyfully under his current circumstances. Most certainly the apostle depended on the Lord's Spirit to deliver him from any situation that brought hardship to him. Whatever the Roman authorities decided to do with Paul, God Himself would vindicate the apostle.

B. Living and Dying for the Savior: vss. 20-24

I eagerly expect and hope that I will in no way be ashamed, but will have sufficient courage so that now as always Christ will be exalted in my body, whether by life or by death. For to me, to live is Christ and to die is gain. If I am to go on living in the body, this will mean fruitful labor for me. Yet what shall I choose? I do not know! I am torn between the two: I desire to depart and be with Christ, which is better by far; but it is more necessary for you that I remain in the body.

As Paul awaited his trial, his major concern was not whether the Father would save his life, but whether the apostle would present himself in such a way that the Son would be exalted. In fact, Paul was both eager and hoping to bring glory and not shame to the Lord. The Greek word rendered "eagerly expect" (Phil. 1:20) provides a vivid picture of one who cranes his or her neck to catch a glimpse of what lies ahead. The apostle was letting his readers know that, while ignoring all other interests, he keenly anticipated honoring of the Lord during his trial.

Paul realized that the verdict could mean life or death for him physically. That is why he referred to "my body" in verse 20. Throughout the long ministry in which he preached the Gospel, whether to friendly crowds or hostile ones, the apostle always sought to exalt the Messiah in his body. Now, whether the Romans released or executed Paul, he desired above all else that his Lord still be exalted in him. In a few words the apostle beautifully summed up the no-lose situation of belonging to Jesus: "For to me, to live is Christ and to die is gain" (vs. 21). This immortal affirmation expresses a believer's faith and hope. To Paul the gain meant much more than the eternal benefit of heaven. The profit was that the Gospel of Christ would be further advanced if the apostle was martyred for his faith and hope in the Son.

Paul was confident that he would continue to be fruitful in his ministry if the Romans did not execute him. In fact, even if he was forced to serve more time in prison, he would continue to proclaim the Gospel. He remained certain that nonbelievers would turn to faith in the Messiah because of his preaching. Indeed, due to Paul's strategic position in Rome, he would have additional opportunities to be God's instrument in bringing more people into the kingdom (vs. 22).

Nonetheless, to be with the Son in heaven was also appealing to the apostle. In fact, if he were given a choice to continue to minister God's Word or be in the presence of Christ, Paul confessed that the decision would be difficult to make. Yet he stated that he would choose to be with the Savior, for the apostle would have a much deeper intimacy with Jesus in heaven, though Paul already enjoyed a close relationship with the Son here on earth (vs. 23). Despite the apostle's own inclination to depart, he believed it was more important for him to remain. In fact, his whole reason for staying was for the sake of tending to other people's spiritual welfare, specifically for the pastoral care of his friends in the church at Philippi (vs. 24).

C. Rejoicing in the Savior: vss. 25-26

Convinced of this, I know that I will remain, and I will continue with all of you for your progress and joy in the faith, so that through my being with you again your joy in Christ Jesus will overflow on account of me.

With bold confidence, Paul told the Philippians that he was certain he would live in order to fulfill his duties in bringing them to spiritual maturity. Perhaps the great responsibility he had in caring for so many young believers throughout the Mediterranean world convinced him that it was too soon for him to die. Evidently, the Lord gave the apostle a premonition or an assurance that he would not be executed. Maybe word was passed to him that the Roman authorities looking at his case were favorable to him.

Whatever the reason, Paul was now unmistakably upbeat (Phil. 1:25). Moreover, the apostle thought that the Romans would not only spare his life but also give him his freedom, for he promised the Philippians that he would visit with them once again (vs. 26). We do not know whether this joyous meeting ever occurred. If it did, the Philippian Christians would have been thrilled to see their friend and mentor. They would have listened carefully to his stirring account of how the Lord was glorified through the apostle's harrowing yet rewarding experiences in Rome.

Having been in Philippi and encountered persecution because of his faith, Paul knew what the believers in the city were up against. Also, since the apostle was deeply concerned for their individual and corporate welfare as a church, he sought to encourage and instruct them with a love and tenderness unique among his known letters. Whatever difficulties might arise against the Philippians, Paul exhorted them to be faithful to the teachings about the Messiah. This demanded a high standard of godly behavior (vs. 27). Only by maintaining this high calling toward one another would they be worthy examples of the Christian life.

Once again, Paul reminded the Philippians of his possible return. In the same way, much as the apostle asked Philemon to prepare a guest room for him (see Philem. 22), Paul's mention of visiting Philippi was a subtle way of applying pressure on his readers to comply with his instructions. It was also typical of the apostle to make it evident to his readers that their obedience would be of tremendous encouragement to him. In this case, the Philippians could bring him supreme joy, especially as he endured the ordeal of Roman confinement. By adding that he would hear reports about them even if he was unable to visit them, he was urging them to heed his words immediately (vs. 27).

Paul expected his readers to be united in spirit and be of one mind. Of course, he wasn't insisting that they all have the same personality or share the exact same views about everything when he told them to be "as one man." Nor did he want them to be carbon copies of himself. Different people have different gifts with which to serve God, and all are equally valuable to Him. There is also a wide range of personalities within the church, each integral to the health of the Messiah's spiritual body. Even so, Paul was concerned with the rivalry and conflict that were apparently dividing the church in Philippi. For this reason the apostle emphasized the importance of unity.

Discussion Questions

1. What were some of the impure motives some had for proclaiming the Gospel?
2. How was it possible for Paul to continue to rejoice while under house arrest in Rome?
3. What did Paul recognize as the advantage to being set free at his trial?
4. How strongly do you believe that God is involved in your current circumstances?
5. Why is it important for us, as Jesus' disciples, to remain calm when we are harassed for our faith in Christ?

Contemporary Application

In Philippians 1:21, Paul said that "to live is Christ and to die is gain." Perhaps the apostle's simple testimony sounds otherworldly to us. *He can't be real,* we think. How could he possibly rejoice while wearing chains and locked in a prison? How could he be so bold and confident about his life's purpose and destiny? What a contrast to the aimlessness we see in people all around us.

The church stands as a beacon of brightness to people lost in the fog of meaninglessness. How encouraging it is to hear the testimonies of people who say that the Lord Jesus filled the emptiness in their lives. Perhaps at times we are afraid or ashamed to say this in our own life. It takes faith to recognize that with each passing day, Jesus is making a real difference for us.

Paul knew that the Savior works through other believers. Indeed, Jesus helps us to find joy in our tough experiences through the prayers, support, and encouragement of fellow Christians. When believers are motivated by the Spirit's promptings, they become agents of healing. At the same time, the Spirit Himself also ministers to our emotional needs.

Paul faced his imprisonment with courage and creativity. Because of the Savior, a situation that could have resulted in the apostle's being depressed and benefiting no one instead resulted in an event that produced much fruit for the kingdom. This is what the Lord Jesus wants to do in our lives. As believers, we need to see every difficulty through His perspective. The world is in the hands of the master designer, who creates each day full of new possibilities and the potential to serve Him.

Jesus' Humility and Exaltation

Scripture

Background Scripture: *Philippians 2:1-13*
Scripture Lesson: *Philippians 2:5-11*
Key Verse: *Your attitude should be the same as that of Christ Jesus.* Philippians 2:5.
Scripture Lesson for Children: *Matthew 13:1-9*
Key Verse for Children: *[Some] seed fell on good soil, where it produced a crop—a hundred, sixty or thirty times what was sown.* Matthew 13:8.

Lesson Aim

To consider the importance of showing biblical humility to others.

Lesson Setting

Time: A.D. *61*
Place: Rome

Lesson Outline

Jesus' Humility and Exaltation

    I. The Glory of the Son: Philippians 2:5-6
       A. *The Son's Example of Humility: vs. 5*
       B. *The Son's Equality with the Father and the Spirit: vs. 6*
   II. The Exaltation of the Son: Philippians 2:7-11
       A. *The Son's Humiliation: vss. 7-8*
       B. *The Son's Exaltation: vss. 9-11*

Introduction for Adults
Topic: *Attitude Counts*

Paul wanted the believers in the Philippian church to radically change their attitude. The apostle did not call for a conference on management. Instead, he called for a fresh look at the suffering Savior. Until His followers took Him seriously, they would not discover genuine and joyful humility.

A Christian pastor said, "A person who profoundly changed my life was not a preacher or the leader of a big organization. She was a cheerful office worker at the local bus company. She never married. She used her home and her slim resources to develop Christian maturity among college students. Many of them—including myself—went into the ministry at home and abroad."

Few of us recognize the power of humble, exuberant Christian service. But when the books are revealed, we may be surprised to learn that the major influences in God's kingdom came from believers whose attitude was unselfish and compassionate. Our own lives and our churches are immeasurably enriched when we follow the mind of Christ.

Introduction for Youth
Topic: *Similar Minds*

Imagine trying to herd a barn full of stray cats. No matter how hard we strive, these independent-minded animals will not be corralled. It often seems just as impossible to get adolescent church members to adopt a similar mind-set when it comes to serving one another in their congregation.

Paul reminded us in Philippians 2:5-11 that the Lord Jesus and His priorities are supposed to be number one in the lives of believers and in the church. This remains true regardless of whether we are ministers, deacons, trustees, Sunday school teachers, or other church officers. This knowledge calls for humble servanthood in Jesus' name.

Often, however, we are like the woman in a certain congregation who was asked to prepare a snack for her children and others in her church youth group for one evening. She retorted in a scalding tone, "You mean you are asking me to come up to the church and do the work of a servant?" Exactly!

Concepts for Children
Topic: *Soil That Bears Good Crops*

1. Jesus said that some seed fell on a path and was eaten by birds.
2. Some seed fell on a thin layer of soil, sprang up, and died in the hot sun.
3. Some seed fell among thorns and was choked out.
4. Some seed fell on good soil and produced a rich harvest.
5. God wants us to obey His Word, and in this way bear spiritual fruit.

Lesson Commentary

I. THE GLORY OF THE SON: PHILIPPIANS 2:5-6

A. The Son's Example of Humility: vs. 5

Your attitude should be the same as that of Christ Jesus.

In Philippians 2:1-4, Paul called the recipients of his letter to unity, humility, and obedience. As long as the congregation remained divided, they would not be able to resist the opposition they faced from antagonists (see 1:28). Although the Jewish population in Philippi was small, the problems in the city could have been caused by antagonistic Jews from other cities who sometimes followed Paul and made trouble for his ministry in the towns he visited (see Acts 17:13). However, the opposition referred to in Philippians 1:28 was probably the resistance of the pagan populace in general. They had created a mob scene in which Paul and Silas were arrested on their initial visit to Philippi (see Acts 16:16-24).

The persecution Paul's readers encountered undermined their Christian unity. Well aware of how this problem was manifesting itself among his friends, the apostle appealed to them in four stirring ways. First, Paul noted the united position of his readers in the Messiah (Phil. 2:1). As believers, our starting point is always who we are in the Son—that is, we are all saved sinners because of what He has done for us on the cross. What can be more encouraging to us than being delivered from the condemnation of the Father? Also, what can be more unifying than for all of us to receive the same mercy?

Second, the apostle reminded his readers about the Messiah's love. Jesus died for each one of them because He loved each one of them. This knowledge should always give us comfort. Being so loved should naturally prompt us to be loving as well. In fact, Jesus Himself exhorted His followers to love one another and prayed that we be one (see John 15:17; 17:21). Third, Paul stressed the indwelling of the Holy Spirit in each of his readers. Since there is one Spirit, there is one body of believers of which the Philippian believers were a part. Consequently, sharing the one Spirit of God should have compelled them to avoid any action or attitude that would divide the body of Christ.

Fourth, Paul spoke about the tender feelings and deep sympathy his readers were to have for one another (Phil. 2:1). This was prompted by the apostle's strong desire for these believers to be drawn together. Yet, rather than command the Philippians to bury their resentment toward one another and behave as good Christians should, Paul appealed to their hearts in such a way as to motivate them to be loving and forgiving toward one another. Although the apostle had zealously persecuted the earliest followers of Jesus Christ, the Lord still called this passionate Pharisee from Tarsus to be an important messenger to the Gentiles of the Gospel of love and forgiveness. Paul accomplished his God-appointed mission by both personally establishing churches throughout Greece and Asia Minor and writing divinely inspired letters to Christians throughout the Mediterranean world—including those living in Philippi.

Just as the apostle made four appeals to his readers, so he listed four results from such an effort to be united. First, the Philippians would be of the same mind. This does not mean they would always think the exact same thoughts. Instead, Paul meant they would be in agreement about laboring together for the glory of the Messiah. Second, they would experience the love for one another they each had in the Savior. Third, they would be wholeheartedly of one accord. Fourth, they would be of one mind in purpose as a church (vs. 2). Paul warned his readers not to succumb to those spiritual viruses that damage Christian unity. "Selfish ambition" (vs. 3) and "vain conceit" were evils that had evidently stricken some of the Philippian believers. Perhaps there were some who were engaging in party strife and petty squabbles because of their self-centeredness. Instead, the apostle admonished them to be humble, not like one who cringes before others, but like one who treats others as being more worthy than himself or herself.

In ancient times, the Greeks disdained the quality of humility, regarding it as shameful. It was something to be avoided and overcome with positive thoughts and actions. Believers, however, operated differently. God wanted them to recognize their true sinful condition and need for His grace. This is in keeping with the Greek noun rendered "humility," which means to think rightly about one's position in life. Here we see that humility is a continual appreciation of our need for the Savior and of our need to always depend on Him. This was the opposite of the Greek concept of freedom, which called for a person to not be subject to anyone or anything, including God.

For the Son, humility meant a recognition of His role as a servant in becoming human. Since He was sinless, recognition of His true condition did not involve the presence of iniquity. He did, however, demonstrate the need to depend daily on the Father for strength. In light of what has been said, how can we demonstrate such Christlike humility? Paul advised that believers should look to the interests of other Christians, not just address their own concerns (vs. 4). Without ignoring what is important to us, we can daily show others that we value and appreciate what is important to them. The supreme example of humility was the attitude that Jesus had when He rescued us from sin. If we truly are to be in the Messiah, then we should also have this attitude of loving humility in relationship with others and self-sacrificing obedience to God. This was the attitude that Paul wanted the Philippians to embrace (vs. 5).

B. The Son's Equality with the Father and the Spirit: vs. 6

Who, being in very nature God, did not consider equality with God something to be grasped.

Paul characterized the Son's humble attitude in what some scholars have suggested was originally a hymn sung in the early church. Even then, believers sang songs expressing their devotion and faith in the Messiah (see Col. 3:16). Most of these hymns are now lost to us, but a few are probably preserved in the apostle's letters. Besides the possibility of Philippians 2:6-11, parts of other probable hymns may be found in Ephesians 5:14, Colossians 1:15-20, and 1 Timothy 3:16. Those in favor of this view maintain that Paul quoted the song in Philippians 2:6-11 to provide an example of humility. These experts note the solemn tone of the apostle's words, the way they fit together, and the manner in which they were carefully chosen.

When read aloud in the Greek, the rhythmical quality of Paul's words provides further evidence that this passage could have easily been sung. There is no problem in seeing these verses as an incorporation of an early hymn. The words definitely reflect the apostle's thought and support his point, which would make their inclusion natural. On the other hand, Paul was capable of writing poetic passages (1 Cor. 13, for example), and he should not be dismissed as the author just because of style. Either way, these verses provide a wonderfully concise theology of the person of Christ and accurately reflect other statements of Scripture regarding the Savior. In particular, we learn about the humility and exaltation of the Son, which Paul wanted to convey to his readers.

In his Letter to the Philippians, the apostle wrote some of his most enduring statements about faith and hope and shared his most penetrating insights about the divine nature of the Messiah. Succinctly put, this letter provides believers in Christ with timely encouragement and godly wisdom. Indeed, the sacred truths revealed in Philippians came from the heart and mind of a man who had learned the Father's truths through many years of sacrificial service to the Son. Throughout the Philippian letter, Paul's deep affection for the believers who had supported him with their prayers and financial aid is evident. Though these Macedonian Christians were being persecuted for their faith in the Savior, they had not abandoned Paul's teachings nor discarded his friendship. Their steadfast devotion to the Lord and to Paul compelled the apostle to pour out his heart to them, confessing his longing to be with them and his special love for them.

With respect to Philippians 2:6, we discover that prior to the Son's incarnation, He eternally existed as God with the Father and the Spirit. One of the key doctrines of the Christian faith is that Jesus is, always was, and always will be God. In fact, Paul declared in Colossians 2:9 that in the Lord Jesus all the fullness of the Godhead dwelt in bodily form. Philippians 2:6 reveals that even though Jesus is God, He decided not to use His privileges as God to seize His share of divine glory and honor. Instead, He chose the path of lowly obedience.

II. THE EXALTATION OF THE SON: PHILIPPIANS 2:7-11

A. The Son's Humiliation: vss. 7-8

But made himself nothing, taking the very nature of a servant, being made in human likeness. And being found in appearance as a man, he humbled himself and became obedient to death—even death on a cross!

The Son acted upon His decision to be obedient to the Father by emptying Himself. This is the literal meaning of the Greek phrase that the NIV translates as "made himself nothing" (Phil. 2:7). In this selfless act, Jesus did not give up His divinity but laid aside His kingly privileges as God to become a human being. He also did not choose to be an earthly monarch, a wealthy merchant, a powerful military leader, an idolized athlete or entertainer, or even a renowned philosopher. Jesus became a servant. Once Jesus became fully human through His incarnation, people who knew Him could see that He possessed the full nature of a human being—except that He was without sin. He hungered as any human would. He felt the discomfort of hot and cold weather as any person would. He became tired after a long walk in the same way His fellow travelers became exhausted.

In verse 7, Paul described three steps in Jesus' mission. He "made himself nothing"; He took "the very nature of a servant"; and He was "made in human likeness." From birth to death, Jesus lived in humility. He was born in a stable. His parents were refugees in Egypt. Jesus grew up in obedience to His parents. He worked at a humble trade, that is, as a carpenter. Jesus cried with those who grieved. He washed the feet of His disciples. Paul summarized the Messiah's self-emptying this way: "Though he was rich, yet for your sakes he became poor, so that you through his poverty might become rich" (2 Cor. 8:9). Because of Jesus' sinlessness, however, He could choose whether to die. All individuals are subject to physical death unless the Father decrees differently. But the Son could conceivably have rejected this final conclusion to His earthly life. Jesus, however, chose to die—not to just leave this life peacefully like Enoch, but to perish on the cross in anguish and humiliation so that we might live in renewed and eternal communion with the Father (Phil. 2:8).

The Son lived completely obedient to His Father. This included the Son voluntarily permitting Himself to die like a common criminal for our sins. The enormous pain of Jesus' humiliation was described by Old Testament prophets, psalmists, and the writers of the four Gospels. To the Jews of Jesus' day, crucifixion was the epitome of shame. This gruesome form of execution showed that the victim was languishing in disgrace outside the blessing of God's covenant (see Deut. 21:23; Gal. 3:13). To the Romans, crucifixion was repulsive and reserved it for foreigners and slaves. Believers today tend to know little, if anything, about this kind of humiliation. In Philippians, Paul did not dwell on the details of Jesus' unjust trials and the way He was mocked, beaten, and nailed to the cross. Rather, the apostle emphasized the stigma of being executed in this way. His provision of this key information enables us to grasp the horror connected with Jesus' atoning sacrifice.

Admittedly, when Jesus' executioners dragged Him to the cross, He could have called down legions of angels (see Matt. 26:53). Yet Jesus did not do this. Against the backdrop of His humility, how do we attain the high ambition Paul had for Christ's spiritual body, the church? One way is for us to lay aside our personal rights for the sake of ministering to others. Another way is for us to practice looking at our lives and circumstances—as well as the lives of our fellow believers—from the perspective of Jesus. We do this because we are one through faith in the Messiah. Here we discover that Jesus is not an abstract philosophical example. Instead, He is a living person who, through the Holy Spirit, dwells in us and empowers us to live according to this high standard. Consequently, it is possible for believers to foster the same humble disposition modeled by the Savior. We look to Him for our inspiration and example. In short, genuine humility comes from allowing the fullness of the Son to be expressed in our daily lives.

B. The Son's Exaltation: vss. 9-11

Therefore God exalted him to the highest place and gave him the name that is above every name, that at the name of Jesus every knee should bow, in heaven and on earth and under the earth, and every tongue confess that Jesus Christ is Lord, to the glory of God the Father.

Paul could not end his extended illustration with the Messiah on the cross. The place of honor that Jesus willingly forsook was given back to Him with the added glory of His triumph over sin and death. In response to the Son's humility and obedience, the Father supremely exalted Jesus to a place where His triumph will eventually be recognized by all living creatures (Phil. 2:9). The apostle emphatically tells us that every person who has ever lived will someday recognize the Son for who He is, namely, the supreme Lord revealed in the Old Testament as Yahweh (see Acts 2:33-36). The "name of Jesus" (Phil. 2:10) signifies the majestic office or position the Father bestowed on the Son, not His proper name. By bowing their knees, every human being and angel will acknowledge Jesus' deity and sovereignty. Also, everyone will confess that Jesus is Lord—some with joyful faith, others with hopeless regret and anguish (vs. 11). Centuries earlier, the prophet Isaiah had announced the words of the Messiah: "Before me every knee will bow; by me every tongue will swear" (Isa. 45:23; see Rom. 14:11; Rev. 5:13). Philippians 2:6-11 affirms that this universal acknowledgment of Jesus' lordship will ultimately come to pass.

Following Paul's description of the supreme humility and obedience of Jesus' servanthood, the apostle charged his friends in Philippi to be as obedient as the Messiah was. When Paul labored among them, they obeyed his instructions. Moreover, they had followed the apostle's teachings after he had left. Now Paul told them to maintain their diligence in submitting themselves to God's Word. This was not so that they might earn their salvation but that they would express their salvation in such a way that the spiritual health of their Christian community would grow in unity. The apostle characterized how he expected them to act by adding the phrase "with fear and trembling" (vs. 12). He was not saying they should comply strictly out of fear of what God would do to them if they weren't obedient, but that they should strive to be Christlike while having reverence for the Lord. It is God who gives us the desire and power necessary to do His will (vs. 13).

Our great comfort in the Christian life is that God continually works His good and perfect will in us. We always live in tension between laboring for God and His kingdom as faithfully and diligently as we can, and allowing God to inspire and train us to do what He desires. We are not alone in the spiritual battle. After all, the Lord is present in our lives to build our confidence and give us the hope we need to fulfill His purposes for us and for His church. This is why we must be completely dependent upon God, especially if we are to be faithful to Paul's charge. While salvation is entirely a work of God and a free gift of His grace, it does require a response of obedient faith on our part. Also, while God deserves all the glory for our deliverance from sin, we are not totally passive in how the inner change affects our daily activities. Paul set a high standard for Christian humility, love, and unity. And the apostle knew that the Lord works in us, His spiritual children, to reach that standard successfully.

Discussion Questions

1. What effects does Jesus' humiliation have on the Christian's outlook on life? On the life of the church?
2. Why is it hard to live by the principle that exaltation follows humiliation?
3. Which is easier—to be humble before God or before other people?
4. How do we develop humility and dispose of selfish ambition?
5. How might your church's business meetings be different if Philippians 2:6-11 was read thoughtfully before the meeting started?

Contemporary Application

Have you ever seen an advertisement for a seminar on humility? There are lots of ads about how to be successful, how to get ahead, and how to be number one. But how to be humble? Forget it.

We need to understand the part humility should play in our daily interactions with people. When we are humble, we will pay closer attention to those around us and regularly ask God such questions as the following: How can I see this person's concerns as being as important as mine? What can I say to this person that would show Your love? How do You want me to use my time to serve his or her needs? Then we wait on the Lord to give us the answers, and we reach out in His name.

Admittedly, when we, as Christians, take seriously the high standards of the Gospel, we run smack into the world's way of thinking. That's why one of our most powerful influences in society is our model of humility. When people see Christians following the humility of the Savior, they cannot deny that Jesus makes a difference.

Our churches would also find larger responses if they were known as communities where people put the interests of others ahead of their own. Too often, it appears, the public sees more fighting than humility among God's people. Having the mind of Christ shapes the church and shakes the world.

Gaining in Jesus Christ

Scripture

Background Scripture: *Philippians 3:1-11*
Scripture Lesson: *Philippians 3:7-11*
Key Verse: *Whatever was to my profit I now consider loss for the sake of Christ.* Philippians 3:7.
Scripture Lesson for Children: *Matthew 18:10-14*
Key Verse for Children: *Your Father in heaven is not willing that any of these little ones should be lost.* Matthew 18:14.

Lesson Aim

To recognize the supreme value of knowing the Messiah as Lord.

Lesson Setting

Time: A.D. *61*
Place: Rome

Lesson Outline

Gaining in Jesus Christ

   I. Eternal Gains Outweighing Temporal Losses: Philippians 3:7-8
      A. *Counting Assets as Liabilities: vs. 7*
      B. *Regarding Everything As a Complete Loss: vs. 8*
  II. Fully Experiencing the Messiah: Philippians 3:9-11
      A. *Receiving Righteousness from the Messiah: vs. 9*
      B. *Personally Knowing the Messiah: vss. 10-11*

Introduction for Adults

Topic: *Gain and Loss*

Where do we meet the Lord today? Some people claim they can encounter Him in nature or experience Him by taking drugs (among various options). Gaining access to God is somehow thought to be a mystical experience reserved for a few privileged people who are into religion. Supposedly, all others are at a loss when it comes to knowing the Lord.

However, when we examine God's Word, we discover that the Savior wants all people to be in a personal relationship with Him. That's why the Father sent the Son to earth over two thousand years ago. Jesus loved us, died for us, and rose from the dead for us. In doing so, He made it possible for each of us to experience Him fully in our lives (Phil. 3:8, 10). This is no religious secret reserved for an elite class of individuals. It is plainly made known in the Bible.

In turn, our task is to help others come to know Jesus as their personal Savior. We can encourage them to put their trust in the Son and receive eternal life. When they do so, they will be given the righteousness that freely comes from God on the basis of faith (vs. 9).

Introduction for Youth

Topic: *Win or Lose?*

The only restrictions on youth used to be the age of driving, drinking, and voting. Today, the situation is different. The rules now extend to what adolescents can't wear to school, the weapons and drugs they can't carry into the building, the hours they can't keep, and the portable media devices they aren't allowed to use.

It seems as if teens have lost more privileges than they have won. Of course, it's no use arguing that the reason for some of these rules is to ensure the safety and well-being of young people. It's common knowledge that if some youth had not started to carry the habits of adult lawbreakers into high school, the rules would not be necessary.

Despite this seemingly restrictive situation, there's good news for Christian youth (as well as all other believers). Whatever they feel they've lost up to this point in their lives is more than offset by the eternal gains belonging to them as Jesus' followers. In fact, nothing this world has to offer or threatens to take away can compare with the treasure of personally knowing the Messiah as Lord.

Concepts for Children

Topic: *Finding the Lost One*

1. Jesus cares about each of us.
2. Even though Jesus is in heaven, He gives us His attention.
3. Jesus does not want bad things to happen to us.
4. Jesus is happy when we trust in Him.
5. Jesus wants us to ask others to believe in Him.

Lesson Commentary

I. ETERNAL GAINS OUTWEIGHING TEMPORAL LOSSES: PHILIPPIANS 3:7-8

A. Counting Assets as Liabilities: vs. 7

But whatever was to my profit I now consider loss for the sake of Christ.

Paul began Philippians 3 with the exhortation to his readers to "rejoice in the Lord" (vs. 1). Joy is a major theme that is stressed throughout the apostle's letter. In this instance, Paul encouraged his fellow Christians to rejoice because they belonged to the Lord Jesus. Such an experience would aid in protecting the apostle's readers from the legalism of his doctrinal enemies. He referred to them as "dogs" (vs. 2), those who do "evil," and "mutilators of the flesh." These words are harsh, yet they convey the seriousness with which Paul viewed the imminent threat to his spiritual children in Philippi.

"Judaizers" is the term used to refer to the enemies of the Gospel proclaimed by the apostle. These were legalistic Jews who insisted that all believers, regardless of their ethnicity, had to observe the ceremonial practices of the Old Testament in order to gain and maintain salvation. The Judaizers also declared that converted Gentiles had to be circumcised before they could be received into the church (see Acts 15:1-2). Moreover, the Judaizers rejected Paul's claim to be an apostle, arguing that he had diluted the Gospel by ignoring the requirements and customs of the Mosaic law (see 21:20-21).

Against this backdrop we can understand why Paul called the Judaizers "dogs" (Phil. 3:2). This was the term that orthodox Jews would call Gentiles, for they considered both Gentiles and dogs to be unclean, vicious scavengers. In a way, the apostle reversed the use of this derogatory term by applying it to those who insisted that Gentiles subject themselves to Jewish cleansing rites before they could become true Christians. Paul also may have used this word because these people harassed him at times during his missionary journeys (see 2 Cor. 11:13-15; Gal. 5:12). Perhaps this is what prompted the apostle to refer to his antagonists as doers of "evil" (Phil. 3:2). After all, the upshot of their troublesome actions and heretical teachings was injurious to the spiritual well-being of Jesus' followers.

Moreover, Paul called the legalists "mutilators of the flesh," in which the Greek word translated "mutilators" (literally, "to cut down or off") is an ironic play on the term rendered "circumcision" (literally, "to cut around"; vs. 3). This brings to mind the disfiguring injuries pagans inflicted on themselves as they participated in frenzied rituals (see 1 Kings 18:28). The apostle's sarcasm was appropriate, for the religious frauds demanded that all Christians be physically circumcised as a prerequisite for becoming holy and acceptable to God. The apostle did not attack circumcision itself, but rather the significance that the Judaizers placed upon it. On the one hand, Paul affirmed the propriety of the Jews to be circumcised. In fact, on at least one occasion he circumcised a believer when he thought it was appropriate (see Acts 16:3). On the other hand, the apostle objected to anyone teaching that righteousness comes through obeying a Jewish ceremony such as circumcision.

Paul transformed the meaning of circumcision from an external mutilation of the flesh, which could be done only to men, to the internal work of God's Spirit that marks every believer's union with the Father based on the Son's redemptive work (see Col. 2:11, 13). Paul declared that it is Jesus' disciples—namely, everyone worshiping and serving God by the power of His Spirit (see John 4:23-24)—who are the true "circumcision" (Phil. 3:3) and the real people of God (see Gal. 3:6–4:7). This included both believing Jews and Gentiles. Instead of bragging about what they have attained, they exulted in what the Lord Jesus had accomplished on their behalf through His atoning sacrifice at Calvary, resurrection from the dead, and ascension into heaven. Expressed differently, believers did not put any trust in their pious observance of religious rituals. Instead, they rejoiced in the fact that they had eternal life in spiritual union with the Redeemer (see 1 Cor. 1:31; 2 Cor. 10:17).

Paul indicated that he had plenty of reasons to put confidence in his personal ancestry and professional achievements, especially based on the Judaizers' standard of righteousness. As a matter of fact, no one was a more zealous defender of the Jewish laws and customs than had been the apostle. Moreover, whatever credentials the Judaizers claimed they had, Paul contended that he was far more qualified than any of them to speak as a Jew on matters of observing the Torah (Phil. 3:4). He began by noting that he was circumcised on the eighth day after his birth (vs. 5). The implication is that Paul's parents were devout Jews, who faithfully followed the Mosaic laws (see Gen. 17:12; 21:4; Lev. 12:3) and trained their son in his religious duties from the time he was an infant. How many of the apostle's detractors could say the same?

Next, Paul stressed his birthright as a Jew. Not only was he a member of God's chosen people by birth (see Rom. 9:3-4; 11:1), but he was also from the tribe of Benjamin. Jacob was the son of Isaac and the grandson of Abraham, and together these three men were the patriarchs of the nation of Israel. Jacob had twelve sons, two by his beloved wife, Rachel. The older was Joseph, and the younger was Benjamin (see Gen. 35:18, 24; 46:19; 1 Chron. 1:28; 2:1-2; Matt. 1:2; Luke 3:34). One of the twelve tribes of Israel was descended from Benjamin. Israel's first king was Saul, a Benjamite (see 1 Sam. 9:1-2; 10:20-21; Acts 13:21). When Israel divided into the northern kingdom of Israel and the southern kingdom of Judah, the tribe of Benjamin remained loyal to the tribe of Judah (see 1 Kings 12:20-24). Furthermore, Jerusalem and the temple in the holy city were located within the district of Benjamin (see Josh. 18:15-16).

Paul's list of credentials included being "a Hebrew of Hebrews" (Phil. 3:5). This meant, in part, that he was the Hebrew son of Hebrew parents (rather than merely a proselyte to the faith). In more contemporary parlance, one might say that Paul was a true or pure-blooded Hebrew—if one could ever be found. He was part of an elite group who had been taught Hebrew (or Aramaic), the ethnic language of the Jewish people, and schooled in the Jewish traditions (see Acts 22:2-3; Gal. 1:14). To his birth and training as a Jew, Paul added three personal achievements. Foremost, he was a Pharisee. Within the Jewish community, no group of people was more highly esteemed as strict observers of the law of Moses. In fact, Gamaliel, one of the most respected rabbis in the Pharisee party of the day, was Paul's mentor (see Acts 22:3; 23:6; 26:5).

Additionally, the former Pharisee demonstrated his fervor for the law by zealously persecuting Christians, whom he once believed were God's enemies (see 1 Cor. 15:9). The zealot not only denounced the followers of Jesus but also actively hunted them down in order to imprison and execute them (Phil. 3:6). As a matter of fact, before Paul's conversion, he would settle for nothing less than the total destruction of the church (see Acts 8:3; Gal. 1:13). In a way, Paul was even more blind to the truth of the Gospel than were the Judaizers. Finally, he said he was "faultless" (Phil. 3:6) according to the righteousness stipulated in the law. Put another way, if the law could produce righteousness in a person, then Paul would qualify, for by any human measure he was blameless in his observance of the Jewish commands and rituals.

Despite Paul's impeccable credentials, he rejected as inconsequential everything he had accomplished as an upstanding Jew before his dramatic encounter with Jesus the Messiah on the road to Damascus. In light of the Savior's work in the apostle's life, Paul considered his birth as a Benjamite Jew, his high standing in the party of the Pharisees, and even his scrupulous adherence to the Mosaic law to be ineffectual in securing his redemption. All that had been a "profit" (vs. 7) to Paul (and which the Judaizers prized) he counted as a "loss" due to his devotion to the Messiah. Expressed differently, what the apostle once regarded as sterling personal assets he now regarded as grave liabilities.

B. Regarding Everything as a Complete Loss: vs. 8

What is more, I consider everything a loss compared to the surpassing greatness of knowing Christ Jesus my Lord, for whose sake I have lost all things. I consider them rubbish, that I may gain Christ.

Paul candidly admitted that every single thing about which he once boasted as a Jew he now considered to be a "loss" (Phil. 3:8). This was especially so when compared to the far greater value of knowing the Messiah as "Lord." Likewise, the apostle welcomed, rather than resented, suffering the loss of "all things." Indeed, he regarded them as "rubbish." The underlying Greek noun was used in the vernacular of the day for fecal matter—that is, detestable excrement or worthless dung meant to be discarded in a sewer (see Isa. 64:6).

In Philippians 3:8, the Greek noun that Paul chose for "knowing" expresses the idea of understanding and perceiving an object in an intelligent manner. The word implies personal acquaintance, experience, and familiarity. Thus, when Paul spoke about "knowing" Jesus, the apostle was not just referring to gathering theological facts about the Son. More importantly, Paul had in mind *experientially* knowing the Messiah. In other words, the apostle desired to know Jesus in an ever-deepening personal union on a day-to-day basis. Furthermore, Paul wanted to have an ongoing relationship through his encounter with the Redeemer, especially as He worked in the apostle's life (see Jer. 31:34; Hos. 6:3; 8:2; John 10:27; 17:3; 2 Cor. 4:6; 1 John 5:20).

II. FULLY EXPERIENCING THE MESSIAH: PHILIPPIANS 3:9-11

A. Receiving Righteousness from the Messiah: vs. 9

And be found in him, not having a righteousness of my own that comes from the law, but that which is through faith in Christ—the righteousness that comes from God and is by faith.

Paul was now ready to press his point home. As righteous as he might have appeared in his relentless zeal to obey the Mosaic law, he now realized that true righteousness can come only "through faith in Christ" (Phil. 3:9). The latter refers to trusting in the Messiah for salvation. A less likely option is to translate the original as "through the faith [or faithfulness] of Christ," which emphasizes the steadfast obedience of the Savior (see 2:6-11).

The Judaizers had demanded that believers be ritually purified through circumcision. Paul's argument was that he was circumcised and did far more in his efforts to be justified under the Mosaic law. And yet none of that was of any value to God. The upshot is that no one can attain righteousness. Only God can offer it, and it is received when people believe in the Lord Jesus. The implication is that the merit arising from Jesus' atoning sacrifice is the basis of salvation. Moreover, faith is the means by which believers are joined to the Son and His merit. These truths were at the heart of Paul's teaching, and he wanted his Philippian friends to permanently establish them as the doctrinal cornerstone of their church.

In the New Testament, the Greek noun translated "righteousness" comes from a root term that means "straightness" and refers to that which is in accordance with established moral norms. In a legal sense, righteousness means to be vindicated or treated as just. From a biblical perspective, God's character is the definition and source of righteousness. As a result, the righteousness of human beings is defined in terms of God's holiness. Because the Lord solely provides righteousness, it cannot be produced or obtained by human efforts. God makes His righteousness available to all people without distinction. Just as there is no discrimination with Him in universally condemning all people as sinners, so God does not show partiality by offering righteousness to one particular ethnic group. The Lord freely gives it to all people—regardless of their race or gender—when they trust in the Messiah.

In the New Testament, a related Greek word is translated "justified." In Paul's day, it signified a court setting, with a judge declaring an individual to be "not guilty." The idea of justification comes from a judge pronouncing someone to be righteous or innocent of a crime. The word had a technical application of a one-time rendering of a positive judicial verdict. Paul used the term to refer to God's declaration that the believing sinner is righteous because of the atoning work of the Messiah on the cross. Without question, then, faith in the Lord Jesus was the sole basis for repentant sinners to be justified in God's sight (see Rom. 1:17; 3:21-26; 9:30-32; Gal. 2:16; 3:22).

B. Personally Knowing the Messiah: vss. 10-11

I want to know Christ and the power of his resurrection and the fellowship of sharing in his sufferings, becoming like him in his death, and so, somehow, to attain to the resurrection from the dead.

Amazingly, Paul wanted to know more about both Jesus' sufferings and His resurrection power. While many believers want more of His power, few would seem to crave "sharing in his sufferings" (Phil 3:10). Paul, however, regarded suffering for Christ as a sought-after privilege (see Rom. 8:17; 2 Cor. 12:10). The apostle understood that the power of Jesus' resurrection was rooted in His self-denial, which led to the cross. The Son taught that His followers would have to take up their own crosses (see Matt. 16:24; Mark 8:34; Luke 9:23). Paul realized there was spiritual power in participating in Jesus' sufferings. This was the reason the apostle willingly faced incredible hardships for the sake of the Gospel.

There were two realms, then, in which Paul wanted to grow in his knowledge of the Savior. The first included a personal awareness of the power that raised Jesus from the dead. To be specific, the apostle wanted to experience that power daily working in his life in order to bring about Jesus' righteousness in him (see Rom. 6:1-14; 2 Cor. 12:1-10; Eph. 1:18-23). Second, the apostle wanted to have fellowship with Jesus in His sufferings. The idea is that through Paul's own sharing in the adversity and anguish that came with being a committed believer, he would understand more fully the anguish Jesus endured on the cross. In the process, the Father would transform the apostle into the image of His Son (see Col. 1:24; 1 Thess. 1:6; Heb. 10:34; Jas. 1:2; 1 Pet. 4:12-16).

In all this, Paul wanted to conform to Jesus' death. The latter consisted of the apostle divesting himself of personal gains and regarding them as complete losses (Phil. 3:7-8). Being conformed to the Savior also involved crucifying the "sinful nature with its passions and desires" (Gal. 5:24). Paul's goal was not to languish moribund in a state of lifelessness. Rather, it was to be raised from the dead along with other believers on the day appointed by God (Phil. 3:11). At the Messiah's second advent, Paul would completely know Jesus as supreme Ruler and Redeemer.

On the one hand, the apostle was uncertain about the outcome of his current situation as a prisoner in Rome and how boldly he would witness for Christ in the face of impending execution. On the other hand, Paul had no doubt that he (and all believers) would be raised from death to life at the end of the age (see Dan. 12:2; John 5:29; Acts 24:15; Rom. 8:30-31; 1 Cor. 15:20-23; 1 Thess. 4:13-17; 2 Tim. 1:12; Rev. 20:4-15). In short, the apostle's confession of faith in the Messiah made it clear that salvation totally and without question depended on the atoning work of the Lord Jesus.

Discussion Questions

1. Which aspects of Paul's former life as a Pharisee would he have once considered to be an advantage?
2. How would you compare personal losses to gains that have resulted from your decision to follow Jesus?
3. Why did Paul supremely value knowing the Messiah as Lord?
4. What type of righteousness does a person need to possess in order to be saved?
5. What motivates you to serve Jesus and His followers?

Contemporary Application

A common practice is to divide the fundamental issues of human existence into three areas of investigation: (1) where we come from (that is, the origin of our existence); (2) why we are here (that is, the purpose of our existence); and (3) where we are going (that is, the ultimate destiny of our existence). This triad of issues deals, respectively, with the past, present, and future aspects of every individual's life.

The preceding breakdown can be seen in the faith journey of Paul, especially as he described it in Philippians 3. For instance, in the past, before he put his faith in Christ, Paul trusted in his human attainments (vss. 1-6). Then, after encountering the risen Lord on the road to Damascus (see Acts 9:3-5; 22:6-11; 26:12-18), the apostle wanted growing in the knowledge of Christ to be the central focus of his existence in the present (Phil. 3:7-11). Moreover, with the future looming over the horizon, Paul set his sights on increasing in Christlikeness (vss. 12-14).

While the apostle never forgot the lessons learned from his past (including his mistakes), he did not let these stymie his present efforts to know the Messiah more deeply and one day arrive at his future home in heaven. Indeed, Paul's discussion of the past, present, and future aspects of his life represents an affirmation of the lordship and centrality of the Savior in every area of human existence.

If we are honest with ourselves, we have to admit that our past personal and professional accomplishments are rubbish, or waste material. This is especially so when our present situation is focused on genuinely knowing the Lord Jesus. Indeed, experiencing Him fully in our lives has the potential to open the door to limitless future spiritual possibilities. As we allow the Savior's resurrection power to be at work in us, we are inspired to live uprightly, offer praise to the Lord, and serve others in a humble and sacrificial manner.

Stand Firm

Scripture

Background Scripture: *Philippians 3:12–4:1*
Scripture Lesson: *Philippians 3:12-16*
Key Verse: *Let us live up to what we have already attained.*
Philippians 3:16.
Scripture Lesson for Children: *Matthew 25:1-13*
Key Verse for Children: *Keep watch, because you do not know the day or the hour [when the Lord will come].*
Matthew 25:13.

Lesson Aim

To appreciate the necessity of moving ahead and maturing as Christians.

Lesson Setting

Time: A.D. *61*
Place: Rome

Lesson Outline

Stand Firm

I. Hastening Toward the Goal: Philippians 3:12-14
   A. *Pressing On to Christlike Maturity: vs. 12*
   B. *Maintaining a Single-Minded Determination: vss. 13-14*
II. Remaining Objective in Outlook: Philippians 3:15-16
   A. *Affirming the Biblical Perspective: vs. 15*
   B. *Heeding the Truth of Scripture: vs. 16*

Introduction for Adults

Topic: *Gaining the Prize*

Sadly, when people talk about "church," they often focus on programs, staff, buildings, and denominational differences. There's more than enough criticism to go around, which means outsiders are frequently turned off by what they see and hear.

However, the essence of the Christian life is none of these. Indeed, the previously mentioned concerns often get in the way of genuine, saving faith. The reality of the latter is demonstrated by trusting in Jesus and focusing one's life on obeying His will. In the case of Paul, he had to jettison a lot of religious baggage that kept him from knowing and serving the Lord. Saved adults have to do the same.

Striving to be Christlike is more important than anything else. If we find something in our lives that distracts us from anticipating the prize of spending eternity with the Savior, we have to discard it. This may mean radical changes for some people who have been in church for years. Regardless of the adjustments that need to be made, it is well worth it in order to become more conformed to Christ's glorious image.

Introduction for Youth

Topic: *Press On!*

Today's society puts a premium on knowledge. Futurists state that we are relentlessly pressing on from an industrial society to a paperless, information-based one. The image of this age is no longer the foundry or the assembly line but the microprocessor chip. Silicon, not steel, is the new king.

However, the question to this age is not "How do we process information now that computers have made it so plentiful and so easy?" but "How do we acquire knowledge? How do we learn?" Christians have always believed in sharing knowledge. In fact, it's known as witnessing. Paul, through his testimony, shared with the Philippians his knowledge of the Messiah. Saved teens can also share what they know with their peers by pointing the way to Jesus.

Concepts for Children

Topic: *Be Prepared*

1. One day, Jesus will return.
2. We want to be ready for Jesus' return.
3. The Holy Spirit is here to help us get ready.
4. We can tell others to get ready for Jesus' return.
5. Jesus is pleased when we help others to get ready.

Lesson Commentary

I. HASTENING TOWARD THE GOAL: PHILIPPIANS 3:12-14

A. Pressing On to Christlike Maturity: vs. 12

Not that I have already obtained all this, or have already been made perfect, but I press on to take hold of that for which Christ Jesus took hold of me.

In Philippians 3:7-11, Paul described the kind of knowledge about the Messiah the apostle desired to experience. Paul also wanted to correct any misconceptions the Philippians might have had about what he had previously said. He noted that he had not yet acquired a perfect knowledge concerning the Savior, nor was the apostle insinuating that he had reached a state of spiritual flawlessness. Instead, Paul was pursuing the redemption that the Son had attained for him—the redemption that the apostle would fully possess when the Father raises believers from the dead. On the one hand, the Messiah had already redeemed Paul. On the other hand, he recognized the need to "press on" (vs. 12) to the goal of reaching the level of Christlike maturity the Son had set for all His followers.

Paul used the metaphor of a race to illustrate what it means to wholeheartedly follow the Messiah. Both the Greeks and the Romans were avid fans of sporting contests. Sometimes the Roman games were violent and cruel, but often combatants merely engaged in feats of strength, endurance, and speed. Running was one of the more popular sports. When runners won their races, they may have won prizes of wealth. Of far more value to most of them, however, was the honored recognition they received. After each contest, a herald proclaimed the victor and his hometown, and a judge presented the athlete with a palm branch. At the conclusion of the games, each victor received a wreath made of olive or laurel leaves (see 3:14). According to Greek tradition, an oracle from the god Delphi had established this custom.

B. Maintaining a Single-Minded Determination: vss. 13-14

Brothers, I do not consider myself yet to have taken hold of it. But one thing I do: Forgetting what is behind and straining toward what is ahead, I press on toward the goal to win the prize for which God has called me heavenward in Christ Jesus.

Paul repeated his statement that he had not yet attained the spiritual perfection that comes only with the final resurrection. Moreover, the apostle emphasized to his "brothers" (Phil. 3:13) in Christ that human credentials are powerless in meriting God's favor. Assuredly, if Paul did not claim to be spiritually complete, then the Christians in Philippi (as well as the Judaizers) could not make such a boast. The latter notwithstanding, there still remained two initiatives that Paul and all other believers could undertake, especially as they strove with single-minded determination for the lofty goal of Christlike maturity held out before them.

First, believers could put their past behind them. For Paul, this included his abandoned career as a Jewish zealot and all his successes up to that point. Despite his outward attainments and dedication to the Mosaic law, he had failed to acquire God's favor or personal righteousness. Paul was not talking about obliterating the memories of his former life. Instead, he did not want to recall his bygone achievements with the intention of noting how they had contributed to his spiritual progress. Nor did the apostle want to dwell on his past sins (which may have included the execution of Christians), for God no longer held these transgressions against him.

Second, Paul and his fellow Christians in Philippi could strive for the future prize that awaited them, namely, the culmination or consummation of their salvation. The apostle used specific Greek words to draw a picture in the minds of his readers of an athlete who is participating in a running contest. Just as sprinters exert all of their efforts to push forward and reach the finish line, so Paul used every effort to drive himself forward in becoming more conformed to Christ's glorious image (see Rom. 8:29; 2 Thess. 2:14; 1 John 3:2). The great difference between races in a sporting event and the race Christians are running in is that a sporting event has only one winner. In the case of the Christian life, all who finish the race win (see 1 Cor. 9:24-27; 1 Tim. 6:12; Heb. 12:1).

Paul's utmost effort to win the prize was not to run faster or longer than all other Christians but to reach a common objective of being conformed to the glorious image of the Son. Expressed differently, the apostle was not trying to excel above all other believers but to win a prize that Jesus will award to all who run for Him (Phil. 3:14). Paul did not say exactly what the prize would be, but he did indicate that he would receive it in heaven in the presence of his Lord and Savior, Jesus Christ. Moreover, God was the one who called Paul to press on toward this objective (see Rom. 8:30; Gal. 1:15), which especially included becoming more Christlike. Furthermore, it was God who enabled the apostle to run the race (Phil. 1:6; 2:12-13). Thus, Paul fully participated in the race of the Christian life for the glory and honor of God.

Here we see that Paul's concept of the Christian life was that of a mountain climber who continually worked his way to the summit. He was not content to stop at a lower level of spiritual maturity. Moreover, the apostle regarded salvation not as an entry pass into a life of ease but as the beginning of a lifelong pursuit to achieve the Lord's will. Such a view transforms a dull, static concept of Christian living. We routinely ask ourselves whether we are becoming what Jesus wants us to be and achieving what He wants us to do. Behind these concerns is the reason Jesus saves us and makes us righteous. It's not for our self-fulfillment but for the accomplishment of His purposes. Jesus takes hold of every believer for a specific, lifelong objective. And when we discern and fulfill that aim, we enjoy the God-given blessing of ultimate satisfaction.

II. REMAINING OBJECTIVE IN OUTLOOK: PHILIPPIANS 3:15-16

A. Affirming the Biblical Perspective: vs. 15

All of us who are mature should take such a view of things. And if on some point you think differently, that too God will make clear to you.

Paul had plumbed new depths of spiritual insight and maturity, perhaps too deep for some of his fellow Christians to follow. Could everyone be as intense as he was in his pursuit of becoming more like the Savior and achieving His will? Possibly not. But those who had reached some degree of spiritual maturity could accept the apostle's testimony and teachings. Apparently, he was aware of some Philippian Christians who believed they had arrived spiritually. They may have looked down upon those who did not share their belief about themselves. In the apostle's subtle manner of rebuking this group, his statement about maturity was his way of regarding them as spiritually immature (Phil. 3:15). Paul was convinced that if a Christian was sincere in his or her desire to faithfully serve the Son, in time the Father would show that believer that everything the apostle said was true. In fact, he was so confident about the biblical basis for his teaching that he called upon God to correct those who disagreed with him.

B. Heeding the Truth of Scripture: vs. 16

Only let us live up to what we have already attained.

Undoubtedly, most of the Philippians agreed with Paul's primary teaching on the importance of pursuing Christlike maturity. But some might have questioned, or could not understand, the secondary points of what he had written. Again, the apostle felt that those who truly seek God's truth will be rewarded with the full measure of understanding. Paul recognized that God had imparted varying levels of spiritual insight to the members of the Philippian church. His instruction was that they put into practice the truths they had already learned (Phil. 3:16). In other words, he admonished them to walk according to what the Lord had taught them.

Neither the apostle nor anyone else can expect more from a Christian. In fact, to demand more is to overstep what the Holy Spirit is doing in that believer's life. This truth notwithstanding, Paul was confident that in time the Father would graciously help His spiritual children advance in their comprehension of what it means to know and serve the Son. This included all believers pressing on to spiritual maturity in light of what they already understood. The apostle's main point is that we must not quit. Neither should we give up our pursuit of conforming to the Son's glorious image. In short, the race goes on, one Spirit-empowered step at a time. As we live in obedient faith, the Son makes clear to us the full scope of why He has called us to Himself.

Paul trusted in God's sovereignty. For instance, the apostle believed God was in control not only of his life but also of the lives of the Christians in Philippi. Though some of the Philippians might have disagreed with Paul, he was confident that God would enlighten them to the truths he declared and change their behavior accordingly. Nevertheless, Paul's strong belief in God's sovereignty did not silence him. Put another way, the apostle did not think the best solution was to stand back and let the misunderstanding somehow resolve itself. Instead, since Paul knew that he had the gift of communicating God's truth, he voiced his views so these Christians would have the tools to advance in their walk with the Lord. Whether they used these tools was up to them.

Paul's plan was to humbly provide direction for God's flock in Philippi, while trusting that the Lord would use the apostle's efforts to bear fruit for the kingdom. For those who might think they had arrived at spiritual perfection, Paul pointed to his example as someone who had room to grow. Undoubtedly, the apostle had set an excellent example in these areas during the time he had spent laboring in the church in Philippi. So the Philippians clearly understood what he meant when he told them to consider him as a godly role model (vs. 17). Of course, they saw much more of him than is recorded in the Book of Acts. Nevertheless, Luke did provide us with an invaluable account of Paul's activities in Philippi, which the believers there could recall and imitate.

We learn that the apostle proclaimed the Gospel to nonbelievers and led them to the Lord (Acts 16:14-15). Furthermore, Paul combated evil and delivered a girl from a demon (vss. 16-18). Despite being unjustly flogged and imprisoned, the apostle prayed and sang praises to God (vss. 23-25). Paul showed compassion and concern toward his non-Christian jailer, who also became a believer because of the apostle's preaching (vss. 27-34). Though Paul suffered hardship, he encouraged his Christian brothers and sisters, thinking of their needs before his own (vs. 40).

In Philippians 3:18, Paul warned his readers about those whose lives dishonored "the cross of Christ." The identity of the antagonists remains uncertain. They could have been the Judaizers, who were a constant thorn in Paul's side. It is also possible that these enemies were professing believers who taught that the Messiah's work on the cross freed them from any moral restraints. Since Jesus had died for all of their sins and had saved their souls, these people reasoned, they then had a license to transgress with their bodies. They believed carnal sins could no longer stain their souls. If Paul had these people in mind, it would explain why he said they were obsessed with their appetites and lusts, prided themselves on their immorality, and were entirely focused on their sensual pursuits (vs. 19). Another uncertainty about these opponents is whether they were actually members of the Philippian church. It's conceivable that the apostle was warning the Philippians about a potential threat to their Christian community.

In any case, these bad examples were such a blight to the spread of the Gospel that Paul felt compelled to alert the Philippians to the danger in their midst. The fact that Paul had to tell his readers this once more in this letter was so grievous to him that it brought tears to his eyes. Whoever these enemies were, their fate was severe. If they continued to be unrepentant antagonists of the Son, the Father would eventually destroy them. In contrast to such an eternal future, heaven is the destiny of Jesus' true followers. Unlike His enemies, who are preoccupied with earthly things and pleasing themselves, Jesus' followers are focused on heavenly things, particularly on the Savior. Moreover, we anticipate that day when we will be with Him. For this reason Paul declared, "Our citizenship is in heaven" (vs. 20).

The apostle described Christians as pilgrims or colonists here on earth, yearning to be with our Savior in our true eternal home. Because heaven is the eventual dwelling place of believers, they should not live like those who fight against the Messiah by their immoral living. The believers' hope of the Son's return gives meaning and purpose to their Christian experience. Their focus is on Him, for they belong to Him and His kingdom. Likewise, they seek to obey the Savior and live in a godly manner, especially as they anticipate His return. Despite what enemies of the cross might assert to the contrary, Jesus' true followers remain firm in their conviction that being a citizen of heaven makes a difference here and now.

In Paul's day, most people in the Mediterranean world prized being a citizen of Rome because of the high status and favorable benefits conferred on Roman citizens. In fact, the people of Philippi were appreciative of this label since Philippi was officially a Roman colony and its citizens enjoyed special Roman privileges. When the apostle was beaten and arrested in Philippi and he disclosed that he was a Roman citizen, the magistrates of the city were alarmed by what they had done to him and therefore tried to appease him (see Acts 16:37-39). Yet Paul did not place the highest value on his Roman citizenship. The only citizenship that had lasting meaning to him was his citizenship in heaven (Phil. 3:20).

The apostle assured his readers that their hope of one day being in heaven was not wishful thinking. Indeed, the power that will make our hope a reality is that associated with Jesus' commands, and His power is absolute. In fact, the Redeemer will wield His power to subdue all earthly authorities and spiritual forces, placing all things under His command on the day of our homecoming in heaven. Moreover, the Savior will use His power to change us. We will no longer have a body with a sinful nature, but we will have a new body like the one belonging to the Messiah. It will be a truly wonderful day when Jesus transforms our bodies into the likeness of His glorious body so we can be free from all sins and bodily weaknesses (vs. 21).

In 4:1, Paul addressed his readers in Philippi with several endearing phrases. He called them his "brothers" and "dear friends." The apostle told them that he loved them and longed to see them. He described them as his joy and crown. Paul could have commanded them to stand firm in the Lord. Instead, based on the preceding truths he shared, he encouraged them with fatherly affection to be strong and faithful in the Lord Jesus, even in the midst of all their troubles and hardships. The way Paul instructed the Philippians is a powerful example of how Christians can build one another up in their unity in the Messiah.

Discussion Questions

1. Why would it have been inappropriate for Paul to claim he had achieved full spiritual maturity?
2. What are some ways that believers can press on to spiritual maturity?
3. Why is it important for believers to put their pasts behind them, especially as they become more Christlike?
4. What was the nature of the heavenly "prize" (Phil. 3:14) that Paul strove to receive?
5. How would you summarize the biblical point Paul was making to his readers in verse 15?

Contemporary Application

Today, when journalists write about Charles Colson, many refer to him as an indicted former member of President Richard Nixon's White House, a man who served time in prison for his role in the Watergate scandal. Watergate, however, was almost four decades ago, and Charles Colson has done much in the intervening years.

After becoming a believer in prison, Colson wrote a string of bestselling books about the Christian life, founded the International Prison Fellowship Ministries, became a highly regarded speaker, and received the prestigious Templeton Prize for Progress in Religion. Those are some incredible achievements. But the media seems stuck in the past.

Sometimes Christians can also remain stuck in the past. Unless we learn to leave the failings of our past behind, we risk overlooking the rewards God has for our future. These are the eternal, heavenly blessings Paul had in mind in the Scripture passage for this week's lesson.

If anyone had a past to dwell on, it was Paul. As a former persecutor of Christians, Paul had dragged believers off to jail and stood by approvingly as Stephen, the first recorded Christian martyr, was stoned to death. Paul once tried to destroy the church he later helped to build. It took an encounter with the risen Lord Jesus to turn Paul's life around. Thankfully, Paul had learned not to dwell on the failings of his past. Instead, he said, "I press on" (Phil. 3:14) while keeping his eyes on heaven and the future.

Likewise, God has called us to run for Him. He wants us to strive for the prize that awaits us in Christ Jesus and to put forth every ounce of effort to attain the goal God has set before us. The Lord will reward us with a prize of far greater worth than anything we could possibly receive on earth.

The Supremacy of Christ

DEVOTIONAL READING

Ephesians 1:17-23

DAILY BIBLE READINGS

Monday January 28
  *Ephesians 1:17-23 Christ,
  the Head of the Church*

Tuesday January 29
  *Revelation 1:1-6 Christ, the
  Firstborn of the Dead*

Wednesday January 30
  *John 17:20-26 Christ, One
  with the Father*

Thursday January 31
  *2 Corinthians 5:16-21
  Christ, the Reconciler to God*

Friday February 1
  *Romans 5:15-21 Christ, the
  Channel of God's Grace*

Saturday February 2
  *Matthew 4:18-25 The
  Compelling Call of Christ*

Sunday February 3
  *Colossians 1:15-20 The
  Person and Work of Christ*

Scripture

Background Scripture: *Colossians 1:15-20*
Scripture Lesson: *Colossians 1:15-20*
Key Verse: *For God was pleased to have all his fullness dwell in him.* Colossians 1:19.
Scripture Lesson for Children: *Matthew 4:18-22*
Key Verse for Children: *[Jesus said to Simon and Andrew],
"Come, follow me." . . . At once they . . . followed him.*
Matthew 4:19-20.

Lesson Aim

To emphasize that reconciliation to the Father is possible only through faith in the Son.

Lesson Setting

Time: A.D. 60
Place: Rome

Lesson Outline

The Supremacy of Christ

  I. Jesus, the Sovereign: Colossians 1:15-18
     A. *The Image of God: vs. 15*
     B. *The Creator and Sustainer of All Things: vss. 16-17*
     C. *The Head of the Church: vs. 18*

  II. Jesus, the Peacemaker: Colossians 1:19-20
     A. *The Divine-Human Messiah: vs. 19*
     B. *The Reconciler of All Things: vs. 20*

Introduction for Adults

Topic: *Awed by Greatness*

Tony had a business associate who wanted to discuss religion in general. Tony, though, gently refused. Instead, he faithfully talked about his awe for the greatness of Jesus, whom Paul revealed is the "firstborn over all creation" (Col. 1:15).

During one conversation, Tony left his peer with the question, "Do you have eternal life?" Tony explained that the issue is new life through faith in the Creator, not religion (see vs. 16). One day several months later, the same individual came to Tony and exclaimed, "I've got life!" He meant he had trusted in Jesus for salvation.

The supremacy of the Son in our lives begins when we put our faith in Him as our Lord and Savior. After all, no other person could have died for our sins and reconciled us to the Father (see vs. 20). Because Jesus is God the Son, the Father accepted nothing less than the sacrifice of His Son. Therefore, only through Jesus can we become members of God's spiritual family.

Introduction for Youth

Topic: *Eternal Ruler*

One day a disciple of Jesus named Philip said, "Lord, show us the Father and that will be enough for us" (John 14:8). Many young people are asking for the same sort of thing. They want to see authentic Christianity lived by those who claim to be followers of the eternal Creator and Ruler (see Col. 1:16). They are not directly demanding to see the "invisible God" (vs. 15), but they rightly expect to see Him in the lives of those who say they are believers.

The Son is the only one who perfectly bore the Father's glorious "image." Even so, Paul revealed that in union with the Messiah, we likewise can be regarded as God's holy children. As others see the presence of the Son in us, they get a taste of what it means to see the Father's image.

Jesus said that He would unveil Himself to others by living in us. He promised to show Himself when we love and obey Him. The implication is that younger and older believers alike stand in the gap between God and an unbelieving world.

Concepts for Children

Topic: *A Hero to Follow*

1. For some time, Jesus told people about the Good News of the kingdom.
2. One day, Jesus walked along the shore of Lake Galilee.
3. Jesus invited several people to become His followers.
4. These people were excited to follow Jesus.
5. Jesus also wants us to become His followers.

Lesson Commentary

I. JESUS, THE SOVEREIGN: COLOSSIANS 1:15-18

A. The Image of God: vs. 15

He is the image of the invisible God, the firstborn over all creation.

The Greek historian Herodotus once called Colossae "a great city of Phrygia." His statement is understandable since Colossae was situated on the most important trade route between Ephesus and the Aegean Sea to the west, and the Euphrates River to the east. Traders and armies journeyed on this route. In addition, Colossae was built near the southern bank of the Lycus River, an ideal region for grazing sheep. Consequently, its chief commercial business was the weaving industry.

By Paul's day, however, Colossae had declined in its importance. By the first century B.C., it was simply a market town in the Roman province of Asia (near the modern town of Denizli in Turkey). Its population comprised people from Greek, Phrygian, and Jewish backgrounds. Meanwhile, the neighboring cities of Laodicea and Hierapolis had far surpassed Colossae in prosperity and political importance. Laodicea was about 10 miles from Colossae, while Hierapolis was 13 miles away. Christians established churches in all three towns (see Col. 4:13).

Paul wrote Colossians while under house arrest in Rome. The apostle began this letter with thanksgiving for what the Father had done in raising up the church at Colossae (1:3-8). Paul reminded the believers in the city about their priceless spiritual heritage. Then he penned a magnificent prayer for them (vss. 9-14). He concluded his prayer with thanksgiving for the Father's deliverance of believers from the power of darkness, as well as for redeeming and forgiving them in the Son. This majestic spiritual reality led the apostle to comment on the supremacy of the Messiah over all creation (vss. 15-28).

Paul's teaching about the person and work of the Son was needed at Colossae because the church was plagued by religious frauds. They tried to convince believers to venerate a cadre of inferior created beings and angelic mediators, rather than the Savior (see 2:8, 18). The apostle reminded his readers that the Son is the full and final revelation of the Father and that all human ideas must be brought into subjection to the Son. In brief, the only adequate response to heretical teaching is a correct understanding of, and commitment to, Jesus as the supreme Creator and Redeemer (see Eph. 1:20-23; Phil. 2:6-11).

Some experts think Colossians 1:15-20 was originally part of an ancient Christian hymn or poem. If so, it may have been used as a creedal confession during worship. Paul may have expanded certain parts of the hymn to clarify the truth about the Messiah that the counterfeit teachers in Colossae were disputing. There is considerable debate as to how many stanzas there are in this hymn and how the lines should be broken down. The following arrangement has been suggested by several Bible scholars. Stanza one (vss. 15-16) praises Jesus Christ as the one who brought the universe into existence. He is the Lord over all things. Stanza two (vss. 17-18a) professes Jesus Christ as the one who unifies the universe. He is the Head of the church. Stanza three (vss. 18b-20) proclaims Jesus Christ as the one who reconciles the universe through the sacrifice of His life on the cross. He is our Redeemer.

In verse 15, Paul declared the personhood of the Messiah, namely, that "He is the image of the invisible God." The Son is not merely a reflection or copy of the Father, whom no one can see with their physical eyes. Nor does the Son simply represent the Father. The Greek noun rendered "image" means "likeness" or "manifestation of" and indicates that the Son is the perfect embodiment of the Father's character and nature. In contrast, human beings are made in the image of God (see Gen. 1:26-27; 5:1; 9:6). In this sense, we reflect the Father's character in finite ways. For example, God is all-powerful, but we have some power; God is all-knowing, while our knowledge is limited; and God is everywhere, yet we can be in only one place at one time. While Jesus' human nature is characterized by these sorts of limitations, His divine nature has no such limitations. This is the difference between people being made in the image of God and Jesus being the visible image of the unseen God.

Moreover, the Son is "the firstborn over all creation" (Col. 1:15). In some contexts, the Greek adjective rendered "firstborn" denoted what was first in order of time. By way of example, in Paul's day the term was used to refer to a firstborn child. In other contexts, the term referred to someone who was preeminent in rank. For instance, when Isaiah spoke about "the poorest of the poor" (Isa. 14:30), he used a Hebrew noun that literally means "firstborn." The second usage best fits the context of Colossians 1:15, in which Paul emphasized the priority of the Son's rank over creation. So, when the apostle referred to the Messiah as "the firstborn over all creation," he did not mean that the Son was the first creature the Father brought into being, but rather that the Son reigns supreme over all that exists.

B. The Creator and Sustainer of All Things: vss. 16-17

For by him all things were created: things in heaven and on earth, visible and invisible, whether thrones or powers or rulers or authorities; all things were created by him and for him. He is before all things, and in him all things hold together.

In Paul's song, he continued to praise the Son by declaring His unique creative powers. Nothing that has been brought into existence—whether dwelling in heaven or inhabiting the earth, whether visible or imperceptible to our eyes—has come into being without the Son's involvement. Moreover, the apostle stressed the Son's preeminence over the angelic realm. As noted earlier, within the Colossian heresy was the worship of angels. By listing the perceived hierarchy of angels ("thrones or powers or rulers or authorities," Col. 1:16), Paul attacked the systematic division of the angelic realm. Since the apostle referred to the visible as well as the invisible, this hierarchy probably includes human institutions. Paul exposed as foolish any homage to human or angelic authority because, in fact, Jesus is Lord over them all.

Indeed, the Father formed the creation not only through His Son but also for His Son. Thus, the ultimate purpose of creation is the Messiah Himself. According to God's redemptive plan, He designed the world in such a way that it can have real meaning only in the Son.

Paul noted two more traits about the Son's divine nature in relationship to creation. First, He eternally preexisted before the Father made all things (vs. 17). Several times in this hymn the apostle used the phrase "all things" or words to that effect (see vss. 15, 16, 17, 18, 20). Paul was repeatedly stressing that the Messiah is supreme over whatever exists, and in this instance the Son was forever with the Father and the Spirit prior to the creation event.

Second, the apostle affirmed the Son as the sustainer of all creation (vs. 17). The writer of Hebrews also elaborated on this theme when he noted that the Son is the outshining of the Father's glory, perfectly represents His essence, and upholds the cosmos by His "powerful word" (Heb. 1:3). Deists believe that God created the world and then left it alone, allowing it to run on its own. In direct contradiction to this belief, Scripture makes it clear that the Son maintains His creation and bears it along to its divinely appointed destiny. If He were to abandon it, utter chaos would result and the world would simply stop existing.

C. The Head of the Church: vs. 18

And he is the head of the body, the church; he is the beginning and the firstborn from among the dead, so that in everything he might have the supremacy.

Next in Paul's hymn, the apostle praised the Son for His character and redemptive work. The false teachers in Colossae denied the supreme importance of the Messiah. The apostle may have expanded on the original poem to spotlight the Messiah's preeminent position as the ruler over God's people and the Son's incomparable work as the reconciler of all creation. By doing this, Paul assured his readers that their faith in the Lord Jesus was not in vain, despite the clever yet deceptive doctrines of the Colossian heretics.

In Ephesians 5:23, Paul noted that "Christ is the head of the church, his body." But in Colossians 1:18, Paul reversed the order of the objects of "the head." Here, the "body" is listed before what it represents, namely, the church. In the context of the Ephesian letter, Paul was making an analogy between a husband's relationship with his wife and the Messiah's relationship with His church. But in the context of the Colossian letter, the apostle was pointing to Jesus' sovereignty—first, as He relates to the church, and second, as He relates to everything else. Nonetheless, both passages stress Jesus' divine authority, under which we are all His subjects.

Paul noted that the Son marks a new beginning for humanity. In a sense, Jesus was like Reuben, who was the patriarch Jacob's "firstborn" (Gen. 49:3). As Reuben was the beginning of Jacob's children, so the Son is the beginning of a new generation of redeemed people. In Romans 8:29, Paul noted that those whom the Father "foreknew" He additionally decided from the outset to become like His Son, so that

He would be the first among a cohort of spiritual brothers and sisters. Furthermore, the apostle noted in Colossians 1:18 that the Son was the first to be raised from the dead. In fact, He will never die again. Because of the resurrection of Jesus' body, those who trust in the Messiah for salvation will also be raised from the dead. This corresponds to what Paul declared in 1 Corinthians 15:20. We learn that the risen Lord is "the firstfruits of those who have fallen asleep." Moreover, the Son reigns supreme because He conquered all of the Father's enemies, the last being death (vss. 25-27). In short, the Messiah holds first place in all things (Col. 1:18).

II. JESUS, THE PEACEMAKER: COLOSSIANS 1:19-20

A. The Divine-Human Messiah: vs. 19

For God was pleased to have all his fullness dwell in him.

Paul next articulated another key doctrine, that is, the deity of the Son. The apostle reaffirmed this central truth of the Christian faith later in this letter (see Col. 2:9). When Paul said the Father was pleased to have all the fullness of the Godhead dwell in the Son, the apostle implied that Jesus completely and permanently possesses all the attributes of God. Expressed differently, the Redeemer is God. Yet, in 1:19, Paul was not merely stating a Christian creed but also deepening its theological meaning. The apostle noted the Father's pleasure in having His full divine nature reside in His Son, the Lord Jesus.

B. The Reconciler of All Things: vs. 20

And through him to reconcile to himself all things, whether things on earth or things in heaven, by making peace through his blood, shed on the cross.

Furthermore, Paul praised the Messiah not only as divine ruler but also as supreme reconciler (Col. 1:20). What the Messiah accomplished is equally important as who He is. It is only through the Son that the Father reconciled everything to Himself. No imagined deity, no mythical angel, and no celebrated human being could have achieved what the Savior did. This statement was a reminder to the Colossians to rebuke any self-stylized expert who taught otherwise. In this ancient hymn, Paul declared that the Lord Jesus is the reconciler of all things. The apostle probably added the phrase "whether things on earth or things in heaven" to this Christian sonnet. It is a further defining of the "all things" just mentioned and Paul's way of affirming that the Messiah's reconciling work affects everything. In short, nothing is beyond the reaches of the Son's redemptive work.

Some modern interpreters of the Bible understand verse 20 to mean that Jesus has saved everyone who has and ever will be born. In fact, they use this verse to support their doctrine of universalism—namely, the teaching that the Messiah will redeem every human being and even all angels, including those who have fallen. Paul, however, was not speaking about everlasting redemption but of the subjugation of all human and heavenly beings to their rightful position as God's subjects.

Thus, the Son has rendered all the Father's enemies powerless. And where does this event take place? It occurs at the cross, where the Son shed His blood and gave His life so that we might have peace with the Father. Indeed, Jesus accomplished two goals on the cross. First, He cleansed us of our sins in order to bring us into His kingdom. Second, He defeated all our enemies so that nothing can stand between us and the Father (see Rom. 8:38-39).

Paul's theology of the cross is that believers now have peace with the Father and that nothing can disturb that peace. The Son has also overcome the world and reconciled it to the Father. Where once the terrible prospect of the Father's wrath remained (see John 3:36; Rom. 9:22; Eph. 2:3), now through the Son's reconciliation, peace is made and remains (see Rom. 5:1; 8:1). Hostility is canceled out. The fact that Paul started every one of his letters with a greeting of grace and peace highlights the importance of this theological truth. Our peace with the Father is not a truce. After all, a truce is passive, implying that the parties cease and desist from their antagonistic actions. Peace, however, is active. The Father wants us to be mindful of the activity of His peace in our lives whenever we're anxious (see Phil. 4:6-7) or afraid or discouraged (see John 14:27). Our peace with the Father affects our peace with each other. And peace becomes one of the guiding rules of conduct in our relationships (see Rom. 12:18; 1 Thess. 5:13).

After Paul recorded the preceding Christian hymn, along with his expanded statements, he applied its theological professions to the personal lives of his readers in Colossae. To the apostle, the doctrine of reconciliation must have a practical application in terms of how we relate to the Father and to one another. This must happen if the power of the cross is to have real meaning in the lives of believers. In addition, Paul probably wanted to demonstrate the sharp contrast between the impersonal speculations of the Colossian heretics and the relational transformations produced by the Gospel. In stressing how his readers were to identify with the doctrinal declarations of the hymn, the apostle began by calling the Colossians' attention to their previous spiritual condition. In fact, he noted three descriptive aspects of their past lostness.

Paul's readers were once "alienated from God" (Col. 1:21). Like these believers before their conversion, non-Christians today are estranged from God, entirely unimpressed with His holiness and persistently divorced from His righteousness. Second, the apostle's readers were formerly "enemies in [their] minds." They were not just indifferent to the Father but hostile to Him and everything He stood for. They were not just passive in their rejection of the Messiah but were actively opposing His will and commandments. Their minds plotted against the Father, which fallen human nature invariably does when people are estranged from the Creator.

Third, the recipients of Paul's letter were previously engaged in "evil behavior." Being separated from God and opposed to His will naturally led them to acts of disobedience. People today may not worship pagan idols, but they may have devoted their lives to acquiring wealth, seeking the perfect human relationship, and other unstable forms of security. Evil deeds and bad thinking always result from a life lived apart from the Messiah.

Discussion Questions

1. In what sense is Jesus the visible "image" (Col. 1:15) of the unseen God?
2. Why is it important for believers to emphasize that Jesus created all things?
3. How can Jesus' followers draw comfort from the truth that He is the Head of the church?
4. How does reconciliation between the Father and His spiritual children occur?
5. What sort of "peace" (vs. 20) did Jesus' shed blood establish?

Contemporary Application

The Samurai is one of the most widely acclaimed novels in Japan. It takes place in seventeenth-century Japan, just before the military rulers of that era outlawed Christianity there. The story focuses on a European monk and a Japanese warrior by the name of Hasekura Rokuemon, who has no control over the political forces that ultimately destroy his life.

Toward the beginning of the book is a memorable scene in which Hasekura gazes at an image in a monastery of Jesus on the cross and is repulsed by this sight. In Hasekura's mind, it was beyond comprehension that Christians could worship such a pathetic figure—supposedly a God who allowed Himself to be humiliated in such a shameful way. Indeed, the warrior reasons, dying in this way proved that Jesus was no God. He was certainly not worthy to be anyone's Lord.

Later, Hasekura realizes that his superiors have plotted his ruin and disgrace in order to achieve their own ends. It is then that the samurai's understanding of Jesus begins to change. With the help of the Portuguese monk, Hasekura puts his faith in the Messiah for salvation. The Japanese warrior has come to see that only through Jesus' death on the cross could he triumph over his own social dishonor and finally be at peace with the heavenly Father.

The shame of the cross is real. In fact, while Jesus died, people scorned and ridiculed Him. They also challenged Him to demonstrate His divine powers and liberate Himself from the agony of crucifixion. That Jesus refused is, indeed, the power and glory of His atonement.

Full Life in Christ

Scripture

Background Scripture: *Colossians 2:6-15*

Scripture Lesson: *Colossians 2:6-15*

Key Verse: *You have been given fullness in Christ, who is the
head over every power and authority.* Colossians 2:10.

Scripture Lesson for Children: *Matthew 8:1-4*

Key Verse for Children: *Jesus reached out his hand and
touched the [leper]. . . . Immediately he was cured of his lep-
rosy.* Matthew 8:3.

Lesson Aim

To recognize that the truth about the Son exposes false
religious ideas.

Lesson Setting

Time: A.D. *60*
Place: Rome

Lesson Outline

Full Life in Christ

I. Spiritual Fullness in the Son: Colossians 2:6-10
    A. *Living in the Son: vs. 6*
    B. *Becoming Rooted and Grounded in the Son: vs. 7*
    C. *Rejecting False Teachings: vs. 8*
    D. *Affirming the Son's Deity: vss. 9-10*

II. Spiritual Victory in the Son: Colossians 2:11-15
    A. *Deliverance from the Sinful Nature: vss. 11-12*
    B. *Forgiveness of Sins: vss. 13-14*
    C. *Triumph over Rulers and Authorities: vs. 15*

Introduction for Adults

Topic: *It's a Wonderful Life!*

A young father of two children lost his wife when their second child was born. One night as the grieving father was praying for strength, God directed him to Colossians 2:10. The Lord reminded him through this verse that he was spiritually complete in the Savior, despite the death of his wife.

The Holy Spirit touched this struggling believer. He confessed that he did not need anything more than what he had in Jesus—not even a wife and mother for his children. God comforted the young father with the wonderful fullness of life he already had through faith in the Son. The believer's heart and mind came to rest and peace.

Too often, it seems, we come to God with complaining spirits. That's why we need to bolster our minds with the truths of God's Word about our spiritual resources. Sometimes the Father has to strip us spiritually bare (as it were) before we come to grips with the fact that the Son is more than sufficient to meet all of our needs.

Introduction for Youth

Topic: *360° of Living*

Both inside and outside the church the presence of commitment is seriously lacking. People shun obligation because they think it will prevent them from doing what they want in order to enjoy a whole or complete life. This attitude is extremely harmful among Christians who profess to believe in the vital doctrines of the faith.

For instance, a hesitancy to stand firmly on the truth of the Gospel can lead to spiritual confusion. It is only when we, as believers, preserve the integrity of the Good News that the doctrinal foundation of the church will withstand the attacks of spiritual frauds.

That is why Paul warned the Colossians not to turn away from the Savior and be taken in by the false teachings of the world. The apostle declared that the Son is God. In Him is the power to cleanse people of their sins and raise them from the dead into everlasting fellowship with the Father. Moreover, Jesus triumphed over evil when He willingly gave Himself up on the cross.

Concepts for Children

Topic: *The Divine Healer*

1. Jesus came down from being on a mountain.
2. There were many people following Jesus.
3. A man with a skin disease asked Jesus to heal him.
4. Jesus said He would heal the man.
5. Jesus also wants to help us with our problems.

Lesson Commentary

I. SPIRITUAL FULLNESS IN THE SON: COLOSSIANS 2:6-10

A. Living in the Son: vs. 6

So then, just as you received Christ Jesus as Lord, continue to live in him.

Paul was primarily concerned with a heresy that had crept into the Colossian church. Some false teachers were evidently promoting an extreme form of Judaism, which demanded strict adherence to rituals and regulations. Other false teachers were introducing elements of early Gnosticism, a belief system that diminished the supremacy of the Messiah. Paul argued brilliantly in this letter that the Son is indeed truly divine, uniquely sovereign, and entirely capable as the reconciler of sinful humanity to the Father.

Colossians 2:3 states that the Son is the reservoir of all of the Father's wisdom and knowledge. The embodiment of this invaluable knowledge, which Paul called "the mystery of God" (vs. 2), is Jesus Christ. The apostle was referring to knowing who the Messiah truly is and what He has really accomplished. Here we see that Paul's objective in ministry was to reveal the Father's eternal plan of redemption in the Son. As was noted in lessons 1 and 5, the Greek noun rendered "mystery" is a truth that was once undisclosed but has now been made known through the Messiah. With His advent, the divine secret is meant to be understood by all believers (see Rom. 16:25-27; Col. 1:25-27). In Paul's day, so-called "mystery" cults were widespread throughout the Western world. The apostle often used the Greek noun rendered "mystery" to provide a counterpoint to the false doctrine that only a small circle of initiates possessed ultimate truth. Instead, he taught that the Son's earthly ministry, death, burial, and resurrection have fully unveiled the Father's once mysterious plan. According to the apostle, this mystery included various aspects of the truth that is found in the Messiah: (1) the incarnation of the Son (1 Tim. 3:16); (2) the eternal ramifications of Jesus' death and resurrection (1 Cor. 15:51); and (3) the comprehensiveness of Jesus' atoning work (Eph. 3:2-6).

In Colossians 2:4, Paul rebuked the heretics. They prided themselves on being spiritually wiser, aggressively promoted their false doctrines about the Messiah, and verbally assaulted Paul's reputation and teachings among the Colossian believers. However convincing these determined troublemakers were with their seemingly credible assertions, the apostle warned his readers not to be tricked into believing their claims. Undoubtedly, Paul would have preferred to be with the believers living in Colossae so that he could deal directly with their problems. But, of course, his Roman imprisonment prohibited him from performing this pastoral duty. Presumably, the apostle was confident that his spiritual presence would arouse their respect for his authority. Hopefully, this respect would spur them on to follow his written instructions eagerly and carefully. Therefore, he reminded them that he was among them, not physically, but certainly in spirit (Col. 2:5).

For the time being, Paul expressed his pleasure with the "orderly" conduct of his readers. The apostle was drawing from a military image to describe how they unified their ranks against the Messiah's foes. As a matter of fact, the religious frauds were not able to break the morale of the Colossians. In addition, Paul commended them on how they stood steadfastly in their faith in the Son. It is evident from the apostle's remarks that the heresies he condemned in this letter had not engulfed the Colossian congregation. However, Paul was intent on equipping them with doctrinal arguments that would demolish the theological claims of the false teachers among them. A unified front, empowered by the Holy Spirit, is by far the strongest weapon against falsehood that Christians have at their disposal.

Despite Paul's praise for the believers in Colossae, he still felt compelled to admonish them to keep away from the forces that wanted to lead them astray. When the apostle's readers first heard the Good News about the Savior, they embraced it with joy and zeal. But perhaps their initial enthusiasm had started to fade. For this reason, Paul urged them to draw upon deeper spiritual resources as they continued to anchor their lives in the Son (vs. 6). It is all too common for many believers to go through a so-called "honeymoon period" just after conversion. During this time, the new believers might begin to feel invulnerable to emotional or spiritual pain and expect these feelings to last a lifetime. After a while, however, as the pressures of following the Savior begin to mount, the pain inevitably comes. A mark of spiritual maturity is to let go of false expectations and to keep growing despite temporary discomforts.

B. Becoming Rooted and Grounded in the Son: vs. 7

Rooted and built up in him, strengthened in the faith as you were taught, and overflowing with thankfulness.

What does it mean to live our spiritual lives in the Son? Paul provided three answers to this question. First, we are to be "rooted and built up" (Col. 2:7) in the Redeemer. This phrase brings two pictures to mind. One is of a plant rooted in the ground. The other is of a structure being built above ground. This mixed metaphor actually combines two important features of the growth of one's Christian faith. At the same time we are growing upward in the Savior, our roots in the faith should also be deepening. Second, we are to be "strengthened in the faith." Specifically, Paul was exhorting the Colossian believers to rely on the teachings Epaphras had given them. These instructions were consistent with what the apostle had taught and were certainly in harmony with other biblical teachings. Expressed differently, they were to stay committed to the truth of the Gospel, which empowered them to live in harmony with the Father's will.

Third, we are to be "overflowing" with gratitude. This includes being thankful that Jesus died for our sins and now lives in us. For these and other reasons, we should show our appreciation to the Father and the Son (along with the Spirit) in all that we do. Paul prayed that this attitude would mark the lives of the Christians in Colossae. This attitude should most certainly mark the lives of believers today, too. As before, Paul's objective in giving this much emphasis to the Messiah was so that people would come to know Him and devote their lives to Him. With respect to the Colossian believers, the apostle wanted them to understand who Jesus truly is and what He had done for them. This knowledge would protect them from doctrinal error and invigorate their faith. This type of knowledge can do the same for us who are rooted and grounded in Christ.

C. Rejecting False Teachings: vs. 8

See to it that no one takes you captive through hollow and deceptive philosophy, which depends on human tradition and the basic principles of this world rather than on Christ.

Paul warned the believers in Colossae not to be fooled into believing the deceitful doctrines of the false teachers who had slipped in among them. Quite possibly, these heretics were present when the apostle's letter was read to the church members and were livid at hearing his censure of them. Nevertheless, Paul was not one who made any effort to spare the feelings of those who tried to lead believers into doctrinal or moral error. The apostle's language in Colossians 2:8 vividly portrays the consequence of being misled by a philosophy that is empty of any value and deceptive in its intent. Those who were captivated by it are like people who are kidnapped or captured during a war. In short, the false teachers were spiritual enemies who treacherously preyed upon Jesus' followers.

Paul went on to characterize this evil philosophy as being man-made. God had not revealed this doctrine. Rather, it was the product of corrupted human minds. Moreover, this philosophy was based on the strictly human ideas found in the world. They consisted of instructions on acquiring secret knowledge and codes, angel worship, eating and drinking practices, and religious rituals. Yet very little of it reflected the well-known public teachings of the Savior. It would be incorrect to conclude that Paul was arguing against the study of philosophy as an academic discipline. Instead, the apostle was warning against adopting any point of view or teaching that was contrary to the Gospel (see Gal. 1:6-9).

The precise meaning of the Greek noun rendered "basic principles" (Col. 2:8) is debated among scholars. One option is that it refers to the rudimentary teachings of fallen humanity. A second option is that the focus is on how elemental spiritual forces operated in and controlled the world (under the permission and authority of God). In any case, Paul and the other apostles were attacking the foundations of Gnosticism during the first century A.D. Despite their efforts, this heretical doctrine flourished in the second and third centuries A.D. Famous second-century Gnostics such as Marcion and Valentinus taught that the Messiah was one of many angels who got past forces of darkness to bring the secrets of the spiritual realm to an unenlightened world. Following the apostles' example, the church fathers Irenaeus (A.D. 130–200), Tertullian (A.D. 160–225), and Hippolytus (A.D. 170–236) devoted much of their writing to exposing this philosophy, which seemed so compelling to many believers of the day. Irenaeus compared a Gnostic commentator to one who tore up the portrait of a king and put it back together to resemble a fox. Even today, many modern occultic and cultic groups claim to be influenced by second-century Gnosticism.

D. Affirming the Son's Deity: vss. 9-10

For in Christ all the fullness of the Deity lives in bodily form, and you have been given fullness in Christ, who is the head over every power and authority.

At this point in his letter, Paul sensed the importance of affirming the deity of the Son. Previously, in Colossians 1:19, the apostle declared that the Father was "pleased" to have His full divine nature reside in the Son. As was noted in lesson 10, this is a permanent dwelling, not a temporary one. Again, in 2:9, the apostle stated that the inner essence of the Godhead in its entirety resided in the Messiah—even in His human body. This statement unequivocally rejects the view that the Son did not have a bodily form and that the human body is evil. More importantly, this verse affirmed both the divine and human natures of the Savior. He is God who has lived as a human being.

Paul declared in verse 10 that believers have been brought to "fullness in Christ." By this the apostle meant they were complete through their spiritual union with Him. Paul dismissed the claim of the false teachers who said believers are deficient and therefore need further spiritual enlightenment. The apostle also rejected the idea that believers must practice additional religious rituals in order to reach spiritual perfection. The Son, who is Lord over all the powers and forces in the supernatural and natural realms, has already provided everything we need for salvation and spiritual growth. Jesus is not one of many spirit beings or angels, but the supreme commander over every power and authority.

II. SPIRITUAL VICTORY IN THE SON: COLOSSIANS 2:11-15

A. Deliverance from the Sinful Nature: vss. 11-12

In him you were also circumcised, in the putting off of the sinful nature, not with a circumcision done by the hands of men but with the circumcision done by Christ, having been buried with him in baptism and raised with him through your faith in the power of God, who raised him from the dead.

Before the advent of the Messiah, the Israelites were members of a special covenant with God (see Rom. 9:4-5). Their males affirmed this covenant by being physically circumcised. Now, following the coming of the Savior, there is a new sign that indicates who God's people are. It is no longer a physical mark but a spiritual one that the Savior has performed, and not just for men but for all people who put their faith in Him. That sign is a circumcision of the heart in which the whole self ruled by the flesh is cut away and discarded (see Deut. 10:16; Jer. 4:4; Rom. 2:28-29; Phil. 3:3). In turn, believers are freed from the power of the "sinful nature" (Col. 2:11). Indeed, the apostle said, it is "circumcision done by Christ," and it is by this that we enter into a covenant of grace with God—both Jew and Gentile (see Eph. 2:11-19; 1 Pet. 2:10).

Next, Paul associated baptism with circumcision (Col. 2:12). The apostle vividly paralleled the act of baptism with the dramatic events at the end of Jesus' earthly ministry. After the Son died on the cross, His friends buried His body. But then the Father raised Him from the dead never to physically die again. In baptism, we are symbolically buried and raised from the dead never to experience spiritual death. In truth, Jesus has washed away our sins with the blood He shed on the cross. As a result of our identification with Him by faith, our old sinful selves, along with their passions and desires, were nailed to the cross (see Rom. 6:6; Gal. 5:24). We can now be in a right relationship with the Father because the Son's redemptive work at Calvary atoned for our sins completely.

B. Forgiveness of Sins: vss. 13-14

When you were dead in your sins and in the uncircumcision of your sinful nature, God made you alive with Christ. He forgave us all our sins, having canceled the written code, with its regulations, that was against us and that stood opposed to us; he took it away, nailing it to the cross.

Paul continued to pile up more facts about the complete nature of the victory we have in union with the Messiah. The apostle noted that before our conversion, we were spiritually lifeless because of our transgressions and the unregenerate condition (or "uncircumcision," Col. 2:13) of our flesh. At this point, we stood judged and condemned by God. Then, when we trusted in the Son for our salvation, the Father spiritually regenerated us and pardoned us of all our trespasses. This inner re-creation of our fallen human nature is known as the new birth. We experience passing from spiritual death to new life, for Jesus took the judgment due us because of our sins. In the Messiah's resurrection, He conquered the death penalty, which enabled us to receive forgiveness of our transgressions.

Because we were born in a state of sin and committed innumerable iniquities, the Mosaic law declared us to be guilty and demanded our punishment. It was as if there was a certificate listing the divine decrees we had violated and tallying up the full extent of our indebtedness to God. In a manner of speaking, the Father wiped out the unfavorable record of our debts. Another way of putting it is that He took that long list of charges against us and nailed every last one of them to the cross (vs. 14). The Father could do this because the Son's atoning sacrifice fully satisfied the law's demands. At Calvary, Jesus took our judgment on Himself. Now that we are united to the Messiah by faith, the law's power to condemn us is taken away.

C. Triumph over Rulers and Authorities: vs. 15

And having disarmed the powers and authorities, he made a public spectacle of them, triumphing over them by the cross.

The cross signifies the Son's complete and lasting victory over all spiritual "powers and authorities" (Col. 2:15) arrayed against the Father. As a result of what Jesus did at Calvary, He "disarmed" every evil entity, both in heaven and on earth. He also disgraced and humiliated them publicly. The image is that of an ancient post-battle victory procession in which spectators witness the return home of a conqueror. Trailing behind him are his defeated enemies, now stripped and in chains. Because of our union with the Son by faith, we can join His victory procession and offer praises to Him as our conquering King (see 2 Cor. 2:14). In order for the Father to bring about this amazing triumph over evil, the Son had to experience the horror of crucifixion. In turn, Satan's eternal doom was sealed when the Father raised His Son from the dead.

Discussion Questions

1. Why is it important for us not only to believe in Jesus but also to live in union with Him?
2. What real danger is there in allowing Christians to be misled by spiritual frauds?
3. How can we tell if supposedly "new" teaching is in agreement with the Gospel or is of purely human origin?
4. How is it possible for the Messiah to be divine and human at the same time?
5. What has the Father done for those who put their faith in the Son?

Contemporary Application

The Father has made every provision for our spiritual vitality, yet many believers often appear to be defeated. Or if not defeated, they do not seem to reflect much enthusiasm about their Christian commitment.

It's one thing to lose a battle if we lack adequate resources, but quite another if we have the resources but refuse to use them. Perhaps one reason for the church's lack of spiritual power is that too many believers are not aware of all they possess through faith in the Son. They lack the passion for discovering the wealth of their spiritual riches.

When we confess Jesus as Lord, we acknowledge that He alone can win our battles. Yet we seem to go on as if everything depends on our own cleverness and ingenuity. We find it difficult to trust Jesus alone for every aspect of our spiritual well-being. We also find it hard to discard useless human philosophies and traditions (see Col. 2:8).

Let us affirm that Jesus made a "public spectacle" (vs. 15) of all our spiritual enemies. Indeed, the cross is our sign of triumph! Moreover, our sins are forgiven, our old nature has been crucified, and we are raised to new life in union with the Son (vss. 11-13). There is no excuse for settling for anything less than a victorious life as followers of the Lord Jesus (see vs. 6).

Clothed with Christ

Scripture

Background Scripture: *Colossians 3:1-17*

Scripture Lesson: *Colossians 3:5-17*

Key Verse: *Over all these virtues put on love, which binds them all together in perfect unity.* Colossians 3:14.

Scripture Lesson for Children: *Matthew 14:22-33*

Key Verse for Children: *[Peter] was afraid and, beginning to sink, cried out, "Lord, save me!" Immediately Jesus reached out his hand and caught him.* Matthew 14:30-31.

Lesson Aim

To follow God's principles for holy living.

Lesson Setting

Time: A.D. 60

Place: Rome

Lesson Outline

Clothed with Christ

I. Living as God's Transformed People: Colossians 3:5-11
    A. *Forsaking Immorality: vss. 5-6*
    B. *Abandoning Vice: vss. 7-8*
    C. *Being Spiritually Renewed: vss. 9-11*
II. Living as God's Chosen People: Colossians 3:12-14
    A. *Being Clothed with Christian Virtues: vs. 12*
    B. *Binding Christian Virtues with Love: vss. 13-14*
III. Living as God's Grateful People: Colossians 3:15-17
    A. *Ruled by Christ's Peace: vs. 15*
    B. *Indwelt by Christ's Message: vs. 16*
    C. *Undergirded by Heartfelt Thanks: vs. 17*

Introduction for Adults

Topic: *Breaking Bad Habits*

If you've been in a supermarket recently, you might have noticed the numerous shelves of natural food supplements. In recent years, these products have become big business. People pay soaring prices because they put a high priority on their physical health.

In contrast, you find the purveyors of so-called junk food are also doing quite well. They cater to people who have the bad habit of eating and drinking anything, as long as it's filling and tastes good to them. They spend money, too, but not according to the rules of good nutrition. They go for whatever appeals to them, no matter if it is bad for them. Their priority is satisfying their taste buds.

In the supermarket of life, we have to make wise spiritual choices that enable the "word of Christ" (Col. 3:16) to abide in and among us. Some people place a higher priority on godly living than others do. Paul made it clear what our choices must be if we profess to be Jesus' followers (see vss. 5-14). We can't go on consuming a diet of sin that will ruin us. The Bible tells us what those poisons are, as well as the overwhelming benefits of a healthy diet of Christian virtues.

Introduction for Youth

Topic: *Clothed with Love*

A missionary wrote to a friend about her son: "Isaac, at 6'3" and 180 lbs., is looking forward to Duke basketball camp and hopes to get on his high school team this year. He just returned from a church mission trip to Jamaica. He'll be in the eleventh grade next year and hopes to maintain his straight-A record."

Isaac illustrates life on a higher level. What makes the difference? For one thing, his values and choices have been solidly anchored in the Lord Jesus. Does this mean Isaac has been spared problems and hardships? Not at all. He recently has been through some very rough patches.

Colossians 3:9-10 clearly explains what we have to do to achieve life on a higher level. There are vices we need to discard like an old, filthy garment, and some new virtues (such as Christlike love) we need to clothe over our regenerate selves. If we are serious about following Jesus, we have to study these truths and ask the Holy Spirit to lead us in paths of obedience.

Concepts for Children

Topic: *A Friend in Our Need*

1. Jesus' followers were in a boat on the Sea of Galilee.
2. Early in the morning, they saw Him walking on the water.
3. At first, they were scared.
4. When Jesus spoke to His followers, they calmed down.
5. When we feel afraid, Jesus can give us peace.

Lesson Commentary

I. LIVING AS GOD'S TRANSFORMED PEOPLE: COLOSSIANS 3:5-11

A. Forsaking Immorality: vss. 5-6

Put to death, therefore, whatever belongs to your earthly nature: sexual immorality, impurity, lust, evil desires and greed, which is idolatry. Because of these, the wrath of God is coming.

In the first two chapters of Colossians, Paul carefully explained what to believe about the Messiah, especially who He is and what He has done. This instruction was necessary in view of the gains made by the heretical teaching infiltrating Colossae that minimized the Savior's person and work. Now, in chapters 3 and 4 of his letter, the apostle shifted the focus on how to live in response to who Jesus is and what He has done. Noteworthy are the occurrences of the adverbs "then" (3:1) and "therefore" (vss. 5, 12) that precede Paul's listings of ungodly and godly activity. These terms refer back to what the apostle wrote in chapters 1 and 2, since those teachings are the underlying theological foundation for the behaviors advanced in chapters 3 and 4. Succinctly put, what believers know about the Messiah determines how they live in and for Him.

In 3:1, Paul reiterated what he stated in 2:12, namely, that believers have been spiritually raised to new life in union with the Son. When they recognize all the eternal blessings He bestows on them—including forgiveness, righteousness, and peace with the Father—it is only logical for Jesus' followers to focus their hearts (3:1) and minds (vs. 2) on the eternal realities of heaven, not just on temporal, earthly concerns. In Scripture, the heart and mind are closely connected (see Ps. 26:2; Matt. 15:19; Acts 4:32). Accordingly, the lives of believers should be so intertwined with the presence of the Savior that while they remain in a real world, all their thinking and acting should be transformed by the heavenly realm. This is not, as the old saying goes, "becoming so heavenly minded that we're of no earthly good," but exactly the opposite. The more we aspire to God's holy standards, the more our earthly lives count for what's best.

At the moment of conversion, believers are transformed from what characterized their former unredeemed life to the new life the Lord graciously bestows on them (Col. 3:3). It is as if they are dead to this world's attractions due to their union with the Son (see Gal. 2:20; Col. 2:20). They are now totally secure in Jesus' love, wisdom, and power. When He who is the basis for their existence is revealed (at His second coming), then His followers will also share in His glory (Col. 3:4). In light of these truths, Paul urged believers to discontinue sinning and being enslaved to evil. Figuratively speaking, they are to "put to death" (vs. 5) whatever earthly desires lurk within them. There is a sense of decisive urgency as believers exterminate the cravings of the old self, not just suppress them or try to control them.

The apostle listed five vices that are indicative of the old fallen nature. These included "sexual immorality," or illicit sexual relations; "impurity," or moral uncleanness; "lust," or carnal cravings; "evil desires," or depraved covetousness; and "greed," or the insatiable hunger for material possessions—which is idolatry. Paul followed his admonition with a stern warning. The Father will not ignore unrepented sins. Instead, He will show His displeasure with these vices on the day of judgment when the Son returns. Divine retribution will fall on everyone who has sold themselves out to such wickedness (vs. 6). All of us are tempted by these vices somewhere in the course of our earthly lives. When enticements to sin hit us, we have to kill them right away and not even think about indulging them.

B. Abandoning Vice: vss. 7-8

You used to walk in these ways, in the life you once lived. But now you must rid yourselves of all such things as these: anger, rage, malice, slander, and filthy language from your lips.

Most of Paul's readers were Gentiles from pagan backgrounds. They had probably indulged in the sins he just described. Now, however, Jesus had forgiven and renewed them and given them a new way in which to live. Therefore, they were not to be characterized by their former pagan existence (Col. 3:7). After all, this old way of life was buried in the past for the true follower of the Messiah. To reinforce the apostle's point, he listed a second catalog of vices that have more to do with verbal offenses (vs. 8). Paul commanded his readers to get rid of "anger," or outbursts of temper; "rage," or the violent expression of hatred; "malice," or vindictive spite; "slander," or destructive gossip; and "filthy language," or vulgar speech.

These common sins are powerful roadblocks on the way to righteousness. Too often, though, we think they are not as bad as the vices Paul cited in verse 5. Nevertheless, the transgressions the apostle recorded in verse 8 can just as easily cut off our fellowship with the Father and with each other. In too many cases, believers find it easy to excuse misconduct as simply bad habits. They claim these tendencies are just part of the way they are made. Evidently, in their opinion Jesus does not care to set them free from obnoxious attitudes and actions. Or they simply like their sins and refuse to put them to death.

C. Being Spiritually Renewed: vss. 9-11

Do not lie to each other, since you have taken off your old self with its practices and have put on the new self, which is being renewed in knowledge in the image of its Creator. Here there is no Greek or Jew, circumcised or uncircumcised, barbarian, Scythian, slave or free, but Christ is all, and is in all.

Paul urged believers to discontinue lying to one another (Col. 3:9). The apostle may have been noting actual spiritual maladies within the congregation at Colossae. The problem could have been a source of mistrust and conflict that was beginning to flare up in the church. Paul presented a vivid picture of what it means to turn away from a life of sin and walk in newness of life in the Savior. It is like taking off old, dirty clothes and putting on new, clean garments. Expressed differently, we are to strip off all the disgusting habits we had when we were nonbelievers and clothe ourselves with godly behavior that reflects the character of the Son. This is possible only as the Holy Spirit empowers us to do so. As a result of putting on a new self in the Messiah, believers are "renewed in knowledge" (vs. 10). In turn, they come to understand their Creator better and conduct themselves in a manner that is pleasing to Him.

For the remainder of the believers' sojourn on earth, the Son renews their minds and transforms their thinking, with the result that they choose to do the Father's perfect will (see Rom. 12:2). In this new way of living, there are no distinctions between any of us who belong to the Son. To reinforce this truth, Paul gave examples from his day of social barriers that separated groups of people (Col. 3:11). Between Gentiles and Jews, race was an issue. Differing religious practices divided the circumcised from the uncircumcised. The elites of society regarded barbarians and Scythians as being uncivilized brutes. Class distinctions separated slaves from those who were free. Against this backdrop, it must have seemed quite radical for Paul to declare, "Christ is all, and is in all." By this the apostle meant that Jesus unites all of us, despite our vast differences, because He dwells in all believers (see Gal. 3:28).

II. LIVING AS GOD'S CHOSEN PEOPLE: COLOSSIANS 3:12-14

A. Being Clothed with Christian Virtues: vs. 12

Therefore, as God's chosen people, holy and dearly loved, clothe yourselves with compassion, kindness, humility, gentleness and patience.

Paul did not just tell his readers to abandon all forms of sin. He also exhorted them to demonstrate and cultivate Christlike virtues. The motivation for doing so was their status as "God's chosen people" (Col. 3:12). Put another way, they were the elect of God. As such, the Lord considered them to be His "holy and dearly loved" spiritual children. By putting to death the vices of the old self and putting on Christian love, they demonstrated the reality of the new life they had in the Son. They also promoted harmony within their fellowship. It was not enough for them as individual Christians to be like the Savior. In fact, it was more important for them to be like the Son as a unified church. In this way, they collectively represented themselves as the Messiah's bride to the world, "without stain or wrinkle or any other blemish, but holy and blameless" (Eph. 5:27).

To further encourage a holy way of life, Paul listed five virtues that should spiritually clothe believers (Col. 3:12). The apostle's purpose was to remind his readers that they were to practice what the Son had taught His followers and measure up to what the Father created them to be. Paul first urged the Colossians to array themselves with a heart of "compassion," or mercy. This refers to an affectionate sympathy for others, especially for those in need. Second, the apostle affirmed the value of kindness. His readers were to have a generous and helpful regard in their dealings with others. Humility was third on Paul's list. He certainly was not advocating self-mortification, as the false teachers had done, but was speaking about meekness in behavior and attitude that is respectful and not haughty or pretentious.

Fourth, the apostle wanted the believers in Colossae to exhibit gentleness. By this he meant showing congenial consideration toward others. Although people regard humility as a sign of weakness, Paul did not view this trait as a flaw, especially since Jesus Himself had the characteristic. The Redeemer said, "Take my yoke upon you and learn from me, for I am gentle and humble in heart" (Matt. 11:29). Finally, the apostle stressed the importance of "patience" (Col. 3:12). He wanted his readers to have a tolerant and forgiving spirit toward those who wronged them. All of these characteristics have relational aspects to them. As we exercise and cultivate these virtues in our relationships with other believers, we will individually and collectively become more Christlike.

B. Binding Christian Virtues with Love: vss. 13-14

Bear with each other and forgive whatever grievances you may have against one another. Forgive as the Lord forgave you. And over all these virtues put on love, which binds them all together in perfect unity.

Paul's next admonition pertained to forgiveness. Even within the church, believers often rub each other the wrong way, and it's easy to harbor a grudge against a Christian brother or sister. The apostle, however, instructed the Colossians to resist such a temptation and instead be forbearing and forgiving when they felt they had been mistreated (Col. 3:13). Furthermore, making allowance for the faults of others and being willing to overlook an offense were the means by which believers clothed themselves with the Christian virtues listed in verse 12. Paul then recalled how the Lord forgave us. The implication is that if Jesus could pardon us, who have wronged Him infinitely more than we have been mistreated, how much easier it should be for us to forgive those who have frustrated us.

Of course, Paul knew that forgiving is not easy to do. Yet the apostle also believed that the Son empowers us to be like Him, especially as the Holy Spirit conforms us to the Savior's image. This gives us the ability to be patient with one another no matter how great a loss someone has caused in our lives. Most of all, Paul asked the Colossians to clothe themselves with "love" (vs. 14). Metaphorically speaking, Christlike compassion is like an overcoat that rests on top of all the other virtues. When Jesus' followers are dressed in this manner, they will enjoy perfect unity. The Messiah will have knit us all together in a single multicolored, multipatterned tapestry by His transforming love.

III. LIVING AS GOD'S GRATEFUL PEOPLE: COLOSSIANS 3:15-17

A. Ruled by Christ's Peace: vs. 15

Let the peace of Christ rule in your hearts, since as members of one body you were called to peace. And be thankful.

After Paul described the kind of conduct the Colossian believers should maintain, especially within their fellowship, he explained how it was possible for them to obey his instructions. In essence, he said they must live day by day totally under the lordship of the Savior. This involved letting the peace that He supplied control their thoughts, emotions, and actions. The Greek noun rendered "peace" (Col. 3:15) denoted the presence of harmony and tranquility. Unlike worldly forms of concord, this peace was a special, personal gift from the Savior (see John 14:27). Moreover, this peace is the embodiment of the Messiah, "for he himself is our peace" (Eph. 2:14).

Since the biblical writers thought of the heart as the center of a person's being, Paul, in effect, was calling upon believers to submit their entire being to the control of the Son's peace. The reason for doing so is that the Father has "called [us] to peace" (Col. 3:15). Moreover, the Father wants His spiritual children to live in harmony, not as separate individuals, but as a unified community of believers. Since we are all members of one spiritual body, of which Jesus is the appointed Head (see 1:18; 2:19), we must not let our selfishness disrupt the health of His body. Paul also directed us to be thankful. He didn't ask us to just express gratitude to the Father but to have a constant attitude of thankfulness for being a redeemed member of the Son's spiritual body. The apostle wanted believers to be a grateful people who appreciated what the Savior was doing within them.

B. Indwelt by Christ's Message: vs. 16

Let the word of Christ dwell in you richly as you teach and admonish one another with all wisdom, and as you sing psalms, hymns and spiritual songs with gratitude in your hearts to God.

Living as the Father's grateful children includes letting the message about the Son, in all its richness, fill our lives (Col. 3:16). This admonition means more than just a simple reading and rote memorization of the Bible. It is allowing the Word of God to affect every aspect of our existence. For instance, we allow Scripture to shape our decisions and determine our thinking patterns. We also seek to live by it on a daily basis. As Jesus' message dwells in us richly, we are better able to instruct and exhort one another in a prudent and discerning manner. Moreover, the Spirit enables us to draw upon all the wisdom provided by the Savior as we go about our daily lives. Indeed, the "word of Christ" is the basis for our singing "psalms, hymns and spiritual songs . . . to God" with our "hearts" filled with "gratitude."

The "psalms" were probably the canticles found in the Old Testament Psalter. "Hymns" most likely were lyrics composed by Christians to honor God. "Songs" may have been called "spiritual" either to distinguish them from similar compositions by non-Christians or because they referred to spontaneous singing in the Spirit. The idea is that the words in our worship songs are meant to express the compassion and truth of the Savior. These hymns can either be taken from the Old Testament psalms or be newly written lyrics of praise. Whatever the type of music, it is clear that the Spirit should guide the words, the music, and the singer. Furthermore, we are to praise the Father and the Son in song not just with our lips but more importantly with all our heart—that is, our whole being.

C. Undergirded by Heartfelt Thanks: vs. 17

And whatever you do, whether in word or deed, do it all in the name of the Lord Jesus, giving thanks to God the Father through him.

Paul concluded this part of his instructions with an admonition that the believers in Colossae were to do everything in Jesus' name (Col. 3:17). Put differently, they were to think, behave, and minister in light of the Messiah's supreme authority and character. Since the Lord has claimed us with His atoning blood, we belong to and are dependent on Him. Accordingly, His name should be stamped on all that we do and say as His representatives to the unsaved. This includes our expressing gratitude through the Son to the Father.

Discussion Questions

1. Why is it important for believers to put to death the cravings of their earthly nature?
2. How can believers develop spiritual goals that keep Jesus at the center?
3. How can believers keep their families unsullied from sexual defilement found in print and electronic media?
4. What are some ways the "word of Christ" (Col. 3:16) abides in believers?
5. How does "giving thanks to God" (vs. 17) regulate what believers do?

Contemporary Application

Every day we seem to be confronted by a new crisis of some kind. What would the evening news be if there were no predicaments to report? But perhaps the most significant crisis of all never makes the news. Our churches must realize that a crisis exists when believers fail to follow God's principles for holy living. It's a dilemma when believers adopt a ho-hum attitude toward the standards of godliness revealed in the Bible.

The Lord has provided all we need to throw off the old life and put on the new one. There can be no doubts about His governing principles. But until we realize the danger of neglecting the Father's spiritual resources made available in union with the Son, we will not swing into action.

Action begins by evaluating how much time we spend feeding our souls on the truths of the Gospel. Confession and repentance are demanded. We also have to regularly use Paul's checklist of virtues and vices. Where we fall short, we must acknowledge the error of our ways. We should also seek the help of others to keep us on the road to godly living. As we rejoice and praise the Lord together, we allow the words of the Savior to penetrate our hearts and minds.

Spiritual Disciplines

Scripture

Background Scripture: *Colossians 4:2-17*
Scripture Lesson: *Colossians 4:2-6*
Key Verse: *Tell Archippus: "See to it that you complete the work you have received in the Lord."* Colossians 4:17.
Scripture Lesson for Children: *Matthew 20:29-34*
Key Verse for Children: *Jesus . . . touched [the two blind men's] eyes. Immediately they received their sight and followed him.* Matthew 20:34.

Lesson Aim

To encourage living faithfully and responsibly for the Lord.

Lesson Setting

Time: A.D. *60*
Place: Rome

Lesson Outline

Spiritual Disciplines

   I. Devotion to Prayer: Colossians 4:2-4
      A. *Being Diligent in Prayer: vs. 2*
      B. *Remembering to Pray for Others: vss. 3-4*
  II. Godly Deeds and Words: Colossians 4:5-6
      A. *Acting Wisely Among Unbelievers: vs. 5*
      B. *Maintaining Gracious Speech: vs. 6*

Introduction for Adults

Topic: *Support through Mentoring*

Paul urged the believers in Colossae to be known to others for their godly deeds and words (Col. 4:5-6). This included behaving wisely and being gracious in how they treated others. At first, their role model was Paul's beloved coworker Epaphras, who told them about the Lord Jesus (see 1:7). Later, there were other godly mentors who encouraged them to remain faithful in their Christian commitment (see 4:7-9).

In 2004, Peter Lane Taylor, a correspondent for *National Geographic Adventure Magazine,* did a story on how a small group of Ukrainian Jews avoided "being captured by Nazis." It was 1942, and the Stermer family faced a grim outcome at the hands of the Germans advancing on their small village of Korolówka.

To stay alive, the matriarch of the family, Esther Stermer, told one of her sons to "find a place" where all of them could safely "hide in the forest." The adolescent succeeded in discovering a labyrinth of local caves "about five miles to the north." Next, as a result of Esther's leadership and mentorship, 38 people decided to cooperate with one another. This decision proved crucial to their survival.

Introduction for Youth

Topic: *Get Spiritually Fit*

Until his death in 2011, Jack LaLanne was known as the "godfather of fitness" due to his expertise in exercise and nutrition. But it wasn't always that way for him. As a young adolescent, he recalled being addicted to sugar and junk foods.

Then, when LaLanne was 15, he heard a pioneer in America's wellness movement, Paul Bragg, give a lecture on health and nutrition. That speech motivated LaLanne to radically change his lifestyle. He began to eat properly and exercise regularly. In time, he became physically fit. He also gained recognition as a weightlifter and bodybuilder. He devoted the rest of his life to encouraging people to better themselves through exercise and fitness.

For saved teens, even more important than physical wellness is their spiritual fitness (see 1 Tim. 4:8). And one of the ways they can become more spiritually healthy and robust is by means of prayer. This includes devoting themselves to praying regularly and remaining alert and thankful as they petition God on behalf of themselves and others (see Col. 4:2-4).

Concepts for Children

Topic: *A Leader Worth Following*

1. Jesus and His followers left a city named Jericho.
2. Many people were also with Jesus.
3. Two blind men asked Jesus for help.
4. Jesus gave the two men their sight.
5. Jesus loves us and will also help us.

Lesson Commentary

I. DEVOTION TO PRAYER: COLOSSIANS 4:2-4

A. Being Diligent in Prayer: vs. 2

Devote yourselves to prayer, being watchful and thankful.

Colossians 3:18–4:1 records Paul's instructions to Christian households. These exhortations parallel what the apostle wrote in Ephesians 5:21–6:9. There he directed married couples to be kind and considerate to one another (5:21). In Colossians 3, Paul specified that wives were to understand and affirm their husbands (vs. 18). In turn, the apostle urged husbands to be loving, rather than resentful, toward their wives (vs. 19). In regard to children, Paul said they would please the Lord by obeying their parents (vs. 20). Also, parents were not to exasperate their children and cause them to lose heart (vs. 21).

Slavery was a stark reality in the ancient world. At least one-third of the population in the Roman Empire was in bondage, and some historians put the percentage at over one-half. Most slaves labored in private homes. God never ordained slavery as He sanctioned marriage and the family. Eventually, Christian influence helped remove the blight of slavery from human society. But the day when that would be possible came long after Paul's time. And so, since slavery existed, the apostle tried to counsel believers who were involved in it. Specifically, the apostle instructed Christian slaves to be obedient and respectful to their human masters. Slaves were to do so wholeheartedly due to their reverent fear of the Lord (vs. 22).

In many instances, slaves did their work grudgingly and out of compulsion. They cared little if their efforts made their masters more prosperous or increasingly comfortable. Slaves did just enough work to keep from being beaten or otherwise mistreated. Paul urged Christian slaves to adopt a different attitude. Regardless of the work they performed, they were to do so with enthusiasm. The apostle also advised genuine submission to human masters, not because the latter deserved it, but because the slaves were actually serving a heavenly Master (vs. 23). He was none other than the Lord Jesus. Paul promised that when the Messiah returned, He would bestow on Christian slaves (as well as all believers) an eternal inheritance as their reward (vs. 24). Moreover, the apostle assured his fellow enslaved Christians that everyone who acted unjustly or wickedly would receive the consequences of their wrongdoing, and there would be no exceptions (vs. 25).

In the early Christian church, slaves probably outnumbered masters, but obviously there were some in the latter category. For example, Philemon of Colossae (to whom Paul wrote one of the New Testament letters) certainly was a slaveholder. The apostle did not tell the Christian masters to free their slaves. Instead, he directed them to treat their slaves in a just and fair manner, for slaveholders likewise were accountable to their "Master in heaven" (4:1). Put another way, the masters were not independent rulers over their slaves. Paul's admonition constituted a major break from the usual superior attitude of masters to slaves. Perhaps in this way, the apostle helped pave the way for an end to slavery.

It would be incorrect to assume that maintaining Christlike relationships is just a simple process of following specific rules. While human initiative and effort are involved, all of it must be bathed in prayer (4:2). The Greek verb rendered "devote" means "to persevere in" or "to be steadfastly attentive to" and indicates that prayer is to be a consistent part of every believer's life. Furthermore, being vigilant in prayer requires earnestness, readiness, and determination. Paul directed his readers both to pray diligently and to maintain an attitude of thankfulness and praise. This is the opposite of being filled with anxiety, irritation, or smugness.

B. Remembering to Pray for Others: vss. 3-4

And pray for us, too, that God may open a door for our message, so that we may proclaim the mystery of Christ, for which I am in chains. Pray that I may proclaim it clearly, as I should.

Paul wanted his readers to do more than pray for themselves. He also wanted them to remember to offer prayer to God on behalf of him and his colleagues in ministry. In particular, the believers in Colossae were to petition God to give the evangelistic team new and increased opportunities to herald His message to the lost. This was the Good News about the "mystery of Christ" (Col. 4:3). The latter phrase referred to the truth that the Father intended for salvation through faith in His Son to be made available to Jews and Gentiles alike (see 2:2).

In Ephesians 3:2-6, Paul explained more fully what he meant by the Greek noun rendered "mystery." (See also the comments made on this term in lessons 1, 5, and 11.) We learn that the apostle regarded himself as a steward whom God appointed to serve as a missionary to the lost (vs. 2). By preaching the Gospel to the Gentiles, Paul had become a means by which God extended the message of grace to people who previously had been without hope for salvation. The apostle himself had told the early converts of Ephesus about his role. Later converts would have heard about him from others. The Lord disclosed His will to Paul "by revelation" (vs. 3). This refers to Paul's meeting with the risen Messiah on the road to Damascus. At that time, the Savior charged Paul with taking the Gospel to the Gentiles (see Acts 9:15; 26:16-18).

One aspect of the divine secret is God's plan to bring all things under the Messiah's authority, including the entire cosmos (see Eph. 1:9-10). A second aspect is that God's grace includes Gentiles as well as Jews (3:6). According to the Father's redemptive plan, the time had arrived to disclose His compassion toward those Gentiles who became devoted followers of the Son. Indeed, all the blessings enjoyed by saved Jews have also been bestowed upon believing Gentiles. The Messiah dwells in them as assuredly as He lives in Jewish believers, and both possess the same "hope of glory" (Col. 1:27).

Previously in Ephesians, Paul had written about God's grace for the Gentiles (see 2:11-22, which was covered in lesson 2). As the Ephesians reread those earlier parts of the letter, they could understand Paul's insight into the "mystery" (3:4). The apostle wanted his readers to appreciate his knowledge and understanding of the divine plan regarding the Messiah, not so that they would admire Paul, but so that they would accept his teachings. He explained that what God had not disclosed about His redemptive plan to former generations, the Holy Spirit "revealed . . . to God's holy apostles and prophets" (vs. 5) of the early church so that everyone might hear about it.

Paul explained that by means of the Gospel, Gentiles were now "heirs together with Israel" (vs. 6). In other words, Gentile and Jewish believers alike could inherit the kingdom of God. Also, by believing the Good News, Gentiles became "members together of one body." That is, Gentile and Jewish believers were part of one united body with the Messiah as its Head. Moreover, the Gospel has given Gentiles a share "in the promise in Christ Jesus." This meant both Gentile and Jewish believers could enjoy the covenant blessings.

To us, it may seem obvious that Gentiles needn't convert to Judaism to be acceptable in God's sight, but that's because we live long after Paul. For the early Jewish Christians, who were raised with the idea that only Jews could have a serious relationship with God, this was a radical concept. Still, God had intended Gentile inclusion all along. Perhaps no one in the early church understood the change that had occurred in the Son as thoroughly as did Paul. Now that Gentile believers are a major part of the church, we may find it easy to forget our spiritual heritage is Jewish. But if we consider how Jews would have perceived a Gentile's eternal status before the divine secret was revealed, we should be all the more grateful for God's abundant grace.

As Paul and his colleagues freely shared the Gospel with Jews and Gentiles alike, the missionaries encountered stiff opposition from those who were antagonistic to their message. This is one reason why, as the apostle wrote to the believers in Colossae, he did so while imprisoned in Rome and awaiting trial (Col. 4:3). Despite his sobering circumstance, Paul refused to shirk his God-given responsibility to tell others about the Savior. Even so, the apostle did not operate in his own strength. Instead, he made the truth plainly and clearly known in the power of the Holy Spirit. This is one reason why Paul asked his readers to keep him in prayer as he shared the Good News with whomever would listen (vs. 4).

II. GODLY DEEDS AND WORDS: COLOSSIANS 4:5-6

A. Acting Wisely Among Unbelievers: vs. 5

Be wise in the way you act toward outsiders; make the most of every opportunity.

Paul encouraged his readers to conduct themselves with wisdom toward "outsiders" (Col. 4:5), namely, unbelievers. The Greek word rendered "wise" denoted the presence of skill in managing a broad range of responsibilities, as well as displaying prudence in one's interpersonal relationships. So instead of the believers in Colossae wasting their time and energy on frivolous pursuits, the apostle urged them to make good use of "every opportunity" the Lord gave them to share the Gospel (for example, while at work, at civic forums, and at the marketplace).

In 1 Thessalonians 4:11-12, Paul also offered counsel regarding the best way to live among non-Christians. He urged his readers to strive earnestly to lead quiet lives, mind their own affairs, and earn their own living. Probably these were three areas in which some Thessalonians were deficient. In the apostle's first directive, the Greek verb translated "make" (vs. 11) indicates a wholehearted pursuit of an objective. The result is a paradox, something like "work energetically to be still." The first directive ("lead a quiet life"), when taken with the second ("mind your own business"), suggests that some of Paul's readers were meddling in the affairs of others, stirring up trouble, or gossiping around town. Such behavior—unfortunately, still known among believers today—is wrong and reflects badly on the Savior and His church. If the Thessalonians had kept themselves busy at useful labor, they would not have had time to get into trouble by meddling, troublemaking, or gossiping (compare 2 Thess. 3:11).

Based on that reasoning, Paul told his spiritual children, "Work with your hands" (1 Thess. 4:11). This means they were to be diligent about pursuing their jobs and household chores. Greeks despised manual labor, thinking it fit only for slaves. For Jews, however, manual labor had dignity. In the mind of the apostle, a Jew, respect for hard work had a place in the church's tradition. Paul had argued for the value of manual labor while he was with the Thessalonians in person. He had given them the rule that anyone who was unwilling to work would not eat (see 2 Thess. 3:10). The apostle, as a tentmaker by trade, had also modeled a productive lifestyle while he was with the new converts (see vss. 7-9).

In 1 Thessalonians 4:12, Paul offered two reasons why his readers were to work with their hands. First, they would live in a decent manner in the presence of "outsiders." In turn, this godly lifestyle might earn the respect of the unsaved. Second, the apostle's spiritual children would not have to depend on others to satisfy their ongoing daily needs. As a result, the believers in Thessalonica could offer the Gospel without charge and remain free from the possibility of being manipulated by unscrupulous donors. We may not always realize it, but unbelievers are watching us to see how we behave. If we have joy and love, and if we live on a high plane of morality, then the unsaved are more likely to be favorably impressed with the Christian faith. However, if we fail to live consistent with what we teach, then unbelievers will conclude that Christianity is full of hypocrisy.

With respect to the unsaved living in Thessalonica, they saw that some of the believers were busybodies and idlers. Thus, the resident pagans could hardly be blamed for concluding that the new religion in town, Christianity, had nothing special to offer. *If that's what it means to be a follower of Jesus, I don't want to be one!* they might have thought. In contrast, if the believers began to work diligently, then others would start to respect them and might even become interested in learning more about the Savior.

Verse 12 also emphasizes the importance of being self-supporting. As long as the believers in Thessalonica earned their own living, they would "not be dependent on anybody." Evidently, some of them were living off the charity of others. The idle Christians had become a burden to others and could not know the self-respect that comes from taking care of oneself. We should do whatever we can to take care of our own needs before going to others for help. Men and women who are diligent in doing all they can to take care of their family's needs deserve our respect. As far as they are able, they are "not . . . dependent on anybody" but God for their material well-being.

B. Maintaining Gracious Speech: vs. 6

Let your conversation be always full of grace, seasoned with salt, so that you may know how to answer everyone.

Paul instructed his readers to ensure that their speech was gracious. By this he meant their "conversation" (Col. 4:6) was to be characterized by compassion and kindness. This is possibly one reason why, in Ephesians 5:4, the apostle said believers are to have nothing to do with obscenity, foolish talk, and coarse joking (compare 4:29). These kinds of speech are sinful because they harm both those who speak them and those who hear them. In place of improper speech, believers are to give thanks to God. Expressing gratitude is beneficial to all who speak and hear it.

Moreover, the speech of Jesus' followers is to be "seasoned with salt" (Col. 4:6). Insight into the meaning of this phrase can be found in Matthew 5:13, where Jesus compared believers to salt. In ancient times, the Jews obtained their salt from the shores of the Dead Sea and the Hill of Salt (Jebel Usdum). The salinity of the chemical could be lost due to overexposure to the sun and excessively damp conditions. People used salt to season and preserve their food and to bring out its flavor. Ingesting salt also helped people to maintain their electrolytes and prevent dehydration from occurring. Jesus noted that when salt becomes contaminated with foreign substances, it could lose its distinctive flavor and preservative qualities. When this happened, people would discard such a worthless chemical.

Jesus was figuratively referring to the spiritual qualities that should be present in His disciples. In other words, they needed to have a wholesomeness about them that enabled them to be a blessing and a moral preservative in the world. In a similar way, Paul encouraged stimulating and vibrant speech that brought out the best in others. Rather than being insipid and dull in their conversation, believers sought to be winsome and engaging. Admittedly, there were times when this would be difficult to do, especially when the unsaved challenged the faith of Jesus' followers. Still, as Colossians 4:6 indicates, the Lord can help believers know when and how to give a fitting response to others about their faith.

In 1 Peter 3:15, the author of the epistle noted that his readers would not be able to predict when others would persecute them. That is why Peter urged them to always be ready to give an answer when someone asked them about their hope in the Messiah. Hostile questions were prominent in the apostle's mind. If his readers were unprepared when the inquiries came, they might be either speechless or unable to articulate clearly why they had devoted themselves to the Lord. The Greek word translated "to give the reason" can also be rendered "to make a defense." The English word *apology* is derived from it and refers to vindicating the Christian faith. Some argue that Peter was referring only to formal interrogations. Others, however, think he included informal questioning. Either way, the apostle wanted his readers to hold fast to the Gospel and fearlessly proclaim it to others.

Discussion Questions

1. Why do you think it is sometimes a challenge for believers to be persistent in prayer?
2. Who are some devoted Christian ministers the Lord might want you to keep in prayer?
3. What reason did Paul give for being imprisoned in Rome?
4. Why did Paul think it was important for him to "proclaim the mystery of Christ" (Col. 4:3)?
5. Why would it be detrimental for believers to act foolishly around the unsaved?

Contemporary Application

When basketball superstar Michael Jordan was at the peak of his career, an ad campaign for a product encouraged kids to "Be like Mike." All who aspired to be like their sports hero would, of course, pester their parents to buy the product he endorsed. If Mike ate it, drank it, or wore it, that decision was simply the right thing to do.

Believers need to be devoted even more so to their hero, the Lord Jesus. This means, in part, that they take all their cues from Him. And a key to being like Him is carefully tending their relationships in a loving, biblical manner.

Being persistent in prayer is a good place to start. This includes keeping alert while praying to the Lord and maintaining a grateful attitude (Col. 4:2). From there, believers can uphold one another in prayer (vs. 3). This entails petitioning God for each other's spiritual and physical well-being. It also includes asking the Lord for ongoing opportunities to share the Gospel.

Because Christians live among the unsaved, the Lord wants His spiritual children to be characterized by godly deeds and words. For instance, instead of believers acting in shortsighted and inconsiderate ways, they are to be known by the unregenerate as individuals who are thoughtful, prudent, and diligent (vs. 5). Moreover, the Savior is honored when His followers respond to their unsaved peers in ways that are gracious and engaging (vs. 6).

Daniel's Vision of Change

Scripture

Background Scripture: *Daniel 7*

Scripture Lesson: *Daniel 7:9-14*

Key Verse: *"His dominion is an everlasting dominion that will not pass away, and his kingdom is one that will never be destroyed."* Daniel 7:14.

Scripture Lesson for Children: *Daniel 6:11-13, 16, 19-23*

Key Verse for Children: *When Daniel was lifted from the den, no wound was found on him, because he had trusted in his God.* Daniel 6:23.

Lesson Aim

To recognize that God is building a kingdom that will never be destroyed.

Lesson Setting

Time: 553 B.C.
Place: Babylon

Lesson Outline

Daniel's Vision of Change

   I. The Ancient of Days: Daniel 7:9-12
       A. *The Glorious Throne: vss. 9-10*
       B. *The Slaying of the Beast: vss. 11-12*
  II. The Son of Man: Daniel 7:13-14
       A. *The Arrival of the Son of Man: vs. 13*
       B. *The Authority of the Son of Man: vs. 14*

Introduction for Adults

Topic: *Better Days Ahead*

On March 11, 2011, a 9.0-magnitude undersea earthquake occurred off the coast of Japan. This event triggered a massive tsunami. Within minutes, waves as high as 124 feet crashed into the Japanese coast and in some areas sea water traveled up to 6 miles inland. Along with causing hundreds of billions of dollars in property damage, the horrific natural disaster claimed the lives of tens of thousands of victims.

News such as this is enough to convince most people that we live in uncertain times. And as we get older, we are eventually touched (either directly or indirectly) by disease and loss of loved ones. Other personal hardships we may encounter include financial loss, marital upheaval, and deep psychological turmoil.

What are we to do in a world filled with so much uncertainty? To whom should we turn for help and the hope of better days ahead? The Book of Daniel (which is the focus of this week's lesson) urges us to put our hope in the "Ancient of Days" (7:9), who alone is all-powerful. Even in our moments of crisis, we can draw strength and encouragement, guidance and help from the Creator and Lord of the universe. When we rest our confidence in Him, we will never be disappointed.

Introduction for Youth

Topic: *The Future Is Sure*

There's a certain company that markets its product by claiming that it can keep battery-operated devices going and going and going. This self-assured optimism is reflected throughout society in the West. It doesn't seem to matter whether we're talking about young people, middle-aged people, or people heading into retirement. Individuals from each age group seem to have this durable confidence that their future is guaranteed to turn out right. And so they can do whatever they want, however they want, and whenever they want.

A study of the Book of Daniel exposes the folly of such thinking. Even young people are not the captains of their own destinies (in a manner of speaking), though they might like to think they are. Ultimately, the future course of our lives falls under the rule of God. He determines when we are born and when we will die. Even such things as the shape of our hands and the size of our feet are controlled by Him. Isn't it time we begin to acknowledge this in the way we live?

Concepts for Children

Topic: *Daniel Keeps the Faith*

1. Despite what others said, Daniel continued his practice of prayer.
2. Daniel's faith in God helped him stand firm even in the face of death.
3. God stood with Daniel in the lions' den and saved his life.
4. Daniel influenced the king to proclaim the power of God.
5. God can help us do what is best in changing situations.

Lesson Commentary

I. THE ANCIENT OF DAYS: DANIEL 7:9-12

A. The Glorious Throne: vss. 9-10

"As I looked, thrones were set in place, and the Ancient of Days took his seat. His clothing was as white as snow; the hair of his head was white like wool. His throne was flaming with fire, and its wheels were all ablaze. A river of fire was flowing, coming out from before him. Thousands upon thousands attended him; ten thousand times ten thousand stood before him. The court was seated, and the books were opened."

The Book of Daniel contains historical accounts known and loved by generations of believers and unbelievers alike. What child who has spent any time in Sunday school cannot tell the episode of Daniel in the lions' den? Or who does not know at least the basic elements of the deliverance of Daniel's friends, Shadrach, Meshach, and Abednego from Nebuchadnezzar's fiery furnace? Miraculous events such as these have given Daniel a welcomed place in many people's hearts.

As a member of the Israelite nobility in Judah and Jerusalem, Daniel was among those taken captive to Babylon (see 1:6). Early on, he was given the name of Belteshazzar and trained for the king's service (see vs. 7). Daniel was also given a position of prominence in the successive governments of Nebuchadnezzar, Belshazzar, and Darius. Though Daniel was highly favored and greatly honored by various kings, his ministry at the highest levels of government was characterized by humility and a complete lack of interest in personal power or prestige. Daniel's long diplomatic career (605–530 B.C.) was also marked by his interpretation of visions and by his own spectacular vision of Israel's future messianic kingdom. Furthermore, it was on his knees that he conquered kings and prophesied the rise and fall of world empires. Daniel's life is a model of what persistent prayer and unwavering faith can accomplish.

We learn that as new arrivals in Babylon, Daniel and his companions passed the test of diet and learning. After refusing the king's food for 10 days, they appeared healthier than the young men who had eaten the royal food (see 1:8-16). Verse 17 states that to "these four young men God gave knowledge and understanding of all kinds of literature and learning. And Daniel could understand visions and dreams of all kinds" (vs. 17). Later on, three of them were cast into a fiery furnace for refusing to worship Nebuchadnezzar's golden image; but God preserved them (chap. 3). Many years later, jealous officials charged Daniel himself with praying to his God, despite King Darius's decree against doing so. For this infraction, Daniel was thrown into a den of lions; but God protected Daniel from any harm (chap. 6).

These historical accounts are what most of us remember about Daniel. In one sense, they are incidental to his prophecies, though they do spotlight the faith and character of the Hebrew captives. We discover that God has been, and is, in the business of using human institutions (for example, empires, nations, companies, and cities) to accomplish His will. Chapter 7 of the book is a case in point. It concerns Daniel's dream involving four beasts. The "first year of Belshazzar" (vs. 1) would be about 553 B.C. when Daniel saw in his vision a "lion" (vs. 4), a "bear" (vs. 5), a "leopard" (vs. 6), and a hideous, exceedingly strong creature (vs. 7). These beasts were graphic depictions of four successive empires, namely, Babylonia, Medo-Persia, Greece, and Rome (see 7:17; 11:30).

The fourth beast seemed to capture Daniel's attention the most (see vs. 19). He was riveted by the huge iron teeth this brute used to trample and consume its prey (see vs. 23). We learn from ancient history that the legions of Rome used their superior military might to overrun and assimilate other nations, including the remnants of the once powerful but later divided kingdom of Greece. The "ten horns" (vs. 20) Daniel saw in his dream represent the vast sweep of the beast's authority, which was manifested either in ten monarchs or kingdoms arising from the Roman empire (see vs. 24). It is debated whether these entities existed at the same time as Rome or came after its demise. For instance, one common view is that the horns symbolize a second phase of the fourth kingdom, namely, a revived Roman empire that will materialize in the last days. This view notwithstanding, there is no direct evidence in the biblical text to support such a distinction.

A parallel passage is 2:41-42, which is part of the interpretation Daniel gave to Nebuchadnezzar's dream in which he saw an "enormous, dazzling statue" (vs. 31). The head of the figure was made out of pure gold, its chest and arms were comprised of silver, and its belly and thighs were composed of bronze (vs. 32). These sections of the breathtaking statue corresponded (respectively) to Babylonia, Medo-Persia, and Greece. In turn, the figure's legs made from iron and feet comprised of an iron-clay mixture symbolized Rome (vs. 33). Daniel explained that the feet and toes Nebuchadnezzar saw represented the divided nature of the kingdom (vs. 41). Some parts of the realm would be as strong as iron, while other parts would be as brittle as baked clay (vs. 42). This mixture of iron and clay also showed that these kingdoms would try to strengthen themselves (for example, by forming alliances with each other through intermarriage). Despite such efforts, though, they would fail, just as iron and clay do not mix (vs. 43).

As with the ten horns on the hideous beast mentioned in 7:7 and 20, some interpreters view the mixture of iron and clay in the feet of the statue as representing a second phase of the fourth kingdom that is different from the legs of solid iron (for instance, a later federation of states occupying the region previously controlled by the Roman Empire). Another possibility is that the iron represents the culture and laws of imperial Rome, while the clay represents the divergent political and social traditions of its many parts. In either case, it's clear that the elements of the fourth kingdom cannot preserve their union. Thus, while this entity has a measure of strength, it is temporary and to be replaced by the eternal kingdom of God.

In 7:8, Daniel noted that while he was contemplating the ten horns, a smaller horn suddenly appeared. In turn, three of the earlier horns were plucked up by their roots to make room for the formidable newcomer (see vss. 20, 24). One view is that this entity symbolizes the rise of the Antichrist (see vs. 21). This individual not only deceives the earth, but also seeks to control it through the military, economic, and religious systems of the world (see 2 Thess. 2:1-10; 1 John 2:18, 22; 4:1-4; 2 John 7; Rev. 19:19). Another view is that the smaller horn represents an evil world system that embodies the Antichrist's wicked characteristics. Ancient Rome would be one example of a human government that endorsed the persecution of believers, the spread of immorality, and the proliferation of heretical ideas.

Regardless of which option is preferred, the despicable nature of the smaller horn is unmistakable. Daniel 7:8 says this entity had humanlike eyes that could never be satiated and a mouth that spouted arrogant claims. Verses 21 and 25 reveal that the imposing horn was allowed to wage war for a set time period against God's holy people, as well as oppress and defeat them. Verses 9 and 10 record Daniel's vision of a heavenly courtroom scene, the immediate backdrop of which is God's plan for judging the wicked and vindicating the upright (see vss. 22, 26). As was noted earlier, the broader literary context of these verses is the elder statesman's dream concerning the four world empires of Babylon, Medo-Persia, Greece, and Rome.

It's worth noting that verses 9 and 10 are characterized by symmetry and balance, which is consistent with the beauty and order that distinguishes the supreme Judge of the cosmos. This situation contrasts sharply with the churning of the sea and its beasts, which represents the agitation found in the tyrannical waters of human rebellion (see vss. 2-8). Despite the pompous claims and defiant actions of the anti-God forces in the world, none of them can withstand the judgment of the Lord (see vs. 27). From this truth redeemed humanity learns that all would-be antagonists are completely muzzled and condemned by the God of glory.

In his vision, Daniel saw thrones being set up, followed by the "Ancient of Days" (vs. 9) taking His place to administer justice. In this verse, God is portrayed in human form as a revered, prudent, and authoritative judge. Paul referred to Him as the "King of kings and Lord of lords" (1 Tim. 6:15), the one who alone possesses immortality, who dwells in "unapproachable light" (vs. 16), and upon whom no human is able to look directly. Daniel noticed that the attire of the eternal God was white as snow, and His hair was white like pure lamb's wool. The chariot-like throne on which the ancient one sat was ablaze and mounted on fiery wheels (see Pss. 50:3; 68:4; 97:3; 104:3-4; Isa. 6:1-4; 19:1; 66:15; Ezek. 1:27; Nah. 1:3). A "river of fire" (Dan. 7:10) streamed out from the all-glorious throne. It was as if flames emanated like solar flares from all around Him. The heavenly host who attended to the Creator-King and served Him were countless in number. This was the awe-inspiring backdrop for convening the divine tribunal (see Pss. 82:1; 94:2; 96:13).

B. The Slaying of the Beast: vss. 11-12

"Then I continued to watch because of the boastful words the horn was speaking. I kept looking until the beast was slain and its body destroyed and thrown into the blazing fire. (The other beasts had been stripped of their authority, but were allowed to live for a period of time.)"

As Daniel's dream continued to unfold, he was captivated by the arrogant remarks mouthed by the small horn (Dan. 7:11). This entity somewhat resembles the beast emerging from sea recorded in Revelation 13:1. That grotesque creature had ten horns and seven heads. On each horn there was a crown, and on each head there was a pretentious name that was an insult to God. In ancient times, people used horns to symbolize the military, economic, and religious power of their kings. People also used crowns to represent the exalted status of their rulers. The ten horns and crowns of the beast suggest that it is characterized by unequaled power and preeminence.

Ancient people used the head as a symbol of control and intelligence. John may have been indicating that the seven-headed beast was cunning and influential. Rulers in the ancient world often assumed titles of deity. Likewise, the beast from the sea took upon itself designations that God has reserved exclusively for Himself. Although the beast looked like a leopard, it had the feet of a bear and the mouth of a lion. People in those days associated agility with the leopard, bone-crushing strength with the bear, and swiftness and stealthy force with the lion. Evidently, the beast had all these characteristics, making it extremely deadly (Rev. 13:2). There have been and continue to be those who oppose the Savior and promote evil. God has called us to be salt and light in such an ungodly environment.

With respect to Daniel's vision, as he watched, he noticed that the small-horned beast was eventually put to death. Next, its corpse was cremated in an intense fire (Dan. 7:11). The elder statesman noted that the Lord had already removed the authority belonging to the rest of the beasts Daniel described earlier. Be that as it may, God permitted them to go on living for a "period of time" (vs. 12). It's unclear why the Lord allowed the preceding kingdoms to continue for an indefinite span, along with their inhabitants and customs. What is certain is that God will one day judge all evil. Likewise, no matter how dark things may appear, believers have the assurance that the Lord will watch over them and bring them through their trials.

II. THE SON OF MAN: DANIEL 7:13-14

A. The Arrival of the Son of Man: vs. 13

"In my vision at night I looked, and there before me was one like a son of man, coming with the clouds of heaven. He approached the Ancient of Days and was led into his presence."

Daniel 7:13 spotlights the coronation of the "son of man." The preceding phrase emphasizes that this person was a representative of the people of God. In contrast to the grotesque and arrogant small horn, the individual Daniel saw was characterized by divine power and holiness. To the elder statesman it appeared as if the "son of man" was being carried along by the clouds of the sky, just as a triumphant monarch might ride in his chariot to vanquish his foes. A procession of angels escorted the "son of man" into the presence of the Ancient One.

The New Testament identifies the "son of man" as Jesus of Nazareth. During His trial before the Sanhedrin, the high priest demanded to know whether Jesus claimed to be the Messiah, the "Son of God" (Matt. 26:63). In response, He affirmed His identity. Moreover, Jesus declared that a future day was coming in which everyone would see the divine Savior seated in the place of power at the Father's right hand. The onlookers would also see the "Son of Man" (vs. 64) arriving on the "clouds of heaven" (see Ps. 110:1; Mark 14:62; Luke 22:69).

In Revelation 1:7, John made a similar statement about the second coming of the Messiah. The apostle echoed two prophetic passages from the Old Testament, one of which is Daniel 7:13. The other is Zechariah 12:10, which reads, "They will look on me, the one they have pierced, and they will mourn for him." At Jesus' second coming, none will doubt that He is Lord. People will mourn either because of the judgment that is about to fall on them or because of the sins they have committed (see Matt. 24:30; 25:31-33).

In Revelation 1:8, the Lord Jesus declared that He is the "Alpha and the Omega" (see 22:13). Alpha and omega are the first and last letters of the Greek alphabet. In other words, the Messiah is the beginning and the ending of all things. Furthermore, He is sovereign over all that takes place in human history. In point of fact, His lordship encompasses the past, the present, and the future. Throughout history, believers have endured abuse from enemies of the faith. Jesus' promise that He is "coming soon" (22:12) has been a source of comfort for His followers down through the centuries.

B. The Authority of the Son of Man: vs. 14

"He was given authority, glory and sovereign power; all peoples, nations and men of every language worshiped him. His dominion is an everlasting dominion that will not pass away, and his kingdom is one that will never be destroyed."

Daniel 7:14 says that to the Son of God was conferred ruling "authority," along with honor and royal sovereignty, so that all people of every race, nation, and language would worship and serve Him. Unlike earthly rulers and empires, the "dominion" of the Messiah is eternal, His authority will never cease, and His "kingdom" will never be "destroyed." In Revelation 5:11-14, we find similar truths being emphasized. John recounted hearing the singing of countless numbers of angels around God's throne, along with the voices of the living creatures and of the elders (vs. 11). The heavenly choir praised the Lamb for His worthiness. It was fitting for Him to receive glory, power, and praise for who He is and what He has done. In particular, He is the Son of God, the one who died on the cross so that those who trust in Him might become His servants in His kingdom (Rev. 5:12).

John next heard every creature in heaven, on earth, under the earth, and in the sea sing hymns in adoration to the Father and the Son. The idea in verse 13 is that all the creatures in the universe united their voices to give unending praise to God and His Son, the Messiah. The four living creatures affirmed their praise by declaring "Amen" (vs. 14), and the 24 elders responded appropriately by prostrating themselves in worship before the throne. We live in uncertain times and there are days when the future seems bleak. We should not lose hope, however, for the Savior was worthy to take the scroll (mentioned in verses 1-9) and open its seals. This means God allowed Him to carry out His plan for the world. The future is not in doubt, for the Son will bring to pass all that the Father has planned for His people.

Discussion Questions

1. How do you think Daniel felt when he saw the "Ancient of Days" (Dan. 7:9) take His seat on the throne?
2. In what way are believers called to offer the sort of praise given by the multitude of attendants before God's throne?
3. What are some reasons for identifying the "son of man" (vs. 13) with Jesus of Nazareth?
4. How is your attitude toward life affected by the prospect of the Son's future return?
5. What are some indications of the Son's eternal reign that you can see in the present?

Contemporary Application

Daniel wrote his book to teach that the God of Israel is sovereign, even over the powerful nations that surrounded His people. Jerusalem was destroyed and its temple lay in ruins. God's people were in exile and wicked rulers seemed triumphant. Nevertheless, Daniel emphasized through his writings that the Lord remained in supreme control.

This truth is still applicable today. Even when we endure hardship for the cause of Christ, or suffer loss for seemingly no clear reason, or witness untold suffering in the lives of others, we need to remember that the Lord is in control of all things. Yes, this world is filled with tragedy and turmoil, and at times it seems unfair. Nevertheless, as Paul declared in Romans 8:18, "I consider that our present sufferings are not worth comparing with the glory that will be revealed in us." May we take comfort in these words.

Daniel's Prayer

Scripture

Background Scripture: *Daniel 9:3-19*

Scripture Lesson: *Daniel 9:4b-14*

Key Verse: *"The Lord our God is merciful and forgiving, even though we have rebelled against him."* Daniel 9:9.

Scripture Lesson for Children: *Daniel 2:2, 10-13, 17-19, 23, 27-28, 44*

Key Verse for Children: *"I thank and praise you, O God of my fathers: You have given me wisdom and power."* Daniel 2:23.

Lesson Aim

To affirm that God holds people responsible for their own behavior.

Lesson Setting

Time: 539–538 B.C.

Place: Babylon

Lesson Outline

Daniel's Prayer

  I. Daniel's Candid Admission: Daniel 9:4-6
     A. *The Faithfulness of the Lord: vs. 4*
     B. *The Transgressions of God's People: vss. 5-6*
 II. Daniel's Ardent Confession: Daniel 9:7-14
     A. *The Shame of God's People: vss. 7-8*
     B. *The Mercy and Forgiveness of the Lord: vss. 9-10*
     C. *The Punishment of God's People: vss. 11-12*
     D. *The Obstinacy of God's People: vss. 13-14*

Introduction for Adults

Topic: *Have Mercy!*

Not one of us is immune from disobeying the Lord. Spiritual waywardness is something all believers struggle with at some point in their journey of faith (see 1 John 1:8-10).

Even when we go through the painful process of repentance, we must never forget that God shows mercy and graciously bestows blessings upon us because it pleases Him to do so, not because we deserve it. Many people, believers and unbelievers alike, act as if God is somehow obligated to grant any and all requests made of Him. But since sin placed all humanity under a death sentence, it would be unwise indeed to demand that a just and holy God give us what we deserve.

Daniel was well aware of God's righteousness (see Dan. 9:7, 14). Moreover, the elder statesman affirmed the faithfulness and compassion of the Lord (see vss. 4, 9). This week's study of Daniel's prayer on behalf on the chosen people can become an opportunity for your students to seek the Lord's forgiveness for transgressions in their lives. When they do, they will discover that He is ready and willing to lavish them with His mercy and grace.

Introduction for Youth

Topic: *Prayer of Confession*

Daniel knew how to pray. Unreserved confession of sin opened his heart to the Lord. Complete submission to God's will also prepared the prophet for divine direction. Like Daniel, we should first go to the Lord in confession, then listen with an attitude of submission and openness to hear what He wants to say to us.

At first, the idea of admitting personal sins might be difficult for some believing teens to accept. Most likely, they have not seen this humble attitude in their peers. And perhaps many of the adults in their life are more inclined to blame others for their misdeeds.

In situations such as this, you can remind your students of the example Daniel set. He was not told to identify with the sins of God's people. Yet Daniel humbly did so. Likewise, he did not hesitate to confess his own transgressions to the Lord. Like him, when saved adolescents do so, they will experience the blessing of God's forgiveness.

Concepts for Children

Topic: *Daniel Prays to God*

1. A king named Nebuchadnezzar was troubled by his dreams and looked for someone to explain their meaning.
2. Daniel offered to help.
3. Daniel asked his friends to join him in seeking God's help through prayer.
4. God responded by revealing to Daniel the king's dream and its meaning.
5. God is always available to hear and respond to our prayers.

Lesson Commentary

I. DANIEL'S CANDID ADMISSION: DANIEL 9:4-6

A. The Faithfulness of the Lord: vs. 4

"O Lord, the great and awesome God, who keeps his covenant of love with all who love him and obey his commands."

The events of Daniel 9 took place during the first year of the reign of Darius the Mede (Dan. 9:1). That began in 539 B.C., the year Babylon was conquered by the Medo-Persians. Daniel had been in captivity for 66 years, since 605 B.C. At this time, he would have been about 82 years old. The last date recorded in the Book of Daniel is 536 B.C., "the third year of Cyrus king of Persia" (see 10:1). Media was a region northeast of Babylon (which is today part of northwest Iran). Almost nothing is known about the origins of the ancient Indo-European people known as the Medes, and only a few words of their language have survived. Persia, modern Iran, was located south of Media.

While the kings of Persia and Media had made joint military campaigns into southwest Asia in 559 B.C., 20 years later Darius overthrew Belshazzar to gain control of the Babylonian empire. Belshazzar knew about his own fall in advance because of a handwritten message inscribed on his palace wall (see Dan. 5). The rise of the Medo-Persians was a providential act of God. Daniel apparently knew that the rise of Darius paved the way for the return of the Israelites to their homeland. Daniel understood from Jeremiah's prophecies (which the elder statesman regarded as being verbally inspired) that the 70-year exile begun by the "desolation of Jerusalem" (9:2), was nearing its end (see Jer. 25:11-12; 29:10).

The writer of Chronicles saw those 70 years as the sabbath rest for the promised land, time accumulated during 490 years when the people had neglected to allow the land to rest every seventh year, according to the law (see 2 Chron. 36:20-23; compare Lev. 25:1-7). With no specific way to measure the 70 years, some interpret this as a round number, perhaps denoting either a complete generation or an entire human lifetime (see Ps. 90:10). Others see it as the time period extending from 605 B.C. (the first attack on Jerusalem) to 536 B.C. (when Jerusalem was resettled). Still others calculate the 70 years from 586 B.C. (when the temple was destroyed) to 516 B.C. (when Zerubbabel dedicated the new temple; Ezra 6:13-18; Zech. 1:12).

In any case, Daniel's expectation for his people drove him to his knees in prayer. Two distinct terms appear in Daniel 9:3. The first, simply rendered "prayer," was a general word often used in intercessory entreaties. The second word, translated "petition," denoted a supplication for mercy and compassion. On behalf of his people, Daniel pleaded with God for mercy. Daniel also cried out to the Lord first in confession, and then in petition.

In describing how he prayed, Daniel said that he turned his face to the Lord. This could mean Daniel set aside his normal routine and devoted himself entirely to prayer. It may also allude to the practice of praying in the direction of Jerusalem. Earlier in this book, we read how Daniel prayed in his upstairs room, where the latticed windows opened toward Jerusalem (6:10). Daniel approached the throne of grace with fasting, adorned in sackcloth (a rough material similar to burlap) and ashes. All three of these were signs of deep repentance or personal grief and loss (Dan. 9:3; see Ezek. 27:29-31).

Daniel recognized that the exile in Babylon was God's judgment for Israel's sin. The prophet also understood what God's covenant with His people required if they were to receive forgiveness, restoration, and divine blessing. The people of the nation had to confess their sin and obey the commands of God (Dan. 9:4-5). In this knowledge, Daniel confessed the sins of the people, not once but four times (vss. 5, 8, 11, 15). He included himself as if he were personally involved in Israel's wickedness, rebellion, and disobedience. Even though God had graciously sent the prophets to turn His people back, the nation as a whole had ignored their message. According to Daniel, all Israel was guilty before God (vss. 6, 8-11).

The elder statesman began his prayer by affirming that the sovereign Lord is both "great and awesome" (vs. 4). Additionally, God was faithful to fulfill His covenant promises with those who loved and obeyed Him. These truths formed the theological foundation of Daniel's confession. As he prayed, he made reference to the "LORD" (vs. 4), a term that renders the four Hebrew letters making up the divine name, YHWH (or *Yahweh*). Incidentally, it appears eight times in this chapter, but nowhere else in the rest of the book. This special name for the covenant-keeping God of Israel emphasizes His eternal existence, supreme power, and active involvement in human history. In short, He is the ever-present, ever-living God (see Exod. 3:13-14). The second Hebrew term rendered "Lord" in Daniel 9:4 is *adonai*. It emphasizes the authority, rule, and majesty of Yahweh over all creation.

"God" is the rendering for *elohim* in the Hebrew. In addition to being used for rulers, judges, and pagan deities, the word is the most common way the writers of the Old Testament referred to God. Despite the plural form of the noun, it is consistently used in the Hebrew sacred writings as a singular term. As a matter of fact, when used as a proper name for the divine, *elohim* portrays the Lord as the one, true, and unique God. The totality of Scripture leaves the impression that He is unique in His being or essence, the fountain and source of all things, and the one who unifies all the forces of time and eternity.

B. The Transgressions of God's People: vss. 5-6

"We have sinned and done wrong. We have been wicked and have rebelled; we have turned away from your commands and laws. We have not listened to your servants the prophets, who spoke in your name to our kings, our princes and our fathers, and to all the people of the land."

Daniel did not hesitate to affirm the Lord's faithfulness to the Mosaic covenant. As it happened, God remained more loyal in His devotion to His chosen people than they had been with Him. In Daniel 9:5, the elder statesman acknowledged that the faith community had sinned against its Creator and Redeemer in every imaginable way. The people were guilty of committing iniquity and participating in wicked acts. They also rebelled by scorning His commands and dodging His teachings. Moreover, the chosen people refused to heed the Lord's prophets, who humbly served Him. The latter spoke as His representatives in the authority of His name to a wide audience of people, including monarchs and princes who ruled the inhabitants of the promised land (vs. 6).

II. DANIEL'S ARDENT CONFESSION: DANIEL 9:7-14

A. The Shame of God's People: vss. 7-8

"Lord, you are righteous, but this day we are covered with shame—the men of Judah and people of Jerusalem and all Israel, both near and far, in all the countries where you have scattered us because of our unfaithfulness to you. O LORD, we and our kings, our princes and our fathers are covered with shame because we have sinned against you."

Daniel affirmed the righteousness of the Lord in His person and actions. Expressed differently, God was characterized by equity, justice, and truthfulness in His dealings with the faith community. His chosen people, though, suffered public disgrace as a result of their disloyalty to God. The shame was carried by the leaders of Judah, the citizens of Jerusalem, and all the rest of the inhabitants of Israel. Because they transgressed God's ways, He was in the right to scatter them far and wide (Dan. 9:7). All the chosen people experienced the humiliation of being dragged away to foreign lands because of their extensive and repeated acts of sin against the Lord (vs. 8).

B. The Mercy and Forgiveness of the Lord: vss. 9-10

"The Lord our God is merciful and forgiving, even though we have rebelled against him; we have not obeyed the LORD our God or kept the laws he gave us through his servants the prophets."

If it had been any lesser ruler, that monarch would have immediately punished his subjects for a single act of insurrection. Yet despite the faith community's ongoing rebellion, the sovereign Lord remained "merciful and forgiving" (Dan. 9:9). His compassion was evident when He gave the Mosaic law. Also, despite the chosen people's violations of God's edicts, He freely pardoned them. Sadly, the recipients of His favor refused to heed His stipulations and listen to His teachings, as set before them through His prophets (vs. 10).

Prior to the destruction of Jerusalem by the Babylonians, many people of Judah did not believe that God would destroy His own temple and His holy city until it actually happened. They continued in their worship of other gods. The prophets repeatedly pointed out that the people's unfaithfulness would bring judgment, and it did, namely, their 70-year exile in Babylon. The people's rejection of the prophets proved the unfaithfulness of those whom God had chosen. Although the Lord's representatives occasionally foretold future events, their primary responsibility was calling the nation to obey God in the present. They spoke to Israel's leaders and, through them, to all the people.

C. The Punishment of God's People: vss. 11-12

"All Israel has transgressed your law and turned away, refusing to obey you. Therefore the curses and sworn judgments written in the Law of Moses, the servant of God, have been poured out on us, because we have sinned against you. You have fulfilled the words spoken against us and against our rulers by bringing upon us great disaster. Under the whole heaven nothing has ever been done like what has been done to Jerusalem."

Tragically, the entire nation was guilty of violating God's injunctions and stubbornly refusing to follow His will (Dan. 9:11). Because the Lord is just in everything He does (see vs. 7), He had no other option but to pour out on His wayward people the judgment solemnly threatened in the Mosaic law (see Deut. 28:15-68). God had given His people a very straightforward choice—either obey Him and be blessed or disobey Him and suffer terrible curses. Because Israel had chosen the latter course, the Lord kept His word by doing exactly what He had forewarned. The calamity referred to in Daniel 9:12 is the destruction of Jerusalem and the exile of the chosen people to Babylon. As far as the faith community was concerned, no other disaster on record seemed as horrendous as the tragedy the inhabitants of Judah experienced at the hands of their enemies in 586 B.C.

D. The Obstinacy of God's People: vss. 13-14

"Just as it is written in the Law of Moses, all this disaster has come upon us, yet we have not sought the favor of the LORD our God by turning from our sins and giving attention to your truth. The LORD did not hesitate to bring the disaster upon us, for the LORD our God is righteous in everything he does; yet we have not obeyed him."

Centuries earlier, the Mosaic law forewarned the chosen people about the unimaginable horrors they would endure if they rebelled against the Lord. These alarming calamities were meant to bring God's people back to Him, but they refused to entreat the Lord's "favor" (Dan. 9:13). Moreover, despite the unparalleled "disaster" brought upon the nation, the people were still not turning away from their sin and submitting themselves to God's well-founded moral standards recorded in the law. Because the sovereign Lord of Israel is characterized by justice and rectitude, He intentionally allowed His wayward people to experience catastrophe at the hands of their foes (vs. 14).

Daniel's petition for divine favor was grounded in an awareness of how God had faithfully acted throughout the course of Israel's history. The premier example of this was the Lord's deliverance of His people out of the land of Egypt with great power. Because of that mighty act, God brought lasting honor to His name. But this did not prevent His chosen people from sinning and behaving wickedly (vs. 15). As a consequence of this sobering truth, the only thing Daniel could do was appeal to the Lord on the basis of His justice.

In view of all of God's faithfulness and mercy in connection with His covenant promises, the elder statesman humbly asked the Lord to turn His raging anger away from Jerusalem. It was the chosen city built on His holy mountain (vs. 16) and thus the place where God decided to dwell and reign (see Pss. 43:3; 68:16; Isa. 24:23). As such, it was intended to be the sacred site where the people could enjoy a transcendent encounter with God, in addition to finding refuge, peace, and joy in His presence (see Isa. 2:1-5; Mic. 4:1-5).

In short, Daniel was entreating the Lord to end Jerusalem's condition as an object of scorn among the surrounding nations. Suggested here is the idea that the fortunes of a country, whether good or bad, were an indicator of its deity's power and might. A positive outcome for Judah would require God to forgive the sins of the current generation of Jews and the iniquities committed by their ancestors (Dan. 9:16). With humility and courage, Daniel petitioned God to "hear" (vs. 17) the prayer of His servant. Expressed differently, the prophet asked the Lord to graciously accept his request to show favor on His devastated sanctuary. Daniel was convinced that God would bring honor to His name by smiling once again (in a manner of speaking) on His temple. Though it lay in ruins, the Lord could enable His people to rebuild it.

Daniel concluded with an entreaty to God to "give ear" (vs. 18) to his prayer, as if the Lord would turn His ear to listen attentively to the prophet's request. The elder statesman also asked God to open His eyes and see the ruined condition of Jerusalem. The Hebrew word translated "desolation" usually describes devastation that results from divine judgment. Daniel was not implying that God was not listening or had closed His eyes to the exiles' problems. The Lord was fully aware of these issues. This prayer, however, came from the human perspective on the circumstances. It appeared to the Jews still in exile in Babylon as if God had stopped listening and had closed His eyes.

Although Daniel hoped God would show compassion, the prophet recognized that Israel deserved its current suffering. Therefore, his prayer request appealed to divine mercy. But the petition also showed a concern for God. Daniel reminded Him that both the city of Jerusalem and His people carried His "Name" as a mark of ownership. The Hebrew word can signify reputation or renown, as in God's name being praised and known for what He has done (see 2 Sam. 7:25-26). The Lord's deliverance of His people from Babylon would show who He was to the people who were called by His name. Also, since God's reputation rested with His people and His holy city, the neighboring peoples would recognize who the Lord is by His deliverance of the Jews and restoration of Jerusalem and its temple.

Daniel acknowledged that he was not basing his requests on his own righteous deeds or those of his fellow Jews, whether they were living in the past or present. Rather, it was due to the Lord's abundant compassion (Dan. 9:18). Moreover, Daniel was not trying to manipulate God. Instead, the prophet showed a concern for the glory of the Lord. The elder statesman realized that God's reputation was inevitably tied to the fortunes of His exiled people. Thus, the prophet was convinced that even though they had disowned God, He would not disown them. This truth emboldened Daniel to plead with the Lord to hear his request and forgive the sins of His people. The prophet entreated God to act quickly in restoring the exiles to the promised land and enable them to bring honor to His name by rebuilding their sanctuary and capital (vs. 19).

Daniel reviewed the content of his prayer once again. He had started by confessing his own sins and the sins of Israel. While nothing negative is recorded about the prophet in Scripture, he still identified himself with the sins of Israel. In his petition, he asked God to consider the state of "his holy hill" (vs. 20), meaning Jerusalem. Daniel also requested that the Lord not delay in acting upon his prayer. The divine response could hardly have come more quickly.

Discussion Questions

1. In what ways had the Lord remained faithful to His covenant?
2. What role did God's prophets serve in the life of the faith community?
3. In what sense were the chosen people of Daniel's day experiencing humiliation?
4. What usually moves you to pray?
5. How willing are you to identify in prayer with the sins of other believers?

Contemporary Application

If you were to interview the students in your class, you would discover that they shoulder a wide variety of personal responsibilities. Many are married, have children, and hold at least one job. The class members have to deal with financial obligations, work-related deadlines, and health matters.

Your students have a multitude of complex and controversial decisions to make as they deal with their responsibilities. For instance, administrators in large organizations often have to make decisions about who to hire or fire, what projects to begin or end, and how to expand or contract certain business ventures.

What happens when a decision that is made backfires? When things go wrong, it is all too common for people to shift the blame to others. It is much rarer to find individuals who hold themselves accountable for their actions. One reason for this is that people do not want to endure the negative consequences associated with a mistake or error in judgment they have made.

In this week's lesson, we discover that it is wrong to blame others for mistakes we have made. God wants us to take personal responsibility for our own lives. When we do, He is glorified and immensely pleased.

Gabriel's Interpretation

Scripture

Background Scripture: *Daniel 8*
Scripture Lesson: *Daniel 8:19-26*
Key Verse: *"The vision of the evenings and mornings that has been given you is true."* Daniel 8:26.
Scripture Lesson for Children: *Daniel 8:19-26*
Key Verse for Children: *While I, Daniel, was watching the vision, [I tried] to understand it.* Daniel 8:15.

Lesson Aim

To clarify that the future of God's people rests in His hands.

Lesson Setting

Time: 551 B.C.
Place: Babylon

Lesson Outline

Gabriel's Interpretation
I. The Kingdoms of Medo-Persia and Greece: Daniel 8:19-22
   A. *Gabriel's Intent: vs. 19*
   B. *Three Kingdoms Depicted: vss. 20-22*
II. The Reign of Antiochus IV Epiphanes: Daniel 8:23-26
   A. *The Emergence of Antiochus IV Epiphanes: vs. 23*
   B. *The Schemes of Antiochus IV Epiphanes: vss. 24-25*
   C. *The Command to Seal Up the Vision: vs. 26*

Introduction for Adults

Topic: *Dreams for a Better Tomorrow*

A U.S. Army officer told about the contrast in his pupils during two different eras of teaching at the artillery training school at Fort Sill, Oklahoma. In 1958–60, the attitude was so lax that the instructors had a problem getting the men to stay awake to listen. During the 1965–67 classes, however, the men, hearing the same basic lectures, were alert and took copious notes. The reason? These men knew that in less that six weeks they would be facing the enemy in Vietnam.

The vision Daniel saw of a ram and a goat was not one he would have ignored or taken lightly. After all, it concerned the future of God's chosen people. Both during and after the experience, Daniel pondered the meaning and significance of the vision (see Dan. 8:5, 15, 27).

When we approach the prophetic portions of God's Word, what is our typical response? Is it one of ambivalence or intense interest? Hopefully, it will be the latter. After all, the Bible's predictions about the future concern us. This is one reason why the class members are wise to sit up and take notice as you guide them through this week's lesson.

Introduction for Youth

Topic: *A Curious Dream*

In 2010, the movie thriller *A Nightmare on Elm Street* hit the theaters. In this remake of a 1984 film with the same title, a serial killer named Freddy Krueger murders people in their dreams. This results in their actual death in real life.

What a contrast the above is to the vision recorded in Daniel 8! The prophet's dream was about the future of God's chosen people. While it was a disturbing experience for the elder statesman, he not only successfully woke up from the dream, but also lived to record what he had seen and heard.

Scripture contains a number of prophecies such as Daniel's about the future. The Bible records these not to shock us, but to encourage us to live faithfully for the Lord. Saved teens need to know that they can use the truths they glean from this week's lesson to prepare themselves for the many spiritual battles they will face from the forces of darkness.

Concepts for Children

Topic: *Daniel Receives Help to Understand His Dream*

1. Daniel had a dream that he did not understand.
2. God sent an angel named Gabriel to Daniel.
3. Gabriel told Daniel what his dream meant.
4. Daniel learned that God would be with His people even in hard times.
5. God is also with us no matter what we are experiencing.

Lesson Commentary

I. THE KINGDOMS OF MEDO-PERSIA AND GREECE: DANIEL 8:19-22

A. Gabriel's Intent: vs. 19

He said: "I am going to tell you what will happen later in the time of wrath, because the vision concerns the appointed time of the end."

Daniel was born in the middle of good King Josiah's reign, and grew up under his religious reforms (see 2 Kings 22–23). During that time, Daniel probably heard Jeremiah, whom he later quoted (see Dan. 9:2). When Judah fell and Josiah was killed in a battle with Egypt in 609 B.C., Josiah's eldest son, Jehoiakim, was made king of Judah by Pharaoh Neco. For four years, Judah was an Egyptian vassal nation until Nebuchadnezzar defeated Egypt at Carchemish in 605 B.C. That same year, the Babylonian king swept into Judah and captured Jerusalem. He had Jehoiakim, who was in the third year of his reign, carried off to Babylon. Nebuchadnezzar also ordered treasures from the temple in Jerusalem sent back home and placed in "the temple of his god" (1:1-2). The "god" referred to was probably Bel (also called Marduk), the chief Babylonian deity.

The reign of Nebuchadnezzar lasted until 562 B.C. After his death, the empire he established and built experienced a steady decline. His successor was his son, Amel-Marduk, who is referred to as Evil-Merodach in 2 Kings 25:27 and Jeremiah 52:31. He ruled only two years, being overthrown in 560 B.C. by a son-in-law of Nebuchadnezzar, Nerglissar. He is referred to as Nergal-Sharezer in Jeremiah 39:3, and his reign lasted four years. In 556 B.C., he was followed by his weak son, Labashi-Marduk, whose reign lasted just two months due to an army coup led by Nabonidus in 556 B.C. Previously, he was a chief official of a Babylonian city during the reign of Nebuchadnezzar and had married one of his daughters.

Because Nabonidus was deeply religious, he launched a campaign to restore the ancient temples of Babylon. Also, because of his interests and involvement in military campaigns, he spent long periods of time away from Babylon (especially 10 years at Teima in northwest Arabia). In his absence, his eldest son, Belshazzar (about 553–539 B.C.), governed in his place as coregent and commander of the Babylonian army. Belshazzar's name means "Bel, protect the king." As the second-in-command in the empire, the highest honor he could grant to a subordinate was to be the third most powerful ruler in the kingdom (see Dan. 5:7). The events of chapters 7 and 8 chronologically took place between those of chapters 4 and 5.

The episode recorded in this week's lesson occurred in 551 B.C., which was two years after the dream recorded in chapter 7. In 8:1, Daniel said he experienced a vision. According to verse 2, he saw himself in the walled city of Susa. The latter was located about 230 miles east of Babylon. In his dream, he was at the Ulai Canal. This broad artificial waterway connected two rivers flowing into the Persian Gulf and was used by local residents for irrigation. Daniel remembered lifting his eyes and seeing a ram standing on the bank of the canal. This unusual animal had two long horns. One of them was longer than the other, even though the longer one began to grow later than the shorter one (vs. 3). Daniel noticed the creature butting westward, northward, and southward, and no other beast was able to stop it or help its victims. The ram did whatever it wanted and acted arrogantly (vs. 4).

While Daniel pondered the meaning of what he had seen, suddenly a male goat with a conspicuous horn between its eyes appeared. It was moving so fast out of the west that its feet did not even seem to touch the ground (vs. 5). The goat attacked the ram with savage force (vs. 6). In fact, the goat was so enraged that when it smashed into the ram, the goat broke off the ram's two horns and the latter was powerless to resist the attack. The goat threw the ram to the ground and trampled on it, and no one could deliver the ram from being overpowered (vs. 7). For a while, the goat acted even more arrogantly. But when its horn was at the height of its power, it was broken off. In its place arose four other conspicuous horns, with each one extending in the four directions of the earth (vs. 8).

Out of these four prominent horns Daniel saw a small horn emerge. Soon, however, it became exceedingly large, with its enormous power extending toward the south, the east, and the "Beautiful Land" (vs. 9). The latter is a reference to Israel (see 11:16, 41). Eventually, the horn grew strong enough to attack the "host of the heavens" (8:10). In this context, the reference most likely is to God's faithful remnant, who valiantly try to resist their wicked foe (see Gen. 15:5; Exod. 12:41; Dan. 12:3). Moreover, the horn challenged the "Prince" (Dan. 8:11) of the chosen people by profaning the Jerusalem temple. This included stopping the regular burnt offering and then pillaging and desecrating the entire shrine. In the course of the horn's sinful rebellion against God, the horn was able to commit barbarous acts against His chosen people. The horn even succeed in trampling on God's truth by authorizing the destruction of copies of the Mosaic law. It seemed as if the horn succeeded in whatever it did (vs. 12).

At this point, Daniel heard one angel ask another angel how long the events in the vision would last (vs. 13). Daniel learned that it would be "2,300 evenings and mornings" (vs. 14) before the temple was restored (see vs. 26). Some consider this to be a reference to the evening sacrifice and the morning sacrifice (see Exod. 29:38-42; Num. 28:3-5; Dan. 9:21). In this case, the elapsed time would be 1,150 days (or 3 years and 55 days). Others consider the phrase in Daniel 8:14 to be reminiscent of the creation account in Genesis 1. In this case, the reference to evening and morning would be equivalent to an entire day. Hence, the expression denotes 2,300 days (or 6 years and 111 days). In either case, it is difficult to pinpoint a specific event within ancient Jewish history that marked the outset of this horrific period. In contrast, the cleansing and rededicating of the Jerusalem temple (following the sacrilegious acts committed by Antiochus IV Epiphanes) signaled the end of this period. The latter occurred on December 14, 165 B.C., when Judas Maccabeaus lead a group of his fellow Jews to liberate the shrine.

This victory is commemorated each year by the observance of the Jewish holiday of Hanukkah.

As Daniel watched the vision unfold, he struggled to make sense of it. Just then, he saw a humanlike creature standing in front of him (Dan. 8:15). The elder statesman remembered hearing a voice calling out from the Ulai Canal. The voice referred to the supernatural messenger in Daniel's presence as "Gabriel" (vs. 16) and directed him to explain to Daniel what he had seen in the vision. In Hebrew, the angel's name means "man of God," "God has shown Himself strong," or "God is my hero." The greatness of this messenger from heaven is seen in the fact that Gabriel stood in the presence of the Lord (see Dan. 9:21; Luke 1:19, 26).

When Gabriel approached Daniel, the elder statesman became so terrified that he fell facedown on the ground (Dan. 8:17). Gabriel, in referring to Daniel as "son of man," was drawing attention to his existence as a mortal human being. The angel stated that the vision pertained to the "time of the end." In some contexts, this expression deals with the absolute end of history, while in other circumstances, the phrase is more chronologically limited in its focus (see 11:27, 35). As Gabriel was speaking, Daniel lapsed into a trancelike state in which he lay face down. Then, when the angel touched the elder statesman, he was able to stand upright (8:18). Next, Gabriel revealed that the vision related to the divinely appointed end of time and that it would be a period characterized by indignation (vs. 19).

B. Three Kingdoms Depicted: vss. 20-22

"The two-horned ram that you saw represents the kings of Media and Persia. The shaggy goat is the king of Greece, and the large horn between his eyes is the first king. The four horns that replaced the one that was broken off represent four kingdoms that will emerge from his nation but will not have the same power."

Gabriel explained that the double-horned ram Daniel noticed symbolized the rulers of the Medes and Persians (Dan. 8:20; see vss. 3-4). As was noted in last week's lesson, the Medes were an ancient group of people who lived in what is today part of northwest Iran. They were assimilated by the rise of Persia in the seventh century B.C. The latter group of ancient people occupied land that stretched from southwest Asia to the east of Babylonia. It is approximately the same territory controlled today by the country of Iran. Next, Gabriel stated that the male goat represented the future "king of Greece" (vs. 21; see vs. 5). Initially, the territory of the latter included the south Balkan Peninsula, along with the islands and adjoining coasts of the Aegean Sea.

The huge horn between the male goat's eyes symbolized Alexander the Great (356–323 B.C.). The goat's swift movement (see 7:6) depicted the meteoric rise of the Greek empire under Alexander's leadership. In fact, in three major battles spanning just three years (334–331 B.C.), he was able to defeat the once powerful Persian empire (see 8:6-7). The first engagement, which took place in 334 B.C. at the Granicus River, opened Asia Minor to Alexander. The second battle, which occurred in 333 B.C. at Issus, enabled him to take control of Syria, Canaan, and Egypt. The third battle, which took place in 331 B.C. at Arbela, resulted in the routing of the remaining Persian army.

From there, Alexander and his forces made their push toward what is today territory belonging to Afghanistan, Pakistan, and India. At this point, the extent of his control exceeded that of the Persian empire. Be that as it may, Alexander's troops were exhausted and they refused to advance farther eastward. He then decided to return to Babylon, where he suffered an untimely death at the age of 33 (see vs. 8). As a result, the empire founded by Alexander divided into four parts under the control of his regional commanders (see vs. 22): (1) Macedonia and Greece under Antipater and Cassender; (2) Thrace and Asia Minor under Lysimachus; (3) Syria under Seleucus I; and (4) Egypt under Ptolemy I. Historical records indicate that these four kingdoms were not as strong as the empire established by Alexander, both in terms of the territory they controlled and the military power they wielded.

II. THE REIGN OF ANTIOCHUS IV EPIPHANES: DANIEL 8:23-26

A. The Emergence of Antiochus IV Epiphanes: vs. 23

"In the latter part of their reign, when rebels have become completely wicked, a stern-faced king, a master of intrigue, will arise."

Daniel 8:23 skips ahead about 150 years to a time when rebellious acts had run their course. This verse points to the emergence of a wicked ruler from one of the four Greek kingdoms (see vs. 9). The king whose beginning was seemingly lackluster is Antiochus IV Epiphanes, who ruled the Seleucid empire from 175 to 164 B.C. Initially, his kingdom lacked cohesion, being politically fragmented and financially weak. Antiochus addressed this issue by aggressively implementing a program of Hellenization. The latter refers to the spread of ancient Greek culture and language. Antiochus also sponsored the worship of Zeus. This was the god of the sky and thunder in Greek mythology and the chief deity of the Greek pantheon.

Throughout much of his reign, the relationship between Antiochus and the Jewish inhabitants of Palestine was terse and violent. He ended up trying unsuccessfully to wipe out the Jewish people and their faith. Verse 23 describes him as "stern-faced," which points to someone who was insolent and rash. Antiochus was also a "master of intrigue," which suggests he was deceitful and adept in devising sinister schemes.

B. The Schemes of Antiochus IV Epiphanes: vss. 24-25

"He will become very strong, but not by his own power. He will cause astounding devastation and will succeed in whatever he does. He will destroy the mighty men and the holy people. He will cause deceit to prosper, and he will consider himself superior. When they feel secure, he will destroy many and take his stand against the Prince of princes. Yet he will be destroyed, but not by human power."

Antiochus was not the lawful successor to the Seleucid throne. That is why, as Daniel 8:24 predicted, he used underhanded techniques to obtain control of the empire. His tumultuous reign resulted in extraordinary amounts of death and destruction. In fact, he ended up slaughtering many who were oblivious to his ploys. Verse 25 adds that Antiochus was characterized by arrogance, and he tried to advance his agenda by means of treachery and deceit. For instance, he took the name Ephiphanes (which literally means "God manifest") because he mistakenly considered himself to be the human embodiment of Zeus. Some think the description of Antiochus prefigures the Antichrist, who will arise in the end times to oppose God and persecute His chosen people (see 2 Thess. 2:3-4; 1 John 4:3).

Daniel 8:9 draws attention to the armed conflict Antiochus waged against the Jewish inhabitants of Palestine. Historical records indicate that Antiochus unceasingly persecuted the Jewish people. This included banning their right to practice longstanding ceremonial practices connected with their worship of the Lord in the Jerusalem temple. Antiochus was also guilty of entering the most holy place of the shrine and ransacking the silver and gold vessels. Furthermore, in the temple court, he built an altar to Zeus on top of the bronze altar to the Lord and had swine slaughtered there (see 8:11-12; 11:31). These profane acts against the Jewish people (especially their warriors and priests) amounted to an attack against the God of Israel, the "Prince of princes" (8:25). The demise of Antiochus did not occur by any human agency. For instance, he did not perish in battle and he was not assassinated by any of his foes. Instead, Antiochus died in 164 B.C. in Tabae in Persia as a result of a sudden psychological or physical malady.

C. The Command to Seal Up the Vision: vs. 26

"The vision of the evenings and mornings that has been given you is true, but seal up the vision, for it concerns the distant future."

Gabriel affirmed that the "vision" (Dan. 8:26) concerning the 2,300 "evenings and mornings" (see vs. 14) was correct. Moreover, what this celestial messenger declared about the "distant future" (vs. 26; at least from Daniel's perspective) proved to be historically accurate. For the time being, though, Daniel was directed to "seal up the vision" he had written on a scroll. In ancient times, seals often were in the form of signet rings or cylinders and inscribed with the owner's name or with a distinctive design.

On some occasions, a seal authenticated or certified an item (such as an official, royal document). On other occasions, a seal was used to keep an item fastened shut because it was confidential and needed to be preserved. In keeping with the second usage, Gabriel explained that the vision Daniel recorded needed to remain a secret, for it concerned a series of events occurring centuries after his lifetime. Understandably, the elder statesman was emotionally and physically "exhausted" (vs. 27) from his visionary experience. Indeed, he felt sick for several days after that astonishing episode. Nevertheless, once Daniel felt better, he resumed his official duties in service to the king.

Discussion Questions

1. What is the "time of wrath" referred to in Daniel 8:19?
2. What was distinctive about the double-horned ram Daniel saw?
3. What will characterize the "stern-faced" ruler mentioned in verse 23?
4. In addition to fortune-teller and psychics, what other individuals might try to mislead believers about the future? Why is it unwise for believers to trust what these frauds claim to "predict"?
5. Why must the Bible be the lens through which we look at the future?

Contemporary Application

The vision Daniel experienced was about future historical events concerning God's people. On the one hand, Daniel would live to see the overthrow of Babylon by the Medes and Persians, who were represented by the "two-horned ram" mentioned in Daniel 8:20. On the other hand, the sudden rise of Alexander the Great, who was symbolized by the "shaggy goat" recorded in verse 21, would take place many years after Daniel's death. The elder statesman learned that regardless of how difficult the situation became for God's chosen people, their foes would eventually be "destroyed" (vs. 25) by the Lord, who is the "Prince of princes."

In modern times, many movies typically conclude their story with "The End." Sometimes we're glad, and sometimes we wish for more fun, excitement, and drama. Our physical lives on earth also have an ending. For some it comes sooner, for others later. No one knows when "The End" will pop up on our life's script. Nevertheless, we can be sure that the Father knows and that He has prepared the best possible ending for those who believe in the Son and serve Him.

As Paul reminded us in Romans 8:28, "In all things God works for the good of those who love him." How wonderful it is to be loved by God! There are moments when we may doubt His love. But then we should remember what Paul said in verses 38-39: "For I am convinced that neither death nor life, . . . nor anything else in all creation, will be able to separate us from the love of God that is in Christ Jesus our Lord."

So, if God is inviting us to be a part of His great plans and purposes, where do we sign up? According to Ephesians 2:1-10, anyone who has experienced the Lord's saving grace is already on the list. What, then, can we expect as participants in God's plans? We can know that the Lord will cause us to will and to act according to His good pleasure (Phil. 2:13), and that He will be working through us to make His love and greatness known to the unsaved (1 Pet. 2:9-10). God can and will use us in extraordinary ways to carry out His eternal purposes.

The Lord's Supper

Scripture

Background Scripture: *Luke 22:14-30*

Scripture Lesson: *Luke 22:14-30*

Key Verse: *"The greatest among you should be like the youngest, and the one who rules like the one who serves."* Luke 22:26.

Scripture Lesson for Children: *Luke 22:14-30*

Key Verse for Children: *"I am among you as one who serves."* Luke 22:27.

Lesson Aim

To discover the joy of serving others unconditionally and unselfishly.

Lesson Setting

Time: A.D. *30*

Place: Jerusalem

Lesson Outline

The Lord's Supper

I.   The Lord's Supper: Luke 22:14-23
   A. *The Intent of Jesus: vss. 14-16*
   B. *The Bread and the Cup: vss. 17-20*
   C. *The Betrayal by Judas: vss. 21-23*

II. The Disciples' Dispute: Luke 22:24-30
   A. *The Argument about Greatness: vs. 24*
   B. *The Nature of True Greatness: vss. 25-27*
   C. *The Promise of God's Kingdom: vss. 28-30*

Introduction for Adults

Topic: *The Privilege of Serving*

Military heroes stand out in our history as great people, and many of them were. Yet, in every conflict there are examples of greatness among those who never rose to leadership. For example, during World War II, four chaplains found greatness, not in leading, but in setting an example; not in being served, but in serving; and not in being first, but in being last.

These chaplains—George Fox, Alexander Goode, Clark Poling, and John Washington—were on a troopship headed for Europe when the vessel was torpedoed. Rather than use their life jackets themselves, the four chaplains handed them to others. They went down with the ship, for they had caught the spirit of what Jesus taught concerning greatness.

Though we may not aspire to be president, commanding officer, or even mayor, we are still tempted to shun what Jesus said about greatness. We would rather spend lots of time and energy advancing our personal fortunes. This is pointless, however, for unselfish, humble service is the only path to true and lasting greatness in God's kingdom (see Mark 10:43).

Introduction for Youth

Topic: *A Lesson in Service*

Youth often wonder who among them is the greatest, and they answer that question in several different ways. Some consider intelligence, while others think about athletic ability. There are adolescents who define greatness either in terms of what they have, who they know, or how they look.

In the hustle and bustle of making a name for themselves, youth can become mean and selfish. It's no wonder, then, that Christian young people struggle with Jesus' concept of true greatness. He taught that thinking of others counts the most. Also, our desire for worldly greatness must be supplanted by the higher goal of growing in Christlikeness (see 2 Pet. 3:18).

The young people in your church should be encouraged to let their attitude of greatness mirror that of the Savior. They can do so knowing that He loves and accepts them just as they are. And if we also treat them that way, they will see true greatness in action.

Concepts for Children

Topic: *Serving Others*

1. Jesus and His followers sat down together to eat one last meal.
2. Jesus knew that He would soon be arrested and crucified.
3. Jesus said that the Lord's Supper would be a reminder of what He did on the cross.
4. Jesus wants us to reach out and help others.
5. Jesus is ready to help us find ways to serve others.

Lesson Commentary

I. THE LORD'S SUPPER: LUKE 22:14-23

A. The Intent of Jesus: vss. 14-16

When the hour came, Jesus and his apostles reclined at the table. And he said to them, "I have eagerly desired to eat this Passover with you before I suffer. For I tell you, I will not eat it again until it finds fulfillment in the kingdom of God."

Matthew, Mark, and Luke clearly tie the Last Supper to celebrating the Passover. This festival was one of three that all Jews came to Jerusalem to observe, the other two being the Feasts of Pentecost and Tabernacles (see Exod. 23:14-17). The Passover commemorated the Hebrews being "passed over" by the angel of death in Egypt when they marked the doorposts of their houses with the blood of a lamb (see 12:13).

God specified that the Passover meal was to be eaten on the fourteenth day of the first month of the Jewish calendar (see Lev. 23:5). Since the Jewish calendar is based on the cycles of the moon, the date for Passover varies. Therefore, our date for Easter does as well. Moses instituted the first Passover observance the night before God freed Israel from the nation's bondage in Egypt. God commanded that Israel continue to celebrate the Passover in remembrance of His great saving work (see Exod. 12:21-28). Similarly, the night before Jesus' crucifixion, He celebrated the Passover with His disciples in an upper room specially prepared for the occasion.

An unblemished lamb would be selected prior to Passover, then killed and roasted in the afternoon before that evening meal. The lamb was to be eaten with bread, wine, and a sauce made with bitter herbs. The lamb would remind the Jews of the blood on the doorposts in Egypt, the unleavened bread of their haste in leaving Egypt, and the bitter herbs of their suffering as Pharaoh's slaves (see Exod. 12:8-20, 39).

Sometime in the centuries after the Exodus, the Jews had added the drinking of at least four cups of diluted wine to the Passover meal. Each of these cups related to one of God's four promises to His people found in 6:6-7. The head of the household would pronounce special blessings over the bread and wine during the meal and be responsible for explaining to the family the significance of the feast (see 13:8). The whole reason for having the meal was to remember that God had led His people out of slavery. In Jesus' day, the people were looking for a new Moses to lead them out of bondage to Rome. Instead, Jesus became the new sacrificial Lamb for the sins of the world (see John 1:29).

During Passover week, thousands of Jews from all over the known world made the pilgrimage to Jerusalem. Thus, an unusually large crowd was on hand to take part in the events surrounding Jesus' entry into the city (see Luke 19:37-39) and His arrest, trial, and crucifixion (see 23:18, 27, 35, 48). Evidently, many stayed on until the Feast of Pentecost, when they heard Peter's moving sermon (see Acts

2:1-41). The celebration of the feast of "Unleavened Bread" (Luke 22:7) lasted eight days, beginning with the Passover meal. The celebrations were so close together that at times the names of both were used interchangeably. Part of the observance involved the sacrifice of the Passover lamb. As the Jews gathered for the Passover celebration in A.D. 30, little did they realize that as they sacrificed their Passover lambs, the Lamb of God was about to be sacrificed to set people free from spiritual slavery (see John 1:29).

As the time drew near, Jesus sent Peter and John ahead into Jerusalem to prepare the Passover meal (Luke 22:8). They were to look for a man carrying a water pitcher and follow him (vss. 9-10). Since women in ancient Jewish culture usually carried these jars, it would have been no problem for Peter and John to recognize the man Jesus was referring to. The owner of the house to which Peter and John were led was evidently expecting them. Upon their inquiry (vs. 11), he showed them a second-floor room complete with furniture (vs. 12).

Next, the disciples—who probably gained access to the upper room by stairs on the outside of the house—prepared the Passover meal (vs. 13). Perhaps Jesus used the question recorded in verse 11 to keep the exact location of the meal a secret from His numerous enemies. Some think Jesus prearranged the meeting as a way for one of His Jerusalem followers to encounter Peter and John at the city gate. Others, however, think the meeting demonstrates Jesus' supernatural knowledge. In any case, at the time designated by Jesus, He gathered with the Twelve to eat the Passover meal (vs. 14). He told them how much He wanted to share the celebration with them before His time of suffering (vs. 15). The Redeemer explained that this would be the last time He would eat the Passover "until it finds fulfillment in the kingdom of God" (vs. 16).

B. The Bread and the Cup: vss. 17-20

After taking the cup, he gave thanks and said, "Take this and divide it among you. For I tell you I will not drink again of the fruit of the vine until the kingdom of God comes." And he took bread, gave thanks and broke it, and gave it to them, saying, "This is my body given for you; do this in remembrance of me." In the same way, after the supper he took the cup, saying, "This cup is the new covenant in my blood, which is poured out for you."

Luke says that the day of the Passover meal was the same as that of the Lord's Supper (Luke 22:7), and Matthew and Mark also imply that the Lord's Supper involved Jesus' celebrating the Passover meal with His disciples. John, however, says that the Last Supper was before the Passover meal (John 13:1). Many attempts have been made to explain this time difference, such as the Lord's Supper's being a separate fellowship meal, but regardless of the time of the supper, it had elements of the Passover meal attached to it, including the bread and the wine.

The Passover that Jesus ate with His disciples followed a well-established Jewish pattern for celebrating this feast. A Jewish family normally purchased a lamb several days before the festival. They then took the animal to the temple to be sacrificed by the priests. The family would next take the lamb home, where they roasted it in the afternoon. Passover began at sunset on that day, and the Passover meal was eaten sometime that evening. Before the actual meal was eaten, all the participants washed their hands.

During an opening prayer, the first of four cups of diluted wine was blessed and passed around. Each person reclining at the table then took herbs and dipped them in salt water. (The diners would lean on their left elbow, facing the table with their feet away from it, and eat with their right hand.) Next, the host took one of three flat cakes of unleavened bread, broke it, and laid some of it aside. Thanksgiving was made to God, and more of the bread was broken apart. The host dipped bread in a sauce usually made of stewed fruit, and then distributed a portion to each person gathered at the table. Finally, the time for the main meal arrived. Eating a roasted lamb was the high point of the evening.

It was after Jesus and His disciples had eaten the Passover meal that He instituted the Lord's Supper. Jesus took the third cup (which was known as the "cup of blessing") and uttered a prayer of thanks to God. He then instructed each of His disciples to take the cup and share its contents among themselves (vs. 17). Jesus emphasized the solemnity of the occasion by stating that He would not "drink again from the fruit of the vine until the kingdom of God comes" (vs. 18).

The Savior next took a flat cake of unleavened bread, broke it, and passed it around so that each of His disciples could eat a portion of it. Perhaps while this was still occurring, He noted that the bread represented His body, which He was offering on their behalf (vs. 19). Jesus then took the fourth cup and said that its contents represented His blood, which He was pouring out through His atoning death on the cross. Jesus' sacrifice of Himself made it possible for God to establish a new covenant in which forgiveness and knowledge of Him would be possible for all who believed (vs. 20; see Jer. 31:31-34).

C. The Betrayal by Judas: vss. 21-23

"But the hand of him who is going to betray me is with mine on the table. The Son of Man will go as it has been decreed, but woe to that man who betrays him." They began to question among themselves which of them it might be who would do this.

Jesus declared that one of the Twelve would betray Him. In fact, His betrayer was reclining at the table with the group (Luke 22:21). No one but Jesus knew that Judas Iscariot was the turncoat, and so they all began to suspect each other. They found it hard to believe that they had a traitor in their midst (vs. 23). Jesus' upcoming crucifixion had been decreed by God (see Rev. 13:8). This truth, however, did not erase the guilt that rested on Judas for betraying the Messiah. Judas willingly cut a deal with the religious leaders, and he would justly suffer the eternal consequences of his crime (Luke 22:22).

Prior to the start of Jesus' farewell meal, Satan had put it into the mind of Judas to betray his loyalty to the Savior (see John 13:2). Judas is identified as the son of

245

Simon (see 6:71; 13:26). Most likely, the term "Iscariot" refers to the town of Kerioth, which was located near Hebron in southern Judah (see Josh. 15:25). Among Jesus' 12 disciples, Judas was their treasurer. He carried the moneybag and sometimes would steal from it (see John 12:6).

The three Synoptic Gospels detail how Judas plotted with the Jewish leaders to bring about Jesus' arrest. Judas received a payment of 30 silver coins (see Matt. 26:14-16; Mark 14:10-11; Luke 22:3-6) for leading the authorities to Jesus (see John 18:1-2). It's unlikely that Jesus felt any personal sense of defeat about this, for He was aware that the Father had given Him authority over everything. Jesus also knew that nothing could happen to Him apart from the will of God, from whom He had come and to whom He was returning (see 13:3).

II. THE DISCIPLES' DISPUTE: LUKE 22:24-30

A. The Argument about Greatness: vs. 24

Also a dispute arose among them as to which of them was considered to be greatest.

The disciples' discussion about who would betray Jesus may have turned into a debate about who among them was the most loyal. If so, this degenerated into an argument about who was the best, or greatest, disciple (Luke 22:24). Of course, the betrayer was the worst. But who among the others was acting sensibly? More importantly, why would they even argue over the issue? Peter, James, and John comprised the inner circle of disciples. Did that make them the best? Or was it those who had healed the most, or who garnered the largest number of followers for Jesus? The disciples looked at greatness the way we usually do, that is, in terms of supposedly grand accomplishments for God's kingdom, not in terms of humble and sacrificial service.

B. The Nature of True Greatness: vss. 25-27

Jesus said to them, "The kings of the Gentiles lord it over them; and those who exercise authority over them call themselves Benefactors. But you are not to be like that. Instead, the greatest among you should be like the youngest, and the one who rules like the one who serves. For who is greater, the one who is at the table or the one who serves? Is it not the one who is at the table? But I am among you as one who serves."

Jesus had dealt with the oversized egos of His disciples before. Now as He faced the cross, He again had to stop their arguing. John wrote that at some point in the evening, Jesus wrapped a towel around His waist and washed the feet of the Twelve, taking on the role of a lowly servant (see John 13;1-17). Perhaps initially, none of the disciples dared to ask Jesus why He had chosen to wash their feet. Despite all His teaching on servanthood, He may have felt the need to do this task because the Twelve still did not understand the concept of being a servant. Although Jesus knew He was in His last hours before His death on the cross, He remained calm, reflective, and serious. He took the time to show His followers how much He loved them and how much they were to love others.

During the farewell meal, the Savior noted that the kings of the world ordered their subjects around, even though these rulers loved to be called "benefactors" (Luke 22:25). The intent was to portray the rulers as champions of their people. But the title had a condescending ring to it, especially since so many "benefactors" were ruthless tyrants who measured greatness by the nations they conquered and the people they enslaved. In contrast, Jesus told His followers they were to treat one another differently. He urged them to "be like the youngest" (vs. 26), namely, the ones to whom the least favorable duties were often assigned. The Messiah also stated that normally the master sits at the table and is served by his underlings. But Jesus had humbly served His followers. This was to remind them that their greatness would be equal to the services they rendered unconditionally and unselfishly to others (vs. 27).

In the Old Testament, servanthood is a common concept. In many places, Scripture mentions hired laborers and slaves. But more important are the references to servants of God. People who were in covenant with the Lord considered Him their master. For example, Elijah declared to God, "I am your servant" (1 Kings 18:36). And when God spoke, He sometimes called one of His followers "my servant" (for instance, see 2 Kings 21:8). This servant-master relationship between a person and God is also in the New Testament. Believers are servants of the Son, who is Himself the servant of His Father. But in the New Testament, a related idea occurs. Believers are not only servants of God, but also servants of one another (see Mark 10:43; 2 Cor. 4:5).

If any of Jesus' followers thought they were too good to stoop to any menial task of serving others, they did so only by placing themselves above their Lord. He was the suffering Servant, who had come to minister to others and give His life as a ransom for the sins of the world (see Mark 10:45). Jesus solemnly assured the Twelve (and all who trust in Him for eternal life) that slaves are not greater than their master. Likewise, messengers are not greater than the person who sends them (see John 13:16). Jesus' use of the word "sent" reminded His disciples that He had been sent to them by the Father. In turn, Jesus was sending His followers out to serve others, beginning with the proclamation of the Gospel (see 20:21-23).

The Lord Jesus, by example as well as by precept, introduced His followers to this principle of servanthood toward one another. Therefore, He is the believers' model of unselfish service. Those who willingly, consistently, and wholeheartedly follow His example are promised blessings (see John 13:17). Thus, the only way for believers to be truly fulfilled and satisfied in their relationship with the Savior is for them to be willing to accept and perform the role of a servant.

C. The Promise of God's Kingdom: vss. 28-30

"You are those who have stood by me in my trials. And I confer on you a kingdom, just as my Father conferred one on me, so that you may eat and drink at my table in my kingdom and sit on thrones, judging the twelve tribes of Israel."

Jesus had commanded His disciples to serve one another rather than seek individual greatness. This did not mean, however, they would go unnoticed. Jesus made it clear that He knew how they had stood with Him in His various trials (Luke 22:28), which included temptations (see 4:1-13), hardships (see 9:58), sorrows (see 19:41), and rejection (see John 1:11). The Messiah promised His followers future blessings and authority at the end of the age. The image is one of a victory banquet in which Jesus' followers would rejoice in His triumph (see Rev. 19:9). They also would be given the right to rule at His return (see Matt. 19:28; 2 Tim. 2:12). In fact, the authority that the Son would bestow on them was like the authority that the Father had bestowed on Him (see Luke 22:29-30).

Discussion Questions

1. Why was Jesus so eager to eat the Passover meal with the Twelve?
2. How did Jesus respond when the disciples argued about who was the greatest among them?
3. What promise to the disciples did Jesus make about the future kingdom?
4. Why is it important for us to serve others unconditionally and unselfishly?
5. Why do we sometimes struggle to serve in this way?

Contemporary Application

The world's system of leadership is quite different from leadership in God's kingdom. Pagan leaders are often selfish and arrogant, especially as they claw their way to the top. But Jesus said that among Christians, the leader is the one who serves others. This isn't done with arrogance or resentment, but rather with humility and sensitivity.

There are different styles of leadership in the church. Some lead through public speaking, some through managing, and some through relationships (to name a few examples). Regardless of the method, every Christian leader needs a servant's heart.

Each time we observe the Lord's Supper, we not only remember Jesus' atoning sacrifice but also His call to humble Christian service. We renounce our pride and love of status, and we ask Jesus to strip us of worldly ambitions. By doing these things, we show we are true followers of the Savior, who is the humblest servant of all.

The Lord Has Risen!

Scripture

Background Scripture: *Luke 24:1-35*

Scripture Lesson: *Luke 24:13-21, 28-35*

Key Verse: *Then their eyes were opened and they recognized [Jesus], and he disappeared from their sight.* Luke 24:31.

Scripture Lesson for Children: *Luke 24:13-21, 28-35*

Key Verse for Children: *"It is true! The Lord has risen and has appeared to Simon."* Luke 24:34.

Lesson Aim

To witness to the reality of Jesus' resurrection.

Lesson Setting

Time: A.D. 30

Place: Jerusalem

Lesson Outline

The Lord Has Risen!

   I. Jesus Appears to Two Disciples: Luke 24:13-21
      A. *Traveling to Emmaus: vss. 13*
      B. *Encountering Jesus: vss. 14-16*
      C. *Responding to Jesus' Questions: vss. 17-21*
  II. Jesus Reveals His Identity: Luke 24:28-35
      A. *The Invitation Offered by the Two Disciples: vss. 28-29*
      B. *The Two Disciples' Recognition of Jesus: vss. 30-32*
      C. *The Report Made by the Two Disciples: vss. 33-35*

Introduction for Adults

Topic: *Hope Restored*

Each of the Gospels tells many engaging accounts about people who met Jesus. But after His death and resurrection, the nature and focus of the disciples' encounters with Him changed dramatically. He both calmed their fears and removed their doubts about His resurrection,

There are times when believers feel confused or doubtful about whether Jesus is truly alive. In those moments of uncertainty, He restores their hope with His reassuring presence. He helps them to see that He is no longer in the grave, but has risen from the dead. This gives them the confidence to believe the truth and to affirm it to others, even skeptical family members and friends.

When believers encounter obstacles to faith, we can encourage them to look afresh at the evidence surrounding Jesus' resurrection. They need to know that believing in Him is of eternal importance. They can also be told that Jesus will never reject them, for He is full of grace, truth, and love. When they believe in Him, they receive new life, forgiveness, hope, and peace.

Introduction for Youth

Topic: *A Mystery Guest*

To many young people the idea of a person's rising from the dead seems either mysterious or far-fetched. This is why it is important for saved adolescents to be reliable witnesses for Christ to their peers. One need not possess an advanced degree in theology to be a spokesperson for the risen Lord. The only qualification is knowing Him by faith.

These days, young people face so many conflicting claims made by members of different world religions that they are often turned off by invitations to come to church. Thankfully, there are times when they are willing to listen to believers give a clear and simple presentation of the Gospel. The issue is not joining a religion, but rather coming to know the risen Lord in a personal way.

These same people are also willing to study the Bible in small groups. They respond favorably when asked, "Have you ever read about Jesus and His resurrection from the dead?" Such an inquiry may open the door to a group discussion about the Savior's life and teachings. When the Lord makes this opportunity available, Christian teens are wise to take full advantage of it!

Concepts for Children

Topic: *Jesus Appears!*

1. Jesus spent some time with two followers walking to the village of Emmaus.
2. Jesus showed them that He really was alive.
3. Jesus helped them to understand better what the Bible says about Him.
4. Jesus wants us to accept the truth that He is alive from the dead.
5. Jesus wants us to let others know that He has conquered death.

Lesson Commentary

I. JESUS APPEARS TO TWO DISCIPLES: LUKE 24:13-21

A. Traveling to Emmaus: vss. 13

Now that same day two of them were going to a village called Emmaus, about seven miles from Jerusalem.

After Jesus died on the cross, Joseph of Arimathea and Nicodemus had prepared the Savior's body in the traditional way (see John 19:39-40). But some of Jesus' followers—women from Galilee—wanted to honor Him in a more personal way. After the Sabbath (which ended Saturday at sunset), they bought spices to anoint Jesus' body (see Mark 16:1). Then early Sunday morning, the women headed for the tomb (Luke 24:1). They knew where to go because they had watched Jesus' burial (see 23:55). When the women arrived at the tomb, the first sign of something unusual was that the stone had been rolled away from the sepulcher's opening (24:2). After going inside, they were even more shocked to discover that Jesus' body was gone (vs. 3). While the women were wondering about this, two men in shining clothes—namely, angels (vs. 4; see vs. 23)—appeared.

The pair of heavenly emissaries asked the women at the empty tomb why they were looking "among the dead" (vs. 5) for someone who is alive. The angels, by referring to Jesus as "the living," indicated that He had risen from the dead. The emissaries were straightforward and direct in declaring that, due to the Savior's resurrection, He was not at the abandoned sepulcher. The angels reminded the women what Jesus had previously said to them while He was ministering in Galilee (vs. 6). Verse 7 brings to mind what the Messiah had previously foretold, namely, that He, as the "Son of Man," was appointed by the Father to be betrayed into the hands of sinners. The latter included the "elders, chief priests and teachers of the law" (9:22). In 17:25, Jesus foretold that the people of that day ("this generation") would reject Him.

Jesus not only predicted His rejection and crucifixion, but also His resurrection from the dead "on the third day" (24:7). On other occasions, Pharisees and teachers of the law demanded to see Jesus perform a sign to authenticate His divine authority. In response, He declared that the only certifying mark they would receive was that of Jonah. The prophet was facing certain death during the three-day period in which he lay entombed in the belly of a huge sea creature (see Jonah 1:17). The Lord restored Jonah to life by setting him free from his predicament.

This historical incident foreshadowed Jesus' spending a similar amount of time buried in the depths of the earth. His own resurrection from the dead would be the supreme validation of His messianic power and authority and serve as a sign that He was superseding the old temple order (see Matt. 12:38-41; 16:1-4; Luke 11:16, 29-32; John 2:19-21). After Jesus' body was raised from the dead, the Holy Spirit enabled the disciples to remember what the Redeemer had said, including the meaning and significance of His teachings (John 2:22; 14:26). Of course, the angels' words to the women at the empty tomb helped them to recall what Jesus had foretold (Luke 24:8).

As proof that Jesus was truly alive, the women were invited to inspect the spot where the Savior's body had rested (Matt. 28:6). After the women had taken some time to examine the empty tomb, they were told to deliver an important message to the remainder of Jesus' disciples. Luke 24:9 indicates that it was the "Eleven," which reflects the fact that Judas was no longer among them. Other disciples were gathered with the remaining eleven. The women were to declare to the entire group that the one who had risen from the dead was going ahead of them to Galilee (Mark 16:7). There the disciples would find the risen Lord (Matt. 28:7). This is what Jesus had told His followers prior to His crucifixion and resurrection (26:32).

That Jesus would appear to His disciples in Galilee seems appropriate when we consider His earthly ministry. For all practical purposes, Galilee was His home (21:11), and the place where He called most of His disciples. It is also possible that the disciples, in a sense, retreated there for a while after the Resurrection to wait and wonder what was next. Would they go back to fishing in the Sea of Galilee (John 21:1-3), or would they continue to fish for people (so to speak), as Jesus had said they would (Matt. 4:19)?

The statement "Now I have told you" (Matt. 28:7) implies that the message from God's emissaries was extremely important and the women were not to delay in reporting it. As true servants of God, the women followed the angels' instructions by hurrying from the tomb. At this time, they were feeling both fear and joy (vs. 8). Perhaps these conflicting emotions spurred them to go as fast as possible to the disciples. While the women were en route, though, Jesus suddenly appeared and said, "Greetings" (vs. 9), which also can be translated "Rejoice." The sight of the risen Lord was a good reason to be filled with delight, for He had conquered death. Upon seeing the Messiah, the women approached Him, fell at His feet, and worshiped Him. Paying such homage to Jesus was an entirely appropriate response.

Evidently, there was a strong sense of fear in the women as they prostrated themselves in the presence of the Savior. Like the angels, Jesus directed the women not to be afraid. In His presence, they were to be courageous. The Messiah also repeated the same basic message the angels had given to the women. Perhaps this was to emphasize the urgency of their telling the disciples to go to Galilee, where they would see Him (vs. 10). It was gracious of Jesus to call the disciples "my brothers," for just a few days earlier they had denied and abandoned Him (see 26:56). Despite what they had done, Jesus was willing to forgive them and to allow them to serve Him.

Because the four Gospels have some differing details about Jesus' resurrection, some critics have dismissed the event as a false or embellished story. However, a close look at the four accounts shows that the differences give each one the flavor of eyewitness testimony, and all of them agree that Jesus rose from the dead. One point of difference is which women went to the tomb that Sunday morning. Luke

24:10 mentions Mary Magdalene, Joanna, and Mary the mother of James. Matthew 28:1 mentions the two Marys, while Mark 16:1 omits Joanna and adds Salome. John 20:1 only identifies Mary Magdalene as going to the tomb.

One likely explanation for the differences is that several women went to the sepulcher, in different groups and at different times. John, for example, reports at least two visits of Mary Magdalene to the tomb (John 20:1, 11). Her first visit seems to have been with the other women, for she told Peter and John, "They have taken the Lord out of the tomb, and we don't know where they have put him!" (vs. 2). Peter and John then went back with Mary to the tomb to look for themselves. John's Gospel also focuses on Mary Magdalene's account of the events because she seems to be the spokesperson for the group of women. Matthew, Mark, and Luke all refer to her first in their reports of who was there that morning.

Those who doubt the Resurrection today should consider that skeptics in the first century A.D. were able to check out the facts with eyewitnesses. For instance, the disciples were at first doubters. Despite the women's excitement, the Eleven did not accept what the women reported. Even the women's enthusiasm seemed like pure nonsense to the Eleven, that is, like the crazy babbling of someone hallucinating with a fever (Luke 24:11). Verse 12 reveals that Peter was the first to respond by running to the tomb to check it out for himself. Next, John outran Peter and reached the tomb first, but he waited for Peter before entering the sepulcher (see John 20:3-6). Peter saw the empty graveclothes, but still could not bring himself to believe (Luke 24:12). He was not yet capable of realizing what had taken place.

In all, the Bible records 11 appearances of the resurrected Messiah, but there may have been other instances (see Acts 1:3). The first episode Luke wrote about was the risen Lord's encounter with two disciples walking from Jerusalem to Emmaus (Luke 24:13). The latter town has not been positively located, but in Jesus' time, it was about seven miles (possibly northwest) from Jerusalem. One of the disciples Jesus encountered on the road to Emmaus was named Cleopas (see vs. 18). All attempts to identify him further have been unsuccessful. He apparently was a faithful follower of Jesus, for he was present with the disciples in the upper room when the women reported on their trip to the empty tomb (see vs. 23). We have no information at all on the other disciple. Possibly this person was the wife of Cleopas, since it appears they lived at the same place (see vss. 28-29). But it's also possible that traveling companion of Cleopas was his son, his brother, or his friend.

B. Encountering Jesus: vss. 14-16

They were talking with each other about everything that had happened. As they talked and discussed these things with each other, Jesus himself came up and walked along with them; but they were kept from recognizing him.

These two disciples were talking about what had recently happened to Jesus (Luke 24:14). No doubt, the two disciples were disappointed and depressed. Suddenly, their conversation was interrupted by a wonderful turn of events. Jesus came up

253

and joined in their discussion (vs. 15). But amazingly, they were "kept from recognizing" (vs. 16) the Savior. One possibility is that the two never really got a good look at Jesus as they walked toward the west, perhaps as the sun was setting on the horizon (see vs. 29). A second option is that the two failed to recognize Jesus because they weren't really expecting to see Him. A third option is that Jesus intentionally prevented the two from identifying Him so that He could first explain the meaning of the Scriptures to them.

C. Responding to Jesus' Questions: vss. 17-21

He asked them, "What are you discussing together as you walk along?" They stood still, their faces downcast. One of them, named Cleopas, asked him, "Are you only a visitor to Jerusalem and do not know the things that have happened there in these days?" "What things?" he asked. "About Jesus of Nazareth," they replied. "He was a prophet, powerful in word and deed before God and all the people. The chief priests and our rulers handed him over to be sentenced to death, and they crucified him; but we had hoped that he was the one who was going to redeem Israel. And what is more, it is the third day since all this took place.

The stranger asked the two disciples what matters they were deliberating so intently as they made their way to Emmaus. The pair, whose faces were disheartened, paused for a moment in their walking (Luke 24:17). Both were astounded that this stranger was unaware of the momentous events that had recently taken place in Jerusalem (vs. 18). When the stranger asked for more information, the two explained that Jesus of Nazareth was recognized by many as being a "prophet" (vs. 19), that is, an anointed spokesperson for God to others. This is evident by the "powerful" deeds He performed and the message He proclaimed.

The pair further noted that the religious leaders delivered Jesus to the civil authorities to be condemned to death and crucified (vs. 20). The two, along with many others, previously held onto the hope that Jesus was the Messiah, that is, the person who would "redeem Israel" (vs. 21). That aspiration, though, seemed to be shattered when Jesus died on the cross. And now it was the third day since that tragic event had occurred. The Jewish desire for the nation's redemption came from a misconception about the Messiah taken from selected Hebrew prophecies. Most first-century A.D. Jews looked for the Messiah to come as a political hero who would deliver their nation from Roman rule and reestablish the throne of David. They knew about the glory, but they didn't recognize the suffering of the Messiah.

II. JESUS REVEALS HIS IDENTITY: LUKE 24:28-35

A. The Invitation Offered by the Two Disciples: vss. 28-29

As they approached the village to which they were going, Jesus acted as if he were going farther. But they urged him strongly, "Stay with us, for it is nearly evening; the day is almost over." So he went in to stay with them.

The two disciples continued their story. Just that morning they heard startling news (Luke 24:22). Some women returned from the tomb and claimed that Jesus' body was gone and the sepulcher was empty. The women also said they saw a "vision of angels" (vs. 23), who announced that Jesus was not dead but alive. Moreover, the two disciples told Jesus about the visit made by Peter and John to the empty tomb. But they had not yet personally seen the risen Lord (vs. 24). Just then, Jesus rebuked the two disciples for being so foolish in failing to believe the prophecies recorded in the Old Testament about the promised Messiah (vs. 25). In essence, their understanding was incomplete, for they knew only one side of what the prophets had foretold.

Next, Jesus declared that it was the Father's sovereign will for His Son first to "suffer" (vs. 26) the crucifixion and death before being raised to "glory." Then, Jesus guided the two disciples through the Scriptures by explaining how the events of the past few days had been foretold and fulfilled (vs. 27). By this point the group was nearing the outskirts of Emmaus. Perhaps Jesus signaled by His body language that He intended to continue His journey down the road (vs. 28). The two, however, implored Jesus to accept their hospitality to lodge with them for the night at their residence. They explained that it was early evening and the darkness of nighttime, with all its potential dangers, was fast approaching. In turn, Jesus decided to accept their offer (vs. 29).

B. The Two Disciples' Recognition of Jesus: vss. 30-32

When he was at the table with them, he took bread, gave thanks, broke it and began to give it to them. Then their eyes were opened and they recognized him, and he disappeared from their sight. They asked each other, "Were not our hearts burning within us while he talked with us on the road and opened the Scriptures to us?"

After the travelers reached the home of the two disciples, the latter most likely prepared a simple but adequate meal for themselves and their guest. While they reclined at the table, the stranger took some bread, blessed and broke it, and started to give the two disciples some of the bread (Luke 24:30). Instantly, they were enabled to recognize that the risen Lord was in their presence. As soon as the pair knew who Jesus was, He vanished out of their sight (vs. 31). As the two began to process this encounter with Jesus, they admitted they felt as though their hearts were on fire with new life. This was especially so while they walked on the road and listened to Jesus explain to them the messianic passages of the Old Testament (vs. 32).

C. The Report Made by the Two Disciples: vss. 33-35

They got up and returned at once to Jerusalem. There they found the Eleven and those with them, assembled together and saying, "It is true! The Lord has risen and has appeared to Simon." Then the two told what had happened on the way, and how Jesus was recognized by them when he broke the bread.

The two disciples couldn't wait to tell Jesus' other followers back in Jerusalem what had happened. So they hurried out into the night, prepared to hike the seven miles through darkness (Luke 24:33). When the pair arrived in Jerusalem, the others were talking about another appearance of the risen Savior to Peter (vs. 34). Undoubtedly, the group was thrilled to learn that the disciple who previously had denied the Lord was one of the first Jesus wanted to see again. At this point, the two Emmaus disciples described their encounter with Jesus while they were walking on the road. They also told how they finally realized His identity when "he broke the bread" (vs. 35) during the meal the two had prepared.

Discussion Questions

1. How do you think the two Emmaus disciples were feeling as they walked along the road?
2. How did Jesus get the two disciples to share their thoughts?
3. What fueled the excitement of the two disciples as they hurried back to Jerusalem?
4. What does it mean to be a witness to the reality of the risen Messiah?
5. What role does the Spirit serve in the witness believers bear concerning Jesus?

Contemporary Application

The early followers of the Messiah would have disappeared as insignificant footnotes to history had it not been for Jesus' resurrection. Like many others who had trusted in false saviors, they would have been ridiculed and perhaps murdered. Instead, their witness changed the course of history.

The Messiah's resurrection and ascension remains the key to the proclamation of the Gospel, the spread of the church, and the spiritual growth of believers. The living Savior confronts the world of unbelief and demands repentance. Growing churches draw power from Him and declare the Gospel with boldness. And individual Christians find the strength and courage to tell others about their faith in the Lord.

By means of the Holy Spirit, Jesus changes lives and delivers people from sin, guilt, and despair. He helps the weak and discouraged. He meets people when they have given up hope. Because Jesus lives and reigns in heaven, people can find forgiveness from God.

The joy of Jesus' presence ignites our praise and worship. Jesus was raised from the dead, returned to the Father, and abides in us and in His church forever (see John 15:4-5; Eph. 2:21-22). Therefore, we as believers are not ashamed of declaring to others the good news about the Savior.

The Lord Appears

Scripture

Background Scripture: *Luke 24:36-53*

Scripture Lesson: *Luke 24:36-53*

Key Verse: *[Jesus] said to [the disciples], "This is what I told you while I was still with you: Everything must be fulfilled that is written about me in the Law of Moses, the Prophets and the Psalms."* Luke 24:44.

Scripture Lesson for Children: *Luke 24:36-50*

Key Verse for Children: *"Look at my hands and my feet. It is I myself!"* Luke 24:39.

Lesson Aim

To make the proclamation of the Gospel a high priority.

Lesson Setting

Time: A.D. 30

Place: Jerusalem

Lesson Outline

The Lord Appears

  I. The Evidence for Jesus' Resurrection:
     Luke 24:36-43
     A. *The Appearance of Jesus: vs. 36*
     B. *The Alarm of the Disciples: vss. 37-38*
     C. *The Reassurance of Jesus: vss. 39-43*

  II. The Explanation of Scripture: Luke 24:44-49
     A. *The Facts Presented: vss. 44-47*
     B. *The Promise of the Spirit: vss. 48-49*

  III. The Ascension of Jesus: Luke 24:50-53
     A. *The Departure of Jesus: vss. 50-51*
     B. *The Disciples' Return to Jerusalem: vss. 52-53*

Introduction for Adults

Topic: *Promises Kept*

Promises have fallen on hard times. Once, a person's word was as certain a guarantee as you could get. Then spoken words became suspect, and the written contract was born. Now we've spurned even that symbol of trust. Today, it seems there is no contract that can't be broken in the name of money, better business deals, or more pressing priorities.

How different the situation is with the promises recorded in Scripture. Long ago, the Father spoke through the Old Testament prophets about the advent of His Son. These promises were literally fulfilled, including the truth that Jesus would suffer, die, and be raised from the dead.

Even today, God is faithful to fulfill His promises in the lives of His spiritual children. As the students in your class live in the hope of that truth, God will again bring about His pledges to them. Though they might not always understand His ways, they will discover that He remains true to His Word concerning them.

Introduction for Youth

Topic: *From Fear to Faith*

Does heaven exist? A young man asked the pastor of his church that question after a funeral service had been given for the young man's mother. It is also a question that Americans were asked in a telephone survey by *TIME/CNN.* Eighty-one percent of Americans said that they believed in heaven, while 66 percent claimed that they believed a person has both a body and soul in heaven.

Perhaps the more important question concerns the reality of the resurrection. Luke's Gospel leaves no doubt. Jesus rose from the dead, and it is the reason His first disciples went from being fearful to filled with faith. Jesus' resurrection is also the basis for the believer's hope of eternal life. Because the Son has conquered sin and death, His followers can also have victory over them. And Jesus has given believers the wonderful privilege of sharing this good news with the entire world!

Concepts for Children

Topic: *Jesus Appears Again!*

1. Jesus' followers heard He was alive from the dead.
2. Jesus' followers were amazed when He appeared to them.
3. Jesus showed His followers His hands and feet.
4. Jesus reminded His followers about the promises in the Bible concerning Him.
5. Jesus wants us to be filled with joy because He has risen from the dead.

Lesson Commentary

I. THE EVIDENCE FOR JESUS' RESURRECTION: LUKE 24:36-43

A. The Appearance of Jesus: vs. 36

While they were still talking about this, Jesus himself stood among them and said to them, "Peace be with you."

At this time, Jesus' followers were gathered behind locked doors because they feared what the religious authorities might do to them (see John 20:19). They had legitimate concerns in light of what had happened to Jesus. Despite the locked doors, though, Jesus had no problem entering the room and standing in the midst of His disciples. The Savior's resurrection body, while real and tangible, nonetheless possessed certain properties that indicate it was glorified, or altered in some unknown way. Not only could Jesus appear and disappear bodily, but also He could pass through solid objects. Jesus greeted His disciples by saying, "Peace be with you" (Luke 24:36). In light of His resurrection, this statement took on new significance. Through faith in Him, peace with God was possible (see Rom. 5:1). The Savior's greeting also complemented His statement recorded in John 19:30 ("It is finished"), for His work on the cross was the basis of peace between God and believers (see Eph. 2:14-17).

B. The Alarm of the Disciples: vss. 37-38

They were startled and frightened, thinking they saw a ghost. He said to them, "Why are you troubled, and why do doubts rise in your minds?

The disciples were terrified, troubled, and perplexed by Jesus' sudden appearance. In fact, they thought they were seeing a ghost (Luke 24:37). We can easily understand why they were so alarmed, for they had not expected to see Jesus in bodily form. Jesus didn't berate His disciples for their lack of faith. Instead, He gently confronted their fears and doubts by asking them two simple and direct questions (vs. 38). This prompted them to think more objectively about the situation. The Savior wasted no time targeting the doubts of His followers. His goal was to replace their uncertainty with faith. This was important, since faith was the basis for being in a saving relationship with Him (see 2 Cor. 5:7).

C. The Reassurance of Jesus: vss. 39-43

"Look at my hands and my feet. It is I myself! Touch me and see; a ghost does not have flesh and bones, as you see I have." When he had said this, he showed them his hands and feet. And while they still did not believe it because of joy and amazement, he asked them, "Do you have anything here to eat?" They gave him a piece of broiled fish, and he took it and ate it in their presence.

Perhaps someone else would have scolded the disciples for their confusion, fear, and doubt. Thankfully, Jesus took a different approach. He pointed to His body as factual evidence that He had physically risen from the dead (Luke 24:39). The disciples knew that disembodied spirits could not be touched. Jesus, however, could and that's why He invited them to look at His hands and feet, which carried the scars of His crucifixion. They could see that Jesus was no hallucination or figment of their imagination (vs. 40). Here was indisputable proof that Jesus had conquered death. Despite this, some critics still speak of a so-called spiritual resurrection, for they deny the bodily resurrection of the Son. Their assertions, however, do not square with the evidence.

After examining Jesus' body, the disciples were overcome with joy and amazement. Though the proof of His resurrection was clear, they still remained baffled. They could not deny that Jesus was standing before them, but His resurrection did not fit their preconceptions (vs. 41). Rather than get annoyed and impatient, Jesus remained calm with His disciples. The Savior asked for something to eat (vs. 42). After being given a piece of fish, He ate it, thereby proving that He was not a ghost (vs. 43). Through this and other appearances, Jesus thoroughly convinced His disciples that He had indeed risen from the dead. John 20:20 adds that once the disciples recognized their Lord, they were "overjoyed."

II. THE EXPLANATION OF SCRIPTURE: LUKE 24:44-49

A. The Facts Presented: vss. 44-47

He said to them, "This is what I told you while I was still with you: Everything must be fulfilled that is written about me in the Law of Moses, the Prophets and the Psalms." Then he opened their minds so they could understand the Scriptures. He told them, "This is what is written: The Christ will suffer and rise from the dead on the third day, and repentance and forgiveness of sins will be preached in his name to all nations, beginning at Jerusalem.

Jesus reminded His followers that while He was previously with them, He told them how the messianic promises recorded in the Old Testament were ordained by God to be fulfilled. The Law, the Prophets, and the Psalms—the three major sections of the Hebrew Scriptures—reveal truths about the Redeemer that had to occur. Luke 24:44 affirms that there is a strong interrelationship between the Old and New Testaments. Succinctly put, the triune God brought the universe into existence; humankind sinned, bringing moral and spiritual corruption to themselves and their world; and now the Godhead has made redemption possible through the atoning work of the Son. The divine plan of redemption began at Calvary, continues even now, and will one day be complete when God creates a new heaven and new earth.

At this point, Jesus opened the minds of the disciples to comprehend the Scriptures (vs. 45). While the specific texts are not listed in this verse, it's possible they included the many Old Testament passages appearing elsewhere in the Gospel of Luke and the Book of Acts. The threefold thrust of those prophecies was that the Messiah had to die on the cross (see Pss. 22; 31; 69; 118; Isa. 53), rise from the dead (see Pss. 16:10; 110:1), and have the good news of salvation heralded to the lost (Luke 24:46-47; see Matt. 28:19; Mark 13:10).

Part of the Gospel proclamation included an emphasis on repentance for the forgiveness of sins (Luke 24:47). This Hebrew concept included the idea of turning from wrongdoing as a prelude to experiencing the Father's offer of pardon through faith in the Son. Beginning at Jerusalem (the initial center and focus of the Gospel), the followers of the Savior were to announce the Good News to the nations of the world (see Isa. 49:6; Luke 2:32; Acts 13:47). Acts 2 records how this began on the day of Pentecost.

The disciples must have been surprised at Jesus' words. Generally, Jews believed that Gentiles were outside the favor of God, or that if Gentiles were to receive God's favor, they first had to become Jews. But here was Jesus telling His disciples to disperse into the world and make disciples of people from all nations (see Matt. 28:19). The Father had opened His arms wide to graciously receive all people who love and believe in His Son.

B. The Promise of the Spirit: vss. 48-49

"You are witnesses of these things. I am going to send you what my Father has promised; but stay in the city until you have been clothed with power from on high."

Jesus declared to His followers that they were witnesses of all that had occurred (Luke 24:48). The idea of proclaiming everything that happened in connection with the Savior is a key concept in the Book of Acts (see 1:22; 2:32; 3:15; 5:32; 10:39, 41; 13:31; 22:15, 20; 26:16). In 1:8, for instance, the risen Lord told His disciples that they and future believers would testify about Him in Jerusalem, in all Judea and Samaria, and to the farthest regions of the earth. They would not do this alone and in their own strength. Instead, the Holy Spirit would empower them for effective Christian service.

The Greek noun translated "witnesses" (*martus*; Luke 24:48; Acts 1:8) is the origin of the English word *martyr* and means to testify to something on the basis of what one has seen or heard. After Jesus' ascension, the Eleven plus other disciples gathered to choose someone to replace Judas as an apostle. Peter said that this person should be a "witness" (Acts 1:22) to the resurrection and someone who had been with Jesus since His baptism. In one sense, then, a witness was someone who actually saw the risen Lord and could testify, as in a courtroom, to the reality of the resurrection. Nonetheless, the writer of Hebrews also called anyone who perseveres for the faith a witness, and says all believers are surrounded by a "great cloud of witnesses" (Heb. 12:1). These witnesses include those who have testified to the reality of the Gospel, and their witness encourages us to testify today.

At the start of his first letter, John drew attention to his role as a witness who possessed the authority of experience and was competent to tell about what he had seen, heard, and touched. John and the other apostles (the "we" of 1 John 1:1) had a face-to-face encounter with the Lord. They heard Jesus speak and watched Him perform miracles. They witnessed His life and even touched His body. This touching may refer to one of the Savior's postresurrection appearances, where the Lord allowed His disciples to verify that He was not a phantom or a ghost.

First John 1:2 again emphasized the apostle's part in testifying about the "life" that was with the Father. The Son, who had existed for all eternity, became flesh and blood and gave His life so that we might possess eternal life through faith in Him. The immediate purpose of this life-giving message is our fellowship with the triune God and one another. The Greek noun rendered "fellowship" (vs. 3) assumes our reconciliation to God. It also assumes the common birthright that believers share through God's grace, which draws us all into a special, supernatural unity not possible apart from the Savior. That unity brings the "joy" that John mentioned in verse 4.

In Luke 24:49, Jesus referred to the Spirit as the one whom the Son was sending and whom the Father had previously promised to His people. This divine pledge is rooted in Old Testament passages such as Jeremiah 31:31 and Ezekiel 36:26-27. Also, when John prepared the way for the advent of the Messiah, the messenger declared that Jesus would baptize people with the Holy Spirit (Luke 3:16). As the disciples heralded the Good News, they helped to fulfill what God had promised to do. Moreover, Jesus pledged to clothe His followers with "power from on high" (24:49). This is a reference to the Holy Spirit, who would enable them to bear much fruit by leading many lost people to put their trust in the Redeemer for salvation.

The provision of the Spirit inaugurates a new era centered in the Messiah. We learn from John's Gospel that one must be "born of the Spirit" (3:8) to enter the kingdom of God. Jesus identified the Spirit with the living water of salvation (7:37-38; see 4:10-14). Jesus clarified that while "the flesh counts for nothing" (6:63), it is the Spirit who gives eternal life. The Spirit is the "Counselor" (14:16, 26; 15:26; 16:7) whom Jesus promised to send to His disciples after His resurrection from the dead and ascension into heaven. The third member of the Trinity, as the "Spirit of truth" (14:17), bears witness to Jesus, makes the meaning of His teaching clear to His disciples, and guides them into all the truth (14:26; 15:26; 16:13-14). The Spirit proves the world to be in the wrong about "sin and righteousness and judgment" (16:8). In anticipation of the Spirit's permanent indwelling and empowerment of believers, Jesus gave His disciples an anticipatory endowment of the Spirit on the evening of the first Easter Sunday (20:22).

Jesus' victory over death is the foundation of our faith, the source of our hope, and the basis for our Spirit-empowered witness. Paul stressed to the Corinthians that they could "stand" (1 Cor. 15:1) on these unshakable facts: Jesus died for our sins and was resurrected the third day (vss. 3-4). If that victory over death had not happened, Paul added, our faith is futile and those who die are truly lost (vss. 17-18). But the apostle declared that Jesus was raised from the dead, and His is just the first, for all believers will follow in His path (vs. 20). Through the Son's resurrection, the

Father has rewritten the presumed ending of our life history. Death is just the beginning of a new chapter in our life with the Lord. The resurrection hope should shine in our moments of darkness, reminding us that the tomb was indeed empty. Also, we should join Paul in crying out, "Thanks be to God! He gives us the victory through our Lord Jesus Christ" (vs. 57).

III. THE ASCENSION OF JESUS: LUKE 24:50-53

A. The Departure of Jesus: vss. 50-51

When he had led them out to the vicinity of Bethany, he lifted up his hands and blessed them. While he was blessing them, he left them and was taken up into heaven.

The ascension of Jesus took place 40 days after His first postresurrection appearance to His disciples (see Acts 1:3, 12). In Acts, Luke gave us a fuller account of the event and described Jesus' activities during the 40 days. Luke 24:50 states that when Jesus ascended, the disciples were with Him at Bethany. This was a small village located two miles southeast of Jerusalem on the road to Jericho. The town was on the eastern slope of the Mount of Olives. Bethany was the home of Mary, Martha, and Lazarus, and it was there that Jesus raised Lazarus from the dead (see John 11:17-44). In the house of Simon the leper, a resident of Bethany, a woman anointed Jesus with an expensive jar of perfume (see Mark 14:3-9). At the time of Jesus' ascension, He blessed His disciples. Then, they watched spellbound as Jesus rose upward until they could no longer see Him (Luke 24:51).

B. The Disciples' Return to Jerusalem: vss. 52-53

Then they worshiped him and returned to Jerusalem with great joy. And they stayed continually at the temple, praising God.

After Jesus ascended to heaven, His disciples worshiped their glorified Lord and returned to Jerusalem full of joy (Luke 24:52). As the years went by and the disciples recalled the sight of His departure, they must have been thrilled to realize He would be returning in the same way (see Acts 1:11).We know from verse 13 that in the days following the ascension, Jesus' disciples were staying in the upper room. So when Luke says "they stayed continually at the temple" (Luke 24:53), he meant they went to the Jerusalem shrine at the regular times for prayer (see Acts 3:1).

Why did Jesus leave the earth in such a dramatic fashion? We may never know for sure, but one view is that it was important for His earthly ministry to come to a definite conclusion. Put another way, the disciples needed to experience a specific point in time when Jesus returned to heaven. Also, by leaving this earth, Jesus was in a position to dispatch the Holy Spirit to minister through all believers everywhere (see John 16:7). The Lord Jesus is now seated at the right hand of His Father (see Eph. 1:20). He "speaks to the Father in our defense" (1 John 2:1) and is our great High Priest (see Heb. 7:26). In addition, Jesus is preparing a place for us to join Him someday (see John 14:2-3).

Discussion Questions

1. Why was it necessary for the Old Testament prophecies concerning the Messiah to be fulfilled?
2. What specific things did the Old Testament reveal would happen to the Messiah?
3. What relationship is there between repentance and forgiveness of sins?
4. How would you convince an unbeliever that Jesus literally rose from the dead?
5. Why is it important to rely on the power of the Spirit when telling others about the risen Savior?

Contemporary Application

Jesus' resurrection motivated the disciples to put their lives on the line for Him. For instance, after Saul met the risen Lord, the convert became a powerful preacher. Despite the prospect of death, Saul was willing to affirm to others the reality of Jesus' resurrection.

Jesus still transforms lives. We come to Him first for our salvation, an act that is dependent on His power and grace alone. Then, as the Spirit of God works through our obedience and submission, day by day, the risen Lord is changing us into His image (see Rom. 12:1-2). As we study God's Word, the Holy Spirit helps us to recognize the life changes that we need to make. Our Lord is very gentle and patient as He transforms the areas of our lives that we surrender to Him.

Moreover, as Jesus' followers, we need to recognize the importance of affirming to others that His resurrection actually took place. But how do we do it? We start by cultivating a personal relationship with the risen Lord in our daily life. This should then prompt us to share the Good News of Jesus' resurrection with others.

Expression may take the form of evangelism, but also it may take the form of song or prayer. In fact, there are many ways we can express our faith in Jesus' resurrection. But regardless of the approach we take, God is pleased when we show our trust and hope in the risen Savior.

The Holy Spirit Comes

Scripture

Background Scripture: *Acts 2:1-36*

Scripture Lesson: *Acts 2:1-13*

Key Verse: *All of them were filled with the Holy Spirit and began to speak in other tongues as the Spirit enabled them.* Acts 2:4.

Scripture Lesson for Children: *Acts 2:1-13*

Key Verse for Children: *All of them were filled with the Holy Spirit and began to speak in other tongues as the Spirit enabled them.* Acts 2:4.

Lesson Aim

To encourage believers to rely upon the Holy Spirit as they live for the Messiah.

Lesson Setting

Time: A.D. *30*

Place: Jerusalem

Lesson Outline

The Holy Spirit Comes

  I. The Arrival of the Spirit: Acts 2:1-4
      A. *The Meeting of Jesus' Followers: vs. 1*
      B. *The Appearance of the Tongues of Fire: vss. 2-4*
  II. The Manifestation of the Spirit: Acts 2:5-13
      A. *The Presence of Devout Jews: vs. 5*
      B. *The Crowd's Confusion: vss. 6-8*
      C. *The Crowd's Composition: vss. 9-11*
      D. *The Crowd's Mixed Reaction: vss. 12-13*

Introduction for Adults

Topic: *Power to Change*

People are usually skeptical if they cannot see evidence of a claim. The motto of the state of Missouri (the "Show Me State") reflects the attitude of many adults. If we claim that God's Spirit is dwelling in us, then we need to give evidence of His presence. One way to show we have had a genuine and lasting encounter with the Spirit is by the powerful changes in behavior He has made in us (for example, by our trusting in the Savior, shunning sin, and remaining united with our fellow believers).

This was the central thrust of Peter's message on the day of Pentecost. Adults need to know that Peter's promise of forgiveness and the indwelling Holy Spirit extended beyond his current audience to future generations and to those living in other lands. Although Peter may not have realized it at the time, his words included the Gentiles as well.

Introduction for Youth

Topic: *Hope for Power*

Some of the most interesting conversion stories I have heard involve people studying to be ministers. The standard assumption is that these people are already saved. Occasionally, this isn't the case.

There are many reasons why individuals want to train for church leadership. Even teens are known to wrestle with this issue. Often, though, the desire— whether it is to help others, exercise abilities in teaching and counseling, enjoy a position of respect and influence, and so on—is void of God's presence and power.

As we learn in this week's lesson, an individual claiming to be a Christian, regardless of his or her age, is spiritually powerless when not connected with the Savior and operating in the Spirit. What a dynamic change occurs when a young person stops trying to live for God in his or her own strength and starts faithfully serving Him with the limitless resources of the Spirit!

Concepts for Children

Topic: *The Holy Spirit Comes*

1. The believers were together when God's Spirit came to them.
2. When Jesus' followers spoke in other languages, it caught the crowd's attention.
3. Jews from every nation heard the Gospel in their own languages.
4. Many heard Peter's message and became believers.
5. God can give us the courage to tell others about Jesus.

Lesson Commentary

I. THE ARRIVAL OF THE SPIRIT: ACTS 2:1-4

A. The Meeting of Jesus' Followers: vs. 1

When the day of Pentecost came, they were all together in one place.

The Gospel of Luke focuses on all the things that Jesus did and taught (see 1:1-4). The Book of Acts picks up where the third Synoptic Gospel left off (see Acts 1:1). Indeed, the Greek verb translated "began" implies that the works and teachings of the Savior continued after He ended His earthly ministry. From Luke's perspective, the actions of the "apostles" (vs. 2) after Jesus' resurrection and ascension were an extension of His ministry, carried on through the power of the Holy Spirit. Prior to Jesus' ascension, He appeared to the Eleven, as well as to some of His other disciples, on several occasions over a period of 40 days. One of the purposes of these appearances was to prove to His followers that He had truly risen from the dead in bodily form. In addition, Jesus taught them about the kingdom of God (vs. 3).

In Acts, the original core group of disciples are usually called "apostles" (vs. 2), which means "those who are sent." In ancient times, the word referred to both messengers and ambassadors. During Jesus' ministry, He appointed 12 of His followers to be distinctive representatives (see Luke 6:12-16). Moreover, He gave them the most intensive training and poured His life into them. They became known as the "Twelve" (8:1; 9:1). These chosen followers came to have special authority in the church (see Eph. 2:20). Although the early church recognized other believers (such as Paul, Barnabas, and Jesus' brother James) as apostles, only Paul attained the same unquestioned status at the forefront as the Twelve regarding matters pertaining to Christian life and doctrine.

Last week, we learned that the Lord's teaching during the 40-day period before His ascension included a command that the apostles were to wait in Jerusalem until they had received the gift of the Holy Spirit (see Luke 24:49; Acts 1:4-5). With the Spirit's power, they would become witnesses to the world of Jesus' work and His message of forgiveness. The Spirit would enable the disciples to perform mighty deeds and work in the hearts of their listeners to convince them of the truth of the Gospel. Jesus described expanding zones of influence, beginning at Jerusalem, spreading throughout Judea and Samaria, and eventually reaching to the "ends of the earth" (Acts 1:8). Interestingly, the literary movement of Acts follows this general pattern of expansion. The events recorded in chapters 1 through 7 occurred in Jerusalem; those of chapters 8 and 9 took place in Judea and Samaria; and the action of chapters 10 through 28 progressed from Caesarea to Rome.

After Jesus' ascension (vss. 9-11), His disciples returned to Jerusalem (vs. 12), where they met in an upper room (vs. 13). Such spaces were desired in Palestine because they were above the noise and prying eyes of those walking by on the street. Furthermore, upper rooms of large homes were often rented out to the poor. It is possible that this was the same location where Jesus had celebrated His final meal with the disciples. With the exception of Judas Iscariot, all the apostles and several of the women who had followed Jesus were gathered for prayer. Mary, the mother of Jesus, and His brothers were also present (vs. 14).

Along with the 12 disciples, Jesus had a faithful band of women who followed Him throughout His ministry. Unlike most Jewish teachers, Jesus permitted women to travel with Him and even support Him (see Luke 8:1-3). These women also saw His crucifixion and were the first to witness His resurrection (see 24:1). The women mentioned in Acts 1:14 probably also included the wives of the apostles, along with these other women who had remained loyal to Jesus all through His ministry, death, and resurrection. The reference to Jesus' mother is the last time she is mentioned in Scripture. These women waited with the disciples and other followers of the Savior and shared in the initial outpouring of the Holy Spirit on the day of Pentecost.

Acts 2:1 reveals that the Holy Spirit came upon Jesus' disciples while they were assembled in one place. In addition to the fact that they gathered together in a single location, this verse implies that the disciples were in agreement in their thinking and purpose on Pentecost. This Jewish festival, which means "fiftieth," was the second of three main yearly feasts. Passover and Tabernacles were the other two annual festivals requiring the presence of all Jewish males. Pentecost was also known as the feast of Weeks, the day of first fruits, and the feast of Harvest. The festival was always on a Sabbath day. The feast was celebrated 50 (*pente* in Greek) days after the Passover (Lev. 23:15-16). Some have seen a connection between Pentecost and the giving of the law on Mount Sinai, which may have occurred on the fiftieth day after the Exodus.

Pentecost was basically a celebration of the grain harvest, a period that lasted about seven weeks. Barley and wheat were the primary harvest foods. The poor and strangers were especially welcome during this festival. During Pentecost, the people would bring their offerings of first fruits to the Lord. A special sacrifice was presented in the temple during this time. A wave offering of new bread made from the recently harvested wheat was presented before the Lord, along with sin and peace offerings. No celebrating was to occur until after this ceremony. Every male Israelite was to appear in the sanctuary. Jews from all over the known world would come to Jerusalem to celebrate this feast of thanksgiving.

B. The Appearance of the Tongues of Fire: vss. 2-4

Suddenly a sound like the blowing of a violent wind came from heaven and filled the whole house where they were sitting. They saw what seemed to be tongues of fire that separated and came to rest on each of them. All of them were filled with the Holy Spirit and began to speak in other tongues as the Spirit enabled them.

All at once and unexpectedly, the disciples heard a sound from heaven that was similar to that of a turbulent "wind" (Acts 2:2). The noise filled the entire house where they were meeting. In the context of this incident, the wind was a physical indication of the presence of the Spirit. In Scripture, wind and breath are common symbols of God's Spirit (see Ezek. 37:9, 14; John 3:8).

The sight of "tongues of fire" (Acts 2:3) was even more unusual than the sound of the wind, perhaps being reminiscent of the thunder and lighting that accompanied God's giving of the law to Moses on Mount Sinai (see Exod. 19:16-19). The tongue-shaped flames appeared to stand over each disciple's head (Acts 2:3). This incident was significant, for it indicated that God's presence was among Jesus' followers in a more powerful and personal way than they had ever experienced before. The disciples could sense the Spirit's coming audibly (through wind) and visibly (through fire). Moreover, they were filled with the Holy Spirit (vs. 4). As evidence of His presence, the Spirit enabled them to speak in other tongues. Apparently these were actual languages or dialects being voiced by the disciples to the visitors from many countries in Jerusalem. The Spirit had come to empower Jesus' followers to reach out to the lost with the saving message of the Gospel.

Some think Jesus' followers were at that moment in one of the courts of the Jerusalem temple (Luke 24:52-53). In a few instances, Luke uses the Greek word for "house" in Acts to refer to the temple, and Luke's Gospel closes with the statement that the disciples "stayed continually at the temple, praising God" (24:53). Those who hold this view also suggest that the disciples had the best chance of attracting a large crowd in the temple precincts than in the upper room. Those who think the Spirit came upon the disciples in the upper room of a house argue that "one place" (Acts 2:1) more naturally refers to the space mentioned in 1:13. They also point out that Luke more often uses the common Greek word for temple rather than the word for house. With the entire city of Jerusalem filled with pilgrims, the disciples could have attracted a large crowd by coming down to the street after the Holy Spirit had come upon them.

II. THE MANIFESTATION OF THE SPIRIT: ACTS 2:5-13

A. The Presence of Devout Jews: vs. 5

Now there were staying in Jerusalem God-fearing Jews from every nation under heaven.

The disciples, being enthusiastic in their baptism of power, spilled out into the streets of Jerusalem. As was noted earlier, the population of Jerusalem swelled with pilgrims attending the festival of Pentecost (Acts 2:5). This event proved to be a strategic time for the Father and Son to send the Holy Spirit. Visitors who heard God being miraculously praised in their own languages—and were perhaps among that day's 3,000 converts (see vs. 41)—could take the good news of salvation in the Messiah back with them to their homelands.

B. The Crowd's Confusion: vss. 6-8

When they heard this sound, a crowd came together in bewilderment, because each one heard them speaking in his own language. Utterly amazed, they asked: "Are not all these men who are speaking Galileans? Then how is it that each of us hears them in his own native language?"

While the Spirit operates quietly, God sometimes sends visible and audible signs of His work. The wind, fire, and inspired speech all have their roots in Jewish tradition as signs of God's presence. This did not escape the notice of the foreign Jews who heard the sound of tongues-speaking. They were amazed that locals could fluently speak languages from around the Roman Empire (Acts 2:6). With their curiosity aroused, crowds of people quickly gathered together to discuss what could be behind all the commotion. They could tell by the distinctive accent of Jesus' followers that they were mainly from Galilee (vs. 7). In general, the Jews living in Jerusalem looked down upon those from Galilee because it was so far away from the religious center of the nation (see John 7:52).

Evidently, the throng operated under the assumption that the disciples spoke only one or two languages. Consequently, they were perplexed that these simple, uneducated Galileans could speak fluently in so many different native dialects, which in turn could be understood by the diverse group of pilgrims (Acts 2:8). In this amazing turn of events, the Lord began to reverse the confusion that occurred at the tower of Babel thousands of years earlier (see Gen. 11:1-9). Whereas then God scattered the human race over all the earth, on the day of Pentecost He brought all sorts of different people back together to hear the message of salvation.

C. The Crowd's Composition: vss. 9-11

"Parthians, Medes and Elamites; residents of Mesopotamia, Judea and Cappadocia, Pontus and Asia, Phrygia and Pamphylia, Egypt and the parts of Libya near Cyrene; visitors from Rome (both Jews and converts to Judaism); Cretans and Arabs—we hear them declaring the wonders of God in our own tongues!"

Both ethnic Jews and converts to Judaism heard the Messiah's disciples using the crowds' own languages to declare to them the wonderful things God had done. These visitors came from all across the Roman Empire (Acts 2:9-11). At the time when the New Testament was written, the entire civilized world (with the exception of the little known kingdoms of the Far East) was under the domination of Rome. From the Atlantic Ocean on the west to the Euphrates River and the Red Sea on the east, from the Rhone, the Danube, the Black Sea, and the Caucus mountains on the north, and to the Sahara on the south, stretched one vast empire under the headship and virtual dictatorship of the emperor.

"Parthians" (vs. 9) lived in the region that constitutes what is today modern Iran. As was noted in lessons 2 and 3, "Medes" refers to the ancient Indo-European inhabitants in what is today part of northwest Iran. "Elamites" denotes those living in the region located north of the Persian Gulf, with the Tigris River forming its western boundary. "Mesopotamia" (modern-day Iraq) is the region located between the Tigris and the Euphrates. "Judea" is the Greco-Roman name for the land of Judah. "Cappadocia" was a large region in Asia Minor bordered on the north by the Kingdom of Polemon, in the south by Cilicia and Syria, in the west by Galatia and Lycaonia, and in the east by Armenia and Syria. "Pontus," located along the southern shore of the Black Sea, was bordered on the west by Bithynia and on the southeast by Galatia. "Asia" refers to a Roman province located in western Asia Minor.

"Phrygia" (vs. 10) was a tract of land centered on the great Anatolian plateau of Asia Minor. "Pamphylia," located on the southern coast of Asia Minor, was bordered on the west by Lycia and on the east by Cilicia Tracheia. The kingdom of "Egypt," located in northeastern Africa, extended south about 550 miles from the Mediterranean Sea. "Libya" was the stretch of territory encompassing north Africa west of Egypt. Most of the Jews who lived there resided in "Cyrene," which was the capital of a region called Cyrenaica. "Rome" was located about 15 miles from the mouth of the Tiber River on the Italian peninsula. The city was a sprawling metropolis of about one million people and the imperial capital of the empire. "Cretans" (vs. 11) were residents of an oblong shaped island located 60 miles southeast of the mainland of Greece. "Arabs" were residents of Arabia, which was located between the Red Sea and the Euphrates River.

D. The Crowd's Mixed Reaction: vss. 12-13

Amazed and perplexed, they asked one another, "What does this mean?" Some, however, made fun of them and said, "They have had too much wine."

The pilgrims were excited but confused by the tongues-speaking episode unfolding before them. The crowds kept asking one another what its significance might be (Acts 2:12). Regrettably, some in the throng took a less charitable view. They crassly joked that Jesus' disciples were drunk from having ingested too much wine (vs. 13). The Savior would use the bewilderment of the pilgrims as an opportunity to shine the light of the Gospel into their sin-filled lives.

Just a few months earlier, Peter had denied being a disciple of the Lord (see John 18:15-18, 25-27). Thankfully, the Savior reinstated His repentant disciple to Christian service (see 21:15-19). On the day of Pentecost, Peter was empowered by the Holy Spirit to stand before an assembled crowd to explain what they were seeing. He was "with the Eleven" (Acts 2:14), suggesting that while Peter was the primary speaker, the others all affirmed what he said. Peter began by asking his fellow Jews, as well as all who lived in Jerusalem, to listen carefully to the explanation he was about to offer about the wonderful things God was doing in their presence.

Peter declared that his fellow disciples were not drunk, as some mistakenly conjectured. In fact, such a theory was not even probable, for it was too early in the morning for drunkenness (vs. 15). Instead, something far more extraordinary was occurring. To explain, Peter quoted from Joel 2:28-32 (Acts 2:16-21). The apostle noted that the outpouring of the Spirit on Jesus' followers (being evidenced by speaking in foreign languages) was a partial fulfillment of what will occur at the second advent of the Messiah. In contrast to the former days of the old covenant, the latter days of the new covenant will be characterized by unique manifestations of the Spirit among God's people. Of course, what occurred at Pentecost will find its ultimate fulfillment in the end-time kingdom of the Son.

Discussion Questions

1. Why were the disciples gathered together on the day of Pentecost?
2. What did Jesus' followers do when they became filled with the Holy Spirit?
3. What utterly amazed the pilgrims about the tongues-speaking episode?
4. How can you promote unity among believers you know who are from a different background or tradition than you?
5. What are some specific ministries the Holy Spirit has empowered you to perform?

Contemporary Application

Jesus' plan for the church was larger than any of the disciples could have imagined. It must have seemed incredible to this small group to hear that their efforts would eventually have a worldwide impact. Such a mission required nothing less than the power of God's own Spirit to ensure its fulfillment.

The emphasis on power in Jesus' promise to the church contrasts with the weakness the disciples must have initially felt after the Savior's crucifixion. Afraid of the authorities and ashamed of their own failure to stand with Jesus in His hour of humiliation, they must have wondered how they could be effective witnesses to the ends of the earth.

This mission could be fulfilled only through God's strength. No amount of natural courage or human resolve could match the empowerment that would come from the outpouring of God's Spirit on the day of Pentecost. The role played by the Holy Spirit in the mission of the early church was so important that the disciples could not even begin to fulfill that mission until the Spirit had come upon them.

What does this mean for us, now that the gift of the Spirit has been given? On the one hand, if we attempt to live our Christian life in our own limited strength, we can expect failure, disappointment, and frustration. On the other hand, if we depend upon the power of the Holy Spirit, the Father Himself will strengthen us to be like the Son and enable us to tell others about Him. The Holy Spirit is as important to the church today as He was to the early church. While there is some disagreement among believers regarding certain details of the Holy Spirit's work, all can agree that virtuous living and effective service are possible only through the Spirit's power.

Living with Hope

Scripture

Background Scripture: *1 Thessalonians 4:13–5:11*
Scripture Lesson: *1 Thessalonians 4:13–5:11*
Key Verse: *God did not appoint us to suffer wrath but to receive salvation through our Lord Jesus Christ.*
1 Thessalonians 5:9.
Scripture Lesson for Children: *1 Thessalonians 4:13–5:3, 6-11*
Key Verse for Children: *God did not appoint us to suffer wrath but to receive salvation through our Lord Jesus Christ.*
1 Thessalonians 5:9.

Lesson Aim

To motivate believers to consider the ways God comforts them in difficult times.

Lesson Setting

Time: A.D. *51*
Place: Written from Corinth to the church in Thessalonica.

Lesson Outline

Living with Hope

  I. The Savior's Return: 1 Thessalonians 4:13-18
    A. *The Antidote to Despair: vs. 13*
    B. *The Certainty of the Resurrection: vs. 14*
    C. *The Order of the Resurrection: vss. 15-17*
    D. *The Need for Mutual Encouragement: vs. 18*
  II. The Preparation for the Savior's Return:
    1 Thessalonians 5:1-11
    A. *False Hopes: vss. 1-3*
    B. *Sons of Light: vss. 4-5*
    C. *Watchful Self-Control: vss. 6-9*
    D. *Christian Anticipation: vss. 10-11*

Introduction for Adults

Topic: *Great Expectations*

The newly married couple set up housekeeping in a ground floor apartment in an old house located on a traditional street with lawns and flowers. For some time they ignored how their place looked. But one day they got word that visitors were coming: the husband's parents, who kept their own place clean and sharp inside and out.

The couple sprang into action cleaning rooms, pulling weeds, and cutting grass. It was almost like the coming of the Lord. In the nick of time they made their place sparkle and it passed inspection.

What would we do differently today if we knew that Jesus would knock on our door tomorrow? It's so easy to dismiss the coming of the Lord, because we get so deeply involved in our own concerns. Our agenda becomes more important than His.

Since we do not get advance word about Jesus' coming, we can take steps to be ready to meet Him. Thinking about that prospect helps us to shape our program more like His and less like ours.

Introduction for Youth

Topic: *Hope for Resurrection*

Psychologists tell us that many teenagers have little sense of their own mortality. They take crazy risks because they think they are immortal. They make career choices based on the best offers, looking for satisfaction in the future based on positions and money.

However, when accidents take the lives of their friends, adolescents are forced to think about life and their future. Christians step up at times like these and offer a totally different perspective on life and its meaning.

Because Jesus died, rose from the grave, and is coming again, we can fit our goals and fears into His good and perfect will. We do not have to be nervous about our future because we know it is with Jesus. Thus, knowing Jesus makes life worthwhile.

Concepts for Children

Topic: *A Future Filled with Hope*

1. Paul's friends in Thessalonica had some questions about Jesus' return.
2. Paul said that all believers will join Jesus when He returns.
3. Paul also said that believers will live with Jesus forever.
4. Paul wanted his friends to be filled with hope and love.
5. We, too, can encourage others by telling them that Jesus will return.

Lesson Commentary

I. THE SAVIOR'S RETURN: 1 THESSALONIANS 4:13-18

A. The Antidote to Despair: vs. 13

Brothers, we do not want you to be ignorant about those who fall asleep, or to grieve like the rest of men, who have no hope.

In 1 Thessalonians 4:13-18, Paul addressed a special concern raised by his readers. Since the apostle had been in their midst, one or more of their number had died. This raised some theological questions, which Timothy evidently had carried to Paul on the Thessalonians' behalf. He assured his readers that believers who have died will in no way fare worse at Jesus' second coming than those who survive until that time. The apostle went on to give the Thessalonians a fuller understanding of the order of events surrounding the Lord's return.

When it came to the death of their fellow Christians, Paul was concerned about both the knowledge and the emotions of his readers. Referring to them affectionately as his dear friends in the Lord, the apostle told his readers he wanted them to know what would happen to the believers who had died so that the surviving Christians would not grieve like people who had no hope. "Fall asleep" (4:13) was a euphemism for physical death that was used by Jews and some non-Jews. The non-Christians among whom the Thessalonian believers lived had no basis to expect anything good for their departed loved ones. They had despair rather than hope for the dead.

Some interpreters take the biblical comparison of death to sleep almost literally. This view, called soul sleep, holds that the souls of dead people remain in a state of unconsciousness until resurrection. The majority of conservative interpreters, however, take another view of the intermediate state between earthly life and resurrection life. According to these interpreters, while the body dies (to be raised later), the soul is alive. During the intermediate period, the souls of believers are with the Lord (see Luke 23:43; Phil. 1:23), while the souls of unbelievers are in a place of punishment (see Luke 16:22-23).

During his short stay in Thessalonica, Paul declared that Jesus will come again. The apostle also taught about the resurrection of the dead. But Paul evidently had not described how the dead will participate in the events surrounding the Lord's second coming. The apostle knew that if he cleared up the Thessalonians' confusion about death, he would in the process reassure them. Believers, Paul said, need not grieve "like the rest of men, who have no hope" (1 Thess. 4:13). The "rest of men" are, of course, unbelievers. Historians attest to the truth of Paul's words about pagan despair in the face of death. The best philosophers and teachers of the ancient world had no real hope to offer their followers. Literature of the time is filled with pictures of hopelessness at death. Inscriptions on tombs reflect the same dread. Ancient myths describe scenes of the utter darkness of the afterlife.

B. The Certainty of the Resurrection: vs. 14

We believe that Jesus died and rose again and so we believe that God will bring with Jesus those who have fallen asleep in him.

Paul argued in 1 Thessalonians 4:14 that since Jesus rose from the dead, believers can be certain they, too, will be resurrected. Moreover, Jesus will bring with Him all the believing dead, in their resurrected form, when He returns as He promised. Because the Messiah survived death, the survival of believers beyond death was as equally certain. Some Bible commentators have suggested that early on in his career, Paul expected to be among those who are still alive at the time of the Lord Jesus' coming. They base this view, first of all, on passages in early letters written by the apostle where he used the word "we," seeming to include himself with those who will be alive (for example, vss. 15, 17).

Furthermore, passages in letters written later in Paul's career seem to indicate that the apostle expected to be among those who would die and be resurrected (for instance, 2 Cor. 4:14). Some commentators who favor this view suggest that the primary incident that changed Paul's mind was his close brush with death in the Roman province of Asia (see 1:8-10). Other commentators believe we cannot know whether the apostle expected to survive until the Savior's return. They point out that Paul regularly identified himself with his readers by saying "we." Therefore, nothing can be proved by his use of that pronoun.

C. The Order of the Resurrection: vss. 15-17

According to the Lord's own word, we tell you that we who are still alive, who are left till the coming of the Lord, will certainly not precede those who have fallen asleep. For the Lord himself will come down from heaven, with a loud command, with the voice of the archangel and with the trumpet call of God, and the dead in Christ will rise first. After that, we who are still alive and are left will be caught up together with them in the clouds to meet the Lord in the air. And so we will be with the Lord forever.

The Thessalonian believers were evidently concerned that their dead loved ones would be at a disadvantage when Jesus returned. But that would not be the case. In fact, Paul stated on the authority of the exalted Messiah that the righteous dead will be the first to join the Savior in a resurrection existence (1 Thess. 4:15). The apostle did not try to specify when the Lord's coming will happen. But Paul did say that when it occurs, three signs will accompany it: (1) "a loud command" (vs. 16), (2) "the voice of the archangel," and (3) "the trumpet call of God." The three signs mean the same thing: an announcement of Jesus' coming.

At that time, deceased believers will be the first to be resurrected from the dead in an immortal and glorified form. Then they, along with Christians alive at the time, "will be caught up . . . in the clouds" (vs. 17). The order of events suggests that at Jesus' return, deceased believers will "rise first" (vs. 16) before the events of verse 17 take place. The Greek verb translated "caught up" can also be rendered "snatched away." This verb carries the ideas of irresistible strength and total surprise. In this case, the event the verb describes what is often called the "rapture," after a word used in the Latin translation of verse 17.

Expressed differently, a time is coming when a whole generation of believers in Christ will be privileged to miss out on death. At Jesus' return, all believers living on the earth will be caught up in the air to meet the Lord. And the bodies of Jesus' followers will be instantaneously glorified, so that they will be like the resurrected believers. The believers who are "caught up" will have a double reunion. They will be reunited with the Savior as well as with their deceased loved ones in the faith. The joy of this gathering is probably beyond our imagination.

This meeting will take place "in the clouds." In the Old Testament, clouds were often associated with God's special activity (see Dan. 7:13). Also, when Jesus ascended to heaven, a cloud hid Him from the apostles' sight, and He will return "in the same way" (Acts 1:11). The clouds will not be a vehicle of the Lord's return. But in some sense, they will be recognized as a sign of God's glory and majesty. The main purpose of the event is to meet the Lord. When a dignitary paid a visit to a Greek city in ancient times, leading citizens went out to meet him and to escort him on the final stage of the journey. Paul similarly pictured Jesus as being escorted by His own people, those newly raised from the dead and those who will have remained alive. Having met the Lord in a glorified existence, they will never have to leave Him again.

Numerous Old Testament prophets spoke of the day of the Lord. Uniformly, they pictured this future day as a time when God will enter history decisively, executing wrath upon the ungodly (for example, Amos 5:18-20). New Testament writers frequently mentioned the day of the Lord, relating it specifically to Jesus' return. For these writers, the day of the Lord retained its wrathful character for the wicked (for instance, 1 Thess. 5:2-3). But they indicated that the day of the Lord is also a time of blessing for the righteous (for example, Eph. 4:30). Theologians today understand the day of the Lord in somewhat differing ways. According to some experts, the Second Coming, the resurrection of the dead, the rapture, and the final judgment all will take place in a brief space of time and together comprise the day of the Lord. Other experts think the day of the Lord is a long period that will begin just after the rapture and will end following a thousand-year reign of Christ on earth.

D. The Need for Mutual Encouragement: vs. 18

Therefore encourage each other with these words.

As the Thessalonians thought about the death of their loved ones or the possibility of their own death before Jesus' return, they might have become discouraged. To counteract discouragement, they needed to recall that one day Jesus will come in glory and gather all His followers to His side forever. In light of that promise, they were to comfort and console one another (1 Thess. 4:18).

II. THE PREPARATION FOR THE SAVIOR'S RETURN: 1 THESSALONIANS 5:1-11

A. False Hopes: vss. 1-3

Now, brothers, about times and dates we do not need to write to you, for you know very well that the day of the Lord will come like a thief in the night. While people are saying, "Peace and safety," destruction will come on them suddenly, as labor pains on a pregnant woman, and they will not escape.

The Thessalonians had two questions related to Jesus' return. First, they wondered whether believers who die before the Messiah's second advent will miss out on the blessings of that time. First Thessalonians 4:13-18 contains Paul's assurance that not only will the dead in Christ participate in those blessings, but also they will join the Lord in a resurrected existence prior to Christians who are alive at the Second Coming. The apostle's readers also wanted to know how and when all the events connected with Jesus' return will happen (5:1). Paul reminded them of what he had told them before, namely, that the timing of that future day is unknown. Paul went on to tell his readers that they ought to keep looking forward to the day of the Lord with confidence.

Evidently, the Thessalonians were engaging in speculation about the "times and dates" of Jesus' return. Paul gently chided his readers for their useless endeavor. He really should not have had to write to them on this subject, because they knew that the day of the Lord's return will come suddenly and unexpectedly, like a "thief in the night" (vs. 2). People will be lulled into false security right up until the day of the Lord. They will be talking about "peace and safety" (vs. 3) when destruction suddenly strikes. Paul made reference to a pregnant woman's going into labor. The apostle's main focus was not on the intense pain of labor, but rather on the rapid and unexpected way in which the experience starts. The unsaved, being surprised by the commencement of the day of the Lord, will not escape this future time of unprecedented travail.

The history of human life on the earth is filled with more scenes of destruction than any of us care to contemplate. But in verse 3, commentators believe Paul was referring to a future time of unprecedented difficulties, usually called the Great Tribulation period. This passage does not necessarily mean that all people will die during the future time of harrowing distress, only that the destruction will be terrible and there will be no avoiding it. The apostle referred to the immediate arrival of a pregnant woman's labor pains to emphasize how quickly God's wrath will strike the wicked. The use of childbirth to illustrate spiritual truth is seen both in the prophets and in the teachings of Jesus (see Isa. 13:6-8; Jer. 4:31; Mark 13:8). In rabbinic writings, the sufferings preceding the establishment of the messianic age are often called labor pains. Sometimes, the point is the intense pain of labor, but in 1 Thessalonians 5:3, Paul's emphasis is on the sudden onset of labor pains.

B. Sons of Light: vss. 4-5

But you, brothers, are not in darkness so that this day should surprise you like a thief. You are all sons of the light and sons of the day. We do not belong to the night or to the darkness.

Paul's readers were not to be taken by surprise by the day of the Lord. While they could not predict its timing, they knew with certainty that it was coming and they could expect it to happen (1 Thess. 5:4). After all, they were "sons of the light" (vs. 5) and "sons of the day." Moral purity and truth characterized them. In contrast, unbelievers belonged "to the night" and "to the darkness." Impurity and falsehood characterized them.

C. Watchful Self-Control: vss. 6-9

So then, let us not be like others, who are asleep, but let us be alert and self-controlled. For those who sleep, sleep at night, and those who get drunk, get drunk at night. But since we belong to the day, let us be self-controlled, putting on faith and love as a breastplate, and the hope of salvation as a helmet. For God did not appoint us to suffer wrath but to receive salvation through our Lord Jesus Christ.

In 1 Thessalonians 5:6-8, Paul further compared the saved and unsaved. Like people who sleep, unbelievers are spiritually insensitive and unaware of the coming of the day of the Lord. Their drunkenness represents their lack of proper self-control. In contrast, believers live in the brightness of spiritual awareness and keep themselves alert and sober. We often think about sobriety in terms of avoiding some form of sin. But in verse 8, Paul had in mind self-control's positive virtues. It means to put on the breastplate of faith and love and to don "as a helmet" the "hope of salvation."

Here the apostle was using parts of a Roman legionnaire's armor to symbolize qualities that make up the believer's spiritual armor and perhaps to stress that the Christian life involves spiritual conflict. There are other places in Paul's writings where he makes use of this analogy. The apostle's most complete description of armor is found in Ephesians 6:10-17, where he mentioned a belt, breastplate, footgear, shield, helmet, and sword. He also used armor symbolism in Romans 13:12 and 2 Corinthians 6:7 and 10:4. Paul may have been influenced by the prophet Isaiah, who spoke about the Lord's breastplate of righteousness and helmet of salvation (see Isa. 59:17). The recurring symbolism of armor in the apostle's writing is vivid evidence that the Christian life involves spiritual conflict.

Faith is the means by which we enter the Christian life, and day by day we trust in the Lord for our care. The love that exists between God and us prompts us to be compassionate and kind to one another. The hope of salvation means that, while divine wrath awaits unbelievers, we who are Christians will abide forever with the Lord. The day of the Lord will indeed bring sudden destruction (1 Thess. 5:3), but this "wrath" (vs. 9) is not meant for Jesus' followers. Yes, we, along with everyone else, deserve God's wrath because of our sin. But instead of receiving judgment for our misdeeds, we will "receive salvation" because of what Jesus has done for us.

D. Christian Anticipation: vss. 10-11

He died for us so that, whether we are awake or asleep, we may live together with him. Therefore encourage one another and build each other up, just as in fact you are doing.

In the end, it does not really matter whether we pass away before Jesus comes, for He died (and rose again from the dead) so that we can abide with Him forever. Moreover, whether we are living or deceased, our eternal future will be the same: "We may live together with him" (1 Thess. 5:10). The everlasting joy we are promised in union with the Son is not a dry biblical truth, but rather a wonderful source of encouragement and edification. Thus, believers are to "encourage one another" (vs. 11) and edify each other in their faith. In fact, this is to continue until Jesus returns.

Discussion Questions

1. What did Paul want the Thessalonians to be informed about?
2. What will happen to Christians who have already died when Jesus comes again?
3. What will happen to Christians who are still alive when Jesus returns?
4. How should we act as we wait for the Savior's return?
5. As you anticipate the day of the Lord, what are some ways you can encourage others to exhibit self-control by living a life of faith, love, and hope?

Contemporary Application

In the midst of the Thessalonians' hardships, Paul reminded them of the Lord's return and urged them to draw comfort from this truth. Even believers face moments of distress and uncertainty, and the reality of Jesus' coming can be a source of consolation for them.

The years of life are filled with change and discovery as well as with emerging talents, aptitudes, and dreams. Nevertheless, the students still struggle with loneliness and depression. There undoubtedly are times when the students, out of the depths of their hearts, cry for something or someone to give them peace and comfort. But before they can experience God's help and consolation, they must first recognize their own human frailty.

Only the Savior can fill the void that exists in the lives of all people. When they invite the living Lord to come into their hearts, He supplies the freeing power from the bondage of evil and sin's oppression. He also helps them deal with the loneliness, depression, and insecurity they might feel at times.

Jesus comforts believers through His presence and the promises of His Word, especially concerning His second advent. He also consoles them through the indwelling Spirit and the loving support of Christian friends. Such evidences of compassion and care undergird the students in their times of need.

Hope from God's Grace

Scripture

Background Scripture: *2 Thessalonians 2*
Scripture Lesson: *2 Thessalonians 2:1-3, 9-17*
Key Verse: *May our Lord Jesus Christ himself and God our Father, who loved us and by his grace gave us eternal encouragement and good hope, encourage your hearts and strengthen you in every good deed and word.* 2 Thessalonians 2:16-17.
Scripture Lesson for Children: *2 Thessalonians 2:1-3, 9-17*
Key Verse for Children: *So then, brothers, stand firm and hold to the teachings we passed on to you.* 2 Thessalonians 2:15.

Lesson Aim

To rely on the Lord for help to stand firm in the faith.

Lesson Setting

Time: A.D. *51 or 52*
Place: Written from Corinth to the church in Thessalonica.

Lesson Outline

Hope from God's Grace
   I.   Countering Erroneous Teaching:
        2 Thessalonians 2:1-3, 9-12
        A. *The False Report: vss. 1-2*
        B. *The Man of Lawlessness: vs. 3*
        C. *The Lawless One: vss. 9-10*
        D. *The Powerful Delusion: vss. 11-12*
   II. Relying on the Lord: 2 Thessalonians 2:13-17
        A. *Being Loved and Sanctified by God: vss. 13-14*
        B. *Standing Firm in the Faith: vss. 15-17*

Introduction for Adults

Topic: *Sure Source of Hope*

We run the risk of skepticism when we read about the physical obstacles the believers in Thessalonica faced and overcame with the help of the Lord. We wonder if we would have responded with the same level of hope to the challenges they endured. Regardless of whether God calls us to go through similar circumstances, the importance of standing firm in the faith remains unchanged.

Jesus' earliest followers succeeded because of their complete commitment to the Savior. They loved Him so much, and they wanted to obey Him so completely, that they persevered and grew in spiritual wisdom and understanding. Through the sanctifying work of the Spirit and belief in the truth of the Gospel, they were able to finish the race of life successfully.

There is no other way for believers today. Despite many popular but false "secrets" on the market, we are challenged to turn to Jesus as our sure source of hope and stand firm in the provision of His grace. When we love and serve Him above everything else, He enables us to rise above our difficulties and setbacks.

Introduction for Youth

Topic: *Hope Grounded in God's Grace*

Power from weakness is an oxymoron in today's culture. Smart people tell us to use power to get ahead and make something of ourselves. The importance of power is the unwritten message that undergirds the media's assault of our minds. We are sold power cars, power computers and mobile devices, and power cosmetics.

However, we learn from the Gospel that "In our own power, we are dead." So teenagers are forced to choose between society's power and Jesus' power. He was dismissed by the crowds because He refused to use His power to overthrow the Romans, who had conquered, subjugated, and persecuted the Jews.

Instead, Jesus showed that real, eternal power comes only through His cross. In today's culture, to remain firmly committed to Him requires enormous courage and faith. But Paul convincingly showed that by Jesus' power, believers could not only endure hardships, but also live with grace, hope, and purpose. The Gospel's power really is better, and it lasts forever.

Concepts for Children

Topic: *Stand Firm with Hope*

1. One day, Jesus is coming back.
2. Before Jesus returns, evil people will do bad things.
3. Paul told us not to be tricked by what evil people say and do.
4. We can pray to God for help whenever we need it.
5. We can also thank God for saving us.

Lesson Commentary

I. COUNTERING ERRONEOUS TEACHING: 2 THESSALONIANS 2:1-3, 9-12

A. The False Report: vss. 1-2

Concerning the coming of our Lord Jesus Christ and our being gathered to him, we ask you, brothers, not to become easily unsettled or alarmed by some prophecy, report or letter supposed to have come from us, saying that the day of the Lord has already come.

At this point in his second letter to the Thessalonian believers, Paul returned to one of the subjects he had discussed in his first letter (1 Thess. 4:13-18): the second coming of the Savior (see 2 Thess. 2:1). At the same time, the apostle expanded on the subject of the coming judgment of God (see 1:7-9). Paul was seriously alarmed by a report—supposedly from him—that was upsetting the church at Thessalonica. He told the people there to recognize that what others told them was false (2:1-2), to know what must happen before Jesus' return (vss. 3-4), to learn about the restrainer of evil (vss. 5-7), to be aware of spiritual counterfeits (vss. 8-10), and to accept the truth of God's judgment (vss. 11-12).

Why were Paul's readers in such turmoil? He blamed it on a message purported to have come from him. Allegedly, the second advent of the Messiah had already occurred, and the Thessalonians had missed it. Paul categorically denounced the interpretation in a disturbing "prophecy, report or letter" (vs. 2) that certain false prophets had made. The apostle firmly declared that nothing he had ever said or written could be correctly interpreted to mean that the Second Coming had already occurred. The Thessalonians, rather than being shaken, troubled, and excited, could hold onto what the apostle had taught them. He had clearly said that they would not miss the return of Christ (see 1 Thess. 4:17).

B. The Man of Lawlessness: vs. 3

Don't let anyone deceive you in any way, for that day will not come until the rebellion occurs and the man of lawlessness is revealed, the man doomed to destruction.

To help his readers stand firm, Paul declared something of what will happen in the end times. First, there will be a rebellion against God. Of course, people have always rebelled against God, but this will be worse than anything that has happened before. The apostle stressed the climactic nature of this apostasy by calling it "the rebellion" (2 Thess. 2:3)—one that will far exceed anything else like it in human history (see also Matt. 24:10-12; 2 Tim. 3:1-9; 1 Tim. 4:1). Second, "the man of lawlessness" (2 Thess. 2:3) will be revealed. This title is appropriate, for he will break God's injunctions. Presumably, this person will be the leader of the rebellion. He will defy everything considered to be holy or sacred and even claim that he himself is God (vs. 4; see Isa. 14:13-14; Ezek. 28:2-9; Dan. 11:36). Despite his bombastic assertions, this person is destined for "destruction" (2 Thess. 2:3).

Paul's spiritual children were distraught because they had forgotten or failed to apply what he had told them in person (vs. 5). He reminded them that the ultimate revelation of the powers of darkness is being held back by someone or something. This implies that the current age is not as bad as it could be. Indeed, the full-fledged manifestation of Satan that will be exhibited through his evil collaborators has not yet occurred. Currently, his appearance is being delayed according to God's sovereign will (vs. 6). There is no agreement concerning the identity of the restrainer of lawlessness. Options include the following: the Roman Empire and its emperor; the principle of law and government; the preaching of the Gospel; the Jewish state; and the Holy Spirit.

In any case, verse 7 says that during the present age, the hidden "power of law-lessness is already at work" in the world. Perhaps this is akin to the "spirit of antichrist" (1 John 4:3). Expressed differently, even though the Antichrist has not yet appeared, many people presently are opposed to God. Be that as it may, the full force of the diabolical one's mysterious power is being held back until the restrain-er is removed. This information implies that a specific series of events must occur prior to the return of the Messiah: (1) a sudden acceleration of apostasy (2 Thess. 2:3); (2) the removal of a restraining influence (vss. 6-7); and (3) the complete unveiling of the lawless one, who will be animated by Satan, oppose God, and attempt to exalt himself above God (vss. 4, 9).

C. The Lawless One: vss. 9-10

The coming of the lawless one will be in accordance with the work of Satan displayed in all kinds of counterfeit miracles, signs and wonders, and in every sort of evil that deceives those who are perishing. They perish because they refused to love the truth and so be saved.

As the present era unfolds, Satan and his operatives continue to clash with Jesus and His followers. Moreover, as the end of the age draws to a close, the battle will reach a point of no return. Regardless of how deplorable the situation becomes, the triumph of the Savior, the vindication of the saints, and the demise of the wicked are assured (2 Thess. 2:8). In the meantime, the devil's agent of lawlessness will use whatever tactics and schemes are at his disposal to persecute believers and undermine the will of God. Paul provided a graphic description of the wicked one's powers. This self-glorifying individual will be under Satan's control. Indeed, the devil will give his henchman unusual abilities to perform miracles, signs, and won-ders. Satan's work will be seen in the most audacious deceptions (vs. 9).

The tragic outcome will be destruction for people who allow themselves to be duped by this Satan-inspired miracle worker. People usually flock after an unusual phenomenon, but a miracle in and of itself proves nothing. Works of power will be used to deceive people into worshiping the lawless one. People will fall into this snare because they find no place in their hearts for the truth of the Gospel, the acceptance of which leads to salvation (vs. 10). The Good News must not only be acknowledged, but also upheld. The latter is demonstrated when converts allow

God's Word to rule their lives. In contrast, to reject the Gospel is to spurn the divine offer of salvation.

D. The Powerful Delusion: vss. 11-12

For this reason God sends them a powerful delusion so that they will believe the lie and so that all will be condemned who have not believed the truth but have delighted in wickedness.

Because the unsaved reject the Good News, God eventually sends on them a deluding influence so that they embrace what is wrong (2 Thess. 2:11). In other words, God will use their sin as a punishment against them. He will let them continue in their profane ways so that they are fooled into believing an assortment of lies. The world is filled with deceivers and falsehoods, all of whom are inspired by Satan, the "father of lies" (John 8:44). But the specific deception Paul was talking about in 2 Thessalonians 2:11 is the counterfeit claim made by the devil's operation.

The lawless one deludes unsaved humanity to believe that he is divine and worthy of veneration (vs. 4). Those taken in by this deceit not only reject the Gospel, but also delight in evil. It's no wonder that God condemns them (vs. 12). This presumably refers to eternal punishment in hell. Here we see that more than intellect is involved in accepting the Gospel. In Scripture, belief always includes the will and the emotions. Paul emphasized the connection between the two. Moreover, refusing to believe the truth and delighting in wickedness are interrelated.

II. RELYING ON THE LORD: *2 THESSALONIANS 2:13-17*

A. Being Loved and Sanctified by God: vss. 13-14

But we ought always to thank God for you, brothers loved by the Lord, because from the beginning God chose you to be saved through the sanctifying work of the Spirit and through belief in the truth. He called you to this through our gospel, that you might share in the glory of our Lord Jesus Christ.

On the one hand, Paul foresaw a time when the Messiah will judge the lawless one, along with all who will follow this satanic deceiver (2 Thess. 2:8-12). But the apostle hastened to assure his readers that they would not be among those judged. They were destined for blessing by God (vss. 13-14). This is why Paul thanked God for the Thessalonian believers—not so much because of who they were in themselves, but because of who they had become through God's grace to them.

The apostle called his spiritual children those who were "loved by the Lord" (vs. 13). God had demonstrated His love for them by choosing them for salvation. This shows that God's love is not a vague, emotion-charged slogan. Put another way, His love is not the basis of some blind hope for a silver lining in the clouds. The Father's love has been verified in history by what He has done for the church. To be specific, He sent His beloved Son as the atoning sacrifice for the sins of the entire world (see 1 John 2:2).

After Paul described the future, when the Messiah will judge lawless people, the apostle turned his attention to the distant past. He noted that from the very "beginning" (2 Thess. 2:13) God chose the believers in Thessalonica to "be saved." Paul made similar claims in other letters (for example, see Eph. 1:4). These passages are understood in different ways by Christians. Some think that God long ago predestined some individuals (but not others) for receiving His salvation. Others say that God formed His plan of salvation long ago, but that the matter of who receives salvation is determined by the exercise of free human will.

In either case, the salvation of the Thessalonians (and that of all believers) came through the work of the Spirit. He enables the lost to believe the Good News and grow increasingly holy in their lives. Paul emphasized both the Spirit's "sanctifying work" and the individual's "belief in the truth." With respect to the apostle's readers, God the Spirit had made unholy people holy, and the people themselves had put their faith in the truth about the Messiah. At this point, we should note the contrast between the Thessalonian believers and the future followers of the lawless one. Those whom God will judge "have not believed the truth" (vs. 12), while the Thessalonians were saved "through belief in the truth" (vs. 13).

On a practical and historical level, Paul's proclamation of the Gospel had been the means by which God called the Thessalonians to salvation. No doubt, the apostle was pleased and overjoyed to be used by the Lord in this important way. One reason God called the Thessalonians to salvation was so that they "might share in the glory" (vs. 14) of Jesus. This was a far different destiny than that awaiting the followers of Satan's wicked confederates. They would be eternally condemned.

Other Bible passages likewise describe believers as sharing the Messiah's glory—now, and even more so in the life to come. For instance, while the Son prayed to the Father, He said of His disciples, "I have given them the glory that you gave me" (John 17:22). Also, consider some of what Paul wrote: (1) "We, who with unveiled faces all reflect the Lord's glory, are being transformed into his likeness with ever-increasing glory, which comes from the Lord, who is the Spirit" (2 Cor. 3:18); (2) "When Christ, who is your life, appears, then you also will appear with him in glory" (Col. 3:4); and (3) "God . . . calls you into his kingdom and glory" (1 Thess. 2:12). Moreover, Peter said the following: (1) "When the Chief Shepherd appears, you will receive the crown of glory that will never fade away" (1 Pet. 5:4); and (2) "The God of all grace . . . called you to his eternal glory in Christ" (vs. 10).

It's hard to comprehend the fact that one day believers will share in Jesus' glory. After all, the Messiah is the sinless Son of God. So who are we to participate in His glory? But out of love, Jesus became as we are so that we might become as He is—and He is glorious. Knowing that God has prepared glory for believers should not make us complacent. On the contrary, it should motivate us to serve the Lord better. Because Christians are destined for glory, we should be concerned about obeying the instructions God has given us in the Scriptures. Also, since believers are destined for glory, we should live as God's hands and mouth in the world—ministering to people's needs and proclaiming the Gospel boldly.

B. Standing Firm in the Faith: vss. 15-17

So then, brothers, stand firm and hold to the teachings we passed on to you, whether by word of mouth or by letter. May our Lord Jesus Christ himself and God our Father, who loved us and by his grace gave us eternal encouragement and good hope, encourage your hearts and strengthen you in every good deed and word.

In light of the Thessalonians' decision to trust in the Lord Jesus for salvation, Paul urged them to remain steadfast in their faith. This included standing firm on the solid ground of the apostolic teaching they had received from the missionaries. Also, rather than be misled by spiritual frauds, they were to maintain a strong grip on the biblical truths Paul and his colleagues had imparted to them. It did not matter whether it took place directly in person or indirectly by means of letters (2 Thess. 2:15). Either way, the proclamation of the Gospel had effectively contributed to the salvation of the Thessalonians. Therefore, it was only logical for them to continue to heed what the missionaries had taught them.

Given the challenges the believers in Thessalonica faced, it would not be easy for them to hold fast to biblical truth. Indeed, they would need help—divine assistance. So at this point in his letter, Paul prayed that God would encourage and strengthen them. In the apostle's prayer, he invoked both the Lord Jesus Christ—God the Son—and God the Father (vs. 16). Perhaps Jesus was mentioned first because the Savior was much in Paul's thoughts. Usually he mentioned the Father first (for example, see 1 Thess. 1:1), but sometimes the apostle reversed the order (for example, see Gal. 1:1). This indicates that the apostle regarded the Father and the Son (along with the Spirit) as equal members of the Godhead.

Paul reminded his readers of what God had done for them. Specifically, He "loved" (2 Thess. 2:16) them and by means of His "grace" bestowed on them everlasting consolation and a firm hope. When speaking of the love of the Father for believers, the apostle may have had in mind the sacrifice of the Son for sinners. Surely no greater evidence of the Father's love could be imagined. Most likely, then, "eternal encouragement" refers to the effects of salvation. Because the Thessalonians had been redeemed, they had received a permanent change of attitude. For similar reasons, the "good hope" was their confident assurance of receiving future kingdom blessings. Put another way, they had every reason to expect kindness from the Lord Jesus at His second coming.

With respect to the Greek noun rendered "encouragement," it literally means "a calling to one's side." That is, one person is called to the side of another to admonish or console. A form of this word is used as a title for the Holy Spirit (see John 14:26). The Greek noun also refers to encouragement that prepares for action. So when Paul said that God "gave us eternal encouragement" (2 Thess. 2:16), he was talking about a continuing process of divine strengthening, exhortation, and aid. It would be natural to see the Holy Spirit's involvement in this process.

The love, encouragement, and hope believers receive from the Father through faith in the Son is the basis for Paul's specific prayer request for the Thessalonians. He wanted God to encourage their hearts and strengthen them in every good thing they did and said (vs. 17). Given their situation, these are the areas the apostle thought they needed God's assistance the most. Because of persecution and false teaching in Thessalonica, and perhaps for other reasons as well, Paul's readers needed encouragement. God could give them the spiritual uplift they required. He could also refresh their hearts and give them the grit they needed to go on believing and obeying the truth. The apostle's spiritual children were already involved in serving others in what they said and did. But as Christians soon find out, ministry can be wearying. So Paul prayed for an injection of new spiritual energy into the Thessalonians as they continued their lives of service.

Discussion Questions

1. In what ways did God show His love to the believers in Thessalonica?
2. How does the Holy Spirit use the proclamation of the Gospel to bring about the salvation of the lost?
3. Why is it important for us, as Jesus' followers, to stand firm in the faith?
4. In what ways has the truth of salvation in Christ provided you with "good hope" (2 Thess. 2:16)?
5. What are some specific ways you can serve the Lord in "every good deed and word" (vs. 17)?

Contemporary Application

Have you ever encountered someone who confesses to have trusted in the Savior in the past, but after suffering or disappointment, admits to little faith? All believers experience times when their ability to stand firm in the faith is tested. Undoubtedly, some in your class are now facing situations in which their faith needs strengthening.

Second Thessalonians was directed to believers whose commitment to the Lord Jesus was being undermined by persecution and false teaching. If these challenges were left unaddressed, Paul's spiritual children faced the possibility of drifting away from their loyalty to the Savior. Just as an anchor is needed to keep a boat from drifting into danger, so the Redeemer is the anchor of our faith. He is also the bedrock that secures our hope so that it can remain firm in the soil of our lives.

The main point of this imagery is that we are to find encouragement and strength in the Lord. When we do so, we are better able to hold fast to biblical truth. The implication is that Christianity must not be for us an off-again, on-again, when-it's-convenient religion. Paul, in his second letter to the Thessalonians, calls us to live consistently close to the Savior. We can do so knowing that when He returns, we will share in His glory.

A Living Hope

Scripture

Background Scripture: *1 Peter 1:1-12*
Scripture Lesson: *1 Peter 1:3-12*
Key Verse: *Praise be to the God and Father of our Lord Jesus Christ! In his great mercy he has given us new birth into a living hope through the resurrection of Jesus Christ from the dead.* 1 Peter 1:3.
Scripture Lesson for Children: *1 Peter 1:3-12*
Key Verse for Children: *In [God's] great mercy he has given us new birth into a living hope through the resurrection of Jesus Christ from the dead.* 1 Peter 1:3.

Lesson Aim

To discover ways to revive a vibrancy of hope in our lives, especially during trials.

Lesson Setting

Time: The early 60s of the first century A.D.
Place: Rome

Lesson Outline

A Living Hope

  I. The Believer's Salvation: 1 Peter 1:3-9
     A. *Future Hope and Inheritance: vss. 3-5*
     B. *Present Joy and Trials: vss. 6-9*
  II. The Prophets' Investigation: 1 Peter 1:10-12
     A. *Searching the Scriptures: vss. 10-11*
     B. *Serving the Saints: vs. 12*

Introduction for Adults

Topic: *Hopeful Living*

A woman fell under an oncoming commuter train and became trapped by the first car. Paramedics came to her rescue, but were frustrated because they could not ease her from under the train. They told the engineer not to move the train. Then they inserted an inflatable airlift bag under the 50-ton car and slowly raised it six inches to release her.

God's strength comes to our rescue like that time and again. We feel crushed under our heavy burdens and no one seems to be able to help us. But when we cry out to God, He lifts the burden and releases us to find joy, hope, and peace for daily living (see 1 Pet. 1:3).

Beyond our immediate release, God also guarantees us a crown of life. We are the firstfruits of His creation and He will not allow us to go under (see vss. 4-5).

Introduction for Youth

Topic: *A Clean Slate*

Years after the end of World War II, a few Japanese soldiers still hid on remote Pacific islands, awaiting the next battle. They had lost touch with the world and assumed that hostilities were still going on. Yet their war had already been lost. What a picture of "dead hope."

But what would a "living hope" (1 Pet. 1:3) look like? We might simply turn the gaze of our faith to the Cross, where a battle has already been won on our behalf. When we trust in the Son, who rose from the dead, He wipes clean the slate of sin in our lives. Now we hopefully await His victory's full manifestation at His return, when He will finally be "revealed" (vs. 5).

Concepts for Children

Topic: *Having Hope*

1. After Jesus died on the cross, He rose from the dead.
2. Because Jesus lives, He wants us to trust in Him.
3. When we do so, He gives us eternal life.
4. No matter what we go through, Jesus will help us.
5. The Father is pleased when we praise Him for the hope we have in His Son.

Lesson Commentary

I. THE BELIEVER'S SALVATION: 1 PETER 1:3-9

A. Future Hope and Inheritance: vss. 3-5

Praise be to the God and Father of our Lord Jesus Christ! In his great mercy he has given us new birth into a living hope through the resurrection of Jesus Christ from the dead, and into an inheritance that can never perish, spoil or fade—kept in heaven for you, who through faith are shielded by God's power until the coming of the salvation that is ready to be revealed in the last time.

A fisherman by trade, Peter was known for his impulsiveness and tendency to speak before thinking. The Lord in part used Peter's mistakes to shape him into a humble but powerful leader for the church. The two letters of Peter represent part of the apostle's effort to fulfill that expectation. He began his first epistle by referring to himself as an "apostle of Jesus Christ" (1 Pet. 1:1). In the New Testament, the term "apostle" is used to refer to God's special envoys who helped lay the foundation for Christian churches. After Jesus' death and resurrection, the term was applied to someone to whom Jesus had appeared and who had received a divine call to preach the Gospel.

Apostolic teaching was to be the norm for the doctrine and fellowship of the church. The apostles' common witness was the yardstick against which all Christian teaching was measured. Some Bible interpreters believe apostleship was restricted to those disciples who had seen Jesus with their own eyes. Others interpreters think the term did not always have such a restricted meaning. As was noted in lesson 7, those whom the New Testament calls or assumes to be apostles include the Twelve (Luke 6:13), Paul (Rom. 1:1), James (Gal. 1:19), Barnabas (Acts 14:14), Silas and Timothy (1 Thess. 1:1; 2:6b), and Andronicus and Junias (Rom. 16:7).

Now for a moment, let's imagine we're holding a beautifully cut diamond up to the light. Each of its sides sparkles as we slowly turn and examine the precious stone. This suggests how beautiful and multifaceted is God's salvation. Peter said in his first letter that he was filled with gratitude as he thought about what it meant to be redeemed through faith in the Messiah. The apostle's outburst of praise following his greeting is distinctively Jewish and Christian in content (see 1 Pet. 1:1-2). Giving thanks to God was a typical feature of Jewish prayer. The blessing in verse 3, however, has a richer conception of God than one would find in traditional writings. The one Peter praised was not just God, but God the Father as revealed by His unique and precious Son.

Peter referred to the Savior in three different ways. As "Lord," His power is absolute and unchallengeable. "Jesus" is the Greek form of Joshua, which means "the Lord saves." "Christ" literally means "Anointed One" and is used to refer to the Messiah promised by God in the Old Testament. In verse 3, Peter praised the Father for His tremendous display of mercy in providing salvation from sin through His Son. Next, the apostle referred to the new-birth experience. When people trust in the Lord Jesus, the Spirit does a work upon their fallen human nature. He completely transforms their inner being so that they want to live for God rather than themselves. As they renounce the ways of the world, their lives manifest the changes made by the Spirit.

Those who are born again have a new life and a living hope. In the Bible, hope is not a desire that has no basis for expecting fulfillment. It is a firm conviction based on the revealed truth of Scripture. The firm conviction of the church is that one day God will raise His people from the dead to live with Him forever in heaven. The hope of being raised is based on Jesus' resurrection from the dead. Through faith, Christians are identified with their Lord's death, burial, and resurrection (see Rom. 6:3-11). His new life makes it possible for them to trust and obey God, not doubt and defy Him.

Peter noted that Christians not only are born again but also are heirs of God. He will give them an eternal, heavenly inheritance that can never be destroyed by time, the elements of nature, or the powers of darkness. God also protects this inheritance from thieves. He preserves it safely in heaven for His people (1 Pet. 1:4). Great corporations, worth millions and billions of dollars, often go bankrupt. Devious people misappropriate funds, causing huge financial empires to crash. But such will never happen to the inheritance God has set aside for His children.

God also watches over those who trust in His Son. The Greek verb rendered "shielded" (vs. 5) conveys the idea of vigilantly defending a fortress. Believers can count on God's protection regardless of the hardships they encounter. The salvation Peter mentioned in this verse refers to the believer's complete deliverance from sin in the future. When Jesus returns, He will raise His people from the dead and give them glorified bodies. Then they will fully enjoy the eternal riches of heaven.

B. Present Joy and Trials: vss. 6-9

In this you greatly rejoice, though now for a little while you may have had to suffer grief in all kinds of trials. These have come so that your faith—of greater worth than gold, which perishes even though refined by fire—may be proved genuine and may result in praise, glory and honor when Jesus Christ is revealed. Though you have not seen him, you love him; and even though you do not see him now, you believe in him and are filled with an inexpressible and glorious joy, for you are receiving the goal of your faith, the salvation of your souls.

The original readers of Peter's first letter could rejoice in all that God would do for them. The Greek verb rendered "greatly rejoice" (1 Pet. 1:6) refers to a jubilant expression of gratitude. The recipients of the apostle's epistle were to maintain a confident expectation of the future. In turn, this forward-looking attitude would sustain them, especially as they endured all sorts of trials that caused them grief. No doubt some of the persecutions were physical, but more likely Peter had in mind social stigma, ridicule, the loss of status, and even the loss of their livelihood. The believers were paying a heavy price for their faithfulness to the Messiah.

Admittedly, no persecution is easy to take. But Peter tried to get his readers to view their troubles from an eternal perspective. These hardships were "for a little while." One day God would bring their suffering to an end and eternally reward them for their faithfulness. In short, a Christian's attitude toward suffering makes all the difference on its effect in that person's life. On the one hand, if hardship and difficult circumstances are constantly viewed as unfair and undeserved, then a root of bitterness can spring up in the heart of the believer that hinders his or her spiritual growth. On the other hand, if a Christian views suffering as normal for the committed follower of the Lord Jesus, then hardship and difficult circumstances become an expected part of life. Also, these afflictions are often viewed as a special time for growth and opportunities to become more like the Messiah in His humility and perseverance.

Peter explained that God allowed the recipients of his letter to experience persecution to refine and verify the genuineness of their faith in the Son (vs. 7). As people used fire to refine precious metals, such as gold, so God used trials to distinguish true faith from superficial profession. At the same time, He used suffering to strengthen faith. Gold is a metal that most societies highly value. Despite this, gold will one day cease to have value. The faith of Christians, however, is enduring. When the Savior is disclosed at His second coming, the believers' trust will result in praise, glory, and honor. The Greek noun translated "revealed" stresses the unveiling of Jesus' glory and greatness.

Peter reminded his readers that God had saved them so that they too might share in the glory of Jesus when He is once again manifested. In this present age, the Father has veiled the presence of the Son. Although the original recipients of Peter's letter had never personally seen the exalted and risen Savior, their love for Him was unquestionable. Despite the fact that they could not visibly see the Messiah, they continued to trust in Him for redemption (vs. 8). This truth is reminiscent of what Jesus said to Thomas, who at first doubted that the Messiah had risen from the dead: "Blessed are those who have not seen and yet have believed" (John 20:29). This certainly includes believers in our day. Even though we have not seen the Savior, we have experienced His powerful work in our lives.

The original readers of Peter's first letter were not depressed about their vexing situation. They were overflowing with a joy that cannot be explained, a joy that was sustained by the hope of future glory. They could be this way because they realized that salvation in the Messiah was the goal or consummation of their faith (1 Pet. 1:9). Although they already enjoyed certain aspects of salvation, their full possession of it awaited the return of the Son.

II. THE PROPHETS' INVESTIGATION: 1 PETER 1:10-12

A. Searching the Scriptures: vss. 10-11

Concerning this salvation, the prophets, who spoke of the grace that was to come to you, searched intently and with the greatest care, trying to find out the time and circumstances to which the Spirit of Christ in them was pointing when he predicted the sufferings of Christ and the glories that would follow.

Peter had just been speaking about the salvation Jesus provides to all who believe. Now the apostle noted that numerous Old Testament prophets had spoken about this grace of God, which He would make available to Gentiles as well as Jews (1 Pet. 1:10). Generally speaking, prophets were God's authorized and accredited representatives. They proclaimed His message of hope and judgment under specific circumstances.

While Abraham (Gen. 20:7) and Moses (Deut. 18:15) are both called prophets, prophets first appear as a group during the time of Samuel. He is referred to as being among the last of the judges and first of the prophets. The prophets often began their oracles with "God spoke" or "God says." The Lord's message sometimes came to a prophet in a vision and was delivered to the people by means of preaching, parables, or poetry. While little is said about the actual way in which God revealed His word to the prophets, they were thoroughly persuaded that the message was indeed of divine origin.

Sometimes God disclosed mysteries through Scripture that were beyond the comprehension of those who recorded them (see Dan. 12:8-9). In this case, the prophets did not completely understand what the Spirit inspired them to write. But in due time, He revealed the meaning to those for whom the information was intended. First Peter 1:10 adds that while these spokespersons for God could see some details of the Lord's redemptive plan, there were many specific facts that eluded their grasp. Be that as it may, these prophets still diligently searched Scripture to learn about God's provision of salvation (see Luke 10:24).

"The Spirit of Christ" (1 Pet. 1:11) refers to the Holy Spirit, whom Jesus sent (see John 16:7). The Spirit revealed to the Old Testament prophets that Jesus would suffer and be glorified (see Ps. 22; Isa. 53; Luke 24:25-27). However, they did not comprehend the whole of God's plan to save Gentiles by means of a suffering Messiah. For instance, the prophets failed to understand that the Redeemer would die during His first coming and that He would return in glory at His second coming.

B. Serving the Saints: vs. 12

It was revealed to them that they were not serving themselves but you, when they spoke of the things that have now been told you by those who have preached the gospel to you by the Holy Spirit sent from heaven. Even angels long to look into these things.

The Spirit had revealed to the Old Testament prophets that they were ultimately serving future generations of believers (1 Pet. 1:12). The prophets ministered to New Testament believers when they foretold the Messiah's sufferings and glories. The messengers of the Gospel related these same truths to the church after Jesus' resurrection and ascension. Looking back, we can see how God was working through these Old Testament prophets, even though they were not fully aware of how God was using them.

Those who proclaimed the Good News did so in the power of the Holy Spirit, whom the Lord had sent from heaven (see John 14:16, 26; Acts 2:33). The same Spirit who inspired the prophets also directed the Gospel messengers. Peter's point seems to be that there is a united message proclaimed in the Old and New Testaments concerning the Messiah and His salvation. The apostle noted that even angels have a strong desire to know the truths of the Gospel. The keen interest angels have in redemption is highlighted by the Greek verb rendered "to look into" (1 Pet. 1:12). It means "to stoop over to inspect intently." First-century Jews believed angels knew more than humans about divine matters, but in this case those who have accepted the Gospel understand far more than even the angels. In short, God ultimately uses the church to make His plan known to angels (see Eph. 3:10).

On the basis of God's wonderful gift of grace, those who have benefited from it should show evidence of their new relationship with God in certain specific ways. That is why Peter exhorted his readers to prepare their minds for action. A more literal rendering of the opening to 1 Peter 1:13 might be the following: "Therefore, gird up the loins of your mind." In Bible times, when people who dressed in loose clothing wished to move about quickly or perform tasks requiring significant freedom of movement, they would prepare themselves by tucking the folds of their robe under their belt. Drawing upon this vivid imagery, Peter admonished his readers to be disciplined in their thinking and prepare themselves for vigorous and sustained spiritual exertion.

Peter also urged his readers to "be self-controlled." The KJV has the rendering "be sober." In other words, believers were to exercise sound judgment in every area of their lives. One way to do this was to submit to the control of the Spirit (see Eph. 5:18). When the mind of the Christian is free from unwholesome thoughts, it is better able to concentrate on what is pure and pleasing to the Lord. Next, Peter directed the original recipients of his letter to fix their hope completely on God's grace, which He would bestow on them at the revelation of Jesus Christ. The "hope" (1 Pet. 1:13) was the believers' confident assurance of being fully and finally delivered from sin's presence. The Father would bring this about at the second coming of the Son. At that time, His followers would also be glorified and dwell forever with Him in heaven.

Peter referred to his readers as obedient children, that is, those who were characterized by a submissive spirit. This disposition contrasted sharply with the way they had thought and acted before trusting in the Messiah. When formerly they were separated from the Father, they knew nothing about His love and law. And when they were lost in spiritual darkness, their evil desires shaped and controlled their lives (vs. 14). Peter stressed that God is holy, which means He is superior to His creatures both physically and morally (vs. 15). Whatever the Lord thinks or does is characterized by purity, goodness, and perfection. There is no trace of evil in God, and He abhors all that is wicked and false.

A similar attitude should characterize those who are the Lord's spiritual children (vs. 16). The holy God, who has called us to salvation, wants us to be holy in every area of life (1 Pet. 1:6; see Lev. 11:44-45; 19:2; 20:7). This means we are to be cleansed from sin to serve the Lord. Our desires, motives, thoughts, words, and acts should be characterized by purity. We should detest sin and love righteousness. The moral perfection of God Himself is the standard we are to follow. In all candor, even after we put our trust in the Son, we continue to struggle with sinful desires. We soon learn from experience that it is impossible on our own to adopt God's focus and priorities. That is why we must rely on the Spirit to help us obey the Lord and enable us to overcome sin. When we call on God's power, He can free us from the grip of sin.

Discussion Questions

1. What do believers receive when they trust in the Messiah?
2. In what way is faith described in 1 Peter 1:8?
3. For whom were the prophets speaking and writing when they spoke about the coming salvation?
4. Do you sometimes find it hard to maintain your focus on the Son as you serve Him and His people? If so, why?
5. What can you do to proclaim God's mighty acts to the unsaved?

Contemporary Application

We have firsthand, written accounts of the Gospel. And so the message of salvation is not as mysterious to us as it was to the Old Testament prophets (see 1 Pet. 1:10-12). Nevertheless, it also may not be as special to us as it was to Peter's first readers. After all, much time has passed since that hope was first realized. Thus, we sometimes become dulled to the spiritual reality that eternal life begins here and now. This leaves us without the hope we need to get through life's trials.

Hope helps us because it tells us that the present is not all there is. Being targeted for ridicule by someone at work, being ignored by family members, or losing someone close to us are crises. But they are not catastrophes in which there is no comfort from God. Trials may cause others to look down on us, but with God no disappointment needs to be final.

This is why hope helps us put trials in the appropriate perspective. We expect trials to occur and we expect them to hurt. Even so, with hope, we do not expect to be devastated by predicaments. We can develop a mind-set of determination in which we can endure anything. After all, we know the future that is coming is better than anything we have known before.

How can we look beyond today and stay open to unknown factors? It is because we have learned that God often uses trials to refine us. We may even be thankful someday for how the hardship has transformed us.

Equipped with Hope

Scripture

Background Scripture: *2 Peter 1*

Scripture Lesson: *2 Peter 1:4-14*

Key Verse: *[The Lord's] divine power has given us everything we need for life and godliness through our knowledge of
him who called us by his own glory and goodness.*
2 Peter 1:3.

Scripture Lesson for Children: *2 Peter 1:4-14*

Key Verse for Children: *[The Lord's] divine power has
given us everything we need for life and godliness through our
knowledge of him who called us by his own glory and goodness. 2 Peter 1:3.*

Lesson Aim

To promote the adoption of a plan for spiritual growth
and commit to following it.

Lesson Setting

Time: Between A.D. 65–68

Place: Rome

Lesson Outline

Equipped with Hope

   I. Being Faithful and Fruitful: 2 Peter 1:4-11

      A. *Living in a Way that Pleases God: vs. 4*

      B. *Growing in Christian Virtues: vss. 5-6*

      C. *Cultivating Christlike Love: vs. 7*

      D. *Opting for Spiritual Growth and Productivity: vss. 8-9*

      E. *Validating the Reality of One's Salvation: vss. 10-11*

  II. Heeding Scripture: 2 Peter 1:12-14

      A. *Being Reminded of the Truth: vss. 12-13*

      B. *Making the Truth Clear: vs. 14*

Introduction for Adults

Topic: *Life Worth Living*

The young woman flew off to see her family in South America. She was meticulous about her preparations. She thought she had everything she needed. But when she arrived, she found that she had forgotten to pack one of her prescription medicines. She called home and her husband took care of the matter.

Our pride tells us that we have everything we need to pursue virtue on our own. But Peter would say that such an attitude is counterproductive. An attitude of pride prevents us from grasping all that the Father has done for us in the Son. As believers, we participate in Jesus' divine nature and His promises. So, we can claim His power and wisdom and be bold about our faith and godliness.

We have everything we need in the Savior to live for Him. The Lord, in turn, has commissioned us to use His resources to grow in His grace for His glory.

Introduction for Youth

Topic: *A Sure Escape Route*

A church was built more than 100 years ago in an affluent Midwestern suburb. It flourished and grew to some 900 members. Facilities were added to accommodate people and programs. But somewhere along the way the congregation stopped growing. Its numbers dwindled to less than 100.

Such stories are not unusual. They testify to the fact that churches don't always have what it takes to remain vibrant. Indeed, it's possible for entire congregations to stop growing, shrink in numbers, and die. We can point to many reasons for this phenomenon, including the possibility that individual members lost their vision for what God had called them to do.

All Christians—regardless of their age, gender, and social or economic status—must keep growing in faith. There's no escaping this truth. That's why Peter's concrete reminders are so important. We can easily become sidetracked. Personality clashes sap our energies. We must keep adding qualities of spiritual power to ourselves and our churches.

Concepts for Children

Topic: *Getting What We Need*

1. God knows that life can sometimes feel hard for us.
2. God is always here to help us.
3. God will be with us when we say *no* to sin.
4. God will give us the strength to grow spiritually.
5. God will help us to be more loving to others.

Lesson Commentary

I. BEING FAITHFUL AND FRUITFUL: 2 PETER 1:4-11

A. Living in a Way that Pleases God: vs. 4

Through these he has given us his very great and precious promises, so that through them you may participate in the divine nature and escape the corruption in the world caused by evil desires.

First and Second Peter belong to a group of New Testament letters called the general epistles because they were addressed to a group of churches and not one specific congregation of believers. The other general epistles include Hebrews, James, John's letters, and Jude. First and Second Peter have clearly different objectives from one another. The first letter is warm and pastoral, and it is written to believers who were facing persecution. The second letter is a warning to be on guard against false teachers. No generation of believers has been exempt from the dangers of persecution and false teaching. So the messages of 1 and 2 Peter are as relevant today as they were for the church in the first century A.D.

The recipients of 2 Peter are not as easy to identify. In the salutation of the epistle, the apostle did not address his readers by name. If the wording in 3:1 is referring to 1 Peter, then the same churches probably received the "second letter." In that case, the salutation, or introductory greeting, of 1 Peter indicates that the initial recipients lived in Asia Minor (present-day Turkey), particularly in its eastern, central, and western regions and in the territory that bordered the Black Sea. Although Peter traditionally has been referred to as "the apostle to the Jews" (Gal. 2:7-9), we know that he also preached to Gentiles, such as Cornelius (see Acts 10). Second Peter concentrates on the need for spiritual growth among believers and taking an aggressive stand against false doctrine and those who teach it. The letter also touches upon end-time events, such as the day of the Lord and the judgment of the unrepentant.

The call to holiness that is so evident in 1 Peter also resonates strongly in 2 Peter. In 1:2, the apostle stressed getting to know the Father and Son more and more. Then, in verse 3, Peter noted that, through our increased knowledge of the Lord, we become more responsive to His "divine power." The emphasis here is on living in a godly way. The apostle explained that our knowledge of the Son and His provision of the Father's own power make it possible for us to pursue "life and godliness." Further incentive can be found in the truth that the Lord has invited us to share in His own "glory and goodness."

There is also an emphasis on having "everything we need" to be godly. A heretical group known as the gnostics were telling Christians that they did not have everything necessary to live in a reverent manner. Supposedly, they also needed to be enlightened by a secret, mystic knowledge. Many cults today claim to lay hold of an exclusive saving knowledge that can be obtained only through various levels of teaching. In contrast, the revelation that God has provided is sufficient, not only for our salvation, but for an abundant life as well.

Ultimately, our focus is not on acquiring the world's fame and fortune, for these are fleeting. Instead, it is to live in a manner that pleases God. The Lord has made this possible by bestowing on us "very great and precious promises" (vs. 4). The Greek noun that is rendered "promise" had a special meaning in ancient Hellenic culture. It was used in connection with public announcements of events that concerned everyone, as in the notification of public games and sacrifices to gods. The word implied some type of emphatic, state-sponsored proclamation.

The implication in this verse is that here were promises that were made decidedly and openly for the benefit of all believers (not covertly to an elite few). It was a pledge given voluntarily, without coercion. Perhaps the most profound promise is that we will "participate in the divine nature." The idea here is not that we will gradually become divine, but that we grow in a host of Christian virtues. The more we pursue holiness, the more we will shun our evil desires and the "corruption" of the world that it spawns.

When Peter said that Christians can "participate in the divine nature," he took a risk by using the language of his opponents to express an eternal truth. The gnostics believed a person could become divine through secret knowledge and enlightened thinking. The truth is that though we will never become little gods (so to speak), we can participate fully in the spiritual life offered by the one true God (see Rom. 8:9; Gal. 2:20; Col. 1:27; 1 Pet. 2:23; 1 John 5:1). This is especially so as we worship Him in all His glory (while looking forward to our own glorification) and imitate His goodness.

B. Growing in Christian Virtues: vss. 5-6

For this very reason, make every effort to add to your faith goodness; and to goodness, knowledge; and to knowledge, self-control; and to self-control, perseverance; and to perseverance, godliness.

In light of all the provisions we have in the Redeemer, we can be faithful and fruitful in our lives. We start by making a maximum "effort" (2 Pet. 1:5) to appropriate our God-given blessings. The English phrase "add to" doesn't do justice to the full, rich meaning of Peter's original statement. In that day, the underlying Greek verb described bearing the expense of a chorus of performers to be used in the dramatic presentations of the early Hellenic tragedies. The person selected to do this was responsible for the cost, training, and upkeep of such a chorus. Eventually, the word came to mean providing the cost for any public duty or religious service to make it more than mediocre. Thus the verb meant to supply generously, even lavishly, beyond the bare need.

In the present context, the idea is that believers must dedicate themselves unstintingly to strengthen their faith by the development of the characteristics Peter mentioned. Of central concern is their growth in holiness. At the moment of salvation, Christians are made holy in a legal sense. In other words, they are declared righteous in God's eyes. That event is called justification. Then, throughout their lives, the Holy Spirit works to bring their moral condition into conformity with their legal status. Expressed differently, He helps to make them actually holy. This process is called sanctification.

Sanctification is the work of God (see 1 Thess. 5:23). Nonetheless, the Bible contains many exhortations for believers to do their part in becoming more holy (see Phil. 2:12-13). "Faith" (2 Pet. 1:5) is the starting point, and to it believers are to add "goodness." This is one of several moral excellencies that Peter mentioned. The idea is that, with unwavering trust in the Savior as their foundation, believers press on in a disciplined way to cultivate integrity and rectitude in their lives. Peter next mentioned "knowledge." While an objective understanding of revealed truth is included, the apostle also had in mind a practical application of that truth.

When Jesus' followers heed the teachings of Scripture, it will lead to "self-control" (vs. 6). Peter was referring to a mastering of one's carnal desires. Because believers know God and are empowered by Him, they are able to control their fleshly passions. In turn, they become more patient. They are less likely to be discouraged and succumb to temptation, and more likely to persevere in doing what is right. This ability to endure allows "godliness" to flourish. Christians become more reverent and devoted to the Lord, and less preoccupied with themselves.

C. Cultivating Christlike Love: vs. 7

And to godliness, brotherly kindness; and to brotherly kindness, love.

A heightened loyalty to God results in believers having increased "brotherly kindness" (2 Pet. 1:7). This mutual affection is displayed in serving one another, sharing with one another, and praying for one another. These activities, in turn, foster genuine "love." This form of compassion is not flustered by the personal cost of reaching out to others in need. This sincere love seeks the highest good of others for the glory of the Savior.

D. Opting for Spiritual Growth and Productivity: vss. 8-9

For if you possess these qualities in increasing measure, they will keep you from being ineffective and unproductive in your knowledge of our Lord Jesus Christ. But if anyone does not have them, he is nearsighted and blind, and has forgotten that he has been cleansed from his past sins.

Peter urged believers to continue growing in their life of godliness. Indeed, he wanted to see the various "qualities" (2 Pet. 1:8) he listed earlier to be present and developing in their lives. "Increasing measure" renders a Greek verb that can also be translated "grow in abundance" or "superabound." The tense of the verb indicates that the situation the apostle described is to be an active and ongoing experience for believers.

It would be erroneous to think that the virtues mentioned in verses 5 through 7 can be added in a mathematically precise, sequential fashion. Instead, they are developed together and evidenced gradually over many years of walking with the Lord. The goal, of course, is that these moral excellencies will be present in us without limit (vs. 8). Their abundance indicates spiritual health in Christians. Peter noted that if believers continue to grow in this way, they will become increasingly productive and fruitful, rather than "ineffective" and "unproductive," in their knowledge of the Savior.

Once again, we see that knowing God is more than an intellectual exercise. This truth stands, regardless of what religious frauds might otherwise assert. Knowing more and more about the Lord Jesus is intended to foster spiritual vitality. The other alternative is to fail to develop the graces Peter mentioned, which results in spiritual loss. The apostle declared that those opting for this are blind and short-sighted, for they have failed to fully appreciate the cleansing and forgiveness from "past sins" (vs. 9) secured by the Messiah. "Cleansed" translates a Greek verb that refers to Christians being purged from the guilt associated with their transgressions through the atoning sacrifice of the Son.

E. Validating the Reality of One's Salvation: vss. 10-11

Therefore, my brothers, be all the more eager to make your calling and election sure. For if you do these things, you will never fall, and you will receive a rich welcome into the eternal kingdom of our Lord and Savior Jesus Christ.

Peter was discussing two different mind-set. One is obsessed with the concerns of this present life, while the other is sensitive to eternal, spiritual realities. Though we live in the world, the things of God should be our supreme focus. Thus, we are to make every effort to confirm our "calling and election" (2 Pet. 1:10). In his first letter, Peter pointed out that God's election of His people to salvation was because of His foreknowledge (see 1 Pet. 1:2). So, the apostle urged believers to seize the opportunity to increase their assurance of salvation by cultivating the virtues he had described in 2 Peter 1:5-7.

Peter was not saying that Christians can make their salvation more secure by their works. Good deeds are never to be considered spiritual "fire insurance" (in a manner of speaking). The tense of the Greek verb, which is rendered "make" (vs. 10), can also be translated "to make for oneself." This means that the increasing assurance of salvation is a benefit of consistent obedience to God. With this kind of assurance, God's people can expect a joyous welcome into His eternal kingdom (vs. 11). Here we see that there is more to heaven than just getting through the proverbial pearly gates. Scripture is full of promises of everlasting reward to those who are faithful. The greeting believers will receive when they enter God's presence will be rich because of the blessings the Father has lavished upon those who belong to Him through the redemptive work of His Son.

By remaining loyal to the Father and ministering to our fellow believers, we show that we truly "participate in the divine nature" (vs. 4), that we fully appreciate the atoning sacrifice of the Son, and that we value His "very great and precious promises" to us. Such a consistent life-orientation indicates we will not succumb to doubt or despair concerning our spiritual status. Rather than spiritually stumble and "fall" (vs. 10), we will be assured of our salvation. This assurance also includes our eventual entrance into "the eternal kingdom" (vs. 11) of the Messiah. The Lord, in turn, will honor our life of faithful service with more abundant privileges in heaven.

II. HEEDING SCRIPTURE: 2 PETER 1:12-14

A. Being Reminded of the Truth: vss. 12-13

So I will always remind you of these things, even though you know them and are firmly established in the truth you now have. I think it is right to refresh your memory as long as I live in the tent of this body.

At times, even mature believers can wane in their diligence to grow in the Lord. This is especially true in moments of hardship. Peter, perhaps realizing this, was determined to remind his readers about the truths he had previously shared. The apostle's decision did not mean that his readers were ignorant of the truth or had failed to stand firm in it. Peter's intention was to ensure they remained "firmly established" (2 Pet. 1:12) in the faith and diligent in applying it to their lives. The Greek verb that is rendered "firmly established" can also be translated "to make stable" or "to fix securely in place."

In some way, Peter had become increasingly aware of the short time he had left "in the tent of this body" (vs. 13). This is a metaphorical reference to his body being laid aside like a temporary shelter. John 21:18-19 records a statement Jesus made concerning the way in which Peter would die. Perhaps the apostle had this in mind as he approached the end of his life. The Greek noun that is translated "tent" (2 Pet. 1:13) can also be rendered "tabernacle." It is clarifying to note that Paul literally referred to the physical body we live in as an "earthly house" (2 Cor. 5:1), which we inhabit for a time while we wait to put on our new, heavenly bodies (vs. 4).

Contrary to what the gnostics claimed, neither Peter nor Paul believed the physical body was unimportant or inherently evil. In fact, Paul referred to our bodies as "temple[s] of the Holy Spirit" (1 Cor. 6:19). Peter and Paul used various figurative expressions for the physical body to convey the idea of a temporary dwelling. While he was on earth, Peter would use the tabernacle of his body in obedience to God's will. Death was simply temporarily putting aside the physical dwelling so that the soul could depart to be with God. Assuredly, that physical structure (so to speak) would be raised again at the Messiah's second advent.

B. Making the Truth Clear: vs. 14

Because I know that I will soon put it aside, as our Lord Jesus Christ has made clear to me.

Peter said he knew that his upcoming death was near. He metaphorically referred to the event as a removal of his earthly tabernacle. The Greek verb that is translated "know" (2 Pet. 1:14) refers to a definite awareness of the facts. In the apostle's case, the Messiah previously revealed to him what would eventually happen to him (see John 21:18-19). This impression is reinforced by the past tense of the verb that is rendered "made clear" (2 Pet. 1:14).

"Departure" (vs. 15) translates a Greek noun that figuratively refers to Peter's imminent exit from his current earthly existence. In light of what the apostle realized would happen to him, we can certainly appreciate his strong desire to reinforce to his readers the teaching of Scripture. His goal was to make the truth clear so that they could more readily recall and apply it. The destructive teachings of spiritual frauds made the apostle's task all the more imperative (see 2:1-4).

Discussion Questions

1. What does the Lord's divine power provide for believers?
2. What is the basis for growing in the Christian virtues that Peter listed?
3. Why did Peter want to continue reminding his readers of their hope in the Savior?
4. What can believers do to ensure they are spiritually maturing?
5. How can believers fight the tendency to forget the truths of the faith?

Contemporary Application

Trusting in Jesus as Savior is the beginning of a Christian's growth process. The Holy Spirit then works in our lives to produce the virtues listed in this week's Scripture lesson text. The order of the virtues is not a sequence in time, as if stages of the Christian life were being described. Instead, the qualities Peter enumerated were to occur simultaneously and lead to a well-rounded and productive Christian life.

While the Spirit makes it possible for us to grow and mature as believers, we must also cooperate with Him in the process. That is why Peter urged us to "make every effort" (2 Pet. 1:5) to cultivate the character qualities he listed in verses 5-7. Faith is the starting point, and the climax of the virtues mentioned by the apostle is love, the preeminent fruit of the Christian life. From this we see that the church is not a playpen, but rather a construction area where the Spirit desires to work in the lives of Jesus' followers.

Consequently, the virtues listed in this week's Scripture lesson text are the result of our working together with God. Each time we choose to obey the Lord and not just please ourselves, the fruit becomes more abundant. Also, as we strive to mature, God will do for us what we cannot do for ourselves.

Hope through Stewardship

Scripture

Background Scripture: *1 Peter 4*
Scripture Lesson: *1 Peter 4:1-11*
Key Verse: *Each one should use whatever gift he has received to serve others, faithfully administering God's grace in its various forms.* 1 Peter 4:10.
Scripture Lesson for Children: *1 Peter 4:1-11*
Key Verse for Children: *Each one should use whatever gift he has received to serve others, faithfully administering God's grace in its various forms.* 1 Peter 4:10.

Lesson Aim

To wisely and faithfully use the gifts God has given us.

Lesson Setting

Time: The early 60s of the first century A.D.
Place: Rome

Lesson Outline

Hope through Stewardship
  I. Dying to the Old Life: 1 Peter 4:1-6
      A. *Being Prepared to Suffer: vs. 1*
      B. *Abandoning Sin: vss. 2-3*
      C. *Being Maligned for Virtuous Behavior: vss. 4-6*
  II. Living for God's Glory: 1 Peter 4:7-11
      A. *Earnestly Serving Christ and His People: vss. 7-9*
      B. *Responsibly Exercising Spiritual Gifts: vss. 10-11*

Introduction for Adults

Topic: *Serving One Another*

Often a discussion about spiritual gifts ends up in arguments and division. We don't have to agree on the precise meaning of the special abilities mentioned in 1 Peter 4:10-11 to find common ground in a larger purpose. But many times, our larger purpose and our common bond in Christ get lost in our heated debates.

Meanwhile, some churches are weakened because of a false dichotomy between so-called gifted believers and the rest of the ordinary Christians. We have to make room for all believers to exercise their gifts for the common good. We cannot afford to let some Christians think they are second class just because they might not have some of the more publicly recognized gifts.

Thankfully, Peter emphasized oneness, unity, and harmony. He did not glorify the gifts. He would not tolerate fighting over any special ability, all of which are intended to build Christ's body. The whole point of Peter's admonition was to produce a vital, loving, growing, and unified fellowship, not one shattered by arguments and bickering.

Introduction for Youth

Topic: *A Changed Life*

Youth today are introduced early to the values of working together. They work on class projects, participate in musical groups and plays, and join athletic teams. They all know that if any member slacks off, the team suffers. They also realize that if any player tries to steal the whole show, the team is weakened.

These are the kinds of illustrations adolescents can understand when applied to the church, which is Christ's spiritually gifted team (see 1 Pet. 4:10-11). When teens put their faith in Him, He brings about a profound change in their lives. They now have the Spirit empowering them to serve one another in a loving and sacrificial manner. The beauty of the church is that faith in Jesus is the only requirement to be on His team. It doesn't depend on skill or experience.

Faith in Jesus is also required to accept the contributions of all other team members. Perhaps the final production will not be as stellar as we would prefer it to be. But we have to remember that the church is not just for professionals. It is also for lifelong learners and followers of the Savior. In this regard, we need to coach each other, so that our team can become as strong as possible.

Concepts for Children

Topic: *Being a Good Steward*

1. Jesus died on the cross and rose from the dead for us.
2. Jesus wants us to turn away from sin.
3. Jesus wants us to be loving and kind to others.
4. Jesus wants us to help others.
5. Jesus promises to help us do what He wants.

Lesson Commentary

I. DYING TO THE OLD LIFE: 1 PETER 4:1-6

A. Being Prepared to Suffer: vs. 1

Therefore, since Christ suffered in his body, arm yourselves also with the same attitude, because he who has suffered in his body is done with sin.

First Peter is considered by many Bible scholars to be part of the persecution literature of the New Testament (which also includes Hebrews, Revelation, and possibly James). As part of this collection, 1 Peter would have been written during one of the three periods of Roman persecution endured by early Christians—under Roman emperors Nero (A.D. 62–64), Domitian (A.D. 90–97), and Trajan (A.D. 111). If we hold to Peter's authorship of the letter, the only period that would fit would be the time of Nero. Tradition has it that Peter was crucified outside the city of Rome during the last few years before Nero ended his own life in A.D. 68.

In Scripture, the concept of suffering involves physical and mental pain as well as affliction and agony brought on by a great variety of experiences. While Scripture reveals that some suffering is the direct result of human sin, it is also presented as a tool for shaping Christlike character and testing faith (see 1 Pet. 1:6-7; 5:10). Even Jesus Himself is said to have been greatly influenced by suffering. For instance, suffering perfected Him (see Heb. 2:10) and taught Him obedience (see 5:8). Other Scriptures say that suffering cements the believers' identification with the Savior, especially as they experience persecution for His sake (see Phil. 1:29; 2 Thess. 1:5). Paul even went so far as to say that suffering is inevitable for those who desire to live a godly life and to follow the Redeemer (see 2 Tim. 3:12). If the Master suffered, the servant must expect suffering as well (see John 15:18-21).

In 1 Peter 3:18, the apostle stressed that Jesus, who was innocent, died for the guilty so that they might have the opportunity to be saved. After a brief digression in verses 19-22, Peter returned to the theme of unjust suffering in 4:1. When Peter said that Jesus "suffered in his body," the apostle was referring to the Savior's crucifixion and death. The Messiah did not value His physical life so much that He refused to die on the cross, and His followers were to adopt this same attitude. They were to accept the fact that living and dying for the cause of Christ were more important than preserving their earthly existence. It would have been hard for the believers of northwest Asia Minor to consider the possibility of enduring further mistreatment as followers of the Messiah. Although the prospect was unpleasant, there were spiritual benefits to suffering unjustly. Foremost in Peter's mind was the truth that the Christian "is done with sin."

There are two primary ways of understanding what Peter meant. According to one view, he was referring to the character-building effects of suffering. As enemies of the church persecuted God's people, they were forced to decide what was most important in life. Consequently, the things of the world became less attractive.

According to a second view, Peter was thinking about the spiritual union of believers with the Messiah in His suffering and death. This identification is symbolized by baptism, which the apostle had talked about in 3:21. The Redeemer died to sin in the sense that, after His death and resurrection, He was no longer subject to the power of sin and death. Similarly, believers were dead to the power of sin and alive to the Father through their identification with the Son (see Rom. 6:11).

B. Abandoning Sin: vss. 2-3

As a result, he does not live the rest of his earthly life for evil human desires, but rather for the will of God. For you have spent enough time in the past doing what pagans choose to do—living in debauchery, lust, drunkenness, orgies, carousing and detestable idolatry.

Due to the experience of unjust suffering, the recipients of Peter's letter were more likely to spend their time on earth doing what God wanted, not doing the evil things that people wanted (1 Pet. 4:2). The apostle said his friends had already spent enough time in the past living like pagans, that is, people who did not know the Lord (vs. 3). At one time the Christians followed their evil desires. They participated in lewd activities, got drunk, indulged in orgies, and caroused with others. They even worshiped idols.

In Galatians 5:19-21, Paul offered his own list of sinful acts that represented the variety of ways people do evil. The inventory includes three vices of sensuality (sexual immorality, impurity, debauchery), two vices associated with heathen religions (idolatry, witchcraft), eight vices of interpersonal conflict (hatred, discord, jealousy, fits of rage, selfish ambition, dissensions, factions, envy), and two vices related to the misuse of alcohol (drunkenness, orgies). The acts of the sinful nature that Paul listed are highly varied, but they all are alike in arousing God's wrath.

That being the case, the apostle warned his readers about the consequences of these sins. As Paul had told the Galatians earlier when he was with them, those who practiced such vices would not "inherit the kingdom of God" (vs. 21). This does not mean that every believer who commits a sin is prevented from inheriting God's kingdom. Rather, the apostle's statement indicates that people who continually commit these acts of the sinful nature thereby demonstrate that they are not following the Lord Jesus and have no place in His eternal kingdom. Nevertheless, believers can learn from Paul's warning how seriously God views human sin.

C. Being Maligned for Virtuous Behavior: vss. 4-6

They think it strange that you do not plunge with them into the same flood of dissipation, and they heap abuse on you. But they will have to give account to him who is ready to judge the living and the dead. For this is the reason the gospel was preached even to those who are now dead, so that they might be judged according to men in regard to the body, but live according to God in regard to the spirit.

The readers of Peter's letter were grateful that they no longer lived immorally. Of course, their unsaved acquaintances did not understand why they chose to abandon sin. Those who opposed the faith were shocked that God's people refused to do the wasteful things they did. That is why the former friends of the Asia Minor Christians maligned them for their virtuous behavior (1 Pet. 4:4). Peter knew that it was difficult for his fellow believers to endure such persecution. He explained that one day God would require their enemies to explain their reprehensible actions. The unsaved would stand condemned before the One who will judge the living and the dead (vs. 5).

According to Jesus, unbelievers now live under the threat of God's condemnation and wrath (see John 3:18, 36). Outwardly, they may appear to be secure and comfortable. Nonetheless, God will judge all of humanity (both Jews and Gentiles); the agent of His judgment will be Jesus Christ; and His evaluation will focus on the secrets of people's hearts (see Rom. 2:16). Sometimes people do good things that are actually rooted in selfish intentions. Other times people may appear guilty of a wrongdoing when there was no bad intention. Sometimes people internalize blame for the sins of others. On the great day, all that is hidden will be revealed. There will be no second-guessing when it comes to motives. God's judgment will be impartial, perfect, and absolutely just.

In 1 Peter 4:6, the apostle explained that Jesus' disciples had proclaimed the Gospel to people who were now dead. Some think Jesus, between His death and resurrection, preached and offered salvation to all the dead who had lived in pre-Christian times. Others connect this preaching with 3:19 and 20 and say the dead were the people of Noah's day. A third group says Jesus preached salvation to the righteous of Old Testament times. Each of these views gives the impression that the preaching took place after the people had died. Yet the Bible teaches that once people pass away, there will be no second chance to get saved (see Heb. 9:27). Most likely, then, Peter was referring to people who had died after becoming followers of Christ. In other words, they heard the Good News while they were still alive and then subsequently died.

These believers had experienced the same judgment that eventually falls on all people, namely, death (see Rom. 5:12). When the Father raised His Son from the dead, He triumphed over death (see 6:9). However, the full extent of that victory is not yet manifested in the lives of God's people. Of course, they enjoy new life through union with Christ. And they have the assurance of knowing that one day the Savior's victory over death will extend to their physical bodies (see Rom. 8:11; 1 Cor. 15:25-26).

There are two other ways of understanding the reference to judgment in 1 Peter 4:6. Possibly the apostle was talking about either God's discipline or eternal condemnation (see 1 Cor. 11:30; Rev. 20:11-15). Or possibly the judgment was the unfair way the wicked judged Christians. In the latter case, their evaluation was based on human, not divine, standards of behavior. Whichever view is preferred, Peter's main emphasis remains the same. Those who hear the Gospel preached and who trust in the Messiah are saved from divine wrath. They also enjoy new life with God. The Spirit gives them eternal life, and neither persecution nor death can take it away from the true followers of Christ.

Despite their high moral character, first-century Christians were routinely charged with committing a wide array of crimes—everything from murder to treason against Rome. In reality, they were persecuted for no other crime than bearing the name "Christian." Indeed, Peter told his readers that they would suffer as "Christians" (1 Pet. 4:16). The term "Christian" was a word unsaved Gentiles probably used to slander believers (see Acts 11:26). The word denoted someone who belonged to or followed Christ. Even though outsiders used the term in a derogatory manner, the church adopted it as an appropriate title, for Christians were not ashamed to be associated with Jesus or to be known as His disciples.

II. LIVING FOR GOD'S GLORY: 1 PETER 4:7-11

A. Earnestly Serving Christ and His People: vss. 7-9

The end of all things is near. Therefore be clear minded and self-controlled so that you can pray. Above all, love each other deeply, because love covers over a multitude of sins. Offer hospitality to one another without grumbling.

First Peter 4:7-11 contains a series of practical, everyday principles the apostle laid down for his readers to understand and follow. Peter began by saying that the culmination of the present age was at hand (vs. 7). Some claim this statement is a veiled reference to the destruction of Jerusalem in A.D. 70. A more likely view, however, is that Jesus had ushered in the messianic era. Peter implied that the entire period between the first and second comings of the Son made up the "last times" (1:20; compare Heb. 1:1 and 1 John 2:18).

In light of Jesus' return, the apostle urged his readers to be "clear minded" (1 Pet. 4:7), that is, alert and levelheaded in their thinking. The Christians were to know why they existed, make sensible decisions, and act in a reasonable manner. Peter also encouraged his friends to be "self-controlled," or sober in spirit. They were to maintain mental and moral balance in a sinful and self-indulgent world. A serious and sensible disposition would help the believers do a better job of praying. Scripture teaches that we are always to keep in touch with God through prayer and receive power and strength from Him. Prayer is a vital link with God that strengthens our relationship not only with Him, but also with our fellow Christians.

Verse 8 might contain the most all-embracing of the commands in this section, for it tells the readers to maintain earnest, sincere "love" for one another. The apostle's readers were already exercising Christlike love, but Peter discerned that a reminder would not be amiss. The apostle could give his readers such a command, for godly love is not just an emotion, but also a decision that leads to action. This kind of love makes it possible for one to genuinely care for others regardless of how he or she feels about them. In times of persecution when believers are feeling stressed, there is a greater chance for them to say or do something that is offensive to others. Love becomes a key factor in maintaining unity, for it does not keep track of wrongs. Instead, it continually extends forgiveness to others (see Prov. 10:12; Matt. 18:21-22; 1 Cor. 13:4-7).

As the Christians faced hardship, it would be easy for them to forget the needs of others. Peter reminded his readers to do what they could to extend "hospitality" (1 Pet. 4:9) to their fellow believers without complaining or grumbling. In those days, there weren't many inns, and the lodges that did exist often had an unsavory reputation. So travelers had to rely on households if they were to get good accommodations during a journey. By welcoming people into their home and meeting their needs, believers would show God's love in tangible ways.

When a person came to another individual's home, the following traditions were usually observed. First, the host would show respect by bowing to the guest. Then the host would wish his guest peace, and the guest would respond with the same wish. The two would kiss one another's cheeks. Next, the host would invite the guest to remove his sandals and have the dust washed from his feet. Sometimes the host would anoint the guest's head with olive oil, possibly mixed with spices. Finally, the host would offer the guest a drink of water and prepare a meal for him.

B. Responsibly Exercising Spiritual Gifts: vss. 10-11

Each one should use whatever gift he has received to serve others, faithfully administering God's grace in its various forms. If anyone speaks, he should do it as one speaking the very words of God. If anyone serves, he should do it with the strength God provides, so that in all things God may be praised through Jesus Christ. To him be the glory and the power for ever and ever. Amen.

Peter next mentioned that the Lord had given the Christians of Asia Minor spiritual gifts and that they were to use these to serve others (1 Pet. 4:10). The Greek noun translated "gift" is *charisma*. The plural form of this word is *charismata*—"gifts." Both words are related to the word *charis*, which means "grace" or "favor." Thus *charisma* is a gift of grace. The Holy Spirit bestows on Christians special abilities to accomplish the will of God. They do not own the gifts. Instead, they are stewards of what God has graciously provided for them. These gifts of grace take various forms, and they are to be faithfully used wherever and whenever possible.

The spiritual gifts that Peter mentioned in verse 11 represent only a few of the many that God had given His people in Asia Minor. The apostle noted that some had a special ability to declare the truths of Scripture. This included all forms of speaking (for example, preaching, teaching, prophesying, and speaking in tongues). Peter reminded his readers that they were proclaiming the message of God (as opposed to a mere human message). Others had a unique ability to serve others. Peter exhorted them to minister to people in God's strength, not their own.

Believers often disagree about which gifts, if any, are still given by God's Spirit to Christians today. Some believers argue that all of the gifts described in Scripture are still given to the church because its needs are still the same and because there is evidence of these gifts operating in believers today. Others maintain that one or more of the gifts ended with the early church, while most of the gifts still exist. For example, some people hold that the gift of apostleship died out with the original apostles, but the other gifts are still in operation. Still other Christians think that all of the so-called miraculous gifts—such as miracles, speaking in tongues, and healings—were given only to the early church and not to the church today.

Regardless of which of these views is favored, as the believers diligently help one another and rely on the Father for enabling, they bring Him honor through His Son, the Lord Jesus. For instance, others will see believers ministering in the name of the Son and praise the Father for it. The thought of God's being honored moved Peter to write a doxology of praise at the end of verse 11. Glory and power belonged to the Lord for ever and ever. Peter then affirmed this truth with an "Amen," which might be paraphrased "So be it!"

Discussion Questions

1. What attitude did Jesus display when He suffered and died on the cross?
2. Why does it sometimes feel hard to reject enticements to sin and follow the will of God?
3. What can believers do to remain spiritually alert and sober at all times?
4. In what ways can the presence of Christlike love "cover a multitude of sins" (1 Pet. 4:8)?
5. What are some creative ways you could use your home to minister to others?

Contemporary Application

We learn in 1 Peter 4:9 that every believer has at least one spiritual gift. Moreover, we discover that God expects us to use these special abilities to serve others, regardless of whether they are believers or unbelievers. In short, the students in your class are called to be faithful stewards of "God's grace" as they minister to people around them.

Many people yearn for the kind of human companionship, support, and fellowship offered in Christ's spiritual body, the church. Sadly, many times they don't find it because the church seems to be marked by disunity, cliques, and self-centeredness. That's why many of these folks look elsewhere to get their legitimate needs met. They might join service organizations, community groups, and athletic clubs, or spend a lot of time pursuing frivolous entertainment activities.

When congregations do not offer the kind of hospitality people are looking for, they do not seek the Messiah who is supposed to be at the heart of His church. His spiritual body is supposed to be the one social group that transcends all our differences. It's supposed to bear witness to the lost that Jesus can meet their deepest needs. Our witness is only as valid and strong as our visible unity. Our message is heard when we sublimate our differences and cooperatively use our spiritual gifts in a peaceful manner to show Jesus' love to the lost.

The Day of the Lord

Scripture

Background Scripture: *2 Peter 3*

Scripture Lesson: *2 Peter 3:1-15*

Key Verse: *The Lord is not slow in keeping his promise, as some understand slowness. He is patient with you, not wanting anyone to perish, but everyone to come to repentance.* 2 Peter 3:9.

Scripture Lesson for Children: *2 Peter 3:3-15*

Key Verse for Children: *The Lord is not slow in keeping his promise. . . . He is patient with you, not wanting anyone to perish, but everyone to come to repentance.* 2 Peter 3:9.

Lesson Aim

To stress that we look forward to a new heaven and earth.

Lesson Setting

Time: Between A.D. *65–68*

Place: Rome

Lesson Outline

The Day of the Lord

I. The Certainty of Jesus' Return: 2 Peter 3:1-7
   A. *Reminders of the Truth: vss. 1-2*
   B. *Mockers of the Truth: vss. 3-4*
   C. *Past Examples of Divine Judgment: vs. 5-6*
   D. *A Future Time of Divine Judgment: vs. 7*

II. The Challenge to Be Morally Pure: 2 Peter 3:8-13
   A. *The Patience of God: vss. 8-9*
   B. *The Day of the Lord: vs. 10*
   C. *The Importance of Maintaining a Godly, Holy Lifestyle: vs. 11*
   D. *The Hope of a New Heaven and Earth: vss. 12-13*
   E. *The Exhortation to Virtuous Living: vss. 14-15*

Introduction for Adults

Topic: *Ready and Waiting*

Every believer encounters challenges, frustrations, and opposition. These steps to maturity in the Savior are like foothills that sometimes block the view of the lofty snowcapped peaks. But because the peaks are there, Christians, like a mountain hiker, can push onward and upward.

What is the highest peak of biblical hope? It is the return of Jesus and eternal life in His presence (see 2 Pet. 3:14-15). That hope should lighten every step and quicken the heart of all believers. Most importantly, they realize that the best part of God's plan for them is yet to come. Because the Lord is the "God of hope" (Rom. 15:13), He is able to "fill you with all joy and peace as you trust in him, so that you may overflow with hope by the power of the Holy Spirit."

Introduction for Youth

Topic: *Hope Motivates Holy Living*

The story is told of how a village incorrectly thought a vagrant passing through their town was the government inspector. They not only treated him as royalty, but also quickly set into motion a plan to cover up years of fraud. Their mistaking the man for someone else cost them dearly.

This fable is a reminder of how important it is to search for hope in the right place—namely, the Messiah of the Bible—not some figment of our imagination. Jesus is no longer a newborn baby in a manger. Nor is He merely a wise and loving person. He is the Lord of life, the King of kings, and the Savior of the world.

Down through the centuries, people of faith recognized these truths about Jesus. The returning Savior was for them light, hope, and salvation (see 2 Pet. 3:14-15). In fact, all who receive Jesus by faith can partake of the forgiveness and grace He now offers.

Concepts for Children

Topic: *Living in Hope*

1. Some people do not believe what the Bible says.
2. These people might try to get you to doubt, too.
3. Jesus wants you to believe that He will one day come back.
4. Jesus will help you to be filled with hope as you wait for Him to return.
5. Jesus will also help you to be faithful to Him.

Lesson Commentary

I. THE CERTAINTY OF JESUS' RETURN: 2 PETER 3:1-7

A. Reminders of the Truth: vss. 1-2

Dear friends, this is now my second letter to you. I have written both of them as reminders to stimulate you to wholesome thinking. I want you to recall the words spoken in the past by the holy prophets and the command given by our Lord and Savior through your apostles.

Peter concluded his second letter with words of endearment used four times between this point and the end of the epistle. The Greek noun that is rendered "dear friends" (2 Pet. 3:1) can also be translated "beloved" and is derived from a verb that is often rendered "love." Peter wanted his readers to know that he genuinely cared for them. Peter wrote several times to the Christians living in Asia Minor to warn them about the false teaching of spiritual frauds and remind them about key apostolic truths. The goal was to "stimulate [them] to wholesome thinking."

In short, the apostle wanted to refresh the memory of his readers and thereby encourage them to do some honest consideration of what they had been taught. The latter included all that God's holy prophets had spoken long ago. Their oracles are recorded in the Old Testament, which initially was the primary collection of sacred writings used by believers in the first century A.D. Peter also wanted the Christians in Asia Minor to recall what he and the other apostles taught. This especially concerned what their Lord and Savior, Jesus Christ, had commanded them to do—namely, to be morally vigilant, especially as they awaited His return in glory.

B. Mockers of the Truth: vss. 3-4

First of all, you must understand that in the last days scoffers will come, scoffing and following their own evil desires. They will say, "Where is this 'coming' he promised? Ever since our fathers died, everything goes on as it has since the beginning of creation."

Peter used a tense of the Greek verb that is rendered "you must understand" (2 Pet. 3:3) to emphasize that the issue he was about to discuss was morally imperative for his readers to grasp. It concerned "the last days." The phrase is sometimes used in the Old Testament to refer generally to events that would take place in the future, both near and distant. When the New Testament speaks of "the last days," it refers to events connected with Jesus' return. The phrase also includes the period from the Savior's first advent to His second advent.

Peter literally noted that as the end of the age drew near, "scoffers in their scoffing" would arise. The Greek noun that is translated "scoffers" refers to the fraudulent prophets and teachers mentioned in 2:1. They already had infiltrated the faith community in Asia Minor, and they would continue to plague the body of Christ until His return (see Matt. 24:3-5, 11, 23-26; 2 Tim. 3:1-5; Jude 18). The charlatans were guilty of deriding God's Word and being propelled by their "own evil desires" (2 Pet. 3:3; see 2:13-22). Scoffing in regard to revealed prophetic truth is more than mere jesting. In ignorance, some will speak jokingly about spiritual matters, and this grieves the Spirit of God. Scoffing, however, is a calculated effort to discredit an accepted truth. The mockers Peter warned about were especially menacing, for they were familiar with the Scriptures and the apostles' inspired interpretation of the Lord's commands.

Peter focused with the greatest intensity on the Christian belief attacked by these scoffers, namely, the Messiah's promise of His second advent (see Matt. 10:23; 16:28; 24:3, 32-36; Mark 9:1; Acts 1:11). The early church believed that when Jesus returned, He would bring to fruition the work of salvation. Indeed, believers were characterized by an intense anticipation of the Savior's return. Jesus had laid the groundwork with His teaching on end-time events in Matthew 24 (see Mark 13; Luke 21). The Christians in Peter's day lived with the expectation of the Son's advent, just as believers should do today.

Regrettably, the false teachers mocked the believers' hope, reminding them that nothing had changed "since the beginning of creation" (2 Pet. 3:4). "Our fathers" might refer to the patriarchs (Abraham, Isaac, and Jacob; see Acts 3:13; Rom. 9:5; Heb. 1:1), or perhaps even to the first Christian martyrs such as James and Stephen (see Heb. 13:7). In any case, the religious frauds' implicit argument was that if Jesus had not yet returned, He would never do so.

C. Past Examples of Divine Judgment: vs. 5-6

But they deliberately forget that long ago by God's word the heavens existed and the earth was formed out of water and by water. By these waters also the world of that time was deluged and destroyed.

Peter noted that the spiritual frauds intentionally suppressed some key biblical facts. One truth is that at the dawn of time, God used His powerful utterance to command the heavens and the earth into existence (2 Pet. 3:5; see Pss. 33:6; 148:5). Concerning the planet, Genesis 1:6-10 reveals that God formed it out of water and by means of water. Moreover, He separated the land from the world's oceans, which continue to surround the continents to this day.

The Lord not only had the power to create the earth with the use of water, but also, as the lawful owner of the same planet, He had the right to destroy it by means of water (2 Pet. 3:6). The apostle was referring to the flood that inundated and wiped out all who inhabited the world in Noah's day (that is, except for Noah and his family, who were all safe in the ark). This obliteration was complete, in that "everything on dry land that had the breath of life in its nostrils died" (Gen. 7:22).

D. A Future Time of Divine Judgment: vs. 7

By the same word the present heavens and earth are reserved for fire, being kept for the day of judgment and destruction of ungodly men.

The conclusion Peter drew was that the same God who in the past destroyed the earth with water will one day destroy both the existing "heavens and earth" (2 Pet. 3:7) with fire. Fire is a symbol of destruction and purification. In both the Old and New Testaments, God is said to be "a consuming fire" (Deut. 4:24; Heb. 12:29). The fire of hell is portrayed as unquenchable (see Matt. 3:12; Mark 9:43; Luke 3:17). As well, the work of the Holy Spirit is compared to fire and has the power to renew (see Matt. 3:11; Acts 2:3, 19).

Peter noted that just as the wicked were destroyed in the Flood, so will it be at the end of time, when the entire universe is destroyed by fire (2 Pet. 3:7). It will be a time of "judgment and destruction" reserved specifically for the "ungodly." The Greek noun translated "judgment" refers to a future day in which God tries and sentences fallen humanity. The noun translated "destruction" points to the eternal misery in hell that awaits the wicked. The account of the Flood proved the inevitability of divine judgment and testified to God's patience. Even more importantly, the biblical record was evidence of the reliability of Scripture. Thankfully, just as God preserved Noah and his family from the Flood, so He will deliver those who have trusted in the Messiah for salvation.

II. THE CHALLENGE TO BE MORALLY PURE: 2 PETER 3:8-13

A. The Patience of God: vss. 8-9

But do not forget this one thing, dear friends: With the Lord a day is like a thousand years, and a thousand years are like a day. The Lord is not slow in keeping his promise, as some understand slowness. He is patient with you, not wanting anyone to perish, but everyone to come to repentance.

The religious charlatans had insisted that the delay in the promised coming of the Messiah proved that it was never going to happen. To counter this destructive error, Peter sought to clarify for his readers how God viewed time. Once again, the apostle used words of endearment as he encouraged these believers not to let an important fact escape their notice (2 Pet. 3:8). Evidently, he summarized the words of Moses recorded in Psalm 90:4.

It would be incorrect to conclude that Peter presumed to suggest an exact date when the end of history would come. Jesus made it clear that only the Father knew the precise time of the Son's second advent (see Matt. 24:36). The apostle's point was that God does not regard time as humans do. Whereas people are always conscious of days and months and years, God is above time, and its passing does not affect Him in the ways it affects His creatures.

Peter noted that just because the Son had not yet returned did not mean that the Father was "slow in keeping his promise" (2 Pet. 3:9). "Slow" renders a Greek verb that can also mean "to delay" or "to be hesitant." Despite what the false teachers alleged, Peter considered the apparent delay of Jesus' return, not as a doubt-producing dilemma, but as a means of God's grace. The Greek verb that is rendered "patient" literally means "to be long-spirited" and figuratively refers to a forbearing disposition. The Lord was lengthening the time period in which people could repent and be delivered from eternal destruction.

B. The Day of the Lord: vs. 10

But the day of the Lord will come like a thief. The heavens will disappear with a roar; the elements will be destroyed by fire, and the earth and everything in it will be laid bare.

When God's patience is finally exhausted, "the day of the Lord" (2 Pet. 3:10) will come suddenly, as a thief who strikes in the darkness (see 1 Thess. 5:2; Rev. 3:3; 16:15). Jesus also taught that His second advent would be unexpected, like the intrusion of a burglar (see Matt. 24:42-44; Luke 12:39-40). But unlike the housebreaker, Jesus will have every right to take whatever He wishes.

Peter used strong language typical of end-time passages to describe three events that will happen when the Messiah returns. First, the heavens will vanish with a "roar" (see Isa. 13:10-13; 34:4; Rev. 6:14). The latter renders a Greek adverb that denotes the presence of a horrific noise similar to a whirling, rushing sound. Second, the "elements" (2 Pet. 3:10) will melt away in a fiery blaze. The noun translated "elements" refers to the celestial bodies in the universe as well as the chemical compounds out of which they are made.

Third, the planet and every deed done on it will be "laid bare." The latter renders a Greek verb that points to the truth that one day every human creation will be exposed and judged by God. Another textual reading uses a verb that means "to burn up" or "be consumed by fire." In this case, the idea is that everything on earth will be obliterated. In turn, humanity will be left to stand exposed and accountable before God.

C. The Importance of Maintaining a Godly, Holy Lifestyle: vs. 11

Since everything will be destroyed in this way, what kind of people ought you to be? You ought to live holy and godly lives.

Peter had spelled out in vivid terms the terrifying events that will take place when the Messiah returns. The apostle had not done so to produce a trembling fear in the hearts of his readers, for he had assured them of their hope in the Redeemer. Since eventually all earthly things will be completely destroyed, believers should want all the more to live in a manner that is pleasing to God. Specifically, they are to be "holy and godly" (2 Pet. 3:11) in their conduct. Moreover, because death for any of us is but a heartbeat away, and because the Son could come soon, we should feel an urgency to glorify the Father in our daily living.

D. The Hope of a New Heaven and Earth: vss. 12-13

As you look forward to the day of God and speed its coming. That day will bring about the destruction of the heavens by fire, and the elements will melt in the heat. But in keeping with his promise we are looking forward to a new heaven and a new earth, the home of righteousness.

A difference of opinion exists concerning the phrase "speed its coming" (2 Pet. 3:12) in regard to the "day of God" (which is another way of referring to the day of the Lord). Some think the phrase is merely a description of the eagerness with which believers anticipate the Messiah's return. Others, however, relate Peter's statement to the belief that Christians can do things to hasten the Lord's advent. A recorded prayer of the early Christians, "Maranatha! Come, Lord Jesus" (see 1 Cor. 16:22; Rev. 22:20), corresponds with this perspective.

Peter repeated his earlier declaration that the heavens will be burned up and dissolve, and the celestial bodies will melt in a blaze (2 Pet. 3:12). The apostle quickly reassured Christians that, though the fire would destroy creation, God promised to provide "a new heaven and a new earth" (vs. 13). The latter anticipates John's statement in Revelation 21:1. Both of these verses likely have their roots in the words of Isaiah 65:17 and 66:22.

The Greek adjective that is rendered "new" (2 Pet. 3:13) denotes what is fresh and pristine. The idea is that either the new creation will be a total replacement for its old counterparts or will emerge from the same. The old universe was negatively impacted by the fall of Adam and Eve and by all their descendants. The result is the natural world's inability to fully achieve its God-given purpose and potential (see Gen. 3:17-19; Rom. 8:20-21). The cleansing fire of the Lord's holiness will make everything new at the end of the age, renovating, renewing, and purifying the heavens and the earth. In turn, the new creation will be a place in which one finds "righteousness" (2 Pet. 3:13). The latter translates a noun that points to the presence of such virtues as integrity, purity, and rectitude.

E. The Exhortation to Virtuous Living: vss. 14-15

So then, dear friends, since you are looking forward to this, make every effort to be found spotless, blameless and at peace with him. Bear in mind that our Lord's patience means salvation, just as our dear brother Paul also wrote you with the wisdom that God gave him.

Once more Peter encouraged his readers to accept the glorious anticipation of a new heaven and earth as a challenge to live righteously before God. This is accomplished by following the ethical example of the Savior, who was "without blemish or defect" (1 Pet. 1:19). In turn, believers are to ensure that their lives are morally "spotless [and] blameless" (2 Pet. 3:14). A virtuous person is more likely to be a peaceful one. To emphasize this point, Peter referred again to the meaning of God's patience as an invitation to "salvation" (vs. 15).

In this the apostle was repeating what he knew Paul had already written to his readers. Indeed, this was a common theme in his letters (vss. 15-16). While Peter wanted his readers to note the similarity and harmony between his teachings and those of Paul, Peter admitted that some of the statements Paul wrote were "hard to understand." Untaught and irresponsible people tried to twist and misrepresent these obscure texts (for example, 1 Cor. 5:5; 7:29; 15:29; Col. 1:24; 1 Tim. 2:15). Yet Peter placed Paul's writings on the same level as the Old Testament Scriptures. In this way, Peter showed his high regard for the God-given wisdom and authority of his fellow apostle in the Lord.

Discussion Questions

1. Why did Peter write his second letter?
2. What lessons did Noah's flood offer for those who were troubled by the apparent delay in Jesus' return?
3. If the Father is faithful to His promise, why has the Son not yet returned?
4. If you had only two hours to live before Jesus' return, how would you spend that time?
5. What can you do to prevent believers from being fooled by false teaching?

Contemporary Application

Peter was deeply concerned about the false teachers who had crept into the infant churches and beguiled many weak-minded Christians into believing doctrines that distorted the Gospel. Peter wrote his second epistle to urge his fellow believers to beware of these frauds, who were headed to certain "destruction" (2 Pet. 3:7).

We must be resolute in denouncing any teaching that falsifies the person and work of the Savior. If we remain silent when Jesus is said to be anything less than what He truly is, we permit dishonor to His name. That is something we can never do. Peter was also concerned that believers were losing their eagerness for Jesus' return. In response, the apostle assured his readers that the Lord will keep His promise to come again. So they were not to be dismayed that He had not yet returned.

Now, nearly 2,000 years later, many Christians still think that Jesus' return will occur in the long-distant future. Most importantly, some do not anticipate His coming with excitement and longing. Instead, they occasionally pray about it and discuss it as a theological issue. But do we truly yearn for Jesus' second coming?

Since so much time has passed, and since many of us live quite comfortably, it is understandable that Jesus' return does not impact us as it should. Yet, as Peter said, "with the Lord a day is like a thousand years" (vs. 8). To the Father, the Son's return is imminent, and so it should be to us as well.

We need to always look forward to Jesus' coming again because that thought will help us live godly lives. If we truly love the Lord, none of us want Jesus to return right when we are sinning. Instead, we want Him to find us living holy lives. Then, at His return, He will say to us, "Well done, good and faithful servant!" (Matt. 25:21). In light of these thoughts, what kind of fruit are we bearing in our witness?

Holy, Holy, Holy

Scripture

Background Scripture: *Isaiah 6:1-12*

Scripture Lesson: *Isaiah 6:1-12*

Key Verse: *"Holy, holy, holy is the LORD Almighty; the whole earth is full of his glory."* Isaiah 6:3.

Scripture Lesson for Children: *Isaiah 6:1-8*

Key Verse for Children: *"Holy, holy, holy is the Lord Almighty; the whole earth is full of his glory."* Isaiah 6:3.

Lesson Aim

To encourage living in total commitment to God's plans and will.

Lesson Setting

Time: 740 B.C.
Place: Judah

Lesson Outline

Holy, Holy, Holy

 I. Isaiah's Vision of God: Isaiah 6:1-4
  A. The Lord Seated on His Celestial Throne: vs. 1
  B. The Seraphs in Attendance: vss. 2-3
  C. The Effect on the Heavenly Temple: vs. 4
 II. Isaiah's Commission: Isaiah 6:5-12
  A. The Prophet's Distress: vs. 5
  B. The Prophet's Cleansing from Sin: vss. 6-7
  C. The Prophet's Willingness to Go: vs. 8
  D. The Prophet's Message to Proclaim: vss. 9-10
  E. The Prophet's Lengthy Ministry: vss. 11-12

Introduction for Adults

Topic: *Beyond Description*

The church is a voluntary organization. No one is compelled to join it. Every believer is a volunteer. Thus, we cannot force members to accept duties. Of course, we can ask them to do certain things and pray that they would say yes; and God honors these efforts.

Perhaps that seems like a risky way to run an organization. Yet it's God's way for His church, which is really a spiritual body, not merely a business. Our desire is that believers will be so overwhelmed by the grandeur of God's holiness, love, and mercy, as Isaiah was, that they will gladly volunteer for service at home and abroad. It is a commitment to be changed by God and to be one of His agents of change in a sin-cursed world.

We have to resist the pressure to program believers into slots. Instead, we should encourage them to be sensitive to God's leading and to worship Him in a genuine manner. When they approach Him in this way, they will be spiritually transformed, and the church will grow in God's grace.

Introduction for Youth

Topic: *Awed beyond Words*

The young man was quite an athlete, but he had to spend time on the bench before he was allowed to play in the game. Though he often volunteered to play, other athletes sometimes got the nod from the coach. Later on, when war broke out, the young man was drafted into the army. But in that setting, he never volunteered for frontline duty with the infantry. Instead, he tried to get an easy desk job in headquarters.

Our churches give us nice, comfortable places to worship, pray, and study the Bible. But our devotion to God calls for us to make a deeper, longer-lasting sacrifice. In brief, God wants us to go out into the world with the good news of salvation so that the lost might be saved. God also wants all of us to be ready for action on the front lines of spiritual warfare.

Isaiah felt awed beyond words in the presence of the holy Lord. And in response to God's call, the prophet stepped forward. He didn't know exactly what challenges he would face, but he knew God, and that was enough for him.

Concepts for Children

Topic: *Worthy of Praise*

1. In the year that King Uzziah died, Isaiah saw angels praising God.
2. When Isaiah confessed his sin, God spiritually purified him.
3. Isaiah heard the call of God and answered as a faithful servant.
4. We can find forgiveness with the Father through faith in the Son.
5. God is pleased when we are willing to serve Him, regardless of how hard it might be.

Lesson Commentary

I. ISAIAH'S VISION OF GOD: ISAIAH 6:1-4

A. The Lord Seated on His Celestial Throne: vs. 1

In the year that King Uzziah died, I saw the Lord seated on a throne, high and exalted, and the train of his robe filled the temple.

God dramatically called Isaiah to his prophetic ministry "in the year that King Uzziah died" (Isa. 6:1), namely, 740 B.C. Uzziah was a monarch of Judah, and he helped restore the nation to some of its former glory. Scripture says that Uzziah "did what was right in the eyes of the LORD" (2 Chron. 26:4). He extended Judah's territory and brought the nation to a time of great prosperity. In the south, he maintained control over Edom and rebuilt port facilities at Elath on the Gulf of Aqaba. To the west, he warred against the Philistines, seizing several cities. Apparently, he also defeated and subdued the Ammonites (vss. 6-8).

Because of Uzziah's political and economic successes, many people in Judah became affluent. Sadly, however, the poor were exploited by extortion and injustice. The unparalleled prosperity evidently diverted many from the worship of God and from obedience to His laws. This era of high living came to a crashing halt with the death of Uzziah. He remained leprous until his death because he tried to take over the high priest's duties (vss. 18-21).

Uzziah's death meant that his successors would be Jotham (750–735 B.C.) and then eventually Ahaz (735–715 B.C.), both known for their morally weak characters. The loss of a beloved national leader such as Uzziah and the unsettled situation it created in the palace undoubtedly affected Isaiah at the start of his ministry. While people looked for security in the midst of change, God called Isaiah to arouse them from their spiritual apathy and wickedness.

Isaiah said he "saw the Lord" (Isa. 6:1). The prophet did not physically see God's innermost nature. Rather, Isaiah was able to perceive the Lord in appearance seated upon a heavenly throne with the hem, or fringe, of His robe filling the celestial temple. This description expresses the overwhelming presence of God as both king and judge over all creation. Isaiah's lofty view of God gives us a sense of the Lord's greatness, mystery, and power. The Lord used Isaiah's vision to commission him as God's messenger to His people. Isaiah was given a difficult assignment. He had to tell people who believed they were blessed by God that the Lord was going to destroy them instead because of their disobedience.

B. The Seraphs in Attendance: vss. 2-3

Above him were seraphs, each with six wings: With two wings they covered their faces, with two they covered their feet, and with two they were flying. And they were calling to one another: "Holy, holy, holy is the LORD Almighty; the whole earth is full of his glory."

Accompanying the Lord were "seraphs" (Isa. 6:2), that is, spiritual beings who served as God's attendants. The literal meaning of "seraphs" is "burning ones," which suggests these creatures had a fiery appearance. Evidently, they were bright creatures, even though they had to hide their faces before God's brighter light. Nowhere else are they spoken of in the Old Testament. Scripture is full of references to angels, both fallen and glorified. The Bible reveals that angels are spirit creatures (Heb. 1:14) who live in heaven (Matt. 22:30) but may be sent by God as messengers to earth. They are mighty and powerful (Ps. 103:20; 2 Thess. 1:7) and possess great wisdom (2 Sam. 14:20). Ordinarily, they are invisible to us (2 Kings 6:17), though they have appeared as humans (Luke 24:4).

Angels do not marry or reproduce (Matt. 22:30). Because they are not subject to death (Luke 20:36), they will live forever and remain constant in number. Contrary to popular belief and artistic portrayal, few angels in the Bible are explicitly stated to have wings. In fact, Isaiah 6:2 may be the sole instance. On the other hand, angels are said to have the ability to fly (Dan. 9:21). Angels exist as an organized hierarchy (Col. 1:16). Among their duties are serving God by serving us (Heb. 1:14), providing us protection (Dan. 6:22), guarding us (Ps. 91:11), guiding us (Acts 8:26), and helping us (Dan. 10:13).

The seraphs Isaiah saw had six wings, two of which covered their faces in reverence and awe before the Lord. Because they had no glory to compare with God's, they could not look on Him directly. Two of the seraphs' wings covered their feet, which suggests humbleness. They remained humble before the Lord, even though they engaged in divine service. The seraphs' final two wings were used to fly, which signifies that they existed to do God's bidding.

Drawn against the backdrop of Judah's sin and Isaiah's personal needs, God's holiness came through powerfully in the prophet's vision. God Himself was the focus of this heavenly scene. The angels lauded God with the thunderous chorus, "Holy, holy, holy is the LORD Almighty" (Isa. 6:3). The threefold repetition was the strongest way in the Hebrew language to stress nothing is as holy as God. The basic meaning of "holy" is to be set apart from that which is commonplace. The word also refers to what is special or unique.

That the entire earth is filled with God's glory emphasizes the cosmic perspective of Isaiah's prophecies. He would proclaim that the Lord reigns supreme over all creation and that His salvation and judgment encompass all nations. God's regal position is the basis for His moral authority as the transcendent and sovereign Judge. Also, His holy character establishes the ethical standard for upright conduct and gives Him the right to decree to humankind how they should behave. Moreover, His infinite holiness is the basis for people worshiping Him. Indeed, God's holiness is the theme of worship in heaven (see Rev. 4:8).

C. The Effect on the Heavenly Temple: vs. 4

At the sound of their voices the doorposts and thresholds shook and the temple was filled with smoke.

Often in the Old Testament, phenomena such as earthquakes, smoke, fire, and lightning accompany a manifestation of God. Isaiah noted that the thunderous chorus of the seraphs shook the "doorposts and thresholds" (Isa. 6:4) of the celestial temple. Also, smoke filled the entire heavenly sanctuary. The Hebrew word rendered "smoke" possibly reflects the cloud of God's glory that filled the tabernacle, which Moses had built in the wilderness (Exod. 40:34). Both the shaking and the smoke that Isaiah described were manifestations of God's holiness, especially as it related to judgment.

II. Isaiah's Commission: Isaiah 6:5-12

A. The Prophet's Distress: vs. 5

"Woe to me!" I cried. "I am ruined! For I am a man of unclean lips, and I live among a people of unclean lips, and my eyes have seen the King, the LORD Almighty."

Isaiah's encounter with the Lord proved to be a life-changing experience for him. First, God's presence made him realize the depth of his sinfulness. Second, seeing even the seraphs humbly covering themselves before the Lord must have reminded the prophet of his moral imperfection. These emphases are reflected in the Hebrew term rendered "woe" (Isa. 6:5), which conveys a feeling of great sorrow or distress. When the prophet exclaimed, "I am ruined!," he made it seem as if his destruction had already occurred. Isaiah could have made excuses, pleaded for mercy, or fallen back on his good deeds. But he did none of these things. Instead, he fully accepted God's judgment. Isaiah knew that what he had seen and heard had left him totally helpless before the Lord.

Isaiah confessed that he and his people were guilty of "unclean lips." While this admission possibly included uttering vulgar language, most likely Isaiah had something else in mind. The people's lips were instruments of religious hypocrisy and of false professions of faith in God. Other Old Testament prophets and Jesus consistently charged God's people with worshiping with their lips, while their hearts were far from the Lord. Similarly, though the people of Judah claimed to believe in God, they violated His laws and worshiped idols.

Isaiah was careful to include himself in this indictment. And though he did not have to confess the sins of his people, he did. The prophet realized his need for the Lord to cleanse and purge him of his wrongdoings. In addition, he needed his lips purified so that he could praise the Lord with the seraphs and declare God's message to the people. Isaiah's confession reminds us of those of Peter and John. Peter said, "Go away from me, Lord; I am a sinful man!" (Luke 5:8). Similarly, John's reaction to his vision of the glorified, risen Lord was, "When I saw him, I fell at his feet as though dead" (Rev. 1:17).

Isaiah reported seeing "the King, the LORD Almighty" (Isa. 6:5). The depiction is one of a divine warrior who commanded the hosts of heaven and earth. Scripture tells us that no one has ever seen or can see the Lord (1 Tim. 6:16). Knowing this, how was it possible for Isaiah to have a vision of God? In response, we should remember that God is spirit, and thus invisible (see John 4:24). This means that no one has seen or can see Him in His true essence. However, the Lord has at times chosen to manifest Himself temporarily in one visible form or another. Such a visible manifestation is called a "theophany." This term comes from two Greek words: *theos*, which means "God," and *phaino*, which means "to appear." What Isaiah saw, then, was an appearance of God, not God in His essence.

B. The Prophet's Cleansing from Sin: vss. 6-7

Then one of the seraphs flew to me with a live coal in his hand, which he had taken with tongs from the altar. With it he touched my mouth and said, "See, this has touched your lips; your guilt is taken away and your sin atoned for."

Upon Isaiah's confession of his sinfulness, a seraph flew over him with a hot coal, which had been taken from the celestial altar (Isa. 6:6). This coal symbolized the redeeming power of God to purge and forgive sins. When the angel touched the prophet's lips with the coal, both his iniquity and guilt were removed. Also, his sin was forgiven (vs. 7). Of course, the coal did not atone Isaiah's transgressions. Rather, God did through the offering of a sacrifice, namely, the atoning work of the Messiah on the cross (see Rom. 4:25-26). When we confess our sins before God in true repentance, He forgives us at that moment and restores us into fellowship with Him (see 1 John 1:9). It would be incorrect to think that this incident is an account of Isaiah's conversion. The prophet was already a fervent believer and true servant of God. Isaiah's purification served to prepare him for his future ministry as God's spokesperson.

C. The Prophet's Willingness to Go: vs. 8

Then I heard the voice of the Lord saying, "Whom shall I send? And who will go for us?" And I said, "Here am I. Send me!"

With Isaiah's cleansing over, God moved directly to the business for which He had called Isaiah into His presence. God had seen that the people of Judah were not following His ways, so He wanted someone to tell them of their need for change and to warn them of what to expect. He chose Isaiah for this job. But God did not come right out and tell Isaiah the job He had for him. God wanted Isaiah to volunteer for the assignment. So the Lord asked, "Whom shall I send? And who will go for us?" (Isa. 6:8). Bible scholars have debated the identity of "us" in the second question. Some suggest that this is a reference to the Trinity. Others believe that God was addressing His question to the angelic beings in His royal court (vs. 2).

In either case, it's clear how Isaiah responded to the questions. Though shortly before he felt unfit to serve God as a prophet, now Isaiah was eager. Before, he had said, "Woe to me!" (vs. 5) and "I am ruined!" But now he said, "Here am I. Send me!" (vs. 8). That's just the response God wanted to hear. Even without knowing where God intended to send His messenger, Isaiah was ready to volunteer. We can easily imagine God smiling at Isaiah's enthusiasm. God is pleased with us, too, when we have an eager disposition and declare, "Here am I. Send me!"

D. The Prophet's Message to Proclaim: vss. 9-10

He said, "Go and tell this people: "'Be ever hearing, but never understanding; be ever seeing, but never perceiving.' Make the heart of this people calloused; make their ears dull and close their eyes. Otherwise they might see with their eyes, hear with their ears, understand with their hearts, and turn and be healed."

Now God proceeded to give Isaiah the core of the message he was to deliver to the people. Surprisingly, Isaiah was to tell them that they would hear the truth without understanding it and would see the truth without perceiving it (Isa. 6:9). Isaiah's face must have fallen in disappointment when he heard this assertion. Perhaps he expected to learn that God was going to use him to lead Judah to repentance. But instead, the Lord informed Isaiah that his ministry would have little positive spiritual impact. In fact, the people's hearts would become even more hardened against God. Isaiah's prophecy would lead to the further callousing of their hearts, dulling of their spiritual hearing, and clouding of their spiritual vision (vs. 10). Certainly, God is not pleased when people reject His truth. He wants all sinners to "turn and be healed." But He knew that Isaiah's message would have a hardening effect on the hearts of most Judeans, just as the sun hardens clay.

God's call of Isaiah to render the hearts of the Judeans "calloused" might sound puzzling to us. After all, why would the Lord prevent His people from responding favorably to His pronouncements through Isaiah? The answer is that the chosen people had consistently rebelled against the Lord. They had become stubborn in their thinking and obdurate in their hearts. For instance, during the last 10 years of Uzziah's life, his son Jotham had ruled in his place. Jotham excelled in honoring the Lord, and the time of prosperity continued (2 Chron. 26:21; 27:1-6). But Scripture tells us that despite the leadership of these two godly kings, "the people . . . continued their corrupt practices" (27:2). When Jotham and his son, Ahaz, came to power, the nation turned completely away from God and willfully turned a deaf ear to His decrees (see 2 Kings 16:1-4; 2 Chron. 28:19). As a result, the nation eventually reaped the consequences of moral and spiritual decline.

E. The Prophet's Lengthy Ministry: vss. 11-12

Then I said, "For how long, O Lord?" And he answered: "Until the cities lie ruined and without inhabitant, until the houses are left deserted and the fields ruined and ravaged, until the LORD has sent everyone far away and the land is utterly forsaken."

Isaiah did not object to the commission God had given him. Before knowing his commission, Isaiah had accepted it, and now he would not shrink from it. But understandably, he was curious how long God would want him to minister to people of calloused hearts. So the prophet asked, "For how long, O Lord?" (Isa. 6:11). God's reply was that Isaiah should continue preaching until the land of Judah was devastated and abandoned, and its inhabitants had been taken into exile (vs. 12). Since the Babylonian captivity did not occur for another century and a half, Isaiah would have to keep up his poorly received message for the remainder of his life.

Discussion Questions

1. How did Isaiah feel at the sight of the Lord seated on His celestial throne?
2. When was there a time when you experienced the majesty of God? How did you feel?
3. Why did the seraphs use their wings to cover themselves in the Lord's presence?
4. How did Isaiah react to what he heard and saw in his vision?
5. In what ways has God recently made known His greatness and holiness to you?

Contemporary Application

The application for this week's study is unambiguous. God wants us, His followers, to be steadfast in our devotion to Him. He wants from us the same relinquishing of our plans and will as He had from Isaiah. He desires to be our first priority in life. While we probably won't be having visions of the Lord as the prophet experienced, we have something better. We have God's complete Word, including the record of Isaiah's profound experience.

Through the Bible, countless people have been led to faith in the Messiah. They have been spiritually transformed. And they have been made fully aware of God's holiness, glory, and love. But along with those many who have ears to hear, there are even more who resemble the people of Judah, their hearts only further hardened by the Gospel. Nonetheless, there always remains the remnant, namely, those of us who have received God, who have been cleansed, and who are commissioned. Our orders are clear—herald the Good News with total commitment.

There is one major way in which our ministry differs from that of Isaiah. God sent the prophet to proclaim a message of doom, but we have a message of deliverance. Isaiah's main emphasis in the early part of his book was on God's outraged holiness, while ours is on His outreaching and everlasting love.

Our strategy may be different than the methods Isaiah used, especially since the circumstances are different. The doom and despair that Isaiah foresaw and preached has since come and gone. Yet in many real forms it exists today as devastatingly as ever. Governments and individuals inflict horrific atrocities upon one another. And the personal despair of individuals living independently of God's hope and grace is as palpable. People still desperately need the Lord, and they still need God's followers to stand up and say, "Here I am. Send me!"

Give Thanks

DEVOTIONAL READING

Psalm 92:1-8

DAILY BIBLE READINGS

Monday June 3
  *Psalm 92:1-8 Giving
  Thanks Is Good*

Tuesday June 4
  *Psalm 95:1-7 Coming into
  God's Presence with
  Thanksgiving*

Wednesday June 5
  *1 Chronicles 16:8-13
  Remembering God's
  Wonderful Works*

Thursday June 6
  *1 Chronicles 29:10-18
  Giving Thanks and Praise
  to God*

Friday June 7
  *1 Timothy 4:1-5 Receiving
  God's Goodness with
  Thanksgiving*

Saturday June 8
  *Luke 17:11-19 Where Are
  the Other Nine?*

Sunday June 9
  *Isaiah 12 Giving Thanks to
  the Lord*

Scripture

Background Scripture: *Isaiah 12*
Scripture Lesson: *Isaiah 12*
Key Verse: *In that day you will say: "Give thanks to the
LORD, call on his name; make known among the nations what
he has done, and proclaim that his name is exalted."* Isaiah
12:4.
Scripture Lesson for Children: *Isaiah 12*
Key Verse for Children: *Give thanks to the LORD, . . . make
known among the nations what he has done."* Isaiah 12:4.

Lesson Aim

To consider ways to express thanks to the Lord.

Lesson Setting

Time: 740–700 B.C.
Place: Judah

Lesson Outline

Give Thanks
  I.   The Reason for Offering Praise: Isaiah 12:1-3
      A. *Divine Consolation: vs. 1*
      B. *Divine Deliverance: vss. 2-3*
  II. The Summons to Offer Praise: Isaiah 12:4-6
      A. *Proclaiming God's Mighty Acts: vs. 4*
      B. *Praising God in Song: vss. 5-6*

Introduction for Adults

Topic: *Sing and Shout!*

For seven long years (1985–1991), friends, colleagues, and loved ones brought their petitions to God to deliver Terry Anderson from his captors. Anderson, an Associated Press employee, was one of several Americans who were kidnapped in Lebanon and held hostage.

In his book, *Den of Lions,* Anderson says that despite the beatings and deprivation he suffered, his faith in the Lord remained strong. When he was finally released and asked about his feelings toward his abductors, Anderson said, "I am a Christian. I am required to forgive."

Clearly, God had answered the petitions of those who prayed for Anderson, as well as Anderson's own prayers for release. In the aftermath, the former hostage offered "praise" (Isa. 12:1) to the Lord. Whether in churches, on television, or in print, Anderson declared God to be his source of "salvation" (vs. 2).

Introduction for Youth

Topic: *Wow! Thanks!*

Derek has been a Christian since he was a child. Though he had his rebellious teenage years, as an adult, he has more faithfully loved and served the Lord. If you asked Derek today what was the greatest source of his personal joy in Christ, he would tell you it was found in his praise for the "glorious things" (Isa. 12:5) the Lord has done.

In Derek's early 20s, he read A. W. Tozer's *The Knowledge of the Holy,* on the attributes of God (see the reference in vs. 6 to the "Holy One of Israel"). As Derek read about the various and unique attributes that God possessed, he was continually amazed by the Lord's greatness. When Derek's father died at an early age, and when Derek overcame his own personal challenges and health issues, he found himself praising God, from whom the "wells of salvation" (vs. 3) came.

For Derek, it always seemed right to give thanks and praise to God, regardless of life's circumstances. Derek also believes that praise is the most important gift that a person can give to the Lord. For Derek, it is the obvious expression of one who has seen the greatness of God in some small way.

Concepts for Children

Topic: *Give Praise and Thanks*

1. A future day was coming when God's people would sing.
2. God's people would thank Him for forgiving them.
3. God's people would praise Him for being their Savior.
4. God's people would trust in Him and not be afraid.
5. God's people would tell others how great He is.

Lesson Commentary

I. THE REASON FOR OFFERING PRAISE: ISAIAH 12:1-3

A. Divine Consolation: vs. 1

In that day you will say: "I will praise you, O LORD. Although you were angry with me, your anger has turned away and you have comforted me."

The prophecies recorded in Isaiah 9–12 speak of a coming Deliverer who would bring great blessing. These pronouncements might have applied to the more contemporary King Hezekiah (715–686 B.C.), or to another king of Judah. But they ultimately apply in the fullest sense to the Lord Jesus, the promised Messiah of Israel. Following Isaiah's glorious description of the Savior and His kingdom (see 9:1-7), the prophet immediately switched back to the present. Israel had already tasted judgment, but had not repented from sin. So it would be further judged by God's using Syria and Philistia as instruments. Isaiah warned that captivity was imminent (see 9:8–10:4). Mighty Assyria, another instrument God would use to judge His people, in turn would be judged by the sovereign Lord. Consequently, Assyria would be utterly destroyed (see 10:5-19). In verses 20-23, we find the familiar theme of a faithful remnant of God's people returning from exile. Even in judging His people, the Lord would never forget His purpose of restoration. Next, Isaiah exhorted the faithful not to fear the Assyrians (see vss. 24-34), for God had plans to bring Assyria to a sudden end.

While in Isaiah 9, the promised Messiah appeared as a child, in 11:1, He is depicted as a green shoot breaking through the ground from the roots of a stump. Then, 9:2-5 returns to the theme of Judah's desolation, which was foretold in 6:9-13. The prophet pictured the royal family of God's chosen people as a chopped-down tree. However, unlike the Assyrians (who were cut down, never to rise again), the stump of David's father, Jesse, contained the promise of new life. In fulfillment of 2 Samuel 7:16, this Messiah would continue the dynasty of David. Also, the Spirit of the Lord would rest upon the Savior, empowering Him to establish at long last true righteousness and justice.

The Davidic kings of the Old Testament era were notorious for at least error, if not intentional injustice and oppression. In contrast, the Branch from Jesse's roots was entirely different. He would conduct a righteous, peaceful reign based on unerring reverence for the Lord and His will (Isa. 11:3; see John 8:29). The branch perceived the motive of every heart and yielded judgments that upheld the poor against their oppressors and the meek against the arrogant. Furthermore, His justice was swift and sure: A mere word from the Savior's mouth had the ability to crush an offender (Isa. 11:4). With righteousness as the Messiah's belt and faithfulness as His sash, His kingdom would be in complete harmony with God's perfect moral standards. Finally, then, goodness and fairness would reign (vs. 5).

Indeed, the Messiah's rule would extend beyond the human race to nature itself.

His kingdom would restore the conditions of Eden and make the earth a place of tranquility and harmony. Natural enemies would be at peace: wolf with lamb, leopard with young goat, lion with calf, cow with bear, and infant with cobra (vss. 6-8). Clearly, these prophecies are yet to be fulfilled in a future earthly kingdom. We look from the world's present darkness toward that brilliant light of promise. In that day of peace and joy, nothing harmful would take place on God's holy mountain. But in our present state, the image is almost inconceivable. Just as water filled the sea, so the land would be filled with people who know and honor the Lord (vs. 9).

In verse 10, the dazzling promise of the Messiah's coming extends beyond Israel to shine upon all the nations of the world. The Savior Himself stood as a banner to which the nations rallied. In Him, they would find glorious rest from strife. Moreover, God would gather the exiles of Israel and Judah from every geographical direction (vs. 12). This prophecy goes beyond the return of Jews from Babylonian captivity in 536 B.C., or the establishment of a new Jewish state in 1948. Isaiah's words again would find their fulfillment in the ultimate regathering of the Jewish people to Israel in the future kingdom of the Messiah. In fact, the Lord would remove all obstacles to His people's regathering (vs. 16).

In light of these glorious promises, there was no better way to respond than through songs of praise. After all, the future time of hope would be a "day" (12:1) of victory and joy, especially as the Lord defeated Israel's foes and restored the chosen people to the promised land. Isaiah, in using the personal pronoun rendered "I," spoke as a representative for all the faithful remnant. Centuries earlier, Moses followed a similar approach as he and the Israelites stood on the shoreline of the Red Sea (see Exod. 15:1). For them, it was a moment to celebrate the Lord's vanquishing of Pharaoh and his army. For a future generation of Israelites, the occasion for praise would be God's freeing them from such oppressors as Assyria and Babylon.

The chosen people acknowledged that they did not deserve to experience deliverance from the Lord. After all, for many years they refused to heed His commands, as recorded in the Mosaic law (see Isa. 1:4). Understandably, God was "angry" (12:1) with His people and allowed them to be overrun by foreign powers (see 5:25; 9:12). Eventually, the northern kingdom of Israel fell to the Assyrians in 722 B.C. Then, in 586 B.C., the southern kingdom of Judah ended at the hands of the Babylonians. Amazingly, though, the Lord "turned away" (12:1) from His "anger" and once again "comforted" the faithful remnant (see 40:1-2). God's consolation and compassion were the basis for His people giving Him thanks.

B. Divine Deliverance: vss. 2-3

"Surely God is my salvation; I will trust and not be afraid. The LORD, the LORD, is my strength and my song; he has become my salvation." With joy you will draw water from the wells of salvation.

Isaiah 12:2 reveals that one day, the covenant community would together proclaim that the God of Israel was its deliverer. Because He alone was the true source of His

people's "salvation," they could have faith in Him and not fear any negative reper-
cussions. Indeed, the sovereign Lord was the fountainhead of His people's
"strength" and the basis for their joyous "song." A similar refrain is found in Psalm
118:14, in which the king and the nation joined to express their heartfelt gratitude
for the victory the Lord had given them over their enemies. Assuredly, with Him as
their defender and protector, they could look to the future with renewed hope.

There is a close relationship between praise and singing in the Old Testament.
For instance, Moses and the Israelites sang praise to God in response to the Exodus
(see Exod. 15:1-18). Deborah and Barak sang praise to God in response to being
delivered from the Canaanites (see Judg. 5:1-31). Many of the psalms are songs
of praise that were originally accompanied by music. In the Book of Isaiah, songs of
praise most often focus on God's deliverance of His people from exile and His
future blessings (see 27:2; 30:29; 44:23).

The latter part of Isaiah 12:2 echoes Exodus 15:2. Here, Moses and his fellow
Israelites praised God, whose strength and power had been clear in His overthrow
of the Egyptians. Verse 3 aptly refers to the Lord as a mighty "warrior," for He
deserved the credit for defeating the forces of Egypt. The chosen people also proclaimed that the "LORD is his name." It's possible this statement was a final taunt to
Pharaoh, who had asked earlier, "Who is the LORD, that I should obey him and let
Israel go?" (5:2). The song of Moses then turned to some of the details of God's victory on the Israelites' behalf. For instance, the people sang about Pharaoh and his
army being inundated by the waters of the sea (15:4-7). The faithful remnant also
recalled how the Egyptians drowned: "They sank to the depths like a stone."
Moreover, the upright recounted how the Lord, who is "majestic in power," "shattered" and "threw down" and "consumed" the Egyptians.

Isaiah 12:3 metaphorically refers to God's future act of deliverance as the "wells
of salvation" from which the chosen people would "draw" life-giving and life-
preserving "water." The latter might also be a historical allusion to the Israelites'
time of wandering in the Sinai desert. For example, Exodus 15:22-25 records an
incident at Marah in which the people challenged Moses' leadership. When the
Israelites arrived at this locale, they found they could not drink the water because
it was bitter. So they began to complain, thinking they would soon die of thirst.
Moses cried out to the Lord. And in response to Moses' plea, God instructed
Moses to toss a particular piece of wood into the water. When he did so, the water
became drinkable.

While the Israelites were encamped at Marah, God issued a decree for them. It
was a law that would test them at that moment as well as into the future. The
Israelites had just demonstrated their true nature. Instead of trusting God to provide for their needs (such as drinking water), they had manifested their lack of
belief by grumbling. The point of the decree was that the Israelites were to rely
completely on the Lord. As they did so, He pledged to watch over them, protect
them, and meet their most basic needs (vs. 26). An immediate example of God's

provision would be the time the Israelites spent encamped at Elim. This was a desert oasis with 12 springs and 70 palm trees (vs. 27). The Hebrew word transliterated Elim means "great trees," but earlier it might have meant "gods." Accordingly, some scholars think that Elim could have been a sacred site for nomads who dwelt in that area. In any case, it was here that the Israelites spent some time and were refreshed by the readily available water God provided.

Additional passages of Scripture refer to God in ways that parallel Isaiah 12:3. For example, Psalm 36:9 describes the Lord as the "fountain of life," and Jeremiah 2:13 calls Him the "spring of living water." These are the sorts of truths that Isaiah 12:1 says are one reason for giving thanks to God. Both Old and New Testament Scriptures point out that believers should offer praise to God for His perfections, for His mighty works, and for His gracious benefits. While giving thanks to the Lord is viewed as a mark of His people (see Eph. 1:13-14; Phil. 1:11; 1 Pet. 2:9), one of the marks of unbelievers is their refusal to offer praise and express gratitude to God for His many temporal blessings (see Rom. 1:21; Rev. 16:9).

II. THE SUMMONS TO OFFER PRAISE: ISAIAH 12:4-6

A. Proclaiming God's Mighty Acts: vs. 4

In that day you will say: "Give thanks to the LORD, call on his name; make known among the nations what he has done, and proclaim that his name is exalted."

In the future day of promised deliverance, the members of the covenant community would summon one another to express "thanks" (Isa. 12:4) and offer praise to the Lord. The underlying Hebrew verb means "to declare aloud in public" or "to give open acknowledgment." Moreover, the faithful remnant were directed to "call on his name." This phrase means to invoke God's name, especially when petitioning Him for help. The motivation for doing so can be found in Exodus 3. For instance, in verse 14, God revealed Himself as "I AM WHO I AM." This phrase signified that God is pure being, and that He is the self-existent one. Verse 15 reveals that the ever-living Lord is also the God of Abraham, Isaac, and Jacob. These patriarchal names would have captured the attention of the Israelites. Assuredly, it was to these individuals that God had first revealed His covenant. So, from one generation to the next, God would be known as the Lord who was faithful to the covenant promises He made to the people of Israel.

The righteous remnant were not just to ask God for help. They were also to declare to the "nations" (Isa. 12:4) the Lord's mighty acts and announce that His "name is exalted" (see Pss. 105:1; 148:13). Once more, Moses' song uttered at the Red Sea is brought to mind, in which the faithful remnant chorused that the Lord was "highly exalted" (Exod. 15:1). Also noteworthy in this regard is Revelation 15, in which John reported seeing the "victorious" (vs. 2) people of God "standing" on a celestial "sea of glass mixed with fire." The saints held harps that God had given them, and they sang a chorus of praise to the Lord for His faithfulness in delivering them and judging the wicked. John first labeled the refrain the "song of Moses" (vs. 3) and then the "song of the Lamb." Just as the people of God in ancient times had been victorious over their foe, Egypt, so too the new people of God—the followers of the Messiah—had triumphed over their antagonists. His atoning sacrifice made victory possible for the saints (see 5:6).

As with the refrain recorded in Isaiah 12:4, the one appearing in Revelation 15:3 draws attention to the Lord's "great and marvelous . . . deeds." There is also an affirmation of His "ways" being "just and true." His sovereignty is made clear by the two parallel references to Him—"Lord God Almighty" and "King of the ages." Through the use of a rhetorical question, the saints implied that everyone would "fear" (vs. 4) the Creator and "bring glory" to His "name." After all, He alone was "holy" and so deserving of reverence, obedience, and praise. The Savior's followers noted how the Lord had "revealed" His "righteous acts." In turn, this would prompt "all nations" of the world to "come and worship" in God's presence. From a theological perspective, the redemption epitomized by Israel's exodus from Egypt found its ultimate fulfillment in the end-time exodus led by the Lamb on behalf of His disciples.

B. Praising God in Song: vss. 5-6

"Sing to the LORD, for he has done glorious things; let this be known to all the world. Shout aloud and sing for joy, people of Zion, for great is the Holy One of Israel among you."

Isaiah 12:5 directs the faithful remnant to "sing" praises to God. The reason calls to mind the statement made in verse 4 about God's mighty acts. In verse 5, they are referred to as "glorious things." Put another way, the Lord had acted marvelously in delivering His beleaguered people from their foes. While the covenant community was to encourage one another with this truth, they were not to keep it to themselves. Instead, they were to publicize God's tremendous deeds to "all the world." In other words, even Gentiles needed to know what the Lord had done so that they too could come to saving faith in Him. The implication is that the benefits of God's plan of redemption went beyond Israel to include all the inhabitants of the earth (see 11:10).

In 12:6, God's people are referred as citizens of "Zion." The latter is first mentioned in 2 Samuel 5:7 as a Jebusite fortress on a hill. After being captured by David, this fortress was called the City of David. Here Israel's king brought the ark of the covenant, thereby making the hill a sacred site (see 6:10-12). In the Old Testament, Zion is also called the "city of God" (Ps. 46:4), God's "resting place" (132:14), God's "holy hill" (2:6), the "holy city" (Isa. 48:2), and the "beautiful holy mountain" (Dan. 11:45). Eventually, Zion came to stand for the entire city of Jerusalem. Moreover, in early Christian thought, Zion represented the "heavenly Jerusalem, the city of the living God" (Heb. 12:22).

Isaiah 12:6 instructed the covenant community to cry out and "sing for joy." The reason is that the "Holy One of Israel" was in their midst and acted mightily among them, particularly by setting them free. As 40:1 makes clear, the news of Israel's deliverance was to be a source of comfort to His chosen people. Verse 9 describes it as "good tidings" that were to be proclaimed to "Zion" and "Jerusalem." In view of what the Lord planned to do on behalf of the covenant community, verse 25 asked to whom could anyone "compare" Him? Likewise, who could be His "equal"? The obvious answer is that there was no one like the Lord. After all, He alone was the "Holy One." As such, He ruled unchallenged over the faithful remnant and exercised supreme authority over all the earth. Consequently, there was no power in the entire cosmos that could prevent the Lord from fulfilling His promises of deliverance to His people.

Discussion Questions

1. What are some specific ways believers can give thanks to the Lord?
2. What are a couple of reasons given in Isaiah 12 for offering praise to God?
3. Why was the Lord initially angry with His people?
4. Why did God eventually turn away from His anger?
5. How can proclaiming that God's "name is exalted" (vs. 4) benefit believers spiritually?

Contemporary Application

A key emphasis in this week's lesson is giving thanks to God. For instance, Isaiah 12:1 talks about praising the Lord, while verses 4-6 direct the faith community to make singing for joy and shouting aloud the basis for their expressions of gratitude. In a world filled with stress and anxiety, surely a healthy physical and spiritual alternative is giving God praise.

The high calling of serving and praising God is accompanied by peace in the midst of conflict. Indeed, personal peace and joy are the priceless privileges of believers. In light of this truth, we have to ask why so many of us seem troubled, confused, and worried. The anxiety we carry around in our lives takes a heavy toll on us. Perhaps one reason is that we have missed the simplicity of expressing gratitude to God. We look for many avenues of relief, without realizing that the Lord is the true source of our comfort and strength. We neglect the practice of prayer, failing to recognize that God is the one who sustains and watches over us.

Moreover, we allow our minds to be filled with unworthy ideas. Often, the world pressures us into its distorted way of thinking. When we give in, we rob ourselves of finding contentment in the Lord. We also squander opportunities to demonstrate to the unsaved that He can do great and marvelous things through us. While we prosper outwardly with abundance, our souls are lean. That's why we need God's reminder from Isaiah 12 to allow His presence and joy to control our lives. It's a matter of faith to believe that the Lord wants to give His strength for whatever life might bring. With Him at our side, we have nothing to fear.

Meaningless Worship

DEVOTIONAL READING

Luke 8:9-14

DAILY BIBLE READINGS

Monday June 10
Isaiah 1:10-17 Fruitless Worship

Tuesday June 11
Isaiah 2:5-17 Worshiping Our Own Achievements

Wednesday June 12
Isaiah 58:1-7 Lives Untouched by Religious Observances

Thursday June 13
Jeremiah 13:1-11 Refusing to Listen

Friday June 14
Zechariah 7:8-14 Tuning Out God

Saturday June 15
Luke 8:9-14 Receiving the Word

Sunday June 16
Isaiah 29:9-16 Hearts Far from God

Scripture

Background Scripture: *Isaiah 29*
Scripture Lesson: *Isaiah 29:9-16*
Key Verse: The Lord says: *"These people come near to me with their mouth and honor me with their lips, but their hearts are far from me. Their worship of me is made up only of rules taught by men."* Isaiah 29:13.
Scripture Lesson for Children: *Isaiah 29:9-16*
Key Verse for Children: *"Everyone who exalts himself will be humbled, but he who humbles himself will be exalted."* Luke 18:14.

Lesson Aim

To conduct our lives in a way that's consistent with our faith.

Lesson Setting

Time: 740–700 B.C.
Place: Judah

Lesson Outline

Meaningless Worship

I. Israel's Spiritual Insensitivity: Isaiah 29:9-12
   A. *A Spiritual Stupor: vs. 9*
   B. *A Spiritual Blindness: vs. 10*
   C. *A Refusal to Heed Divine Oracles: vss. 11-12*

II. Israel's Day of Reckoning: Isaiah 29:13-16
   A. *Empty Worship: vs. 13*
   B. *Divine Judgment: vs. 14*
   C. *Deceptive Ways: vss. 15-16*

Introduction for Adults

Topic: *More than Words*

Most of us probably remember the first time we ran afoul of one of the laws of the universe. Perhaps we touched a hot stove and got burned. Or maybe we fell off a bicycle and got some scraped knees and elbows. Or possibly we fell out of a tree and broke an arm.

The result of our pain was discovering how things work in the world. We learned about the qualities of heat and gravity. However, sometimes it takes us awhile to realize that the universe also has moral laws, and that we suffer when we break them.

Biblical history confirms what we learn by experience—we cannot escape God's moral laws. Consider the people of Judah. Though they claimed to worship the Lord, they violated God's commands and thought there would be no consequences (see Isa. 29:13). Civil leaders, religious officials, and common people alike indulged in sin. Then, the Judge of the universe decided to act, and Judah suffered the consequences (see vs. 14).

God's character has not changed. No amount of wishful thinking can remove His holiness and justice. Judah's eventual exile should send us a powerful message to confess and repent before it is too late.

Introduction for Youth

Topic: *Are You for Real?*

A gang of kids sullenly scuffed along the platform at the train station. The train they wanted to board had just pulled away, and they fell into griping and accusing one another. They suffered the consequences of being late.

Like the people of Judah in Isaiah's day, we'll eternally suffer if we fail to realize the importance of obeying God. Serving Him is more than paying lip service (see Isa. 29:13). The Lord wants us to be sincere in the way we honor Him.

When we're young it's easy to think we'll pay attention to God when we get older. However, if we neglect Him now, there is a strong possibility that we may never turn our hearts to Him in faith. Thankfully, God's grace is always available when we reach out to Him in faith. But we must do so now, for we do not know when a time of reckoning will come.

Concepts for Children

Topic: *Out of a Humble Heart*

1. The people of Judah were making poor choices.
2. Despite Isaiah's warnings, the people of Judah continued to disobey God.
3. God punished His people because of their sins.
4. God loves us so much that He wants us to obey Him.
5. God wants us to let others know that it is best to obey Him.

Lesson Commentary

I. ISRAEL'S SPIRITUAL INSENSITIVITY: ISAIAH 29:9-12

A. A Spiritual Stupor: vs. 9

Be stunned and amazed, blind yourselves and be sightless; be drunk, but not from wine, stagger, but not from beer.

This week's Scripture passage is set against the backdrop of a series of "woes" (see 28:1; 29:1). Isaiah's first declaration of doom was against Samaria, the capital of the northern kingdom of Israel, which was designated as "Ephraim" in 28:1. Isaiah's second declaration of doom was against Judah and Jerusalem. The prophet foresaw the crisis of 701 B.C., one in which the Assyrians would destroy dozens of towns in the southern kingdom. Isaiah began by blasting Judah's leaders, who were headquartered in Jerusalem. They scoffed at his prophecies and trusted in their own plans (vss. 14-15). In their "covenant with death," they had made an alliance with Egypt, perhaps even pledging to serve its gods of the underworld as a way of obtaining protection. Regardless, Judah was not as safe as the leaders thought. No matter what form their faithlessness might take, destruction was inevitable.

The Lord declared that there was only one secure foundation upon which to build, namely, faith in Him (vs. 16). And God set up in Zion the firmest foundation stone for His spiritual temple, the Messiah. Only if Judah trusted in the Lord would the nation be saved from evil invaders such as the Assyrians. Yet, as an act of justice, God would use the Assyrian army to chastise His wayward people (vs. 17). Like a deluge, the invaders would inundate and ruin Judah (vss. 18-19). Also, regardless of how much the people resisted and ignored Him, they could not deny the Lord's chastening them for their rebellion (vss. 20-21). So Isaiah warned his listeners not to worsen the judgment by mocking what God would irrefutably do (vs. 22).

Isaiah then introduced an agricultural illustration to show how God would judge Judah (vs. 24). The parable is in two parts, and each one ends with an affirmation of the Lord's wisdom throughout the process and by implication in judgment (vss. 26, 29). Isaiah's point was that God knew how to handle Judah so that the nation would produce a fruitful harvest. While He would send the Assyrians against His people, the Lord would not let the judgment be too severe. After the time of discipline, He would harvest a fruitful, faithful remnant (vss. 24-29).

Chapter 29 continues the prophecy about the coming invasion of Judah. Isaiah now focused on the effects this attack would have on Jerusalem. Verse 1 poetically refers to Judah's capital as "Ariel." This name might mean "lion of God" or "hearth (altar) of God." Jerusalem was the location of the altar on which sacrifices were burned. Also, the name "Ariel" fits the context of judgment, for in verse 2, the capital is called an "altar hearth." The latter renders another Hebrew word that sounds like "Ariel" (see Ezek. 43:15). So devastating would be the coming judgment that the bloodshed and flames would make Jerusalem comparable to an altar on which sacrifices were burned.

In Isaiah 29:1, "Ariel" is called the "city where David settled." Centuries earlier, David conquered the city of Jebus from the Jebusites and renamed it Jerusalem (see 2 Sam. 5:6-9). Since it had been a place of blessing for God's people, Isaiah's pronouncement of doom must have seemed incredible. The prophet sarcastically exhorted Jerusalem's inhabitants to keep performing their religious "festivals" (Isa. 29:1). Evidently, the city's inhabitants saw that life was continuing as usual and knew that they were maintaining the outward displays of their worship. For these reasons, they did not expect divine judgment. But Isaiah's statement implies that a time was coming when invasion would break the "cycle" of religious life.

In verses 2 and 3, God claimed that He would surround and besiege Jerusalem. More specifically, He would work through the Assyrians to accomplish His purposes for the city. As a result of the siege, Jerusalem would be brought to the ground as if it was a buried corpse (vs. 4). From the ground, where the city lay, its voice would "mumble" and "whisper" like a ghost. The Hebrew verb translated "whisper" was often used in the Old Testament times for the communication of mediums and spiritists with the dead. This suggests the inhabitants of Jerusalem would mutter as if from the realm of the dead. Thus God would make a mockery of their "covenant with death" (28:15).

In 29:5-8, Isaiah began speaking about God's gracious deliverance of Jerusalem. As history shows, in 701 B.C., the Assyrians destroyed dozens of towns in Judah and seemed bound to finish the job of demolishing Jerusalem. Undoubtedly, the invaders then would have dissolved the nation. But the Lord did not want the Assyrians to go that far. While they were camped around Jerusalem, God miraculously destroyed a large part of the army in one night (see 2 Kings 19:35-36; 2 Chron. 32:21; Isa. 37:36-37). Isaiah prophesied that before this event, at the very moment the invaders were about to destroy Jerusalem, God would suddenly move against them in judgment, and the city would be saved.

Isaiah 29:5 says the enemies would become "like fine dust." Verse 6 uses dramatic imagery to depict the all-powerful Lord's judgment as being accompanied by thunder, an earthquake, a loud noise, a windstorm, and consuming flames of fire (see Exod. 19:16-19; Ps. 18:7-15; Hab. 3:3-7). The prophet aptly compared Jerusalem's deliverance from the attacking "horde" (Isa. 29:7) to a person waking up from a nightmare. In contrast, when the invaders figuratively "awaken" (vs. 8) from the siege, they would feel as though they had dreamed of eating and drinking, but were still hungry and thirsty. Put another way, even though the aggressor was determined to overrun "Mount Zion" (or Jerusalem), they would leave without achieving their goal. In short, they would feel dissatisfied.

After describing the siege and deliverance of Jerusalem, Isaiah again began discussing the deplorable spiritual condition of the city's inhabitants. This was necessary, for it was their sin that would lead God to use the Assyrians to judge His people. Isaiah exhorted the wayward residents to be "stunned and amazed" (vs. 9) concerning the judgment the Lord would bring on them. After all, from a divine perspective, they were completely "blind," "drunk," and staggering. Expressed differently, the chosen people were in a spiritual stupor when it came to heeding the Lord's directives and being sensitive to His will.

B. A Spiritual Blindness: vs. 10

The LORD has brought over you a deep sleep: He has sealed your eyes (the prophets); he has covered your heads (the seers).

Isaiah 29:10 compares sleep to a liquid that the Lord poured out on His wayward people. The consequence of this divine action was spiritual dullness among Jerusalem's residents. Furthermore, He closed the eyes of the prophets and covered the heads of the seers. The parallel way in which the second half of the verse is arranged indicates that all of the city's acclaimed visionaries were spiritually blind. The indictment is that even the most esteemed religious leaders failed to pay attention to what God repeatedly tried to tell them.

The preceding verse is cited in Romans 11:8. In verse 7, Paul explained that the majority of the Israelites had tried to obtain righteousness by keeping God's law. Yet, because no one could be justified by human effort, the chosen people failed to obtain reconciliation with God. In turn, these individuals became "hardened." To illustrate the dire nature of this condition, Paul quoted from Deuteronomy 29:4 and Isaiah 29:10. These verses indicate that Israel's hardening resulted from spiritual drowsiness, judicial blindness, and deafness to the things of God (Rom. 11:8). Consequently, the people became impervious to spiritual truth. Furthermore, this hardening had continued "to this very day" (that is, from Isaiah's time to Paul's day). To make clear the results of divine hardening, Paul appealed to Psalm 69:22-23 (Rom. 11:9-10). The apostle maintained that because the Israelites did not respond to God's truth in repentance, their eyes were darkened and their backs were bent under the heavy weight of their own guilt and punishment.

C. A Refusal to Heed Divine Oracles: vss. 11-12

For you this whole vision is nothing but words sealed in a scroll. And if you give the scroll to someone who can read, and say to him, "Read this, please," he will answer, "I can't; it is sealed." Or if you give the scroll to someone who cannot read, and say, "Read this, please," he will answer, "I don't know how to read."

"Vision" (Isa. 29:11) denotes the prophetic revelation God had given to Isaiah. "Scroll" refers to documents made from sheets of leather, papyrus, or parchment that people joined together in long rolls (typically from 10 to 12 inches wide and as much as 35 feet long). The ends of these documents were then attached to two wooden cylinders and rolled up from left to right. Isaiah declared that his own messages were like a closed book to the rebellious inhabitants of Jerusalem and Judah.

Isaiah imagined a situation in which a scroll containing his prophetic oracles was handed over to a person who could read (for example, a religious leader). Then, when he was politely asked to disclose the document's contents, he would respond that he was unable to do so because he found the scroll to be "sealed." A variant of this scenario involved giving the document to someone else who could not read (for instance, a common person). And when this individual was asked to do so, he would state that he was illiterate (vs. 12). These two imaginary episodes illustrated the refusal of all the Judahites to pay attention to the divine oracles Isaiah declared. The prophet must have found it frustrating to lay out warnings and instructions that the people needed to know, and then to have them spurn him.

II. ISRAEL'S DAY OF RECKONING: ISAIAH 29:13-16

A. Empty Worship: vs. 13

The Lord says: "These people come near to me with their mouth and honor me with their lips, but their hearts are far from me. Their worship of me is made up only of rules taught by men."

Though the residents of Jerusalem and Judah rejected Isaiah's prophecies, they did maintain their religion. The Lord acknowledged that His people declared with their "mouth" (Isa. 29:13) that they were devoted to Him. And "with their lips" they said all sorts of reverent things about Him. But God declared that the people's ritual honoring of Him was a sham. In particular, they were disloyal in their hearts (that is, the fountain of their thoughts, emotions, aspirations, and endeavors). Moreover, their displays of "worship" consisted of humanly devised rituals. Just as the people had spurned Isaiah's oracles, they also refused to turn to the Lord in heartfelt obedience (see Isa. 58:2-5; Hos. 7:14; 8:1-2; 10:1-2; Mic. 3:11).

Centuries later, Jesus applied Isaiah 29:13 to the Pharisees (see Matt. 15:7-9; Mark 7:6-8). The Savior correctly sized up the religious leaders as being "hypocrites." The underlying Greek term originally referred to actors who wore masks on stage as they played different characters. When applied to the Pharisees and scribes, the term meant they were not genuinely religious. They were merely playing a part for all to watch (see James 1:26-27). Jesus, in quoting Isaiah 29:13, declared that even though the Pharisees venerated God with their words, they showed contempt for Him by their thoughts and actions. They made their worship of God a farce by replacing divine commands with humanly constructed injunctions. Jesus was making it clear that it was wrong to ignore the Lord's specific laws and substitute one's own self-generated traditions.

During their captivity in Babylon (605–445 B.C.), the Jews underwent a rebirth of interest in the Mosaic law. At that time, an unwritten but highly developed body of teachings and commentary about the law began to grow up among religious teachers, who were called rabbis. The original intention was good. The teachers wanted to prevent violations of the law. They tried to do this by setting up regulations for all of life, like a protective hedge around the law. These regulations grew generation by generation until they were gathered in a written collection, called the Mishnah, two centuries after Jesus' death. Even during Jesus' life, the tradition had become overvalued, obscuring the law it was meant to safeguard.

B. Divine Judgment: vs. 14

"Therefore once more I will astound these people with wonder upon wonder; the wisdom of the wise will perish, the intelligence of the intelligent will vanish."

In 1446 B.C., the chosen people saw the wonders of God as He delivered them from Egypt. Now the residents of Jerusalem and the inhabitants of Judah would again be astounded with amazing events. There is a bit of irony in Isaiah 29:14, for the marvelous work of God would involve the judgment, not the deliverance, of the Judahites. In short, the Lord would use His awesome power to deal firmly with their rebellion. In this way, He would disprove the alleged prudence of the "wise" and discredit the supposed insight of the "intelligent." The immediate historical context seems to be counsel given by advisers in Judah's royal court advocating that illicit alliances be made with the nation's powerful, pagan neighbors.

In 1 Corinthians 1:19, Paul cited Isaiah 29:14. Previously, in 1 Corinthians 1:18, the apostle stated that the message he proclaimed centered on the Cross. Paul also revealed that though the good news about the Messiah has the power to save lives eternally, to unbelievers it is sheer folly. Moreover, as long as unbelievers reject the Gospel as being foolish, they are doomed to perish (vs. 18). But to those who are saved through their faith in God, the message of the Cross is a demonstration of God's power. Then, in verse 19, Paul quoted from Isaiah 29:14 to point out that the Father used the good news about His Son to destroy the wisdom of the worldly-wise and to annihilate the understanding of those who imagined themselves clever.

C. Deceptive Ways: vss. 15-16

Woe to those who go to great depths to hide their plans from the LORD, who do their work in darkness and think, "Who sees us? Who will know?" You turn things upside down, as if the potter were thought to be like the clay! Shall what is formed say to him who formed it, "He did not make me"? Can the pot say of the potter, "He knows nothing"?

Once again, Isaiah interjected another "woe" (Isa. 29:15). This time the declaration of doom was upon those corrupt leaders and people who in their skewed thinking actually believed they could second guess the Lord and hide their misdeeds from Him. They falsely imagined that by performing their iniquities in secret, they would remain immune from detection and prosecution (see Pss. 10:11; 64:5-6). Isaiah represented the folly of questioning God in the personification of a pot doubting the potter (Isa. 29:16; see 45:9). The point is that God knew all that the wicked were doing and would judge them for their pride and rebellion.

As before, judgment is couched in the context of God's grace. Isaiah 29:17-24 reminds us to look beyond the dark days of Assyria to a time of future restoration for the faithful remnant of Israel. In the future kingdom of the Messiah, the once devastated land would become fertile. Moreover, the wicked would be banished from the Lord's presence. Also, He would elevate His chosen people and their nation to a place of unparalleled prominence.

In Romans 9:20, Paul cited Isaiah 29:16. Previously, in Romans 9:19, the apostle anticipated a question that might surface in his readers' minds. If God hardens whomever He wishes to harden, then how can He hold individuals responsible for their actions? Also, if God's will is irresistible, then such blame appears misplaced. Paul responded in verse 20 by rebuking the arrogant attitude with which these sorts of questions were asked. The apostle did not condemn honest inquiry. Instead, he reprimanded those who sought to escape personal responsibility by placing the blame for their sin upon God.

Discussion Questions

1. What would cause God's people to be "stunned and amazed" (Isa. 29:9)?
2. Why did Judah's religious leaders fail to pay attention to what God repeatedly tried to tell them?
3. In what sense were Isaiah's messages like a closed book to the rebellious inhabitants of Jerusalem and Judah?
4. How can believers avoid elevating humanly devised traditions over God's Word?
5. What sources of spiritual insight from God can you use to grow stronger in your devotion to Him?

Contemporary Application

The problems of the Israelites began when they failed to behave consistently with their profession of faith. They claimed to believe in the one and only living God, yet they were characterized by spiritual insensitivity and rebellion. Also, despite their claims to follow the Lord, they engaged in empty religious rituals and eventually became totally engaged in a pagan lifestyle.

If we as believers are to address the wickedness of society, we must begin by conducting our lives in a way that is consistent with what we claim to believe. It is not enough to verbally confess our faith. We must also proclaim it by the way we live. As with Israel, we cannot expect to please God or escape His disciplinary judgment if we do not obey His Word. The most effective way to wage war against the evil around us is to become people who display our belief in God by obeying Scripture, praying, and trusting God to change our lives as well as the lives of those around us.

We may not be able to instantly change the direction of our nation, but we can influence its future course with each person we lead to Christ. As we proclaim our faith through our lives, others, seeing our hope and love for one another, will be drawn to our Savior.

The Glorious New Creation

Scripture

Background Scripture: *Isaiah 65*
Scripture Lesson: *Isaiah 65:17-21, 23-25*
Key Verse: *"I will create new heavens and a new earth. The
former things will not be remembered, nor will they come to
mind. But be glad and rejoice forever in what I will create."*
Isaiah 65:17-18.
Scripture Lesson for Children: *Isaiah 65:17-21, 23-25*
Key Verse for Children: *"Be glad and rejoice forever in
what [God] will create."* Isaiah 65:18.

Lesson Aim

To affirm that God's people can count on a great
future.

Lesson Setting

Time: 740–700 B.C.
Place: Judah

Lesson Outline

The Glorious New Creation

  I. The Transformation of Creation: Isaiah 65:17-19
    A. *The Promise of New Heavens and a New Earth:
       vs. 17*
    B. *The Command to Rejoice: vs. 18*
    C. *The Elimination of Sorrow: vs. 19*
  II. The Transformation of Life: Isaiah 65:20, 23-25
    A. *The Promise of Longevity: vs. 20*
    B. *The Promise of Fruitfulness and Blessing:
       vss. 21, 23*
    C. *The Promise of Answered Prayer: vs. 24*
    D. *The Promise of Perfect Peace: vs. 25*

Introduction for Adults

Topic: *Nothing's Going to Be the Same*

On May 22, 2011, an extremely powerful tornado struck Joplin, Missouri. The twister leveled nearly a third of the city, killed scores of people, and injured hundreds of others. Amid the tangled remains of large buildings, residential homes, and cars, an elderly man looked at his ruined house and exclaimed, "This was all I had. Now it's gone!"

For many people life is limited to their possessions. They have no life beyond their homes, furniture, and cars. As Christians, we believe there is more to life than mere possessions, but it's hard to define what we mean. Paul got it right when he noted that, through faith in Christ, we become "a new creation" (2 Cor. 5:17). "The old has gone, the new has come!"

This truth explains why we look at everything in life from a new perspective. It's also what Isaiah urged God's people to do. Through the prophet, God gave His promise to create new heavens and a new earth, and a new Jerusalem. In fact, those in new Jerusalem would have long life, profitable work, answers to their prayers, and peace.

Introduction for Youth

Topic: *In with the New!*

A radical change takes place when adolescents trust in Christ. They experience new life. This means the Spirit graciously replaces their fallen human nature with a new one. Their relationship with God is restored; obedience to and dependence on the Lord supplant their rebelliousness and unbelief; and their hatred is exchanged for unconditional love.

For some youth the idea of being given new life sounds bizarre. For others, the advantages of being born again appear too good to be true. Finally, there are individuals who feel smugly comfortable in their life of sin and do not want to change.

The world might scoff at the idea of receiving new life in Christ and the promise of "new heavens and a new earth" (Isa. 65:17). However, saved teens know from God's Word that it is a reality. They also need to know that inner renewal cannot be purchased with money or earned by doing good deeds. The lost must put their faith in Christ in order to experience the new birth.

Concepts for Children

Topic: *Everything Will Be New*

1. God promised that He is making a new heavens and a new earth.
2. What God is making will be filled with joy.
3. Everyone will live in peace.
4. Everyone will feel safe.
5. When people pray, God will answer their prayers.

Lesson Commentary

I. THE TRANSFORMATION OF CREATION: ISAIAH 65:17-19

A. The Promise of New Heavens and a New Earth: vs. 17

"Behold, I will create new heavens and a new earth. The former things will not be remembered, nor will they come to mind."

The Book of Isaiah reveals that God's chosen people had rebelled against Him. Yet the prophet still prayed that God would not be angry with them forever (64:8-9). Isaiah petitioned the Lord to take pity on His people, their nation, and their temple. Isaiah implored God to glorify Himself by allowing the faithful remnant to return to Judah and rebuild its devastated nation (vss. 10-12). In the remaining two chapters of Isaiah we have the grand conclusion to the entire book. The Lord gives His answer to the prayer of His spokesperson. Israel failed to stay close to the Lord, though the people sought Him in a superficial way. So in response to Isaiah's prayer, the Lord declared that He would reveal Himself to the people who had not even sought Him (namely, the Gentiles; 65:1).

God had repeatedly reached out with love to His stubborn and sinful people. Yet they rebelled against Him by offering sacrifices and burning incense to idols (vs. 3). They sat in burial graves to consult the spirits of the dead, and they devoured ceremonially unclean meat (vs. 4). Despite the people's claims of being pious, they were an irritation to the Lord (vs. 5). Yet, in answer to Isaiah's rhetorical question (64:12), God promised to not remain silent. He would punish His people for their rebellion and idolatry, but He would not destroy the entire nation. Just as there might be a few good grapes in a cluster, so there would be a faithful remnant in Israel (65:6-8).

God assured Isaiah that His chosen people would be blessed with many descendants, they would be restored to their homeland (vs. 9), and the entire region would be transformed (vs. 10). Ironically, those who worshiped the pagan gods of "Fortune" (vs. 11) and "Destiny" would meet theirs, dying by the sword, for they spurned God's love and rejected His commandments (vs. 12). In this chapter, the contrasting fates of those who follow God and those who don't is apparent: The all-powerful Lord would bless the upright with joy, abundance, and life; however, He would bring emptiness, anguish, and death to the wicked (vss. 13-16).

Isaiah's final prophecies most likely applied in part to the exiles returned from Babylon. But his language clearly goes beyond any fulfillment in ancient history. For instance, notice that earlier, while prophesying about end-time judgments, Isaiah had said, "The heavens will vanish like smoke, the earth will wear out like a garment" (51:6). Now the prophet recorded God's declaration that in place of the old heavens and earth He would create "new heavens and a new earth" (65:17). So glorious would the new creation be that God said "the former things will not be remembered, nor will they come to mind." Those former things, such as weeping and crying, would give way to new things, including gladness, rejoicing, and delight.

Isaiah 65:17 reminds us of Revelation 21:1, where the apostle John declared that he saw "a new heaven and a new earth." These are total replacements for their old counterparts, which God had destroyed. He evidently did this to eliminate any corrupting presence or influence of sin (see 2 Pet. 3:7, 10-13, which was covered in lesson 13 from last quarter). But John was not thinking merely of a world free of sin and hardness of heart. More importantly, the apostle's vision was of a creation new in all its qualities.

B. The Command to Rejoice: vs. 18

"But be glad and rejoice forever in what I will create, for I will create Jerusalem to be a delight and its people a joy."

The Lord commanded His people to "be glad and rejoice forever" (Isa. 65:18). They were to express joy over what God would create. He pledged to create the new Jerusalem as a place of happiness, and the people inhabiting it would be a source of joy for the community of the redeemed. We find parallel thoughts in Revelation 21:2, which makes mention of "the Holy City, the new Jerusalem," which God sent down out of heaven. The Lord magnificently adorned the new Jerusalem (the bride) for her husband (the groom). The implication here is that the city surpassed the beauty of everything else God had made. It remains unclear to Bible scholars and students whether this is to be taken as a literal city where God's people dwell for all eternity or a symbol of the redeemed community in heaven. In either case, Scripture clearly reveals that a new world is coming, and it will be glorious beyond imagination.

In the ancient Near East, the wedding ceremony usually took place after dark at the bride's house. Prior to the wedding ceremony, the groom and his friends would form a procession and walk to the home of the bride. After the couple was officially married, the procession would return to the home of the groom or his father. As the procession journeyed along a planned route, friends of the groom would join the group and participate in singing, playing musical instruments, and dancing. The bride would wear an ornate dress, expensive jewelry (if she could afford it), and a veil over her face. The groom typically hung a garland of flowers around his neck. Once the procession arrived at its destination, a lavish feast, lasting up to seven days, would begin. Friends would sing love ballads for the couple and share stories about them. Everyone would consume food and drink in generous quantities. At the end of the first day's festivities, the bride and groom would be escorted to their private wedding chamber.

C. The Elimination of Sorrow: vs. 19

"I will rejoice over Jerusalem and take delight in my people; the sound of weeping and of crying will be heard in it no more."

God, too, would find joy in the new creation. He would "rejoice over Jerusalem, and take delight in [His] people" (Isa. 65:19). What a contrast this is with God's previous dismay over His chosen nation. In the holy city, no one would ever again hear "the sound of weeping and of crying." In the New Testament, John revealed that in the eternal state, God will permanently dwell, or tabernacle, among the redeemed of all ages. They will be His people, and He will be their God. Also, five scourges of human existence will not exist in the eternal state—tears, death, sorrow, crying, and pain. The new order of things will eliminate all these forms of sadness (Rev. 21:3-4).

The apostle Peter, too, mentioned that Christians await with expectancy the new heavens and new earth of the end times (2 Pet. 3:13). He also wrote, "So then, dear friends, since you are looking forward to this, make every effort to be found spotless, blameless and at peace with [the Lord]" (vs. 14). Down through the centuries, the hope for new heavens and a new earth should be a purifying factor in our lives. The return of the Son is the basis for the Father's creation of the new heavens and the new earth described in Isaiah 65:17-25.

In the New Testament, three Greek words are used when referring to the second advent of Christ: (1) *Parousia* carries the ideas of "presence" and "coming," especially the official visit of a person of high rank (for example, a king or emperor). The word implies personal presence and excited states (see 1 Thess. 4:15; 2 Thess. 2:8); (2) *Apokalypsis* means "revelation" or "disclosure." In connection with end-time events, it refers to the unveiling of Christ at His second coming. This may suggest the suddenness of His return (see 1 Cor. 1:7; 2 Thess. 1:7; 1 Pet. 4:13); and (3) *Epiphaneia* means "appearing" or "appearance" and refers to a visible manifestation of a hidden divinity. In Titus 2:13, Christ's "appearing" is said to be "glorious." This idea of divine glory is taken one step further in 2 Thessalonians 2:8, where *epiphaneia* is translated "splendor."

II. THE TRANSFORMATION OF LIFE: ISAIAH 65:20, 23-25

A. The Promise of Longevity: vs. 20

"Never again will there be in it an infant who lives but a few days, or an old man who does not live out his years; he who dies at a hundred will be thought a mere youth; he who fails to reach a hundred will be considered accursed."

In Isaiah 65:20-25, the prophet described what the new creation would be like for God's people. Expositors differ over whether these verses refer to the heavenly state (the metaphorical view) or to a future period in which Christ will rule on earth (the literal view). Regardless of whether one takes the passage metaphorically or literally, it contains four promises of blessing.

Those who would live in the newly created Jerusalem (1) would have long lives, (2) would not labor in vain, (3) would be speedily answered by God when they pray, and (4) would live in an environment without hostility. Seen together, these blessings apparently indicate that the effects of the Fall would be reversed in the new heavens and new earth and new Jerusalem. The first blessing is longevity (vs. 20). The Old Testament reports that lives stretching to hundreds of years was the rule in early human history. Similarly, in the new creation, infant mortality would drop to zero; all would live to adulthood. Moreover, a tombstone recording a life span of 100 years would not be remarkable for denoting a long life, as in our day, but for denoting a short life.

In John's description of the great heavenly city, he referred to the tree of life, first mentioned in the Book of Genesis (Rev. 22:2; see Gen. 2:9). In fact, many themes introduced in Genesis find their fulfillment in Revelation. In Genesis: the sun is created; Satan is victorious; sin enters the human race; people run and hide from God; people are cursed; tears are shed with sorrow for sin; the garden and earth are cursed; paradise is lost; and people are doomed to death. In Revelation: the sun is not needed; Satan is defeated; sin is banished; people are invited to live with God forever; the curse is removed; no more sin, no more tears or sorrow; God's city is glorified; the earth is made new; paradise is regained; death is defeated; and believers live forever with the Lord.

B. The Promise of Fruitfulness and Blessing: vss. 21, 23

They will build houses and dwell in them; they will plant vineyards and eat their fruit. . . . They will not toil in vain or bear children doomed to misfortune; for they will be a people blessed by the LORD, they and their descendants with them. "

The second blessing in the new creation is profitable toil (Isa. 65:21-23). The people of Isaiah's time lived and died with the vagaries of agricultural life. Droughts and pestilence caused great damage. The pagans prayed to fertility and weather gods and goddesses. But the Lord's chosen people were supposed to trust Him to supply all their needs. After the Fall, God's curse on humanity included the declaration that labor to earn food would be difficult (see Gen. 3:17-19). In the new creation, people would continue to work, but they would have no worries about not receiving the fruits of their labor. Others (perhaps unscrupulous rich people or invaders) would never take what they have earned with their own hands. Generation after generation, the people of God would be blessed.

Isaiah related these truths in terms that people living in his day could understand. For instance, God's people would live in the houses they built and eat the fruit of their vineyards (Isa. 65:21). The Lord would prevent invaders from taking these from them. In fact, God would enable His people to live a long life and enjoy the "works of their hands" (vs. 22). The labor of the redeemed community would not be in vain, and their children would not be "doomed to misfortune" (vs. 23). After all, the Lord would bless them and their children with safety, health, and prosperity. Such blessings would be both physical and spiritual in nature.

Both the books of Isaiah and Revelation are characterized by evocative, symbolic descriptions of future events. There are at least three reasons for this. First, the authors sought to convey, rather than conceal, truth. Symbols proved to be an effective means to illuminate, clarify, and explain what was profound and mysterious. Second, the authors sought to portray with vividness the issues at stake and to drive home with greater force the moral and spiritual truths of their respective messages. Third, the authors used various symbols to address the concerns of their beleaguered faith communities. The authors wanted God's people to see that there is more to life than what one experiences physically. In fact, the spiritual realm is the basis for the historical order of existence.

C. The Promise of Answered Prayer: vs. 24

"Before they call I will answer; while they are still speaking I will hear."

The third blessing in the new creation is answered prayer (Isa. 65:24). In the Garden of Eden, Adam and Eve enjoyed the immediate presence and conversation of the Lord. Similarly, while people in the new creation are praying, even before they make the request, God would answer them. This describes a close fellowship between God and people. Such is echoed in Revelation 22:3-4. The apostle John noted that in the new creation the Father and the Son will be seated on their thrones, and the redeemed will worship and serve them continually. God will establish unbroken communion with His people, and He will claim them as His own.

D. The Promise of Perfect Peace: vs. 25

"The wolf and the lamb will feed together, and the lion will eat straw like the ox, but dust will be the serpent's food. They will neither harm nor destroy on all my holy mountain," says the LORD.

Of noteworthy mention is the fourth blessing in the new creation, namely, peace (Isa. 65:25). The Fall introduced hostility into the world, and murder was committed by the next generation. But in the new creation even the animals would stop preying on one another. Perfect harmony would reign. We see this expectation for wellness and wholeness repeated in the New Testament. God promised to give water from the life-giving fountain to everyone who was thirsty (Rev. 21:6). This pledge is a vivid reminder of the refreshment and satisfaction believers would enjoy in heaven. In the eternal state, God would satisfy the yearnings of the soul. This assurance was grounded in the Lord's own nature. Those who overcame in this life would receive an eternal inheritance and an eternal relationship. They would be the eternal children of the eternal God (vs. 7).

In the new Jerusalem, God would be worshiped face-to-face. The city would be a cosmopolitan place, where redeemed humanity in all its cultural diversity would live together in peace. God would vindicate the faith of the redeemed by not permitting anything immoral or wicked to enter the holy city (vss. 22-27). In previous chapters of Isaiah, the prophet had foretold both the demise of Judah and the exile of the nation's inhabitants to Babylon. But he also foresaw their return to Judah. Beyond that, Isaiah saw the glorious future awaiting all the redeemed, namely, intimacy and unbroken communion with the Lord. It's no wonder the apostle Paul declared, "I consider that our present sufferings are not worth comparing with the glory that will be revealed in us" (Rom. 8:18). Currently, we see the world as it is—physically decaying and spiritually infected with sin. But Christians do not need to be pessimistic, for they have hope for future glory. They look forward to the new heavens and new earth that God has promised, and they wait for God's new order that pledges to free the world of sin, sickness, and evil.

Discussion Questions

1. What do you think will happen to this present creation when God brings the new heavens and new earth into existence?
2. What sort of emotions will prevail among the inhabitants of the new Jerusalem?
3. How will the lives of the redeemed be different in the future time of glory?
4. In light of these truths, how might the believers' idea of God sometimes be too small?
5. How can the hope for a new heavens and a new earth become a purifying factor in your life as a Christian?

Contemporary Application

As believers, eternal life does not begin when we die and go to heaven. It starts here and now. God wants us to enjoy to the fullest extent the new vistas of joy, satisfaction, and fruitfulness that the presence of His indwelling Holy Spirit makes possible.

Once we've put our faith in Christ, we are immediately forgiven and redeemed. So we have God's power within us to bring about an amazing transformation in our character and conduct. And that's just a foretaste of the glorious future that awaits us in the eternal state.

Because God has so richly blessed us, we naturally desire to commit ourselves to His cause, both in the present and in the future. We enthusiastically renounce sin and urge others to join us. It's a choice for life, not death. That's why we proclaim the Gospel and implore the lost to accept its message.

Most of all, we give glory to God for the wonderful things He has in store for His spiritual children. That, in essence, is Isaiah's message: The meaning of life and the purpose for which we were created is to glorify God and to exist in His glory. So let us choose life!

Joyful Worship Restored

DEVOTIONAL READING

Matthew 23:29-39

DAILY BIBLE READINGS

Monday June 24
*Matthew 23:29-39 Jesus'
Lament over Jerusalem*

Tuesday June 25
*Jeremiah 7:30–8:3 The
Coming Judgment*

Wednesday June 26
*2 Kings 24:1-12 Jerusalem
Falls to the Babylonians*

Thursday June 27
*2 Chronicles 36:15-21 The
Destruction of Jerusalem*

Friday June 28
*Ezra 1:1-8 Rebuild a House
for God*

Saturday June 29
*Ezra 2:64-70 The People
Respond*

Sunday June 30
*Ezra 3:1-7 Restoring the
Worship of God*

Scripture

Background Scripture: *Ezra 1:1–3:7*
Scripture Lesson: *Ezra 3:1-7*
Key Verse: *In accordance with what is written, they celebrated
the Feast of Tabernacles with the required number of burnt
offerings prescribed for each day. Ezra 3:4.*
Scripture Lesson for Children: *Ezra 3:1-7*
Key Verse for Children: *They built the altar on its foundation and sacrificed burnt offerings on it to the LORD, both the
morning and evening sacrifices. Ezra 3:3.*

Lesson Aim

To recognize God as our ultimate source of power to
live for Him, even in the most challenging of circumstances.

Lesson Setting

Time: 537 B.C.
Place: Jerusalem

Lesson Outline

Joyful Worship Restored
    I. Rebuilding the Altar: Ezra 3:1-3
        A. *The Assembly: vs. 1*
        B. *The Priests: vs. 2*
        C. *The Sacrifices: vs. 3*
        D. *The Feast of Tabernacles: vs. 4*
        E. *The Observance of Sacrifices and Festivals: vs. 5*
   II. Rebuilding the Temple: Ezra 3:6-7
        A. *The Need for a Temple: vs. 6*
        B. *The Building Materials: vs. 7*

Introduction for Adults

Topic: *Celebrating What Is Meaningful*

When their church's minister of worship and music resigned, Craig and Jackie agreed to fill in until a new person could be found. "How hard can it be?" Craig told his wife. "We just pick some hymns and choruses that go with the pastor's sermon theme, arrange for soloists, and lead the congregation." However, after the couple's first Sunday as worship leaders, Craig wasn't too sure.

"Did you notice their faces?" Jackie asked after the worship service. Craig nodded. "I did. They didn't look like they were worshiping. It felt like we were just up there going through the motions." "Exactly," Jackie affirmed. "We did everything that the former worship minister did, but the spirit wasn't there." The couple promised themselves that the next week they would go into the worship service with prayerful hearts and a reverent spirit of their own. They also decided not to worry about how all the logistics of the service were going to fall into place.

As we discover from this week's lesson, God doesn't expect His people to be flawless in their praise or even to sing supposedly "perfect" songs. Instead, as the Jews returning from exile in Babylon did, He wants us to come into His presence with the right hearts, that is, hearts fully prepared to follow His will and offer Him meaningful praise (see Ezra 3:4-6).

Introduction for Youth

Topic: *Let's Get Ready to Celebrate!*

"If the Lord came to many of our congregations today, He would sadly feel out-of-place because what we have today in most cases are not churches but 'restaurants,'" contends the writer of *Africans Reaching Africa* newsletter. The menus of churches, he explained, can become heavy on desserts and light on the meat of the Word.

It's possible for a congregation of believers to stray from its mission of being a worshipful, God-centered house of praise. In contrast would be the Jews who returned to Judah from exile in Babylon. Rather than create an overindulgent smorgasbord of programs, they worshiped the Lord through heartfelt sacrifice and celebration (see Ezra 3:2-4). Likewise, regardless of how young or old we are, the same should be true of the worship we offer to God.

Concepts for Children

Topic: *A Joyous Return*

1. God's people returned to Judah to live.
2. God's people gathered in Jerusalem.
3. God's people built an altar.
4. God's people offered sacrifices on the altar.
5. God is pleased when we obey Him in everything we do.

Lesson Commentary

I. REBUILDING THE ALTAR: EZRA 3:1-3

A. The Assembly: vs. 1

When the seventh month came and the Israelites had settled in their towns, the people assembled as one man in Jerusalem.

Ezra and Nehemiah were originally placed together as one book. In the Hebrew Bible, this document preceded Chronicles, which was the last of the historical books. Esther was grouped with Song of Songs, Ruth, Lamentations, and Ecclesiastes—five small books that are read annually on Jewish holidays. The Song of Songs belongs to the Passover observance, Ruth to Pentecost, Ecclesiastes to the Feast of Tabernacles, Lamentations to the anniversary of the destruction of Jerusalem, and Esther to Purim.

Prior to the events narrated in Ezra and Nehemiah, God had foretold 70 years of captivity for His people because they had persisted, for centuries, in faithlessness to His covenant (see Jer. 25:11-12; 29:10). Jerusalem had suffered minor deportations in 605 and 597 B.C. before Nebuchadnezzar destroyed the city and temple and carried away all the leading families in 586 B.C. Then, in 539 B.C., Cyrus the Persian conquered Babylon, and the Lord began the gracious work of restoring His chosen people to the land of promise. The first full year of Cyrus's reign was 538 B.C. (Ezra 1:1). The Persian emperor instituted a policy of resettling captive peoples in their homelands and promoting native religions in order to gain the favor of every deity everywhere. Cyrus thought he was helping himself, but all the time it was the Lord moving the heart of the Persian emperor to fulfill the restoration promises of Israelite prophets.

The monarch sent heralds to shout his proclamations in the language of each major city of the Persian Empire, which stretched from Egypt and Asia Minor to India. Printed versions followed later, worded in Aramaic, the language of international affairs, to be posted and stored in archives. The version found in Ezra 1:2-4 is worded in Hebrew, while the version quoted in 6:3-5 is written in Aramaic. Cyrus worded his religious tolerance decrees in the language of the particular faith involved. He identified the Lord as "the God of heaven" (1:2), which had become a popular title among the Jews of the Exile as they realized that the Lord controlled much more than the land of Israel. Jewish tradition says that prominent Babylonian Jews showed Cyrus the prophecies of Isaiah, which named him as the shepherd of Israel in captivity (see Isa. 44:28; 45:1). In any case, the emperor was correct when he said that the God of heaven had appointed him a role in rebuilding the temple in Jerusalem.

Cyrus granted every follower of the Lord, in any part of his empire, the right to return to Jerusalem for the purpose of rebuilding the Lord's temple (Ezra 1:3). The emperor's statement of blessing on the Jews who would return to Jerusalem identified God by name ("the LORD") and connected Him to all the people of Israel—not just the tribe of Judah, in whose territory was Jerusalem, the city of God's temple. Finally, Cyrus's proclamation invited all his subjects throughout his realm to participate in rebuilding the Jerusalem temple by giving to those who would return contributions of money, goods, and livestock (vs. 4). When the emperor called those who were returning "survivors," he introduced the prophets' term for a "remnant" into his decree (see Isa. 10:20-22; Zeph. 3:13).

Just as the Lord had stirred up the heart of Cyrus to decree the return from exile, so He stirred the hearts of many families from Judah and Benjamin and from the priests and Levites to go to Jerusalem and rebuild the temple (Ezra 1:5). Probably most Jews remained in their long-established homes in Babylon and other Persian provinces, but they made generous freewill gifts of precious metals, goods, and livestock to the returning exiles (vs. 6). The emperor also restored to the party of returning exiles all the utensils and service vessels that Nebuchadnezzar had plundered from Solomon's temple and warehoused in the temple of Marduk in Babylon (Ezra 1:7; see 2 Kings 24:13; 25:13-15; Dan. 5:1-2).

Cyrus's treasurer, Mithredath, handed over the temple treasures along with a detailed inventory to Sheshbazzar, "the prince of Judah" (Ezra 1:8). This particular title "prince" does not necessarily imply descent from royalty. Sheshbazzar probably was a Jewish deputy of the governor of the Persian province of Samaria, from which a new province, Judah, was being carved to accommodate the returning exiles. The partial inventory of Ezra 1:9-10 likely lists the most significant temple items restored to the exiles. The number of special items adds up to 2,499 out of the total of 5,400 returned temple articles (vs. 11). Sheshbazzar took responsibility for personally delivering the temple treasures to Jerusalem.

Ezra 2 contains a detailed list of the groups of exiles who came back to Jerusalem and rebuilt the temple. Under the initiative of Jeshua (the high priest or representative religious leader) and Zerubbabel (the governor or representative political leader), the first cluster progressively journeyed to their homeland from 537–516 B.C. The census recorded in this chapter may be divided as follows: leaders and families (vss. 1-35); priests and Levites (verses 36-42); temple laborers (vss. 43-58); individuals who had inadequate proof of their family history (vss. 59-63); servants and animals (vss. 64-67). Incidentally, the names Nehemiah and Mordecai (vs. 2) were common among the exiled Jews and thus should not be identified with the later historical figures by the same names.

Key family leaders voluntarily gave a variety of items that would be essential to the restoration of the temple in Jerusalem (Ezra 2:68-69; Neh. 7:70-72). The pioneers then eventually resettled in the places where their ancestors had once lived (Ezra 2:70). The memory of these places had not been dimmed despite the tragedy of extended exile in a foreign land. This chapter is significant because it serves as a tangible reminder of God's dependability. It demonstrates that the Lord was faithful in bringing back to Jerusalem a committed remnant from captivity. It is a sterling testimony to God's watchful care over His people despite seven decades of their living in exile.

Zerubbabel is credited with leading the exiles to rebuild the temple in 537 B.C. Though Sheshbazzar was the Persian-appointed leader of the Jews, Zerubbabel and Jeshua, the high priest, were considered the true leaders of the remnant. Some scholars have speculated that Zerubbabel and Sheshbazzar were the same person, but this is highly improbable. Zerubbabel was likely born during Judah's exile in Babylon. He was a grandson of Jehoiachin, one of the last Davidic kings, who had died in Babylon (see 1 Chron. 3:17-19). Jehoiachin had been honored in exile (see 2 Kings 25:27-30), and it was natural that his descendant would be highly respected in the Jewish community. Through the mouth of the Old Testament prophet Haggai, the Lord said, "I will take you, my servant Zerubbabel son of Shealtiel . . . and I will make you like my signet ring, for I have chosen you" (Hag. 2:23). On the basis of this prophecy, some scholars have speculated that the Jews attempted to make Zerubbabel king. There is no evidence of this happening, however, one way or the other.

In Ezra 3:1, reference is made to the "seventh month" of the Jewish year, namely, Tishri. The latter extended from about mid-September to mid-October. Several important sacred observances and customs occurred during Tishri (for example, the Feast of Trumpets, the Day of Atonement, and the Feast of Tabernacles or Booths; see Lev. 23:23-43). The year was not specific. Thus, it might have been during the first year of Cyrus (538 B.C.) or his second year (537 B.C.). Most scholars favor the second option. The returnees had been in their homeland for about three months. During that period, they settled in the cities surrounding Jerusalem. Before any more time passed, however, the Jews wanted to reestablish the proper worship of God. So the pioneers assembled as a group in Jerusalem (Ezra 3:1).

B. The Priests: vs. 2

Then Jeshua son of Jozadak and his fellow priests and Zerubbabel son of Shealtiel and his associates began to build the altar of the God of Israel to sacrifice burnt offerings on it, in accordance with what is written in the Law of Moses the man of God.

Under the initiative of Jeshua and Zerubbabel as well as their associates, the people gradually built an altar for worshiping the Lord. This task was the first step in their efforts to rebuild the Jerusalem temple. Even as Abraham and Joshua before them, the exiles marked their entrance into the promised land with the construction of an altar to the Lord (see Gen. 12:7; Josh. 8:30-31). In Ezra 3:2, Jeshua was mentioned first because this was primarily a religious matter. The group offered sacrifices in accordance with the Mosaic law. They remembered Moses as God's official representative and messenger.

Either a bull, ram, or male bird (for instance, a dove or young pigeon) without any defect could be used for a sacrifice. When offered, it was to be entirely consumed on the altar (see Lev. 1; 6:8-13; 8:18-21; 16:24). The burnt offerings served several purposes: a voluntary act of worship; atonement for unintentional sin in general; and an expression of devotion, commitment, and complete surrender to God. All of the activities associated with the altar reminded God's people that it was necessary to approach the Lord through the provision of an acceptable atoning sacrifice.

In ancient times, altars were constructed of various materials. The oldest altars were either made out of mud brick or were simply mounds of dirt. The Hebrew people generally used uncut stones for their altars, since to place any hewn stone on an altar symbolized defilement (see Exod. 20:24-25; Deut. 27:5). In the court of Solomon's temple was an altar made out of bronze. It measured about 30 feet in length, about 15 feet in height, and had some type of horns at the corners (see 1 Kings 1:50-51; 2:28-29). There was also an altar made out of gold located just outside the Most Holy Place in the temple (see 7:48). Altars were used for the presentation of sacrifices to God (or to pagan deities). These sacrifices were usually animals. In fact, the Hebrew word for "altar" means "place of slaughter." Nevertheless, fruit or grain was also offered for sacrifice at these altars.

C. The Sacrifices: vs. 3

Despite their fear of the peoples around them, they built the altar on its foundation and sacrificed burnt offerings on it to the LORD, both the morning and evening sacrifices.

The group of returnees succeeded in setting the altar on its base (Ezra 3:3). They did this despite a lingering fear over the presence of non-Jews in the area. Once the altar was finished, God's people sacrificed burnt offerings on it at sunrise and sunset (see Exod. 29:38-42; Num. 28:3-8). This stands as a tribute to the Jews' wholehearted trust in the Lord, despite their apprehensions about living among their pagan neighbors (see Ps. 62:6-8).

D. The Feast of Tabernacles: vs. 4

Then in accordance with what is written, they celebrated the Feast of Tabernacles with the required number of burnt offerings prescribed for each day.

The Jews performed every aspect of their worship in strict accordance with God's Word (Ezra 3:4). Perhaps they wanted to avoid bringing the Lord's displeasure through some violation of the law. God's people observed the Feast of Tabernacles (or Booths, Ingathering). This was typically done between September and October, five days after the Day of Atonement. Tabernacles involved a week of celebration for the harvest, as well as living in booths and offering sacrifices.

The festival was intended to commemorate the journey from Egypt to Canaan and to give thanks for the productivity of Canaan. God's people offered the right number of sacrifices for each day of the festival. Through this celebration, the Jews memorialized their successful journey from Mesopotamia to Palestine. This time it was comparable to a second exodus from a second bondage to carve out a home amid hostile neighbors. The returnees gave thanks for God's abundant provision and protection, and they expressed their gratitude for experiencing a safe return.

E. The Observance of Sacrifices and Festivals: vs. 5

After that, they presented the regular burnt offerings, the New Moon sacrifices and the sacrifices for all the appointed sacred feasts of the LORD, as well as those brought as freewill offerings to the LORD.

The Jews also reestablished all the other various sacrifices, sacred seasons, and feasts associated with the temple (Ezra 3:5). This included the new moon festival. This religious holiday occurred at the beginning of each new month. Through the offering of special sacrifices and the blowing of trumpets, the Jews set apart this time of observance. During the festival, all forms of work and activity were discontinued.

II. REBUILDING THE TEMPLE: EZRA 3:6-7

A. The Need for a Temple: vs. 6

On the first day of the seventh month they began to offer burnt offerings to the LORD, though the foundation of the LORD's temple had not yet been laid.

Fifteen days before the Feast of Tabernacles actually began, the priests had started to sacrifice "burnt offerings" (Ezra 3:6) to God. While the sacrifices and festive seasons of Israel had been restored, the foundation of the Lord's temple had not yet been laid (Ezra 3:6). This was an important matter, for God wanted His people to rebuild the temple. This house of worship would enable them to properly focus their minds and hearts on the Lord. From the preceding information, we can surmise that God's people were sincere and determined to reestablish the proper worship of God in His holy city. They recognized that, while having a sanctuary would have been desirable, it wasn't essential at this point. Be that as it may, the Jews' commitment to rebuilding the temple continued to be strong.

B. The Building Materials: vs. 7

Then they gave money to the masons and carpenters, and gave food and drink and oil to the people of Sidon and Tyre, so that they would bring cedar logs by sea from Lebanon to Joppa, as authorized by Cyrus king of Persia.

God's people allocated funds to purchase building materials and to pay laborers to construct the temple. Specifically, the Jews hired "masons and carpenters" (Ezra 3:7). The people also sent grain, wine, and olive oil to the cities of "Sidon and Tyre" as payment for cedar trees. These logs were bound into ocean-going rafts and floated down the Mediterranean coast from Byblos in Lebanon to Joppa, which served as port for Jerusalem. All this activity was in accordance with Cyrus's decree. This king had inherited the throne of Anshan, a region in eastern Elam, from his father in 559 B.C. It was evident from the beginning of Cyrus's reign that the king was ambitious. One of his first actions was to increase his territory by unifying the

Persian people. And then, in 550 B.C., he attacked and conquered the region of Astyages.

Even with a vast area already under his control, Cyrus was still determined to expand his power by conquering other kingdoms. So he made an alliance with Babylon against Media, a large but weakly ruled kingdom north of Babylon. He succeeded in subjugating Media and then turned his attention west, to Lydia. In 546 B.C. this, too, came under his control. And in the east, Cyrus extended his kingdom to the borders of India. By 539 B.C. Cyrus was ready to deal with the fertile plains of Babylon. His takeover there was relatively peaceful because the Babylonian people were dissatisfied with their own ruler. They welcomed Cyrus as a liberator.

Discussion Questions

1. What set of circumstances led to the Jewish exiles returning to their homeland?
2. What respective roles did the religious and civil leaders play in rebuilding the altar?
3. As the returnees offered sacrifices, why did they think it was important for them to follow the instructions in the Mosaic law?
4. In what ways has God recently shown Himself faithful to you?
5. How might you discern whether the Lord wants you to attempt a new beginning in some area of your life?

Contemporary Application

First steps are often the most difficult. Although the Jewish exiles had been released from captivity, hard work faced them, especially if they were to fulfill the command of King Cyrus to rebuild the temple in Jerusalem. Obviously, the Jews lacked some building materials, but before they started to gather the necessary resources, they took time to resume their sacrifices as prescribed by the laws of Moses.

The people also had to overcome fear of attacks from antagonists in the surrounding area. The returnees courageously overcame their fears and then they offered sacrifices to God. This must have been a powerful witness to their pagan neighbors. After all, many of them possibly resented the worship of Yahweh, and many probably disliked the idea of sharing the land of Judah and Jerusalem with God's people.

There are times when we will be apprehensive about a situation we're facing. We can be encouraged by knowing that as we pray for God's will to be done, He will watch over us. Furthermore, He will move hearts to accomplish His plans and purposes. We should also not ignore when He speaks to our own hearts, especially as opportunities to join in His work come our way.

Temple Restored

DEVOTIONAL READING

Psalm 66:1-12

DAILY BIBLE READINGS

Monday July 1
2 Chronicles 2:1-9 A Great and Wonderful House

Tuesday July 2
1 Kings 8:14-21 Building a House for God's Name

Wednesday July 3
1 Kings 8:22-30 My Name Shall Be There

Thursday July 4
Matthew 21:10-16 A House of Prayer

Friday July 5
Psalm 66:1-12 Make a Joyful Noise to God

Saturday July 6
Psalm 5 Lead Me in Your Righteousness

Sunday July 7
Ezra 3:8-13 Tears of Joy

Scripture

Background Scripture: *Ezra 3:8-13*

Scripture Lesson: *Ezra 3:8-13*

Key Verse: *All the people gave a great shout of praise to the LORD, because the foundation of the house of the LORD was laid.* Ezra 3:11.

Scripture Lesson for Children: *Ezra 3:8-13*

Key Verse for Children: *All the people gave a great shout of praise to the LORD, because the foundation of the house of the LORD was laid.* Ezra 3:11.

Lesson Aim

To remember the past but enjoy God's present.

Lesson Setting

Time: 536 B.C.
Place: Jerusalem

Lesson Outline

Temple Restored

  I. Getting Organized: Ezra 3:8-9
    A. Beginning the Work: vs. 8a
    B. Appointing Supervisors: vss. 8b-9
  II. Laying the Foundation: Ezra 3:10-13
    A. Offering Praise: vss. 10-11
    B. Differing Responses: vss. 12-13

Introduction for Adults

Topic: *Finding Joy in Restoration*

God calls us to lay many foundations in our lives. Some of them are for houses, churches, schools, office buildings, and new factories. Others are for the long-term security of our lives—spiritual foundations that begin with our expressions of joyful commitment to the Lord.

As the returnees to Judah demonstrated in rebuilding the Jerusalem temple (see Ezra 3:8-11), secure foundations are built with faith, prayer, praise, Bible study, witness, and service. Whatever happens in our homes, churches, and communities, we can find stability and hope in God, for He is the anchor of our souls.

Sometimes we neglect our spiritual foundations. Erosion sets in because we have not kept the Lord first in our hearts. This calls for renewal and recommitment. We should take the lead in spiritual renewal in our homes and churches. Then our strong faith will be a joyful witness and encouragement to others (see vs. 13).

Introduction for Youth

Topic: *Let the Good Times Roll!*

Some adolescents tend to separate the Lord's work from His worship. They think worship is what they do on Sunday morning and work (or evangelism) is what they do during the week.

Though not every saved teen actually does evangelism, most seem to feel it is far more important than worship. They think worship is easy—just sit back in the pews and enjoy the emotional excitement generated by the service. But many teens probably feel guilty for not witnessing.

The fact is, we worship God for the very things our witnessing proclaims. And a heartfelt worship of God helps to strengthen the spiritual foundation of our lives. As the Jews sang in Jerusalem, they declared, "He is good; his love to Israel endures forever" (Ezra 3:11). From this we see that God's goodness and mercy are the essence of our spiritual foundation.

Concepts for Children

Topic: *Celebrating a New Beginning*

1. God's people began the work of rebuilding their temple.
2. God's people chose several people to be in charge of the job.
3. God's people worked together to lay the foundation of the temple.
4. God's people thanked Him for helping them do a good job.
5. God also wants us to thank Him because He loves us.

Lesson Commentary

I. GETTING ORGANIZED: EZRA 3:8-9

A. Beginning the Work: vs. 8a

In the second month of the second year after their arrival at the house of God in Jerusalem, Zerubbabel son of Shealtiel, Jeshua son of Jozadak and the rest of their brothers (the priests and the Levites and all who had returned from the captivity to Jerusalem) began the work.

Ancient Jewish and the oldest Christian traditions assigned the authorship of Ezra and Nehemiah to Ezra. Many contemporary scholars continue to support the view that Ezra also wrote the books of Chronicles. Included in the evidence that supports this view is the fact that the last two verses of 2 Chronicles and the first two verses of Ezra are virtually identical. Ezra may have done this to make a smooth chronological flow between the two books. Some scholars have suggested that a "Chronicler," perhaps a disciple of Ezra, brought together the memoirs of Judah's kings, Ezra, and Nehemiah to compose 1 and 2 Chronicles, Ezra, and Nehemiah.

The books of Ezra and Nehemiah present the history of God's people during the years following the destruction of Jerusalem and its temple (586 B.C.). These, together with the prophecies of Haggai and Zechariah (both dated about 520 B.C.), comprise the main Hebrew records of those years. We learn from these ancient, inspired documents that the return of the exiles from Babylonian captivity to Palestine came in three separate stages. The first group went to restore the temple (starting around 537 B.C.; see Ezra 1–3). The work that began then was interrupted for some years (see 4:5-7, 23), but was resumed at the encouragement of the prophets Haggai and Zechariah (see 5:1-2) and completed around 516 B.C. The second return took place around 458 B.C. under Ezra, who called for reform and a return to covenant obligations (see Ezra 7–10). Nehemiah led the third group of returnees (444 B.C.), and spearheaded the rebuilding of Jerusalem's walls.

In last week's lesson, we learned that policies enacted by Cyrus permitted the Jews to return to their homeland from exile in Babylon (see Ezra 1–2). We also found out about the efforts the returnees made to rebuild the altar in Jerusalem (see 3:1-5). While this was a noteworthy achievement, God's people had not yet laid the foundation of His temple (vs. 6). The initial step in dealing with this shortcoming was for the Jews to purchase building materials and to pay laborers to construct the temple (vs. 7).

The next step was to organize the lengthy and complex building operation. Verse 8 reveals that it was under the initiative of Zerubbabel and Jeshua, as well as their associates and fellow Jews, that construction on the temple finally began. This was probably the midspring (that is, about mid-April to mid-May) of 536 B.C. The event corresponded with the timing of Solomon's groundbreaking in 966 B.C., some 430 years earlier (see 2 Chron. 3:1-2). In Ezra 3:8, Zerubbabel was mentioned first because this was initially a civil matter with religious significance.

B. Appointing Supervisors: vss. 8b-9

Appointing Levites twenty years of age and older to supervise the building of the house of the LORD. Jeshua and his sons and brothers and Kadmiel and his sons (descendants of Hodaviah) and the sons of Henadad and their sons and brothers—all Levites—joined together in supervising those working on the house of God.

The leaders gave Levites who were over the age of 20 the responsibility to supervise the rebuilding of the temple (Ezra 3:8). In earlier situations, 30 and 25 (respectively) had been the minimum ages for Levitical activity (see Num. 4:3; 8:24). From this information we see that the exilic band did not include an abundance of Levites. The supervising Levites fell into three groups. The clans of Jeshua and Kadmiel were mentioned in the roster of exiles (see Ezra 2:40). The descendants of Henadad are also included among the Levites in Nehemiah's time who built the wall of Jerusalem and sealed the covenant (3:9; see Neh. 3:18, 24; 10:9).

II. LAYING THE FOUNDATION: EZRA 3:10-13

A. Offering Praise: vss. 10-11

When the builders laid the foundation of the temple of the LORD, the priests in their vestments and with trumpets, and the Levites (the sons of Asaph) with cymbals, took their places to praise the LORD, as prescribed by David king of Israel. With praise and thanksgiving they sang to the LORD: "He is good; his love to Israel endures forever." And all the people gave a great shout of praise to the LORD, because the foundation of the house of the LORD was laid.

Evidently, it did not take long for the builders to complete the foundation of the Lord's temple. Next, God's people commemorated the momentous occasion. The priests, who were ceremonially dressed in their robes, got trumpets. Instead of the traditional ram's horn, "trumpets" (Ezra 3:10) refers to clarionlike instruments that were long, straight, and metallic. Also, the Levites (the sons of Asaph) obtained cymbals. After taking their places, they thanked and praised God for His abundant provision.

Every action was done in strict accordance with the pattern of worship established for the Levites by David and the precedent set by Solomon when he dedicated his completed temple (see 1 Chron. 6:31-49; 2 Chron. 5:13). The people worshiped God for who He is (namely, His personal attributes and characteristics) and thanked Him for what He does (namely, His presence, power, provisions, and preservation). These emphases are seen in the responsive chorus. The returnees praised God for His kindness and His unfailing love to them even after 70 years of captivity. The entire assembly was united in applauding God for enabling it to lay the temple foundation (Ezra 3:11).

In the biblical era, there were three orders in the hierarchy of priests: the high priests, priests, and Levites. Whereas the Levites were subordinate sanctuary officials who supervised the minor duties of the temple, the priests were associates of the high priests. Priests were to come from the tribe of Levi and had to be without any physical defect. They were organized into 24 divisions that served the sanctuary in rotation. Each of the divisions ministered for a week, beginning on the Sabbath, except during the annual feasts, at which time all the priests served together.

The ceremony of consecration of the priests was much like that for the high priest, but not as elaborate. The clothing of the priests included a tunic, breeches, and a turban—all of which were made with white linen, as well as a white linen girdle embroidered with blue, purple, and scarlet. The chief duties of the priests were the care of the sanctuary vessels and the sacrifices at the altar. But the priests also taught the law, watched over the physical health of the nation, and administered justice.

B. Differing Responses: vss. 12-13

But many of the older priests and Levites and family heads, who had seen the former temple, wept aloud when they saw the foundation of this temple being laid, while many others shouted for joy. No one could distinguish the sound of the shouts of joy from the sound of weeping, because the people made so much noise. And the sound was heard far away.

The size and grandeur of the rebuilt temple foundation paled in comparison to the glorious one Solomon had built. Many of the older priests, Levites, and family members who were alive prior to the exile were sad and disappointed at the sight of the smaller, less impressive scene (Ezra 3:12). Both Haggai (Hag. 2:3) and Zechariah would find themselves addressing a segment of the population discouraged by "the day of small things" (Zech. 4:10). Be that as it may, the dominant mood among the returned exiles still was great joy. In fact, the combined sounds of joy and weeping were so loud that they could not be distinguished. Ezra 3:13 notes that even people at a great distance could hear the resounding noise of this community of worshipers. They dared to take the Lord at His word and risk everything they had to go to ruined towns and farms. In short, they trusted Him to take a remnant, plant it, and grow a nation.

Unlike those who returned from exile, Solomon had the resources to construct a grand and lavish temple. His shrine was made out of the most precious building materials available in his day, with many of them being imported: cedar (1 Kings 5:6), quarried stone (vss. 15-18), gold (6:20-22), olive wood (vss. 23-28, 31-33), cypress or pine (vs. 34), and bronze (7:13-16, 27, 38-45). The project employed a massive number of people: 30,000 laborers (5:13), 150,000 stonemasons and haulers (vs. 15), and 3,300 supervisors (vs. 16). Moreover, the work continued nonstop for seven years (6:37-38). Solomon's temple was a remarkable work of art, being built for the glory of God (8:12-13). Also, the Lord evidently approved of the king's work, for God blessed the sanctuary with His holy presence (vss. 10-11). Nonetheless, even as the construction went forward, the Lord reminded His builder that what mattered most was not a house made out of cedar and gold, but rather keeping the Mosaic law (6:11-13).

Ezra 4 reveals that those who attempt to do the will of God inevitably meet with resistance from a sinful world. To be specific, when the Jewish exiles returned to Jerusalem from Babylon, they came because God had commanded it. They had a royal decree and a divine mandate to rebuild the temple of the Lord in the city of God. But just as Christians today face spiritual opposition when they set their minds to obey God, so the exiles found themselves surrounded by powerful enemies when they began to rebuild their holy city and shrine.

From the outset, the writer identified as "enemies" (vs. 1) those who approached the newly returned exiles and offered to help them build the temple. The reason is implied in the way the exiles viewed the temple. It was "a temple for the LORD, the God of Israel." "The LORD," which renders *Yahweh* in the Hebrew text, was God's covenant name, signifying a unique relationship with those who entered into and kept that covenant. An earlier generation had gone into captivity for persistent covenant violation. Understandably, the present generation was committed to observing that covenant.

The residents of the Persian province of Samaria posed a special problem for the returned exiles. The local populace had resulted from intermarriage between Israelites who were left behind when the Assyrians deported the 10 northern tribes and the Mesopotamian peoples who had resettled in the promised land (see 2 Kings 17:24-41). This group claimed to worship the same God and to have sacrificed to Him since the days of the Assyrian king Esarhaddon (681–669 B.C.; Ezra 4:2). Despite their assertions, they indulged in many deviations from what God had revealed to His people in His Word.

Not surprisingly, the Jews refused to grant this request for joint participation. They alone would rebuild the temple in accordance with the Persian king's edict (vs. 3). Because of this decision, the returnees faced even greater opposition from their opponents. God's people were disheartened and tormented through the shrewd intimidation tactics of the enemy (vs. 4). The Samaritans tried to further inhibit the Jews' rebuilding efforts by using counselors. These so-called advisers sought to hamper and confuse the returnees by giving them misleading information and recommendations. This tactic continued through the reign Cyrus (559–530 B.C.; vs. 5). God's people stood firm, however, in their courageous and uncompromising stand.

Verses 6-23 form a chronological gap, historically occurring over half a century later than verse 5. The author inserted it at this point to stress that opposition to the rebuilding efforts of the Jews continued for many years. This opposition was present during the later reign of Xerxes (or, Ahasuerus; 486–465 B.C.). During this time, the enemies of God and His people filed a complaint against the resettlers in Jerusalem and the providence of Judah (vs. 6). Again, another complaint was filed during the reign of Artaxerxes I (465–424 B.C.). The text of the accusation was originally written and translated from Aramaic (vs. 7), the trade language of that time.

Ezra provided the content of the letter that the official leaders of the opposition filed (vs. 8). The document mentions a variety of nationalities and groups whom the Assyrians (possibly under the rule of Ashurbanipal, 669–627 B.C.) had resettled in northern Palestine and west of the Euphrates (vss. 9-10). In the letter, the opposition claimed that the Jews were rebuilding Jerusalem and that when they finished doing so, they would not pay any taxes to the king. The opposition urged the king to check the records to verify that Jerusalem had a history of rebellion. They warned that if the Jews succeeded in rebuilding the city, the king would lose control over the region (vss. 11-16). King Artaxerxes sent a response letter. In it, he authorized the opposition to halt the Jews' rebuilding efforts. As soon as the opposition read the letter, they quickly forced the Jews in Jerusalem to stop rebuilding (vss. 17-23). Perhaps any restoration to the city wall was destroyed (see Neh. 1:3).

Ezra 4:24 returns to the time of Zerubbabel in 536 B.C. The restoration of the temple was discontinued for about 16 years until the second year (or 520 B.C.) of Darius I (522–486 B.C.; see Hag. 1:1-15). Haggai and Zechariah urged God's people to resume their restoration work on the temple. The prophets directed their message to the resettled Jews living in Jerusalem and the region of Judah (Ezra 5:1). As a result of this ministry of encouragement and exhortation, Zerubbabel and Jeshua restarted the work on the sanctuary (vs. 2). It did not take long for Persian officials in the nearby Trans-Euphrates region to question the legitimacy of these restoration efforts (vs. 3). The authorities asked for and received the names of the individuals involved in the work on the temple (vs. 4).

Despite these intimidation tactics, the Lord watched over His people and prospered their efforts. The Persian officials did not stop the Jews in their work. They allowed God's people to proceed until a reply from the monarch was received concerning the matter (vs. 5). Ezra included a copy of the letter that was sent to King Darius. The Persian officials said that the Jews were busy rebuilding their temple at Jerusalem. Part of the letter contains a summary of what the Jewish leaders reported to their interrogators. Most important is the claim that during the first year of King Cyrus, he authorized the Jews to rebuild their temple in Jerusalem. The Persian officials asked Darius to verify these claims and make a decision concerning the matter (vss. 6-17).

God wanted His people to rebuild the Jerusalem temple, and He promised to be with them throughout the project (see Hag. 1:7, 13). The presence of opposition, however, must have initially made the fulfillment of the promise seem impossible to the Jews. When God makes a promise, it shows two aspects of His character. First, we see that He is the sovereign Lord of all. What He declares will come true and nothing can thwart His will. Second, we see that God does not change His mind, rethink His strategy, or apologize for not doing something according to our timetable. He is faithful to His word and will surely bring it to pass. Ultimately, God's promises are encouragements to faith, for they demonstrate the resolve of the Lord's character. His promises give us the courage to face and deal with difficult circumstances.

Discussion Questions

1. Why was it important for God's people to rebuild the temple in Jerusalem?
2. How did the civil and religious leaders organize God's people to rebuild the temple?
3. What are some ways you can encourage your fellow believers to do the Lord's work in an organized manner?
4. Why did God's people feel compelled to praise Him for His kindness and unfailing love?
5. How can believers maintain a balance between remembering the past and enjoying God's present?

Contemporary Application

Once the returnees had brought their offerings to God, they sought help from people living in Lebanon. After getting some construction materials, the Jews started the difficult task that lay before them. The temple foundation was completed to the tune of great rejoicing mixed with sorrow.

There is nothing wrong with fondly remembering the past. However, like some of the Jews, we may long for the past so much that we do not praise God for our continually renewing and changing relationship with Him. It's the relationship, not places or traditions, that should remain the focus and source of our delight in Him.

Amazingly, in the minds of many adults, worship has its time and place, and work has its time and place. Supposedly, these two activities are distinct and separate. The imaginary wall between the two is practically insurmountable. This week's lesson, however, emphasizes to us that work and worship are interconnected.

The Jews were busy constructing the temple in order to worship God properly. And they worshiped God as a result of their building. These observations stress why we should not separate our worship from our work. As we serve the Lord, our work should be an act of worship that brings glory to God.

Dedication of the Temple

DEVOTIONAL READING

Ezra 5:1-5

DAILY BIBLE READINGS

Monday July 8
*Ezra 4:1-5 Resistance to
Rebuilding the Temple*

Tuesday July 9
*Ezra 4:11-16 Accusations of
Sedition*

Wednesday July 10
*Ezra 4:17-24 Temple
Construction Halted*

Thursday July 11
*Ezra 5:1-5 The Eye of God
upon Them*

Friday July 12
*Ezra 5:6-17 Who Gave You
a Decree?*

Saturday July 13
*Ezra 6:1-12 The Temple's
Official Endorsement*

Sunday July 14
*Ezra 6:13-22 The Temple's
Dedication*

Scripture

Background Scripture: *Ezra 6*
Scripture Lesson: *Ezra 6:13-22*
Key Verse: *The people of Israel—the priests, the Levites and
the rest of the exiles—celebrated the dedication of the house of
God with joy.* Ezra 6:16.
Scripture Lesson for Children: *Ezra 6:13-22*
Key Verse for Children: *The people of Israel—the priests,
the Levites and the rest of the exiles—celebrated the dedication
of the house of God with joy.* Ezra 6:16.

Lesson Aim

To recognize that it is good for us to celebrate God's
great acts.

Lesson Setting

Time: 516 B.C.
Place: Jerusalem

Lesson Outline

Dedication of the Temple
  I. The Temple Completed: Ezra 6:13-15
    A. The Decree of Darius: vs. 13
    B. The Finishing of the Work: vss. 14-15
  II. The Temple Dedicated: Ezra 6:16-18
    A. The Celebration: vs. 16
    B. The Sacrifices: vs. 17
    C. The Priests: vs. 18
  III. The Passover Observed: Ezra 6:19-22
    A. The Preparations: vss. 19-20
    B. The Hunger for God: vs. 21
    C. The Feast: vs. 22

Introduction for Adults

Topic: *Celebrating with Joy*

After the completion of the Jerusalem temple, the people celebrated with great joy (see Ezra 6:16, 19, 22). These were not humdrum rituals or ceremonies, since they marked the Jews' return to their homeland.

More recently, during one American town's annual Fourth of July parade, two or three churches made magnificent floats—so good that often one of them took home first prize. It was their way of informing the public that the worship of God was still a viable option for many people. Then, as time went on, the floats these congregations made gradually disappeared. Why? It's because they required too much work to build and there were not enough people who volunteered to make them.

Making floats, of course, is just one way we can share with others the victory we have in the Lord Jesus. Sometimes we can celebrate with music that has a Christian emphasis. On other occasions we can give praise to the Lord through the performance of skits. Regardless of what we do, our focus should remain on God and not ourselves.

Introduction for Youth

Topic: *Praise in the House*

How great it is when our favorite sports team wins and we can celebrate their victory. Nothing excites us quite like winning a championship. For a few moments we can be jubilant. But soon the fizz of excitement evaporates and we have no more zip than old soda pop.

Like the returnees who celebrated the completion of the Jerusalem temple (see Ezra 6:16, 19, 22), as Christians, there are times when we can enter into festivities and special occasions. On other occasions, however, we decide to withdraw because things get out of hand. Knowing when to do so requires discernment.

Our celebrations do not have to be boisterous public displays. We can rejoice in the Lord as we sit by a lake with our Bibles. We can also celebrate with a friend at Bible study or on a retreat. Real celebration takes place in our hearts, not just on the streets or at music concerts.

Concepts for Children

Topic: *A New Worship Place*

1. After much hard work, the people of Judah finished rebuilding the place to worship God.
2. Then the people celebrated that God had helped them rebuild.
3. After this, the people celebrated a holy day called Passover.
4. Then, for seven days, the people celebrated the Feast of Unleavened Bread.
5. We can encourage other people by joyfully praising God.

Lesson Commentary

I. THE TEMPLE COMPLETED: EZRA 6:13-15

A. The Decree of Darius: vs. 13

Then, because of the decree King Darius had sent, Tattenai, governor of Trans-Euphrates, and Shethar-Bozenai and their associates carried it out with diligence.

Last week, we learned how God used the prophets Haggai and Zechariah to get the leaders and people of Judah to resume their work on the temple. When Persian officials heard about what was taking place, they investigated the matter. However, they did not stop the Jews from moving forward with their plans. Instead, the officials sent a letter to King Darius. They explained what was going on and asked him to check the Jews' claim that Cyrus had authorized them to rebuild their temple (see Ezra 5:1-17). A search for the decree of Cyrus was made, but evidently, the records were not found in Babylon. Instead, an important scroll was found in Ecbatana, the former capital of Media and the summer residence of the Persian kings. The official communication verified Cyrus's original command authorizing the rebuilding of the temple and the restoration of its foundation (see 6:1-2).

Verses 3-12 reveal the content of Darius's letter. The king specified the size of the temple and ordered that stolen articles were to be returned. His officials were to permit the Jews to complete their work. In fact, funds from the royal treasury were to be used to pay for building materials and sacrificial animals. Those who opposed the king's edict would be severely punished. He directed that his orders be implemented with care, thoroughness, and diligence. In verse 13, we are told that Tattenai (who was governor of the province west of the Euphrates River), Shethar-Bozenai (another official of the Persian government), and their colleagues, complied at once with the command of King Darius. Clearly, the prophecies the Lord had made through Haggai and Zechariah were coming to pass. God was giving the Jews success in rebuilding and dedicating their temple.

B. The Finishing of the Work: vss. 14-15

So the elders of the Jews continued to build and prosper under the preaching of Haggai the prophet and Zechariah, a descendant of Iddo. They finished building the temple according to the command of the God of Israel and the decrees of Cyrus, Darius and Artaxerxes, kings of Persia. The temple was completed on the third day of the month Adar, in the sixth year of the reign of King Darius.

During years of delay, the people had fallen into deep discouragement. They now needed reminders of God's love. The people also needed consistent exhortation because their work was hindered by more than just their enemies. It was also hindered by their selfishness and fear. When they decided to trust and obey the Lord, they prospered and God took care of their enemies. Since the people needed encouragement, the Lord provided it for them through the messages delivered by Haggai and Zechariah (Ezra 6:14).

Little is known about Haggai apart from the short oracle he wrote. In contrast, there is no ambiguity about the date of Haggai's prophecy. The occasion of his oracles is clearly specified (see 1:1; 2:1, 10, 20). They occurred within a four-month span of time in the second year (520 B.C.) of the Persian king, Darius I. The primary theme of Haggai is the rebuilding of God's temple. The latter goal was not to be an end in itself. Haggai stressed that the sanctuary represented God's dwelling, in which He manifested His glorious and holy presence among His people. If the returnees rebuilt the temple, Haggai reasoned, it would invite the return of God's presence in their midst.

Zechariah, like his contemporary Haggai, encouraged the people of Judah to again start to rebuild the temple in Jerusalem. Zechariah's ministry began about October–November 520 B.C. (see Zech. 1:1). The last date the prophet mentioned is December 7, 518 B.C. (see 7:1). However, a number of scholars generally agree that Zechariah's ministry did not end until sometime between 480 and 470 B.C. This would account for the difference in style of Zechariah's writing between the first eight chapters and the last six chapters of his book. Zechariah was a relatively young man when he began his ministry (see 2:4). He was also the son and grandson of priests, with his grandfather's name being Iddo (see Ezra 6:14; Neh. 12:4; Zech. 1:1). Therefore, Zechariah ministered as both a priest and a prophet, especially as he encouraged God's people to complete the rebuilding of the Jerusalem temple.

Ezra's report of the completion of the temple takes into account all of the layers of responsibility for it (Ezra 6:14). The "elders of the Jews" were responsible for the laborers at the job site. Haggai and Zechariah provided the spiritual motivation that produced success. And the decrees of three Persian emperors—Cyrus, Darius I, and Artaxerxes I—authorized the project at the level of world politics. The latter was an unlikely coalition, but God is the prime mover of earthly rulers. In this case, He worked through pagan kings to bring about the restoration of His people and their worship of Him in Jerusalem. "The sixth year of the reign of King Darius" (vs. 15) occurred long before the time of Artaxerxes I, the third emperor credited with the temple's erection. Artaxerxes I is the one who commissioned Ezra to enhance temple worship and teach the law of Moses (see 7:19-20, 25-26).

From early times, God's people had a calendar that revolved around both the farmer's seasons and the cycles of the moon so that individuals would know when to celebrate the Lord's festivals. The great festivals normally took place in the spring, early summer, and autumn. A month began when the thin crescent of the new moon was first visible at sunset. After the Exile, the calendar months took Babylonian names. A Jewish month spanned about two halves of two months in our modern calendar. The lunar month Adar (the twelfth month in the calendar) corresponds roughly with February-March in our solar calendar. In 516 B.C., the third of Adar would have been March 12. The destruction of Solomon's temple by Nebuchadnezzar had begun on August 14, 586 B.C. (see 2 Kings 25:8). So, about 70 years had elapsed between the destruction of the first temple and the construction of the second.

II. THE TEMPLE DEDICATED: EZRA 6:16-18

A. The Celebration: vs. 16

Then the people of Israel—the priests, the Levites and the rest of the exiles—celebrated the dedication of the house of God with joy.

Having completed their work, the people and their leaders broke into celebration. This was a significant milestone in the nation's history. After all, "the house of God" (Ezra 6:16) was not just another building to His people. It was the place where the Lord manifested His presence. The key to understanding this celebration is the contrast between living in exile in a land saturated with pagan idolatry and being able to worship the one true God in His sanctuary. His people were overcome with joy because they now had the latter opportunity.

The upright remnant had learned the painful lesson of God's judgment for their past idolatries. While in exile in Babylon, they missed so much the opportunity for worship afforded by the Jerusalem temple that they established what later became the synagogue service. This included prayers, Scripture readings, and moral instruction. The completion of the second temple ensured that the worship of the one true God remained a vital part of Jewish national life. His people resumed their daily temple services, their annual feasts and fasts, and their worship.

B. The Sacrifices: vs. 17

For the dedication of this house of God they offered a hundred bulls, two hundred rams, four hundred male lambs and, as a sin offering for all Israel, twelve male goats, one for each of the tribes of Israel.

Having returned from Babylon without much money, the people's sacrifice of 100 bulls, 200 rams, 400 lambs, and 12 goats represented a costly commitment to God (Ezra 6:17). Although the 10 northern tribes of Israel had long since disappeared, they were remembered by the 12 goats, one for each tribe. The dedication of God's house required significant sacrifices for two reasons. First, sacrifices proved the people's commitment to the Lord. Second, sacrifices reminded them of their sin and God's holiness.

Everyone celebrated the dedication of the new temple with great joy. However, this marvelously joyous celebration was tiny compared to the dedicatory service during the reign of Solomon (see 1 Kings 8:5, 63). Moreover, the number of animals sacrificed by the postexilic Jews was considerably smaller than those offered by Hezekiah (see 2 Chron. 30:24) and Josiah (see 35:7). Undoubtedly, this circumstance reflected the poverty of the returnees compared to earlier days. From this we see that true worship is costly. In the New Testament, Christians are called on to give of themselves to the Father because the Son died for them (see Rom. 12:1-2; 1 Cor. 6:19-20). After all, the new covenant ratified by the blood of the Son supersedes the old covenant of animal sacrifices (see Heb. 9:12-14; 10:11-13).

C. The Priests: vs. 18

And they installed the priests in their divisions and the Levites in their groups for the service of God at Jerusalem, according to what is written in the Book of Moses.

After offering sacrifices, the people divided the priests and Levites into their various divisions. They were to serve at the temple of God in Jerusalem in accordance with the instructions "written in the Book of Moses" (Ezra 6:18). Interestingly, Ezra is a book penned in two languages in its earliest manuscripts. The portion of Ezra from 4:8 through 6:18 is not written in Hebrew, but rather in the related language of Aramaic. Since Aramaic served as the trade language of both the Babylonian and Persian empires, it's easy to see why the official letters of the Persian kings found in chapters 5 and 6, along with those recorded in chapters 4 and 7, are in that language. In contrast, when the book describes the Passover celebration, the language reverts to Hebrew (see 6:19-22 below).

III. THE PASSOVER OBSERVED: EZRA 6:19-22

A. The Preparations: vss. 19-20

On the fourteenth day of the first month, the exiles celebrated the Passover. The priests and Levites had purified themselves and were all ceremonially clean. The Levites slaughtered the Passover lamb for all the exiles, for their brothers the priests and for themselves.

The highlight of the temple's completion came with the Passover observance. Since the returned exiles finished the sanctuary in the "month of Adar" (Ezra 6:15), it made sense for them to observe Passover at its appropriate time in the following month of Nisan, the "first month" (vs. 19) of the Jewish year. It is difficult for us to imagine how much the renewal of this ancient ritual meant to the Jews in Bible times. They had not kept it for several generations. With the rebuilding and rededication of the temple in Jerusalem, they now had the opportunity. It was on April 21, 516 B.C., that the returned exiles observed Passover (Ezra 6:19), a holy day that was originally intended to commemorate Israel's deliverance from Egypt.

Years before, during the reign of Josiah (640–609 B.C.), Passover had been celebrated after a restoration of the first temple. At that time, the king provided an immense number of animals for the festival to feed all the people. The peasants ate from the bounty of the king and the temple. This suggests that Josiah's Passover was a public feast, celebrated through the generosity of the monarch and the sanctuary aristocracy of the kingdom. The situation was much different for the returned exiles. Most of the society would have been village peasants who lived at a bare subsistence level. Meat was a luxury for the wealthy. In fact, any animals the Jewish peasants might have owned were too valuable to consume.

The priests and Levites had gone through the purification ritual and so were ceremonially clean. In accordance with the Mosaic law, they slaughtered the Passover lamb for all the returned exiles, for the other priests, and for themselves (vs. 20). The early church connected the Messiah with the Passover lamb. For instance, Paul referred to Christ as "our Passover lamb" (1 Cor. 5:7). Likewise, Peter equated the "precious blood of Christ" (1 Pet. 1:19) to that of a "lamb without blemish or defect" (see Exod. 12:5; Lev. 22:17-25). The apostle also noted that believers have been healed by the Messiah's "wounds" (1 Pet. 2:24).

B. The Hunger for God: vs. 21

So the Israelites who had returned from the exile ate it, together with all who had separated themselves from the unclean practices of their Gentile neighbors in order to seek the Lord, the God of Israel.

Keeping the Passover symbolically marked the end of the Exile for the returnees. Fellowship was once again restored between God and His chosen people. They were joined by other Jews who had renounced pagan worship (Ezra 6:21). The second group consisted of those who remained in Judah during the Exile, but did not participate in the unclean practices of their pagan neighbors. Together, they ate the lamb as a sign that they had repented of their sins and wanted to seek the Lord.

Moreover, by observing Passover, the upright remnant publicly declared their faith in the one true God. This faith set them apart from the ungodly inhabitants of the land. Additionally, the Jews' ceremony stressed the reality of their walk with God. By keeping the Passover, the returnees acknowledged their total dependence on the Lord. They wanted to learn more about Him and demonstrate that He was not just another local tribal deity. Indeed, out of the fires of suffering there emerged within the remnant a new level of interest in the things of God.

C. The Feast: vs. 22

For seven days they celebrated with joy the Feast of Unleavened Bread, because the Lord had filled them with joy by changing the attitude of the king of Assyria, so that he assisted them in the work on the house of God, the God of Israel.

Ezra 6:22 notes that the people celebrated the Feast of Unleavened Bread for seven days. This is one of the Old Testament festivals that God established for the Israelites. It involved eating bread made without yeast, holding several assemblies, and making designated offerings. It commemorated how the Lord rescued His people out of Egypt with rapid speed. This festival was observed at the newly rebuilt temple with the same joy that had marked the sanctuary dedication (see vs. 16).

With some effort, we can imagine how God's people must have felt. It was like returning home after a long absence, or being reunited with a loved one. Elderly persons would have had a mixture of grief and joy, especially as they remembered the temple of Solomon that had been destroyed (see 3:12). In contrast, younger people would have loved the colors, sights, and sounds of the great spectacle (see vs. 11). All the officiating priests would have been filled with awe, especially as some of their peers stood to make sacrifices in God's presence.

The members of the covenant community, who had been restored to their home-land, had just finished constructing the symbol of their national identity. They also had renewed fellowship with the Lord. How great their exuberance must have been! Through the grace of God, the temple was rebuilt and sacrifices once again were offered in the land of their ancestors. It's important to note that this jubilant time of celebration was based on what God had done through the Persian mon-archs. These kings had conquered territory formerly controlled by the Assyrian Empire, which was one of the kingdoms that had exiled God's people (see Neh. 9:32). Because of the Lord's intervention through the Persian emperors, the Jews were strengthened and encouraged to restore the temple in Jerusalem.

Discussion Questions

1. What prompted the Persian officials to allow the Jews to complete the rebuild-ing of the temple?
2. How has God used unbelievers in your life to bring about His will for you?
3. What role did Haggai and Zechariah serve in the rebuilding effort?
4. Who participated in the Passover celebration?
5. What are some ways we can celebrate God's goodness in our lives?

Contemporary Application

A psychologist once said that in a month he could change the outlook, person-ality, and behavior of anyone to a model he had selected. Supposedly, he could manipulate circumstances in such a way that only the desired set of responses would seem possible. This is the nature of temptation and doubt. We are thrust into circumstances that seem either impossible or irresistible.

The account recorded in Ezra 6:13-22 reminds us that God is ready to do the impossible—to bless His people in their weakness and to call them to rely on Him. When we look at the impossible, God is ready to make it possible. We can have confidence, through the Son, that we will receive the spiritual blessings the Father has promised us.

Of course, opposition to God's work is not a thing of the past. Like the Jews who were trying to complete the reconstruction of the temple, Christians face opposition on many fronts. As believers attempt to carry out a task for the Lord, they may encounter people who will actively seek to stop their work.

While we may dislike conflict, the Bible describes the Christian way of life as one that entails conflict with the forces of evil. We can learn from the Book of Ezra how to persevere in our witness despite the opposition of those who resist things that are good and deserving of praise—that is, things that are true, noble, right, pure, lovely, and honorable (see Phil. 4:8). We are also reminded of the value of celebrating God's great acts in our life. Let us not hesitate to do the latter!

Fasting and Praying

DEVOTIONAL READING

2 Chronicles 7:12-18

DAILY BIBLE READINGS

Monday July 15
*2 Chronicles 7:12-18
Humbly Calling on God*

Tuesday July 16
*Psalm 69:9-18 Beseeching
God's Answer to Prayer*

Wednesday July 17
*Isaiah 66:1-4 Humble and
Contrite in Spirit*

Thursday July 18
*Matthew 6:16-18 Fasting
Directed to God*

Friday July 19
*Ezra 7:1-10 Studying and
Keeping the Law*

Saturday July 20
*Ezra 8:15-20 Securing
Servants for the Temple*

Sunday July 21
*Ezra 8:21-23 Praying for
God's Protection*

Scripture

Background Scripture: *Ezra 8:15-23*
Scripture Lesson: *Ezra 8:15-23*
Key Verse: *We fasted and petitioned our God about this, and
he answered our prayer. Ezra 8:23.*
Scripture Lesson for Children: *Ezra 8:21-23;
Matthew 6:16-18*
Key Verse for Children: *We fasted and petitioned our God
about this, and he answered our prayer. Ezra 8:23.*

Lesson Aim

To renew our commitment to pray on a regular basis.

Lesson Setting

Time: 458 B.C.
Place: Ahava Canal

Lesson Outline

Fasting and Praying

   I. Finding Levites to Serve in the Temple:
     Ezra 8:15-20
     A. *Assembling the Group: vs. 15a*
     B. *Searching for Attendants: vss. 15b-17*
     C. *Obtaining Skilled Workers: vss. 18-20*
  II. Leading the People in Fasting and Prayer:
     Ezra 8:21-23
     A. *The Proclamation of a Fast: vs. 21*
     B. *The Reason for the Fast: vss. 22-23*

Introduction for Adults

Topic: *Preparing for the Journey*

As people journey through life, they learn new skills they can use along the way. For instance, people enjoy talking about how they learned to use a new electronic gadget. And they might even laugh about the mistakes they made and how they inadvertently erased some important information. Others share about the refresher courses they took to upgrade their professional skills.

Learning to pray can feel like that, especially because for many of us praying is a new skill. It's not something you fall into. Prayer is also a developed practice. And it takes a considerable level of training and discipline. While we pray, we learn more about it and find new pleasure in it. Yet, it still requires time and commitment from us.

As Ezra and those he led back to Jerusalem prepared for their long trek, they sought the Lord in prayer. Specifically, they petitioned Him to protect them from danger (see Ezra 8:21). Likewise, as we move through our spiritual pilgrimage, we will want to bring all our endeavors to the Lord and ask Him to bless what we do.

Introduction for Youth

Topic: *Preparing for the Journey*

Ezra was about to lead a group of his fellow Jews on a 900-mile journey from Babylon to Jerusalem. But before they began to travel, they remembered to pray to the Lord for safety (see Ezra 8:21).

The concept of prayer as conversation with God has tremendous appeal to teens. We have to take prayer out of the realm of stuffy, pious jargon. We also have to show adolescents that prayer is not limited to people who petition the Lord in public places. Instead, prayer pleases God because it shows that we love Him and His fellowship.

Often, saved teens pray for the first time on retreats, or in small campus and church groups. They touch levels of intimacy in prayer because they are vulnerable to each other, more so than many adults. Therefore, our concern is not with the right words and tone of voice, but with honesty and integrity.

Our goals for youth are to encourage strong daily prayer habits, as well as quality prayer in fellowship groups. Then, as they pray, they can develop the needed fortitude for standing up to the spiritual battles they encounter in life.

Concepts for Children

Topic: *Preparing for the Journey*

1. Ezra was a person who led God's people.
2. Ezra helped some families take a long journey.
3. These families were going from Babylon to Jerusalem.
4. Before the people left, they fasted and prayed.
5. It is helpful for us to pray with our parents and friends.

Lesson Commentary

I. FINDING LEVITES TO SERVE IN THE TEMPLE: EZRA 8:15-20

A. Assembling the Group: vs. 15a

I assembled them at the canal that flows toward Ahava, and we camped there three days.

Ezra finally appears in the seventh chapter of the book that bears his name. After Moses, Ezra was the most important human figure in the shaping of classical Judaism. Moses was considered the giver of the law, while Ezra was considered the teacher of the law. Ezra demonstrated that a godly scholar could do as much, if not more, than a general or a politician to shape the character and destiny of a nation. Chapters 7 through 9 are taken from the memoirs of the great scribe. The memoirs begin abruptly as though no time had elapsed between the completion of the temple in 516 B.C. and the seventh year of Artaxerxes (458 B.C.).

The genealogy of Ezra recorded in 7:1-5 is one of the most extensive (for an individual) in the Old Testament. Sixteen prominent names hit the high spots in the millennium between Ezra and Aaron, the brother of Moses. Ezra brought this impressive heritage with him back to Jerusalem from Babylon (vs. 6). In addition, he was an expert in the law of Moses. Some scholars think that when Ezra brought the law with him from Babylon, he was introducing something new to the religious life of Israel. They even speculate that this was Ezra's own expanded edition of Israelite traditions. However, Ezra viewed himself as a student of, not a contributor to, the ancient body of sacred writing penned by Moses a thousand years earlier.

Ezra referred to the people living in and around Jerusalem as "Israel" rather than "Judah" (unless Ezra was specifically referring to the Persian province). Clearly, Ezra wasn't interested in religious innovation. Instead, he focused on recapturing the covenant that the Lord had made with His people when the 12 tribes of Israel were united under Moses. Ezra mentioned in passing that he had initiated the contact with Artaxerxes. He asked for authorization to teach the law in Jerusalem, to mobilize a party of priests to strengthen worship at the temple, and to gather contributions for improvements within Jerusalem. Ezra played down the courage it must have required to approach an Eastern despot (see Esth. 4:11). On the other hand, he repeatedly emphasized the role of God's blessing on him and others (Ezra 7:6, 9; see also vs. 28; 8:18, 22, 31).

In this summary of Ezra's venture, which he then expanded in 7:11–8:36, the scribe mentioned that he was accompanied by various spiritual leaders, ranging from highly regarded priests to lowly temple servants (7:7). Again, he credited God's hand for the success of the trek. Ezra also stressed the graciousness of the Lord's travel mercies—which become more obvious when the expanded version of the story reveals the size of the party, the wealth it transported, and its vulnerability to robbery (vss. 8-9). Throughout this undertaking, the most obvious quality of

Ezra's personality was devotion (vs. 10). Not surprisingly, this descendant of the high priestly family of Israel had set his heart on studying "the Law of the LORD." Ezra's obedience was not a slavish legalism, but wholehearted devotion to the Lord. Moreover, Ezra did not simply focus on his own personal holiness, but also taught others and motivated them to godly knowledge and living.

In verse 11, Ezra once again noted that he was a priest of Aaron, a teacher, and an expert in the law of Moses. Then, in verses 12-26 an official letter of Artaxerxes is recorded. The document, which authorized Ezra's mission to Jerusalem, is the other portion of this book written in Aramaic (4:6–6:18 is the first). The use of this international language reminds us that God can work through the unwitting emperors of pagan empires just as readily as He uses believers to fulfill His purposes. The content of Artaxerxes' letter was clear evidence to Ezra of the gracious hand of God on his mission to Jerusalem.

It's not surprising that Ezra included the complete text of the royal decree in his memoirs. Persian emperors often employed advisers from the provinces to help draft edicts pertaining to their home territories. They did this in order to write laws that fit the diverse cultures of the empire. Artaxerxes' decree reads as though a priest (perhaps Ezra himself) edited it so that the details about Israelite worship and sacrifice would be accurate. Persian policy was to patronize the religions of each province as the best way to stabilize local social structures. The emperors also required the priesthood of each province to pray to their local deities for the welfare of Persia. They studied and codified the religious customs of every culture and sent experts, such as Ezra, to their homelands to facilitate worship.

In the letter, we learn that Artaxerxes gave the Jews and their priests and Levites permission to travel with Ezra to Jerusalem. The king allowed them to see whether the laws of their God were being obeyed. The returnees were to take the silver and gold they obtained from Artaxerxes and from their own people and use it in the Jerusalem temple. The returnees were to buy sacrificial animals, grain, and wine, and they were free to use leftover money and items as they saw fit. The king directed all the treasurers in the western portion of the empire to make every effort to help Ezra. His orders were to be executed with care, thoroughness, and diligence. Artaxerxes (perhaps superstitiously) did not want the God of the Jews to become offended because of some oversight. Anything that His temple might need was to be provided (vss. 12-23).

The king said the various individuals who served in the temple were excused from any taxes normally collected from the people living in the region west of the Euphrates River. Furthermore, Artaxerxes permitted Ezra to select leaders over the people of Judah. He would have jurisdiction over those committed to the Mosaic law. The king allowed Ezra to instruct those ignorant of the law. He was also allowed to punish those who violated Jewish and Persian laws. Ezra could use execution, banishment from the covenant community of Judah, seizure of property, or imprisonment (vss. 24-26).

In response, Ezra praised God for His control of events. Because of the Lord's involvement, a Gentile king extended favor to the Jewish people. The Jerusalem temple would be further beautified through the decree of Artaxerxes. Ultimately, the Lord obtained the glory. Ezra also praised God for the kindness Artaxerxes and his officials showed to him. Ezra saw this favorable treatment as evidence of God's unfailing love and mercy. The Lord enabled Ezra to select capable people to serve with him as leaders in the job he was commissioned to do (vss. 27-28).

Artaxerxes granted Ezra everything he had asked because the king was convinced that a strong Jewish population in Judah would foster peace and security as well as result in greater loyalty from his Jewish subjects. Artaxerxes gave Ezra the responsibility of leading about 1,750 men (perhaps a total of 5,000 people) in the second return from Babylon to Jerusalem. In 8:1-14, Ezra listed the Jewish people who returned with him from Babylon to Jerusalem. He included various priests, descendants of royal heritage, and common Jews. This last category includes a list of 12 families consistently arranged as follows: the family name, the current head of the family, and the total number of men that relocated.

According to 7:9, the journey from Babylon to Jerusalem began on the "first day of the first month," that is, Nisan. The latter coincided with March-April of our modern calendar. This would have been April 8, 458 B.C. The decision to travel in the spring was sensible, especially since there would have been an ample supply of water available along the route. Ezra and the Jews he led "arrived in Jerusalem on the first day of the fifth month," that is, Ab. The latter coincided with July-August of our modern calendar. This would have been August 4, 458 B.C. This means the entire 900-mile journey (which first headed northwest along the Euphrates River) took four months.

When 7:9 is compared with 8:31, it appears there was an initial delay of 11 days. Part of that delay is accounted for in 8:15. It states that Ezra gathered God's people at a canal that flowed toward the district of Ahava, where they camped in tents for three days. The exact location of this area remains unclear, though the canal might have flowed into either the Tigris or Euphrates rivers. Ezra took this step to organize the caravan for the long journey ahead back to Jerusalem. According to verse 31, the excursion began on the "twelfth day of the first month," that is, Nisan. This means the group first assembled at the "Ahava Canal" on the ninth of Nisan.

B. Searching for Attendants: vss. 15b-17

When I checked among the people and the priests, I found no Levites there. So I summoned Eliezer, Ariel, Shemaiah, Elnathan, Jarib, Elnathan, Nathan, Zechariah and Meshullam, who were leaders, and Joiarib and Elnathan, who were men of learning, and I sent them to Iddo, the leader in Casiphia. I told them what to say to Iddo and his kinsmen, the temple servants in Casiphia, so that they might bring attendants to us for the house of our God.

When Ezra surveyed the assembly, he found there were no Levitical priests in the group to serve the faith community once it had resettled in the promised land (Ezra 8:15). The absence of Levites was a major point of concern, especially given that they performed important routine tasks in the temple and helped with the offering of sacrifices. In response, Ezra sent for nine influential leaders and two teachers known for their insight and discernment (vs. 16).

Ezra wanted these individuals to persuade some of the Levites to journey with their fellow Jews back to Jerusalem. Verse 17 mentions one prominent Levite named Iddo, who was living in Casiphia. This town remains unidentified, though some have speculated it was located north of Babylon on the Tigris River. Ezra directed his representatives to ask Iddo and his relatives to provide God's people with Levites so that they could serve as "attendants" in the temple after the group had arrived in Jerusalem.

C. Obtaining Skilled Workers: vss. 18-20

Because the gracious hand of our God was on us, they brought us Sherebiah, a capable man, from the descendants of Mahli son of Levi, the son of Israel, and Sherebiah's sons and brothers, 18 men; and Hashabiah, together with Jeshaiah from the descendants of Merari, and his brothers and nephews, 20 men. They also brought 220 of the temple servants—a body that David and the officials had established to assist the Levites. All were registered by name.

Ezra 8:18 reveals that it was due to the "gracious" intervention of the Lord that a Levite named Sherebiah and his extended family agreed to join the returnees at their river encampment before making the journey to Jerusalem. Sherebiah is described as a person having skill, insight, and prudence. He was a descendant of Mahli, who in turn traced his lineage back to Levi (see Exod. 6:19; Num. 3:20; 1 Chron. 6:19, 29; 23:21; 24:26, 28). Sherebiah was accompanied by his sons and relatives, who numbered 18 men.

Ezra 8:19 mentions two other prominent individuals named Hashabiah and Jeshaiah. Both of them were descendants of Merari. He was the third son of Levi and the father of Mahli (see Gen. 46:11; Exod. 6:16; 1 Chron. 6:16). Along with Hashabiah and Jeshaiah were 20 of the latter's kinsmen and their sons (Ezra 8:19). In addition, there were 220 "temple servants" (vs. 20), all of whom were listed by name. During the reign of David, their ancestors had been set apart by the king's officials to help the Levites in their work. With only a few days to consider, all the individuals mentioned in verses 18-20 were willing to uproot themselves from life in exile and return to Jerusalem. The providential intervention of God in bringing about this outcome helped to give legitimacy to Ezra's undertaking.

II. LEADING THE PEOPLE IN FASTING AND PRAYER: EZRA 8:21-23

A. The Proclamation of a Fast: vs. 21

There, by the Ahava Canal, I proclaimed a fast, so that we might humble ourselves before our God and ask him for a safe journey for us and our children, with all our possessions.

Ezra announced at the Ahava canal that there would be a mandatory fast to seek the Lord's favor. Through this fast the participants would humbly recognize their inability to safeguard their journey from potential dangers. In addition, they would be able to request that God make the trip level and straight (in other words, free from any life-threatening situations). They would ask the Lord to protect their entire group, including their young children and valuable possessions (Ezra 8:21). The priceless items being transported by the group would be an especially tempting target for marauding bandits.

Fasting refers to abstaining from eating for a limited period of time. In the Bible, we can see that God's people fasted for a variety of reasons: to express grief over the death of a loved one or a leader (see 1 Sam. 31:13), to petition God for a matter of great urgency (see 2 Sam. 12:15-23), to humble oneself before God (see 1 Kings 21:27-29), to seek God's help (see 2 Chron. 20:1-4), to confess sins (see Neh. 9:1-2), and to prepare oneself spiritually (see Matt. 4:1-2). Fasting was difficult, requiring self-discipline and sacrifice. It gave God's people the opportunity to devote more time to spiritual pursuits. It said to God, in effect, that the matter they were bringing before Him was more important than anything else, even eating.

Even today, when we fast quietly and sincerely, God endows our work in the kingdom with spiritual power. This is evident from what Jesus taught His disciples in Matthew 6:16-18. When Jesus made His remarks, He was censuring the hypocritical manner in which the religious leaders of the day fasted. Specifically, when they did so, they would look dreary and gloomy. They deliberately disfigured their faces by heaping ashes on their heads and disheveling their hair and beards. Supposedly, everyone would conclude they were doing something pious. Yet any admiration the pretenders received would be their only reward (vs. 16).

In New Testament times, people would perfume their heads with olive oil and splash their faces with water to help rejuvenate and invigorate themselves. Jesus instructed His followers to put oil on their heads and wash their faces when they fasted (vs. 17). They were to look refreshed and joyful, not sullen and unkempt, so that others might not realize they were fasting. In other words, they were supposed to hide their fasting. But their unseen heavenly Father would know, and whatever they did in private would be rewarded by Him (vs. 18). Whatever righteous acts we do—not only giving, praying, and fasting, but also such things as serving and evangelizing—should be performed out of love for God and not to receive people's applause. Otherwise, whatever acclaim we obtain will be all the benefit we get out of the deal. So instead we should play to an audience of one, namely, God.

B. The Reason for the Fast: vss. 22-23

I was ashamed to ask the king for soldiers and horsemen to protect us from enemies on the road, because we had told the king, "The gracious hand of our God is on everyone who looks to him, but his great anger is against all who forsake him." So we fasted and petitioned our God about this, and he answered our prayer.

The Hebrew verb translated "ashamed" (Ezra 8:22) refers to the presence of embarrassment or disgrace as a result of an awkward circumstance or adverse turn of events. This is how Ezra would have felt had he requested from Artaxerxes a military escort of foot soldiers and mounted troops to safeguard the Jews' trek back to Jerusalem. Previously, the scribe explained to the Persian king that God had displayed His favor on those who were committed to Him. In contrast, God's wrath was displayed against those who rebelled against Him. In light of these comments, Ezra felt he would have brought humiliation upon the name of the Lord (whom he represented) if he had requested a body of armed men to accompany the returnees. For this reason, God's people fasted and prayed to the Lord for a safe journey. In turn, He graciously answered their petition (vs. 23). In contrast, about 13 years later, Nehemiah would request a military escort when he made the journey to Jerusalem (see Neh. 2:7-9).

Discussion Questions

1. Why did Ezra think it was important for the Levites to be part of the group of returnees?
2. How was Ezra able to convince some Levites to uproot and resettle in Jerusalem?
3. How would you characterize your devotion to God?
4. Why did Ezra proclaim a fast?
5. What can believers do to ensure that they have the right motives for serving God?

Contemporary Application

Ezra and his fellow Jews faced a daunting task. They were about to embark on a 900-mile journey from Babylon to Jerusalem. This was not just a trip for the strongest among them. There would also be younger and older individuals. And they would have the added burden of transporting many precious items.

Ezra did not just impulsively charge ahead. Instead, before embarking on a momentous trek, he and the rest of the returnees fasted, humbled themselves in God's presence, and prayed for His protection (see Ezra 8:21). And we learn that the Lord answered their petitions (see vs. 23).

These are important observations. But for us an underlying question needs to be raised: Do we pray at all? That's not a silly question, for surveys show that professing Christians on the whole pray very little. In small group discussions, believers admit that it is hard for them to find time to pray, either by themselves or as families. Invariably, time pressures and other priorities crowd out prayer.

Looking at the church, it is obvious that prayer meetings have virtually vanished. Even many large congregations draw only 20 to 30 people for midweek prayer services. In contrast, some cities have successfully had "concerts of prayer" where hundreds and sometimes thousands of people gather for a united prayer service. In light of these distinctions, let us renew our commitment to pray on a regular basis.

Gifts for the Temple

Scripture

Background Scripture: *Ezra 8:24-30*
Scripture Lesson: *Ezra 8:24-30*
Key Verse: *"You as well as these articles are consecrated to the* LORD. *The silver and gold are a freewill offering to the* LORD, *the God of your fathers."* Ezra 8:28.
Scripture Lesson for Children: *Ezra 8:24-30;
Psalm 27:4-6*
Key Verse for Children: *At his tabernacle will I sacrifice with shouts of joy; I will sing and make music to the* LORD. Psalm 27:6.

Lesson Aim

To dedicate every aspect of our lives in service to God.

Lesson Setting

Time: 458 B.C.
Place: Ahava Canal, Jerusalem

Lesson Outline

Gifts for the Temple
  I. Inventorying the Temple Items: Ezra 8:24-27
      A. *Choosing Twelve Leading Priests: vs. 24*
      B. *Weighing Out the Objects for the Temple: vss. 25-27*
  II. Taking Charge of the Temple Items: Ezra 8:28-30
      A. *Declaring the Sacredness of the Priests and Objects:
          vs. 28-29*
      B. *Receiving the Objects for the Temple: vs. 30*

Introduction for Adults

Topic: *Generous Gifts*

The covenant community was blessed by the dedicated service provided by the 12 leading priests and Levites mentioned in Ezra 8:24 and 30. In *A Call to Excellence,* Gary Inrig describes a similar sacrificial mindset.

In the late 1800s, a group of European pastors came to one of D. L. Moody's Northfield Bible Conferences in Massachusetts. Following the European custom of the time, each guest put his shoes outside his room to be cleaned overnight by the hall servants. But since this was America, there were no hall servants.

That night, while Moody walked through the dormitory halls, he saw the shoes and determined not to embarrass his peers. He mentioned the need to some ministerial students who were there, but met with only silence or pious excuses. Moody returned to the dorm, gathered up the shoes, and, alone in his room, the world-renown evangelist began to clean and polish the shoes.

That episode is a vital insight into why God powerfully used D. L. Moody. He was a believer with a servant's heart.

Introduction for Youth

Topic: *Give It Up!*

The Christian faith is sometimes considered a one-time-only commitment: You make a decision, take the church membership class, get your name on the church roll, and that's it. But the enemy of our souls never stops trying to subvert that decision. He wants us to avoid the tough moral and ethical requirements of committing every aspect of our lives to the Lord and His service.

The devil is especially delighted when saved teens live just like unbelievers. Indeed, many youth find it easier to follow the crowd than to make their own decisions. However, when they are challenged to follow a better way, some of them respond positively.

Ezra's forthright challenge to the 12 leading priests and 12 Levites is what youth prefer to hear (see Ezra 8:24). In contrast, young people do not respond well to exhortations to serve that are blurred by vague statements. Every day, adolescents step forward and answer God's call to Christian service. They don't always know exactly what challenges they will face, but they know God, and that is enough for them.

Concepts for Children

Topic: *Bringing Our Gifts*

1. Ezra chose 12 priests and 12 Levites to do an important job.
2. Ezra told these men to take care of some valuable items.
3. David spoke about his desire to be in the house of God.
4. David also spoke about bringing offerings to the Lord joyfully.
5. God is pleased when we faithfully serve Him.

Lesson Commentary

I. Inventorying the Temple Items: Ezra 8:24-27

A. Choosing Twelve Leading Priests: vs. 24

Then I set apart twelve of the leading priests, together with Sherebiah, Hashabiah and ten of their brothers.

In last week's lesson, we learned that Ezra asked Artaxerxes for permission to return to Jerusalem. He granted Ezra everything he requested because the king was convinced that a strong Jewish population in Judah would foster peace and security as well as result in greater loyalty from his Jewish subjects. Artaxerxes gave Ezra the responsibility of leading about 1,750 men (perhaps a total of 5,000 people) in the second return from Mesopotamia to Jerusalem (see Ezra 7:1-28). Having obtained this authorization from the Persian monarch, Ezra gathered an impressive group of family leaders and their kin who wanted to go with him back to Jerusalem. Two of the clans were priestly families, and most were following relatives who had returned with Jeshua and Zerubbabel (see 8:1-14).

Ezra delayed departure eight days while he found key Levitical families to infuse new vigor into the temple ritual. Also, Ezra would not accept an armed escort for their 900-mile journey. The returnees trusted the Lord to guard them from bandits as they transported tons of precious metals to the temple treasury (see vss. 15-23). To oversee the safe conveyance of the sacred items to the Jerusalem shrine, Ezra appointed 12 leaders from among the Jewish priests, along with 12 Levites (vs. 24; see vs. 30). Two of the Levites—Sherebiah and Hashabiah—were mentioned in verses 18 and 19, respectively. They were part of the group of Levites who had responded to Ezra's request for "attendants" (vs. 17) to serve in the sanctuary in Jerusalem. Sherebiah and Hashabiah were joined by "ten of their brothers" (vs. 24). "Brothers" renders a Hebrew noun that can also mean "relatives" or "colleagues."

B. Weighing Out the Objects for the Temple: vss. 25-27

And I weighed out to them the offering of silver and gold and the articles that the king, his advisers, his officials and all Israel present there had donated for the house of our God. I weighed out to them 650 talents of silver, silver articles weighing 100 talents, 100 talents of gold, 20 bowls of gold valued at 1,000 darics, and two fine articles of polished bronze, as precious as gold.

A huge responsibility was being shouldered by the 12 priests and 12 Levites that Ezra put in charge of the costly items he was transporting to the Jerusalem temple. The catalog of sacred objects included such precious metals as "silver and gold" (Ezra 8:25). There were also numerous vessels intended to be used in the sanctuary of God. These utensils had been contributed by the Persian monarch, his counselors, his overseers, and wealthy Jewish families living in Mesopotamia at the time.

Verse 26 details the enormous quantities of money as well as instruments that had been dedicated for use in the temple. The Hebrew noun rendered "talent" refers to a weight of circular shape, which could be made out of gold, silver, bronze, or iron. In ancient times, the weight of a talent ranged from 62 and 66 pounds. So, "650 talents of silver" was about 40,000 to 43,000 pounds. The "silver articles weighing 100 talents" and the "100 talents of gold" each varied between 6,200 and 6,600 pounds. Verse 27 refers to 20 gold basins worth "1,000 darics" (which was about 19 pounds in weight). The daric was a highly valued Persian gold coin used at that time. There were also two well-crafted vessels made out of finely "polished bronze." These utensils were so exquisitely made that they were considered as valuable as gold.

The importance of the temple for God's people cannot be overstated. To begin, the sanctuary had an indispensable theological function to serve. It was the place where the Lord manifested His holy presence in Israel. It was also the spot where sacrifices were made in response to God's gracious choice of Israel as His people. In the sanctuary, God's people could spend time in prayer. Furthermore, its design, furniture, and customs were object lessons that prepared the people for the Messiah.

Additionally, the temple had important political and economic roles to play in Jewish society. It was the institution that held together the entire covenant community—the past as well as the present and the future. The sanctuary gave political identity to the people. Access to its courts identified who was properly a citizen and who was excluded. From an economic perspective, rooms in the temple functioned as a treasury—in effect, the society's bank. Because of the sanctuary's demands for tithes and offerings, a large portion of the Israelite economy passed through the temple personnel and storehouses. In brief, without the sanctuary, God's people had little opportunity to pull together as a coherent society to face the challenges of the future.

II. TAKING CHARGE OF THE TEMPLE ITEMS: EZRA 8:28-30

A. Declaring the Sacredness of the Priests and Objects: vs. 28-29

I said to them, "You as well as these articles are consecrated to the LORD. The silver and gold are a freewill offering to the LORD, the God of your fathers. Guard them carefully until you weigh them out in the chambers of the house of the LORD in Jerusalem before the leading priests and the Levites and the family heads of Israel."

The Hebrew noun rendered "consecrated" (Ezra 8:28) refers to what has been set apart as sacred or holy to the Lord. In this case, Ezra declared that both those serving in the Jerusalem sanctuary and the objects placed within the holy place were regarded as being specially designated for the temple service. Ezra also noted that the "silver and gold" were a voluntarily "offering" that had been made to the Lord, the God of the returnees' ancestors. Because of the sacredness of the temple ministers and items, it was essential that the utmost caution and care were exercised, especially as God's people made the long and dangerous trek back to Jerusalem.

Accordingly, Ezra directed the 12 priests and 12 Levites mentioned in verse 24 to be careful with and protect the sacred items entrusted to their care. Their vigilance was to be maintained until the precious cargo arrived safely at the Jerusalem temple. At that time, the priests and Levites were to put the "articles" (vs. 28) on scales in the designated storerooms of the sanctuary complex. Moreover, this was to be done in the presence of the chief priests, the Levites, and the family leaders of "Israel" (vs. 29). In turn, they would verify that whatever had been "consecrated" (vs. 28) arrived in Jerusalem safely and intact.

Whether it was the tabernacle or temple, both consisted of three sections. First, there was the outer court, and on its eastern side was the entrance. Second, within the courtyard, facing the entrance, was the altar of burnt offerings. Behind it, toward the west, was the laver for the priests' ceremonial washing. Third, in the western portion of the courtyard was the sanctuary proper. This was divided into two chambers by a hanging curtain.

The first of these was the Holy Place, which only the priests could enter. It contained the table of showbread, the lampstand, and the altar of incense. The second of the chambers was called the Holy of Holies or the Most Holy Place. It contained the ark of the covenant (which was called the mercy seat). The high priest entered this area once a year on the Day of Atonement. Precious metals and finely woven colored materials were employed in the construction of the Most Holy Place. Also, only objects made of rare and costly materials were located near the sacred space. The objects placed farther away were made of bronze and ordinary woven cloths (see Heb. 9:1-7).

B. Receiving the Objects for the Temple: vs. 30

Then the priests and Levites received the silver and gold and sacred articles that had been weighed out to be taken to the house of our God in Jerusalem.

The "priests and Levites" (Ezra 8:30) willingly accepted responsibility for the precious metals and consecrated vessels placed under their care. They would ensure that whatever had been "weighed out" to them was transported safely to the Jerusalem temple. After that, Ezra and the Jews who were with him began the journey from Mesopotamia to Jerusalem. Ezra was convinced that God enabled them to survive the long trek. In fact, the Lord rescued His people from attack and abuse by vandals. After their arrival, they rested and refreshed themselves for three days. Then, on the fourth day, they distributed the money and the items dedicated for use in the temple. Everything was meticulously accounted for (vss. 31-34).

As an expression of worship, the returnees offered various animals to the Lord. They did so because they were thankful for the grace of the Lord in their lives. The sin offering mentioned in verse 35 was an atonement for specific unintentional sins, confession of sins, forgiveness of sins, and cleansing from defilement (see Lev.

4:1–5:13; 6:24-30; 8:14-17; 16:3-22). These temple offerings remind us that it is necessary to approach God through the provision of an acceptable atoning sacrifice. In faithful service to God, the Jewish leaders also delivered the king's directives to his various Persian officials in the Trans-Euphrates region of the empire. In compliance with Artaxerxes' orders, these officials assisted the Jews and their work in the temple (Ezra 8:36).

Within four and a half months of Ezra's arrival in Jerusalem, the leaders told him that many of their fellow Jews had not separated themselves from the surrounding peoples of Canaan (9:1). Some of the Jews had intermarried with pagan women, an act that was abhorrent to the Lord. Not only the common people, but also the priests, Levites, and various rulers and leaders were guilty of this unfaithfulness. This situation placed God's people in serious danger of adopting pagan concepts. Eventually, they would have lost their distinctiveness and been absorbed into other communities (vs. 2). Ezra was shocked at this distressing news and understood the grave implications of the situation. As a sign of horror and outrage, he tore his tunic and cloak, pulled out some of his hair, and sat down until twilight (that is, the time between the decline of the sun and nightfall; vs. 3). Perhaps others also were grieved and dismayed over the infidelity of their fellow Jews. They demonstrated their concern by gathering around Ezra (vs. 4).

In Bible times, God's people expressed their sorrow visibly and audibly. Wearing sackcloth of dark goat or camel hair (see Isa. 32:11; Jer. 6:26), lying in dirt or ashes and putting them in one's hair (see Job 2:12; Ezek. 27:30), tearing one's own clothing (see 2 Sam. 1:11; 3:31), wailing and weeping aloud (see Ezek. 27:30-32), and even lacerating one's body (see Jer. 16:6; 41:5) in violation of the law of God (see Lev. 19:28) marked occasions of deep distress. Men typically shaved their hair or beards to symbolize loss (see 2 Sam. 10:4; Isa. 15:2; Ezek. 7:18). In contrast, full hair and beard represented vigor and prosperity. A Phoenician carving on a sarcophagus older than the time of Ezra shows professional female mourners tearing at their hair. Ezra is the only man whom the Bible tells us spontaneously tore at his hair because his sorrow was so intense he could not wait for a razor. By contrast, when Nehemiah was later confronted with similar sin (see Neh. 13:25), he tore out the offenders' hair.

Ezra humbled himself by refusing to eat until the time of the evening offering. He then changed positions. While still clothed in his torn garments, he fell prostrate on his knees with outstretched arms in prayer before the Lord (Ezra 9:5). Ezra realized that his fellow Jews had brought dishonor to the name of God. The rebellion and guilt of the Jews, with whom he identified, had become immeasurable. If the individual acts of sin could be piled one on top of the other, the stack would pierce the heavens (vs. 6). This situation was a continuation of the compromise that eventually led to the destruction of Israel and the exile of the Jews. When God's people disobeyed their covenant with Him, He allowed them to experience disaster (vs. 7). The Lord had graciously allowed the Jews to resettle in their homeland and rebuild the temple. They could once again learn about His ways and renew their commitment to Him (vs. 8).

Ever since the days of Egypt, God's people had experienced various types of enslavement. God had been merciful in giving them relief from bondage through the Persians. In His unfailing love, He had permitted the Persian monarchs to grant the Jews permission to return to Judah, to rebuild their shrine, and to experience protection and security in Jerusalem and the surrounding region of Judah (vs. 9). Nonetheless, God's people were guilty of violating His directives. By intermarrying with pagan women, they risked the possibility of idolatry and impurity creeping in. After all, Judah was inhabited by people who neither worshiped the Lord nor followed His commandments. Through His representatives, God had directed the returnees to remain set apart from these morally corrupting influences (vs. 12).

It was imperative that God's people not adopt the pagan customs of the unsaved, especially through intermarriage. The Jews were also to avoid making any type of peace treaty, for this would lead to moral and spiritual disaster (see Deut. 23:6). By remaining pure, the Jews would also remain strong as a distinctive community of people. They would experience the blessings of the Lord. And He would honor their commitment by enabling them and their descendants to prosper (Ezra 9:12). Although the Jews had experienced 70 years of exile, this punishment did not match the extent of their rebellion against God (vs. 13).

In His grace, the Lord had permitted a small group of survivors to reclaim their homeland and their temple. In light of this, how could they once again depart from Him? The result of repeated offenses would be the elimination of God's people. The Lord, in His holy wrath, would wipe out His people from existence (vs. 14). God demonstrated His upright character by allowing a small group of survivors to immigrate to Jerusalem. The Lord had also been gracious in permitting the temple to be reconstructed. Ezra confessed the sins of his people and acknowledged God's unfailing commitment to them. The scribe affirmed that their disobedience could have resulted in instant death, if God had so desired (vs. 15).

The law of Moses forbade intermarriage between Israelites and the various nations inhabiting Canaan at the time of the conquest (see Deut. 7:1-3). Further, the law forbade the presence of Ammonites, Moabites, and their descendants in the sanctuary of God (see 23:3). Yet Rahab the Canaanite and Ruth the Moabite both married into the tribe of Judah and the lineage of David and Jesus (see Matt. 1:5). The prohibition seems to have been against marriage with foreign women committed to idolatry, not foreign women who had identified with the God of Israel. The concern of the law was that idolatrous wives "will turn your sons away from following me to serve other gods, and the LORD's anger will burn against you" (Deut. 7:4). Marriage with converts to faith in the Lord was not unlawful and may explain the lengthy interview process preceding the divorces reported in Ezra 10.

Discussion Questions

1. Why did Ezra set apart 12 leading priests?
2. Why had the Persian king and his officials been so generous to the returnees?
3. What sort of donations had been made to furnish the Jerusalem temple?
4. What are some ways we can give generously to the Lord and His work?
5. Why is it important for believers to ensure that whatever is given to God is properly used?

Contemporary Application

Ezra 8:24-30 recounts the appointment of 12 leading priests and 12 Levites to take charge of the temple offering and vessels. Indeed, as noted in the lesson commentary, the Hebrew noun rendered "consecrated" (vs. 28) could also be translated "holy." The term signified distinction, separation, and chosenness.

Ask three friends what image comes to mind when they hear the word *holy*, and you'll likely get three different answers. Maybe one will see the face of a well-known spiritual leader—a person known for an outspoken faith and a lifestyle beyond reproach. Another might imagine monks cloistered in some mountain-top monastery far away from the cares of daily living—people so caught up in visions of heaven that they are removed from the rough-and-tumble struggles faced by "ordinary" folks. On the negative side, a third friend might picture individuals described as "holier than thou"—people so certain of their own righteousness that no one else can measure up to their standards.

But what could be greater than asking your closest friends, "What comes to mind when you hear the word *holy?*" and listening to them sincerely reply "You"? True, relatively few Christians will establish worldwide reputations for their faith or devote every moment of their waking lives to prayer and worship. And yet, God calls every one of His people to be holy. As we learn from this week's lesson, being holy is not an impossibility. Holiness is a natural characteristic of those who fully obey God and keep His covenant.

God still calls believers to a life of holiness. His summons to a consecrated lifestyle is accompanied by His guiding commands, as expressed in His written Word. These commands speak to every aspect of our existence—what we think, how we feel, and the way in which we act. By reviewing what Scripture has to say about holy living, we can do a better job of dedicating every aspect of our lives in service to God.

Festival of Booths

DEVOTIONAL READING

Exodus 23:12-17

Scripture

Background Scripture: *Nehemiah 7:73b–8:18*
Scripture Lesson: *Nehemiah 8:13-18*
Key Verse: *The whole company that had returned from exile built booths and lived in them. . . . And their joy was very great.* Nehemiah 8:17.
Scripture Lesson for Children: *Nehemiah 8:13-18*
Key Verse for Children: *The whole company that had returned from exile built booths and lived in them. . . . And their joy was very great.* Nehemiah 8:17.

Lesson Aim

To discover that recommitment to God's Word produces celebration and confession.

Lesson Setting

Time: 444 B.C.
Place: Jerusalem

Lesson Outline

Festival of Booths

  I. Learning about the Feast of Booths: Nehemiah 8:13-15
     A. *Gathering Together: vs. 13*
     B. *Finding the Directive Concerning the Sacred Day: vss. 14-15*

 II. Observing the Feast of Booths: Nehemiah 8:16-18
     A. *Building Temporary Shelters: vs. 16-17*
     B. *Celebrating the Sacred Day: vs. 18*

Introduction for Adults

Topic: *Great Rejoicing*

We all accept the axiom that ignorance is no excuse when we break the law. Yet we tend to tolerate ignorance of God's laws and wonder why our lives and our churches seem to lack spiritual authority, power, and joy.

A researcher in church growth has noted that preaching is essentially useless unless people first confess their sins. But why should they confess when they have no standard by which to measure their behavior? God's laws are that standard. Unless we know those laws and respect them, there's not much likelihood for confession to occur.

Just as Ezra did in his day (Neh. 8:13), our task is to make God's Word clear and applicable to all of life. Only then will we see spiritual growth and strong discipleship in our lives and in our churches. Likewise, as with God's people in Ezra's day (see vs. 17), that is when we will experience the overwhelming joy of being freed from the guilt of sin.

Introduction for Youth

Topic: *Remembering to Celebrate*

All of us use favorite send-off words to encourage our friends, such as the following: "Live strong," "Keep your chin up," and "Hang in there!" Right words do make a difference. The best words to remember are found in the Bible.

"The joy of the LORD is your strength" (Neh. 8:10) is one of those classic biblical promises. It means a lot more when we recall its original setting. When God's people wept for their sins, Nehemiah told them that it was now time for them to experience God's joy. In turn, this truth enabled the covenant community to celebrate the Feast of Booths with great joy (see vs. 17).

Scripture brings us to confession and joy. Divine words of truth are always the right and best ones for us. When we neglect them, it's like neglecting food and drink for our bodies. The Bible helps us to overcome our sins, to find joy, and to give joy to others.

Concepts for Children

Topic: *A Freedom Celebration*

1. God's people got together to hear Ezra teach.
2. Ezra explained what God's Word said.
3. God's people celebrated the Feast of Booths.
4. God's people were filled with joy when they did so.
5. We can be filled with joy, too, for the wonderful things God has done for us.

Lesson Commentary

I. LEARNING ABOUT THE FEAST OF BOOTHS: NEHEMIAH 8:13-15

A. Gathering Together: vs. 13

On the second day of the month, the heads of all the families, along with the priests and the Levites, gathered around Ezra the scribe to give attention to the words of the Law.

It had taken over 80 years after the Exile for the Jerusalem wall to be completed (see Neh. 6:15). Some of this delay was due to opposition from enemies, but the returnees were as much to blame for the delay as anyone else. They became discouraged when they faced hardship and they also easily fell into sin. Accordingly, while the first half of the Book of Nehemiah concentrated on the physical preservation of God's people, the second half focused on the spiritual preservation. Ezra plays a prominent role in this endeavor. As was noted in lesson 8, he was a Jewish scribe and priest who traced his ancestry back to Aaron (see Ezra 7:1-5). In 458 B.C., he received permission from Artaxerxes I to travel to Jerusalem with thousands of exiles and carry out religious reform.

It was also mentioned in lesson 9 that, while in the capital of Judah, Ezra wept bitterly over the sins of the people. In response, many Jews gathered to confess their transgressions and weep alongside their spiritual leader. The people then made a covenant to obey God and to put away the foreign wives who had caused them to abandon the Lord (see 10:1-4). The efforts of Ezra to initiate a spiritual renewal lasted for a short period. But by the time Nehemiah returned, the spiritual fire had fizzled. As a matter of fact, in the 13 years between the end of the Book of Ezra and the beginning of the Book of Nehemiah, the Jewish people once again fell into their sinful ways. They intermarried into families with foreign religions and neglected to support the temple.

Thankfully, God was at work in the hearts of His people. They had seen the Lord's hand on Nehemiah, and they knew that to survive, they needed God's help. They also understood that to receive God's help, they needed to dedicate themselves to obeying His commands. Rather than waiting for Ezra or Nehemiah to start another spiritual revival, the people started it themselves. The Jews assembled in Jerusalem on October 8, 444 B.C. The event was timed to coincide with the Feast of Trumpets, the New Year's Day of the Jewish civil calendar (later known as Rosh Hashanah; see Neh. 7:73–8:1). This was one of the most noteworthy seasons on Israel's religious calendar (Lev. 23:23-43), and it was celebrated by the blowing of horns or trumpets from morning until evening. After the Exile, the festival was observed by the public reading of the Mosaic law and by general rejoicing.

The people gathered in an open plaza in front of the Water Gate, an entryway leading to the Gihon spring (Jerusalem's primary source of water). The gate was located on the eastern side of the city, slightly south of the wall's midsection, and directly opposite the temple. This area was not considered sacred, which meant laypeople could participate with priests in the gathering. Women and children, who did not always attend temple ceremonies, were present in accordance with Moses' instructions in Deuteronomy 31:10-13 (Neh. 8:2; see 2 Chron. 20:13). The occasion for the assembly was Ezra's reading of the "Book of the Law of Moses" (Neh. 8:1), which the Lord had given Israel to obey.

Several suggestions have been made concerning the identity of the preceding document, but most likely it was a scroll (or scrolls) containing the first five books of the Old Testament—Genesis, Exodus, Leviticus, Numbers, and Deuteronomy. As was noted in lesson 3, scrolls were made from sheets of leather, papyrus, or parchment that people joined together in long rolls. Scribes would use a pen to write in columns on one or both sides of these materials. In the Hebrew canon, these documents are known as the Torah (or Law) and comprise the first of three major divisions of the Jewish sacred writings. The other two are the Prophets and the Writings. Both Jewish and Christian traditions assert that Moses was the human author of the Torah (which is also called the "Pentateuch" or five books). The Law is not only a compilation of the decrees of God entrusted to Moses, but also the history of humanity and the Israelites. Moses probably wrote these books in the fifteenth century B.C. A thousand years later, the Book of Nehemiah was being created as the wall of Jerusalem underwent rebuilding.

The purpose of having Ezra read from the Law was not only to preserve the Torah, but also to encourage every generation to revere and obey God's decrees and teachings. This public reading led the Jews to renew their commitment to God's covenant and to instruct their children to do the same. The Jews did not own personal copies of the Law. The main way they were able to become familiar with it was by hearing it read and explained. This is what Ezra had returned to Jerusalem to do. But during the 52 days when the wall of Jerusalem was being rebuilt, there was little time for an assembly. After the wall's completion, however, the people expressed a desire to hear more instruction from the Torah.

Ezra faced the open square just inside the Water Gate from early morning until noon and read aloud from the Torah scroll to everyone who could understand. In ancient times, this was the customary practice. All the people, in turn, paid close attention to what they heard (Neh. 8:3). Imagine standing for five or six hours in reverential silence while attentively listening to the Bible being read! From this incident comes the modern Jewish tradition of standing as the Torah scroll is read in the synagogue (a ritual some Christian churches also observe). Everything that was done and the way it was reported points to the deep commitment and devotion of God's people. Ezra the scribe was standing on a high wooden platform that had been built for this occasion. He wasn't alone, either. Standing next to him was Nehemiah, and they were flanked on their right and left by priests, Levites, and other Jewish leaders (vs. 4; see vs. 9). They evidently stood alongside Ezra to assist in the long time that it took to read, translate, and interpret God's Word.

Ezra stood on the elevated platform in full view of the people. When they saw the scribe unroll the Torah scroll, they rose to their feet in unison out of respect for the reading and exposition of God's Word (Neh. 8:5). This spontaneous response from the crowd must have warmed the scribe's heart. These Jews were far different from the ones he had addressed years earlier. They were now eager to hear God's Word and willing to do whatever He asked of them. When Ezra gave praise to the Lord, "the great God" (vs. 6), the people chanted "Amen! Amen!" (to indicate emphatic agreement with and acceptance of the law) and lifted their palms heavenward (perhaps in unison, to denote expectation and dependency). Then the attendees bowed down and worshiped the Lord "with their faces to the ground." In this way, the people indicated their humble and willing submission to their God and Creator. As a matter of fact, the Hebrew word translated "worshiped" originally meant "to prostrate oneself on the ground."

As Ezra read the Mosaic law, a number of Levites instructed the people who were standing (vs. 7). Jewish tradition says the Levites were translating the words from ancient Hebrew to Aramaic, the international diplomatic and trade language of the day. Most likely, at intervals between the readings, the assistants circulated freely among the crowd and gave the sense of the text (perhaps paragraph by paragraph and sentence by sentence) so that the people could grasp what was being read (vs. 8). The goal of the expositors was to make the interpretation of God's Word clear and its application understandable. The reading and teaching of the law took place under the watchful eyes of Nehemiah, Ezra, and the Levites, which indicated there was unity among the Jewish leaders. Unexpectedly, something quite remarkable happened. The people began to weep and mourn. The Holy Spirit used the words of the law to bring strong conviction of sin to their hearts and minds (vs. 9).

Perhaps for the first time, the returnees comprehended how far short of God's righteous moral standard they fell (see Rom. 3:23). Incidentally, the Hebrew word rendered "mourn" (Neh. 8:9) often describes the reaction of those who are suddenly aware that they deserve judgment (see Exod. 33:4; Ezra 10:6). Although the people's weeping and confessing of their sin (and possibly the transgressions of their ancestors) was an understandable response, this occasion called for a different reaction. The Jewish leaders encouraged the people not to be sorrowful at this time. Because it was a sacred day before the Lord, the appropriate response was for the community of the redeemed to sing praises to the God of Israel. That's why Nehemiah, in concert with the other officials (vs. 11), urged the people to celebrate the occasion with "choice food and sweet drinks" (vs. 10). The former reference is to festive, tasty morsels prepared with the fat of sacrificial animals. Nehemiah also encouraged the attendees to share gifts of food with those who had nothing prepared. This reflects the Jewish tradition of remembering the disadvantaged on joyous occasions (2 Sam. 6:19; Esth. 9:22).

While the returned exiles experienced a renewed devotion to the law of God and sincerely repented of their sins, this devotion eventually led to close study of the law and then to a legalistic interpretation of it. This phenomenon became the seedbed for the development of the Pharisees and their strict adherence to the Torah. Jesus later rebuked the Pharisees for obeying the letter of the law while neglecting to obey the spirit of the law. Once Ezra and his associates were done, the audience departed to do all that the leaders had said. They ate and drank at a festive meal, shared gifts of food with the disadvantaged, and celebrated the occasion with "great joy" (Neh. 8:12), for they had both heard and understood the Word of God that had been read and expounded to them. The next day, the leaders of each family along with the priests and Levites assembled to meet with Ezra. His goal was to help them understand the law better (vs. 13).

B. Finding the Directive Concerning the Sacred Day: vss. 14-15

They found written in the Law, which the LORD had commanded through Moses, that the Israelites were to live in booths during the feast of the seventh month and that they should proclaim this word and spread it throughout their towns and in Jerusalem: "Go out into the hill country and bring back branches from olive and wild olive trees, and from myrtles, palms and shade trees, to make booths"—as it is written.

Ezra traveled from Babylon to Jerusalem in 458 B.C. (see Ezra 7:8). Nehemiah arrived in Jerusalem from Susa, one of the Persian capitals, in 445 B.C. (see Neh. 1:1). Both accounts appear to have been written soon after the occurrence of the events they describe. The Book of Ezra may date from about 440 B.C., and the Book of Nehemiah from about 430 B.C. With respect to the latter document, it records Nehemiah's determination to rebuild the walls of Jerusalem and renew the commitment of its people to the Lord. This brisk, forceful book emphasizes the importance of faithfulness to God and perseverance in trials.

Even though the books of Ezra and Nehemiah go together, they make a contrasting pair. On the one hand, both documents narrate events in Jerusalem after a remnant of Judah returned from the Babylonian captivity. On the other hand, while Ezra was a meditative scribe who led reforms by means of teaching and holiness of character, Nehemiah was an official in the Persian government who led reforms by means of bold plans and force of character. The personality differences between these two leaders are significant. For example, as was noted in lesson 9, when Ezra heard that some of the Jewish men had taken foreign wives, he tore out his own hair. Oppositely, when Nehemiah confronted the same problem, he tore out the hair of the offenders.

According to Nehemiah 8:14, in 444 B.C., the religious and civil leaders of the covenant community discovered that the Feast of Booths was celebrated during the fall season five days after the Day of Atonement. The leaders announced in Jerusalem and Judah that the people were to observe the sacred day. This involved going out to the hill country and obtaining a variety of branches—from cultivated and wild olive trees, myrtle trees (evergreen shrubs that gave off a pleasant fragrance), date palms, and other leafy trees—to construct temporary shelters for living outside. This was done in accordance with the Mosaic law (vs. 15). The Feast of Booths (also called Tabernacles or Ingathering) was characterized by a week of celebration for the harvest in which God's people lived in booths and offered sacrifices. This observance memorialized the Israelites' journey from Egypt to Canaan (when they lived in tents) and gave them an opportunity to thank the Lord for the productivity of the land (see Exod. 23:16; Lev. 23:33-43; John 7:37).

II. OBSERVING THE FEAST OF BOOTHS: NEHEMIAH 8:16-18

A. Building Temporary Shelters: vs. 16-17

So the people went out and brought back branches and built themselves booths on their own roofs, in their courtyards, in the courts of the house of God and in the square by the Water Gate and the one by the Gate of Ephraim. The whole company that had returned from exile built booths and lived in them. From the days of Joshua son of Nun until that day, the Israelites had not celebrated it like this. And their joy was very great.

The people complied with the directive given them by the religious and civil leaders. The people went out, cut branches, and used them to build shelters in every possible location of Jerusalem, that is, on the flat roofs of their houses, in the courtyards of their homes, in the outer and inner courtyards of God's temple, and in the plazas around the Water Gate and the Ephraim Gate (the latter being on the north side of the city and facing toward the territory of Ephraim; Neh. 8:16). The people living in the surrounding villages also built temporary shelters.

This holiday had not been observed in quite this way and with this much joy since the time of Joshua centuries earlier. The people were once again giving thanks to God for His blessings with the same enthusiasm and zeal as the Israelites of Joshua's day had done (vs. 17). As we have learned, the events that transpire in Nehemiah 8 took place during the celebration of two of Israel's sacred days: the Feast of Trumpets (see vs. 2) and the Feast of Booths. Absent in this account is the celebration of a third feast: the Day of Atonement. The people's prior disobedience and lack of attention to God's law may have caused them to neglect this important day.

B. Celebrating the Sacred Day: vs. 18

Day after day, from the first day to the last, Ezra read from the Book of the Law of God. They celebrated the feast for seven days, and on the eighth day, in accordance with the regulation, there was an assembly.

Understanding of biblical truth is dry without the joy that God produces. Likewise, feasting and joy are meaningless without the firm foundation of God's Word. That is why Ezra read from the Mosaic law each day throughout the entire seven-day period of celebration. On the eighth day, a solemn assembly took place in accordance with the law (Neh. 8:18). The purpose of the reading was not only to preserve the law, but also to encourage every generation to revere and obey God's Word. This public reading led the Jews to renew their commitment to God's covenant and to instruct their children to do the same.

Discussion Questions

1. Why did Ezra, along with the leaders of the covenant community, value the study of God's Word?
2. What was the significance of the Feast of Booths?
3. Why did the covenant community in Ezra's day celebrate the Feast of Booths?
4. What connection do you see between the Word of God and celebration?
5. What can you do to renew a commitment to know and do God's will?

Contemporary Application

Ezra, Nehemiah, and their fellow Jews understood the importance of launching their resolve to obey God with the strongest possible beginning. Do your students have the same attitude about obeying God? This week's lesson stresses that when a strong commitment is absent, believers are more prone to violate His Word.

Missionaries tell stories that resemble Nehemiah's account about the public reading and teaching of God's Word. On the one hand, people who have never heard it before are amazed and overcome. They seek God's forgiveness for their sins and welcome Jesus Christ as their Lord and Savior. On the other hand, people who have heard the Bible read and taught again and again sometimes find it hard to be moved. The Word of God becomes so familiar to them that it loses its initial forcefulness on their consciences.

We also face the problem of Bible ignorance and neglect. Public opinion polls show that among Christians, regular Scripture reading is largely neglected. Yet we can be thankful that local Bible study groups flourish in many churches and communities. Those who hunger and thirst for righteousness will be spiritually satisfied (see Matt. 5:6). When we seek God and put Him first in our lives, we will listen to, study, obey, and teach God's Word. Compared to the upright remnant in Nehemiah's day, we are surfeited with Bibles and Scripture study materials. Therefore, our judgment will be severe if we neglect these gifts and opportunities from the Lord.

Community of Confession

DEVOTIONAL READING

Luke 15:1-10

DAILY BIBLE READINGS

Monday August 5
Acts 3:17-26 Repent and Turn to God

Tuesday August 6
Matthew 21:28-32 A Changed Mind

Wednesday August 7
Job 42:1-6 I Repent in Dust and Ashes

Thursday August 8
Matthew 5:21-26 First Be Reconciled

Friday August 9
Luke 18:9-14 God, Be Merciful to Me

Saturday August 10
Luke 15:1-10 Joy in Heaven

Sunday August 11
Nehemiah 9:2, 6-7, 9-10, 30-36 The Community Confesses Together

Scripture

Background Scripture: *Nehemiah 9:1-37*

Scripture Lesson: *Nehemiah 9:2, 6-7, 9-10, 30-36*

Key Verse: *Those of Israelite descent had separated themselves from all foreigners. They stood in their places and confessed their sins and the wickedness of their fathers.* Nehemiah 9:2.

Scripture Lesson for Children: *Nehemiah 9:1-3, 6-8, 26-28*

Key Verse for Children: *Create in me a pure heart, O God, and renew a steadfast spirit within me.* Psalm 51:10.

Lesson Aim

To recognize our shortcomings and confess them to God.

Lesson Setting

Time: 444 B.C.

Place: Jerusalem

Lesson Outline

Community of Confession

    I. The Faithfulness of God: Nehemiah 9:2, 6-7, 9-10

        A. *Confession of Sins: vs. 2*

        B. *God as the Creator: vs. 6*

        C. *God's Choice of Abraham: vs. 7*

        D. *God's Deliverance of His People from Egypt: vss. 9-10*

    II. The Unfaithfulness of God's People: Nehemiah 9:30-36

        A. *The Mercy of God: vss. 30-31*

        B. *The Hardship Endured by the Returnees: vs. 32*

        C. *The Guilt of the Returnees' Ancestors: vss. 33-35*

        D. *The Servitude Endured by the Returnees: vs. 36*

Introduction for Adults

Topic: *Admitting Shortcomings*

  The presence of sin in the faith community of Ezra's day finds numerous parallels today. The returnees confessed that many, including civic and religious leaders, had violated God's will.

  On a more positive note, the assembled Jews discovered the power of remorse, confession, and repentance at work in their lives. And the entire faith community was willing to acknowledge and renounce its sins. Beyond that, it willingly accepted considerable hardship in order to make things right.

  Confession, repentance, and restoration—these are the sorts of steps to getting back on course spiritually when we sin. No one is exempt, for everyone has sinned. Perhaps it has not been openly or flagrantly, but we have all broken God's laws and have fallen far short of His glory (see Rom. 3:23). That's why we need courageous spiritual leaders who are willing to identify with sinful people. The Holy Spirit honors these leaders, especially when they confront people with the requirements of God's holiness.

Introduction for Youth

Topic: *Fess Up!*

  One day, as I was shopping at the grocery store, I heard a mother firmly say the following to her disobedient child: "What did I tell you to do? Are you making a good choice? Remember what we talked about before we came inside the store." The child needed to know that heeding her mother's warning was the wisest decision to make.

  In ancient Judah, the Lord's spokespersons kept issuing warnings, but God's people ignored them. Despite many years of hearing the prophets' declarations, the people refused to repent. In the end, they experienced sorrow and loss for their disobedience.

  God's warning to us is clear. If we disobey Him, He will discipline us. The good news, of course, is that when we turn away from our sins and seek to obey God, we will be eternally blessed. Just as He did for the Jews who returned to their homeland from exile, so today He also gives us the strength to do His will.

Concepts for Children

Topic: *Saying We Are Sorry*

1. God's people gathered in Jerusalem.
2. God's people said they had disobeyed Him.
3. God's people said they were sorry for their sins.
4. God's people decided they were going to obey Him.
5. God is pleased when we say we're sorry for our sins.

Lesson Commentary

I. THE FAITHFULNESS OF GOD: NEHEMIAH 9:2, 6-7, 9-10

A. Confession of Sins: vs. 2

Those of Israelite descent had separated themselves from all foreigners. They stood in their places and confessed their sins and the wickedness of their fathers.

The ninth chapters of Ezra, Nehemiah, and Daniel all contain prayers of confession dealing with the national sins that led to the Babylonian Captivity and the loss of Israel's sovereignty over its own affairs. These confessions of the sins of people long dead were not requests that the original sinners be forgiven. They were statements of identification with the past. Through the prayer recorded in Nehemiah 9, Ezra helped his contemporaries rehearse the sins of the past, recognize the present results of those sins, and prepare to move into a future marked by faithfulness and blessing. As Christians today, we, too, can find it helpful to face the past in order to understand the present and move into the future with God's fullest blessing.

Two days after the last joyous day of the Feast of Booths, on October 30, 444 B.C., the people of Judah and Jerusalem gathered once again in the holy city (vs. 1). Previously, Ezra and Nehemiah had discouraged mourning over sin during the festival days when the people were to draw spiritual strength from the joy of knowing the Lord (see 8:9-10). Now, they assembled again to explore another aspect of being the people of God through fasting, separation from idolatry, and confession of sin. Most likely, the sackcloth worn by the confessing Jews was a coarsely woven cloth of goat hair (9:1). The participants stood for three hours of reading from the Mosaic law and three hours of confession and worship, just as they had stood all morning on the first of the month to hear Ezra read the law (9:2-3; see 8:3, 5). The people stood in reverence because the law had come through Moses from "the LORD their God" (9:3).

B. God as the Creator: vs. 6

"You alone are the LORD. You made the heavens, even the highest heavens, and all their starry host, the earth and all that is on it, the seas and all that is in them. You give life to everything, and the multitudes of heaven worship you."

Probably the assembly of Judah gathered for confession before the same platform in the square at the Water Gate where Ezra had previously read the Mosaic law (see Neh. 8:1). Most likely, the steps on which the Levites stood as worship and confession guides were the stairs to the platform. Two groups of eight Levites are named in 9:4-5. While the people watched, the first group called on the Lord. The second group led the mass of worshipers in praising God. Five Levites—Jeshua, Bani, Kadmiel, Shebaniah, and Sherebiah—participated in both acts of worship.

The Levites called on the people to stand for worship (vs. 5). This display of reverence consisted of praise that focused on the covenant relationship between God and His people Israel. "The LORD"—Yahweh—was God's covenant name. Indeed, the following recitation of Israel's history is an account of God's covenant faithfulness and Israel's covenant unfaithfulness. Jewish tradition and many Christian commentators attribute to Ezra the beautiful prayer recorded in verses 5-37. The prayer is structured carefully to guide the worshipers of Judah and Jerusalem in contrasting themselves with the Lord. Worship at its best always does that. We stand in awe before God in His infinite majesty and power, while we acknowledge our limitations. We stand mourning because He is pure and holy, while we are stained by the effects of sin. We stand in hope because He is gentle and loving toward undeserving sinners, who cast themselves on His mercy.

The emphasis throughout these verses is on God. The statements are addressed to Him. The pattern is something like the following: "You did this, You did that, and You proved Your faithfulness again and again." No wonder the sequence begins with an exhortation to praise the sovereign Lord, who deserves to blessed from age to age. Moreover, His glorious name was worthy to be praised, even though no human expression of adoration was great enough (vs. 5). Then, the participants affirmed the truth of God as the Creator. The people declared that He alone is the Lord who brought all things into existence. This included the "heavens" (vs. 6), the "highest heavens," and the vast multitude of stars. Furthermore, the Lord created the earth, along with all the plant and animal life found on the land, within the seas, and in the air. Because every living thing owed its existence to God, the angels of heaven worshiped Him.

C. God's Choice of Abraham: vs. 7

"You are the LORD God, who chose Abram and brought him out of Ur of the Chaldeans and named him Abraham."

Nehemiah 9:7 recounts the fact that the sovereign Lord chose Abram while he was living in Ur of the Chaldeans (a city on the Euphrates River in what is today southern Iraq) and summoned him to resettle his family in Canaan. Moreover, God changed the patriarch's name from "Abram," which means "[my] father is exalted," to "Abraham," which means "father of a multitude." In this way, the Lord designated the patriarch in a special way as His servant. This is the only Old Testament reference outside Genesis to God's renaming Abraham (see Gen. 17:5).

Nehemiah 9:8 notes that the Lord found Abraham to be trustworthy and characterized by integrity. God responded to the patriarch's faithful disposition by establishing a covenant with him. In it, the Lord pledged to give the land of Canaan to Abraham's descendants (see Gen. 15:18-20). Later, God promised to make the patriarch "the father of many nations" (17:4). God fulfilled His pledge, for He is "righteous" (Neh. 9:8). The latter renders a Hebrew adjective that emphasizes the integrity and uprightness of the Lord in all His dealings with people.

D. God's Deliverance of His People from Egypt: vss. 9-10

"You saw the suffering of our forefathers in Egypt; you heard their cry at the Red Sea. You sent mirac-ulous signs and wonders against Pharaoh, against all his officials and all the people of his land, for you knew how arrogantly the Egyptians treated them. You made a name for yourself, which remains to this day."

The Jewish assembly next recited God's mighty works of the Exodus. The Lord heeded the anguish of their ancestors in Egypt and at the Red Sea when escape seemed hopeless (Neh. 9:9). God performed awesome acts of power against Egypt's ruler, his officials, and all the inhabitants of the nation. The Lord did so, for He knew how insolently the Egyptians had acted against the ancestors of the Jews. By means of the 10 plagues, God earned a lingering reputation among the nations (vs. 10). Then the Lord opened the barrier of the sea to save Israel and swallow the pursuing Egyptians (vs. 11). The phrase "like a stone into mighty waters" echoes the victory song of Moses and Miriam sung on the shores of the Red Sea (see Exod. 15:5).

In Nehemiah 9:12-14, the Jews confessed how God led their ancestors from the Red Sea to Mount Sinai with a pillar of cloud by day and a pillar of fire by night. The worshipers recalled the way the Lord personally descended to address Israel through Moses. Cloud and fire are often used as symbols of God's presence in the Hebrew Scriptures. For instance, clouds symbolize God's mystery and hidden glory in 1 Kings 8:10-11. Not surprisingly, the Lord gave Moses the 10 Commandments on Mount Sinai in the midst of smoke and fire (see Exod. 19:18). Fire symbolizes God's holiness in Deuteronomy 4:24, His protective presence in 2 Kings 6:17, His wrath against sin in Isaiah 66:15-16, His glory in Ezekiel 1:4-13, and His righteous judgment in Zechariah 13:9.

II. THE UNFAITHFULNESS OF GOD'S PEOPLE: NEHEMIAH 9:30-36

A. The Mercy of God: vss. 30-31

"For many years you were patient with them. By your Spirit you admonished them through your prophets. Yet they paid no attention, so you handed them over to the neighboring peoples. But in your great mercy you did not put an end to them or abandon them, for you are a gracious and merciful God."

The pronouns "you" and "they" interchange throughout Nehemiah 9:16-38, as the Jews compared and contrasted the deeds of God and their ancestors. Despite their deliverance from bondage in Egypt, the revelation of the Mosaic law at Mount Sinai, the guidance and nourishment the Israelites received in the wilder-ness, and the clear instructions God gave them on how to enter and possess the promised land, the nation stubbornly bowed its neck like an ill-tempered ox and rebelled against the Lord (vs. 16). The people disregarded His revealed will and His gracious miracles of deliverance and decided to go back to Egypt and slavery (vs. 17; see Num. 14:1-4). Only God's graciousness and compassion kept Him from abandoning Israel when the people went further and worshiped a golden calf (Neh. 9:18; see Exod. 32:4).

The Jews of Ezra's day confessed that for 40 years, God faithfully furnished Israel with the pillars of fire and cloud, the Holy Spirit (see Num. 11:17; Isa. 63:11), and manna and water as the people wandered in the desert. Neither their clothing nor their feet gave out during that ordeal (Neh. 9:19-21). The assembled citizens of Judah and Jerusalem acknowledged that the Lord gave their ancestors more territory than they had expected. Specifically, He gave them the Transjordanian kingdoms of Sihon and Og. Also, He greatly multiplied the Israelites' number and gave the land of Canaan to the children of those who had left Egypt. Moreover, God drove out the Canaanite nations before Israel and gave them well-established cities, houses, cisterns, and orchards for which they did not have to toil (vss. 22-25).

Ezra's confession on behalf of the assembled congregation admitted that their ancestors fully enjoyed every good gift God gave them in Canaan, even as they rebelled against the Lord by disregarding and disobeying His law. Throughout the period of the judges and into the monarchy, when Israel fell into the habit of killing God's prophets, the people suffered repeatedly though a cycle of sin, punishment, repentance, and divine deliverance (vss. 26-27). The Jews of Ezra's day recognized that the unfaithfulness of their ancestors had amounted to "awful blasphemies" (vs. 26). The worshipers also knew the chastening of God had been just and that His deliverance through the judges revealed His "great compassion" (vs. 27).

The assembled congregation acknowledged that the cycle of sin, punishment, repentance, and deliverance did not end with the era of the judges. Even during the monarchy, peace and prosperity tended to lead to wicked behavior (vs. 28). Then, surrounding enemies oppressed Israel until the nation cried out to God in heaven. Time after time, He delivered His rebellious people because of His compassion. Those gathering in Jerusalem confessed that God warned their ancestors repeatedly through His prophets to return to His law and live (vs. 29).

Tragically, the Israelites became more arrogant, stubborn, and stiff-necked in their refusal to heed the oracles of God. The Lord knew Israel was becoming impervious to His law, but His Spirit patiently kept sending prophetic warnings (vs. 30). Despite God's displays of kindness, His people paid no attention to Him. Consequently, there was no option but to bring upon them the curses threatened in the law for repeated, persistent disobedience (see Deut. 28:15-68). Even then, the Lord, in His abundant "mercy" (Neh. 9:31), prevented Israel's annihilation. And, out of God's great compassion, He refused to forsake His chosen people.

B. The Hardship Endured by the Returnees: vs. 32

"Now therefore, O our God, the great, mighty and awesome God, who keeps his covenant of love, do not let all this hardship seem trifling in your eyes—the hardship that has come upon us, upon our kings and leaders, upon our priests and prophets, upon our fathers and all your people, from the days of the kings of Assyria until today."

Starting in Nehemiah 9:32, the assembled Jews began to focus their prayer of confession to their own time within the Persian Empire. They praised God for being "great, mighty and awesome." The worshipers declared that the Lord remained faithful to His covenant, which was characterized by His steadfast love. In contrast, the returnees bemoaned the distress of their political leaders, spiritual leaders, and tribal structures. They saw a straight line of well-deserved misery starting with the Assyrian conquest of the 10 northern tribes in 722 B.C., through the Babylonian destruction of Jerusalem in 586 B.C., right down to their plight under Persian domination. The people of Judah and Jerusalem asked God not to regard all the adversities they were experiencing as an inconsequential matter.

C. The Guilt of the Returnees' Ancestors: vss. 33-35

"In all that has happened to us, you have been just; you have acted faithfully, while we did wrong. Our kings, our leaders, our priests and our fathers did not follow your law; they did not pay attention to your commands or the warnings you gave them. Even while they were in their kingdom, enjoying your great goodness to them in the spacious and fertile land you gave them, they did not serve you or turn from their evil ways."

The assembly of Jews confessed that whenever the Lord punished His people, He remained righteous. He had dealt with them "faithfully" (Neh. 9:33). In contrast, the ancestors of the returnees were guilty of acting wickedly. Political leaders, spiritual authorities, and tribal heads all had strayed from the Mosaic law and ignored every prophetic warning to repent (vs. 34). Even when it had become a prosperous, independent nation, the covenant community refused to serve the Lord. Moreover, despite the fact that in His "great goodness" (vs. 35), He blessed His chosen people with a "spacious and fertile land," they refused to turn from their wicked practices.

D. The Servitude Endured by the Returnees: vs. 36

"But see, we are slaves today, slaves in the land you gave our forefathers so they could eat its fruit and the other good things it produces."

In the end, the assembled Jews appealed to God's mercy on the basis of their status as "slaves" (Neh. 9:36) in their own country, their own cities, and their own homes. Their livelihood was disappearing to pay the crippling taxes that the Persian emperors imposed on all the provinces (vs. 37). The returnees acknowledged that their own sins were adequate reasons for their subjection to foreign rulers. The worshipers reminded "the great, mighty and awesome God" (vs. 32), who keeps His promises because He is righteous, that they—His repentant servants—were "in great distress" (vs. 37). This had been the sort of thing that moved Nehemiah to leave the palace in Susa to help his people rebuild the walls of Jerusalem (see 1:3). The Jews hoped God would be favorably disposed toward them, too. The Old Testament gives several examples of prayers that reason with

God on the basis of His Word and previous deeds. No one has any right to tell God what to do, but He looks favorably on those of His spiritual children who root their prayers in the Scriptures and in His promises to them.

Discussion Questions

1. Why did the returnees feel the need to confess the sins their ancestors had committed?
2. Why did God choose to make a covenant with Abraham?
3. What are some difficult circumstances that God has enabled you to endure?
4. How did God remain merciful to His people, despite their rebellion?
5. Why is it important for believers to remain faithful to God?

Contemporary Application

The events of Nehemiah 9 took place about two days after the conclusion of the Festival of Booths. The Jews gathered as a group in Jerusalem. They demonstrated their deep sorrow over their unfaithfulness to the covenant by fasting, wearing dark, uncomfortable sackcloth, and placing dirt on their heads. The returnees separated themselves from all non-Jews. For three hours the group stood and listened to the law of God, and then for the next three hours they confessed their sins and worshiped the Lord.

When we think about obeying God, we might say that we want to, while at the same time not do what He wants. Instead, we choose to do only what is convenient for us or does not require much from us. But the Lord wants wholehearted obedience in all things He asks of us. Jesus is our example of wholehearted obedience, and anything less is disobedience.

Obedience to God's will results from an inner decision and a personal commitment. Admittedly, our personal commitment is under continual pressure from outside forces. Daily exposure to those who are living to please themselves can strike hard at our desire to wholeheartedly follow the Lord. Moreover, being surrounded by those whose lives reflect a disregard for God's will can tempt us to compromise. One way we can win the spiritual battle is by altering any aspects of our lifestyle that are compromising to God's will, as revealed in His Word.

Regardless of our age—whether younger or older—it is never too late to deal with the presence of sin in our lives. The prospect of having to renounce ungodly deeds might not be appealing to us. But it is necessary, especially if spiritual health is to be restored to us and encouraged among our peers in church.

Dedication of the Wall

Scripture

Background Scripture: *Nehemiah 12:27-43*

Scripture Lesson: *Nehemiah 12:27-36, 38, 43*

Key Verse: *On that day they offered great sacrifices, rejoicing because God had given them great joy. The women and children also rejoiced. The sound of rejoicing in Jerusalem could be heard far away.* Nehemiah 12:43.

Scripture Lesson for Children: *Nehemiah 12:27-36, 38, 40, 42b-43*

Key Verse for Children: *I had the leaders of Judah go up on top of the wall. I also assigned two large choirs to give thanks.* Nehemiah 12:31.

Lesson Aim

To develop fresh, creative approaches to worship.

Lesson Setting

Time: 444 B.C.

Place: Jerusalem

Lesson Outline

Dedication of the Wall

I. Preparing for the Ceremony: Nehemiah 12:27-30
    A. *Making the Decision: vs. 27a*
    B. *Performing the Ritual Purification: vss. 27b-30*

II. Dedicating the Jerusalem Wall:
    Nehemiah 12:31-36, 38, 43
    A. *The Procession of the First Choir: vss. 31-36*
    B. *The Procession of the Second Choir: vs. 38*
    C. *The Sound of Rejoicing: vs. 43*

Introduction for Adults

Topic: *Taking Pride in Accomplishment*

Rebuilding the Jerusalem wall was quite an accomplishment. This is especially so when we consider all the challenges God's people had to overcome. In the end, though, they realized it was the Lord who enabled them to be successful in their endeavor. And this is why, when they dedicated the wall, they gave thanks to the Lord.

None of the students in your class can truthfully claim to have a problem-free existence. For some, there are health issues; for others, there are financial pressures; and still for others, there are relational setbacks. Ultimately, the only way to overcome these challenges is by the grace of God. In turn, He deserves to be thanked for the amazing ways in which He is working in their lives.

God's desire for worship is part of a reciprocal love relationship He wants to establish with the class members. It is a relationship in which they worship Him exclusively in fresh, creative ways. In fact, setting aside special times of worship is one approach to help develop that relationship.

Introduction for Youth

Topic: *Celebration by Dedication*

Even saved teens experience times when their feelings don't match up with what they know they should be doing. It's similar to those Monday mornings when they just don't feel like going to school, even though they know they should.

It's not uncommon for adolescents to have similar feelings about church and worship. Whether they are tired from a late Saturday night social event, upset with a sibling or peer, or simply not having a good day, it isn't always easy for them to sing songs of praise and thanksgiving.

This is where making worship a priority comes into view. Despite all the hardships God's people in Nehemiah's day had to endure and overcome, they did not let these challenges prevent them from giving thanks to the Lord in worship. Similarly, encourage your students to consider how they can make the worship of God their primary goal.

Concepts for Children

Topic: *Mission Complete!*

1. God's people finished rebuilding the city wall of Jerusalem.
2. God's people got together to give thanks to Him.
3. God's people used musical instruments and singing to thank Him.
4. God's people were very happy for all He had done for them.
5. We can also give thanks to God for everything He does for us.

Lesson Commentary

I. PREPARING FOR THE CEREMONY: NEHEMIAH 12:27-30

A. Making the Decision: vs. 27a

At the dedication of the wall of Jerusalem.

This week's lesson focuses on Nehemiah's dedication of the newly rebuilt wall in Jerusalem (Neh. 12:27). The city, being set on a hill some 2,500 feet above sea level, is 33 miles east of the Mediterranean Sea and 14 miles west of the Dead Sea. Because access was difficult and the city lacked natural resources, it at one time enjoyed a relatively protected location. But when a major regional trade route developed through the city, Jerusalem became commercially and strategically desirable to every subsequent political force that came to power. Jerusalem's wall was one of the city's most distinctive features during the kingdom years. Also, the wall encircling the city provided its best defense against attack. Yet, when the Babylonians demolished the wall in 586 B.C., Jerusalem became defenseless against any invading army.

In 444 B.C., Nehemiah learned that the condition in Jerusalem was not good. This situation moved him to ask to God to intervene on his behalf, especially as he made his request known to Artaxerxes (see Neh. 1). Then, when Nehemiah asked the king for permission to go to Jerusalem and rebuild the city's walls, Artaxerxes agreed (see 2:1-10). While Nehemiah was in his beloved city, he inspected the condition of the wall. He also encouraged the Jews living there to repair and rebuild the demolished stone structure (see vss. 11-20). In Nehemiah 3, the author listed over 40 Jewish groups that helped rebuild the wall (which was not completed until 6:15). The extent of destruction and repair was not uniform. Some sections of the wall and the buildings would demand more time and attention than other areas.

Most of the residents (except the rulers of Tekoa; 3:5) participated in the restoration efforts. Nehemiah assigned each an important job, and they faithfully completed their task. Each team (perhaps involving some family units) worked on a particular area that was of unique concern to them. Advance preparation and planning undoubtedly ensured that the project continued to proceed despite harassment. There are 10 gates listed in chapter 3. Nehemiah started with the Sheep Gate in the northeastern corner and moved in a counterclockwise direction (vss. 1, 32). The other gates include the Fish Gate (vs. 3), the Old or Jeshanah Gate (vs. 6), the Valley Gate (vs. 13), the Refuse or Dung Gate (literally, Gate of Ash Heaps; vs. 14), the Fountain or Spring Gate (vs. 15), Water Gate (vs. 26), the Horse Gate (vs. 28), the East Gate (vs. 29), and the Inspection or Muster Gate (vs. 31).

The emphasis given by Nehemiah on these various gates is instructive. While the wall itself was being rebuilt, more time and resources were spent on the various city gates. This is because an onslaught of the city usually would be focused on the gates, making their fortification crucial. The author also mentioned four towers: the Tower of the Hundred, the Tower of Hananel (vs. 1), the Tower of the Furnaces or Ovens (vs. 11), and the tower projecting from the upper palace of the king (vss. 25-27). Experts are unsure about the exact location of some of these towers. In any case, the wall surrounding Jerusalem symbolized the preservation of God and His faithfulness in reestablishing His people. Its successful restoration indicated that the Jews in the heart of their capital would remain safe. God would protect them from attack and abuse by vandals. Moreover, rebuilding the wall would end Jerusalem's humiliating condition (see 1:3). The city would no longer seem like a disgrace to the Jews and their God.

As the members of the covenant community rebuilt the Jerusalem walls, they encountered stiff opposition from their enemies. Yet, throughout the ordeal, Nehemiah remained calm and levelheaded in his response (see 4:1-23). An internal challenge Nehemiah could not ignore was the fact that the people of Judah were facing economic distress. The biblical record indicates that Nehemiah resolved the issue in a fair and compassionate manner (see 5:1-19). Toward the end of the rebuilding project, Nehemiah's opponents made one last attempt to derail his efforts. Nehemiah, however, remained dedicated to the task of successfully bringing the undertaking to completion.

More specifically, Nehemiah's enemies heard that he had rebuilt the wall and closed the breaches in it, though he had not yet set the doors on the gates. They decided to ask if the governor would meet with them in one of the villages in the plain of Ono. Knowing they were planning to harm him, Nehemiah said he could not come, for he was doing a great work for God. This question and response happened four times (see 6:1-4). The fifth time, a local governor named Sanballat sent his servant to Nehemiah with an unsealed letter. The document alleged that the Jews were rebuilding the wall as part of their plan to rebel against Artaxerxes and install Nehemiah as king. Sanballat used this accusation as a pretext for meeting. Nehemiah, however, said the charges were unfounded. He realized his enemies were trying to frighten and demoralize the Jews. Nehemiah prayed that God would make His people strong (see vss. 5-9).

Next, a supposed friend of Nehemiah named Shemaiah, who was confined to his home, invited Nehemiah to retreat with him to the protective shelter of the temple. Shemaiah informed Nehemiah that his enemies were plotting to murder him at night. Nehemiah, however, did not think it was wise for him to go. He knew that his enemies had paid Shemaiah to trick him. Nehemiah's opponents wanted to see him do something foolish and bring shame on his good name. Nehemiah asked God to punish his enemies for what they had done (see vss. 10-14). Amazingly, despite all these challenges, in just 52 days, the rebuilding of the wall was completed (see vs. 15).

When the Jews' enemies heard the news, they were disheartened and realized God had helped His people. All this time, the Jewish leaders and Tobiah (a government official for the Ammonites) had been writing letters back and forth. There were bonds of loyalty due to strong family ties. These Jewish leaders would praise Tobiah in front of Nehemiah and also report Nehemiah's words back to Tobiah. Tobiah himself tried to intimidate Nehemiah through a series of letters (see vss. 16-19). None of these efforts, though, deterred Nehemiah. He appointed gatekeepers, temple singers, and the Levites to their work. He put his brother, Hanani, and Hananiah, the commander of the citadel, in charge of Jerusalem. The governor told them not to open the city gates until well after sunrise and to close and bar the gates before the guards went off duty at sunset. The leaders were to choose people from Jerusalem to stand guard at different places around the wall and near their own houses (see 7:1-3).

B. Performing the Ritual Purification: vss. 27b-30

The Levites were sought out from where they lived and were brought to Jerusalem to celebrate joyfully the dedication with songs of thanksgiving and with the music of cymbals, harps and lyres. The singers also were brought together from the region around Jerusalem—from the villages of the Netophathites, from Beth Gilgal, and from the area of Geba and Azmaveth, for the singers had built villages for themselves around Jerusalem. When the priests and Levites had purified themselves ceremonially, they purified the people, the gates and the wall.

After the law had been reaffirmed (see Neh. 9–10), the leaders of the Jewish people tackled the practical matter of increasing the population of Jerusalem (see chapters 11:1–12:26). They approached the problem with three strategies: Many leaders settled in the city as an example to the nation; 10 percent of the general population was assigned by lottery to move there; and others volunteered to the applause of their neighbors. The tribe of Benjamin contributed twice as many new residents to Jerusalem as the tribe of Judah. The priests continued to greatly outnumber the Levites. The priests and Levites continued to keep meticulous family records based on the documents created when Zerubbabel and Jeshua led the first exiles from Babylon. Their family records in chapter 11 extend to the days of Darius II, the emperor after Artaxerxes.

Previously, when Nehemiah inquired about the condition of his homeland, he asked about both the people and the place (see 1:2). He did not celebrate the physical rebuilding of the Jerusalem walls until the people who would live within them had been spiritually rebuilt as well. From this observation we see that bricks and mortar are never as important as hearts and lives. Even in our churches today, we need to keep in mind, as Nehemiah did, that every facility we build should advance the work of God in human hearts and lives.

Nehemiah's first-person account of the restoration of Jerusalem had broken off after 7:5. It picks up again at 12:27 and continues through the end of the book. When Nehemiah was ready for an official celebration by the renewed people to dedicate the rebuilt walls of the city, he needed to have Levites available to assist in the ceremony. These individuals had the instrumental and vocal musical skills

413

necessary for a mass celebration (for example, leading songs of thanksgiving accompanied by music played on cymbals, harps, and lyres).

Accordingly, Nehemiah had the Levites brought to Jerusalem from wherever they lived in Judah. Furthermore, the Levitical families of singers and musicians were brought together from the regions around Jerusalem and from the outlying villages of Benjamin and Judah where they lived (vss. 28-29). Before the priests and Levites dedicated the recently completed walls, they conducted purification ceremonies (vs. 30). These rituals were not concerned with physical cleanliness, but with spiritual preparation to be in God's presence. The unspecified ceremonies may have involved washings by the priests and Levites and sacrifices for the people, the gates, and the walls (see Exod. 40:30-32; Lev. 14:49-53).

II. DEDICATING THE JERUSALEM WALL: NEHEMIAH 12:31-36, 38, 43

A. The Procession of the First Choir: vss. 31-36

I had the leaders of Judah go up on top of the wall. I also assigned two large choirs to give thanks. One was to proceed on top of the wall to the right, toward the Dung Gate. Hoshaiah and half the leaders of Judah followed them, along with Azariah, Ezra, Meshullam, Judah, Benjamin, Shemaiah, Jeremiah, as well as some priests with trumpets, and also Zechariah son of Jonathan, the son of Shemaiah, the son of Mattaniah, the son of Micaiah, the son of Zaccur, the son of Asaph, and his associates— Shemaiah, Azarel, Milalai, Gilalai, Maai, Nethanel, Judah and Hanani—with musical instruments prescribed by David the man of God. Ezra the scribe led the procession.

Nehemiah directed all of the community leaders of Judah to ascend the wall for the dedication (Neh. 12:31). He divided the priests and Levitical musicians into two large choirs. The Hebrew text literally says these choirs represented "two thanksgivings." In other words, they embodied what they did. The choirs got in formation atop the wall and marched around the city: The first choir moved in a counterclockwise direction, and the other clockwise.

The starting point was the Dung Gate. This gate (mentioned earlier) was the city exit to the garbage dump in the Valley of Hinnom on the southern tip of the city. Ezra probably led the first procession, followed by singers and instrumentalists (vss. 35-36). The political leaders brought up the rear (vss. 32-34). Old Testament compass points are determined by facing east. So, "to the right" (vs. 31) means "to the south." This choir rounded the southern tip of Jerusalem and processed north atop the eastern wall alongside the ancient City of David and his royal residence (vs. 37).

B. The Procession of the Second Choir: vs. 38

The second choir proceeded in the opposite direction. I followed them on top of the wall, together with half the people—past the Tower of the Ovens to the Broad Wall.

The second choir matched the first in makeup (Neh. 12:38). Nehemiah joined the other civic leaders at the rear. He did not lead this sacred procession because he was not a priest. The people also divided themselves in two masses and followed one or the other choir of thanksgiving around the wall. The second choir marched north atop the western wall, then east atop the northern wall (vs. 39). At the Gate of the Guard (or Prison Gate; see 2 Kings 11:6, 19; Jer. 32:2), in the vicinity of the temple at the northeast corner of Jerusalem, the two choirs of thanksgiving met one another face-to-face and halted. When the Jews dedicated the walls of Jerusalem, purity preceded praise, and praise resulted in faithful service. Today, in our lives, dedication to God should not be isolated from personal purity or joyous service. We praise God best when our lives back up what our lips declare.

C. The Sound of Rejoicing: vs. 43

And on that day they offered great sacrifices, rejoicing because God had given them great joy. The women and children also rejoiced. The sound of rejoicing in Jerusalem could be heard far away.

After encompassing Jerusalem with a parade that claimed the city as God's gift to His people, the two choirs descended from the walls and assembled "in the house of God" (Neh. 12:40). The latter refers to the courtyards of the temple—not in the actual Holy Place, where no one went but the ministering priests and Levites in the course of their daily routines. Nehemiah and half the civil leaders joined the choirs and 15 priests (seven of whom blew trumpets) for a choral festival under the direction of Jezrahiah (vss. 41-42). His name meant "The Lord Shines Forth," and he fulfilled his name's significance by directing the gathered multitude in glad adoration of the Lord.

The leaders, priests, Levites, and ordinary citizens worshiped the Lord with numerous sacrifices on the brazen altar before the temple entrance on its east side (vs. 43). Men, women, and children launched into an extended time of praising God for the joy He had given them and was giving them through His gifts of the city walls and the renewed covenant. Ninety-two years before (that is, 536 B.C.), the exiles who returned under Zerubbabel and Jeshua had made a noise of celebration that could be heard a long way outside the city. They were rejoicing that the foundation of the temple had been laid. As was noted in lesson 6, at that time, sorrow mixed with joy as some old-timers remembered better days (see Ezra 3:10-13). In contrast, as the walls were dedicated in 444 B.C., no sorrow dampened the spirits of the revelers. They had no doubt that God was in their midst and ready to affirm them as His chosen people in His holy city.

Out of the joyous dedication of the walls came a repeated pledge to serve the Lord faithfully and gladly. Stewards were appointed to keep track of the firstfruits and tithes brought to the temple storerooms (Neh. 12:44). At this time, the Jews were pleased with the spiritual labor of the priests and Levites in assisting Ezra in bringing about revival. Moreover, the people were glad to make donations from their fields, orchards, and vineyards to support the work done in the temple. For their part, the priests and Levites were prepared to follow the worship duties spelled out centuries before by kings David and Solomon (vss. 45-46; see 1 Chron. 23–26).

Discussion Questions

1. What challenges had to be overcome to make the rededication of the rebuilt Jerusalem wall possible?
2. Why was it important to seek out Levites for the rededication ceremony?
3. Why were the two choirs so jubilant in giving thanks to God?
4. What are some ways your church celebrates major milestones it achieves?
5. What key events in your life bring you deep and abiding spiritual joy?

Contemporary Application

This week's lesson draws our attention to the rededication of the wall of Jerusalem (see Neh. 12:27). It occurred after God's people had overcome numerous challenges. Part of the preparation included the priests, Levites, and participants purifying themselves ceremonially (see vs. 30). They considered this step to be an essential part of approaching the Lord in heartfelt worship.

I was raised in a traditional kind of church. My worship experiences were all much the same on the outside, since the congregation's approach to worship varied little. What did vary was what happened on the inside, namely, how I approached the worship service.

Sometimes, I was too preoccupied to do more than go through the motions. On other occasions, I felt in need of God's help. Still other times, I just felt glad to belong to God and worshiped because it flowed easily out of my emotions. This kind of corporate worship is probably similar to many of your students' experiences.

But recently, I have stumbled onto something that has breathed new life into worship for me. And, I trust, it has helped me become a better worshiper. A church I have been attending strives first for genuineness and authenticity in worship. This parallels the reverential attitude displayed by God's people in Nehemiah's day as they rededicated the Jerusalem wall.

Moreover, the church I attend values creativity, variety, and excellence in its approach to worship. For instance, it uses drama, lighting, music, video, creative readings, and many other vehicles to draw participants into worship. This attitude can also be seen in the creative way God's people rededicated the Jerusalem wall. Specifically, they divided into two large choirs, circled the wall in opposite directions, and joined together in the temple to express thanks to God (see vss. 31-43).

The Creator must certainly delight in these expressions of creativity. This is especially so as we endeavor in worship to let Him know just what He means to us. Also, as we seek fresh approaches to worship, we become more thoughtful about our relationship with God. And in the process, we become better worshipers.

Sabbath Reforms

DEVOTIONAL READING

Mark 2:23-27

DAILY BIBLE READINGS

Monday August 19
Exodus 16:13-26 A Sabbath to the Lord

Tuesday August 20
Exodus 31:12-18 Keep the Sabbath Holy

Wednesday August 21
Isaiah 58:9-14 Honoring the Sabbath

Thursday August 2
Mark 2:23-27 The Lord of the Sabbath

Friday August 23
Mark 3:1-6 Doing Good on the Sabbath

Saturday August 24
Nehemiah 13:4-14 Restoring the Sanctity of the Temple

Sunday August 25
Nehemiah 13:15-22 Restoring the Sanctity of the Sabbath

Scripture

Background Scripture: *Nehemiah 13:4-31*
Scripture Lesson: *Nehemiah 13:15-22*
Key Verse: *I commanded the Levites to purify themselves and go and guard the gates in order to keep the Sabbath day holy.* Nehemiah 13:22.
Scripture Lesson for Children: *Nehemiah 13:15-22*
Key Verse for Children: *When evening shadows fell on the gates of Jerusalem before the Sabbath, I ordered the doors to be shut and not opened until the Sabbath was over.* Nehemiah 13:19.

Lesson Aim

To be responsive to biblical instruction and exhortation.

Lesson Setting

Time: 432 B.C.
Place: Jerusalem

Lesson Outline

Sabbath Reforms

   I. Confronting Sabbath Violations: Nehemiah 13:15-18
      A. *Local Residents Working on the Sabbath: vs. 15*
      B. *Merchants Doing Business on the Sabbath: vss. 16-18*
  II. Enacting Sabbath Reforms: Nehemiah 13:19-22
      A. *Shutting the City Gates: vs. 19*
      B. *Disbanding the Merchants: vss. 20-21*
      C. *Guarding the City Gates: vs. 22*

Introduction for Adults

Topic: *Getting It Right*

God's mandate to His people in Nehemiah's day was very specific. He wanted them to honor Him by observing the Sabbath. This mindset is quite different from our modern way of thinking. Ours is a pick-and-choose society.

Supposedly, we can choose which of God's moral principles to keep and forget the rest. In this kind of cultural climate, it's often hard for believers to be unequivocal about the commands of God's Word. On the one hand, they don't want to be considered narrow-minded, bigoted, and intolerant by their peers. On the other hand, believers know that what the Lord has revealed in Scripture is best for society as well as their individual lives.

Therefore, we cannot afford to explain away the principles and priorities of God's Word. It's also unwise to tone down or make exceptions to His commands just to gain popular approval. After all, so much of society is at risk, and so many people's lives are messed up. So we must insist, as Nehemiah did in his day, that the only way to improvement lies in following the teachings of God's Word.

Introduction for Youth

Topic: *Profane No Gain!*

In Nehemiah's day, the people of Judah and Jerusalem were conducting business on the Sabbath. Nehemiah warned them not to desecrate that holy day. He noted that their ancestors' violation of the Sabbath had displeased God and led to their long exile from their homeland (see Neh. 13:15-18). The decision to follow God's will in every area of life remains just as imperative for young people today.

Jim's best friend and fellow athlete went for a drive one night. Earl seemed like a good guy who went to church. Despite the fact that they were both under the legal drinking age, Earl took a six-pack of beer in his car and urged Jim to drink a can with him. Jim refused. From then on the two drifted apart, Earl into a rather typical pattern of short-term jobs and drinking, and Jim into the ministry.

Of course, that one decision did not determine how the two would live their lives. But it does illustrate the different choices young people have to make, not just about drinking but also about sexual practices, using drugs, cheating in class, and so on. That's why we should teach and demonstrate that Christian ethical values differ sharply from the world's profane moral code.

Concepts for Children

Topic: *Shut the Doors!*

1. God's people were doing work on a special day called the Sabbath.
2. Other people were selling things on this special day.
3. God's people were not supposed to do these things on the Sabbath.
4. Nehemiah asked God for help to do what was right.
5. God will also help us to obey His Word and do what is right.

Lesson Commentary

I. CONFRONTING SABBATH VIOLATIONS: NEHEMIAH 13:15-18

A. Local Residents Working on the Sabbath: vs. 15

In those days I saw men in Judah treading winepresses on the Sabbath and bringing in grain and load-ing it on donkeys, together with wine, grapes, figs and all other kinds of loads. And they were bringing all this into Jerusalem on the Sabbath. Therefore I warned them against selling food on that day.

Nehemiah's book ends on a bittersweet note. In 432 B.C., after spending time back in Persia (see 5:14; 13:6), this extraordinary, forceful man returned to Jerusalem for a second term as governor of Judah. Nehemiah's walls still stood firm, but his spiritual reforms were in disarray. He immediately began to take corrective action. Perhaps Nehemiah's prayers of frustration recorded in chapter 13 are a fitting way for this period of Old Testament history to end. After all, the best human efforts to keep God's commandments usually fail—then as now. The final chapter of Nehemiah virtually calls out to God to send the promised Messiah and make things new.

At some point after the dedication of the walls of Jerusalem, the "Book of Moses" (vs. 1) was being read at a public assembly. Nehemiah's first reforms began when the law was read during the Feast of Tabernacles (see 7:73–8:18). It was appropri-ate that the second set of reforms should begin in the same way. When Deuteronomy 23:3-6 was read, the participants discovered that the Mosaic law banned certain foreigners from the assembly of God's people because of how their ancestors had treated Israel when the nation approached Canaan to conquer it (Neh. 13:2). As before, the public reading of Scripture had a powerful practical impact on its hearers. The Jews began expelling unconverted aliens from their communities (vs. 3).

This policy brought a serious matter to public attention. Tobiah, one of Nehemiah's strongest opponents when the walls were being built, had used his con-nections with the high priest, Eliashib, to convert a storage area on the temple grounds into his Jerusalem living quarters (vs. 4). Long before this, Tobiah had developed his network of supporters in Judah (see 6:17-19). The support of the high priest surely marked the pinnacle of his popularity. Tobiah's name meant "the Lord is good." He may even have been part Jewish, but he apparently had no concern for the Lord or His work. Tobiah gladly put his own interests ahead of the worship of God and the support of the priests and Levites (13:5). Evidently, the expulsion of foreigners from the midst of Judah and Jerusalem started at the bottom of the social ladder and reached up to the point where powerful Jewish friends offered protec-tion. Tobiah probably felt he had little to worry about in his temple apartment.

Nehemiah's name meant "the Lord comforts." He had shown that he could com-fort the afflicted when he cared for the poor of Judah who were being oppressed by the wealthy (see chap. 5). Nehemiah also demonstrated that he could afflict the comfortable. For instance, he readily rebuked those who neglected God's will and work (see 13:11, 17, 25). Nehemiah revealed that he was absent from Jerusalem when information found in the Mosaic law led the people to expel the foreigners. During that time, however, Tobiah was allowed to move into the temple (vs. 7). Nehemiah had come to Jerusalem in the 20th year of Artaxerxes' reign (see 1:1; 2:1) and returned to Persia in the 32nd year. Twelve years was a long time to divert from Nehemiah's duties in Persia to the needs of Jerusalem. Even so, he felt that he needed to do more.

After an unspecified period, Nehemiah petitioned Artaxerxes to send him back to Judah (13:7). One of the first things Nehemiah learned when he got back to Jerusalem was that the high priest, Eliashib, was shielding Tobiah's residence in the temple from public opinion. Armed with imperial authority and an aggressive personality, the governor went to the temple and personally threw Tobiah's furnishings and personal effects out on the pavement (vs. 8). Having done his part, Nehemiah ordered others to ceremonially cleanse the affected temple chambers and restock them with temple gear and worship materials (vs. 9).

Soon Nehemiah heard that temple worship was disrupted by much more than a set of misused rooms. Levites and musicians had left Jerusalem to make a living on farms throughout Judah, for not enough people were supplying firstfruits and tithes to support the temple workers (vs. 10). Sanctuary rituals were impoverished by the absence of these worship leaders. Nehemiah gathered the elders of Judah and Benjamin to reprimand them (vs. 11). He held them responsible for the faithlessness of Jewish worshipers and the defection of the temple workers. Then, Nehemiah gathered the Levites, musicians, and other sanctuary ministers from around the countryside and put them back to work at their designated tasks.

Almost at once, ordinary people began responding to the initiatives of Nehemiah and their local officials. Tithes of various agricultural products flowed in again (vs. 12). Nehemiah devised an interesting approach to administer the materials provided for the temple and its personnel. He appointed a priest, a scribe, and a Levite—people with three different perspectives on temple activities—to share oversight of the storage system (vs. 13). Next, the governor made another man their assistant, which brought a lay point of view to the project. In the same way, Nehemiah had appointed keepers of the gates years earlier (see 7:2), he chose overseers of the temple storerooms based on their integrity and fidelity (13:13). Nehemiah relied on them to care for the material needs of all the temple staff so that the worship of God could proceed without distraction.

Earlier in the book, Nehemiah had asked God to remember his care for the poor and the wickedness of his opponents (see 5:19; 6:14). In the governor's prayer recorded in 13:14, he feared all the advances he had made might be lost. He pleaded with God to preserve the new reforms enacted for the temple and its services. Nehemiah recognized how deviations from the stipulations recorded in the Mosaic law could undermine the spiritual and moral vitality of the covenant community. A case in point would be the observance of the Sabbath. Years before, Nehemiah had faced foreign merchants coming to Jerusalem to sell goods on the Sabbath (see 10:31). At that time, the Jews had decided to accept the practice. After all, they weren't the ones running the shops.

In Nehemiah's absence, disregarding Sabbath violations by foreigners had led to Jewish physical labor as well as Jewish commercial activity on the Sabbath. For instance, on that holy day, Nehemiah saw the local residents of Judah treading wine presses. Others loaded onto their donkeys sacks filled with grain, grapes, figs, and other agricultural products so that these could be brought to Jerusalem and sold in the city. The situation had reached a critical point and Nehemiah decided to take corrective action. Specifically, he directed his fellow Jews to stop selling "food" (13:15) on the Sabbath.

B. Merchants Doing Business on the Sabbath: vss. 16-18

Men from Tyre who lived in Jerusalem were bringing in fish and all kinds of merchandise and selling them in Jerusalem on the Sabbath to the people of Judah. I rebuked the nobles of Judah and said to them, "What is this wicked thing you are doing—desecrating the Sabbath day? Didn't your forefathers do the same things, so that our God brought all this calamity upon us and upon this city? Now you are stirring up more wrath against Israel by desecrating the Sabbath."

"Tyre" (Neh. 13:16) was a port city in Phoenicia on the Mediterranean coast north of Jerusalem. At that time, Tyre was regarded as the commercial capital of the entire region. Nehemiah learned that merchants from the seaport were transporting salted and dried fish, along with a wide variety of other goods, into the city. Then, on the Sabbath, the foreigners sold their merchandise to Jewish residents. Nehemiah dealt with the irreligious Phoenicians by confronting the prominent leaders of Judah. The governor questioned how they could profane the Sabbath day by allowing an evil activity to occur in the holy city (vs. 17). Nehemiah reasoned that the ancestors of the Jewish remnant were guilty of similar transgressions. In turn, these violations of the Mosaic law were the basis for God's bringing about the horror of the Exile and the destruction of Jerusalem. Nehemiah accused the officials of bringing more of God's "wrath" (vs. 18) down on "Israel" by allowing the Sabbath to be profaned.

When God had finished Creation, Genesis 2:2 says that "on the seventh day he rested from all his work." That rest was the model for the Sabbath. It is not known when the Hebrews began keeping the Sabbath. From Exodus 16:27, however, we know that they began before God gave the fourth commandment to require Sabbath observance. Centuries later, while the people of Judah were exiled in Babylon, they had to suspend religious practices that depended on the temple. But since the Sabbath may be observed apart from the temple, it was continued. In fact, it rose in importance during the Exile. Presumably, the Sabbath was at first faithfully observed by Jews who returned to Judah. But as time passed, they again began breaking Sabbath regulations.

In the four or five centuries before the advent of the Messiah, Jewish religious teachers debated at length what actions should and should not be permitted on the Sabbath. They formulated 39 articles prohibiting all kinds of agricultural, industrial, and domestic work. But the teachers also developed ways of getting around their own rules. For example, they taught that no one should travel more than 2,000 cubits (or about 3,000 feet) on the Sabbath. But if people were to deposit food 2,000 cubits from their home before the Sabbath, then on the Sabbath, they could declare the spot a temporary residence and act as though they had not traveled up to that point. It's no wonder that during Jesus' earthly ministry, He decided to put the Sabbath back into theological perspective.

II. ENACTING SABBATH REFORMS: NEHEMIAH 13:19-22

A. Shutting the City Gates: vs. 19

When evening shadows fell on the gates of Jerusalem before the Sabbath, I ordered the doors to be shut and not opened until the Sabbath was over. I stationed some of my own men at the gates so that no load could be brought in on the Sabbath day.

After rebuking the nobles of Judah for allowing the Sabbath to be profaned, Nehemiah did not fall into inactivity. Instead, he waited until the next Sabbath, when he ordered the gates of Jerusalem to be closed and barred. He issued the directive as the shadows of late afternoon darkened the recesses of the doorways (Neh. 13:19). The Sabbath officially began at sundown, but the governor shut the gates early and posted his personal guards to emphasize that business hours were done until the following evening.

B. Disbanding the Merchants: vss. 20-21

Once or twice the merchants and sellers of all kinds of goods spent the night outside Jerusalem. But I warned them and said, "Why do you spend the night by the wall? If you do this again, I will lay hands on you." From that time on they no longer came on the Sabbath.

For the first couple of weeks, merchants showed up outside the locked gates of Jerusalem as they had done before (Neh. 13:20). Either they had not heard or did not believe the Jews were strictly observing the Sabbath. Nehemiah finally confronted the merchants with the pointed question as to why they were camping out during the night by the city wall. Then the governor sent them away with a threat that he would take decisive action if they showed up again before the start of the Sabbath (vs. 21).

C. Guarding the City Gates: vs. 22

Then I commanded the Levites to purify themselves and go and guard the gates in order to keep the Sabbath day holy. Remember me for this also, O my God, and show mercy to me according to your great love.

Nehemiah directed the Levites to go through a ritual purification ceremony. Doing so was in keeping with the sacred nature of the Sabbath day. Afterward, they were to stand guard at the Jerusalem gates during the 24-hour period of the Sabbath to ensure that it was not profaned by any sacrilegious commercial activity. Once more, Nehemiah asked God to "remember" (Neh. 13:22) him. In this case, the petition did not just mean to call to mind, for the governor was not afraid that God would forget about him. Rather, in this context, to "remember" means to intervene. Specifically, Nehemiah asked God to show His servant grace and loving mercy by preserving the work he had done for God's people.

When Nehemiah noticed that the situation was amiss in Judah, he started with a problem in the heart of everything—the integrity of the Jerusalem temple. Then, he attacked the problem of ignoring the Sabbath. Finally, he went after an issue that extended through the whole nation, namely, intermarriage. Nehemiah began in the center and worked out. More than 25 years earlier, Ezra had imposed the drastic measure of sending away foreign wives (see Ezra 9–10). When Nehemiah returned from Persia for his second term as governor, the practice had surfaced again (Neh. 13:23).

In the streets of Jerusalem and other towns or villages of Judah, the governor heard children who spoke the languages of their mothers from the Mediterranean coast or the lands east of the Jordan River (vs. 24). Nehemiah did not approach this problem through the leaders of the people, as he had the previous two problems. Instead, he went directly to the fathers who had arranged these marriages with foreigners, and he did not treat them gently (vs. 25). He scolded the fathers. The governor invoked the curses that accompanied the Mosaic covenant they had made with God (see 10:29). Nehemiah also physically struck some of the offenders and pulled the hair of their beards.

Finally, Nehemiah compelled those who had given their children in marriage to foreigners to swear an oath in God's name that they would not repeat the practice with their younger sons and daughters. The governor preached a short sermon about the dire consequences of King Solomon's prolific intermarriage with foreign women (13:26). Nehemiah reminded his fellow Jews how that national hero—one of Israel's greatest kings, whom God loved—had fallen into grievous sin and led the nation after him to violate the Mosaic law. Nehemiah asked them rhetorically whether they wanted to do the same thing in their generation through their sons and daughters (vs. 27).

The worst incident of intermarriage with a foreigner involved a member of the high priestly family and a daughter of Sanballat—one of Nehemiah's archenemies during the construction of the walls of Jerusalem (vs. 28). It's unclear from the Hebrew text at this point whether Eliashib was still the high priest or if Joiada had already succeeded his father. It made no difference to Nehemiah. He drove the offending son or grandson of the high priest out of Jerusalem and Judah. The governor would not allow that kind of spiritual corruption so close to the high priesthood. As mentioned earlier, Nehemiah had prayed that God would take special note of the wickedness of those who opposed the Lord's will to rebuild the walls of Jerusalem (see 6:14). Now the governor prayed that God would deal in the same way with those who defiled the priesthood (13:29). This kind of depravity immediately touched the entire covenant God made with His people and the Levitical community, who stood between the Lord and His people as servants.

Discussion Questions

1. Why was it important for God's people in the Old Testament to observe the Sabbath?
2. Why did Nehemiah put a stop to foreign merchants' conducting business in Jerusalem on the Sabbath?
3. What reason did Nehemiah give to the leaders of Judah to keep the Sabbath holy?
4. What can you do to encourage the leaders in your church to honor the Lord in their ministerial activities?
5. How can you ensure that your faith is strong enough for you to do the right thing, even if you seem to be the only one doing it?

Contemporary Application

The people of Judah in Nehemiah's day had two clear but opposite choices. They could either put God first by keeping the Sabbath holy or spurn His will by profaning the Sabbath. Nehemiah exhorted his fellow Jews to stop desecrating the Sabbath. This included putting a halt to all forms of commercial activity in Jerusalem on that day (see Neh. 13:15-16).

Popular opinion makers find it hard to accept the idea that we have only two paths to follow in life—God's way or our own. They rebel at the clearly stated biblical truth that our destinies are determined by whether we choose God's will or ours. The world does not like to face such stark alternatives. The world likes to think that we can work our way around God's coming judgment.

Some people no doubt ridiculed Nehemiah's statements about God and the fairness of His justice (see vss. 17-18). It would have been much easier for them to blame God than to submit to His ways and honor and fear His name. Nehemiah clearly warned the leaders of Judah that failure to obey the Lord leads to certain calamity.

God's somber message will not win any popularity contests. In fact, the idea of divine judgment has virtually disappeared as a believable concept. Tragically, some ministers fail to spell out the end of those who reject God. In contrast, Nehemiah stood for the truth. One cannot read about his tenure as Judah's governor and fail to grasp the enormous consequences of right and wrong choices.

See the
Power *of* God

through the stories of ordinary people
facing extraordinary circumstances

This popular digest-sized resource is filled with gripping articles about Christians living out their faith. With a focus on start-up ministries, world missions, and challenging issues, *Power for Living* provides a unique perspective on the power of God in all areas of life.

QUARTERLY EDITIONS FEATURE:

- Thirteen lead articles with a variety of faith-based stories

- *Christian Classics* feature, highlighting perspectives from theologians such as D.L. Moody and Charles Spurgeon

- Daily Bible Readings to encourage daily Bible study

- Coordinates with adult David C Cook curriculums

Great for
personal growth
& evangelism